D1238904

The Options Trading Strategy Of A Lifetime

by William Grandmill

Published by Windsor Books
P.O. Box 280
Brightwaters, N.Y. 11718

Manufactured in the United States of America

ISBN 0-930233-56-5

THE OPTIONS TRADING STRATEGY OF A LIFETIME

Wm Grandmill

THE PURPOSE OF THIS BOOK is to help the soybean option trader to reach the right decision before he buys or sells his option. The bewildering combinations of volatility, time and price can make it difficult to arrive at a decision as to which type of option one should use, and how much profit can be made. In addition, a lot of work is needed and most traders do not have the time to spend on these calculations.

NO WORK IS NEEDED when you use this book. The author has done the work for you. He has calculated hundreds of different option positions, using a multitude of variations of the three factors which influence option values, i.e. volatility, time to expiration and price changes. From all this testing, the author has selected 9 options positions which perform well, both from a safety and a profit perspective.

BY USING THIS BOOK you can select the best option to use in 10 minutes or less. All the calculations have been done for you. In addition, the author has built in a unique defense system, a safety zone, to protect your working capital in case prices should go against you after you have taken your option position.

TABLE OF CONTENTS

PART I

THIS PART CONTAINS THE TOOLS FOR THE JOB

Time (weeks to expiration)
Price (the Forecasting Graphs)
Volatility (the Table Finder)

SOYBEAN DATA

Keep the data up to date
Update from each new crop report

U.S. SOYBEAN DATA – the crop year begins on Sept. 1st and ends on Aug. 31st.

Crop year	73/74	74/75	75/76	76/77	77/78	78/79	79/80	80/81
Acres planted (millions)	56.7	53.5	54.6	50.2	58.8	64.7	71.6	70.0
Acres harvested	55.7	51.3	53.6	49.4	57.6	63.7	70.6	67.9
Yield (bu. per acre)	27.8	23.7	28.9	26.1	30.6	29.5	32.1	26.4
Beginning stocks	60	171	188	245	103	161	173	359
Production (mil. bu.)	1547	1216	1547	1289	1767	1870	2269	1792
Total soybean supply	1607	1387	1735	1534	1870	2031	2442	2151
Domestic use & crush	897	778	936	867	1009	1117	1208	1109
Exports (mil. bu)	539	421	554	564	700	741	875	724
Total soybean use	1436	1199	1490	1431	1709	1858	2083	1833
Carryover (mil.bu.)	171	188	245	103	161	173	359	318
Carryover as % of use	12%	16%	16%	7%	9%	9%	18%	17%
This yr. total supply % last yr. total use %	125%	97%	145%	103%	131%	119%	131%	103%
Nov. soybean data								
Highest price	$9.29	$9.56	$6.53	$7.77	$7.98	$7.31	$8.33	$9.23
date of highest	Aug 14/73	Oct 4/74	Aug 20/75	July 7/76	June 7/77	Oct 30/78	June 22/79	Oct 30/80
Lowest price	$4.44	$5.08	$4.76 cycle lo	$5.04	$4.97	$5.86	$6.25	$6.43
date of lowest	May 17/73	May 7/74	Oct 28/75	May 3/76	Aug 16/77	Aug 8/78	Oct 29/79	May 19/80
May soybean data								
Highest price	$6.90	$9.71	$6.37	$10.76	$7.48	$7.30	$7.90	$10.06
date of highest	Feb 26/74	Oct 4/74	Sep 18/75	Apr 22/77	Mar 1/78	Feb 25/79	Sep 18/79	Nov 20/80
Lowest price	$5.21	$4.87	$4.58	$6.19	$5.23	$6.47	$5.70	$7.20
date of lowest	Nov 5/73	Mar 3/75	Dec 15/75	Oct 18/76	Sep 12/77	Sep 6/78	Apr 2/80	Mar 1/81
Weather conditions								
South American Soybeans Production								
Brazilian soybeans	7.9 mmt	9.9	11.2	12.5	9.5	10.2	15.2	15.1
Argentine's soybeans	.5 mmt	.5	.7	1.4	2.7	3.7	3.6	3.5
Total So.America prod.	8.4 mmt	10.4 mmt	11.9 mmt	13.9 mmt	12.2 mmt	13.9 mmt	18.8 mmt	18.6 mmt

South American Soybeans – millions of metric ton. The harvest is in our springtime, so their harvest is added to our harvest of the following autumn. For example, their 1973 harvest will affect our prices at harvest time for the 73/74 crop year.

U.S. SOYBEAN DATA – the soybean crop year begins on Sep. 1st and ends on Aug. 31st.

Crop year	81/82	82/83	83/84	84/85	85/86	86/87	87/88	88/89
Acres planted (millions)	68.0	71.5	63.5	67.8	63.1	61.5	58.0	58.8
Acres harvested	66.7	69.8	62.2	66.1	61.6	58.3	57.0	57.4
Yield (bu. per acre)	30.4	31.9	25.7	28.1	34.1	33.1	33.7	27.0
Begining stocks	318	266	345	176	316	536	436	302
Production (mil. bu)	2000	2229	1636	1861	2099	1940	1927	1553
Total soybean supply	2318	2495	1981	2037	2415	2476	2263	1855
Domestic use & crush	1121	1179	1065	1123	1140	1283	1276	1146
Exports (mil. bu)	931	895	740	598	739	757	785	527
Total soybean use	2052	2074	1805	1721	1879	2040	2061	1673
Carryover (mil.bu.)	266	345	176	316	536	436	302	182
Carryover as % of use	13%	17%	10%	18%	29%	21%	14%	11%
This year's total supply / Last year's total use %	126%	122%	96%	113%	140%	132%	115%	89%
Nov. soybean data								
Highest price	$8.34	$6.85	$9.67	$7.71	$6.09	$5.52	$6.25	$10.46
date of highest	May 1/81	May 17/82	Aug 25/83	June 20/84	May 1/85	May 8/86	June 1/87	June 1/88
Lowest price	$6.37	$5.50	$5.98	$5.69	$4.97	$4.65cycle low	$5.04	$7.06
date of lowest	Sep 28/81	Oct 14/82	Jun 26/83	Sep 21/84	Oct 16/85	Aug 25/86	Sep 1/87	May 4/88
May soybean data								
Highest price	$7.51	$6.56	$9.96	$6.77	$5.67	$5.35	$6.90	$9.12
date of highest	Sep 16/81	Apr 11/83	Sep 13/83	Nov 1/84	Apr 30/86	May 1/87	May 1/88	Sep 8/88
Lowest price	$6.06	$5.59	$7.06	$5.71	$4.89	$4.89	$5.22	$7.04
date of lowest	Mar 15/82	Oct 4/82	Feb 14/84	Mar 4/85	Nov 21/85	Dec 18/86	Sep 1/87	Apr 10/89
Weather conditions								drought
South American Soybeans								
Brazil's soybeans	12.8	14.8	15.2	18.4	13.9	17.3	18.0	22.0
Argentina's soybeans	4.2	3.6	5.3	6.7	7.3	7.1	9.7	6.6
Total So.America prod.	17.0 mmt	18.4 mmt	18.5 mmt	25.1 mmt	21.2 mmt	24.4 mmt	27.7 mmt	28.6 mmt

South American Soybeans – in millions of metric tons. Their harvest is in our spring time – so their harvest affects our prices at the time of our harvest in the following autumn. Thus, their 1973 harvest affects the prices of our harvest for the 73/74 crop year.

5

U.S. SOYBEAN DATA – the soybean crop year begins on Sep. 1st and ends on Aug. 31st.

Crop year	89/90	90/91	91/92	92/93	93/94	94/95	95/96	96/97
Acres planted (millions)	60.8	57.8	59.2	59.2	60.1	61.7	62.6	64.2
Acres harvested	59.5	56.5	58.0	58.2	57.3	60.9	61.6	63.4
Yield (bu. per acre)	32.3	34.1	34.2	37.6	32.6	41.4	35.3	37.6
Begining stocks	182	239	329	278	292	209	335	184
Production (mil. bu.)	1924	1926	1987	2190	1871	2517	2177	2382
Total soybean supply	2108	2169	2319	2471	2170	2731	2516	2575
Domestic use & crush	1246	1282	1357	1409	1371	1558	1481	1562
Exports (mil. bu.)	623	951	684	770	589	838	851	882
Total soybean use	1869	1839	2044	2179	1960	2396	2332	2444
Carryover (mil.bu.)	239	329	278	292	209	335	184	131
Carryover as % of use	13%	18%	14%	13%	11%	14%	8%	5%
This year's total supply %	126%	116%	126%	121%	100%	139%	105%	110%
Last year's total use								
Nov. soybean data								
Highest price								
date of highest								
Lowest price								
date of lowest								
May soybean data								
Highest price								
date of highest								
Lowest price								
date of lowest								
Weather conditions								

South American Soybeans – in millions of metric tons. Their harvest is in our springtime – so their harvest affects our prices at the time of our Production harvest in the following autumn. Thus, their 1973 harvest affects the prices of our harvest for the 73/74 crop year.

Brazil's soybeans								
Argentina's soybeans								
Total So. American prod.								

6

WESTERN HEMISPHERE SOYBEAN SUPPLY and DEMAND – the Western Hemisphere exports about 90% of the world's exportable soybeans. Therefore world soybean prices are made by the soybean supply in this hemisphere. The combined total supply and demand of the U.S., Brazil, and Argentina in m.m.t.

All supplies are expressed in millions of metric tons.

Crop year	73/74	74/75	75/76	76/77	77/78	78/79	79/80	80/81
Beginning stocks (mmt)	1.7	7.9	10.3	11.8	8.7	8.9	10.1	16.4
Production	50.5	43.5	54.0	49.0	60.3	64.8	80.6	67.4
Total soybean supplies	52.2	51.4	64.3	60.8	69.0	73.7	90.7	83.8
Domestic use & crush	27.9	26.9	34.2	31.8	38.2	40.7	47.1	45.1
Exports	16.4	14.2	18.3	19.2	21.9	22.9	27.2	24.0
Total use	44.3	41.1	52.5	52.0	60.1	63.6	74.3	69.1
Carryover	7.9	10.3	11.8	8.7	8.9	10.1	16.4	14.7
Carryover as % of use	17.8%	25.0%	22.5%	16.7%	14.8%	16.0%	22.0%	21.3%
This year's total supply / Last year's total use		116%	156%	116%	133%	123%	143%	113%
Nov. soybean data								
Highest price	$9.29	$9.56	$6.53	$7.77	$7.98	$7.31	$8.33	$9.23
date of highest	Aug 14/73	Oct 4/74	Aug 20/75	July 7/76	June 7/77	Oct 30/78	June 22/79	Oct 30/80
Lowest price	$4.44	$5.08	$4.76 cycle lo	$5.04	$4.97	$5.86	$6.25	$6.43
date of lowest	May 17/73	May 7/74	Oct 28/75	May 3/76	Aug 16/77	Aug 8/78	Oct 29/79	May 19/80
May soybean data								
Highest price	$6.90	$9.71	$6.37	$10.76	$7.48	$7.30	$7.90	$10.06
date of highest	Feb 26/74	Oct 4/74	Sep 18/75	Apr 22/77	Mar 1/78	Feb 25/79	Sep 18/79	Nov 20/80
Lowest price	$4.44	$4.87	$4.58	$6.19	$5.23	$6.47	$5.70	$7.20
date of lowest	Nov 5/73	Mar 3/75	Dec 15/75	Oct 18/76	Sep 12/77	Sep 6/78	Apr 2/80	Mar 1/81

To change the U.S. bushels to metric tons, divide the U.S. bushels by 36.74.

WESTERN HEMISPHERE SOYBEAN SUPPLY and DEMAND

The Western Hemisphere exports about 90% of the world's exportable soybeans. Therefore world soybean prices are made by the soybean supply in this hemisphere. These numbers are the combined total soybean supplies of the U.S., Brazil, Argentina.

All supplies are expressed in millions of metric tons.

Crop year	81/82	82/83	83/84	84/85	85/86	86/87	87/88	88/89
Beginning stocks (mmt)	14.7	12.1	15.8	11.1	15.1	20.8	17.2	16.6
Production	71.8	78.0	65.4	76.1	78.6	77.5	80.5	70.9
Total soybean supply	86.5	90.1	81.2	87.2	93.7	98.3	97.7	87.5
Domestic use & crush	46.3	47.5	45.2	49.1	49.1	55.7	54.9	54.0
Exports	29.1	26.8	24.9	23.0	23.8	25.4	26.1	19.4
Total use	75.4	74.3	70.1	72.1	72.9	81.1	81.0	73.4
Carryover	12.1	15.8	11.1	15.1	20.8	17.2	16.7	14.1
Carryover as % of use	16.0%	21.3%	15.8%	21.0%	28.5%	21.2%	20.6%	19.2%
This year's total supply / Last year's total use	125%	120%	109%	124%	130%	135%	120%	108%
Nov. soybean data								
Highest price	$8.34	$6.85	$9.67	$7.71	$6.09	$5.52	$6.25	$6.90
date of highest	May 1/81	May 17/82	Aug 25/83	June 20/84	May 1/85	May 8/86	June 1/87	June 1/88
Lowest price	$6.37	$5.50	$5.98	$5.69	$4.97	$4.65 cycle low	$5.04	$7.06
date of lowest	Sep 28/81	Oct 14/82	Jun 26/83	Sep 21/84	Oct 16/85	Aug 25/86	Sep 1/87	May 4/88
May soybean data								
Highest price	$7.51	$6.56	$9.96	$6.77	$5.67	$5.35	$6.90	$9.12
date of highest	Sep 16/81	Apr 11/83	Sep 13/83	Nov 1/84	Apr 30/86	May 1/87	May 1/88	Sep 8/88
Lowest price	$6.06	$5.59	$7.06	$5.71	$4.89	$4.89	$5.22	$7.04
date of lowest	Mar 15/82	Oct 4/82	Feb 14/84	Mar 4/85	Nov 21/85	Dec 18/86	Sep 1/87	Apr 10/89

To change U.S. bushels to metric tons, divide the bushels by 36.74.

WESTERN HEMISPHERE SOYBEAN SUPPLY and DEMAND – The Western Hemisphere exports about 90% of the world's exportable soybeans. Therefore world soybean prices are made by the soybean supply in this hemisphere. These numbers are the combined total soybean supplies of the U.S., Brazil, Argentina.

All supplies are expressed in millions of metric tons.

Crop year	89/90	90/91	91/92	92/93	93/94	94/95	95/96	96/97
Beginning stocks (mmt)	___	___	___	___	___	___	___	___
Production	___	___	___	___	___	___	___	___
Total soybean supply	___	___	___	___	___	___	___	___
Domestic use & crush	___	___	___	___	___	___	___	___
Exports	___	___	___	___	___	___	___	___
Total use	___	___	___	___	___	___	___	___
Carryover	___	___	___	___	___	___	___	___
Carryover as % of use	___	___	___	___	___	___	___	___
This year's total supply / Last year's total use	___	___	___	___	___	___	___	___
Nov. soybean data Highest price	___	___	___	___	___	___	___	___
date of highest	___	___	___	___	___	___	___	___
Lowest price	___	___	___	___	___	___	___	___
date of lowest	___	___	___	___	___	___	___	___
May soybean data Highest price	___	___	___	___	___	___	___	___
date of highest	___	___	___	___	___	___	___	___
Lowest price	___	___	___	___	___	___	___	___
date of lowest	___	___	___	___	___	___	___	___

To change U.S. bushels to metric tons, divide the bushel by 36.74 .

9

TIME

There are 3 different time charts here for finding the "weeks to expiration".

1. A graph - instructions and an example are on the graph.

2. The Day Finder.   This is a precise method.

3. Special tables for the November and the May contracts.
   Because this book uses the November and the May contracts as the usual turning points for the soybean price trend - and consequently these 2 months are used more than the other month contracts - therefore special tables were constructed for November and May so that you can get the "weeks to expiration" quickly.

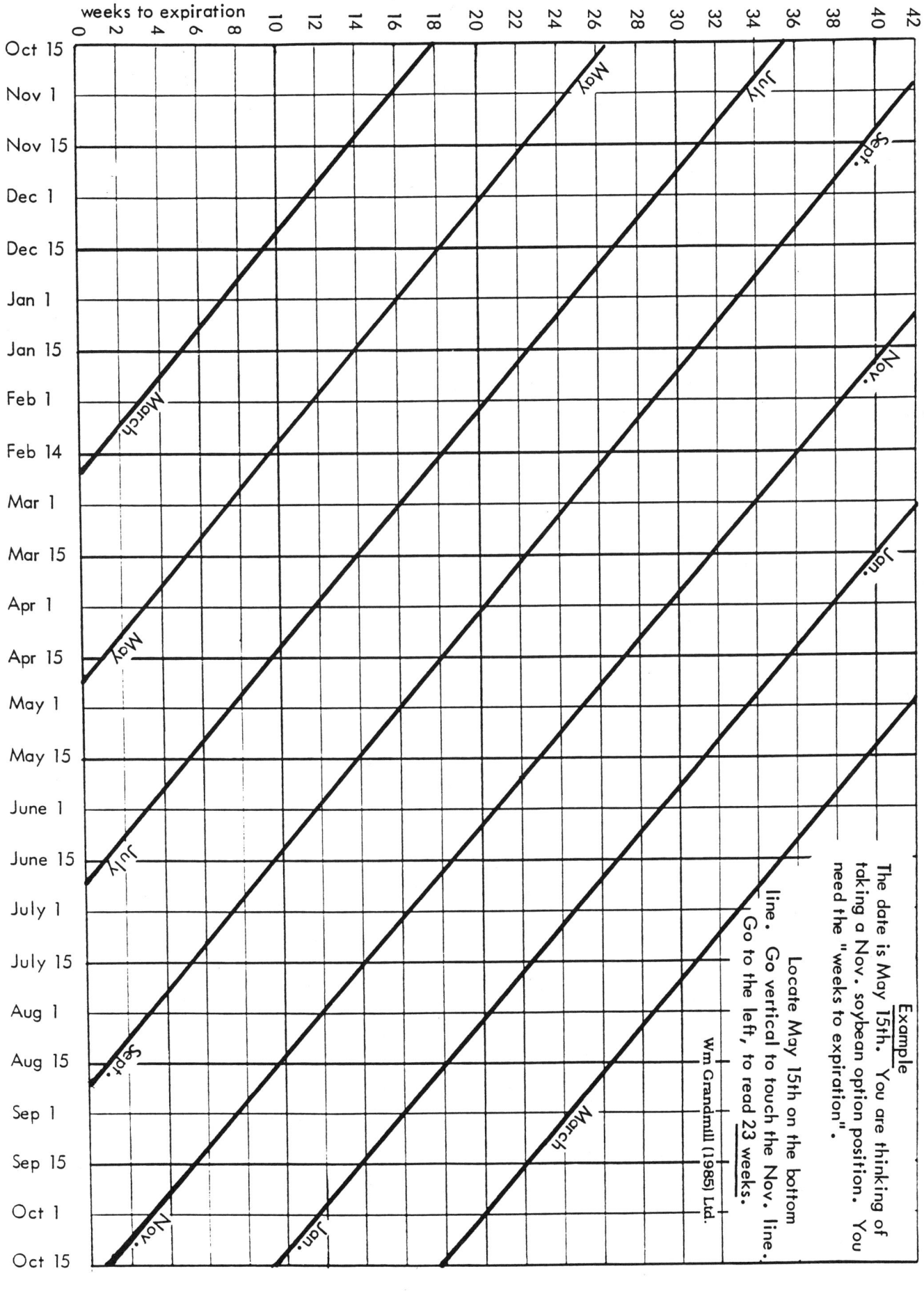

WEEKS TO EXPIRATION for Soybean Options – locate entry date at bottom, go vertical to option month line, then to the left for the weeks.

Example

The date is May 15th. You are thinking of taking a Nov. soybean option position. You need the "weeks to expiration".

Locate May 15th on the bottom line. Go vertical to touch the Nov. line. Go to the left, to read 23 weeks.

11

THE DAY FINDER – FIRST YEAR

TO FIND THE NUMBER OF DAYS BETWEEN TWO DATES

1. Locate the nearest date in the "first year" table.   2. Locate the other date (you may need the "second year" table).   3. Subtract the two amounts.

Day of month	Jan	Feb	Mar	Apr	May	Jun	Jul	Aug	Sep	Oct	Nov	Dec	Day of month
1	1	32	60	91	121	152	182	213	244	274	305	335	1
2	2	33	61	92	122	153	183	214	245	275	306	336	2
3	3	34	62	93	123	154	184	215	246	276	307	337	3
4	4	35	63	94	124	155	185	216	247	277	308	338	4
5	5	36	64	95	125	156	186	217	248	278	309	339	5
6	6	37	65	96	126	157	187	218	249	279	310	340	6
7	7	38	66	97	127	158	188	219	250	280	311	341	7
8	8	39	67	98	128	159	189	220	251	281	312	342	8
9	9	40	68	99	129	160	190	221	252	282	313	343	9
10	10	41	69	100	130	161	191	222	253	283	314	344	10
11	11	42	70	101	131	162	192	223	254	284	315	345	11
12	12	43	71	102	132	163	193	224	255	285	316	346	12
13	13	44	72	103	133	164	194	225	256	286	317	347	13
14	14	45	73	104	134	165	195	226	257	287	318	348	14
15	15	46	74	105	135	166	196	227	258	288	319	349	15
16	16	47	75	106	136	167	197	228	259	289	320	350	16
17	17	48	76	107	137	168	198	229	260	290	321	351	17
18	18	49	77	108	138	169	199	230	261	291	322	352	18
19	19	50	78	109	139	170	200	231	262	292	323	353	19
20	20	51	79	110	140	171	201	232	263	293	324	354	20
21	21	52	80	111	141	172	202	233	264	294	325	355	21
22	22	53	81	112	142	173	203	234	265	295	326	356	22
23	23	54	82	113	143	174	204	235	266	296	327	357	23
24	24	55	83	114	144	175	205	236	267	297	328	358	24
25	25	56	84	115	145	176	206	237	268	298	329	359	25
26	26	57	85	116	146	177	207	238	269	299	330	360	26
27	27	58	86	117	147	178	208	239	270	300	331	361	27
28	28	59	87	118	148	179	209	240	271	301	332	362	28
29	29		88	119	149	180	210	241	272	302	333	363	29
30	30		89	120	150	181	211	242	273	303	334	364	30
31	31		90		151		212	243		304		365	31

THE DAY FINDER – SECOND YEAR

Day of month	Jan	Feb	Mar	Apr	May	Jun	Jul	Aug	Sep	Oct	Nov	Dec	Day of month
1	366	397	425	456	486	517	547	578	609	639	670	700	1
2	367	398	426	457	487	518	548	579	610	640	671	701	2
3	368	399	427	458	488	519	549	580	611	641	672	702	3
4	369	400	428	459	489	520	550	581	612	642	673	703	4
5	370	401	429	460	490	521	551	582	613	643	674	704	5
6	371	402	430	461	491	522	552	583	614	644	675	705	6
7	372	403	431	462	492	523	553	584	615	645	676	706	7
8	373	404	432	463	493	524	554	585	616	646	677	707	8
9	374	405	433	464	494	525	555	586	617	647	678	708	9
10	375	406	434	465	495	526	556	587	618	648	679	709	10
11	376	407	435	466	496	527	557	588	619	649	680	710	11
12	377	408	436	467	497	528	558	589	620	650	681	711	12
13	378	409	437	468	498	529	559	590	621	651	682	712	13
14	379	410	438	469	499	530	560	591	622	652	683	713	14
15	380	411	439	470	500	531	561	592	623	653	684	714	15
16	381	412	440	471	501	532	562	593	624	654	685	715	16
17	382	413	441	472	502	533	563	594	625	655	686	716	17
18	383	414	442	473	503	534	564	595	626	656	687	717	18
19	384	415	443	474	504	535	565	596	627	657	688	718	19
20	385	416	444	475	505	536	566	597	628	658	689	719	20
21	386	417	445	476	506	537	567	598	629	659	690	720	21
22	387	418	446	477	507	538	568	599	630	660	691	721	22
23	388	419	447	478	508	539	569	600	631	661	692	722	23
24	389	420	448	479	509	540	570	601	632	662	693	723	24
25	390	421	449	480	510	541	571	602	633	663	694	724	25
26	391	422	450	481	511	542	572	603	634	664	695	725	26
27	392	423	451	482	512	543	573	604	635	665	696	726	27
28	393	424	452	483	513	544	574	605	636	666	697	727	28
29	394		453	484	514	545	575	606	637	667	698	728	29
30	395		454	485	515	546	576	607	638	668	699	729	30
31	396		455		516		577	608		669		730	31

March	weeks	April	weeks	May	weeks	June	weeks	July	weeks	Aug	weeks	Sept	weeks	Oct	weeks
1	33.4	1	29.0	1	24.7	1	20.3	1	16.0	1	11.6	1	7.1	1	2.9
2	33.3	2	28.9	2	24.6	2	20.1	2	15.9	2	11.4	2	7.0	2	2.7
3	33.1	3	28.7	3	24.4	3	20.0	3	15.7	3	11.3	3	6.9	3	2.6
4	33.0	4	28.6	4	24.3	4	19.9	4	15.6	4	11.1	4	6.7	4	2.4
5	32.9	5	28.4	5	24.1	5	19.7	5	15.4	5	11.0	5	6.6	5	2.3
6	32.7	6	28.3	6	24.0	6	19.6	6	15.3	6	10.9	6	6.4	6	2.1
7	32.6	7	28.1	7	23.9	7	19.4	7	15.1	7	10.7	7	6.3	7	2.0
8	32.4	8	28.0	8	23.7	8	19.3	8	15.0	8	10.6	8	6.1	8	1.9
9	32.3	9	27.9	9	23.6	9	19.1	9	14.9	9	10.4	9	6.0	9	1.7
10	32.1	10	27.7	10	23.4	10	19.0	10	14.7	10	10.3	10	5.9	10	1.6
11	32.0	11	27.6	11	23.3	11	18.9	11	14.6	11	10.1	11	5.7	11	1.4
12	31.9	12	27.4	12	23.1	12	18.7	12	14.4	12	10.0	12	5.6	12	1.3
13	31.7	13	27.3	13	23.0	13	18.6	13	14.3	13	9.9	13	5.4	13	1.1
14	31.6	14	27.1	14	22.9	14	18.4	14	14.1	14	9.7	14	5.3	14	1.0
15	31.4	15	27.0	15	22.7	15	18.3	15	14.0	15	9.6	15	5.1	15	0.9
16	31.3	16	26.9	16	22.6	16	18.1	16	13.9	16	9.4	16	5.0	16	0.7
17	31.1	17	26.7	17	22.4	17	18.0	17	13.7	17	9.3	17	4.9	17	0.6
18	31.0	18	26.6	18	22.3	18	17.9	18	13.6	18	9.1	18	4.7	18	0.4
19	30.9	19	26.4	19	22.1	19	17.7	19	13.4	19	9.0	19	4.6	19	0.3
20	30.7	20	26.3	20	22.0	20	17.6	20	13.3	20	8.9	20	4.4	20	0.1
21	30.5	21	26.1	21	21.9	21	17.4	21	13.1	21	8.7	21	4.3	21	0.0
22	30.4	22	26.0	22	21.7	22	17.3	22	13.0	22	8.6	22	4.1		
23	30.3	23	25.9	23	21.6	23	17.1	23	12.9	23	8.4	23	4.0		
24	30.1	24	25.7	24	21.4	24	17.0	24	12.7	24	8.3	24	3.9		
25	30.0	25	25.6	25	21.3	25	16.9	25	12.6	25	8.1	25	3.7		
26	29.9	26	25.4	26	21.1	26	16.7	26	12.4	26	8.0	26	3.6		
27	29.7	27	25.3	27	21.0	27	16.6	27	12.3	27	7.9	27	3.4		
28	29.6	28	25.1	28	20.9	28	16.4	28	12.1	28	7.7	28	3.3		
29	29.4	29	25.0	29	20.7	29	16.3	29	12.0	29	7.6	29	3.1		
30	29.3	30	24.9	30	20.6	30	16.1	30	11.9	30	7.4	30	3.0		
31	29.1			31	20.4			31	11.7	31	7.3				

November is an important and popular month for soybean options and futures because it occurs just as the soybean harvest is being completed. Therefore this table will make it quicker and easier for you to find the weeks to expiration for the November contract. Just select the date on which you are taking your option and read the weeks to expiration opposite it. Then consult the Forecasting Graphs to get the estimated price direction and the amount of price rise or fall. Then turn to the appropriate option chart to find which option tactic will be the safest and most profitable, and you can get an estimated percentage profit on your investment.

WEEKS TO EXPIRATION FOR MAY SOYBEAN OPTIONS

Day	Sept weeks	Oct weeks	Nov weeks	Dec weeks	Jan weeks	Feb weeks	Mar weeks	Apr weeks
1	33.1	28.9	24.4	20.1	15.7	11.3	7.3	2.9
2	33.0	28.7	24.3	20.0	15.6	11.1	7.1	2.7
3	32.9	28.6	24.1	19.9	15.4	11.0	7.0	2.6
4	32.7	28.4	24.0	19.7	15.3	10.9	6.9	2.4
5	32.6	28.3	23.9	19.6	15.1	10.7	6.7	2.3
6	32.4	28.1	23.7	19.4	15.0	10.6	6.6	2.1
7	32.3	28.0	23.6	19.3	14.9	10.4	6.4	2.0
8	32.1	27.9	23.4	19.1	14.7	10.3	6.3	1.9
9	32.0	27.7	23.3	19.0	14.6	10.1	6.1	1.7
10	31.9	27.6	23.1	18.9	14.4	10.0	6.0	1.6
11	31.7	27.4	23.0	18.7	14.3	9.9	5.9	1.4
12	31.6	27.3	22.9	18.6	14.1	9.7	5.7	1.3
13	31.4	27.1	22.7	18.4	14.0	9.6	5.6	1.1
14	31.3	27.0	22.6	18.3	13.9	9.4	5.4	1.0
15	31.1	26.9	22.4	18.1	13.7	9.3	5.3	0.9
16	31.0	26.7	22.3	18.0	13.6	9.1	5.1	0.7
17	30.9	26.6	22.1	17.9	13.4	9.0	5.0	0.6
18	30.7	26.4	22.0	17.7	13.3	8.9	4.9	0.4
19	30.6	26.3	21.9	17.6	13.1	8.7	4.7	0.3
20	30.4	26.1	21.7	17.4	13.0	8.6	4.6	0.1
21	30.3	26.0	21.6	17.3	12.9	8.4	4.4	0.0
22	30.1	25.9	21.4	17.1	12.7	8.3	4.3	
23	30.0	25.7	21.3	17.0	12.6	8.1	4.1	
24	29.9	25.6	21.1	16.9	12.4	8.0	4.0	
25	29.7	25.4	21.0	16.7	12.3	7.9	3.9	
26	29.6	25.3	20.9	16.6	12.1	7.7	3.7	
27	29.4	25.1	20.7	16.4	12.0	7.6	3.6	
28	29.3	25.0	20.6	16.3	11.9	7.4	3.4	
29	29.1	24.9	20.4	16.1	11.7		3.3	
30	29.0	24.7	20.3	16.0	11.6		3.1	
31		24.6		15.9	11.4		3.0	

May is an important and popular month in soybean futures and options because the effect of the South American soybean crop becomes evident as their soybean harvest gains full momentum in late April and May. Therefore this table will make it easier and quicker for you to find the "weeks to expiration" for this important month. The size of the South American soybean production will greatly affect our soybean prices from April to August. But from September to April, it is the U.S. soybean crop which dominates the Chicago prices.

PRICE

How to use the Forecasting Graphs.

1. Locate the carryover % at the left side of the graph for the desired contract month.

2. Move to the right to touch the heavy curved line.

3. Go straight down to the bottom line to read the estimated "right price".

4. By "right price" is meant the price at which soybeans should be in the future, based on the present supply and demand data.   But soybean prices are fickle – so the final price is not likely to correspond exactly with the "right price", but it should be close.

5. In this book, "price change" is important.   By "price change" is meant the amount of price movement as indicated by the Forecasting Graphs.   For example, the date is Nov. 15th and you are going to take a May soybean option.   The present price of May beans on Nov. 15th is $6.   The May Forecasting Graph indicates that the price should rise to $7 on May 1st.   Therefore, the "price change" is estimated at $1.

Estimated SEPT. SOYBEAN PRICE on Sept. 1st.

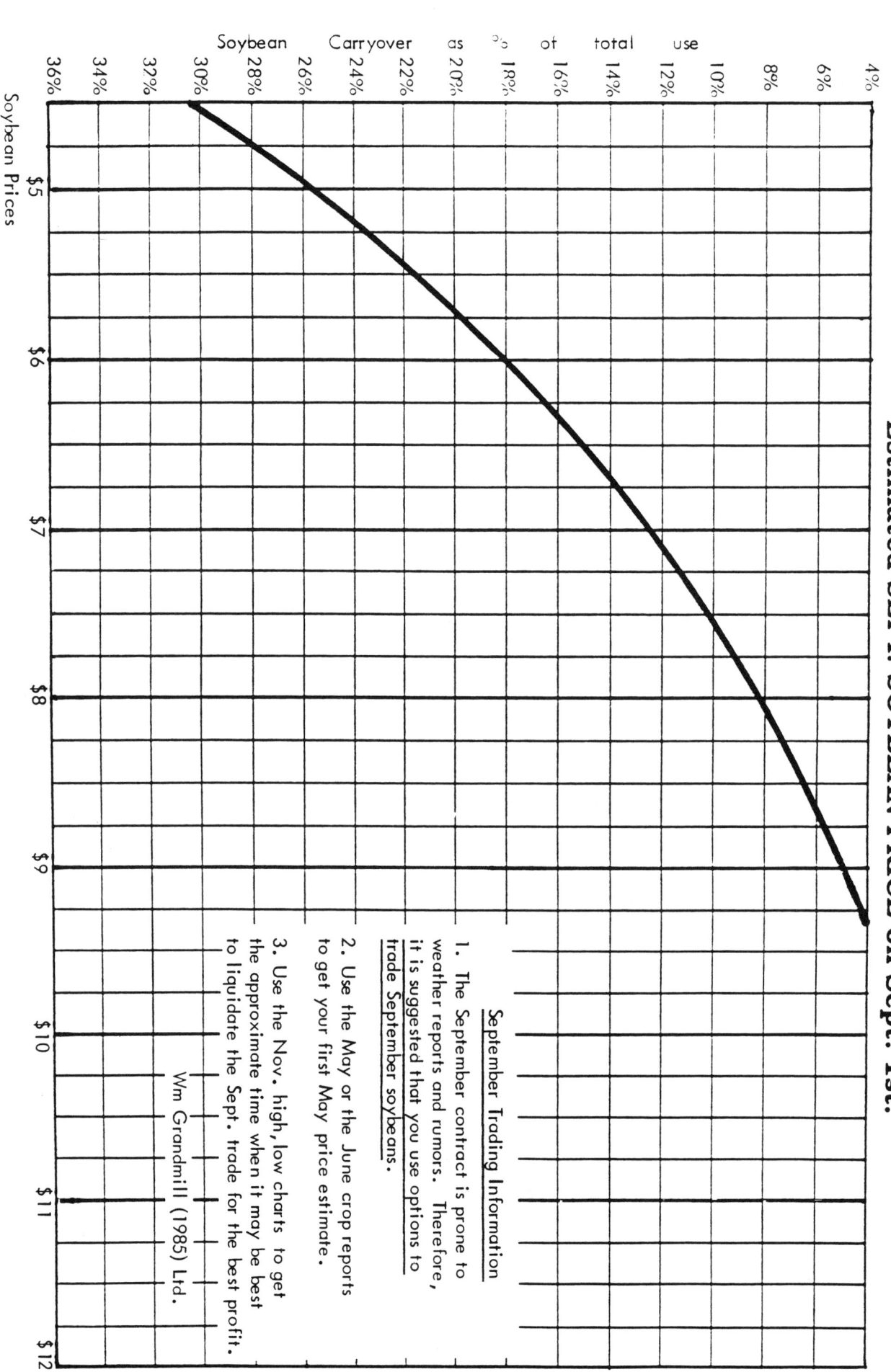

Soybean Carryover as % of total use

Soybean Prices

$5 $6 $7 $8 $9 $10 $11 $12

4% 6% 8% 10% 12% 14% 16% 18% 20% 22% 24% 26% 28% 30% 32% 34% 36%

September Trading Information

1. The September contract is prone to weather reports and rumors. Therefore, it is suggested that you use options to trade September soybeans.

2. Use the May or the June crop reports to get your first May price estimate.

3. Use the Nov. high, low charts to get the approximate time when it may be best to liquidate the Sept. trade for the best profit.

Wm Grandmill (1985) Ltd.

Estimated NOV. SOYBEAN PRICE on Nov. 1st.

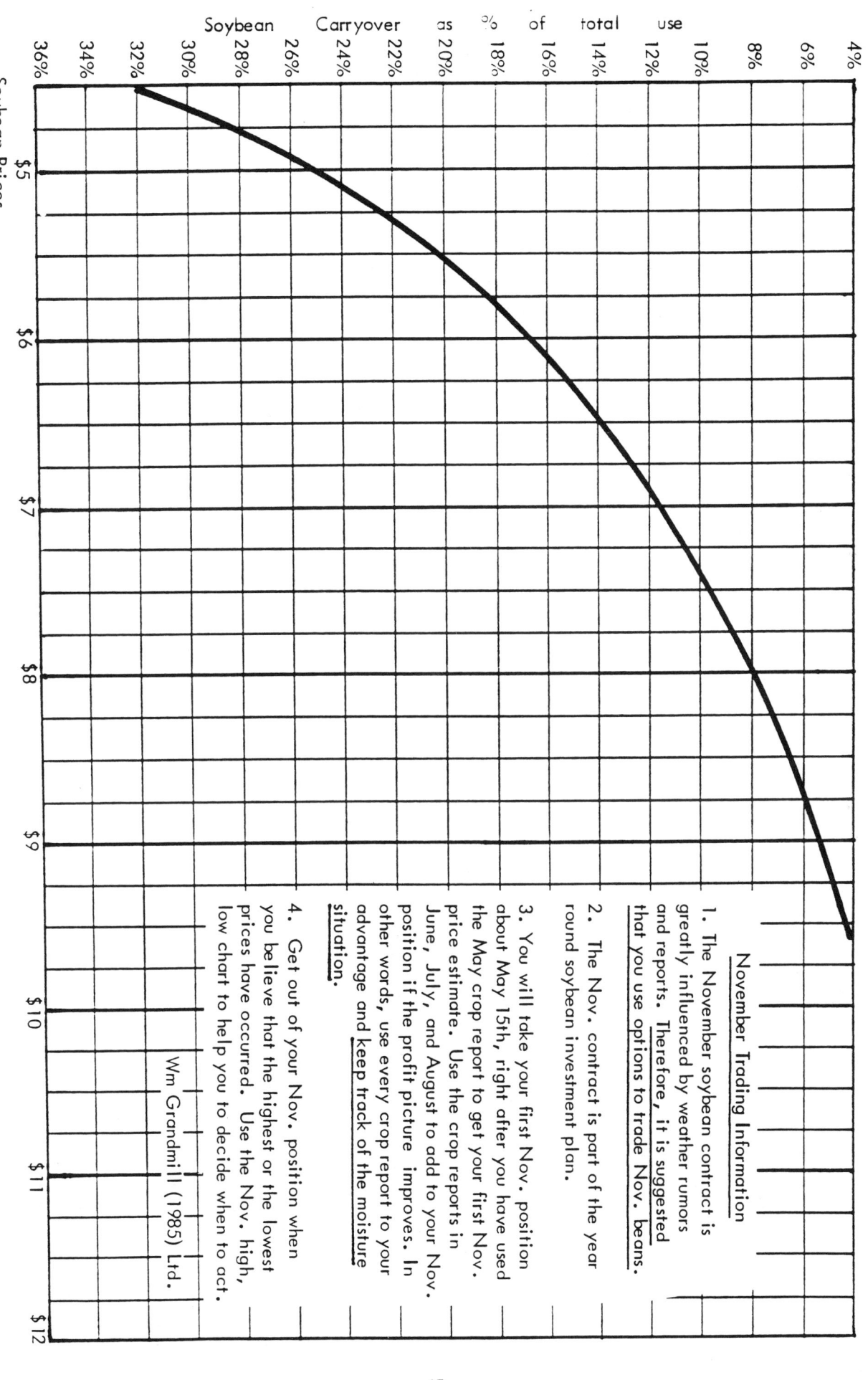

Soybean Carryover as % of total use % Soybean Prices

4%
6%
8%
10%
12%
14%
16%
18%
20%
22%
24%
26%
28%
30%
32%
34%
36%

$5
$6
$7
$8
$9
$10
$11
$12

November Trading Information

1. The November soybean contract is greatly influenced by weather rumors and reports. Therefore, it is suggested that you use options to trade Nov. beans.

2. The Nov. contract is part of the year round soybean investment plan.

3. You will take your first Nov. position about May 15th, right after you have used the May crop report to get your first Nov. price estimate. Use the crop reports in June, July, and August to add to your Nov. position if the profit picture improves. In other words, use every crop report to your advantage and keep track of the moisture situation.

4. Get out of your Nov. position when you believe that the highest or the lowest prices have occurred. Use the Nov. high, low chart to help you to decide when to act.

Wm Grandmill (1985) Ltd.

17

Estimated JAN. SOYBEAN PRICE on Jan. 1st.

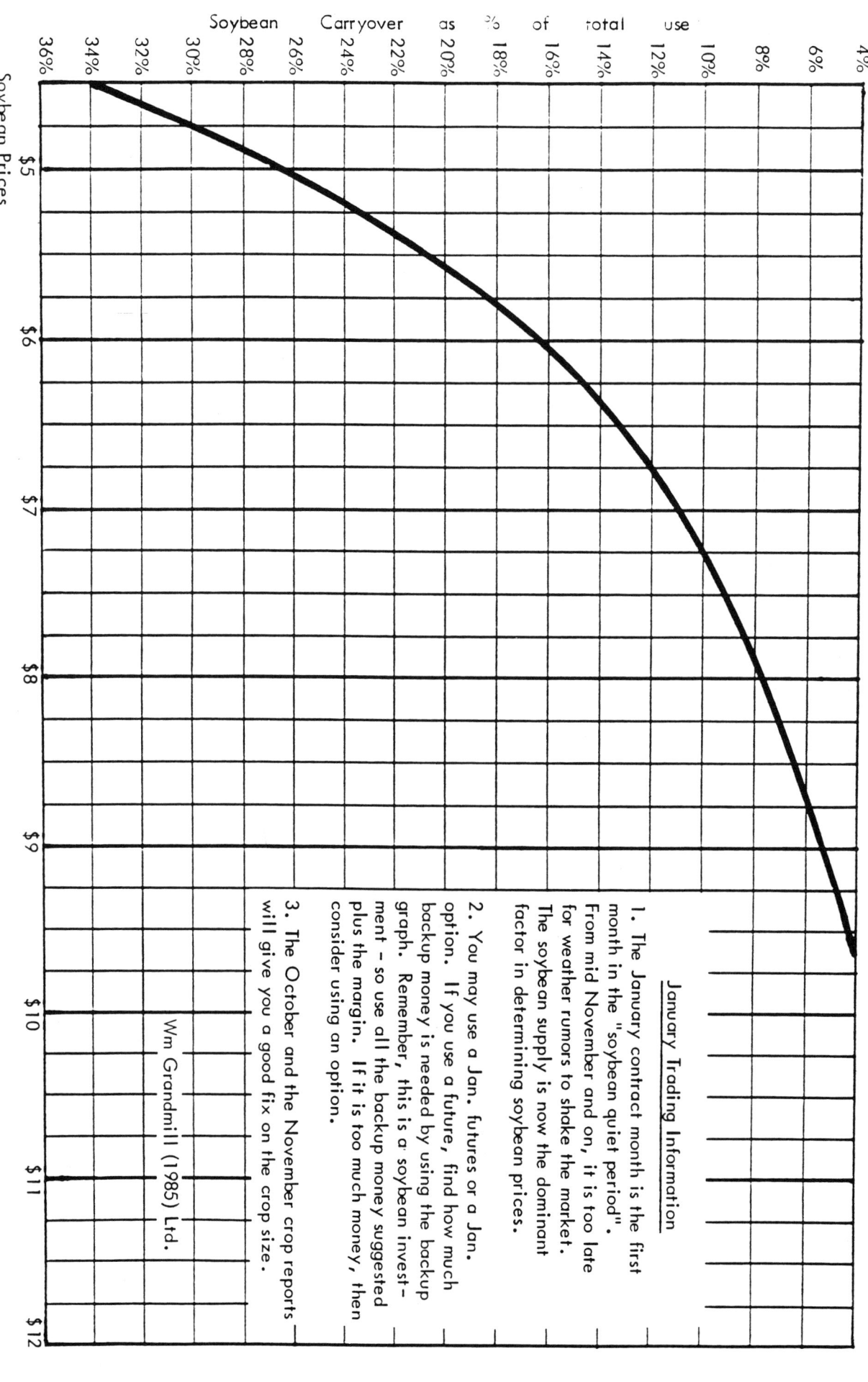

January Trading Information

1. The January contract month is the first month in the "soybean quiet period". From mid November and on, it is too late for weather rumors to shake the market. The soybean supply is now the dominant factor in determining soybean prices.

2. You may use a Jan. futures or a Jan. option. If you use a future, find how much backup money is needed by using the backup graph. Remember, this is a soybean investment - so use all the backup money suggested plus the margin. If it is too much money, then consider using an option.

3. The October and the November crop reports will give you a good fix on the crop size.

Wm Grandmill (1985) Ltd.

Estimated MARCH SOYBEAN PRICE on March 1st.

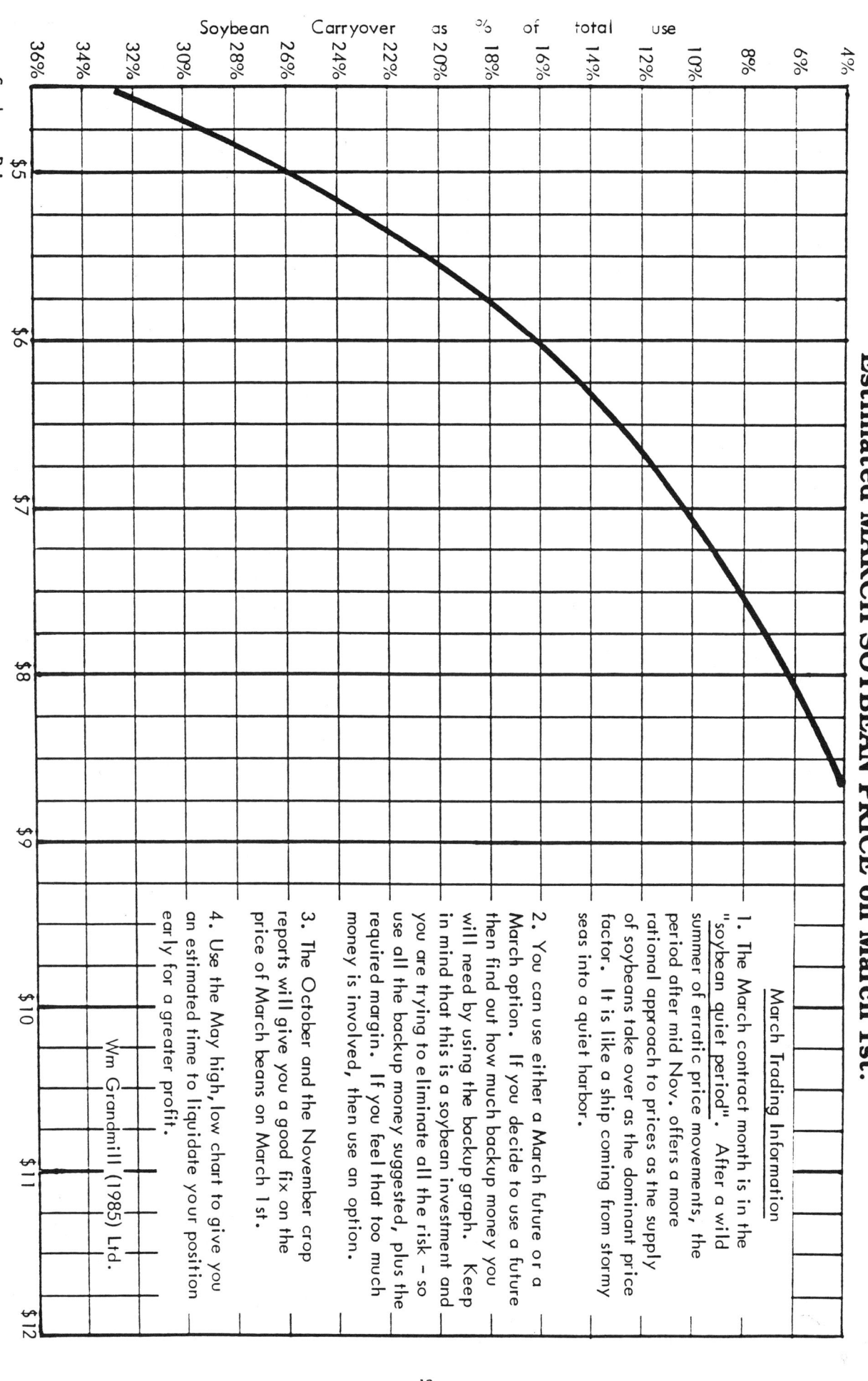

Carryover Soybean use as % of total use

Soybean Prices

Wm Grandmill (1985) Ltd.

March Trading Information

1. The March contract month is in the "soybean quiet period". After a wild summer of erratic price movements, the period after mid Nov. offers a more rational approach to prices as the dominant price factor. It is like a ship coming from stormy seas into a quiet harbor.

2. You can use either a March future or a March option. If you decide to use a future then find out how much backup money you will need by using the backup graph. Keep in mind that this is a soybean investment and you are trying to eliminate all the risk – so use all the backup money suggested, plus the required margin. If you feel that too much money is involved, then use an option.

3. The October and the November crop reports will give you a good fix on the price of March beans on March 1st.

4. Use the May high, low chart to give you an estimated time to liquidate your position early for a greater profit.

Estimated MAY SOYBEAN PRICE on May 1st.

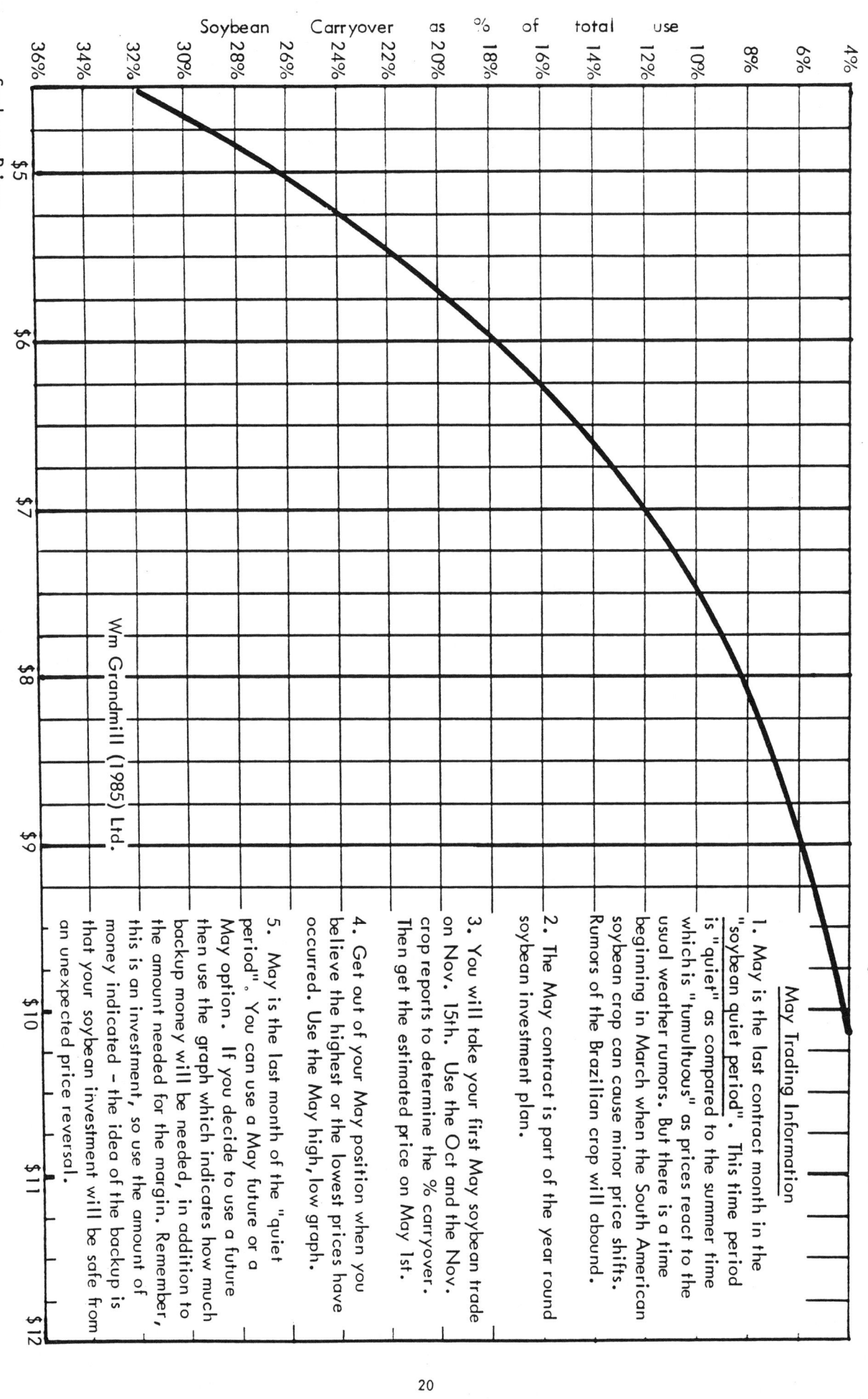

Soybean Carryover as % of total use

Soybean Prices

$5 $6 $7 $8 $9 $10 $11 $12

4% 6% 8% 10% 12% 14% 16% 18% 20% 22% 24% 26% 28% 30% 32% 34% 36%

Wm Grandmill (1985) Ltd.

<u>May Trading Information</u>

1. May is the last contract month in the "soybean quiet period". This time period is "quiet" as compared to the summer time which is "tumultuous" as prices react to the usual weather rumors. But there is a time beginning in March when the South American soybean crop can cause minor price shifts. Rumors of the Brazilian crop will abound.

2. The May contract is part of the year round soybean investment plan.

3. You will take your first May soybean trade on Nov. 15th. Use the Oct and the Nov. crop reports to determine the % carryover. Then get the estimated price on May 1st.

4. Get out of your May position when you believe the highest or the lowest prices have occurred. Use the May high, low graph.

5. May is the last month of the "quiet period". You can use a May future or a May option. If you decide to use a future then use the graph which indicates how much backup money will be needed, in addition to the amount needed for the margin. Remember, this is an investment, so use the amount of money indicated – the idea of the backup is that your soybean investment will be safe from an unexpected price reversal.

Estimated JULY SOYBEAN PRICE on July 1st.

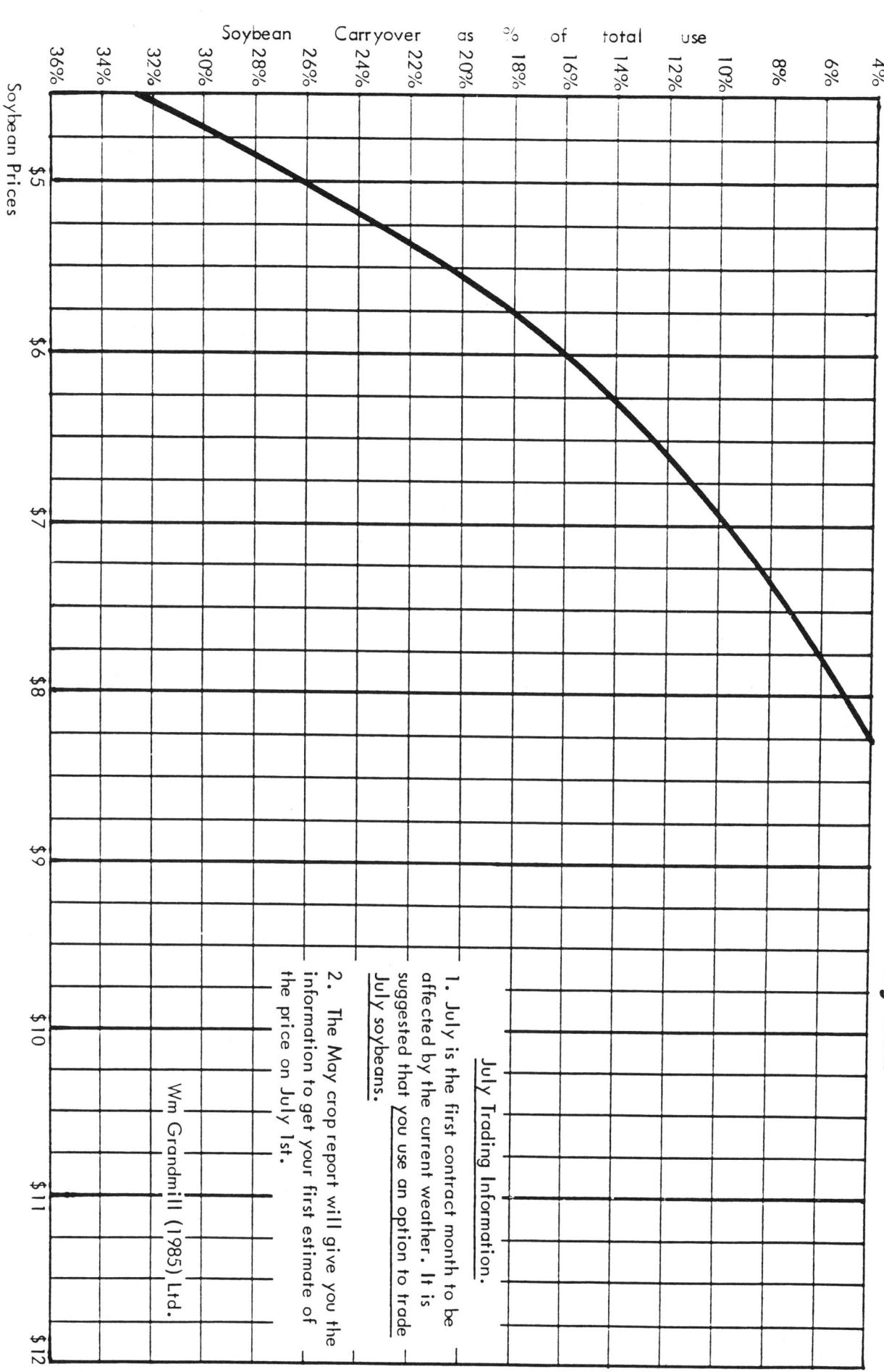

Carryover Soybean as % of total use

Soybean Prices

36% 34% 32% 30% 28% 26% 24% 22% 20% 18% 16% 14% 12% 10% 8% 6% 4%

$5 $6 $7 $8 $9 $10 $11 $12

July Trading Information.

1. July is the first contract month to be affected by the current weather. It is suggested that _you use an option to trade July soybeans._

2. The May crop report will give you the information to get your first estimate of the price on July 1st.

Wm Grandmill (1985) Ltd.

Estimated NOV. SOYBEAN PRICE on Nov. 1st using

New Total Supply
Last year's Total Use

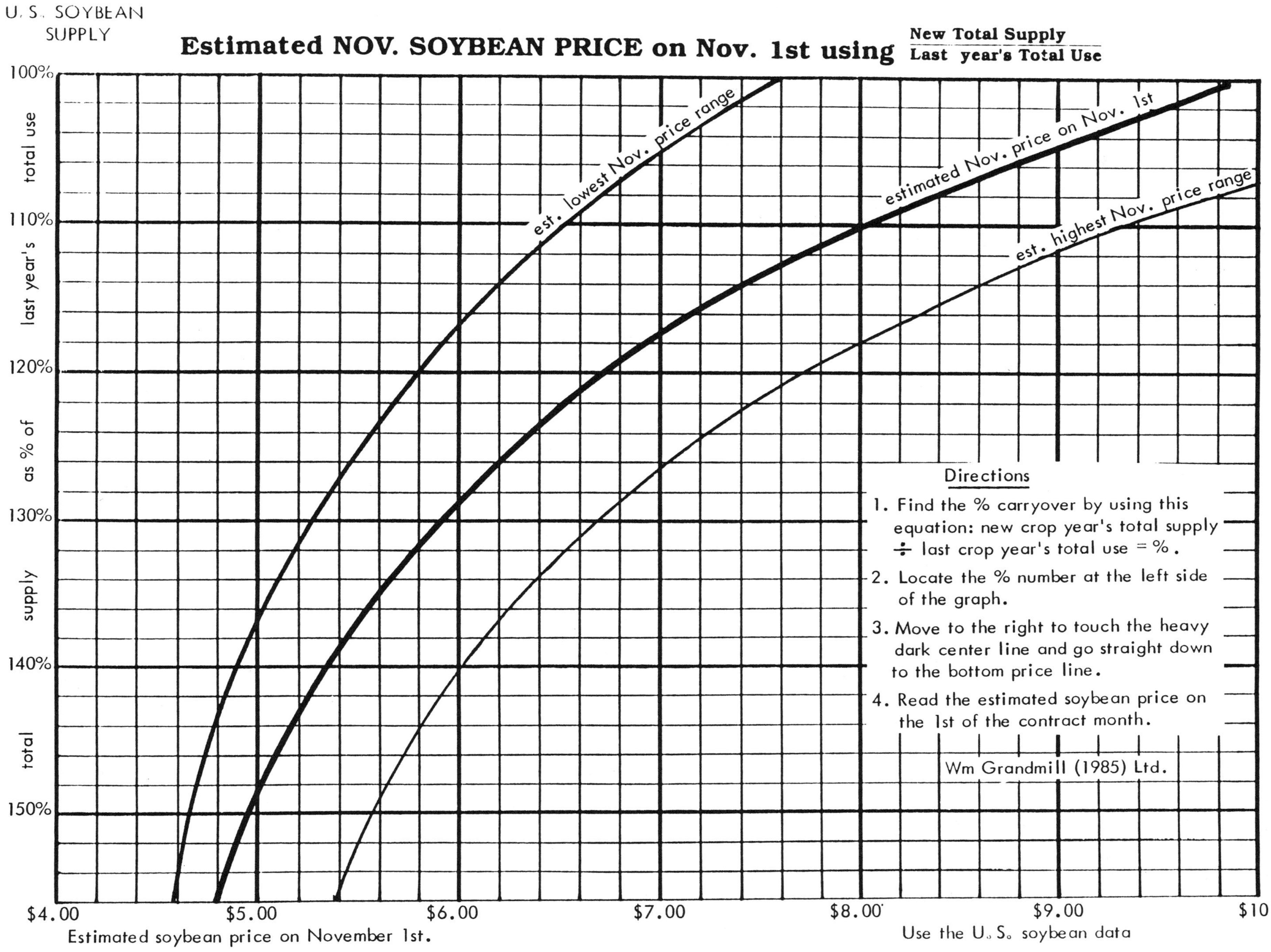

100%

total use

110%

last year's

120%

as % of

130%

supply

140%

total

150%

$4.00

$5.00

$6.00

$7.00

$8.00

$9.00

$10

Estimated soybean price on November 1st.

est. lowest Nov. price range

estimated Nov. price on Nov. 1st

est. highest Nov. price range

Use the U.S. soybean data

Directions

1. Find the % carryover by using this equation: new crop year's total supply ÷ last crop year's total use = %.

2. Locate the % number at the left side of the graph.

3. Move to the right to touch the heavy dark center line and go straight down to the bottom price line.

4. Read the estimated soybean price on the 1st of the contract month.

Wm Grandmill (1985) Ltd.

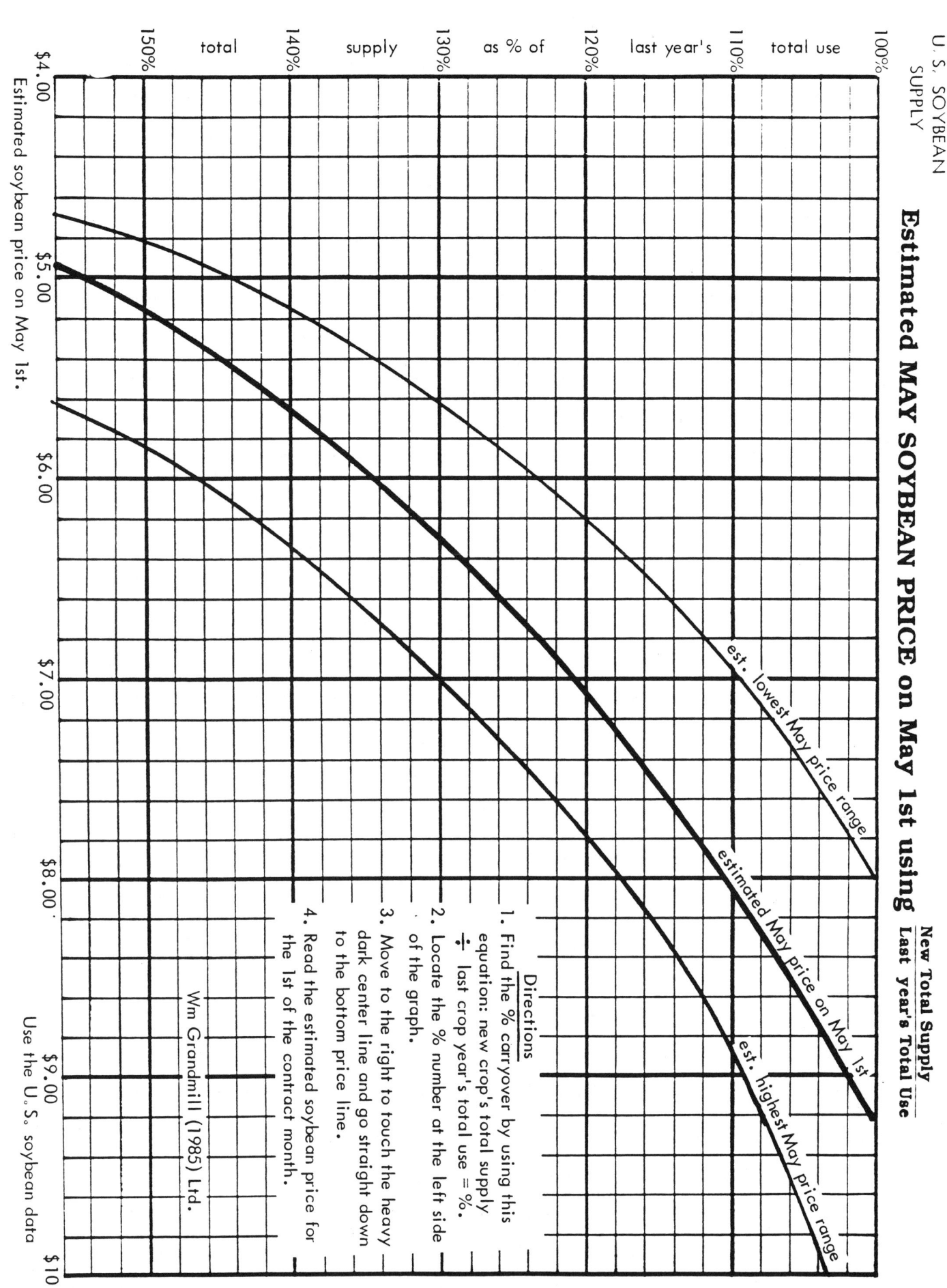

U. S. SOYBEAN SUPPLY

Estimated MAY SOYBEAN PRICE on May 1st using $\dfrac{\text{New Total Supply}}{\text{Last year's Total Use}}$

total use

last year's

as % of

supply

total

100% 110% 120% 130% 140% 150%

Estimated soybean price on May 1st.

$4.00 $5.00 $6.00 $7.00 $8.00 $9.00 $10

est. lowest May price range

estimated May price on May 1st

est. highest May price range

Directions

1. Find the % carryover by using this equation: new crop's total supply ÷ last crop year's total use = %.

2. Locate the % number at the left side of the graph.

3. Move to the right to touch the heavy dark center line and go straight down to the bottom price line.

4. Read the estimated soybean price for the 1st of the contract month.

Wm Grandmill (1985) Ltd.

Use the U.S. soybean data

23

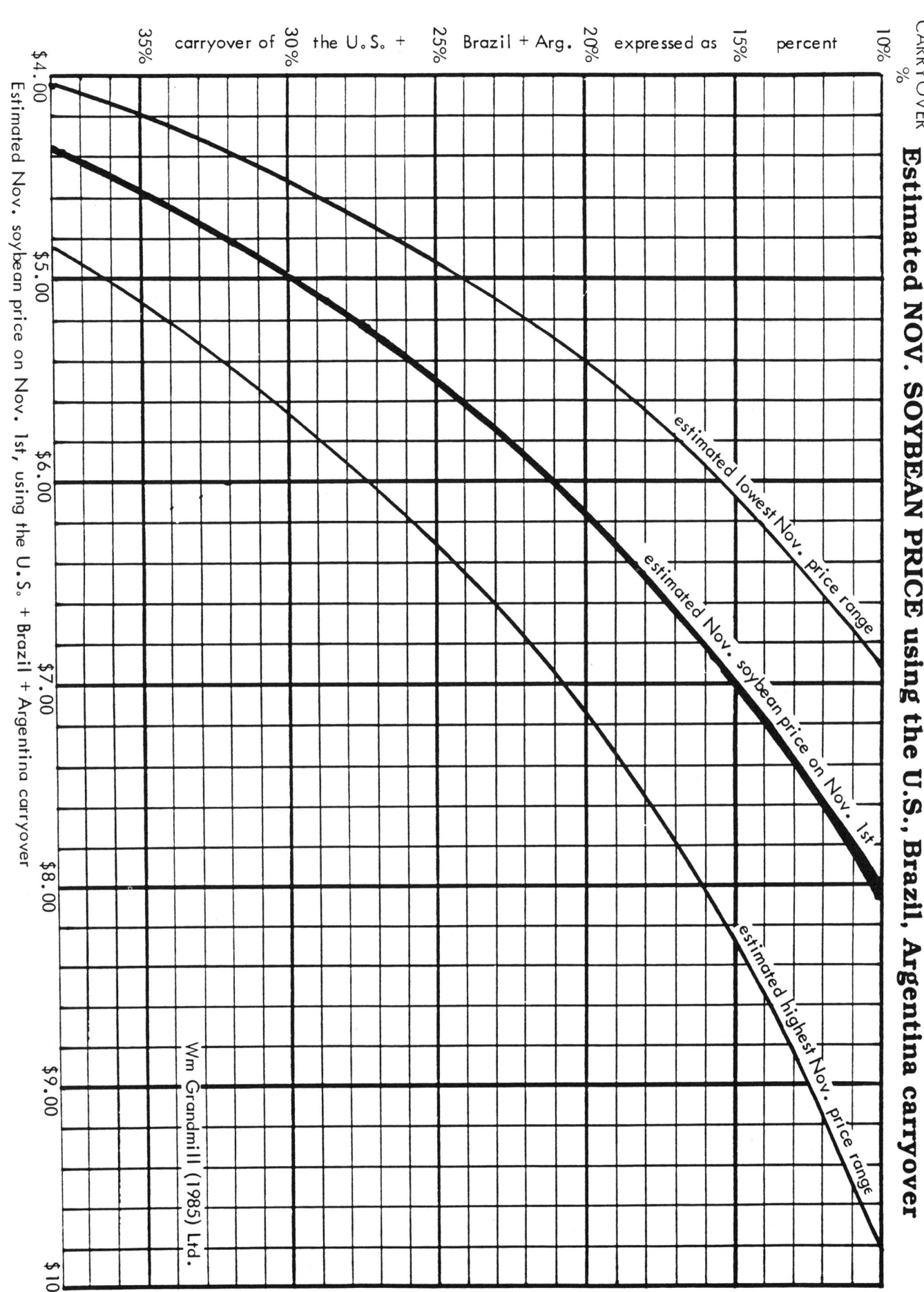

Estimated NOV. SOYBEAN PRICE using the U.S., Brazil, Argentina carryover

USING THE CARRYOVER %

carryover of the U.S. + Brazil + Arg. expressed as percent

estimated lowest Nov. price range

estimated Nov. soybean price on Nov. 1st

estimated highest Nov. price range

Estimated Nov. soybean price on Nov. 1st, using the U.S. + Brazil + Argentina carryover

Wm Grandmill (1985) Ltd.

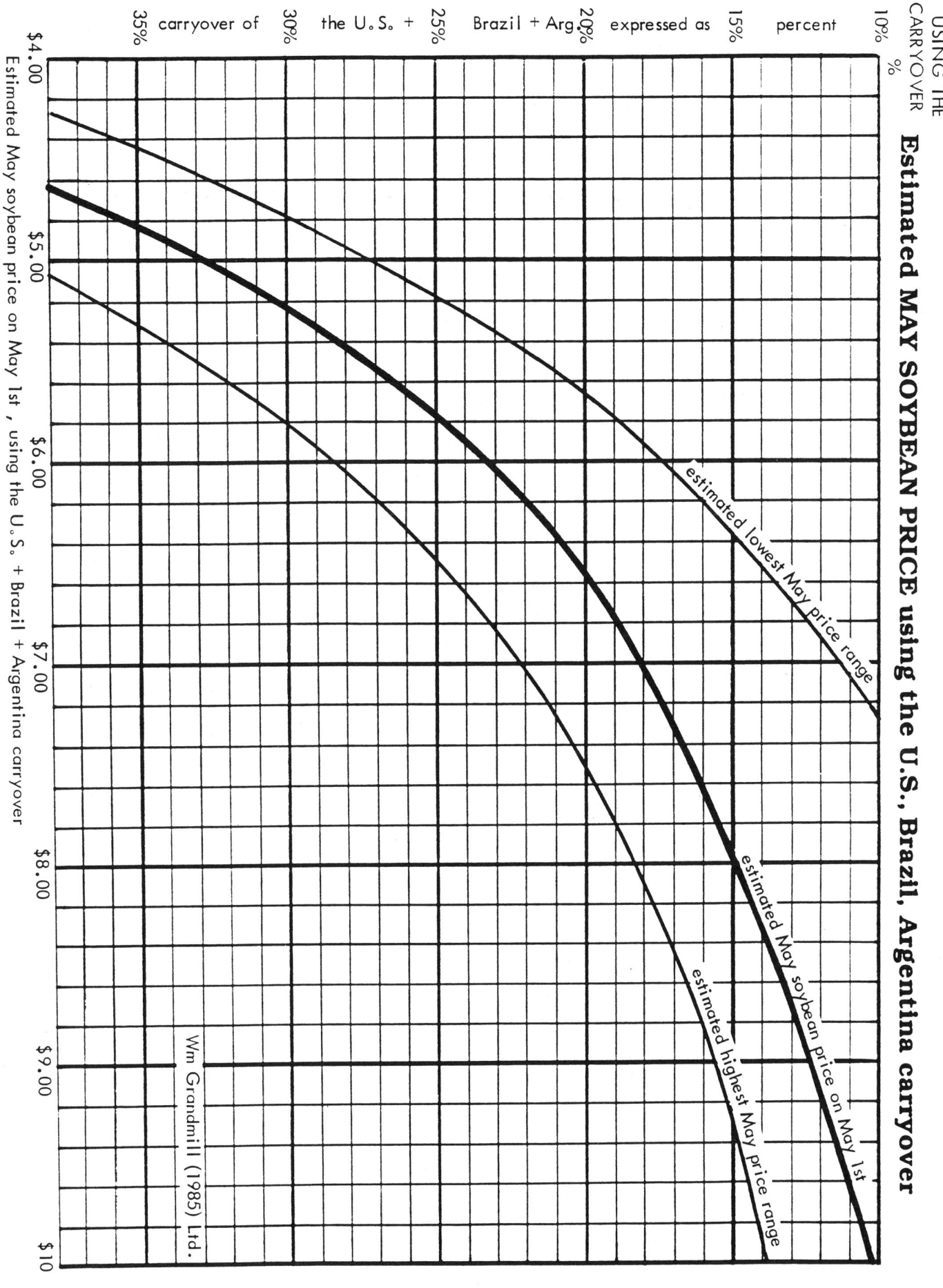

Estimated MAY SOYBEAN PRICE using the U.S., Brazil, Argentina carryover

USING THE CARRYOVER %

carryover of the U.S. + Brazil + Arg. expressed as percent

estimated lowest May price range

estimated May soybean price on May 1st

estimated highest May price range

Estimated May soybean price on May 1st, using the U.S. + Brazil + Argentina carryover

Wm Grandmill (1985) Ltd.

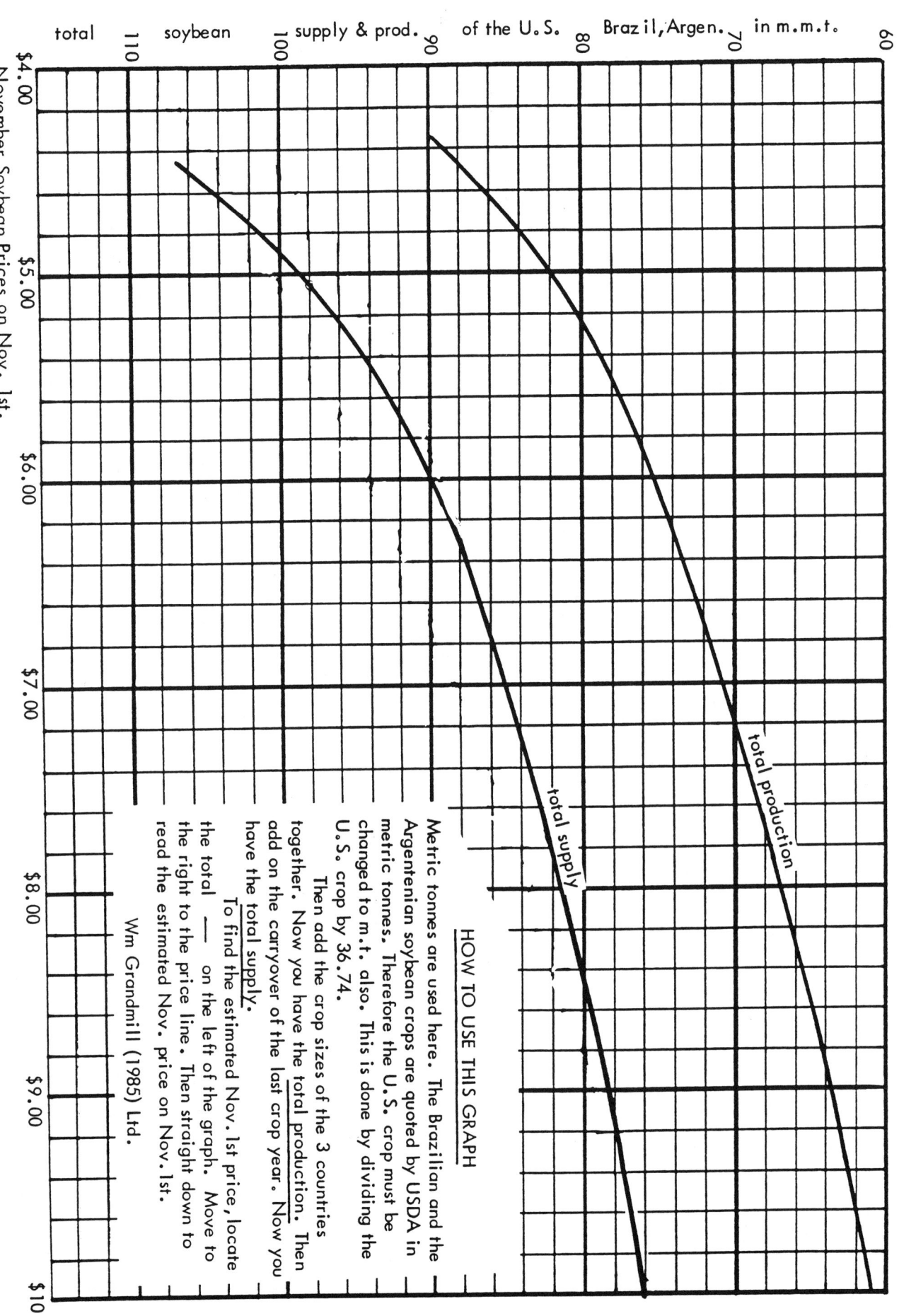

NOV. SOYBEANS   Finding the Nov. Soybean price by using the <u>Total Production</u> & <u>Total Supply</u> of the U.S., Brazil, Argentina in million metric tonnes

total   soybean   supply & prod.   of the U.S.   Brazil, Argen.   in m.m.t.

November Soybean Prices on Nov. 1st.

$4.00 $5.00 $6.00 $7.00 $8.00 $9.00 $10

total production

total supply

HOW TO USE THIS GRAPH

Metric tonnes are used here. The Brazilian and the Argentenian soybean crops are quoted by USDA in metric tonnes. Therefore the U.S. crop must be changed to m.t. also. This is done by dividing the U.S. crop by 36.74.

Then add the crop sizes of the 3 countries together. Now you have the total production. Then add on the carryover of the last crop year. Now you have the <u>total supply</u>.

To find the estimated Nov. 1st price, locate the total ⸺ on the left of the graph. Move to the right to the price line. Then straight down to read the estimated Nov. price on Nov. 1st.

Wm Grandmill (1985) Ltd.

VOLATILITY

This is where we deal with the volatility of the soybean market at the time when we are taking a position in either futures or in options.

What is "volatility"?   It is the speed at which the soybean prices change. For example, in a dull listless market, volatility is said to be low.   Whereas in a wild market, such as one might see in the summer when a drought threatens and prices are jumping all over the place, then one would say that the volatility is high.

Volatility affects the option premium. Here's a valid comparison.   When the vilatility is low, then one would see a 18¢ premium for a 20 weeks to expiration. But when the volatility is high, then one could expect a 42¢ premium for a 20 weeks to expiration option.   There is a saying, "Be a buyer when the volatility is low, and be a seller when the volatility is high".

How is "volatility" expressed?   Most books just use words such as "low, high, very high, etc". But that wasn't accurate enough for this author.   By doing months of research on every soybean option from the date of their conception, and by using the prices of the time and for every "weeks to expiration" time interval, this author put all the data together to construct option tables which told an option trader not only what would occur at the date of expiration, but, more importantly, what happens to the value of the option "in between"- between the time the trader takes the option, to the date of expiration.   This is an important area because very few traders hold their option to the expiration date – instead, they get out early if their profit target is touched. But up until my option tables were constructed, as far as I know, there were no tables or information which told a trader what happened to the option value "in between" as prices and time were changing the option's value.

Ninety – six option tables were constructed, numbered 1 to 96.   Table 1 represented a "very low" volatility, and Table 96 represented a "very high" volatility.   Just to put the tables in perspective, Table 1 has such a low volatility that you will never use that table in your lifetime; and Table 96 represents such a high volatility that you might , maybe, use it once in your lifetime. These tables are in my book "Make Money With Soybean Options", published and sold by Windsor Books, P.O. Box 280, Brightwaters, N.Y. 11718.

The Soybean Option Tables were used to calculate the option values in this book.   The Table Finder pages will be used to find the appropriate Table Number which represents the degree of the volatility at the time that you are taking your option position.   To use these pages, you will need to calculate the "at the money" option value, which means that you will have to interpolate between the strike prices displayed in your morning paper or on your quote screen.   The instructions are given on the Table Finder page.

TABLE FINDER

It is important that you select the appropriate table of option values – the table which best reflects the implied volatility of the option month you are using. To select the table, do this:

1. Find the "Weeks to Expiration" of the option month you are using.
2. Find the "at the money" option price.
3. Look vertically in the selected "weeks to expiration" column until you come as close as possible to the "at the money" price found in (2.) above.
4. Look to the right to find the Table number.

35	34	33	32	31	30	29	28	27	26	25	24	23	22	21	20	19	Table
7.3	7.2	7.1	7.0	6.9	6.8	6.7	6.6	6.5	6.4	6.3	6.2	6.1	6.0	5.9	5.8	5.7	1
8.1	8.0	7.9	7.8	7.7	7.6	7.5	7.4	7.3	7.2	7.1	7.0	6.9	6.8	6.7	6.6	6.5	2
8.9	8.8	8.7	8.6	8.5	8.4	8.3	8.2	8.1	8.0	7.9	7.8	7.7	7.6	7.5	7.3	7.2	3
9.9	9.8	9.7	9.6	9.5	9.3	9.2	9.1	9.0	8.8	8.7	8.6	8.5	8.4	8.2	8.1	7.9	4
10.7	10.6	10.5	10.4	10.3	10.1	10.0	9.9	9.8	9.6	9.5	9.4	9.3	9.1	9.0	8.8	8.6	5
11.7	11.6	11.5	11.3	11.2	11.0	10.8	10.7	10.6	10.5	10.3	10.2	10.0	9.9	9.7	9.6	9.4	6
12.5	12.4	12.3	12.1	12.0	11.8	11.7	11.5	11.4	11.3	11.1	11.0	10.8	10.6	10.5	10.3	10.1	7
13.5	13.4	13.2	13.0	12.9	12.7	12.5	12.4	12.2	12.1	11.9	11.7	11.6	11.4	11.2	11.0	10.8	8
14.3	14.2	14.0	13.8	13.6	13.5	13.4	13.2	13.0	12.9	12.7	12.5	12.3	12.2	12.0	11.8	11.5	9
15.2	15.1	14.9	14.8	14.6	14.4	14.2	14.0	13.8	13.7	13.5	13.3	13.1	12.9	12.7	12.5	12.2	10
16.0	15.9	15.7	15.6	15.4	15.2	15.0	14.8	14.7	14.5	14.3	14.1	13.9	13.7	13.5	13.2	13.0	11
16.8	16.7	16.5	16.4	16.2	16.0	15.9	15.7	15.5	15.3	15.1	14.9	14.7	14.4	14.2	14.0	13.7	12
17.8	17.7	17.5	17.3	17.1	16.9	16.7	16.5	16.3	16.1	15.9	15.7	15.5	15.2	15.0	14.7	14.4	13
18.6	18.5	18.3	18.1	17.9	17.7	17.5	17.3	17.1	16.9	16.7	16.5	16.2	16.0	15.7	15.4	15.1	14
19.5	19.3	19.1	18.9	18.7	18.5	18.3	18.1	17.9	17.7	17.5	17.2	17.0	16.7	16.4	16.1	15.8	15
20.4	20.2	20.0	19.8	19.6	19.4	19.2	19.0	18.8	18.5	18.3	18.0	17.8	17.5	17.2	16.9	16.6	16
21.2	21.0	20.8	20.6	20.4	20.2	20.0	19.8	19.6	19.3	19.1	18.8	18.5	18.2	17.9	17.6	17.3	17
22.1	21.9	21.7	21.5	21.3	21.1	20.9	20.6	20.4	20.1	19.9	19.6	19.3	19.0	18.7	18.4	18.4	18
23.0	22.8	22.6	22.4	22.2	21.9	21.7	21.4	21.2	20.9	20.6	20.3	20.0	19.7	19.4	19.1	18.7	19
35	34	33	32	31	30	29	28	27	26	25	24	23	22	21	20	19	

WEEKS TO EXPIRATION

WM GRANDMILL (1985) LTD.

TABLE FINDER

It is important that you select the appropriate table of option values – the table which best reflects the implied volatility of the option month you are using. To select the table, do this:

1. Find the "Weeks to Expiration" of the option month you are using.
2. Find the "at the money" option price.
3. Look vertically in the selected "weeks to expiration" column until you come as close as possible to the "at the money" price found in (2.) above.
4. Look to the right to find the Table number.

18	17	16	15	14	13	12	11	10	9	8	7	6	5	4	3	2	Table
5.6	5.5	5.4	5.2	5.1	5.0	4.8	4.6	4.4	4.2	4.0	3.7	3.5	3.2	2.7	2.2	1.6	1
6.3	6.2	6.0	5.9	5.7	5.6	5.4	5.2	5.0	4.8	4.5	4.2	3.9	3.6	3.0	2.4	1.8	2
7.0	6.9	6.8	6.6	6.4	6.2	6.0	5.8	5.6	5.3	5.0	4.7	4.4	4.0	3.4	2.7	2.0	3
7.7	7.6	7.4	7.2	7.0	6.8	6.6	6.4	6.1	5.8	5.5	5.2	4.8	4.3	3.7	3.0	2.2	4
8.5	8.3	8.1	7.9	7.7	7.5	7.2	6.9	6.6	6.3	6.0	5.6	5.2	4.7	4.0	3.2	2.4	5
9.2	8.9	8.7	8.5	8.3	8.1	7.8	7.5	7.2	6.9	6.5	6.1	5.6	5.1	4.4	3.5	2.6	6
9.9	9.6	9.4	9.2	9.0	8.7	8.4	8.1	7.9	7.4	7.0	6.6	6.1	5.5	4.7	3.5	2.8	7
10.6	10.3	10.1	9.8	9.6	9.3	9.0	8.7	8.3	7.9	7.5	7.0	6.5	5.8	5.0	4.1	3.0	8
11.3	11.0	10.8	10.5	10.2	9.9	9.6	9.2	8.8	8.4	8.0	7.5	7.0	6.3	5.4	4.3	3.2	9
12.0	11.7	11.4	11.1	10.8	10.5	10.2	9.8	9.4	9.0	8.5	8.0	7.4	6.7	5.7	4.6	3.4	10
12.7	12.4	12.1	11.8	11.5	11.2	10.8	10.4	10.0	9.5	9.0	8.4	7.8	7.1	6.0	4.9	3.6	11
13.4	13.1	12.8	12.5	12.1	11.8	11.4	11.0	10.5	10.0	9.5	8.9	8.3	7.5	6.4	5.1	3.8	12
14.1	13.8	13.5	13.1	12.8	12.4	12.0	11.6	11.1	10.6	10.0	9.4	8.6	7.7	6.7	5.4	4.0	13
14.8	14.5	14.2	13.8	13.4	13.0	12.6	12.1	11.6	11.1	10.5	9.8	9.0	8.1	7.0	5.7	4.2	14
15.5	15.2	14.8	14.4	14.0	13.6	13.2	12.7	12.2	11.6	11.0	10.3	9.4	8.5	7.3	6.0	4.4	15
16.2	15.8	15.5	15.1	14.7	14.3	13.8	13.3	12.7	12.1	11.5	10.8	9.9	8.9	7.6	6.2	4.6	16
16.9	16.5	16.2	15.7	15.3	14.9	14.4	13.9	13.3	12.7	12.0	11.2	10.3	9.3	8.0	6.5	4.8	17
17.6	17.2	16.8	16.4	16.0	15.5	15.0	14.4	13.8	13.2	12.5	11.7	10.8	9.7	8.3	6.8	5.0	18
18.3	17.9	17.5	17.0	16.6	16.1	15.6	15.0	14.4	13.7	13.0	12.2	11.2	10.0	8.6	7.0	5.2	19
18	17	16	15	14	13	12	11	10	9	8	7	6	5	4	3	2	

WEEKS TO EXPIRATION

35	34	33	32	31	30	29	28	27	26	25	24	23	22	21	20	19	Table
24.0	23.8	23.6	23.4	23.1	22.8	22.5	22.2	22.0	21.7	21.4	21.1	20.8	20.5	20.2	19.8	19.4	20
24.8	24.6	24.4	24.2	23.9	23.6	23.4	23.1	22.8	22.5	22.2	21.9	21.6	21.3	20.9	20.5	20.1	21
25.7	25.5	25.3	25.1	24.8	24.5	24.2	23.9	23.6	23.3	23.0	22.7	22.4	22.0	21.7	21.3	20.9	22
26.6	26.4	26.2	25.9	25.6	25.3	25.0	24.7	24.4	24.1	23.8	23.5	23.1	22.8	22.4	22.0	21.6	23
27.5	27.2	27.0	26.7	26.4	26.1	25.8	25.5	25.2	24.9	24.6	24.3	23.9	23.6	23.2	22.8	22.3	24
28.4	28.2	27.9	27.6	27.3	27.0	26.7	26.4	26.1	25.7	25.4	25.1	24.7	24.3	23.9	23.5	23.0	25
29.2	29.0	28.7	28.4	28.1	27.8	27.5	27.2	26.9	26.5	26.2	25.9	25.5	25.1	24.7	24.2	23.7	26
30.2	29.9	29.6	29.3	29.0	28.7	28.4	28.0	27.7	27.3	27.0	26.6	26.2	25.8	25.4	25.0	24.5	27
31.0	30.7	30.4	30.1	29.8	29.5	29.2	28.8	28.5	28.2	27.8	27.4	27.0	26.6	26.2	25.7	25.2	28
31.9	31.6	31.3	31.0	30.7	30.4	30.1	29.8	29.4	29.0	28.6	28.2	27.8	27.4	26.9	26.4	25.9	29
32.7	32.4	32.1	31.8	31.5	31.2	30.9	30.6	30.2	29.8	29.4	29.0	28.6	28.1	27.6	27.1	26.6	30
33.6	33.3	33.0	32.7	32.4	32.1	31.7	31.3	31.0	30.6	30.2	29.8	29.3	28.9	28.4	27.9	27.3	31
34.5	34.2	33.9	33.6	33.3	32.9	32.6	32.2	31.8	31.4	31.0	30.6	30.1	29.6	29.1	28.6	28.1	32
35.4	35.1	34.8	34.5	34.2	33.8	33.4	33.0	32.6	32.2	31.8	31.3	30.9	30.4	29.9	29.4	28.8	33
36.2	35.9	35.6	35.3	35.0	34.6	34.2	33.8	33.4	33.0	32.6	32.1	31.6	31.1	30.6	30.1	29.5	34
37.1	36.8	36.5	36.2	35.9	35.4	35.0	34.6	34.2	33.8	33.4	32.9	32.4	31.9	31.4	30.8	30.2	35
38.1	37.8	37.5	37.1	36.7	36.3	35.9	35.4	35.0	34.6	34.2	33.7	33.2	32.7	32.1	31.5	30.9	36
38.9	38.6	38.3	37.9	37.5	37.1	36.7	36.2	35.8	35.4	34.9	34.4	33.9	33.4	32.9	32.3	31.7	37
39.9	39.6	39.1	38.8	38.4	38.0	37.5	37.1	36.7	36.2	35.7	35.2	34.7	34.2	33.6	33.0	32.4	38
40.7	40.3	40.0	39.6	39.2	38.8	38.4	38.0	37.5	37.0	36.5	36.0	35.5	34.9	34.4	33.8	33.1	39
41.5	41.2	40.8	40.4	40.0	39.6	39.2	38.8	38.3	37.8	37.3	36.8	36.3	35.7	35.1	34.5	33.8	40
42.5	42.1	41.7	41.3	40.9	40.5	40.1	39.6	39.1	38.6	38.1	37.6	37.1	36.5	35.9	35.2	34.5	41
43.4	43.0	42.6	42.2	41.8	41.4	40.9	40.4	39.9	39.4	38.9	38.4	37.8	37.2	36.6	36.0	35.3	42
44.2	43.8	43.4	43.0	42.6	42.2	41.7	41.2	40.7	40.2	39.7	39.2	38.6	38.0	37.7	36.7	36.0	43
45.0	44.6	44.2	43.8	43.3	43.0	42.5	42.0	41.5	41.0	40.5	39.9	39.3	38.7	38.1	37.4	36.7	44
46.0	45.6	45.2	44.8	44.4	43.9	43.4	42.9	42.3	41.8	41.3	40.7	40.1	39.5	38.9	38.2	37.4	45
46.8	46.4	46.0	45.6	45.2	44.7	44.2	43.7	43.2	42.6	42.1	41.5	40.9	40.3	39.6	38.9	38.1	46
47.6	47.2	46.8	46.4	46.0	45.5	45.0	44.5	44.0	43.5	42.9	42.3	41.7	41.0	40.3	39.6	38.8	47
48.5	48.1	47.7	47.3	46.9	46.4	45.9	45.3	44.8	44.2	43.7	43.1	42.5	41.8	41.1	40.4	39.6	48
49.4	49.0	48.6	48.2	47.7	47.2	46.7	46.1	45.6	45.0	44.5	43.9	43.2	42.5	41.8	41.1	40.3	49
50.3	49.9	49.5	49.1	48.6	48.1	47.6	47.0	46.4	45.8	45.2	44.6	44.0	43.3	42.6	41.8	41.0	50
51.4	51.0	50.5	50.0	49.5	49.0	48.4	47.8	47.2	46.6	46.0	45.4	44.7	44.0	43.3	42.6	41.8	51
52.2	51.8	51.3	50.8	50.3	49.8	40.2	48.6	48.0	47.4	46.8	46.2	45.5	44.8	44.1	43.3	42.5	52

WM GRANDMILL (1985) LTD.

18	17	16	15	14	13	12	11	10	9	8	7	6	5	4	3	2	Table
19.0	18.6	18.1	17.7	17.2	16.7	16.2	15.6	14.9	14.2	13.5	12.7	11.7	10.4	9.0	7.3	5.4	20
19.7	19.3	18.8	18.3	17.9	17.4	16.8	16.2	15.5	14.8	14.0	13.1	12.1	10.8	9.3	7.6	5.6	21
20.4	20.0	19.5	19.0	18.5	18.0	17.4	16.7	16.0	15.3	14.5	13.6	12.5	11.1	9.6	7.8	5.8	22
21.1	20.6	20.2	19.7	19.2	18.6	18.0	17.3	16.6	15.8	15.0	14.0	13.0	11.5	10.0	8.1	6.0	23
21.8	21.3	20.8	20.3	19.8	19.2	18.6	17.9	17.2	16.4	15.5	14.5	13.4	11.9	10.3	8.4	6.2	24
22.5	22.0	21.5	21.0	20.4	19.8	19.2	18.5	17.7	16.9	16.0	15.0	13.8	12.3	10.7	8.7	6.4	25
23.2	22.7	22.2	21.6	21.1	20.5	19.8	19.1	18.3	17.4	16.5	15.5	14.3	12.7	11.0	8.9	6.6	26
24.0	23.4	22.8	22.3	21.7	21.1	20.4	19.6	18.8	18.0	17.0	15.9	14.7	13.1	11.3	9.4	6.8	27
24.7	24.1	23.5	22.9	22.3	21.7	21.0	20.2	19.4	18.5	17.5	16.4	15.1	13.5	11.7	9.5	7.0	28
25.4	24.8	24.2	23.6	23.0	22.3	21.6	20.8	19.9	19.0	18.0	16.9	15.6	13.8	12.0	9.7	7.2	29
26.1	25.5	24.9	24.2	23.6	22.9	22.2	21.4	20.5	19.5	18.5	17.2	16.0	14.2	12.3	10.0	7.4	30
26.8	26.2	25.5	24.9	24.3	23.6	22.8	21.9	21.0	20.1	19.0	17.8	16.4	14.6	12.7	10.3	7.6	31
27.5	26.9	26.2	25.6	24.9	24.2	23.4	22.5	21.6	20.6	19.5	18.3	16.8	15.0	13.0	10.6	7.8	32
28.2	27.5	26.9	26.2	25.5	24.8	24.0	23.1	22.1	21.1	20.0	18.7	17.4	15.8	13.4	10.8	8.0	33
28.9	28.2	27.6	26.9	26.2	25.4	24.6	23.7	22.7	21.6	20.5	19.2	17.7	15.7	13.7	11.1	8.2	34
29.6	28.9	28.2	27.5	26.8	26.0	25.2	24.2	23.3	22.2	21.0	19.7	18.1	16.1	14.0	11.4	8.4	35
30.3	29.6	28.9	28.2	27.5	26.7	25.8	24.8	23.8	22.7	21.5	20.1	18.6	16.5	14.3	11.6	8.6	36
31.0	30.3	29.6	28.8	28.1	27.3	26.4	25.4	24.4	23.2	22.0	20.6	19.0	16.9	14.7	11.9	8.8	37
31.7	31.0	30.3	29.5	28.7	27.9	27.0	26.0	24.9	23.8	22.5	21.1	19.5	17.8	15.1	12.2	9.0	38
32.4	31.7	30.9	30.1	29.4	28.5	27.6	26.6	25.5	24.3	23.0	21.6	19.9	17.8	15.3	12.4	9.2	39
33.1	32.4	31.6	30.8	30.0	29.1	28.2	27.1	26.0	24.8	23.5	22.0	20.3	18.0	15.7	12.7	9.4	40
33.8	33.0	32.2	31.4	30.6	29.8	28.8	27.7	26.6	25.3	24.0	22.5	20.7	18.4	16.0	13.0	9.6	41
34.5	33.7	32.9	32.1	31.3	30.4	29.4	28.3	27.1	25.9	24.5	23.0	21.2	18.8	16.3	13.3	9.8	42
35.2	34.4	33.6	32.8	31.9	31.0	30.0	28.9	27.7	26.4	25.0	23.8	21.6	19.2	16.7	13.5	10.0	43
35.9	35.1	34.3	33.4	32.5	31.6	30.6	29.4	28.2	26.9	25.5	23.9	22.0	19.6	17.0	13.5	10.2	44
36.6	35.8	35.0	34.1	33.2	32.2	31.2	30.0	28.8	27.5	26.0	24.4	22.5	20.0	17.3	14.1	10.4	45
37.3	36.5	35.6	34.7	33.8	32.8	31.8	30.6	29.4	28.0	26.5	24.8	22.9	20.4	17.6	14.3	10.6	46
38.0	37.2	36.3	35.4	34.5	33.5	32.4	31.2	29.9	28.5	27.0	25.3	23.3	20.7	18.0	14.6	10.8	47
38.7	37.9	37.0	36.1	35.1	34.1	33.0	31.8	30.5	29.0	27.5	25.8	23.8	21.1	18.3	14.9	11.0	48
39.4	38.5	37.6	36.7	35.7	34.7	33.6	32.3	31.0	29.6	28.0	26.3	24.2	21.5	18.6	15.2	11.2	49
40.2	39.3	38.4	37.4	36.4	35.3	34.2	32.9	31.6	30.1	28.5	26.7	24.6	21.9	19.0	15.4	11.4	50
40.9	40.0	39.0	38.0	37.0	35.9	34.8	33.5	32.1	30.6	29.0	27.2	25.1	22.3	19.3	15.7	11.6	51
41.5	40.6	39.7	38.7	37.7	36.6	35.4	34.1	32.7	31.2	29.5	27.6	25.5	22.7	19.6	16.0	11.8	52
18	17	16	15	14	13	12	11	10	9	8	7	6	5	4	3	2	

WEEKS TO EXPIRATION

35	34	33	32	31	30	29	28	27	26	25	24	23	22	21	20	19	Table
53.1	52.6	52.1	51.6	51.1	50.6	50.0	49.4	48.8	48.2	47.6	47.0	46.3	45.6	44.9	44.1	43.2	53
54.0	53.5	53.0	52.5	52.0	51.5	50.9	50.3	49.7	49.1	48.4	47.8	47.1	46.3	45.6	44.8	43.9	54
54.8	54.3	53.8	53.3	52.8	52.3	51.7	51.1	50.5	49.9	49.2	48.5	47.8	47.1	46.3	45.5	44.6	55
55.6	55.1	54.6	54.1	53.6	53.1	52.5	51.9	51.3	50.7	50.0	49.3	48.6	47.9	47.1	46.2	45.3	56
56.6	56.1	55.6	55.1	54.6	54.0	53.4	52.7	52.1	51.5	50.8	50.1	49.4	48.6	47.8	47.0	46.1	57
57.5	57.0	56.5	56.0	55.5	54.9	54.2	53.6	52.9	52.3	51.6	50.9	50.2	49.4	48.6	47.7	46.8	58
58.4	57.9	57.4	56.9	56.3	55.7	55.0	54.4	53.7	53.1	52.4	51.7	50.9	50.1	49.3	48.4	47.5	59
59.3	58.8	58.3	57.8	57.2	56.6	55.9	55.3	54.6	53.9	53.2	52.5	51.7	50.9	50.1	49.2	48.2	60
60.4	59.8	59.2	58.6	58.0	57.4	56.7	56.0	55.4	54.7	54.0	53.3	52.5	51.7	50.8	49.9	48.9	61
61.3	60.7	60.1	59.5	58.9	58.3	57.6	56.9	56.2	55.5	54.8	54.0	53.2	52.4	5'.5	50.5	49.5	62
62.1	61.5	60.9	60.3	59.7	59.1	58.4	57.7	57.0	56.3	55.6	54.8	54.0	53.2	52.3	51.4	50.4	63
71.9	71.3	70.7	70.1	60.5	59.9	59.2	58.5	57.8	57.1	56.4	55.6	54.8	53.9	53.0	52.1	51.1	64
63.6	63.1	62.5	61.9	61.3	60.7	60.0	59.3	58.6	57.9	57.2	56.4	55.6	54.7	53.8	52.8	51.8	65
64.5	63.9	63.3	62.7	62.1	61.5	60.8	60.1	59.4	58.7	57.9	57.1	56.3	55.4	54.5	53.5	52.5	66
65.5	64.9	64.3	63.7	63.1	62.4	61.7	61.0	60.3	59.5	58.7	57.9	57.1	56.2	55.3	54.3	53.2	67
66.3	65.7	65.1	64.5	63.9	63.2	62.5	61.8	61.1	60.3	59.5	58.7	57.9	57.0	56.1	55.1	54.0	68
67.1	66.5	65.9	65.3	64.7	64.0	63.3	52.6	61.9	61.1	60.3	59.5	58.6	57.7	56.8	55.8	54.7	69
68.1	67.5	66.9	66.3	65.6	64.9	64.2	63.5	62.7	61.9	61.1	60.3	59.4	58.5	57.5	56.5	55.4	70
69.2	68.6	68.0	67.3	66.6	65.9	65.1	64.3	63.5	62.7	61.9	61.1	60.2	59.3	58.3	57.3	56.1	71
70.0	69.4	68.8	68.1	67.4	66.7	65.9	65.1	64.3	63.5	62.7	61.8	60.9	60.0	59.0	58.0	56.8	72
70.9	70.3	69.6	68.9	68.2	67.5	66.7	65.9	65.1	64.3	63.5	62.6	61.7	60.8	59.8	58.7	57.5	73
71.8	71.1	70.4	69.7	69.0	68.3	67.5	66.7	65.9	65.1	64.3	63.4	62.5	61.6	60.6	59.5	58.3	74
72.7	72.0	71.3	70.6	69.9	69.2	68.4	67.6	66.8	65.9	65.1	64.2	63.3	62.3	61.3	60.2	59.0	75
73.6	72.8	72.1	71.4	70.7	70.0	69.2	68.4	67.6	66.7	65.9	65.0	64.0	63.0	62.0	60.9	59.7	76
74.5	73.8	73.1	72.4	71.7	70.9	70.1	69.2	68.4	67.5	66.7	65.8	64.8	63.8	62.8	61.7	60.4	77
75.3	74.6	73.9	73.2	72.5	71.7	70.9	70.1	68.3	68.4	67.5	66.6	65.6	64.6	63.5	62.4	61.1	78
76.2	75.5	74.8	74.1	73.4	72.6	71.7	70.9	70.0	69.2	68.3	67.3	66.3	65.3	64.2	63.0	61.8	79
77.0	76.3	75.6	74.9	74.2	73.4	72.6	71.7	70.8	70.0	69.1	68.1	67.1	66.1	65.0	63.8	62.6	80
77.8	77.1	76.4	75.7	74.9	74.1	73.3	72.5	71.7	70.8	69.9	68.9	67.9	66.8	65.7	64.6	63.3	81
78.6	77.9	77.2	76.5	75.8	75.0	74.2	73.4	72.5	71.6	70.7	69.7	68.7	67.6	66.5	65.4	64.0	82
79.6	78.9	78.2	77.5	76.8	76.0	75.1	74.2	73.3	72.4	71.5	70.5	69.5	68.4	67.3	66.1	64.8	83
80.5	79.8	79.1	78.4	77.6	76.8	75.9	75.0	74.1	73.2	72.2	71.2	70.1	69.1	68.0	66.8	65.5	84

WM GRANDMILL (1985) LTD.

18	17	16	15	14	13	12	11	10	9	8	7	6	5	4	3	2	Table
42.3	41.3	40.3	39.3	38.3	37.2	36.0	34.6	33.2	31.7	30.0	28.1	25.9	23.0	20.0	16.2	12.0	53
42.9	42.0	41.0	40.0	38.9	37.8	36.6	35.2	33.8	32.2	30.5	28.6	26.4	23.4	20.3	16.2	12.2	54
43.6	42.6	41.6	40.6	39.6	38.4	37.2	35.8	34.3	32.7	31.0	29.1	26.8	23.8	20.6	16.8	12.4	55
44.3	43.4	42.4	41.3	40.2	39.0	37.8	36.4	34.9	33.3	31.4	29.5	27.2	24.2	21.0	17.0	12.5	56
45.1	44.1	43.1	41.9	40.9	39.7	38.4	36.9	35.4	33.8	31.0	30.0	27.6	24.6	21.3	17.3	12.7	57
45.8	44.8	43.7	42.6	41.5	40.3	39.0	37.5	36.0	34.3	42.4	30.5	28.1	25.0	21.6	17.6	12.9	58
46.5	45.4	44.3	43.2	42.1	40.9	39.6	38.1	36.6	34.8	32.9	30.9	28.5	25.3	22.0	17.9	13.1	59
47.2	46.1	45.0	43.9	42.8	41.5	40.2	38.7	37.1	35.4	33.4	31.4	28.9	25.7	22.3	18.1	13.3	60
47.9	46.8	45.7	44.6	43.4	42.2	40.8	39.3	37.7	35.9	33.9	31.9	29.4	26.1	22.6	18.4	13.5	61
48.5	47.5	46.4	45.2	44.0	42.8	41.4	39.8	38.2	36.4	34.4	32.3	29.8	26.5	23.0	18.7	13.7	62
49.3	42.8	47.1	45.9	44.7	43.4	42.0	40.4	38.8	37.0	34.9	32.8	30.2	26.9	23.3	18.9	13.9	63
50.0	48.9	47.7	46.5	45.3	44.0	42.6	41.0	39.3	37.5	35.4	33.3	30.7	27.3	23.6	19.2	14.1	64
50.7	49.6	48.4	47.2	46.0	44.6	43.2	41.6	39.9	38.0	35.9	33.7	31.1	27.6	24.0	19.5	14.3	65
51.4	50.3	49.1	47.9	46.6	45.2	43.8	42.1	40.4	38.5	36.4	34.2	31.5	28.0	24.3	19.8	14.5	66
52.1	50.9	49.7	48.5	47.2	45.9	44.4	42.7	41.0	39.1	36.9	34.7	32.0	28.4	24.6	20.0	14.7	67
52.8	51.6	50.4	49.2	47.9	46.5	45.0	43.3	41.5	39.6	37.4	35.1	32.4	28.8	25.0	20.3	14.9	68
53.5	52.3	51.1	49.8	48.5	47.1	45.6	43.9	42.1	40.1	37.6	35.6	32.8	29.2	25.3	20.6	15.1	69
54.2	53.0	51.7	50.4	49.1	47.7	46.2	44.4	42.6	40.7	38.4	36.1	33.3	29.6	25.6	20.8	15.3	70
54.9	53.7	52.4	51.1	49.8	48.3	46.8	45.0	43.2	41.2	38.9	36.6	33.7	30.0	26.0	21.1	15.5	71
55.6	54.4	53.1	51.8	50.4	49.0	47.4	45.6	43.8	41.7	39.4	37.0	34.1	30.3	26.3	21.4	15.7	72
56.3	55.1	53.8	52.4	51.1	49.6	48.0	46.2	44.3	42.2	39.9	37.5	34.6	30.7	26.6	21.6	15.9	73
57.0	55.7	54.4	53.1	51.7	50.2	48.6	46.8	44.9	42.8	40.4	38.0	35.0	31.1	26.9	21.9	16.1	74
57.7	56.5	55.1	53.7	52.3	50.8	49.2	47.3	45.4	43.3	41.0	38.4	35.4	31.5	27.3	22.2	16.3	75
58.4	57.1	55.8	54.4	53.0	51.4	49.8	47.9	46.0	43.8	41.5	38.9	35.9	31.9	27.6	22.5	16.5	76
59.1	57.8	56.4	55.0	53.6	52.1	50.4	48.5	46.5	44.4	42.0	39.4	36.3	32.3	28.0	22.7	16.7	77
59.8	58.5	57.1	55.7	54.3	52.7	51.0	49.1	47.1	44.9	42.4	39.8	36.7	32.6	28.3	23.0	16.9	78
60.5	59.2	57.8	56.4	54.9	53.3	51.6	49.6	47.6	45.4	43.0	40.3	37.1	33.0	28.6	23.3	17.1	79
61.3	59.9	58.5	57.1	55.6	54.0	52.2	50.2	48.2	45.9	43.5	40.8	37.6	33.4	29.0	23.5	17.3	80
61.9	60.6	59.2	57.7	56.2	54.6	52.8	50.8	48.7	46.4	44.0	41.2	38.0	33.8	29.3	23.8	17.5	81
62.8	61.3	59.9	58.4	56.9	55.2	53.4	51.4	49.3	47.0	44.5	41.7	38.4	34.2	29.6	24.1	17.7	82
63.4	62.0	60.5	59.0	57.5	55.8	54.0	51.9	49.8	47.5	45.0	42.2	38.9	34.6	30.0	24.4	17.9	83
64.1	62.7	61.2	59.7	58.2	56.5	54.6	52.5	50.4	48.0	45.5	42.6	39.3	34.9	30.3	24.6	18.1	84

18	17	16	15	14	13	12	11	10	9	8	7	6	5	4	3	2	

WEEKS TO EXPIRATION

33

If you are trading in an area which indicates that you should use tables 85 to 92, then you are trading options which are overpriced and speculative . The market is erratic here , and often the future's price will make limit moves, either up or down.   A prudent trader would withdraw from the market here, and wait for the situation to cool down.

If you are using tables 93 and up, then you are trading in a very seriously overpriced market and speculative to the extreme.

Up until now, you have chosen the table number which is closest to the "at the money" price. But, here, you may have to interpolate between tables to get the values you need if there is a big difference between the "at the money" price and the nearest option value in the selected column.

35	34	33	32	31	30	29	28	27	26	25	24	23	22	21	20	19	Table
					WEEKS TO EXPIRATION												
83.3	82.5	81.7	80.9	80.1	79.3	78.4	77.5	76.6	75.6	74.6	73.6	72.5	71.4	70.2	69.0	67.6	85
85.5	84.7	83.9	83.1	82.3	81.5	80.6	79.7	78.8	77.7	76.7	75.7	74.6	73.4	72.2	70.9	69.5	86
88.9	88.0	87.1	86.2	85.3	84.4	83.4	82.4	81.4	80.4	79.4	78.3	77.2	76.0	74.7	73.4	71.9	87
91.7	90.8	89.9	89.0	88.1	87.2	86.2	85.1	84.1	83.1	82.0	80.9	79.7	78.5	77.2	75.8	74.3	88
94.4	93.5	92.6	91.7	90.8	89.9	88.9	87.9	86.9	85.8	84.7	83.5	82.3	81.0	79.6	78.2	76.7	89
97.3	96.4	95.5	94.6	93.7	92.8	91.7	90.6	89.5	88.4	87.3	86.1	84.9	83.6	82.2	80.7	79.1	90
99.9	99.0	98.1	97.2	96.3	95.4	94.4	93.4	92.3	91.2	90.0	88.7	87.4	86.1	84.7	83.2	81.5	91
102.9	102.0	101.1	100.2	99.3	98.4	97.3	96.2	95.0	93.8	92.6	91.3	90.0	88.6	87.1	85.6	83.9	92
110.1	109.2	108.3	107.4	106.4	105.4	104.2	103.0	101.8	100.5	99.2	97.9	96.5	95.0	93.4	91.8	89.9	93
117.2	116.3	115.4	114.5	113.5	112.5	111.2	109.9	108.6	107.2	105.8	104.4	102.9	101.3	99.6	97.9	95.9	94
132.6	131.4	130.2	129.0	127.8	126.6	125.1	123.6	122.1	120.6	119.1	117.5	115.7	113.9	112.1	110.2	107.9	95
146.8	145.6	144.4	143.2	142.0	140.7	139.0	13713	135.7	134.0	132.3	130.5	128.6	126.6	124.5	122.4	119.9	96
35	34	33	32	31	30	29	28	27	26	25	24	23	22	21	20	19	
					WEEKS TO EXPIRATION												

WM GRANDMILL (1985) LTD.

If you are trading in an area which indicates that you should use tables 85 to 92, then you are trading options which are overpriced and speculative . The market is erratic here , and often the future's price will make limit moves, either up or down. A prudent trader would withdraw from the market here, and wait for the situation to cool down.

If you are using tables 93 and up, then you are trading in a very seriously overpriced market and speculative to the extreme.

Up until now, you have chosen the table number which is closest to the "at the money" price. But, here, you may have to interpolate between tables to get the values you need if there is a big difference between the "at the money" price and the nearest option value in the selected column.

18	17	16	15	14	13	12	11	10	9	8	7	6	5	4	3	2	Table
66.2	64.7	63.2	61.7	60.1	58.3	56.4	54.3	52.1	49.6	47.0	44.0	40.6	36.1	31.3	25.4	18.7	85
68.0	66.5	65.0	63.5	61.8	60.0	58.0	55.8	53.5	51.0	48.3	45.3	41.8	37.1	32.2	26.2	19.3	86
70.4	68.8	67.2	65.6	63.9	62.0	60.0	57.7	55.4	52.8	50.0	46.9	43.2	38.4	33.3	27.1	19.9	87
72.7	71.1	69.5	67.8	66.0	64.1	62.0	59.6	57.2	54.6	51.6	48.4	44.6	39.7	34.4	28.0	20.6	88
75.1	73.4	71.7	70.0	68.2	66.2	64.0	61.6	59.1	56.3	53.3	50.0	46.1	41.0	35.5	28.9	21.2	89
77.4	75.7	74.0	72.2	70.3	68.2	66.0	63.5	60.9	58.1	55.0	51.5	47.5	42.2	36.6	29.8	21.9	90
79.7	77.9	76.1	74.3	72.4	70.3	68.0	65.4	62.8	59.8	56.6	53.1	49.0	43.5	37.7	30.7	22.6	91
82.1	80.2	78.4	76.6	74.6	72.4	70.0	67.3	64.6	61.6	58.3	54.7	50.4	44.8	38.9	31.6	23.2	92
88.0	86.0	84.0	82.0	79.9	77.6	75.0	72.2	69.2	66.0	62.5	58.6	54.0	48.0	41.6	33.8	24.9	93
93.8	91.7	89.6	87.4	85.2	82.7	80.0	77.0	73.8	70.4	66.6	62.5	57.6	51.2	44.4	36.1	26.6	94
105.6	103.1	100.8	98.4	95.8	93.1	90.0	86.6	83.1	79.2	75.0	70.3	64.8	57.6	50.0	40.6	29.9	95
117.3	114.6	112.0	109.3	106.5	103.4	100.0	96.2	92.3	88.0	83.3	78.1	72.0	64.0	55.5	45.1	33.2	96
18	17	16	15	14	13	12	11	10	9	8	7	6	5	4	3	2	

WEEKS TO EXPIRATION

PART II

WHICH SOYBEAN OPTION IS THE BEST ONE TO USE?

Many were tested but few were chosen

INTRODUCTION and EXPLANATION

WHAT IS HERE?

1. In this section you will find the answers to the questions:

Which soybean options are the safest to trade?

Which soybean options are the most profitable?

Which soybean options are the best to trade for the long term?

Which soybean options are the best to trade when there is a high rate of volatility?

2. Dozens of different option positions were calculated to find the answers to the questions above. They were tested to find which options were safe and profitable. They were tested by using varying degrees of volatility, from high to low volatility. They were tested by using varying length of time to the expiration date. They were tested by using different amounts of the future's price movement – from a big price move of $1.25 to no price change at all. They were tested by using combinations of volatility, time, and price.

3. After testing dozens of option positions under the multitude of conditions mentioned above, nine were selected as the best of the many. They were considered to be the best because they offered a good degree of safety to one's working capital, and at the same time they gave a fair to good profit.

4. The 9 option positions selected and written up in this book are :

Buy a call or a put at the money

Buy a call or a put at 50¢ out of the money

Sell a call or a put at the money

Sell a call or a put at 50¢ out of the money

Bull or Bear spread #1 - buy a call or put at the money, and sell a call or put at 25¢ out of the money

Bull or Bear spread #2 -buy a call or put at money, and sell 2 calls or puts at 50¢ out of the money

Straddle – sell a call and sell a put, both at the money

Strangle #1 - sell a call and sell a put, both at 50¢ out of the money

Strangle #2 - sell a call and sell a put, both at $1.00 out of the money

5. Selecting the 9 best options was just the start. The main objective of this book is to save you from the need to do a lot of work and calculations. Therefore the profit and loss of each of the 9 positions mentioned above were calculated and presented in a convenient chart. The calculations for each of the 9 positions were done by using 4 different degrees of volatility – high, above average, average, and low volatility. Also the calculations were done by using different time periods, ranging from 35 weeks to expiration to 4 weeks to expiration. Also calculations for the profit and loss were done by using the future's price move of $1.25 to 0¢. All these calculations were done by using the soybean option tables from the book "Make Money From Soybean Options", mentioned previously.

Then the net profit area of each chart was outlined so that you could see at a glance whether the option was worth considering, under the market conditions prevailing at that time.

Below is an example which shows what was explained above.

6. Example – Suppose you were thinking of selling a call at the money. Let's say that the Table Finder page showed that Table 60 was the correct soybean option table to use. Let's also say that the time to expiration is 20 weeks. Here, then, is what the profit and loss chart will look like for "selling a call at the money", using a volatility represented by Table 60, and a time represented by 20 weeks.

changes in the soybean future's price in 25¢ increments		20	18	16	14	12	10	8	6	4	2	0	weeks to expiration
	+125	-82.7	-81.3	-79.8	-78.5	-77.2	-76.5	-76.3	-76.3	-76.3	-76.3	-76.3	
	+100	-58.9	-57.7	-56.3	-54.9	-53.8	-53.0	-52.2	-51.6	-51.3	-51.3	-51.3	
	+75	-38.6	-37.4	-36.1	-34.9	-33.5	-32.0	-30.5	-28.8	-27.0	-26.3	-26.3	
	+50	-24.6	-22.9	-21.2	-19.3	-17.2	-14.9	-12.3	-9.3	-5.5	-1.8	-1.3	
	+25	-10.8	-9.0	-7.1	-5.0	-2.7	0.1	3.4	7.4	13.2	20.1	23.7	
	0	-0.5	1.5	3.7	5.9	8.5	11.6	15.3	19.8	26.4	35.4	48.7	net profit area, in cents
	-25	9.0	10.9	13.0	15.3	17.8	20.8	24.4	28.8	35.0	43.2	48.7	
	-50	17.4	19.2	21.1	23.1	25.5	28.2	31.4	34.9	40.0	46.2	48.7	
	-75	21.4	23.3	25.4	27.4	29.8	32.5	35.7	39.2	43.7	47.9	48.7	
	-100	27.9	29.4	31.1	33.0	35.0	37.1	39.3	42.0	45.2	48.3	48.7	
	-125	33.6	34.8	36.2	37.6	39.1	40.7	42.5	44.5	46.9	48.6	48.7	

TABLE 60

The estimated credit is: + 49.2¢ premium − 0.5¢ comm. = + 48.7¢

7. Look at the chart above.

(a) See the heavy line which represents the "net profit area, in cents". Note the size of the profit area and see how it extends downward

(b) This is a "sell a call at the money" option position. Therefore you will sell a <u>call</u> only when you believe that soybean future prices will <u>decline</u>. The Forecasting Graphs will help you to make the decision of whether prices will likely rise or fall. By selling a call when prices are likely to fall, the person who buys your call will not make any money from it – which means that you will be able to keep all the premium for yourself. That's why the main part of the profit area is in the part where prices decline.

(c) Note the line at the bottom of the chart. It shows the premium gained from the sale and it shows the discount commission of $25 being subtracted, to give a net profit of 48.7¢ ($2435). Therefore the 48.7¢ will be the maximum amount of profit which you can earn. That's a good profit. But there is more good news. It also means that you could survive a price reversal of 48.7¢ and you would not lose any money. So you see that you have a limited profit protection if prices should rise, rather than decline as you were expecting.

(d) Look at the junction of -25¢ and 16 weeks. There you see 13.0¢. This means that if after 4 weeks time from the time you sold this call, you decided to get out of the position then you could do so and earn a net profit of 13.0¢. Look at the junction of +25 and 16 weeks. There you see -7.1¢. That means that is prices rose by 25¢ after 4 weeks into the position, and if you decided to bail out, then you would have a 7.1¢ loss.

(e) Therefore this example would be called a <u>safe and profitable</u> option. It is called a safe option because (1) the Forecasting Graphs indicated that prices would decline (2) there is a 48.7¢ safety margin in case prices go against you temporarily. It is called a profitable option because it will earn well over 150% on your investment in only 20 weeks (your investment is the amount of margin money which you must deposit into your account)

(f) Take another look at the chart above. Note the black line at the top of the chart. It shows the amount of time remaining in your option, and under each passing week you'll see the profit or loss which you would get if you decided to liquidate the position at that point in time.

(g) Down the left side of the chart you see the future's price changes.

8. <u>Another Example</u>. Sell a strangle #1 – sell a call at 50¢ out of the money and sell a put at 50¢ out of the money.   Let's say that the correct soybean option table to use is Table 40, and let's say that the time to expiration is 20 weeks.

TABLE 40 — changes in the soybean future's price in 25¢ increments	weeks to expiration										
	20	18	16	14	12	10	8	6	4	2	0
+125	-45.3	-44.4	-43.5	-42.7	-42.0	-41.3	-40.5	-39.8	-39.4	-39.4	-39.4
+100	-30.0	-28.4	-26.7	-25.1	-23.3	-21.5	-19.7	-17.9	-15.5	-14.5	-14.4
+75	-17.4	-15.4	-13.5	-11.4	-9.0	-6.3	-3.1	0.3	5.0	9.2	10.6
+50	-8.9	-6.7	-4.3	-1.7	1.0	4.3	8.1	12.6	18.8	16.2	35.6
+25	-3.7	-1.2	1.5	4.3	7.4	10.8	15.1	19.9	26.3	33.5	35.6
0	-1.0	1.4	3.8	6.4	9.2	12.4	16.4	21.0	27.4	34.6	35.6
-25	-3.7	-1.2	1.5	4.3	7.4	10.8	15.1	19.9	26.3	33.5	35.6
-50	-8.9	-6.7	-4.3	-1.7	1.0	4.3	8.1	12.6	18.8	16.2	35.6
-75	-17.4	-15.4	-13.5	-11.4	-9.0	-6.3	-3.1	0.3	5.0	9.2	10.6
-100	-30.0	-28.4	-26.7	-25.1	-23.3	-21.5	-19.7	-17.9	-15.5	-14.5	-14.4
-125	-45.3	-44.4	-43.5	-42.7	-42.0	-41.3	-40.5	-39.8	-39.4	-39.4	-39.4

net profit area , in cents

Est. credit is: +18.3¢ premium +18.3¢ premium -1.0¢ comm. = + 35.6¢

(a) Look at the estimated credit at the bottom of the chart.   It says that you will have a net amount of 35.6¢ ($1780) credited to your account as the result of selling the call and the put.   This 35.6¢ represents your maximum profit.

(b) Look at the size of the net profit area.   It is quite large and you can earn a reasonable profit even if prices go against you.   The strategy to use for this option is to take this position when the Forecasting Graphs indicate that there will be little or no price change in the weeks ahead.   Therefore this large net profit area will give you limited protection in case prices change much more than you expected.   Even though you are hoping for 0¢ price change, the price could change by as much as 85.6¢ and you still not lose money – so there is limited protection here.

(c) As mentioned above, this option should be used when you expect little or no price change after you have taken the position.   But if the Forecasting Graphs should indicate that

40

there will likely be a medium or large price movement, then you should use one of the other 9 option positions which are outlined in this book. There is an option for every situation.

(d) Look at the chart and you can see what profit or loss to expect for any price change and change in time after you have taken this option position.   For example, if the future's price fell by 50¢ and if you decided to abandon your position at the 6th week, then you can expect a net profit of about 12.6¢ – look at the junction of –50 and 6 weeks.

9. In the pages ahead you will see a description of each of the 9 option positions chosen for this book.   Then you will see profit and loss charts for each of the 9 option trades, as determined by a variety of volatility rates and time changes.

10. To use the profit and loss charts to the best advantage, follow these steps : (1) determine the weeks to expiration.   (2) Turn to that particular weeks to exp. charts.   (3) Having done that, you will see laid out before you each of the 9 option positions, using Tables 80, 60, 40, and 20 which offer a good variety of volatility.   Table 80 represents high volatility, Table 20 represents low volatility.   If the Table Finder indicates a table other than the 4 tables on the page, then you will have to interpolate.   For example, if Table 50 is the correct one to use, then you will have to interpolate between Tables 60 and 40 to find the proper profit and loss amounts.   (4) then by looking at each of the 9 options, you can select the best one to use.

BUY A CALL or BUY A PUT

AT THE MONEY

This is the most popular of all option trades. Anyone who has traded options has taken this position many times. Likely it was the first option position which you took when you began trading in options.

But even though it is popular, it can also be a difficult one from which to earn a good profit. Therefore this is the place to give you an important rule : never take an option position unless you believe that you can earn 100% or more on your investment, over the time of the contract. The time of the contract can be as long as 35 weeks or as short as 4 weeks – but you should be able to earn 100% or more in that time – otherwise, don't take it.

What is the investment? Your investment in the option is your cost of buying the call or buying the put, plus the commission paid to your broker. For example, if you paid 20¢ premium to buy a call option and if you paid a $25 discount commission, then your investment is 20.5¢. Therefore if you wish to earn 100% on your investment in this example, then your long call option will have to increase in value to 41¢ or more , at or before the expiration date.

Example. The date is Nov. 15th and you are thinking of buying a May call option. The premium for the May call is 24.5¢, and the commission cost is 0.5¢, making a total cost of 25.0¢. You check out the May Forecasting Graphs and they indicate that the May soybean price should increase by 60¢ at or before May 1st. This would be a worthwhile investment. According to the Forecasting Graphs you would earn $60 \div 50 \times 100 = 120\%$ in the 22 weeks of the contract , at the expiration date. By the way, it is a good policy to liquidate your position a day or more before the last trading day (which is a Friday) because you might forget at the last moment to sell your call and then there could be complications. A call option is really an opportunity to buy 5000 bushels of soybeans at a lower price, hopefully. And if you don't get out before the expiration date, then you might have to do that very thing.

The Forecasting Graphs will be a big help to you in all the 9 options outlined in this book. But there is one thing they cannot do – and that is to know if there is a dry spell comming up. The Graphs are constructed on the basis that there will be "average" weather. Therefore, it is up to you to keep an eye on the weather during the summer months, and to act accordingly. Weather rumors , both true and false, will float through the soybean market during June, July, August and September, causing prices to move up or down unexpectedly. In other words, volatility increases.

HOW VOLATILITY AFFECT THE NET PROFIT

There are two factors which greatly affect an option's profitability. They are: (1) the rate of volatility (2) time, the weeks to expiration.

Volatility will be demonstrated first. Below are two profit and loss charts. One is using Table 80 (high volatility) and the other uses Table 20 (low volatility) . The time factor is constant – both are for 35 weeks.

Just by a glance you can easily see the effects of volatility on the net profit area of the two charts. Later in this book you will see which options will work better in a high rate of volatility and which options work better in a low volatility rate.

TABLE 80

changes in the soybean future's price in 25¢ increments	35	30	25	20	18	16	14	12	10	8	6	4	2	0	weeks to expiration
+125	79.2	75.6	71.3	65.7	63.2	60.7	58.3	55.9	53.1	50.0	47.7	47.4	47.4	47.4	net profit
+100	56.5	52.6	48.0	42.2	39.7	37.1	34.8	32.1	29.4	26.9	24.2	22.8	22.4	22.4	
+75	34.8	31.0	26.5	21.2	18.9	16.4	14.1	11.7	9.1	6.3	3.4	0	-2.5	-2.6	
+50	21.9	18.6	14.3	9.0	6.5	3.9	1.3	-1.8	-5.2	-9.0	-13.6	-19.5	-25.9	-27.6	
+25	10.5	7.5	3.1	-2.8	-5.5	-8.6	-11.7	-15.1	-19.0	123.2	128.5	-36.2	-46.1	-52.6	
0	-0.5	-4.4	-8.5	-13.6	-16.3	-19.1	-22.0	-25.4	-29.4	-34.1	-40.0	-48.6	-60.3	-77.6	
-25	-10.5	-13.8	-18.1	-23.4	-25.9	-28.7	-31.6	-34.9	-38.8	-43.4	-49.2	-57.6	-68.5	-77.6	
-50	-19.6	-22.8	-27.0	-32.2	-34.7	-37.4	-40.2	-43.5	-47.2	-51.4	-56.7	-63.7	-72.4	-77.6	
-75	-24.4	-27.2	-31.0	-36.2	-38.7	-41.3	-44.2	-47.5	-51.2	-55.7	-60.9	-68.0	-75.4	-77.6	
-100	-31.7	-34.4	-38.1	-43.2	-45.6	-48.2	-51.0	-54.1	-57.6	-61.4	-65.7	-70.8	-75.9	-77.6	
-125	-39.8	-42.4	-46.2	-51.1	-53.4	-55.8	-58.1	-60.5	-63.1	-66.1	-69.3	-73.3	-77.1	-77.6	

The estimated cost is: -77.1¢ premium - 0.5¢ comm.= -77.6¢

TABLE 20

changes in the soybean future's price in 25¢ increments	35	30	25	20	18	16	14	12	10	8	6	4	2	0	weeks to expiration
+125	100.5	100.5	100.5	100.5	100.5	100.5	100.5	100.5	100.5	100.5	100.5	100.5	100.5	100.5	net profit area, in cents
+100	75.5	75.5	75.5	75.5	75.5	75.5	75.5	75.5	75.5	75.5	75.5	75.5	75.5	75.5	
+75	51.5	51.3	51.1	50.9	50.8	50.7	50.6	50.6	50.5	50.5	50.5	50.5	50.5	50.5	
+50	30.6	30.0	29.3	28.5	28.1	27.6	27.2	26.8	26.4	26.1	25.8	25.6	25.5	25.5	
+25	12.5	11.5	10.3	9.1	8.4	7.7	7.0	6.2	5.3	4.2	3.1	1.8	0.9	0.5	
0	-0.5	-1.7	-3.1	-4.7	-5.5	-6.4	-7.3	-8.3	-9.6	-11.0	-12.8	-15.5	-19.1	-24.5	
-25	-9.2	-10.3	-11.6	-13.0	-13.8	-14.7	-15.5	-16.4	-17.5	-18.8	-20.5	-22.6	-23.7	-24.5	
-50	-14.5	-15.4	-16.4	-17.5	-18.1	-18.7	-19.3	-20.0	-20.9	-21.8	-23.1	-24.1	-24.5	-24.5	
-75	-18.5	-19.2	-20.0	-20.9	-21.3	-21.9	-22.3	-22.8	-23.2	-23.6	-24.2	-24.5	-24.5	-24.5	
-100	-20.3	-20.8	-21.4	-22.0	-22.3	-22.6	-22.9	-23.2	-23.6	-24.0	-24.4	-24.5	-24.5	-24.5	
-125	-22.2	-22.5	-22.9	-23.3	-23.5	-23.8	-24.0	-24.1	-24.3	-24.4	-24.5	-24.5	-24.5	-24.5	

The estimated cost is: -24.0 premium - 0.5 comm. = -24.5¢

1. Look at the net profit area of each. Note that you can get into the net profit area of Table 20 with a much smaller price increase than for Table 80.

2. Look at the size of the investment (the cost) for each. Table 80 requires an investment of about 77.6¢, whereas Table 20 requires an investment of about 24.5¢.

3. Note that in Table 80 (high volatility) the future's price would have to change by 155.2¢ in the next 35 weeks to earn a 100% profit. That would be difficult to do.

4. But in Table 20, where the cost is 24.5¢, the future's price would need to change by only 49¢ in order to earn a 100% profit. That would be no problem over a 35 week period.

5. You can see from the two volatility extremes above that you would have a better chance for a successful investment of 100% when volatility is low or below average.

6. There is a saying in the options trade which goes like this, "Be a buyer when volatility is low, and be a seller when volatility is high". You will see that it is good advice as you learn more about each of the other 9 positions which are written up in this book.

The 100% Rule – Is It Necessary?

You may have wondered why the rule of earning 100% on your investment is so important. The answer is : it's a safety precaution.

The author of this book has a penchant for the safety of one's working capital. To break even on a trade is not disastrous because one still has his money to try again. But if one loses his money, then his chances for future success is diminished when his capital becomes less than is needed to do the job.

Therefore, this book and other written by this author have safety standards injected into the investment methods outlined. The safety standard for this section of this book is to attempt to earn 100% or more when you take an option position.

Why the caution? Well, if you are an experienced futures or option trader, you will know that a trade will rarely turn out exactly as you have estimated it. Many unexpected events can occur about which you have no knowledge when you take the position. The beginning of the oil crisis in August 1990 is an example. Or a drought. Therefore, no matter how careful you are in estimating how much the future's price might change, it will sometimes fall short of the objective. So if the objective is a reasonable distance away, like 100%, then a shorter future's price movement than expected may bring only a small profit rather than a loss.

And if the "Buy a Call or Put" will not earn 100% profit, then try one of the other 8 options. Nearly always you will find one or more which will fulfill the safety standard.

And if you can't earn a 100% profit in soybeans, try wheat or corn. It is almost a certainty that you can find a safe option trade in one of the grains. This author believes that grain prices are predictable in the long and medium term, based on the supply and demand. In fact, grain is one of the few commodities by which the supply and demand can be used to forecast future prices with a fair degree of accuracy. But unexpected events can change things - hence the 100% rule.

How Can The Same Chart Show The Profits For Both A Call And A Put?

Look at Table 80. Look at the left side of the chart and you see the title

"Changes in the soybean future's price, in 25¢ increments". Also you see the price changes of +25, +50 etc. and -25, -50, etc.

Here's the point. For this particular option, +25 does not mean that prices have risen by 25¢. Instead it means that prices have changed in your favor, have moved in the direction that you want them to move, by 25¢. In other words, if you were buying a call, then a +25 means that prices have risen by 25¢ because to rise means to go in your favor, to your benefit.

On the other hand, if you were buying a put , then a +25 means that prices have fallen by 25¢ because falling prices are what you need when you buy a put. Therefore, in this case, a +25 is 25¢ in your favor, to your benefit. To repeat, a +25 means that prices rise by 25¢ when you buy a call, and it also means that prices fall by 25¢ when you are buying a put. Likewise, a -25 means that prices have fallen by 25¢ if you have bought a call, or that prices have risen by 25¢ if you have bought a put because a -25 means that prices have gone against you. Thus, one chart will show the net profit area for both calls and puts.

HOW A TIME CHANGE AFFECTS THE NET PROFIT

To show the effect of a change in time on the net profit, two tables of similar volatility will be used, but at different time periods . Table 40 will be used in both examples because Table 40 represents about the average volatility over the past 5 years for soybean options.

One chart will be of 35 weeks to expiration and the other will be of 6 weeks to expiration. These two charts will show how the net profit is affected by a change in time.

changes in the soybean future's price in 25¢ increments	35	30	25	20	18	16	14	12	10	8	6	4	2	0
+125	84.4	83.7	83.2	83.0	83.0	83.0	83.0	83.0	83.0	83.0	83.0	83.0	83.0	83.0
+100	60.8	60.2	59.7	59.2	58.9	58.7	58.5	58.3	58.1	58.0	58.0	58.0	58.0	58.0
+75	41.3	40.0	38.8	37.6	37.1	36.5	35.9	35.3	34.7	34.0	33.4	33.0	33.0	33.0
+50	25.3	23.5	21.8	19.7	18.8	17.7	16.7	15.6	14.3	12.8	11.2	9.1	8.1	8.0
+25	11.0	8.9	6.8	4.3	3.0	1.8	0.3	-1.3	-3.2	-5.5	-8.1	-11.7	-15.6	-17.0
0	-0.5	-2.4	-4.7	-7.5	-8.9	-10.4	-12.0	-13.8	-16.0	-18.5	-21.7	-26.3	-32.2	-42.0
-25	-9.7	-11.7	-13.9	-16.7	-18.0	-19.5	-21.1	122.8	-24.7	-27.2	-30.1	-34.3	-39.9	-42.0
-50	-17.3	-19.3	-21.4	-23.7	-24.9	-26.1	-27.4	-28.8	-30.4	-32.4	-34.7	-37.9	-41.5	-42.0
-75	-21.9	-23.6	-25.6	-28.0	-29.2	-30.4	-31.6	-33.0	-34.5	-36.3	-38.2	-40.4	-42.0	-42.0
-100	-27.0	-28.6	-30.3	-32.0	-32.8	-33.7	-34.7	-35.6	-36.7	-38.0	-39.3	-40.9	-42.0	-42.0
-125	-31.6	-32.7	-33.9	-35.3	-36.0	-36.7	-37.3	-38.1	-38.9	-39.8	-40.6	-41.7	-42.0	-42.0

weeks to expiration

net profit area

TABLE 40

The estimated cost is: -41.5¢ premium - 0.5¢ comm. = -42.0¢

45

		weeks to expiration			
		6	**4**	**2**	**0**
T A B L E 4 0	**+125**	104.2	104.2	104.2	104.2
	+100	79.2	79.2	79.2	79.2
	+75	54.6	54.2	54.2	54.2
	+50	32.4	30.2	29.3	29.2
	+25	13.1	9.5	5.6	4.2
	0	-0.5	-5.1	-11.4	-20.8
	-25	-8.9	-13.1	-18.7	-20.8
	-50	-13.5	-16.7	-20.3	-20.8
	-75	-17.0	-19.2	-20.8	-20.8
	-100	-18.1	-19.7	-20.8	-20.8
	-125	-19.5	-20.5	-20.8	-20.8

changes in the soybean future's price in 25¢ increments

net profit area , in cents

Est.cost:-20.3¢-0.5¢=-20.8¢

1. Look at the 35 weeks to expiration chart.   See that the net cost is 42.0¢.   That means that prices must change by 84¢ to earn a 100% net profit.   That's a possibility during the summer months, but unlikely during the winter and spring because Table 40 represents a market where there will not likely be any strong price surges as you would get with high volatility.

2. Look at the 6 week chart.   The net cost here is 20.8¢.   So soybean futures would have to change by 41.6¢ to earn 100% on the investment.   Six weeks is a short time so a 41.6¢ move is unlikely except during the summer months.

3. The two charts above shows how a change in time will affect the size of the net profit area.

4. To sum up: the best condition for buying a call or put is: low volatility and a. long term.

BUY A CALL or BUY A PUT

AT 50¢ OUT OF THE MONEY

This option maneuver is a popular one with all option traders.   But, unfortunately, it is the least profitable of all the 9 options outlined in this book.

It is popular mainly because the premium is much cheaper than buying a call or a put at the money.   But there are drawbacks with this option.   The first one is that the soybean future's price must change by 50¢ just to get into the money.   That's a fairly big move.   Then the future's price must change again by the size of the cost of the option just so that you can break even.   Then the future's price must change again by the size of the cost, so that you can earn a 100% profit.   Add all those price changes together and it comes to a big price change which will be needed to earn 100%.

Is there an advantage to buying a call at 50¢ out of the money, as compared to buying a call at the money?

Yes, but only when a very large price move is expected.   If the Forecasting Graphs indicated that prices would rise by $1.50 in the next 6 months, for example, then one would be better off to buy a call at 50¢ out of the money than to buy a call at the money.   There would be a better percentage return on the investment by buying at 50¢ out of the money when a very large price move is expected.

	35	30	25	20	18	16	14	12	10	8	6	4	2	0
+125	53.9	50.1	45.6	40.3	38.0	35.5	33.2	30.8	28.2	25.4	22.5	19.1	16.6	16.5
+100	41.0	37.7	33.4	28.1	25.6	23.0	20.4	17.3	13.9	10.1	5.5	-0.4	-6.8	-8.5
+75	30.0	26.6	22.2	16.3	13.6	10.5	7.4	4.0	0.1	-4.0	-9.4	-17.1	-27.0	-33.5
+50	18.3	14.9	10.6	5.3	2.8	0.0	-2.9	-6.3	-10.3	-15.0	-20.9	-29.5	-41.2	-58.5
+25	8.6	5.3	1.0	-4.3	-6.8	-9.6	-12.5	-15.8	-19.7	-24.3	-30.1	-38.5	-49.4	-58.5
0	-0.5	-3.7	-7.9	-13.1	-15.6	-18.3	-21.1	-24.4	-28.1	-32.3	-37.6	-44.6	-53.2	-58.5
-25	-5.3	-8.1	-11.9	-17.1	-19.6	-22.2	-25.1	-24.8	-32.1	-36.6	-41.8	-48.9	-56.3	-58.5
-50	-12.6	-15.3	-19.0	-24.1	-26.5	-29.1	-31.9	-35.0	-38.5	-42.3	-46.6	-51.7	-56.8	-58.5
-75	-20.6	-23.3	-27.1	-32.0	-34.3	-36.7	-39.0	-41.4	-44.0	-47.0	-50.2	-54.2	-58.0	-58.5
-100	-29.9	-32.5	-35.5	-39.5	-41.6	-43.5	-46.0	-48.9	-50.5	-52.4	-54.5	-56.8	-58.5	-58.5
-125	-37.0	-39.4	-42.4	-46.3	-48.1	-49.7	-51.4	-53.2	-55.0	-56.0	-57.1	-57.7	-58.5	-58.5

weeks to expiration

TABLE 80 — changes in the soybean future's price in 25¢ increments

The estimated cost is: -58.0¢ premium - 0.5¢ comm. = -58.5¢

47

changes in the soybean future's price in 25¢ increments	35	30	25	20	18	16	14	12	10	8	6	4	2	0 (weeks to expiration)
+125	65.5	65.3	65.1	64.9	64.8	64.7	64.6	64.6	64.5	64.5	64.5	64.5	64.5	64.5
+100	44.6	44.0	43.3	42.5	42.1	41.6	41.2	40.8	40.4	40.1	39.8	39.6	39.5	39.5
+75	26.5	25.5	24.3	23.1	22.4	21.7	21.0	20.2	19.3	18.2	17.1	15.3	14.9	14.5
+50	13.5	12.3	10.9	9.3	8.5	7.6	6.7	5.7	4.4	3.0	1.2	-1.5	-5.1	-10.5
+25	4.8	3.7	2.4	1.0	0.2	-0.7	-1.5	-2.4	-3.5	-4.8	-6.5	-8.6	-9.7	-10.5
0	-0.5	-1.4	-2.4	-3.5	-4.1	-4.7	-5.3	-6.0	-6.9	-7.9	-9.1	-10.1	-10.5	-10.5
-25	-4.5	-5.2	-6.0	-6.9	-7.3	-7.8	-8.3	-8.8	-9.2	-9.6	-10.2	-10.5	-10.5	-10.5
-50	-6.3	-6.8	-7.4	-8.0	-8.3	-8.6	-8.9	-9.2	-9.6	-10.0	-10.4	-10.5	-10.5	-10.5
-75	-8.2	-8.5	-8.9	-9.3	-9.5	-9.8	-10.0	-10.1	-10.3	-10.4	-10.5	-10.5	-10.5	-10.5
-100	-9.2	-9.5	-9.8	-10.1	-10.2	-10.3	-10.4	-10.4	-10.5	-10.5	-10.5	-10.5	-10.5	-10.5
-125	-9.8	-10.1	-10.3	-10.4	-10.5	-10.5	-10.5	-10.5	-10.5	-10.5	-10.5	-10.5	-10.5	-10.5

TABLE 20

net profit area

The estimated cost is: -10.0¢ premium - 0.5¢ comm. = -10.5¢

You can tell at which price level it is advantageous to buy a call or put "at 50¢ out of the money" rather than "at the money" just by looking at the net profit charts of each. Then do a calculation to find the percentage return on each of the investments. There is a point at which it pays to switch from one to the other to get a greater % return on your investment.

To sum up : "Buying a call or a put at 50¢ out of the money" is the least useful of the nine options listed in this book. A large price move is needed to make it worthwhile to do.

Volatility – Let's see how a change in volatility will affect profits. See the two tables above. Table 80 represents a high volatility. Table 20 represents a low volatility.

1. Look at the costs of the options above. For Table 80, the future's price at expiration would have to change by 167¢ in the next 35 weeks to earn a 100% profit (the "at the money" option needed 155.2¢ price change to earn 100%, for Table 80 at 35 weeks).

2. For Table 20, prices would have to change by 71¢ in the next 35 weeks to earn a 100% profit. (in comparison, the "at the money" option needed only 49¢ change to earn a 100% profit)

Time – Let's see how a change in time will affect the profits for "Buying a call or put at 50¢ out of the money".

Look at the two charts below. They are both using Table 40, an average volatility.

TABLE 40

changes in the soybean future's price in 25¢ increments	weeks to expiration														net profit
	35	30	25	20	18	16	14	12	10	8	6	4	2	0	
+125	58.1	56.8	55.6	54.4	53.9	53.3	52.7	52.0	51.5	50.8	50.2	49.8	49.8	49.8	
+100	42.1	40.3	38.6	36.5	35.6	34.5	33.5	32.4	31.1	29.6	28.0	25.9	24.9	24.8	
+75	27.8	25.7	23.6	21.1	19.8	18.6	17.1	15.5	13.6	11.3	8.7	5.1	1.2	-0.2	
+50	16.3	14.4	12.1	9.3	7.9	6.4	4.8	3.0	0.8	-1.7	-4.9	-9.5	-15.8	-25.2	
+25	7.1	5.1	2.9	0.1	-1.2	-2.7	-4.3	-6.0	-7.9	-10.4	-13.3	-17.5	-23.1	-25.2	
0	-0.5	-2.5	-4.6	-6.9	-8.1	-9.3	-10.6	-12.0	-13.6	-15.6	-17.9	-21.1	-24.7	-25.2	
-25	-5.1	-6.8	-8.8	-11.2	-12.4	-13.6	-14.8	-16.2	-17.7	-19.5	-21.4	-23.6	-25.2	-25.2	
-50	-10.2	-11.8	-13.5	-15.2	-16.0	-16.9	-17.9	-18.8	-19.9	-21.2	-22.5	-24.1	-25.2	-25.2	
-75	-14.8	-15.9	-17.1	-18.5	-19.2	-19.9	-20.5	-21.3	-22.1	-23.0	-23.8	-24.9	-25.2	-25.2	
-100	-18.3	-19.3	-20.3	-21.3	-22.0	-22.6	-23.2	-23.9	-24.4	-24.7	-24.9	-25.2	-25.2	-25.2	
-125	-21.6	-22.3	-23.1	-23.9	-24.2	-24.5	-24.8	-24.9	-25.0	-25.1	-25.2	-25.2	-25.2	-25.2	

The estimated cost is: -24.7¢ premium - 0.5¢ comm. = -25.2¢

TABLE 40

changes in the soybean future's price in 25¢ increments	weeks to expiration				net profit
	6	4	2	0	
+125	67.6	67.2	67.2	67.2	
+100	45.4	43.3	42.3	42.2	
+75	26.1	22.5	18.6	17.2	
+50	12.5	7.9	1.6	-7.8	
+25	4.1	-0.1	-5.7	-7.8	
0	-0.5	-3.7	-7.3	-7.8	
-25	-4.0	-6.2	-7.8	-7.8	
-50	-5.1	-6.7	-7.8	-7.8	
-75	-6.4	-7.5	-7.8	-7.8	
-100	-7.5	-7.8	-7.8	-7.8	
-125	-7.8	-7.8	-7.8	-7.8	

Est. cost: -7.3¢ - 0.5¢ = -7.8¢

1. Note the size of the two profit areas. There is not much difference in them.

2. The 35th week chart would need a price change of 100.4¢ to earn a 100% profit. The 6th week chart needs a price change of 65.6¢ in 6 weeks to earn a 100% profit. That's a big move for both and it is unlikely to happen except in a weather market in the summer.

SELL A CALL or SELL A PUT

AT THE MONEY

This is a popular soybean position and also a profitable one.

As you know, when you <u>sell</u> an option, the premium is put into your account and it remains there untouched until the option is liquidated. Then the money is yours to keep if your option trade has been successful. Also, you must deposit a margin into your account.

Your investment for this option is the margin money which you must deposit into your account, and which you will get back if your trade is successful. The size of the margin will vary from about $800 to $2000, depending on the volatility rate at the time. The average seems to be about $1000. The higher the volatility, the higher the margin requirements.

Also your broker has the right to ask you to put more money into your account if the future's price should go against you. Remember, when the buyer of your call or put makes money, he makes it from you. That's why you may have to deposit more money. But this book is cognizant of that possibility. So it shows ways and means by which you can protect your working capital when there is a possibility of prices going against you. One of the ways is the rule below.

<u>RULE</u> - Always sell an option opposite to the direction to which you believe the soybean price is headed. Use the Forecasting Graphs to help you reach the decision.

<u>Example</u> - The date is Nov. 15th, just after the USDA crop report where you will get the latest information of the soybean supply and demand. The Forecasting Graphs indicate that May soybeans should <u>rise</u> by $1.00. Therefore you will sell a <u>put</u>. In other words, the buyer of your put will need falling prices to make money. But you are sure that prices will rise. If you are correct in estimating the price direction, then the other fellow will not make any money from you - and you will be able to keep all of his premium.

You may be one of those kind, soft-hearted persons who thinks that selling a put to someone when prices will rise, is a mean and unethical thing to do because the other fellow will lose his money for sure. At first glance it does look like a mean trick to play on someone. But it's business. Anyway, you can be sure that a person would only buy your put if he believed that soybean prices will fall. So it's your belief against his. But you have the edge - you have the Forecasting Graphs to help you and you have the charts in this book to help you to do the right thing. So go ahead and do it - make some money!

It's easy to earn a 100% net profit with "Selling a call or put at the money" if you get the market direction right. Here is an example, and everything will be average - average volatility, average time to expiration, and an average price change. You could meet this kind anytime.

<u>Example</u> : we will use Table 40, with 18 weeks to expiration, and the Forecasting Graphs indicate that prices will fall by 60¢ before the expiration date. Everything is average. We will sell a call because prices are expected to fall. Look now at the 18 weeks to expiration page in the charts in the following pages. Look at Table 40. Look at the line at the bottom of the chart and you see that there is a net credit of 32.6¢ which will go directly into the commodity account and stay there untouched until this transaction is completed. The margin required for a Table 40 volatility will be

$1000 (20¢).   That works out to be a net return of 163% on the investment of 20¢, in only 18 weeks.

Many large scale option traders who deal in hundreds or thousands of options, are mainly sellers.   Because that's where the money is!   After you have looked carefully at all 9 options outlined in this book, you will see by the net profit areas that there is more money to be made by selling calls and puts than by buying them.   But selling is more dangerous than buying, as explained above.

Volatility –   Let's see how a change in volatility will affect the net profit.

TABLE 800

changes in the soybean future's price in 25¢ increments / net profit area, in cents

	weeks to expiration 35	30	25	20	18	16	14	12	10	8	6	4	2	0
+125	-80.2	-76.6	-72.3	-66.7	-64.2	-61.7	-59.3	-56.9	-54.1	-51.0	-48.7	-48.4	-48.4	-48.4
+100	-57.5	-53.6	-49.0	-43.2	-40.7	-38.1	-35.8	-33.1	-30.4	-27.9	-25.2	-23.8	-23.4	-23.4
+75	-35.8	-32.0	-27.5	-22.2	-19.9	-17.4	-15.1	-12.7	-10.1	-7.3	-4.4	-1.0	1.5	1.6
+50	-22.9	-19.6	-15.3	-10.0	-7.5	-4.9	-2.3	0.8	4.2	8.0	12.6	18.5	24.9	26.6
+25	-11.5	-8.5	-4.1	1.8	4.5	7.6	10.7	14.1	18.0	22.2	27.5	35.2	45.1	51.6
0	-0.5	3.4	7.5	12.6	15.3	18.1	21.0	24.4	28.4	33.1	39.0	47.6	59.3	76.6
-25	9.5	12.8	17.1	22.4	24.9	27.7	30.6	33.9	37.8	42.4	48.2	56.6	67.5	76.6
-50	18.6	21.8	26.0	31.2	33.7	36.4	39.2	42.5	46.2	50.4	55.7	62.7	71.4	76.6
-75	23.4	26.2	30.0	35.2	37.7	40.3	43.2	46.5	50.2	54.7	59.9	67.0	74.4	76.6
-100	30.7	33.4	37.1	42.2	44.6	47.2	50.0	53.1	56.6	60.4	64.7	69.8	74.9	76.6
-125	38.8	41.4	45.2	50.1	52.4	54.8	57.1	59.5	62.1	65.1	68.3	72.3	76.1	76.6

The estimated credit is: +77.1 premium – 0.5 comm. = + 76.6¢

TABLE 200

changes in the soybean future's price in 25¢ increments / net profit area, in cents

	weeks to expiration 35	30	25	20	18	16	14	12	10	8	6	4	2	0
+125	-101.5	-101.5	-101.5	-101.5	-101.5	-101.5	-101.5	-101.5	-101.5	-101.5	-101.5	-101.5	-101.5	-101.5
+100	-76.5	-76.5	-76.5	-76.5	-76.5	-76.5	-76.5	-76.5	-76.5	-76.5	-76.5	-76.5	-76.5	-76.5
+75	-52.5	-52.3	-52.1	-51.9	-51.8	-51.7	-51.6	-51.6	-51.5	-51.5	-51.5	-51.5	-51.5	-51.5
+50	-31.6	-31.0	-30.3	-29.5	-29.1	-28.6	-28.2	-27.8	-27.4	-27.1	-26.8	-26.6	-26.5	-26.5
+25	-13.5	-12.5	-11.3	-10.1	-9.4	-8.7	-8.0	-7.2	-6.3	-5.2	-4.1	-2.8	-1.9	-1.5
0	-0.5	0.7	2.1	3.7	4.5	5.4	6.3	7.3	8.6	10.0	11.8	14.5	18.1	23.5
-25	8.2	9.3	10.6	12.0	12.8	13.7	14.5	15.4	16.5	17.8	19.5	21.6	22.7	23.5
-50	13.5	14.4	15.4	16.5	17.1	17.7	18.3	19.0	19.9	20.8	22.1	23.1	23.5	23.5
-75	17.5	18.2	19.0	19.9	20.3	20.9	21.3	21.8	22.2	22.6	23.2	23.5	23.5	23.5
-100	19.3	19.8	20.4	21.0	21.3	21.6	21.8	22.2	22.6	23.0	23.4	23.5	23.5	23.5
-125	21.2	21.5	21.9	22.3	22.5	22.8	23.0	23.1	23.3	23.4	23.5	23.5	23.5	23.5

The estimated credit is: +24.0¢ premium –0.5¢ comm. = +23.5¢

1. Both of the charts above use the same "weeks to expiration". Consequently you will be able to see how a change in volatility will affect the net profit.

2. There is no doubt that a high volatility works to the benefit of "sell a call or put at the money". Look at Table 80. It would require a margin of between 30¢ and 40¢ on account of its high rate of volatility. But its large credit premium of 76.6¢ works out to be a net profit of 200% or more in only 35 weeks. That's a very good return on the investment.

3. Another point. As you know, this book teaches that you must prevent a loss to your working capital. Well, there are two safeguards to your working capital in this option. First, there is the usual one – which is, you will sell a call only when you believe that prices will fall. Second, you have additional protection from the premium which you will collect when you sell the option. For example, the premium collected in Table 80 is 76.6¢. This means that prices could go against you by as much as 76.6¢ and you still would not lose any money at expiration. You can see by looking inside the net profit area, week by week, just how much profit you can make at any time.

4. In contrast, look at Table 20 (low volatility). You can see that the net profit area is much smaller than in Table 80. In this chart, the maximum profit is 23.5¢ would earn a net profit of about 100% on the investment.

Time – Lat's see how a change in time will affect profits.

TABLE 40 — changes in the soybean future's price in 25¢ increments — net profit area, in cents

	35	30	25	20	18	16	14	12	10	8	6	4	2	0
+125	-85.4	-84.7	-84.2	-84.0	-84.0	-84.0	-84.0	-84.0	-84.0	-84.0	-84.0	-84.0	-84.0	-84.0
+100	-61.8	-61.2	-60.7	-60.2	-59.9	-59.7	-59.5	-59.3	-59.1	-59.0	-59.0	-59.0	-59.0	-59.0
+75	-42.3	-41.0	-39.8	-38.6	-38.1	-37.5	-36.9	-36.3	-35.7	-35.0	-34.4	-34.0	-34.0	-34.0
+50	-26.3	-24.3	-22.8	-20.7	-19.8	-18.7	-17.7	-16.6	-15.3	-13.8	-12.2	-10.1	-9.1	-9.0
+25	-12.0	-9.9	-7.8	-5.3	-4.0	-2.8	-1.3	0.3	2.2	4.5	7.1	10.7	14.6	16.0
0	-0.5	1.4	3.7	6.5	7.9	9.4	11.0	12.8	15.0	17.5	20.7	25.3	31.6	41.0
-25	8.7	10.7	12.9	15.7	17.0	18.5	20.1	21.8	23.7	26.2	29.1	33.3	38.6	41.0
-50	16.3	18.3	20.4	22.7	23.9	25.1	26.4	27.8	29.4	31.4	33.7	36.9	40.5	41.0
-75	20.9	22.6	24.6	27.0	28.2	29.4	30.6	32.0	33.5	35.3	37.2	39.4	41.0	41.0
-100	26.0	27.6	29.3	31.0	31.8	32.7	33.7	34.6	35.7	37.0	38.3	39.9	41.0	41.0
-125	30.6	31.7	32.9	34.3	35.0	35.7	36.3	37.1	37.9	38.8	39.6	40.7	41.0	41.0

The estimated credit is: +41.5 premium – 0.5 comm. = +41.0¢

TABLE 40

changes in the soybean future's price in 25¢ increments	weeks to expiration			
	6	**4**	**2**	**0**
+125	-105.2	-105.2	-105.2	-105.2
+100	-80.2	-80.2	-80.2	-80.2
+75	-55.6	-55.2	-55.2	-55.2
+50	-33.4	-31.3	-30.3	-30.2
+25	-14.1	-10.5	-6.6	-5.2
0	-0.5	4.1	10.4	19.8
-25	7.9	12.1	17.7	19.8
-50	12.5	15.7	19.3	19.8
-75	16.0	18.2	19.8	19.8
-100	17.1	18.7	19.8	19.8
-125	18.5	19.5	19.8	19.8

net profit area, in cents

Est. credit: +20.3¢ -0.5¢ = 19.8¢

1. Note the comparitive sizes of the net profit areas. There is not much of a difference.

2. Note also that the net profit at 6 weeks is about half the profit at 35 weeks. That's a moderate decline when compared to the profit decline caused by a change in volatility, as shown a page or more back.

To sum up:

     "Selling a call or a put at the money" can be a very profitable investment. Selling an option can be dangerous if prices go against you. But this book points out two safeguards which help to protect your working capital against a loss (1) use the Forecasting Graphs to sell an option against the likely future price trend (2) The premium received from the sale will act as a safety margin in case prices go against you temporarily.

SELL A CALL or SELL A PUT

AT 50¢ OUT OF THE MONEY

This is the safest of all the 9 options which are written up in this book — and it is a profitable option. It also works well with any rate of volatility and with any time period. It works well anywhere and anytime. This one could turn out to be your favorite option trade.

Here's why this option is safer than the one just previously written up, namely "sell a call or put at the money". As you know, the expiration date is the day of reckoning for options. It's the end of the line and on that day you must take your profit or pay your loss if you have one. Now it will be shown to you that, at expiration day, it is safer to be selling an option at "50¢ out of the money" instead of an option "at the money".

Example. Let's say that you sold a call "at the money". Let's say that the soybean price rose by 30¢ (that's bad news because you need prices to fall so that you can keep all the premium). The expiration date arrives and prices are still up by 30¢. Therefore your commodity account will be reduced by 30¢ (the other fellow's gain is your loss). That's what happens when you sell a call "at the money". The buyer gained because the price settled at 30¢ "in the money".
Now let's use the same conditions as above for selling a call "at 50¢ out of the money". (1) you sell a call at "50¢ out of the money". (2) the premium gained goes into your account. (3) soybean prices rise by 30¢ and stay there at the expiration date. (4) you keep all the premium and the buyer gets nothing back, unlike what happened in the paragraph above. Why? The answer is: the final settlement was "out of the money". For the buyer to collect, the final price must be "in the money". So you can see that that extra 50¢ protection which was gained by selling "at 50¢ out of the money" provided an extra 50¢ safety zone to protect your profit.

The maximum profit which you can earn with this option is the amount of the premium. No matter how much the soybean price may move in your favor, you will never make any more money than the size of the premium. Suppose, for example, that the Forecasting Graphs indicated that the soybean price would rise by $1.50. Then you should use some other option because if you sold a put here you might gain only about a 30¢ premium, whereas if you bought a call instead, you would earn a much greater profit safely. The point is: even though selling "at 50¢ out of the money" is a nice, safe, profitable move, you would be better off to use some other option for a large price change. Even selling a call or put "at the money" would earn about twice as much profit and it would be quite safe when a large price change is indicated.

If you want to get ahead in the option market, you will have to get into the selling part of it because that's where the money is. Just buying a call or a put is not enough. You have to sell or mix buying and selling together, as you will see in the next two options in the pages ahead.

The nice thing about selling a call or a put is that you can make money even if the soybean price does not change at all. This makes it a good option to use if the Forecasting Graphs indicate that there will be little or no price movement.

Volatility – Let's see how a change in volatility will affect the profit.

TABLE 80

changes in the soybean future's price in 25¢ increments / net profit area, in cents

	35	30	25	20	18	16	14	12	10	8	6	4	2	0 (weeks to expiration)
+125	-54.9	-51.1	-46.6	-41.3	-39.0	-36.5	-34.2	-31.8	-29.2	-26.4	-23.5	-20.1	-17.6	-17.5
+100	-42.0	-38.7	-34.4	-29.1	26.6	-24.0	-21.4	-18.3	-14.9	-11.1	-6.5	-0.6	5.8	7.5
+75	-31.0	-27.6	-23.2	-17.3	-14.6	-11.5	-8.4	-5.0	-1.1	3.0	8.4	16.1	26.0	32.5
+50	-19.3	-15.9	-11.6	-6.3	-3.8	-1.0	1.9	5.3	9.3	14.0	19.9	28.5	40.2	57.5
+25	-9.6	-6.3	-2.0	3.3	5.8	8.6	11.5	14.8	18.7	23.3	29.1	37.5	48.4	57.5
0	-0.5	2.7	6.9	12.1	14.6	17.3	20.1	23.4	27.1	31.3	36.6	43.6	52.2	57.5
-25	4.3	7.1	10.9	16.1	18.6	21.2	24.1	27.4	31.1	35.6	40.8	47.9	55.3	57.5
-50	11.6	14.3	18.0	23.1	25.5	28.1	30.9	34.0	37.5	41.3	45.6	50.7	55.8	57.5
-75	19.6	22.3	26.1	31.0	33.3	35.7	38.0	40.4	43.0	46.0	49.2	53.2	57.0	57.5
-100	28.9	31.5	34.5	38.5	40.6	42.5	45.0	47.9	49.5	51.4	53.5	55.8	57.5	57.5
-125	36.0	38.4	41.4	45.3	47.1	48.7	50.4	52.2	54.0	55.0	56.0	56.7	57.5	57.5

The estimated credit is: +58.0¢ premium – 0.5¢ comm. = +57.5¢

TABLE 20

changes in the soybean future's price in 25¢ increments / net profit area, in cents

	35	30	25	20	18	16	14	12	10	8	6	4	2	0 (weeks to expiration)
+125	-66.5	-66.3	-66.1	-65.9	-65.8	-65.7	-65.6	-65.6	-65.5	-65.5	-65.5	-65.5	-65.5	-65.5
+100	-45.6	-45.0	-44.3	-43.5	-43.1	-42.6	-42.2	-41.8	-41.4	-41.1	-40.8	-40.6	-40.5	-40.5
+75	-27.5	-26.5	-25.3	-24.1	-23.4	-22.7	-22.0	-21.2	-20.3	-19.2	-18.1	-16.3	-15.9	-15.5
+50	-14.5	-13.3	-11.9	-10.3	-9.5	-8.6	-7.7	-6.7	-5.4	-4.0	-2.2	0.5	4.1	9.5
+25	-5.8	-4.7	-3.4	-2.0	-1.2	-0.3	0.5	1.4	2.5	3.8	5.5	7.6	8.7	9.5
0	-0.5	0.4	1.4	2.5	3.1	3.7	4.3	5.0	5.9	6.9	8.1	9.1	9.5	9.5
-25	3.5	4.2	5.0	5.9	6.3	6.8	7.3	7.8	8.2	8.6	9.2	9.5	9.5	9.5
-50	5.3	5.8	6.4	7.0	7.3	7.6	7.9	8.2	8.6	9.0	9.4	9.5	9.5	9.5
-75	7.2	7.5	7.9	8.3	8.5	8.8	9.0	9.1	9.3	9.4	9.5	9.5	9.5	9.5
-100	8.2	8.5	8.8	9.1	9.2	9.3	9.4	9.5	9.5	9.5	9.5	9.5	9.5	9.5
-125	8.8	9.1	9.3	9.4	9.5	9.5	9.5	9.5	9.5	9.5	9.5	9.5	9.5	9.5

The estimated credit is: +10.0¢ premium – 0.5¢ comm. = +9.5¢

Look at Table 80. Look at the size of the net profit area. It shows that one would have a very wide safety margin here when selling a call or a put at 50¢ out of the money. Prices could go against you by 107.5¢ and you would not lose any money. That's gives you lots of protection when you consider that you have used the Forecasting Graphs to help to get the trend right in the first place.

The rate of profit is good, too. Note that the net profit is 57.5¢. A $2000 margin would likely be needed here because of the high volatility (Table 80 represents high volatility). The rate of net profit would be: 57.5¢ ÷ 40¢ x 100 = 144% in 35 weeks.

Look at Table 20. The size of the net profit area is much smaller than Table 80's profit area. The net profit here is only 9.5¢ which gives a moderate but satisfactory profit rate. Table 20 represents low volatility which means that the margin is likely only $1000 (20¢) to $800 (16¢). That would result in about a 45% rate of profit in 35 weeks.

Time – Let's see how a change in time will affect the net profit.

Table 40 is used in both examples because Table 40 represents about the average volatility of the past 5 years. The weeks to expiration of 35 and 6 are used to show you what happens in the long term and in the short term.

TABLE 40 — changes in the soybean future's price in 25¢ increments — net profit area, in cents

	weeks to expiration													
	35	30	25	20	18	16	14	12	10	8	6	4	2	0
+125	-59.1	-57.8	-56.6	-55.4	-54.9	-54.3	-53.7	-53.0	-52.5	-51.8	-51.2	-50.8	-50.8	-50.8
+100	-43.1	-41.3	-39.6	-37.5	-36.6	-35.5	-34.5	-33.4	-32.1	-30.6	-29.0	-26.9	-25.9	-25.8
+75	-28.8	-26.7	-24.6	-22.1	-20.8	-19.6	-18.1	-16.5	-14.6	-12.3	-9.7	-6.1	-2.2	-0.8
+50	-17.3	-15.4	-13.1	-10.3	-8.9	-7.4	-5.8	-4.0	-1.8	0.7	3.9	8.5	14.8	24.2
+25	-8.1	-6.1	-3.9	-1.1	0.2	1.7	3.3	5.0	6.9	9.4	12.3	16.5	22.1	24.2
0	-0.5	1.5	3.6	5.9	7.1	8.3	9.6	11.0	12.6	14.6	16.9	20.1	23.7	24.2
-25	4.1	5.8	7.8	10.2	11.4	12.6	13.8	15.2	16.7	18.5	20.4	22.6	24.2	24.2
-50	9.2	10.8	12.5	14.2	15.0	15.9	16.9	17.8	18.9	20.2	21.5	23.1	24.2	24.2
-75	13.8	14.9	16.1	17.5	18.2	18.9	19.5	20.3	21.1	22.0	22.8	23.9	24.2	24.2
-100	17.3	18.3	19.3	20.3	21.0	21.6	22.2	22.9	23.4	23.7	23.9	24..2	24.2	24.2
-125	20.6	21.3	22.1	22.9	23.2	23.5	23.8	23.9	24.0	24.1	24.2	24.2	24.2	24.2

The estimated credit is: +24.7¢ premium - 0.5¢ comm. = + 24.2¢

TABLE 40

changes in the soybean future's price in 25¢ increments	weeks to expiration				
		6	4	2	0
+125		-68.6	-68.2	-68.2	-68.2
+100		-46.4	-44.3	-43.3	-43.2
+75		-27.1	-23.5	-19.6	-18.2
+50		-13.5	-8.9	-2.6	6.8
+25		-5.1	-0.9	4.7	6.8
0		-0.5	2.7	6.3	6.8
-25		3.0	5.2	6.8	6.8
-50		4.1	5.7	6.8	6.8
-75		5.4	6.5	6.8	6.8
-100		6.5	6.8	6.8	6.8
-125		6.8	6.8	6.8	6.8

net profit area , in cents

Est. credit: +7.3¢ -0.5¢ = +6.8¢

1. Both of the above appear to be safe trades. The 35 week (long term) trade can take a price reversal of 74.2¢ without lasing money. The long term investment should earn about 100% in 35 weeks, or to put it another way, about 149% on an annual basis.

2. The 6 week (short term) chart shows that it is a safe trade. It can absorb a 56.8¢ price reversal without lasing money. At first glance it may appear that it doesn't earn much profit. The 6.8¢ net profit, however, represents about a 28% return in 6 weeks. Or to put it another way, it earns about a 243% on an annual basis, an excellent return on the investment.

3. To sum up.

"Selling a call or a put at 50¢ out of the money" is the safest of all the 9 options which are outlined in this book. And it pays a good profit. Just be sure that you get the market direction right - whether prices will likely rise or whether they might fall in the weeks ahead. The summer months always bring erratic price movements - so keep an eye on the weather. This trade pays well for any time period - long term or short term.

BULL or BEAR SPREAD – #1

BUY A CALL AT THE MONEY
and SELL A CALL AT 25¢ OUT OF THE MONEY
OR
BUY A PUT AT THE MONEY
and SELL A PUT AT 25¢ OUT OF THE MONEY

This option is different from all the others and it has an attractive feature. That feature is this : it will either earn 15¢ or it will lose 10¢ no matter what the volatility rate is, and no matter whether you are trading in the long term or the short term.

In other words, you know where you stand with this one. If you get the market direction right, then you will earn about 15¢. If you get the market direction wrong, you will lose about 10¢. And that's what happens no matter whether the soybean market is turbulent as in the summer, or quiet as in the winter. And it happens no matter whether you take the position at 36 weeks or at 6 weeks. And no matter whether the prices change by 25¢ or by $1.25.

Therefore, if this option earns the same amount of money at 6 weeks as it does at 36 weeks, then this is a good option to use for the short term. Good trades are hard to find which are suitable for the short term – so this one is a welcome addition to that short list.

The "investment" for this option is the amount of money which you pay for the option plus the commission. The premium which you obtained from the sale of the call or put is to remain in your account untouched. Therefore, to calculate the rate of profit, use: net profit in cents ÷ the net cost x 100 = % return on your investment.

The point being made is this: the <u>annual</u> rate of return in the short term is much greater than the annual rate of return in the long term.

<u>Example</u> : Table 40 at 35 weeks has a cost of 42.5¢ and a net profit of 14.8¢. therefore, the rate of return for 35 weeks is about 35%, or about 52% on an annual basis. But Table 40 at 6 weeks has a cost of 21.3¢ and a net profit of 15.6¢. That calculates to about a 73% profit in 6 weeks, or about 635% on an annual basis. This shows that it is an excellent option to use for the short term.

<u>Volatility</u> –

Let's see how a change in volatility will affect the net profit.

The option positions which have been described so far have all been affected by a change in volatility. But this option is different – there is almost no effect on the net profit or on the net profit area. You can see it for yourself on the two charts. (Table 80 represents high volatility and Table 20 represents low volatility).

TABLE 80

changes in the soybean future's price in 25¢ increments

net profit area, in cents

		weeks to expiration												
	35	**30**	**25**	**20**	**18**	**16**	**14**	**12**	**10**	**8**	**6**	**4**	**2**	**0**
+125	12.4	12.6	12.7	12.8	12.9	13.0	13.1	13.2	13.4	13.6	13.8	14.0	14.4	14.4
+100	6.4	6.7	7.0	7.4	7.8	8.2	8.6	9.1	9.6	10.3	11.1	12.8	14.4	14.4
+75	3.8	4.0	4.2	4.4	4.7	5.0	5.3	5.7	6.2	6.8	7.8	9.4	12.8	14.4
+50	1.9	1.9	1.9	2.0	2.1	2.2	2.4	2.7	3.1	3.6	4.3	6.1	9.6	14.4
+25	0.3	0.4	0.4	0.5	0.5	0.6	0.6	0.7	0.8	0.9	1.1	1.8	3.6	14.4
0	-1.0	-1.0	-1.0	-1.0	-1.0	-1.0	-1.0	-1.1	-1.2	-1.3	-1.4	-1.6	-2.6	-10.6
-25	-1.5	-1.6	-1.7	-1.8	-1.8	-1.9	-2.0	-2.1	-2.2	-2.6	-3.3	-4.5	-6.7	-10.6
-50	-1.8	-1.9	-2.0	-2.1	-2.1	-2.2	-2.4	-2.7	-3.1	-3.7	-4.6	-5.7	-7.6	-10.6
-75	-2.1	-2.2	-2.3	-2.4	-2.5	-2.6	-2.8	-3.4	-4.2	-5.0	-6.0	-7.0	-8.6	-10.6
-100	-2.3	-2.4	-2.5	-2.6	-2.7	-3.0	-3.5	-4.2	-5.0	-5.9	-7.0	-8.1	-9.4	-10.6
-125	-2.5	-2.6	-2.7	-2.8	-3.0	-3.3	-3.8	-4.6	-5.4	-6.6	-7.8	-9.1	-10.1	-10.6

The estimated cost is: -77.1¢ premium + 67.5¢ premium - 1.0¢ comm. = -10.6¢

TABLE 20

changes in the soybean future's price in 25¢ increments

net profit area, in cents

		weeks to expiration												
	35	**30**	**25**	**20**	**18**	**16**	**14**	**12**	**10**	**8·**	**6**	**4**	**2**	**0**
+125	15.3	15.3	15.3	15.3	15.3	15.3	15.3	15.3	15.3	15.3	15.3	15.3	15.3	15.3
+100	14.3	14.5	14.7	14.9	15.0	15.1	15.2	15.2	15.3	15.3	15.3	15.3	15.3	15.3
+75	11.2	11.6	12.1	12.7	13.0	13.4	13.7	14.1	14.4	14.7	15.0	15.2	15.3	15.3
+50	8.4	8.8	9.3	9.6	9.9	10.2	10.5	10.9	11.4	12.2	13.0	14.1	14.9	15.3
+25	3.3	3.5	3.7	4.0	4.3	4.4	4.6	4.8	5.1	5.5	6.2	7.6	10.3	15.3
0	-1.0	-1.1	-1.2	-1.3	-1.4	-1.4	-1.5	-1.6	-1.8	-1.9	-2.0	-2.6	-3.1	-9.7
-25	-4.4	-4.6	-4.9	-5.2	-5.4	-5.7	-5.9	-6.1	-6.3	-6.7	-7.1	-8.1	-9.1	-9.7
-50	-5.7	-5.9	-6.1	-6.3	-6.5	-6.6	-6.7	-6.9	-7.3	-7.9	-8.6	-9.3	-9.7	-9.7
-75	-6.9	-7.0	-7.2	-7.3	-7.4	-7.5	-7.7	-7.9	-8.2	-8.8	-9.5	-9.7	-9.7	-9.7
-100	-7.9	-8.0	-8.1	-8.2	-8.3	-8.4	-8.6	-8.8	-9.0	-9.3	-9.6	-9.7	-9.7	-9.7
-125	-8.7	-8.7	-8.8	-8.9	-9.0	-9.2	-9.3	-9.4	-9.5	-9.6	-9.7	-9.7	-9.7	-9.7

The estimated cost is: -24.0 ¢ premium + 15.3 ¢ premium - 1.0 ¢ comm. = -9.7 ¢

–   Let's see how a difference in time will affect the net profit.

TABLE 40

changes in the soybean future's price in 25¢ increments / net profit area, in cents

	35	30	25	20	18	16	14	12	10	8	6	4	2	0 weeks to expiration
+125	13.2	13.3	13.4	13.6	13.9	14.1	14.3	14.5	14.7	14.8	14.8	14.8	14.8	14.8
+100	9.3	10.0	10.7	11.4	11.7	12.0	12.4	12.8	13.2	13.8	14.4	14.8	14.8	14.8
+75	6.0	6.3	6.8	7.4	8.0	8.6	9.0	9.5	10.2	11.0	12.0	12.7	13.5	14.8
+50	4.1	4.4	4.8	5.1	5.4	5.7	6.2	6.7	7.3	8.1	9.1	10.6	13.5	14.8
+25	0.9	1.1	1.3	1.6	1.8	2.0	2.1	2.3	2.6	2.8	3.4	4.4	6.8	14.8
0	-1.0	-1.0	-1.0	-1.0	-1.1	-1.1	-1.1	-1.2	-1.4	-1.6	-1.8	-2.2	-3.0	-10.2
-25	-2.4	-2.6	-2.8	-3.1	-3.3	-3.6	-3.9	-4.2	-4.5	-5.0	-5.6	-6.6	-8.6	-10.2
-50	-4.7	-4.8	-5.0	-5.3	-5.6	-5.8	-5.9	-6.0	-6.1	-6.3	-6.7	-7.7	-9.7	-10.2
-75	-5.0	-5.3	-5.6	-6.1	-6.6	-6.9	-7.2	-7.5	-7.8	-8.2	-8.6	-9.0	-10.2	-10.2
-100	-5.6	-5.9	-6.3	-6.7	-7.0	-7.3	-7.6	-7.8	-8.1	-8.4	-8.9	-9.4	-10.2	-10.2
-125	-6.4	-6.7	-7.0	-7.2	-7.4	-7.6	-7.8	-8.0	-8.3	-8.6	-9.1	-9.9	-10.2	-10.2

The estimated cost is: -41.5¢ premium +32.3¢ premium – 1.0 ¢ comm. = -10.2¢

TABLE 40

changes in the soybean future's price in 25¢ increments / net profit area, in cents

	6	4	2	0 weeks to expiration
+125	15.6	15.6	15.6	15.6
+100	15.2	15.6	15.6	15.6
+75	12.8	13.5	14.3	15.6
+50	9.9	11.4	14.3	15.6
+25	4.2	5.2	7.6	15.6
0	-1.0	-1.4	-2.2	-9.4
-25	-4.8	-5.8	-7.8	-9.4
-50	-5.9	-6.9	-8.9	-9.4
-75	-7.8	-8.2	-9.4	-9.4
-100	-8.1	-8.5	-9.4	-9.4
-125	-8.3	-9.1	-9.4	-9.4

Cost: -20.3+11.9-1.0=-9.4¢

You can see that the net profit area in unaffected by the long terms and the short term. But the _rate_ of return on the investment is greater in the short term as explained a couple of pages back.

To sum up

This is a nice relaxing trade to use because you know where you stand with this one before you take the position – you will either earn about 15¢ or you will lose about 10¢.

This option is one of the best earners for the short term.

Even though it is a relaxing, profitable option position, the "Bull or bear spread #1" should not be used on every occassion. Suppose, for example, that the Forecasting Graphs showed that the soybean price would rise by about $1.25. Then it makes no sense to try for a 15¢ profit by using the "Bull Spread #1". More money can be made with some other option, in this case.

Use 2 criteria when deciding which option to use : (1) calculate the % return on the investment (2) then check for safety because you must protect your working capital. To repeat – the amount of profit and safety are the 2 criteria.

An important point. Because the "Bull or bear spread #1" is so safe, it is unlikely that you will have to deposit a margin (as it is customary to do when selling an option). Therefore your "investment" will be the amount which you pay for the call "at the money".

BULL or BEAR SPREAD – #2

BUY A CALL AT THE MONEY
and SELL 2 CALLS AT 50¢ OUT OF THE MONEY
OR
BUY A PUT AT THE MONEY
and SELL 2 PUTS AT 50¢ OUT OF THE MONEY

This is yet another unique soybean option. The title is similar to the "Bull or bear spread #1 ", but that's where the similarity ends. The profits here form a different pattern than do the profits of spread #1.

Also this spread is expensive to take because there are 3 commissions to pay. If you are paying a full commission, then you should knock off about 8¢ from the profits shown in the charts. If you knocked 8¢ off the low volatility charts, then the remaining net profit might be so small that the option may no longer be worth doing. As mentioned before, the net profits which are showing in the charts were calculated by using a discount commission of $25 round trip. Therefore, if you are using a full commission, then you must expect smaller profits.

Also your "investment " is large for this option. For example, let's say that a "bull spread #2 " is being done because it is expected that prices will rise in the next weeks. First, you are buying a call – so the premium which you pay for the call will be part of your "investment ". Second, you are going to sell 2 calls at 50¢ out of the money. Normally, when you sell a option, you must deposit a margin into your account. There are 2 call being sold here. But you get a break. You will likely have to deposit only <u>one</u> margin into your account. Why? Think back to "bull spread #1 " where you did not need any margin at all because it was so safe. Well, "bull spread #2 " is similar except that there is an extra call being sold. So you will need a margin for that extra call sold. Thus, your total investment will be made from (1) the cost of the call at the money (2) the margin needed for selling the second call. (You need to know the amount of your investment so that you can calculate the net profit percentage.)

Look at the net profit charts below. You will see that the largest profit at the expiration date is on the +50 line. Notice how the profit become smaller as you move away from that +50 line. Therefore, the +50 line is the bull's eye of the profit target. Aim for it.

The ideal situation, then, would be for the Forecasting Graphs to indicate a price change of 50¢ – that way, you would hit or come close to the maximum profit at line +50, at expiration. But conditions are not always ideal and so you should expect a price change which is greater or less than the ideal. If, for example, the Forecasting Graphs indicated that the price would rise by $1.25, then you would overshoot the target and get only a small profit from such a large price move. Look at Table 80 and you will see that you would get only 12.4¢ profit. Normally we all like a big price change because it brings a good profit. But not with this option.

The paragraph above brings out the point that each option is unique in a way. That's a good thing for us because we can use the option which is best suited to a certain situation. One or more of the 9 options outlined in this book can be used to cover any eventuallity which may arise.

Let's see how a change in the volatility rate will affect the profit.

TABLE 80 — changes in the soybean future's price in 25¢ increments — net profit area, in cents

	35	30	25	20	18	16	14	12	10	8	6	4	2	0 (weeks to expiration)
+125	-30.6	-26.6	-21.9	-16.9	-14.7	-12.4	-10.1	-7.7	-5.3	-2.8	0.7	7.2	12.2	12.4
+100	-28.3	-24.8	-20.8	-16.0	-13.5	-10.9	-8.0	-4.5	-0.4	4.7	11.2	21.6	34.0	37.0
+75	-27.9	-24.2	-19.9	-13.4	-10.3	-6.6	-2.7	1.7	6.9	12.5	20.2	32.2	49.5	62.4
+50	-17.3	-13.2	-8.9	-3.6	-1.1	1.9	5.1	8.8	13.4	19.0	26.2	37.5	54.5	87.4
+25	-9.1	-5.1	-0.9	3.8	6.1	8.6	11.3	14.5	18.4	23.4	29.7	38.8	50.7	62.4
0	-1.5	1.2	5.3	10.4	12.9	15.5	18.2	21.4	24.8	28.5	33.2	38.6	44.3	37.4
-25	-1.5	0.4	3.7	8.8	11.3	13.7	16.6	19.9	23.4	27.8	32.4	38.2	42.1	37.4
-50	3.6	5.8	9.0	14.0	16.3	18.8	21.6	24.5	27.8	31.2	34.5	37.7	39.2	37.4
-75	14.8	17.4	21.2	25.8	27.9	30.1	31.8	33.3	34.8	36.3	37.5	38.4	38.6	37.4
-100	23.9	25.6	28.4	31.0	33.7	35.2	36.7	37.9	39.0	40.1	41.3	39.1	38.2	37.4
-125	32.8	34.6	36.8	38.9	40.8	41.8	42.8	43.9	44.9	43.9	42.7	40.1	37.9	37.4

The estimated credit: -77.1¢ premium + 58.0¢ premium + 58.0¢ premium - 1.5¢ comm. = + 37.4¢

TABLE 20 — changes in the soybean future's price in 25¢ increments — net profit

	35	30	25	20	18	16	14	12	10	8	6	4	2	0 (weeks to expiration)
+125	-32.5	-32.1	-31.7	-31.3	-31.1	-30.9	-30.7	-30.6	-30.5	-30.5	-30.5	-30.5	-30.5	-30.5
+100	-15.7	-14.5	-13.1	-11.5	-10.7	-9.7	-8.9	-8.1	-7.3	-6.7	-6.1	-5.7	-5.5	-5.5
+75	-3.5	-1.7	0.5	2.7	3.8	5.1	6.6	8.2	9.9	12.1	14.3	16.9	18.7	19.5
+50	1.6	3.4	5.5	7.9	9.1	10.4	11.8	13.4	15.6	18.1	21.4	26.6	33.7	44.5
+25	0.9	2.1	3.5	5.1	6.1	7.1	8.0	9.0	10.3	11.9	14.1	16.7	18.3	19.5
0	-1.5	-0.9	-0.3	0.3	0.7	1.0	1.3	1.7	2.2	2.6	3.4	3.1	-0.1	-5.5
-25	-2.2	-1.9	-1.6	-1.3	-1.2	-0.9	-0.9	-0.8	-1.1	-1.6	-2.1	-3.6	-4.7	-5.5
-50	-3.9	-3.8	-3.6	-3.5	-3.5	-3.5	-3.5	-3.6	-3.7	-3.9	-4.3	-5.1	-5.5	-5.5
-75	-4.1	-4.2	-4.2	-4.3	-4.3	-4.3	-4.4	-4.5	-4.6	-4.8	-5.2	-5.5	-5.5	-5.5
-100	-4.3	-4.3	-4.4	-4.4	-4.5	-4.5	-4.6	-4.7	-4.9	-5.1	-5.3	-5.5	-5.5	-5.5
-125	-4.4	-4.5	-4.6	-4.7	-4.8	-4.9	-5.0	-5.1	-5.3	-5.4	-5.5	-5.5	-5.5	-5.5

The estimated cost is: -24.0¢ premium + 10.0¢ premium + 10.0¢ premium - 1.5¢ comm. = -5.5¢

Look at the net profit area of Table 80.   It is enormous.   It extends to +137.4¢ on the upside to infinity on the downside.

It is not often that you hear of a profit extending to infinity, but it is true in this case and in most cases of above average volatility.   The volatility makes the difference.

Look at Table 20 above.   You can see that this is a risky trade because the profit area is small and it is doubtful that you could finish up on expiration day inside the net profit area because this chart is for 35 weeks and a lot of thing could happen to the trade in 35 weeks.   Spread #1 would be much better than spread #2, in this case.

Trading a sure thing!   Oh, how often we have heard that siren song, and just as often we have been dashed upon the rocks!

If there is an Impossible Dream in the commodity business, it is likely the dream of finding the perfect trade – the sure thing – a trade which earns a profit for sure with no chance for a loss.   But all you commodity veterans know that it is impossible to find a trade which is both 100% safe and profitable.   But would you settle for 99%?   Or for 95%?   Or for 90%?

Well, you are about to hear of one which is limited in scope, but which this author thinks is 90% to 99% safe and profitable.

But first you should be reminded that there is an unwritten rule in commodity and option trading which says,"Less risk brings less profit".   Most of us have some good, solid Blue Chip stocks which are the epitome of safety because the stocks represent companies which have been in business for years and will be in business for decades more.   It is true that some of them lose a bit of money now and then, but one still keeps them because they have a good future.   It is also true that many Blue Chip stocks have not averaged a 20% increase in value each year for the past 10 years. But these stocks are considered to be a safe investment so we are satisfied with a small net return.

The option position which you are about to see, is considered to be safer than most Blue Chip stocks and much more profitable.   You should earn an annual net return of between 25% and 50%.

Table 80 with 35 weeks to expiration will be used for the example – but any above average volatility will work with a long term or medium term time period. Follow this closely.

1. This example will be a Bull Spread – buy a call at the money & sell 2 calls at 50¢ out of the money – using Table 80 at 35 weeks to expiration.

2. Look at the profit area of Table 80 above and note that the largest profit is 87.4¢ on line +50.   This is a bull spread so it was taken when the Forecasting Graphs indicated that the soybean prices would rise.   Therefore the profit will likely be in the top half of the chart.

3. But what if prices fell instead of rising as was expected?

4. Look at the bottom half of the Table 80.   This is the area where we would be if prices fell. A profit would be made here, too.   A 37.4¢ profit.   And the profit extend to infinity. This is a very safe area to be in because there is ample protection both above and below.

5. Follow this closely.   Suppose that we deliberately tried to get our option into the bottom half of the chart where the "37.4¢ to infinity" profit is situated.   In other words, we deliberately brush aside our chances for getting into the big profit area in the top half of Table 80, and choose instead to go to the safe area in the bottom half of the chart where the profit goes on to infinity.

6. But how to do it?   Answer : by deliberately trying to fail.

7. Trying to fail?   Yes, that's what it amounts to.   If the Forecasting Graphs indicated that soybean prices would rise, for example, then normally we would go for a bull spread. But instead we will go for a bear spread , meaning that we will finish up in the bottom half of the chart where there is the ultimate in safety and a profit.   In other words, even though prices will rise, we do the opposite and "buy a put at the money and sell 2 puts at 50¢ out of the money".

8. Example.
   (a) The date is May 15 and USDA's soybean crop estimate has just been published.   The estimate is for a larger crop this year – so prices will likely decline to harvest.

   (b) The Forecasting Graphs indicate that the Nov. price should decline by 75¢.

   (c) Usually we buy puts and, or sell calls when prices decline.   But not this time.   We will do the opposite.

   (d) We will "Buy a call at the money and sell 2 calls at 50¢ out of the money"

   (e) Now if prices do indeed fall as predicted by the Forecasting Graphs, we will find find ourselves in the safe area in the bottom half of the chart.   But how safe are we?

   (f) Look at Table 80 above.   Let's say that the soybean Nov. price did fall by 75¢ as predicted.   Locate our position in Table 80 at the end of the –75 line.   Got it? Look above and below our location.   We are surrounded by safety!   Look downward. You can see that the 37.4¢ net profit goes to infinity.   Look upward.   You can see that the soybean price would have to reverse its trend and rise by 212.4¢ to cause a loss to your working capital – almost impossible to happen.   The option is very safe.

   (g) You will notice, in this example, that the option was taken on May 15th, just after the USDA crop report (it is important that you use the latest USDA crop report when taking a future or an option position).   In this example we are heading into the summer months and every year we get weather scares.   In June, July, and August there are rumors of drought, and in August and September there are rumors of an early frost. These rumors keep the market on edge, resulting in erratic price swings.

   (h) Let's say, in this example, that the weather scares actually caused the soybean price to rise by 75¢, instead of falling by 75¢ as expected.   What is the situation now?   Look at the +75 line and you will see that we would get a 62.4¢ profit at expiration.

   (i) The point being made is this : we aim for a low, safe return on our investment.   But if prices go against us, then there is a good chance that we will get a larger profit.

(j)   To Sum Up

What has been shown here is a very safe way to trade soybean options where we deliberately seek safety and security for our working capital, knowing that a smaller rate of return will result from it.

This type of trading will likely appeal to only about 30% of option traders – the cautious ones.   This book goes out of its way to teach about the importance of protecting one's capital from loss – so it seemed a good idea to include this safe method.

Most commodity traders, though, are risk takers and will go for the big prize and the risks that go with it.

(k)   Not every volatility will work for this safe method. Here's how to tell if this safe method can be used. Look at the charts for "Bull or Bear Spread #2". If you see a profit in the bottom half of the chart, then that particular volatility and time period will be satisfactory.

Time

How does a change in time affect the profit for spread #2 ?

1. Look at the two charts below – they represent the long term investment and the short term investment at an average volatility rate.

2. Note the change in the size of the net profit area.

3. Even with a smaller net profit area, the 6 week chart is a good one because (a) Table 40 is of moderate volatility , so there will not be much price change in 6 weeks (except in those turbulent summer months) (b) it gives an excellent rate of return, on an annual basis.

		35	30	25	20	18	16	14	12	10	8	6	4	2	0
	+125	-33.8	-31.9	-30.0	-27.8	-26.8	-25.6	-24.4	-23.2	-22.0	-20.6	-19.4	-18.6	-18.6	-18.6
	+100	-25.4	-22.4	-19.5	-15.8	-14.1	-12.3	-10.5	-8.5	-6.1	-3.2	0.0	4.2	6.2	6.4
	+75	-16.3	-13.4	-10.4	-6.6	-4.6	-2.7	-0.3	2.3	5.5	9.4	14.0	20.8	28.6	31.4
	+50	-9.3	-7.3	-4.4	-0.9	1.0	2.9	5.1	7.6	10.7	14.2	19.0	26.1	37.7	56.4
	+25	-5.2	-3.3	-1.0	1.7	3.4	5.2	6.9	8.7	10.6	13.3	16.5	21.3	28.6	31.4
	0	-1.5	0.6	2.5	4.3	5.3	6.2	7.2	8.2	9.2	10.7	12.1	13.9	14.8	6.4
	-25	-1.5	-0.1	1.7	3.7	4.8	5.7	6.5	7.6	8.7	9.8	10.7	10.9	8.5	6.4
	-50	1.1	2.3	3.6	4.7	5.1	5.7	6.3	6.8	7.4	8.0	8.2	8.3	6.9	6.4
	-75	5.8	6.2	6.6	7.0	7.2	7.3	7.4	7.6	7.7	7.6	7.4	7.3	6.4	6.4
	-100	8.4	8.7	9.0	9.3	9.4	9.5	9.5	9.0	8.5	8.1	7.6	6.8	6.4	6.4
	-125	9.6	9.9	10.2	10.5	10.6	10.5	10.3	9.7	9.1	8.4	7.8	6.7	6.4	6.4

weeks to expiration

TABLE 40

changes in the soybean future's price in 25¢ increments

net profit area , in cents

The estimated credit is: -41.5¢ premium + 24.7¢ premium + 24.7¢ premium - 1.5¢ comm. = +6.4¢

changes in the soybean future's price in 25¢ increments	weeks to expiration			
	6	**4**	**2**	**0**
+125	-33.0	-32.2	-32.2	-32.2
+100	-13.6	-9.4	-7.4	-7.2
+75	0.4	7.2	15.0	17.8
+50	5.4	12.5	24.1	42.8
+25	2.9	7.7	15.0	17.8
0	-1.5	0.3	1.2	-7.2
−25	-2.9	-2.7	-5.1	-7.2
−50	-5.4	-5.3	-6.7	-7.2
−75	-6.2	-6.3	-7.2	-7.2
−100	-6.0	-6.8	-7.2	-7.2
−125	-5.8	-6.9	-7.2	-7.2

net profit area

-20.3+7.3+7.3-1.5=-7.2¢

SELL A STRADDLE

SELL A CALL AT THE MONEY
and SELL A PUT AT THE MONEY

The ideal situation for this option is to have no price change at all because the largest profit is made on line 0.   Therefore, the option position should be taken when the Forecasting Graphs indicate that there will be little or no price change in the weeks ahead.

But even though you may be aiming for the largest profit on line 0, there are still good profits to be made even if you misjudge the price change by 50¢ to 75¢ – which gives you a reasonable safety margin in case some unexpected event may occur which will alter the price trend.

You will notice that the safety margin works in both directions – by that is meant that once you have taken the straddle, an unexpected event could send prices either up or down. But the straddle has a safety margin in both directions – so you have coverage no matter which direction the price trend may change.

Volatility   Let's see how a change in volatility will affect profits.

Below are two charts. One at a high volatility rate (Table 80) and one at a low rate (Table 20) and both are at the same weeks to expiration.

		35	30	25	20	18	16	14	12	10	8	6	weeks to expiration 4	2	0
	+125	-41.5	-35.2	-27.1	-16.6	-11.8	-6.9	-2.2	2.6	8.0	14.1	19.6	23.9	27.7	28.2
	+100	-26.8	-20.2	-11.9	-1.0	3.9	9.1	14.2	20.0	26.2	32.5	39.5	46.0	51.5	53.2
	+75	-12.4	-5.8	2.5	13.0	17.8	22.9	28.1	33.8	40.1	47.4	55.5	66.0	75.9	78.2
	+50	-4.3	2.2	10.7	21.2	26.2	31.5	36.9	43.3	50.4	58.4	68.3	81.2	96.3	103.2
T A B L E	+25	-2.4	4.3	13.0	24.2	29.4	35.3	41.3	48.0	55.8	64.6	75.7	91.8	112.6	128.2
	0	-1.0	6.4	15.0	25.6	30.6	36.2	42.0	48.8	56.8	66.2	78.0	95.2	118.6	153.2
8 0	-25	-2.4	4.3	13.0	24.2	29.4	35.2	41.3	48.0	55.8	64.6	75.7	91.8	112.6	128.2
	-50	-4.3	2.2	10.7	21.2	26.2	31.5	36.9	43.3	50.4	58.4	68.3	81.2	96.3	103.2
	-75	-12.4	-5.8	2.5	13.0	17.8	22.9	28.1	33.8	40.1	47.4	55.5	66.0	75.9	78.2
	-100	-26.8	-20.2	-11.9	-1.0	3.9	9.1	14.2	20.0	26.2	32.5	39.5	46.0	51.5	53.2
	-125	-41.5	-35.2	-27.1	-16.6	-11.8	-6.9	-2.2	2.6	8.0	14.1	19.6	23.9	27.7	28.2

changes in the soybean future's price in 25¢ increments

net profit area , in cents

The estimated credit is: +77.1¢ premium + 77.1¢ premium – 1.0¢ comm. = +153.2¢

changes in the soybean future's price in 25¢ increments	weeks to expiration													
	35	**30**	**25**	**20**	**18**	**16**	**14**	**12**	**10**	**8**	**6**	**4**	**2**	**0**
+125	-80.3	-80.0	-79.6	-79.2	-79.0	-78.7	-78.5	-78.4	-78.2	-78.1	-78.0	-78.0	-78.0	-78.0
+100	-57.0	-56.6	-56.1	-55.5	-55.2	-54.9	-54.6	-54.3	-53.9	-53.5	-53.1	-53.0	-53.0	-53.0
+75	-34.9	-33.9	-33.0	-32.0	-31.4	-30.8	-30.3	-29.8	-29.3	-28.9	-28.3	-28.0	-28.0	-28.0
+50	-18.1	-16.6	-14.9	-13.0	-12.0	-10.9	-9.9	-8.8	-7.5	-6.2	-4.7	-3.5	-3.0	-3.0
+25	-5.3	-3.2	-0.7	1.9	3.3	5.0	6.5	8.2	10.2	12.6	15.4	18.8	21.5	22.0
0	-1.0	1.4	4.2	7.4	9.0	10.8	12.6	14.6	17.2	20.0	23.6	29.0	36.2	47.0
-25	-5.3	-3.2	-0.7	1.9	3.3	5.0	6.5	8.2	10.2	12.6	15.4	18.8	21.5	22.0
-50	-18.1	-16.6	-14.9	-13.0	-12.0	-10.9	-9.9	-8.8	-7.5	-6.2	-4.7	-3.5	-3.0	-3.0
-75	-35.0	-33.9	-33.0	-32.0	-31.4	-30.8	-30.3	-29.8	-29.3	-28.9	-29.3	-28.0	-28.0	-28.0
-100	-57.0	-56.6	-56.1	-55.5	-55.2	-54.9	-54.6	-54.3	-53.9	-53.5	-53.1	-53.0	-53.0	-53.0
-125	-80.3	-80.0	-79.6	-79.2	-79.0	-78.7	-78.5	-78.4	-78.2	-78.1	-78.0	-78.0	-78.0	-78.0

TABLE 20

net profit area

The estimated credit is: +24.0¢ premium + 24.0¢ premium - 1.0¢ comm. = + 47.0¢

   The straddle works better with a larger than average volatility rate.   Look at the size
of the net profit area in Table 80 - it extend away off the chart.

   In Table 80, the future's price would have to change by more than 153.2¢ in either
direction before you would lose money.   That's plenty of protection - especially since you take this
position only if the Forecasting Graphs indicate little or a moderate price change (it would be
unrealistic to expect no price change because the time to expiration is 35 weeks and a lot can happen
in that time).

   Also, if you wish to get out of the position early, there is plent of opportunity to get out
with a profit .   For example, suppose that by week 20 the price had risen by 50¢ and that fact worried
you - then you could liquidate the straddle at that point and earn a net profit of 21.2¢ (locate line
+50 's juncture with the 20th week column in Table 80).

   The net profit area of all the 9 positions outlined in this book will show you the size
of the net profit at any time if you wish to get out of the position early.

   Look at Table 20.   Note how small the net profit area is.   This would be a risky trade
to do because (1) the time to expiration is 35 weeks, and you need no price change or very little
change to keep inside the small net profit area - and that would be unlikely because a lot of
unexpected events can happen in 35 weeks (2) all low volatility positions have too small a profit area.

Time - Let's see how a change from long term to short term will affect profits.   Table 40 is used with
   both charts because Table 40 represents about the average volatility of the past 5 years.

TABLE 40

changes in the soybean future's price in 25¢ increments	35	30	25	20	18	16	14	12	10	8	6	4	2	0 (weeks to expiration)
+125	-54.8	-53.0	-51.3	-49.7	-49.0	-48.3	-47.7	-46.9	-46.1	-45.2	-44.3	-43.3	-43.0	-43.0
+100	-35.8	-33.6	-31.4	-29.2	-28.1	-27.0	-25.8	-24.7	-23.4	-22.0	-20.6	-19.1	-18.0	-18.0
+75	-21.4	-18.4	-15.2	-11.4	-9.9	-8.1	-6.3	-4.3	-2.1	0.3	2.8	5.4	7.0	7.0
+50	-9.0	-5.8	-2.4	2.0	4.1	6.4	8.7	11.2	14.1	17.6	21.5	26.8	31.4	32.0
+25	-3.3	0.8	5.1	10.4	13.0	15.7	18.8	22.1	25.9	30.7	36.2	44.0	53.5	57.0
0	-1.0	2.8	7.4	13.0	15.8	18.8	22.0	25.6	30.0	35.0	41.4	50.6	63.2	82.0
-25	-3.3	0.8	5.1	10.4	13.0	15.7	18.8	22.1	25.9	30.7	36.2	44.0	53.5	57.0
-50	-9.8	-5.4	-2.4	2.0	4.1	6.4	8.7	11.2	14.1	17.6	21.5	26.8	31.4	32.0
-75	-21.4	-18.4	-15.2	-11.4	-9.9	-8.1	-6.3	-4.3	-2.1	0.3	2.8	5.4	7.0	7.0
-100	-35.8	-33.6	-31.4	-29.2	-28.1	-27.0	-25.8	-24.7	-23.4	-22.0	-20.6	-19.1	-18.0	-18.0
-125	-54.8	-53.0	-51.3	-49.7	-49.0	-48.3	-47.7	-46.9	-46.1	-45.2	-44.3	-43.3	-43.0	-43.0

net profit area , in cents

The estimated credit is: + 41.5¢ premium + 41.5¢ premium − 1.0 comm. = + 82.0¢

TABLE 40

changes in the soybean future's price in 25¢ increments	6	4	2	0 (weeks to expiration)
+125	-86.7	-85.7	-85.4	-85.4
+100	-63.0	-61.5	-60.4	-60.4
+75	-39.6	-37.0	-35.4	-35.4
+50	-20.9	-15.6	-11.0	-10.4
+25	-6.2	1.6	11.1	14.6
0	-1.0	8.2	20.8	39.6
-25	-6.2	1.6	11.1	14.6
-50	-20.9	-15.6	-11.0	-10.4
-75	-39.6	-37.0	-35.4	-35.4
-100	-63.0	-61.5	-60.4	-60.4
-125	-86.7	-85.7	-85.4	-85.4

net profit area

Credit:+20.3+20.3-1.0=+39.6¢

These two charts show that a medium to a high volatility rate is needed to trade the straddle profitable in the long, medium, and short term.

The 6 week chart is reasonably safe and it will show an excellent return on the investment, on an annual basis.

To sum up   The straddle is a safe, very profitable trade for average volatility or higher. There is a high percentage return on your investment with this one. Your investment may be only one margin which you must deposit into your account. This trade probably has the highest percentage return on the investment of all the 9 positions outlined in this book.

SELL A STRANGLE – #1

SELL A CALL AT 50¢ OUT OF THE MONEY
and SELL A PUT AT 50¢ OUT OF THE MONEY

This option position has a wider safety margin than has the straddle position but the profit percentage is less than the straddle's. In other words, a trader must accept a lower rate of profit if he wishes for more safety for his working capital.

But more safety is a desirable factor and here is how the Strangle #1 illustrates that extra safety. Look at the charts below. You will see that there are 5 lines with the maximum profit at the expiration date – whereas, only 1 line in the Straddle has the maximum profit.

The extra lines with the maximum profit offer a larger target to aim at. In other words, it is possible to actually get the maximum profit in this trade because one would take this trade when the Forecasting Graphs indicated little or no price movement – and here there is a 50¢ leeway, up and down, in case some unexpected event changed the price trend.

This 50¢ leeway exists in all the strangle #1 positions, in all volatility rates and in the long term or short term.

The Strangle #1 earns the second best percentage return of the 9 positions which are outlined in this book. The Straddle has the best return.

Volatility – Let's see how a change in the volatility rates will affect the profit.

changes in the soybean future's price in 25¢ increments	35	30	25	20	18	16	14	12	10	8	6	4	2	0 (weeks to expiration)
+125	-18.9	-12.6	-5.1	4.2	8.1	12.2	16.2	20.4	24.6	28.6	32.5	36.6	39.9	40.0
+100	-13.1	-7.2	0.1	9.4	13.9	18.5	23.6	28.9	34.6	40.4	47.0	55.2	63.3	65.0
+75	-11.0	-5.3	2.9	13.7	18.7	24.2	29.6	35.4	42.2	49.1	57.6	69.3	83.0	90.0
+50	-8.0	-1.6	6.4	16.8	21.7	27.1	32.8	39.3	46.8	55.3	65.5	79.2	96.0	115.0
+25	-5.7	0.8	8.9	19.4	24.4	29.8	35.6	42.2	49.8	58.9	69.9	85.4	103.7	115.0
0	-1.0	5.4	13.8	24.2	29.2	34.6	40.2	46.8	54.2	62.6	73.2	87.2	104.6	115.0
-25	-5.7	0.8	8.9	19.4	24.4	29.8	35.6	42.2	49.8	58.9	69.9	85.4	103.7	115.0
-50	-8.0	-1.6	6.4	16.8	21.7	27.1	32.8	39.3	46.8	55.3	65.5	79.2	96.0	115.0
-75	-11.0	-5.3	2.9	13.7	18.7	24.2	29.6	35.4	42.2	49.1	57.6	69.3	83.0	90.0
-100	-13.1	-7.2	0.1	9.4	13.9	18.5	23.6	28.9	34.6	40.4	47.0	55.2	63.3	65.0
-125	-18.9	-12.6	-5.1	4.2	8.1	12.2	16.2	20.4	24.6	28.6	32.5	36.6	39.9	40.0

TABLE 80

net profit area, in cents

The estimated credit is: + 58.0¢ premium + 58.0¢ premium – 1.0¢ comm. = + 115.0¢

changes in the soybean future's price in 25¢ increments	35	30	25	20	18	16	14	12	10	8	6	4	2	0
+125	-57.8	-57.3	-56.8	-56.5	-56.3	-56.2	-56.1	-56.1	-56.0	-56.0	-56.0	-56.0	-56.0	-56.0
+100	-37.4	-36.5	-35.5	-34.4	-33.9	-33.3	-32.8	-32.4	-31.9	-31.6	-31.3	-31.1	-31.0	-31.0
+75	-20.3	-19.0	-17.4	-15.8	-14.9	-13.9	-13.0	-12.1	-11.0	-9.8	-8.6	-7.3	-6.4	-6.0
+50	-9.0	-7.5	-5.5	-3.3	-2.2	-1.0	0.2	1.5	3.2	5.0	7.2	10.0	13.6	19.0
+25	-2.3	-0.5	1.6	3.9	5.1	6.5	7.8	9.2	10.7	12.4	14.7	17.1	18.2	19.0
0	-1.0	0.8	2.8	5.0	6.2	7.4	8.6	10.0	11.8	13.6	16.2	18.2	19.0	19.0
-25	-2.3	-0.5	1.6	3.9	5.1	6.5	7.8	9.2	10.7	12.4	14.7	17.1	18.2	19.0
-50	-9.0	-7.5	-5.5	-3.3	-2.2	-1.0	0.2	1.5	3.2	5.0	7.2	10.0	13.6	19.0
-75	-20.3	-19.0	-17.4	-15.8	-14.9	-13.9	-13.0	-12.1	-11.0	-9.8	-8.6	-7.3	-6.4	-6.0
-100	-37.4	-36.5	-35.5	-34.4	-33.9	-33.3	-32.8	-32.4	-31.9	-31.6	-31.3	-31.1	-31.0	-31.0
-125	-57.8	-57.3	-56.8	-56.5	-56.3	-56.2	-56.1	-56.1	-56.0	-56.0	-56.0	-56.0	-56.0	-56.0

weeks to expiration

TABLE 20

net profit area

The estimated credit is: + 10.0¢ premium + 10.0¢ premium - 1.0¢ comm. = + 19.0¢

The ideal situation for the Straddle #1 is for the Forecasting Graphs to indicate that there will likely be no or little price movement in the weeks ahead.

Look at Table 80 (high volatility). Look at the size of the net profit area. It shows that one could be wrong about the price trend by as much as 165¢, either up or down, and still not lose any money. That's a wide safety range – much wider than the average soybean future's price move over a 35 week period.

Look at Table 20. Even though it has low volatility, it still has a reasonable wide net profit area.

Time – Let's see how the net profit is affected by the long term and the short term.

Look at the two charts below. They illustrate the effects of the long and short term on the profit. As you can see, the profits are good in both the long and short terms.

In fact, at the 6th week the Stangle #1 option trade seems to be very safe and offers an excellent net profit on an annual basis. As far as safety is concerned, one would need a price change of 63.6¢ before one would lose money – an unlikely event in 6 weeks except in the summer. The net profit return of the 6 week chart below, on an annual basis, is about 590 %.

Therefore Strangle #1 seems like a good option to use in the short term.

TABLE 40

changes in the soybean future's price in 25¢ increments — net profit area in cents

	35	30	25	20	18	16	14	12	10	8	6	4	2	weeks to expiration 0
+125	-38.5	-36.5	-34.5	-32.5	-31.6	-30.7	-29.9	-29.2	-28.5	-27.7	-27.0	-26.6	-26.6	-26.6
+100	-25.8	-23.0	-20.3	-17.2	-15.6	-13.9	-12.3	-10.5	-8.7	-6.9	-5.1	-2.7	-1.7	-1.6
+75	-15.0	-11.8	-8.5	-4.6	-2.6	-0.7	1.4	3.8	6.5	9.7	13.1	17.8	22.0	23.4
+50	-8.1	-4.6	-0.6	3.9	6.1	8.5	11.1	13.8	17.1	20.9	25.4	31.6	39.0	48.4
+25	-4.0	-0.3	3.9	9.1	11.6	14.3	17.1	20.2	23.6	27.9	32.7	39.1	46.3	48.4
0	-1.0	3.0	7.2	11.8	14.2	16.6	19.2	22.0	25.2	29.2	33.8	40.2	47.4	48.4
-25	-4.0	-0.3	3.9	9.1	11.6	14.3	17.1	20.2	23.6	27.9	32.7	39.1	46.3	48.4
-50	-8.1	-4.6	-0.6	3.9	6.1	8.5	11.1	13.8	17.1	20.9	25.4	31.6	39.0	48.4
-75	-15.0	-11.8	-8.5	-4.6	-2.6	-0.7	1.4	3.8	6.5	9.7	13.1	17.8	22.0	23.4
-100	-25.8	123.0	-20.3	-17.2	-15.6	-13.9	-12.3	-10.5	-8.7	-6.9	-5.1	-2.7	-1.7	-1.6
-125	-38.5	-36.5	-34.5	-32.5	-31.6	-30.7	-29.9	-29.2	-28.5	-27.7	-27.0	-26.6	-26.6	-26.6

The estimated credit is: +24.7¢ premium + 24.7¢ premium − 1.0¢ comm. = +48.4¢

TABLE 40

changes in the soybean future's price in 25¢ increments — net profit area, in cents

	weeks to expiration 6	4	2	0
+125	-61.8	-61.4	-61.4	-61.4
+100	-39.9	-37.5	-36.5	-36.4
+75	-23.7	-17.0	-12.8	-11.4
+50	-9.4	-3.2	4.2	13.6
+25	-2.2	4.2	11.4	13.6
0	-1.0	5.4	12.6	13.6
-25	-2.2	4.2	11.4	13.6
-50	-9.4	-3.2	4.2	13.6
-75	-23.7	-17.0	-12.8	-11.4
-100	-39.9	-37.5	-36.5	-36.4
-125	-61.8	-61.4	-61.4	-61.4

Credit: +7.3 +7.3 −1.0 = +13.6¢

SELL A STRANGLE – #2

SELL A CALL AT $1.00 OUT OF THE MONEY
and SELL A PUT AT $1.00 OUT OF THE MONEY

This option trade was added to the list of profitable trades because it is one of the safest trades. It is important to protect your working capital – otherwise you will be out of the game permanently. Unfortunately, one must also accept a lower rate of profit with greater safety.

Look at Table 80 below. Note that the maximum profit target is very wide, much wider than in Strangle #1. This is an important safety feature.

Another thing. As you know, if you were selling a call, for example, the purchaser of your call has the right to change his long call into a long future <u>when his long call gets into the money</u>. It's not often such a conversion happens because most traders are satisfied to stick with a profitable option rather than convert it into a future. But it can happen and you, as the seller, must take evasive action – such as liquidating or buying a long future.

Here's where Strangle #2 helps out in the situation mentioned above. When you sell a call and a put at $1 out of the money, then the purchaser of the call or put will not likely be able to convert to a future because prices would have to change by $1 before one of the purchasers got "into the money". Because you would take a Strangle #2 position only when the Forecasting Graphs indicated only a moderate price change, then it is unlikely that prices will ever change by more than $1. Anyway it's a rare event for someone to convert an option to a future.

TABLE 80 — changes in the soybean future's price in 25¢ increments — net profit area, in cents

| | weeks to expiration | | | | | | | | | | | | | |
	35	**30**	**25**	**20**	**18**	**16**	**14**	**12**	**10**	**8**	**6**	**4**	**2**	**0**
+125	-2.5	1.5	6.8	13.7	16.8	20.3	23.8	27.5	31.6	36.0	41.5	49.4	59.3	65.8
+100	0.8	6.8	13.4	20.9	24.3	28.0	31.8	36.1	40.8	46.0	52.6	61.5	73.5	90.8
+75	1.8	8.0	15.3	24.6	28.7	33.1	37.7	42.8	48.5	54.1	60.9	70.0	81.7	90.8
+50	4.2	10.0	17.2	26.4	30.9	35.6	40.9	46.5	52.4	58.6	65.9	75.2	85.6	90.8
+25	-0.3	5.2	12.8	22.9	27.7	32.7	37.9	43.6	49.9	57.4	65.8	76.9	88.1	90.8
0	-1.0	4.4	11.8	22.0	26.8	32.0	37.6	43.8	50.8	58.4	67.0	77.2	87.4	90.8
-25	-0.3	5.2	12.8	22.9	27.7	32.7	37.9	43.6	49.9	57.4	65.8	76.9	88.1	90.8
-50	4.2	10.0	17.2	26.4	30.9	35.6	40.9	46.5	52.4	58.6	65.9	75.2	85.6	90.8
-75	1.8	8.0	15.3	24.6	28.7	33.1	37.7	42.8	48.5	54.1	60.9	70.0	81.7	90.8
-100	0.8	6.8	13.4	20.9	24.3	28.0	31.8	36.1	40.8	46.0	52.6	61.5	73.5	90.8
-125	-2.5	1.5	6.8	13.7	16.8	20.3	23.8	27.5	31.6	36.0	41.5	49.4	59.3	65.8

The estimated credit is: + 45.9¢ premium + 45.9¢ premium – 1.0¢ comm. = + 90.8¢

		35	30	25	20	18	16	14	12	10	8	6	weeks to expiration 4	2	0
	+125	-30.1	-29.1	-27.8	-26.6	-26.0	-25.2	-24.5	-23.7	-22.8	-21.7	-20.6	-19.3	-18.4	-18.0
	+100	-17.3	-16.0	-14.5	-12.8	-12.0	-11.1	-10.2	-9.2	-7.9	-6.5	-4.7	-2.0	1.6	7.0
	+75	-9.0	-7.7	-6.1	-4.6	-3.7	-2.8	-2.0	-1.1	0.0	1.3	3.0	5.1	6.2	7.0
	+50	-4.3	-3.1	-1.8	-0.4	0.3	1.0	1.7	2.5	3.4	4.3	5.6	6.6	7.0	7.0
T	+25	-1.3	-0.3	0.9	2.2	2.9	3.6	4.3	4.9	5.5	6.1	6.7	7.0	7.0	7.0
A B L E	0	-1.0	-0.4	0.8	2.0	2.6	3.2	3.8	4.4	5.2	6.0	6.8	7.0	7.0	7.0
2 0	-25	-1.3	-0.3	0.9	2.2	2.9	3.6	4.3	4.9	5.5	6.1	6.7	7.0	7.0	7.0
	-50	-4.3	-3.1	-1.8	-0.4	0.3	1.0	1.7	2.5	3.4	4.3	5.6	6.6	7.0	7.0
	-75	-9.0	-7.7	-6.1	-4.6	-3.7	-2.8	-2.0	-1.1	0.0	1.3	3.0	5.1	6.2	7.0
	-100	-17.3	-16.0	-14.5	-12.8	-12.0	-11.1	-10.2	-9.2	-7.9	-6.5	-4.7	-2.0	1.6	7.0
	-125	-30.1	-29.1	-27.8	-26.6	-26.0	-25.2	-24.5	-23.7	-22.8	-21.7	-20.6	-19.3	-18.4	-18.0

TABLE 20 — changes in the soybean future's price in 25¢ increments (left axis); net profit area, in cents (right axis).

The estimated credit is: + 4.0¢ premium + 4.0¢ premium – 1.0¢ comm. = +7.0¢

Volatility – Let's see how a change in volatility will affect the profit.

A Strangle #2 is a nice safe trade with a reasonable profit. Look at the size of the net profit area in Table 80. It's huge, with almost no place to lose money! Prices would have to move by more than 190.8¢ at expiration before you would lose any money.

Table 20 also has a large net profit area but the profits are small. A low volatility may make the option produce such a small profit that it is not worthwhile to take.

Time – Let's see how a change in time will affect profits. Below are two charts using Table 40, but with different time periods – one long term and the other is a short term trade.

Note the differnce in size of the net profit area of each. Note the maximum net profit of each.

The 35 week chart below earns at an annual rate of 215% on the investment of a 20¢ margin. The 6 week chart earns at an annual basis of about 190%. So you can see that there is no particular advantage in trading in the short term.

To sum up. There is plenty of safety in using Strangle #2 but the profits are moderate to low. Also, one might have a bit of difficulty in putting this option together. It is not easy to sell a call or a put at $1 out of the money. It is much easier to find buyers at 50¢ out of the money. But if it is safety you are after, it is hard to beat Strangle #2.

TABLE 40

changes in the soybean future's price in 25¢ increments	weeks to expiration: 35	30	25	20	18	16	14	12	10	8	6	4	2	0
+125	-24.9	-22.6	-20.4	-17.6	-16.2	-14.9	-13.3	-11.7	-9.8	-7.5	-4.9	-1.3	2.6	4.0
+100	-14.3	-12.1	-9.5	-6.2	-4.6	-2.9	-1.2	0.7	2.9	5.5	8.7	13.3	19.6	29.0
+75	-6.9	-4.2	-1.2	2.4	4.1	5.9	7.7	9.5	11.5	14.1	17.1	21.3	26.9	29.0
+50	-2.6	0.4	3.5	6.8	8.7	10.5	12.4	14.5	16.6	18.9	21.4	24.9	28.5	29.0
+25	-1.5	1.3	4.5	8.3	10.2	12.1	13.9	16.1	18.4	21.1	23.8	27.1	29.0	29.0
0	-1.0	2.2	5.6	9.0	10.6	12.4	14.4	16.2	18.4	21.0	23.6	26.8	29.0	29.0
-25	-1.5	1.3	4.5	8.3	10.2	12.1	13.9	16.1	18.4	21.1	23.8	27.1	29.0	29.0
-50	-2.6	0.4	3.5	6.8	8.7	10.5	12.4	14.5	16.6	18.9	21.4	24.9	28.5	29.0
-75	-6.9	-4.2	-1.2	2.4	4.1	5.9	7.7	9.5	11.5	14.1	17.1	21.3	26.9	29.0
-100	-14.3	-12.1	-9.5	-6.2	-4.6	-2.9	-1.2	0.7	2.9	5.5	8.7	13.3	19.6	29.0
-125	-24.9	-22.6	-20.4	-17.6	-16.2	-14.9	-13.3	-11.7	-9.8	-7.5	-4.9	-1.3	2.6	4.0

net profit area , in cents

The estimated credit is: + 15.0¢ premium + 15.0¢ premium - 1.0¢ comm. = +29.0¢

TABLE 40

changes in the soybean future's price in 25¢ increments	weeks to expiration: 6	4	2	0
+125	-29.5	-25.9	-22.0	-20.6
+100	-15.9	-11.3	-5.0	4.4
+75	-7.9	-3.7	1.9	4.4
+50	-3.2	0.3	3.9	4.4
+25	-0.8	2.5	4.4	4.4
0	-1.0	2.2	4.4	4.4
-25	-0.8	2.5	4.4	4.4
-50	-3.2	0.3	3.9	4.4
-75	-7.9	-3.7	1.9	4.4
-100	-15.9	-11.3	-5.0	4.4
-125	-29.5	-25.9	-22.0	-20.6

net profit area , in cents

Credit: +2.7+2.7-1.0= +4.4¢

PART III

HOW DID EACH OF THE 9 SELECTED OPTION POSITIONS PERFORM UNDER VARYING CONDITIONS OF TIME, PRICE, AND VOLATILITY?

Here you will see how the 9 options performed, using 35 to 4 weeks to expiration.
Here you will see how the 9 options performed when the soybean price changed.
Here you will see how the 9 options performed under different degrees of volatility.

As for the volatility, each of the 9 selected option values was calculated by using Table 20 (which represents low volatility), Table 40 (which represents an average volatility), Table 60 (which represents an above average degree of volatility), and Table 80 (which represents a high degree of volatility). Therefore if you wished to see the net profit for Table 50, then you would interpolate between Table 40 and 60, for example.

The following charts show you how much net profit or net loss each of the 9 options will earn or lose. The net profit areas are outlined. The net profits and losses are shown in cents. Thus, a 10¢ profit translates into a $500 profit.

FOLLOW THESE STEPS.
1. First, find the weeks to expiration of the option position which you are considering, then turn to that "wks. to exp." area in the following pages.
2. Second, use the Table Finder tables to find which table you will use to represent the volatility. Now look at the appropriate charts in the designated "wks. to exp." pages, to see the net profit area for each of the 9 selected option positions.
3. See which of the 9 options will be the best one to use.

See the example on the next page.

Example

1. The date is Dec. 1st and you are thinking of taking a May soybean option. At this point you don't know which of the 9 options will be the best one for you. But by looking at the profit and loss charts of each of the 9 options, you can see which one may be the best one.

2. The first step is to find the "weeks to expiration". Turn to the "weeks to exp." section in Part I. Look at the May table, and you can see that the "weeks to exp." for an option taken on Dec. 1st is 20.1 weeks – (use 20 weeks).

3. Turn to the "20 weeks to expiration" charts in the following pages. Here you will see 9 charts with "20 weeks to exp." – one for each of the 9 selected options , each using Tables 20 to 80 which represent the degree of volatility.

4. The second step is to find whether May soybean prices are likely to rise or to fall in the months ahead. This is a job for the May Forecasting Graph. Let's say that the present that the May future's price on Dec. 1st is $6.10, and let's say that the carryover percentage is 12%. Using 12% on the May Forecasting Graph, we get an estimated price of $7 for May beans on May 1st. That means that prices are expected to rise by 90¢.

5. The third step is to find the volatility of the time at which you take the option. The degree of the volatility is expressed by the "Table Number". This is a job for the Table Finder. But, in order to use the Table Finder, you need to know the "at the money option value for a May call", found in your morning newspaper on the commodity option page (you will use the "call" side of the option quotes because prices are rising). Because the future's price is $6.10, then you will have to interpolate between the $6.00 and the $6.25 strike price option values, to get the "at the money" May option value. Let's say that the "at the money" option value is 34.6¢, for this example.

    Follow these steps: (1) In the Table Finder pages, locate the "20 weeks to exp." column (2) search up and down the 20 wk. column to locate 34.6¢ or as close to it as you can get (3) You find 34.5¢, and you look to the right to see that Table 40 is it .

6. Look again at the 9 option charts (each with 20,40,60,80 Table numbers) in the "20 wks. to exp." group. Concentrate on Table 40 in each (as found in the paragraph above). Remember, prices are expected to rise by 90¢. Also remember the safety rule: take an option only if you can earn a 100% profit or better. Now, let's look at each of the 9 options.

    1. Buy a call. This one is worth doing – can earn about 157% net profit.

    2. Buy a call at 50¢ out of the money. Can earn just over 100%.

    3. Sell a put. Very safe. Can earn about 170% net profit.

    4. Sell a put at 50¢ out of the money. Very safe. Can earn about 89% net profit.

    5. Bull Spread #1. Very safe. Should earn about 42% net profit.

    6. Bull Spread #2. No, too risky. A 90¢ rise goes to the edge of the profit area.

    7. Sell a straddle. No. A 90¢ rise goes outside the profit area.

    8. Sell a strangle #1. No. A 90¢ rise goes outside the net profit area.

    9. Sell a strangle #2. No because it can earn only about 95% net profit.

    The Best: Number 3 and 1. But number 4 is worth taking because it is very safe.

BUY A CALL or BUY A PUT

AT THE MONEY

4

weeks to expiration

TABLE 8

changes in the soybean future's price in 25¢ increments	weeks to expiration		
	4	2	0
+125	95.5	95.5	95.5
+100	70.9	70.5	70.5
+75	48.1	45.6	45.5
+50	28.6	22.2	20.5
+25	11.9	2.0	-4.5
0	-0.5	-12.2	-29.5
-25	-9.5	-20.4	-29.5
-50	-15.6	-24.3	-29.5
-75	-19.9	-27.3	-29.5
-100	-22.7	-27.8	-29.5
-125	-25.2	-29.0	-29.5

Cost: -29.0-0.5=-29.5¢

net profit area

TABLE 6

changes in the soybean future's price in 25¢ increments	weeks to expiration		
	4	2	0
+125	102.2	102.2	102.2
+100	77.2	77.2	77.2
+75	50.9	50.2	50.2
+50	31.4	27.7	27.2
+25	12.7	5.8	2.2
0	-0.5	-9.5	-22.8
-25	-9.1	-17.3	-22.8
-50	-14.1	-20.3	-22.8
-75	-17.8	-22.0	-22.8
-100	-19.3	-22.4	-22.8
-125	-21.0	-22.7	-22.8

Cost: -22.3-0.5=-22.8¢

net profit area , in cents

TABLE 4

changes in the soybean future's price in 25¢ increments	weeks to expiration		
	4	2	0
+125	108.8	108.8	108.8
+100	83.8	83.8	83.8
+75	58.8	58.8	58.8
+50	34.9	33.9	33.8
+25	14.1	10.2	8.8
0	-0.5	-6.8	-16.2
-25	-8.5	-14.1	-16.2
-50	-12.1	-15.7	-16.2
-75	-14.6	-16.2	-16.2
-100	-15.1	-16.2	-16.2
-125	-15.9	-16.2	-16.2

Cost: -15.7-0.5=-16.2¢

net profit area , in cents

TABLE 2

changes in the soybean future's price in 25¢ increments	weeks to expiration		
	4	2	0
+125	115.5	115.5	115.5
+100	90.5	90.5	90.5
+75	65.5	65.5	65.5
+50	40.6	40.5	40.5
+25	16.8	15.9	15.5
0	-0.5	-4.1	-9.5
-25	-7.6	-8.7	-9.5
-50	-8.9	-9.5	-9.5
-75	-9.5	-9.5	-9.5
-100	-9.5	-9.5	-9.5
-125	-9.5	-9.5	-9.5

Cost: -9.0-0.5=-9.5¢

net profit area , in cents

Wm Grandmill (1985) Ltd.

BUY A CALL or BUY A PUT
AT 50¢ OUT OF THE MONEY

4 weeks to expiration

TABLE 8

changes in the soybean future's price in 25¢ increments	weeks to expiration 4	2	0
+125	63.2	60.7	60.6
+100	43.7	37.3	35.6
+75	27.0	17.1	10.6
+50	14.6	2.9	-14.4
+25	5.6	-5.3	-14.4
0	-0.5	-9.1	-14.4
-25	-4.8	-12.2	-14.4
-50	-7.6	-12.7	-14.4
-75	-10.1	-13.9	-14.4
-100	-12.7	-14.4	-14.4
-125	-13.6	-14.4	-14.4

net profit

Cost: -13.9-0.5=-14.4¢

TABLE 0

changes in the soybean future's price in 25¢ increments	weeks to expiration 4	2	0
+125	66.5	65.8	65.8
+100	45.0	41.3	40.8
+75	26.3	19.4	15.8
+50	13.1	4.1	-9.2
+25	4.5	-3.7	-9.2
0	-0.5	-6.7	-9.2
-25	-4.2	-8.4	-9.2
-50	-5.7	-8.8	-9.2
-75	-7.4	-9.1	-9.2
-100	-8.5	-9.2	-9.2
-125	-9.2	-9.2	-9.2

net profit

Cost: -8.7-0.5=-9.2¢

TABLE 0

changes in the soybean future's price in 25¢ increments	weeks to expiration 4	2	0
+125	70.4	70.4	70.4
+100	46.5	45.5	45.4
+75	25.7	21.8	20.4
+50	11.1	4.8	-4.6
+25	3.1	-2.5	-4.6
0	-0.5	-3.7	-4.6
-25	-3.0	-4.3	-4.6
-50	-3.7	-4.6	-4.6
-75	-4.3	-4.6	-4.6
-100	-4.6	-4.6	-4.6
-125	-4.6	-4.6	-4.6

net profit

Cost: -4.1-0.5=-4.6¢

TABLE 2

changes in the soybean future's price in 25¢ increments	weeks to expiration 4	2	0
+125	74.1	74.1	74.1
+100	49.2	49.1	49.1
+75	24.9	24.5	24.1
+50	8.1	4.5	-0.9
+25	1.0	-0.1	-0.9
0	-0.5	-0.9	-0.9
-25	-0.9	-0.9	-0.9
-50	-0.9	-0.9	-0.9
-75	-0.9	-0.9	-0.9
-100	-0.9	-0.9	-0.9
-125	-0.9	-0.9	-0.9

net profit area

Cost: -0.4-0.5=-0.9¢

Wm Grandmill (1985) Ltd.

SELL A CALL or SELL A PUT

AT THE MONEY

4 weeks to expiration

TABLE 8

changes in the soybean future's price in 25¢ increments

	weeks to expiration 4	2	0
+125	-96.5	-96.5	-96.5
+100	-71.9	-71.5	-71.5
+75	-49.1	-46.6	-46.5
+50	-26.9	-22.2	-21.5
+25	-12.9	-2.0	3.5
0	-0.5	11.2	28.5
-25	8.5	19.4	28.5
-50	14.6	23.3	28.5
-75	18.9	26.3	28.5
-100	21.7	26.8	28.5
-125	24.2	28.0	28.5

credit:29.0-0.5=+28.5¢

net profit area , in cents

TABLE 6

changes in the soybean future's price in 25¢ increments

	weeks to expiration 4	2	0
+125	-103.2	-103.2	-103.2
+100	-78.2	-78.2	-78.2
+75	-53.9	-53.2	-53.2
+50	-32.4	-28.7	-28.2
+25	-13.7	-6.8	-3.2
0	-0.5	8.5	21.8
-25	8.1	16.3	21.8
-50	13.1	19.3	21.8
-75	16.8	21.0	21.8
-100	18.3	21.4	21.8
-125	20.0	21.7	21.8

credit:22.3-0.5=21.8¢

net profit area , in cents

TABLE 4

changes in the soybean future's price in 25¢ increments

	weeks to expiration 4	2	0
+125	-109.8	-109.8	-109.8
+100	-84.8	-84.8	-84.8
+75	-59.8	-59.8	-59.8
+50	-35.9	-34.9	-34.8
+25	-15.1	-11.2	-9.8
0	-0.5	5.8	15.2
-25	7.5	13.1	15.2
-50	11.1	14.7	15.2
-75	13.6	15.2	15.2
-100	14.1	15.2	15.2
-125	14.9	15.2	15.2

credit:15.7-0.5=15.2¢

net profit area , in cents

TABLE 2

changes in the soybean future's price in 25¢ increments

	weeks to expiration 4	2	0
+125	-116.5	-116.5	-116.5
+100	-91.5	-91.5	-91.5
+75	-66.5	-66.5	-66.5
+50	-41.6	-41.5	-41.5
+25	-17.8	-16.9	-16.5
0	-0.5	3.1	8.5
-25	6.6	7.7	8.5
-50	8.9	8.5	8.5
-75	8.5	8.5	8.5
-100	8.5	8.5	8.5
-125	8.5	8.5	8.5

credit:9.0-0.5=8.5¢

net profit area , in cents

Wm Grandmill (1985) Ltd.

SELL A CALL or SELL A PUT
AT 50¢ OUT OF THE MONEY

4 weeks to expiration

TABLE 8

changes in the soybean future's price in 25¢ increments	weeks to expiration 4	2	0
+125	-64.2	-61.7	-61.6
+100	-44.7	-38.3	-36.6
+75	-28.0	-18.1	-11.6
+50	-15.6	-3.9	13.4
+25	-6.6	4.3	13.4
0	-0.5	8.1	13.4
-25	3.8	11.2	13.4
-50	6.6	11.7	13.4
-75	9.1	12.9	13.4
-100	11.7	13.4	13.4
-125	12.6	13.4	13.4

credit:13.9-0.5=13.4¢

net profit area , in cents

TABLE 8

changes in the soybean future's price in 25¢ increments	weeks to expiration 4	2	0
+125	-67.5	-66.8	-66.8
+100	-46.0	-42.3	-41.8
+75	-27.3	-20.4	-16.8
+50	-14.1	-5.1	8.2
+25	-5.5	2.7	8.2
0	-0.5	5.7	8.2
-25	3.2	7.4	8.2
-50	4.7	7.8	8.2
-75	6.4	8.1	8.2
-100	7.5	8.2	8.2
-125	8.2	8.2	8.2

credit:8.7-0.5=8.2¢

net profit area , in cents

TABLE 4

changes in the soybean future's price in 25¢ increments	weeks to expiration 4	2	0
+125	-71.4	-71.4	-71.4
+100	-47.5	-46.5	-46.4
+75	-26.7	-22.8	-21.4
+50	-12.1	-5.8	3.6
+25	-4.1	1.5	3.6
0	-0.5	3.1	3.6
-25	2.0	3.6	3.6
-50	2.5	3.6	3.6
-75	3.3	3.6	3.6
-100	3.6	3.6	3.6
-125	3.6	3.6	3.6

credit:4.1-0.5=3.6¢

net profit area , in cents

TABLE 2

changes in the soybean future's price in 25¢ increments	weeks to expiration 4	2	0
+125	-75.1	-75.1	-75.1
+100	-50.2	-50.1	-50.1
+75	-25.9	-25.5	-25.1
+50	-9.1	-5.5	-0.1
+25	-2.0	-0.9	-0.1
0	-0.5	-0.1	-0.1
-25	-0.1	-0.1	-0.1
-50	-0.1	-0.1	-0.1
-75	-0.1	-0.1	-0.1
-100	-0.1	-0.1	-0.1
-125	-0.1	-0.1	-0.1

cost:0.4-0.5=-0.1¢

Wm Grandmill (1985) Ltd.

BUY A CALL AT THE MONEY
and SELL A CALL AT 25¢ OUT OF THE MONEY
OR
BUY A PUT AT THE MONEY
and SELL A PUT AT 25¢ OUT OF THE MONEY

4
weeks to expiration

TABLE 0

changes in the soybean future's price in 25¢ increments	cks to expiration		
	4	2	0
+125	14.6	15.0	15.0
+100	13.4	15.0	15.0
+75	10.0	14.9	15.4
+50	6.7	10.2	13.4
+25	2.4	4.2	15.0
0	-1.0	-2.0	-10.0
-25	-3.9	-6.1	-10.0
-50	-5.1	-7.0	-10.0
-75	-6.4	-8.0	-10.0
-100	-7.5	-8.8	-10.0
-125	-8.5	-9.5	-10.0

cost:-29.0+20.0-1.0=-10.

net profit area , in cents

TABLE 0

changes in the soybean future's price in 25¢ increments	4	2	0
+125	15.4	15.4	15.4
+100	14.7	15.4	15.4
+75	11.9	14.9.	15.4
+50	9.1	12.3	15.4
+25	3.6	5.8	15.4
0	-1.0	-1.8	-9.6
-25	-4.6	-6.6	-9.6
-50	-5.9	-7.9	-9.6
-75	-7.9	-9.2	-9.6
-100	-8.0	-9.3	-9.6
-125	-8.3	-9.5	-9.6

cost:-22.3+13.7-1.0=-9.6¢

TABLE 0

changes in the soybean future's price in 25¢ increments	cks to expiration		
	4	2	0
+125	16.0	16.0	16.0
+100	16.0	16.0	16.0
+75	13.9	14.7	16.0
+50	11.8	14.7	16.0
+25	5.6	8.0	16.0
0	-1.0	-1.8	-9.0
-25	-5.4	-7.4	-9.0
-50	-6.5	-8.5	-9.0
-75	-7.8	-9.0	-9.0
-100	-8.2	-9.0	-9.0
-125	-8.7	-9.0	-9.0

cost:-15.7+7.7-1.0=-9.0¢

net profit area , in cents

TABLE 2

changes in the soybean future's price in 25¢ increments	4	2	0
+125	16.9	16.9	16.9
+100	16.9	16.9	16.9
+75	16.8	16.9	16.9
+50	15.7	16.5	16.9
+25	9.2	11.9	16.9
0	-1.0	-1.5	-8.1
-25	-6.6	-7.5	-8.1
-50	-7.7	-8.1	-8.1
-75	-8.1	-8.1	-8.1
-100	-8.1	-8.1	-8.1
-125	-8.1	-8.1	-8.1

cost:-9.0+1.9-1.0=-8.1¢

Wm Grandmill (1985) Ltd.

BULL or BEAR SPREAD – #2

BUY A CALL AT THE MONEY
and SELL 2 CALLS AT 50¢ OUT OF THE MONEY

OR

BUY A PUT AT THE MONEY
and SELL 2 PUTS AT 50¢ OUT OF THE MONEY

4 weeks to expiration

TABLE 0

changes in the soybean future's price in 25¢ increments

	weeks to expiration 4	2	0
+125	-32.9	-27.9	-27.7
+100	-18.5	-6.1	-2.7
+75	-7.9	9.4	22.3
+50	-2.6	14.4	47.3
+25	-1.3	10.6	22.3
0	-1.5	4.2	-2.7
-25	-1.9	2.0	-2.7
-50	-2.4	-0.9	-2.7
-75	-1.7	-1.5	-2.7
-100	-1.0	-1.9	-2.7
-125	-0.2	-2.2	-2.7

net profit area

-29.0+13.9+13.9+1.5=-2.7¢

TABLE 0

changes in the soybean future's price in 25¢ increments

	weeks to expiration 4	2	0
+125	-32.8	-31.4	-31.4
+100	-14.8	-5.4	-6.4
+75	-1.7	11.4	18.6
+50	3.2	17.5	43.6
+25	1.7	11.2	18.6
0	-1.5	1.9	
-25	-2.7	-2.5	-6.4
-50	-4.7	-4.7	-6.4
-75	-5.0	-4.8	-6.4
-100	-4.8	-5.5	-6.4
-125	-4.6	-6.3	-6.4

net profit area

-22.3+8.7+8.7+1.5=-6.4¢

TABLE 0

changes in the soybean future's price in 25¢ increments

	weeks to expiration 4	2	0
+125	-34.0	-34.0	-34.0
+100	-11.2	-9.2	-9.0
+75	5.4	13.2	16.0
+50	10.7	22.3	41.0
+25	5.9	13.2	16.0
0	-1.5	-0.6	-9.0
-25	-4.5	-6.9	-9.0
-50	-7.1	-8.5	-9.0
-75	-8.1	-9.0	-9.0
-100	-8.6	-9.0	-9.0
-125	-8.7	-9.0	-9.0

net profit area

-15.7+4.1+4.1-1.5=-9.0¢

TABLE 2

changes in the soybean future's price in 25¢ increments

	weeks to expiration 4	2	0
+125	-34.7	-34.7	-34.7
+100	-9.9	-9.7	-9.7
+75	12.7	14.5	15.3
+50	22.4	29.5	40.3
+25	12.5	14.1	15.3
0	-1.5	-4.3	-9.7
-25	-7.8	-8.9	-9.7
-50	-9.3	-9.7	-9.7
-75	-9.7	-9.7	-9.7
-100	-9.7	-9.7	-9.7
-125	-9.7	-9.7	-9.7

net profit area

-9.0+0.4+0.4-1.5=-9.7¢

Wm Grandmill (1985) Ltd.

SELL A STRADDLE

SELL A CALL AT THE MONEY and SELL A PUT AT THE MONEY

4 weeks to expiration

TABLE 0

changes in the soybean future's price in 25¢ increments	weeks to expiration 4	2	0
+125	-72.3	-68.5	-68.0
+100	-50.2	-44.7	-43.0
+75	-30.2	-20.3	-18.0
+50	-15.0	0.1	7.0
+25	4.4	16.4	32.0
0	-1.0	22.4	57.0
-25	4.4	16.4	32.0
-50	-15.0	0.1	7.0
-75	-30.2	-20.3	-18.0
-100	-50.2	-44.7	-43.0
-125	-72.3	-68.5	-68.0
	+29.0	+29.0-1.0→	-57.0¢

net profit area , in cents

TABLE 8

changes in the soybean future's price in 25¢ increments	weeks to expiration 4	2	0
+125	-83.2	-81.5	-81.4
+100	-59.9	-56.8	-56.4
+75	-37.-	-32.2	-31.4
+50	-19.3	-9.4	-6.4
+25	-5.6	9.5	18.6
0	-1.0	17.0	43.6
-25	-5.6	9.5	18.6
-50	-19.3	-9.4	-6.4
-75	-37.1	-32.2	-31.4
-100	-59.9	-56.8	-56.4
-125	-83.2	-81.5	-81.4
	+22.3	+22.3-1.0→	+43.6¢

net profit area

TABLE 0

changes in the soybean future's price in 25¢ increments	weeks to expiration 4	2	0
+125	-94.9	-94.6	-94.6
+100	-70.7	-69.6	-69.6
+75	-46.2	-44.6	-44.6
+50	-24.8	-20.2	-19.6
+25	-7.6	1.9	5.4
0	-1.0	11.6	30.4
-25	-7.6	1.9	5.4
-50	-24.8	-20.2	-19.6
-75	-46.2	-44.6	-44.6
-100	-70.7	-69.6	-69.6
-125	-94.9	-94.6	-94.6
	+15.7	+15.7-1.0→	+30.4¢

net profit area

TABLE 2

changes in the soybean future's price in 25¢ increments	weeks to expiration 4	2	0
+125	-108.0	-108.0	-108.0
+100	-83.0	-83.0	-83.0
+75	-58.0	-58.0	-58.0
+50	-33.5	-33.0	-33.0
+25	-11.2	-8.5	-8.0
0	-1.0	6.2	17.0
-25	-11.2	-8.5	-8.0
-50	-33.5	-33.0	-33.0
-75	-58.0	-58.0	-58.0
-100	-83.0	-83.0	-83.0
-125	-108.0	-108.0	-108.0
	+9.0	+9.0-1.0→	+17.0¢

profit

Wm Grandmill (1985) Ltd.

SELL A STRANGLE – #1

SELL A CALL AT 50¢ OUT OF THE MONEY
and SELL A PUT AT 50¢ OUT OF THE MONEY

TABLE 8

changes in the soybean future's price in 25¢ increments	weeks to expiration		
	4	2	0
+125	-51.6	-48.3	-48.2
+100	-33.0	-24.9	-23.2
+75	-18.9	-5.2	1.8
+50	-9.0	7.8	26.8
+25	-2.8	15.5	26.8
0	-1.0	16.4	26.8
-25	-2.8	15.5	26.8
-50	-9.0	7.8	26.8
-75	-18.9	-5.2	1.8
-100	-33.0	-24.9	-23.2
-125	-51.6	-48.3	-48.2

net profit area , in cents

+13.9+13.9-1.0=26.8¢

TABLE 8

changes in the soybean future's price in 25¢ increments	weeks to expiration		
	4	2	0
+125	-59.3	-58.6	-58.6
+100	-38.5	-34.1	-33.6
+75	-20.9	-12.3	-8.6
+50	-9.4	2.7	16.4
+25	-2.3	10.1	16.4
0	-1.0	11.4	16.4
-25	-2.3	10.1	16.4
-50	-9.4	2.7	16.4
-75	-20.9	-12.3	-8.6
-100	-38.5	-34.1	-33.6
-125	-59.3	-58.6	-58.6

net profit area , in cents

+8.7+8.7-1.0=+16.4¢

TABLE 4

changes in the soybean future's price in 25¢ increments	weeks to expiration		
	4	2	0
+125	-67.8	-67.8	-67.8
+100	-43.9	-42.9	-42.8
+75	-23.4	-19.2	-17.8
+50	-9.6	-2.2	7.2
+25	-2.1	5.1	7.2
0	-1.0	6.2	7.2
-25	-2.1	5.1	7.2
-50	-9.6	-2.2	7.2
-75	-23.4	-19.2	-17.8
-100	-43.9	-42.9	-42.8
-125	-67.8	-67.8	-67.8

net profit area , in cents

+4.1+4.1-1.0=+7.2¢

TABLE 2

changes in the soybean future's price in 25¢ increments	weeks to expiration		
	4	2	0
+125	-75.2	-75.2	-75.2
+100	-50.3	-50.2	-50.2
+75	-26.5	-25.6	-25.2
+50	-9.2	-5.6	-0.2
+25	-2.1	-1.0	-0.2
0	-1.0	-0.2	-0.2
-25	-2.1	-1.0	-0.2
-50	-9.2	-5.6	-0.2
-75	-26.5	-25.6	-25.2
-100	-50.3	-50.2	-50.2
-125	-75.2	-75.2	-75.2

+0.4+0.4-1.0=-0.2¢

Grandmill (1985) Ltd.

SELL A STRANGLE – #2

SELL A CALL AT $1.00 OUT OF THE MONEY
and SELL A PUT AT $1.00 OUT OF THE MONEY

4 weeks to expiration

TABLE 8

changes in the soybean future's price in 25¢ increments	weeks to expiration 4	2	0
+125	-28.8	-18.9	-12.4
+100	-16.7	-4.7	12.6
+75	-8.2	3.5	12.6
+50	-3.0	7.4	12.6
+25	-1.3	9.9	12.6
0	-1.0	9.2	12.6
-25	-1.3	9.9	12.6
-50	-3.0	7.4	12.6
-75	-8.2	3.5	12.6
-100	-16.7	-4.7	12.6
-125	-28.8	-18.9	-12.4

6.8+6.8-1.0= +12.6¢

net profit area , in cents

TABLE 8

changes in the soybean future's price in 25¢ increments	weeks to expiration 4	2	0
+125	-29.5	-22.6	-19.0
+100	-16.3	-7.3	6.0
+75	-7.7	0.5	6.0
+50	-3.4	3.5	6.0
+25	-0.8	5.1	6.0
0	-1.0	5.1	6.0
-25	-0.8	5.1	6.0
-50	-3.4	3.5	6.0
-75	-7.7	0.5	6.0
-100	-16.3	-7.3	6.0
-125	-29.5	-22.6	-19.0

3.5+3.5-1.0= +6.0¢

net profit area , in cents

TABLE 4

changes in the soybean future's price in 25¢ increments	weeks to expiration 4	2	0
+125	-29.1	-25.2	-23.8
+100	-14.5	-8.2	1.2
+75	-6.5	-0.9	1.2
+50	-2.9	0.7	1.2
+25	-0.7	1.2	1.2
0	-1.0	1.2	1.2
-25	-0.7	1.2	1.2
-50	-2.9	0.7	1.2
-75	-6.5	-0.9	1.2
-100	-14.5	-8.2	1.2
-125	-29.1	-25.2	-23.8

+1.1+1.1-1.0= +1.2¢

net profit area , in cents

TABLE 2

changes in the soybean future's price in 25¢ increments	weeks to expiration 4	2	0
+125	-27.3	-26.4	-26.0
+100	-10.0	-6.4	-1.0
+75	-2.9	-1.8	-1.0
+50	-1.4	-1.0	-1.0
+25	-1.0	-1.0	-1.0
0	-1.0	-1.0	-1.0
-25	-1.0	-1.0	-1.0
-50	-1.4	-1.0	-1.0
-75	-2.9	-1.8	-1.0
-100	-10.0	-6.4	-1.0
-125	-27.3	-26.4	-26.0

0.0+0.0-1.0= -1.0¢

Wm Grandmill (1985) Ltd.

BUY A CALL or BUY A PUT

AT THE MONEY

6	weeks to
	expiration

TABLE 6 0

changes in the soybean future's price in 25¢ increments	weeks to expiration			
	6	4	2	0
+125	95.6	95.6	95.6	95.6
+100	70.9	70.6	70.6	70.6
+75	48.1	46.3	45.6	45.6
+50	28.6	24.8	21.1	20.6
+25	11.9	6.1	-0.8	-4.4
0	-0.5	-7.1	-16.1	-29.4
-25	-9.5	-15.7	-23.9	-29.4
-50	-15.6	-20.7	-26.9	-29.4
-75	-19.9	-24.4	-28.6	-29.4
-100	-22.7	-25.9	-29.0	-29.4
-125	-25.2	-27.6	-29.3	-29.4

net profit area

Est. cost: -28.9¢-0.5¢=-29.4¢

TABLE 8 0

changes in the soybean future's price in 25¢ increments	weeks to expiration			
	6	4	2	0
+125	87.2	86.9	86.9	86.9
+100	63.7	62.3	61.9	61.9
+75	42.9	39.5	37.0	36.9
+50	25.9	20.0	13.6	11.9
+25	11.0	3.3	-6.6	-13.1
0	-0.5	-9.1	-20.8	-38.1
-25	-9.7	-18.1	-29.0	-38.1
-50	-17.2	-24.2	-32.9	-38.1
-75	-21.4	-28.5	-35.9	-38.1
-100	-26.2	-31.3	-36.4	-38.1
-125	-29.8	-33.8	-37.6	-38.1

net profit area

Est. cost: -37.6¢-0.5¢=-38.1¢

TABLE 2 0

changes in the soybean future's price in 25¢ increments	weeks to expiration			
	6	4	2	0
+125	112.8	112.8	112.8	112.8
+100	87.8	87.8	87.8	87.8
+75	62.8	62.8	62.8	62.8
+50	38.1	37.9	37.8	37.8
+25	15.4	14.1	13.2	12.8
0	-0.5	-3.2	-6.8	-12.2
-25	-8.2	-10.3	-11.4	-12.2
-50	-10.8	-11.8	-12.2	-12.2
-75	-11.9	-12.2	-12.2	-12.2
-100	-12.1	-12.2	-12.2	-12.2
-125	-12.2	-12.2	-12.2	-12.2

net profit area, in cents

Est. cost: -11.7¢-0.5¢=-12.2¢

TABLE 4 0

changes in the soybean future's price in 25¢ increments	weeks to expiration			
	6	4	2	0
+125	104.2	104.2	104.2	104.2
+100	79.2	79.2	79.2	79.2
+75	54.6	54.2	54.2	54.2
+50	32.4	30.2	29.3	29.2
+25	13.1	9.5	5.6	4.2
0	-0.5	-5.1	-11.4	-20.8
-25	-8.9	-13.1	-18.7	-20.8
-50	-13.5	-16.7	-20.3	-20.8
-75	-17.0	-19.2	-20.8	-20.8
-100	-18.1	-19.7	-20.8	-20.8
-125	-19.5	-20.5	-20.8	-20.8

net profit area, in cents

Est. cost: -20.3¢-0.5¢=-20.8¢

Wm Grandmill (1985) Ltd.

BUY A CALL or BUY A PUT
AT 50¢ OUT OF THE MONEY

weeks to expiration

6

TABLE 8

changes in the soybean future's price in 25¢ increments	weeks to expiration 6	4	2	0
+125	59.6	56.2	53.7	53.6
+100	42.6	36.7	30.3	28.6
+75	27.7	20.0	10.1	3.6
+50	16.2	7.6	-4.1	-21.4
+25	7.0	-1.4	-12.3	-21.4
0	-0.5	-7.5	-16.1	-21.4
-25	-4.8	-11.8	-19.2	-21.4
-50	-9.5	-14.6	-19.7	-21.4
-75	-13.1	-17.1	-20.9	-21.4
-100	-17.4	-19.7	-21.4	-21.4
-125	-20.0	-20.6	-21.4	-21.4

net profit

Est.cost:-20.9¢-0.5¢=-21.4¢

TABLE 0

changes in the soybean future's price in 25¢ increments	weeks to expiration 6	4	2	0
+125	63.2	61.4	60.7	60.7
+100	43.7	39.9	36.2	35.7
+75	27.0	21.1	14.3	10.7
+50	14.6	8.0	-0.6	-14.3
+25	5.6	-0.6	-8.8	-14.3
0	-0.5	-5.6	-12.8	-14.3
-25	-4.8	-9.3	-13.5	-14.3
-50	-7.6	-10.8	-13.9	-14.3
-75	-10.1	-12.2	-14.2	-14.3
-100	-12.4	-13.6	-14.3	-14.3
-125	-13.8	-14.3	-14.3	-14.3

net profit

Est.cost:-13.8¢-0.5¢=-14.3¢

TABLE 4

changes in the soybean future's price in 25¢ increments	weeks to expiration 6	4	2	0
+125	67.6	67.2	67.2	67.2
+100	45.4	43.3	42.3	42.2
+75	26.1	22.5	18.6	17.2
+50	12.5	7.9	1.6	-7.8
+25	4.1	-0.1	-5.7	-7.8
0	-0.5	-3.7	-7.3	-7.8
-25	-4.0	-6.2	-7.8	-7.8
-50	-5.1	-6.7	-7.8	-7.8
-75	-6.4	-7.5	-7.8	-7.8
-100	-7.5	-7.8	-7.8	-7.8
-125	-7.8	-7.8	-7.8	-7.8

net profit

Est.cost:-7.3¢-0.5¢=-7.8¢

TABLE 2

changes in the soybean future's price in 25¢ increments	weeks to expiration 6	4	2	0
+125	73.1	73.1	73.1	73.1
+100	48.4	48.2	48.1	48.1
+75	24.7	23.9	23.5	23.1
+50	9.8	7.1	3.5	-1.9
+25	2.1	0.0	-1.1	-1.9
0	-0.5	-1.5	-1.9	-1.9
-25	-1.6	-1.9	-1.9	-1.9
-50	-1.8	-1.9	-1.9	-1.9
-75	-1.9	-1.9	-1.9	-1.9
-100	-1.9	-1.9	-1.9	-1.9
-125	-1.9	-1.9	-1.9	-1.9

net profit

Est.cost:-1.4¢-0.5¢=-1.9¢

Wm Grandmill (1985) Ltd.

SELL A CALL or SELL A PUT

AT THE MONEY

TABLE 8

changes in the soybean future's price in 25¢ increments	weeks to expiration 6	4	2	0
+125	-88.2	-87.9	-87.9	-87.9
+100	-64.7	-63.3	-62.9	-62.9
+75	-43.9	-40.5	-38.0	-37.9
+50	-26.9	-21.0	-14.6	-12.9
+25	-12.0	-4.3	5.6	12.1
0	-0.5	8.1	19.8	37.1
-25	8.7	17.1	28.0	37.1
-50	16.2	23.2	31.9	37.1
-75	20.4	27.5	34.9	37.1
-100	25.2	30.3	35.4	37.1
-125	28.8	32.8	36.6	37.1

net profit area , in cents

Est.credit:+37.6¢-0.5¢=+37.1¢

TABLE 6

changes in the soybean future's price in 25¢ increments	weeks to expiration 6	4	2	0
+125	-96.6	-96.6	-96.6	-96.6
+100	-71.9	-71.6	-71.6	-71.6
+75	-49.1	-47.6	-46.6	-46.6
+50	-29.6	-25.1	-21.3	-21.6
+25	-12.9	-8.4	-2.6	3.4
0	-0.5	6.1	15.1	28.4
-25	8.5	14.7	22.9	28.4
-50	14.6	19.7	25.9	28.4
-75	18.9	23.4	27.6	28.4
-100	21.7	24.9	28.0	28.4
-125	24.2	26.6	28.3	28.4

net profit area , in cents

Est.credit:+28.9¢-0.5¢=+28.4¢

TABLE 4

changes in the soybean future's price in 25¢ increments	weeks to expiration 6	4	2	0
+125	-105.2	-105.2	-105.2	-105.2
+100	-80.2	-80.2	-80.2	-80.2
+75	-55.6	-55.2	-55.2	-55.2
+50	-33.4	-31.3	-30.3	-30.2
+25	-14.1	-10.5	-6.6	-5.2
0	-0.5	4.1	10.4	19.8
-25	7.9	12.1	17.7	19.8
-50	12.5	15.7	19.3	19.8
-75	16.0	18.2	19.8	19.8
-100	17.1	18.7	19.8	19.8
-125	18.5	19.5	19.8	19.8

net profit area , in cents

Est.credit:+20.3¢-0.5¢=19.8¢

TABLE 2

changes in the soybean future's price in 25¢ increments	weeks to expiration 6	4	2	0
+125	-113.8	-113.8	-113.8	-113.8
+100	-88.8	-88.8	-88.8	-88.8
+75	-63.8	-63.8	-63.8	-63.8
+50	-39.1	-38.9	-38.8	-38.8
+25	-16.4	-15.1	-14.2	-13.8
0	-0.5	2.2	5.8	11.2
-25	7.2	9.3	10.4	11.2
-50	9.8	10.8	11.2	11.2
-75	10.9	11.2	11.2	11.2
-100	11.1	11.2	11.2	11.2
-125	11.2	11.2	11.2	11.2

net profit area , in cents

Est.credit:+11.7¢-0.5¢=+11.2¢

Wm Grandmill (1985) Ltd.

SELL A CALL or SELL A PUT
AT 50¢ OUT OF THE MONEY

TABLE 8

changes in the soybean future's price in 25¢ increments	weeks to expiration			
	6	4	2	0
+125	-60.6	-57.2	-54.7	-54.6
+100	-43.6	-37.7	-31.3	-29.6
+75	-28.7	-21.0	-11.1	-4.6
+50	-17.1	-8.6	3.1	20.4
+25	-8.0	0.4	12.3	20.4
0	-0.5	6.5	15.1	20.4
-25	3.8	10.8	18.2	20.4
-50	8.5	13.6	18.7	20.4
-75	12.1	16.1	19.9	20.4
-100	16.4	18.7	20.4	20.4
-125	19.0	19.6	20.4	20.4

Est.credit:+20.9¢-0.5¢=20.4¢

net profit area , in cents

TABLE 6

changes in the soybean future's price in 25¢ increments	weeks to expiration			
	6	4	2	0
+125	-64.2	-62.4	-61.6	-61.7
+100	-44.7	-40.9	-37.2	-36.7
+75	-28.0	-22.2	-15.3	-11.7
+50	-15.6	-9.0	0.0	13.3
+25	-6.6	-0.4	7.8	13.3
0	-0.5	4.6	11.8	13.3
-25	3.8	8.3	12.5	13.3
-50	6.6	9.8	12.9	13.3
-75	9.1	11.5	13.2	13.3
-100	11.4	12.6	13.3	13.3
-125	12.8	13.3	13.3	13.3

Est.credit:+13.8¢-0.5¢=13.3¢

net profit area , in cents

TABLE 4

changes in the soybean future's price in 25¢ increments	weeks to expiration			
	6	4	2	0
+125	-68.6	-68.2	-68.2	-68.2
+100	-46.4	-44.3	-43.3	-43.2
+75	-27.1	-23.5	-19.6	-18.2
+50	-13.5	-8.9	-2.6	6.8
+25	-5.1	-0.9	4.7	6.8
0	-0.5	2.7	6.3	6.8
-25	3.0	5.2	6.8	6.8
-50	4.1	5.7	6.8	6.8
-75	5.4	6.5	6.8	6.8
-100	6.5	6.8	6.8	6.8
-125	6.8	6.8	6.8	6.8

Est.credit:+7.3¢-0.5¢=6.8¢

net profit area , in cents

TABLE 2

changes in the soybean future's price in 25¢ increments	weeks to expiration			
	6	4	2	0
+125	-74.1	-74.1	-74.1	-74.1
+100	-49.4	-49.2	-49.1	-49.1
+75	-25.7	-24.9	-24.5	-24.1
+50	-10.8	-8.1	-4.5	0.9
+25	-3.1	-1.0	-.1	0.9
0	-0.5	0.5	0.9	0.9
-25	0.2	0.9	0.9	0.9
-50	0.9	0.9	0.9	0.9
-75	0.9	0.9	0.9	0.9
-100	0.9	0.9	0.9	0.9
-125	0.9	0.9	0.9	0.9

Est.credit:+1.4¢-0.5¢=0.9¢

net profit area , in cents

Wm Grandmill (1985) Ltd.

BULL or BEAR SPREAD – #1

BUY A CALL AT THE MONEY
and SELL A CALL AT 25¢ OUT OF THE MONEY
OR
BUY A PUT AT THE MONEY
and SELL A PUT AT 25¢ OUT OF THE MONEY

weeks to expiration

6

TABLE 0

changes in the soybean future's price in 25¢ increments	weeks to expiration			
	6	4	2	0
+125	14.2	14.4	14.8	14.8
+100	11.2	13.2	14.8	14.8
+75	8.2	9.8	13.2	14.8
+50	4.7	6.5	10.1	14.8
+25	1.5	2.2	4.0	14.8
0	-1.0	-1.2	-2.2	-10.2
-25	-2.9	-4.1	-6.3	-10.2
-50	-4.2	-5.3	-7.2	-10.2
-75	-5.6	-6.6	-8.2	-10.2
-100	-6.6	-7.7	-9.0	-10.2
-125	-7.4	-8.7	-9.7	-10.2

cost: -37.6+28.4-1.0=-10.2¢

net profit area , in cents

TABLE 0

changes in the soybean future's price in 25¢ increments	weeks to expiration			
	6	4	2	0
+125	14.7	15.0	15.0	15.0
+100	12.8	14.3	15.0	15.0
+75	9.5	11.5	14.5	15.0
+50	6.7	8.7	11.9	15.0
+25	2.4	3.2	5.3	15.0
0	-1.0	-1.4	-2.2	-10.0
-25	-3.9	-5.0	-7.0	-10.0
-50	-5.3	-6.3	-8.3	-10.0
-75	-7.2	-8.3	-9.6	-10.0
-100	-7.5	-8.4	-9.7	-10.0
-125	-7.8	-8.7	-9.9	-10.0

cost: -28.9+19.9-1.0=-10.0¢

TABLE 0

changes in the soybean future's price in 25¢ increments	weeks to expiration			
	6	4	2	0
+125	15.6	15.6	15.6	15.6
+100	15.2	15.6	15.6	15.6
+75	12.8	13.5	15.6	15.6
+50	9.9	11.4	14.3	15.6
+25	4.2	5.2	7.6	15.6
0	-1.0	-1.4	-2.2	-9.4
-25	-4.8	-5.8	-7.8	-9.4
-50	-5.9	-6.9	-8.9	-9.4
-75	-7.8	-8.2	-9.4	-9.4
-100	-8.1	-8.5	-9.4	-9.4
-125	-8.3	-9.1	-9.4	-9.4

Cost: -20.3+11.9-1.0=-9.4¢

net profit area , in cents

TABLE 2

changes in the soybean future's price in 25¢ increments	weeks to expiration			
	6	4	2	0
+125	16.3	16.3	16.3	16.3
+100	16.0	16.3	16.3	16.3
+75	16.0	16.2	16.3	16.3
+50	14.0	15.1	15.9	16.3
+25	7.2	8.6	11.3	16.3
0	-1.0	-1.6	-2.1	-8.7
-25	-6.1	-7.2	-8.1	-8.7
-50	-7.6	-8.3	-8.7	-8.7
-75	-8.5	-8.7	-8.7	-8.7
-100	-8.6	-8.7	-8.7	-8.7
-125	-8.7	-8.7	-8.7	-8.7

cost: -11.7+4.0-1.0=-8.7¢

net profit area , in cents

Wm Grandmill (1985) Ltd.

BULL or BEAR SPREAD – #2

BUY A CALL AT THE MONEY
and SELL 2 CALLS AT 50¢ OUT OF THE MONEY
OR
BUY A PUT AT THE MONEY
and SELL 2 PUTS AT 50¢ OUT OF THE MONEY

6 weeks to expiration

TABLE 8

changes in the soybean future's price in 25¢ increments	weeks to expiration 6	4	2	0
+125	-34.0	-27.5	-22.5	-22.3
+100	-23.5	-13.1	-0.7	2.7
+75	-14.5	-2.5	14.8	27.7
+50	-8.5	2.7	19.7	52.7
+25	-5.0	4.1	16.0	27.7
0	-1.5	3.9	9.6	2.7
-25	-2.3	3.5	7.4	2.7
-50	-0.2	3.0	4.5	2.7
-75	2.8	3.7	3.9	2.7
-100	6.6	6.1	4.4	2.7
-125	8.0	5.4	3.2	2.7

net profit area , in cents
-37.6+20.9+20.9-1.5=+2.7¢

TABLE 6

changes in the soybean future's price in 25¢ increments	weeks to expiration 6	4	2	0
+125	-32.8	-29.2	-27.8	-27.8
+100	-18.5	-11.2	-3.8	-2.8
+75	-7.9	1.9	15.0	22.2
+50	-2.6	6.8	21.1	47.2
+25	-1.3	5.3	14.8	22.2
0	-1.5	2.1	5.5	-2.8
-25	-1.9	0.7	0.9	-2.8
-50	-2.4	-1.1	-1.1	-2.8
-75	-1.7	-1.4	-1.2	-2.8
-100	-0.7	-1.0	-1.9	-2.8
-125	-0.4	-1.0	-2.7	-2.8

net profit area
-28.9+13.8+13.8-1.5=-2.8¢

TABLE 4

changes in the soybean future's price in 25¢ increments	weeks to expiration 6	4	2	0
+125	-33.0	-32.2	-32.2	
+100	-13.6	-9.4	-7.4	-7.2
+75	0.4	7.2	15.0	17.8
+50	5.4	12.5	24.1	42.8
+25	2.9	7.7	15.0	17.8
0	-1.5	0.3	1.2	-7.2
-25	-2.9	-2.7	-5.1	-7.2
-50	-5.4	-5.3	-6.7	-7.2
-75	-6.2	-6.3	-7.2	-7.2
-100	-6.0	-6.8	-7.2	-7.2
-125	-5.8	-6.9	-7.2	-7.2

net profit area
-20.3+7.3+7.3-1.5=-7.2¢

TABLE 2

changes in the soybean future's price in 25¢ increments	weeks to expiration 6	4	2	0
+125	-35.4	-35.4	-35.4	-35.4
+100	-11.0	-10.6	-10.4	-10.4
+75	9.4	12.0	13.8	14.6
+50	16.5	21.7	28.8	39.6
+25	9.2	11.8	13.4	14.6
0	-1.5	-1.8	-5.0	-10.4
-25	-7.0	-8.5	-9.6	-10.4
-50	-8.2	-10.0	-10.4	-10.4
-75	-10.1	-10.4	-10.4	-10.4
-100	-10.2	-10.4	-10.4	-10.4
-125	-11.7	-10.4	-10.4	-10.4

net profit area
-11.7+1.4+1.4-1.5=-10.4¢

Wm Grandmill (1985) Ltd.

SELL A STRADDLE
SELL A CALL AT THE MONEY
and SELL A PUT AT THE MONEY

TABLE 8

changes in the soybean future's price in 25¢ increments

	weeks to expiration			
	6	4	2	0
+125	-59.4	-55.1	-51.3	-50.8
+100	-39.5	-33.0	-27.5	-25.8
+75	-23.5	-13.0	-3.1	-0.8
+50	-10.7	2.2	17.3	24.2
+25	-3.3	12.8	33.6	49.2
0	-1.0	16.2	39.6	74.2
-25	-3.3	12.8	33.6	49.2
-50	-10.7	2.2	17.3	24.2
-75	-23.5	-13.0	-3.1	-0.8
-100	-39.5	-33.0	-27.5	-25.8
-125	-59.4	-55.1	-51.3	-50.8

net profit area, in cents

Credit:+37.6+37.6-1.0=+74.2¢

TABLE 6

changes in the soybean future's price in 25¢ increments

	weeks to expiration			
	6	4	2	0
+125	-72.4	-70.0	-68.3	-68.2
+100	-50.2	-46.7	-43.6	-43.2
+75	-30.2	-23.9	-19.0	-18.2
+50	-15.0	-6.1	3.8	6.8
+25	-4.4	7.6	22.7	31.8
0	-1.0	8.0	21.2	56.8
-25	-4.4	7.6	22.7	31.8
-50	-15.0	-6.1	3.8	6.8
-75	-30.2	-23.9	-19.0	-18.2
-100	-50.2	-46.7	-43.6	-43.2
-125	-72.4	-70.0	-68.3	-68.2

net profit area, in cents

Credit:+28.9+28.9-1.0=+56.8¢

TABLE 4

changes in the soybean future's price in 25¢ increments

	weeks to expiration			
	6	4	2	0
+125	-86.7	-85.7	-85.4	-85.4
+100	-63.0	-61.5	-60.4	-60.4
+75	-39.6	-37.0	-35.4	-35.4
+50	-20.9	-15.6	-11.0	-10.4
+25	-6.2	1.6	11.1	14.6
0	-1.0	8.2	20.8	39.6
-25	-6.2	1.6	11.1	14.6
-50	-20.9	-15.6	-11.0	-10.4
-75	-39.6	-37.0	-35.4	-35.4
-100	-63.0	-61.5	-60.4	-60.4
-125	-86.7	-85.7	-85.4	-85.4

net profit area

Credit:+20.3+20.3-1.0=+39.6¢

TABLE 2

changes in the soybean future's price in 25¢ increments

	weeks to expiration			
	6	4	2	0
+125	-102.6	-102.6	-102.6	-102.6
+100	-77.7	-102.6	-102.6	-102.6
+75	-52.9	-77.6	-77.6	-77.6
+50	-29.3	-52.6	-52.6	-52.6
+25	-9.2	-28.1	-52.6	-52.6
0	-1.0	4.4	11.6	22.4
-25	-9.2	-5.8	-3.1	-2.6
-50	-29.3	-28.4	-27.6	-27.6
-75	-52.9	-52.6	-52.6	-52.6
-100	-77.7	-77.6	-77.6	-77.6
-125	-102.6	-102.6	-102.6	-102.6

net profit

Credit:+11.7+11.7-1.0=+22.4¢

Wm Grandmill (1985) Ltd.

SELL A STRANGLE – #1

SELL A CALL AT 50¢ OUT OF THE MONEY
and SELL A PUT AT 50¢ OUT OF THE MONEY

	6
weeks to expiration	6

TABLE 8

changes in the soybean future's price in 25¢ increments	6	4	2	0
+125	-41.7	-37.6	-34.3	-34.2
+100	-27.2	-19.0	-10.9	-9.2
+75	-16.6	-4.9	8.8	15.8
+50	-8.7	5.0	21.8	40.8
+25	-4.3	11.2	29.5	40.8
0	-1.0	13.0	30.4	40.8
-25	-4.3	11.2	29.5	40.8
-50	-8.7	5.0	21.8	40.8
-75	-16.6	-4.9	8.8	15.8
-100	-27.2	-19.0	-10.9	-9.2
-125	-41.7	-37.6	-34.3	-34.2

net profit area , in cents

Credit:+20.9+20.9-1.0=+40.8¢

TABLE 8

changes in the soybean future's price in 25¢ increments	6	4	2	0
+125	-51.4	-49.1	-48.4	-48.4
+100	-33.3	-28.3	-23.9	-23.4
+75	-18.9	-10.7	-2.1	1.6
+50	-9.0	0.8	12.9	26.6
+25	-2.8	7.9	20.3	26.6
0	-1.0	9.2	21.6	26.6
-25	-2.8	7.9	20.3	26.6
-50	-9.0	0.8	12.9	26.6
-75	-18.9	-10.7	-2.1	1.6
-100	-33.3	-28.3	-23.9	-23.4
-125	-51.4	-49.1	-48.4	-48.4

net profit area , in cents

Credit:+13.8+13.8+1.0=+26.6¢

TABLE 4

changes in the soybean future's price in 25¢ increments	6	4	2	0
+125	-61.8	-61.4	-61.4	-61.4
+100	-39.9	-37.5	-36.5	-36.4
+75	-23.7	-17.0	-12.8	-11.4
+50	-9.4	-3.2	4.2	13.6
+25	-2.2	4.2	11.4	13.6
0	-1.0	5.4	12.6	13.6
-25	-2.2	4.2	11.4	13.6
-50	-9.4	-3.2	4.2	13.6
-75	-23.7	-17.0	-12.8	-11.4
-100	-39.9	-37.5	-36.4	-36.4
-125	-61.8	-61.4	-61.4	-61.4

net profit area , in cents

Credit:+7.3+7.3-1.0=+13.6¢

TABLE 2

changes in the soybean future's price in 25¢ increments	6	4	2	0
+125	-73.2	-73.2	-73.2	-73.2
+100	-48.5	-48.3	-48.2	-48.2
+75	-25.8	-24.5	-23.6	-23.2
+50	-10.0	-7.2	-3.6	1.8
+25	-2.5	-0.1	1.0	1.8
0	-1.0	1.0	1.8	1.8
-25	-2.5	-0.1	1.0	1.8
-50	-10.0	-7.2	-3.6	1.8
-75	-25.8	-24.5	-23.6	-23.2
-100	-48.5	-48.3	-48.2	-48.2
-125	-73.2	-73.2	-73.2	-73.2

net profit area , in cents

Credit:+1.4+1.4-1.0=+1.8¢

Wm Grandmill (1985) Ltd.

SELL A STRANGLE – #2

SELL A CALL AT $1.00 OUT OF THE MONEY
and SELL A PUT AT $1.00 OUT OF THE MONEY

weeks to expiration: 6

TABLE 8

changes in the soybean future's price in 25¢ increments	6	4	2	0
+125	-26.5	-18.6	-8.7	-2.2
+100	-15.4	-6.5	5.5	22.8
+75	-7.1	2.0	13.7	22.8
+50	-2.2	7.2	17.6	22.8
+25	-2.2	8.9	20.1	22.8
0	-1.0	9.2	19.4	22.8
-25	-2.2	8.9	20.1	22.8
-50	-2.1	7.2	17.6	22.8
-75	-7.1	2.0	13.7	22.8
-100	-15.4	-6.5	5.5	22.8
-125	-26.5	-18.6	-8.7	-2.2

weeks to expiration · net profit area , in cents

Credit:+11.9+11.9=1.0→22.8¢

TABLE 6

changes in the soybean future's price in 25¢ increments	6	4	2	0
+125	-28.9	-23.1	-16.2	-12.6
+100	-16.5	-9.9	-0.9	12.4
+75	-8.0	-1.3	6.9	12.4
+50	-3.3	3.0	9.9	12.4
+25	-1.3	5.6	11.5	12.4
0	-1.0	5.4	11.6	12.4
-25	-1.3	5.6	11.5	12.4
-50	-3.3	3.0	9.9	12.4
-75	-8.0	-1.3	6.9	12.4
-100	-16.5	-9.9	-0.9	12.4
-125	-28.9	-23.1	-16.2	-12.6

weeks to expiration · net profit area , in cents

Credit:+6.7+6.7-1.0= +12.4¢

TABLE 4

changes in the soybean future's price in 25¢ increments	6	4	2	0
+125	-29.5	-25.9	-22.0	-20.6
+100	-15.9	-11.3	-5.0	4.4
+75	-7.9	-3.7	1.9	4.4
+50	-3.2	0.3	3.9	4.4
+25	-0.8	2.5	4.4	4.4
0	-1.0	2.2	4.4	4.4
-25	-0.8	2.5	4.4	4.4
-50	-3.2	0.3	3.9	4.4
-75	-7.9	-3.7	1.9	4.4
-100	-15.9	-11.3	-5.0	4.4
-125	-29.5	-25.9	-22.0	-20.6

weeks to expiration · net profit area , in cents

Credit:+2.7+2.7-1.0= +4.4¢

TABLE 2

changes in the soybean future's price in 25¢ increments	6	4	2	0
+125	-28.4	-27.1	-26.2	-25.8
+100	-12.5	-9.8	-6.2	-0.8
+75	-4.8	-2.2	-1.2	-0.8
+50	-2.2	-1.2	-1.6	-0.8
+25	-1.1	-0.8	-0.8	-0.8
0	-1.0	-0.8	-0.8	-0.8
-25	-1.1	-0.8	-0.8	-0.8
-50	-2.2	-1.2	-1.6	-0.8
-75	-4.8	-2.2	-1.2	-0.8
-100	-12.5	-9.8	-6.2	-0.8
-125	-28.4	-27.1	-26.2	-25.8

weeks to expiration

Credit:+0.1+0.1-1.0= -0.8¢

Wm Grandmill (1985) Ltd.

weeks to expiration **6**

BUY A CALL or BUY A PUT

AT THE MONEY

TABLE 8

changes in the soybean future's price in 25¢ increments

	weeks to expiration				
	8	6	4	2	0
+125	83.6	81.8	81.0	81.0	81.0
+100	60.5	57.8	56.4	56.0	56.0
+75	39.9	37.0	33.6	31.1	31.0
+50	24.6	20.0	14.1	7.7	6.0
+25	10.4	5.1	-2.6	-12.5	-19.0
0	-0.5	-6.4	-15.0	-26.7	-44.0
-25	-9.8	-15.6	-24.0	-34.9	-44.0
-50	-17.8	-23.1	-30.1	-38.8	-44.0
-75	-22.1	-27.3	-34.4	-41.8	-44.0
-100	-27.8	-32.1	-37.2	-42.3	-44.0
-125	-32.5	-35.7	-39.7	-43.5	-44.0

Est. cost: -43.5¢ prem. -0.5¢= -44.0¢

net profit area

TABLE 6

changes in the soybean future's price in 25¢ increments

	weeks to expiration				
	8	6	4	2	0
+125	91.1	91.1	91.1	91.1	91.1
+100	67.0	66.4	66.1	66.1	66.1
+75	45.3	43.6	41.8	41.1	41.1
+50	27.1	24.1	20.3	16.6	16.1
+25	11.4	7.4	1.6	-5.3	-8.9
0	-0.5	-5.0	-11.6	-20.6	-33.9
-25	-9.6	-14.0	-20.2	-28.4	-33.9
-50	-16.6	-20.1	-25.2	-31.4	-33.9
-75	-20.9	-24.4	-28.9	-33.1	-33.9
-100	-24.5	-27.2	-30.4	-33.5	-33.9
-125	-27.7	-29.7	-32.1	-33.8	-33.9

Est. cost:-33.4¢ prem. -0.5¢= -33.9¢

net profit area

TABLE 4

changes in the soybean future's price in 25¢ increments

	weeks to expiration				
	8	6	4	2	0
+125	101.0	101.0	101.0	101.0	101.0
+100	76.0	76.0	76.0	76.0	76.0
+75	52.0	51.4	51.0	51.0	51.0
+50	30.8	29.2	27.1	26.1	26.0
+25	12.5	9.9	6.3	2.4	1.0
0	-0.5	-3.7	-8.3	-14.6	-24.0
-25	-9.2	-12.1	-16.3	-21.9	-24.0
-50	-14.4	-16.7	-19.9	-23.5	-24.0
-75	-18.3	-20.2	-22.4	-24.0	-24.0
-100	-20.0	-21.3	-22.9	-24.0	-24.0
-125	-21.8	-22.7	-23.7	-24.0	-24.0

Est. cost: -23.5¢ prem. -0.5¢=-24.0¢

net profit area , in cents

TABLE 2

changes in the soybean future's price in 25¢ increments

	weeks to expiration				
	8	6	4	2	0
+125	111.0	111.0	111.0	111.0	111.0
+100	86.0	86.0	86.0	86.0	86.0
+75	61.0	61.0	61.0	61.0	61.0
+50	36.6	36.3	36.1	36.0	36.0
+25	14.7	13.6	12.3	11.4	11.0
0	-0.5	-2.3	-5.0	-8.6	-14.0
-25	-8.3	-10.0	-12.1	-13.2	-14.0
-50	-11.3	-12.6	-13.6	-14.0	-14.0
-75	-13.1	-13.7	-14.0	-14.0	-14.0
-100	-13.5	-13.9	-14.0	-14.0	-14.0
-125	-13.9	-14.0	-14.0	-14.0	-14.0

est. cost:-13.5¢ prem. -0.5¢=-14.0¢

net profit area , in cents

Wm Grandmill (1985) Ltd.

TABLE

changes in the soybean future's price in 25¢ increments	weeks to expiration				
	8	6	4	2	0
+125	57.2	54.3	50.9	48.4	48.3
+100	41.9	37.3	31.4	25.0	23.3
+75	27.8	22.4	14.7	4.8	-1.7
+50	16.8	10.9	2.3	-9.4	-26.7
+25	7.5	1.7	-6.7	-17.6	-26.7
0	-0.5	-5.8	-12.8	-21.4	-26.7
-25	-4.8	-10.3	-17.1	-24.5	-26.7
-50	-10.5	-14.8	-19.9	-25.0	-26.7
-75	-15.2	-18.4	-22.4	-26.2	-26.7
-100	-20.6	-22.7	-25.0	-26.7	-26.7
-125	-24.2	-25.3	-25.9	-26.7	-26.7
					net profit

Est.cost:-26.2¢ prem. -0.5¢=-26.7¢

TABLE

changes in the soybean future's price in 25¢ increments	weeks to expiration				
	8	6	4	2	0
+125	61.4	59.7	57.9	57.2	57.2
+100	43.2	40.2	36.4	32.7	32.2
+75	27.5	23.5	17.7	10.8	7.2
+50	15.6	11.1	4.5	-4.5	-17.8
+25	6.5	2.1	-4.1	-12.3	-17.8
0	-0.5	-4.0	-9.1	-15.3	-17.8
-25	-4.8	-8.3	-12.8	-17.0	-17.8
-50	-8.4	-11.1	-14.3	-17.4	-17.8
-75	-11.6	-13.6	-16.0	-17.7	-17.8
-100	-14.4	-15.9	-17.1	-17.8	-17.8
-125	-16.4	-17.3	-17.8	-17.8	-17.8

Est.cost:-17.3¢ prem. -0.5¢= -17.8¢

TABLE

changes in the soybean future's price in 25¢ increments	weeks to expiration				
	8	6	4	2	0
+125	65.9	65.3	64.9	64.9	64.9
+100	44.7	42.1	41.0	40.0	39.9
+75	26.4	23.8	20.2	16.3	14.9
+50	13.4	10.2	5.6	-0.7	-10.1
+25	4.7	1.8	-2.4	-8.0	-10.1
0	-0.5	-2.8	-6.0	-9.6	-10.1
-25	-4.4	-6.3	-8.5	-10.1	-10.1
-50	-6.1	-7.4	-9.0	-10.1	-10.1
-75	-7.9	-8.7	-9.8	-10.1	-10.1
-100	-9.6	-9.8	-10.1	-10.1	-10.1
-125	-10.0	-10.1	-10.1	-10.1	-10.1
					net profit

Est.cost: -9.6¢ prem. -0.5¢=-10.1¢

TABLE

changes in the soybean future's price in 25¢ increments	weeks to expiration				
	8	6	4	2	0
+125	71.8	71.8	71.8	71.8	71.8
+100	47.4	47.1	46.9	46.8	46.8
+75	24.5	23.4	22.6	22.2	21.8
+50	10.3	8.5	5.8	2.2	-3.2
+25	2.5	0.8	-1.3	-2.4	-3.2
0	-0.5	-1.8	-2.8	-3.2	-3.2
-25	-2.3	-2.9	-3.2	-3.2	-3.2
-50	-2.7	-3.1	-3.2	-3.2	-3.2
-75	-3.1	-3.2	-3.2	-3.2	-3.2
-100	-3.2	-3.2	-3.2	-3.2	-3.2
-125	-3.2	-3.2	-3.2	-3.2	-3.2
					net profit

Est.cost: -2.7¢ prem. -0.5¢= -3.2¢

Wm Grandmill (1985) Ltd.

SELL A CALL or SELL A PUT

AT THE MONEY

TABLE 8

net profit area, in cents

changes in the soybean future's price in 25¢ increments	weeks to expiration 8	6	4	2	0
+125	-84.6	-82.3	-82.0	-82.0	-82.0
+100	-61.5	-58.8	-57.4	-57.0	-57.0
+75	-40.9	-38.0	-34.6	-32.2	-32.0
+50	-25.6	-21.0	-15.1	-8.7	-7.0
+25	-11.4	-6.1	1.6	11.5	18.0
0	-0.5	5.3	14.0	25.7	43.0
-25	8.8	14.6	23.0	33.9	43.0
-50	16.8	22.1	29.1	37.8	43.0
-75	21.1	26.3	33.4	40.8	43.0
-100	26.8	31.1	36.2	41.3	43.0
-125	31.5	34.7	38.7	42.5	43.0

Est. credit:+43.5¢ prem. -0.5¢=+43.0¢

TABLE 6

net profit area, in cents

changes in the soybean future's price in 25¢ increments	weeks to expiration 8	6	4	2	0
+125	-92.1	-92.1	-92.1	-92.1	-92.1
+100	-68.0	-67.4	-67.1	-67.1	-67.1
+75	-46.3	-44.6	-42.8	-42.1	-42.1
+50	-28.1	-25.1	-21.3	-17.6	-17.1
+25	-12.4	-8.4	-2.6	4.3	7.9
0	-0.5	4.0	10.6	19.6	32.9
-25	8.6	13.0	19.2	27.4	32.9
-50	15.6	19.1	24.2	30.4	32.9
-75	19.9	23.4	27.9	32.1	32.9
-100	23.5	26.2	29.4	32.5	32.9
-125	26.7	28.7	31.1	32.8	32.9

Est. credit:+33.4¢ prem. -0.5¢=+32.9¢

TABLE 4

net profit area, in cents

changes in the soybean future's price in 25¢ increments	weeks to expiration 8	6	4	2	0
+125	-102.0	-102.0	-102.0	-102.0	-102.0
+100	-77.0	-77.0	-77.0	-77.0	-77.0
+75	-53.0	-52.4	-52.0	-52.0	-52.0
+50	-31.8	-30.2	-28.1	-27.1	-27.0
+25	-15.5	-10.9	-7.3	-3.4	-2.0
0	-0.5	2.7	7.3	13.6	23.0
-25	8.2	11.1	15.3	20.9	23.0
-50	13.4	15.7	18.9	22.5	23.0
-75	17.3	19.2	21.4	23.0	23.0
-100	19.0	20.3	21.9	23.0	23.0
-125	20.8	21.7	22.7	23.0	23.0

Est. credit:+23.5¢ prem.-0.5¢=+23.0¢

TABLE 2

net profit area, in cents

changes in the soybean future's price in 25¢ increments	weeks to expiration 8	6	4	2	0
+125	-112.0	-112.0	-112.0	-112.0	-112.0
+100	-87.0	-87.0	-87.0	-87.0	-87.0
+75	-62.0	-62.0	-62.0	-62.0	-62.0
+50	-37.6	-37.3	-37.1	-37.0	-37.0
+25	-15.7	-14.6	-13.3	-12.4	-12.0
0	-0.5	1.3	4.0	7.6	13.0
-25	7.3	9.0	11.1	12.2	13.0
-50	10.3	11.6	12.6	13.0	13.0
-75	12.1	12.7	13.0	13.0	13.0
-100	12.5	12.9	13.0	13.0	13.0
-125	12.9	13.0	13.0	13.0	13.0

Est. credit:+13.5¢ prem.-0.5¢=+13.0¢

Wm Grandmill (1985) Ltd.

SELL A CALL or SELL A PUT
AT 50¢ OUT OF THE MONEY

TABLE 8

changes in the soybean future's price in 25¢ increments

price	8	6	4	2	0
-125	23.2	23.3	23.9	25.7	25.7
-100	19.6	21.7	24.0	25.7	25.7
-75	14.2	17.4	21.4	25.2	25.7
-50	9.5	13.8	18.9	24.0	25.7
-25	3.8	9.3	16.1	23.5	25.7
0	-0.5	4.8	11.8	20.4	25.7
+25	-8.5	-2.7	5.7	16.6	25.7
+50	-17.8	-11.9	-3.3	8.4	25.7
+75	-28.8	-23.4	-15.7	-5.8	0.7
+100	-42.9	-38.3	-32.4	-26.0	-24.3
+125	-58.2	-55.3	-51.9	-49.4	-49.3

weeks to expiration · net profit area, in cents

Est. credit: +26.2¢ prem -0.5¢ = 25.7¢

TABLE 8

changes in the soybean future's price in 25¢ increments

price	8	6	4	2	0
-125	-62.4	-60.7	-58.9	-58.2	-58.2
-100	-44.2	-41.2	-37.4	-33.7	-33.2
-75	-28.5	-24.5	-18.7	-11.8	-8.2
-50	-16.6	-12.1	-5.5	3.5	16.8
-25	-7.5	-3.1	3.1	3.1	16.8
0	-0.5	3.0	8.1	11.3	16.8
+25	3.8	7.3	11.8	14.3	16.8
+50	7.4	10.1	13.3	16.0	16.8
+75	10.6	12.6	15.0	16.4	16.8
+100	13.4	14.9	16.1	16.8	16.8
+125	15.4	16.3	16.8	16.8	16.8

weeks to expiration · net profit area, in cents

Est. credit: +17.3¢ prem -0.5¢ = 16.8¢

TABLE 4

changes in the soybean future's price in 25¢ increments

price	8	6	4	2	0
-125	9.0	8.6	9.1	9.1	9.1
-100	8.6	8.8	9.1	9.1	9.1
-75	6.9	7.7	8.8	9.1	9.1
-50	5.1	6.4	8.0	9.1	9.1
-25	3.4	5.3	7.5	8.6	9.1
0	-0.5	1.8	5.0	8.6	9.1
+25	-5.7	-2.8	1.4	7.0	9.1
+50	-14.4	-11.2	-6.6	-0.3	9.1
+75	-27.4	-24.8	-21.2	-17.3	-15.9
+100	-45.7	-43.1	-42.0	-41.0	-40.9
+125	-66.9	-66.3	-65.9	-65.9	-65.9

weeks to expiration · net profit area, in cents

Est. credit: +9.6¢ prem -0.5¢ = 9.1¢

TABLE 2

changes in the soybean future's price in 25¢ increments

price	8	6	4	2	0
-125	-72.8	-72.8	-72.8	-72.8	-72.8
-100	-48.4	-48.1	-47.9	-47.8	-47.8
-75	-25.5	-24.4	-23.6	-23.2	-22.8
-50	-11.3	-9.5	-6.8	-3.2	2.2
-25	-3.5	-1.8	0.3	1.4	2.2
0	-0.5	0.8	1.8	2.2	2.2
+25	1.3	1.9	2.2	2.2	2.2
+50	1.7	2.1	2.2	2.2	2.2
+75	2.1	2.2	2.2	2.2	2.2
+100	2.2	2.2	2.2	2.2	2.2
+125	2.2	2.2	2.2	2.2	2.2

weeks to expiration · net profit area, in cents

Est. credit: +2.7¢ prem -0.5¢ = 2.2¢

Wm Grandmill (1985) Ltd.

BULL or BEAR SPREAD – #1

BUY A CALL AT THE MONEY
and SELL A CALL AT 25¢ OUT OF THE MONEY
OR
BUY A PUT AT THE MONEY
and SELL A PUT AT 25¢ OUT OF THE MONEY

weeks to expiration
8

TABLE 8

changes in the soybean future's price in 25¢ increments

	weeks to expiration				
	8	6	4	2	0
+125	14.1	14.6	14.9	14.9	14.9
+100	11.6	12.7	14.2	14.9	14.9
+75	8.1	9.4	11.4	14.4	14.9
+50	5.6	6.6	8.6	11.8	14.9
+25	1.8	2.3	3.1	5.2	14.9
0	-1.0	-1.1	-1.5	-2.3	-10.1
-25	-3.1	-4.0	-5.1	-7.1	-10.1
-50	-4.7	-5.4	-6.4	-7.4	-10.1
-75	-6.5	-7.3	-8.5	-9.7	-10.1
-100	-6.9	-7.6	-8.5	-9.8	-10.1
-125	-7.3	-7.8	-8.8	-10.0	-10.1

net profit area , in cents

Est. cost: -33.4¢+24.3¢-1.0¢=-10.1¢

TABLE 0

changes in the soybean future's price in 25¢ increments

	weeks to expiration				
	8	6	4	2	0
+125	13.9	14.1	14.3	14.7	14.7
+100	10.6	11.1	13.1	14.7	14.7
+75	7.1	8.1	9.7	13.1	14.7
+50	3.9	4.6	6.4	9.9	14.7
+25	1.2	1.4	2.1	3.0	14.7
0	-1.0	-1.1	-1.3	-2.3	-10.3
-25	-2.3	-3.0	-4.2	-6.4	-10.3
-50	-3.4	-4.3	-5.4	-7.3	-10.3
-75	-4.7	-5.7	-6.7	-8.3	-10.3
-100	-5.6	-6.7	-7.9	-9.1	-10.3
-125	-6.3	-7.5	-8.8	-9.8	-10.3

net profit area , in cents

Est. cost: -43.5¢+34.2¢-1.0¢=-10.3¢

TABLE 4

changes in the soybean future's price in 25¢ increments

	weeks to expiration				
	8	6	4	2	0
+125	15.3	15.3	15.3	15.3	15.3
+100	14.3	14.9	15.3	15.3	15.3
+75	11.5	12.5	13.2	14.0	15.3
+50	8.6	9.6	11.1	14.0	15.3
+25	3.3	3.9	4.9	7.3	15.3
0	-1.0	-1.3	-1.7	-2.5	-9.7
-25	-4.5	-5.1	-6.1	-8.-	-9.7
-50	-5.8	-6.2	-7.2	-9.2	-9.7
-75	-7.7	-8.1	-8.5	-9.7	-9.7
-100	-7.9	-8.4	-8.9	-9.7	-9.7
-125	-8.1	-8.6	-9.4	-9.7	-9.7

net profit area , in cents

Est. cost: -23.5¢+14.8¢-1.0¢=-9.7¢

TABLE 2

changes in the soybean future's price in 25¢ increments

	weeks to expiration				
	8	6	4	2	0
+125	16.2	16.2	16.2	16.2	16.2
+100	16.2	16.2	16.2	16.2	16.2
+75	15.6	15.9	16.1	16.2	16.2
+50	13.1	13.9	15.0	15.8	16.2
+25	6.4	7.1	8.5	11.2	16.2
0	-1.0	-1.1	-1.7	-2.2	-8.8
-25	-5.8	-6.2	-7.3	-8.2	-8.8
-50	-7.0	-7.7	-8.4	-8.8	-8.8
-75	-7.9	-8.6	-8.8	-8.8	-8.8
-100	-8.4	-8.7	-8.8	-8.8	-8.8
-125	-8.7	-8.8	-8.8	-8.8	-8.8

net profit area , in cents

Est. cost: -13.5¢+5.7¢-1.0¢=-8.8¢

Wm Grandmill (1985) Ltd.

BULL or BEAR SPREAD – #2

BUY A CALL AT THE MONEY
and SELL 2 CALLS AT 50¢ OUT OF THE MONEY
OR
BUY A PUT AT THE MONEY
and SELL 2 PUTS AT 50¢ OUT OF THE MONEY

weeks to
expiration

8

TABLE 8

changes in the soybean future's price in 25¢ increments	weeks to expiration				
	8	6	4	2	0
+125	-32.8	-29.3	-22.8	-17.8	-17.6
+100	-25.3	-18.8	-8.4	4.0	7.4
+75	-17.5	-9.8	2.2	19.5	32.4
+50	-11.0	-3.8	7.5	24.5	57.4
+25	-6.6	-0.3	8.7	20.7	32.4
0	-1.5	3.2	8.6	14.3	7.4
-25	-2.2	2.4	8.2	12.1	7.4
-50	1.2	4.5	7.7	9.2	7.4
-75	6.3	7.5	8.4	8.6	7.4
-100	9.5	9.6	9.1	8.2	7.4
-125	13.9	12.7	10.1	7.9	7.4

net profit area , in cents

Est. -43.5¢+26.2¢+26.2¢-1.5¢=7.4¢

TABLE 0

changes in the soybean future's price in 25¢ increments	weeks to expiration				
	8	6	4	2	0
+125	-33.7	-30.3	-26.7	-25.3	-25.3
+100	-21.4	-16.0	-8.7	-1.3	-0.3
+75	-11.7	-5.4	4.4	17.5	24.7
+50	-6.1	-0.1	9.3	23.6	49.7
+25	-3.6	1.2	7.8	17.3	24.7
0	-1.5	1.0	4.6	8.0	-0.3
-25	-2.0	0.6	3.4	3.6	-0.3
-50	-1.6	0.1	1.4	1.4	-0.3
-75	0.3	0.8	1.1	1.3	-0.3
-100	1.5	1.8	1.3	0.6	-0.3
-125	3.1	2.9	1.5	-0.2	-0.3

net profit

Est. -33.4¢+17.3¢+17.3¢-1.5¢=-0.3¢

TABLE 4

changes in the soybean future's price in 25¢ increments	weeks to expiration				
	8	6	4	2	0
+125	-32.6	-31.6	-30.6	-30.8	-30.8
+100	-15.4	-12.2	-8.0	-6.0	-5.8
+75	-2.8	1.8	8.6	16.4	19.2
+50	2.0	6.8	13.9	25.5	44.2
+25	1.1	4.3	9.1	16.4	19.2
0	-1.5	-0.1	1.7	2.6	-5.8
-25	-2.4	-1.5	-1.3	-3.7	-5.8
-50	-4.2	-4.0	-3.9	-5.3	-5.8
-75	-4.6	-4.8	-4.9	-5.8	-5.8
-100	-4.1	-4.6	-5.4	-5.8	-5.8
-125	-3.8	-4.4	-5.5	-5.8	-5.8

net profit

Est. -23.5¢+9.6¢+9.6¢-1.5¢=-5.8¢

TABLE 2

changes in the soybean future's price in 25¢ increments	weeks to expiration				
	8	6	4	2	0
+125	-34.6	-34.6	-34.6	-34.6	-34.6
+100	-10.8	-10.2	-9.8	-9.6	-9.6
+75	8.0	10.2	12.8	14.6	15.4
+50	14.0	17.3	22.5	29.6	40.4
+25	7.8	10.0	12.6	14.2	15.4
0	-1.5	-0.7	-1.0	-4.2	-9.6
-25	-5.7	-6.2	-7.7	-8.8	-9.6
-50	-8.0	-8.4	-9.2	-9.6	-9.6
-75	-8.9	-9.3	-9.6	-9.6	-9.6
-100	-9.2	-9.4	-9.6	-9.6	-9.6
-125	-9.5	-9.6	-9.6	-9.6	-9.6

net profit

Est.-33.5¢+2.7¢+2.7¢-1.5¢=-9.6¢

Wm Grandmill (1985) Ltd.

SELL A STRADDLE
SELL A CALL AT THE MONEY and SELL A PUT AT THE MONEY

TABLE 8

changes in the soybean future's price in 25¢ increments	weeks to expiration				
	8	6	4	2	0
+125	-53.1	-47.6	-43.3	-39.5	-39.0
+100	-34.7	-27.7	-21.2	-15.7	-14.0
+75	-19.8	-11.7	-1.2	8.7	11.0
+50	-8.8	1.1	14.0	29.1	36.0
+25	-2.6	8.5	24.6	45.4	61.0
0	-1.0	10.8	28.0	51.4	86.0
-25	-2.6	8.5	24.6	45.4	61.0
-50	-8.8	1.1	14.0	29.1	36.0
-75	-19.8	-11.7	-1.2	8.7	11.0
-100	-34.7	-27.7	-21.2	-15.7	-14.0
-125	-53.1	-47.6	-43.3	-39.5	-39.0

net profit area , in cents

Est. credit: +43.5¢ + 43.5¢ -1.0¢ = 86.0¢

TABLE 8

changes in the soybean future's price in 25¢ increments	weeks to expiration				
	8	6	4	2	0
+125	-65.4	-63.4	-61.0	-59.3	-59.2
+100	-44.5	-41.2	-37.7	-34.6	-34.2
+75	-26.4	-21.2	-14.9	-10.0	-9.2
+50	-12.5	-5.7	2.9	12.8	15.8
+25	-3.8	4.6	16.6	31.7	40.8
0	-1.0	8.0	21.2	39.2	65.8
-25	-3.8	4.6	16.6	31.7	40.8
-50	-12.5	-5.7	2.9	12.8	15.8
-75	-26.4	-21.2	-14.9	-10.0	-9.2
-100	-44.5	-41.2	-37.7	-34.6	-34.2
-125	-65.4	-63.4	-61.0	-59.3	-59.2

net profit area , in cents

Est. credit: +33.4¢+33.4¢-1.0¢=65.8¢

TABLE 4

changes in the soybean future's price in 25¢ increments	weeks to expiration				
	8	6	4	2	0
+125	-81.2	-80.3	-79.3	-79.0	-79.0
+100	-58.0	-56.6	-55.1	-54.0	-54.0
+75	-35.7	-33.2	-30.6	-29.0	-29.0
+50	-18.4	-14.5	-9.2	-4.6	-4.0
+25	-5.3	0.2	5.4	0.2	21.0
0	-1.0	5.4	14.6	27.2	46.0
-25	-5.3	0.2	8.0	17.5	21.0
-50	-18.4	-14.5	-9.2	-4.6	-4.0
-75	-35.7	-33.2	-30.6	-29.0	-29.0
-100	-58.0	-56.6	-55.1	-54.0	-54.0
-125	-81.2	-80.3	-79.3	-79.0	-79.0

net profit area

Est. credit: +23.5¢+23.5¢-1.0¢=46.0¢

TABLE 2

changes in the soybean future's price in 25¢ increments	weeks to expiration				
	8	6	4	2	0
+125	-99.1	-99.0	-99.0	-99.0	-99.0
+100	-74.5	-74.1	-74.0	-74.0	-74.0
+75	-49.9	-49.3	-49.0	-49.0	-49.0
+50	-27.2	-25.7	-24.5	-24.0	-24.0
+25	-8.4	-5.6	-2.2	0.5	1.0
0	-1.0	2.6	8.0	15.2	26.0
-25	-8.4	-5.6	-2.2	0.5	1.0
-50	-27.2	-25.7	-24.5	-24.0	-24.0
-75	-49.9	-49.3	-49.0	-49.0	-49.0
-100	-74.5	-74.1	-74.0	-74.0	-74.0
-125	-99.1	-99.0	-99.0	-99.0	-99.0

net profit area

Est. credit: +13.5¢+13.5¢-1.0¢=26.0¢

Wm Grandmill (1985) Ltd.

SELL A STRANGLE – #1

SELL A CALL AT 50¢ OUT OF THE MONEY
and SELL A PUT AT 50¢ OUT OF THE MONEY

8 weeks to expiration

TABLE (Est. credit: +26.2¢ +26.2¢ –1.0 = +51.4¢)

changes in the soybean future's price in 25¢ increments	weeks to expiration				
	8	6	4	2	0
+125	-35.0	-31.1	-27.0	-23.7	-23.6
+100	-23.2	-16.6	-8.4	-0.3	1.4
+75	-14.5	-6.0	5.7	19.4	26.4
+50	-8.3	1.9	15.6	32.4	51.4
+25	-4.7	6.3	21.8	40.1	51.4
0	-1.0	9.6	23.6	41.0	51.4
-25	-4.7	6.3	21.8	32.4	51.4
-50	-8.3	1.9	15.6	19.4	26.4
-75	-14.5	-6.0	1.9	5.7	1.4
-100	-23.2	-16.6	-8.4	-0.3	1.4
-125	-35.0	-31.1	-27.0	-23.7	-23.6

net profit area , in cents

TABLE (Est. credit: +17.3¢ +17.3¢ –1.0¢ = +33.6¢)

changes in the soybean future's price in 25¢ increments	weeks to expiration				
	8	6	4	2	0
+125	-47.0	-44.4	-42.1	-41.4	-41.4
+100	-30.8	-26.3	-21.3	-16.9	-16.4
+75	-17.9	-11.9	-3.7	4.9	8.9
+50	-9.2	-2.0	7.8	19.9	33.6
+25	-3.7	4.2	14.9	27.3	33.6
0	-1.0	6.0	16.2	28.6	33.6
-25	-3.7	4.2	14.9	27.3	33.6
-50	-9.2	-2.0	7.8	19.9	33.6
-75	-17.9	-11.9	-3.7	4.9	8.6
-100	-30.8	-26.3	-21.3	-16.9	-16.4
-125	-47.0	-44.4	-42.1	-41.4	-41.4

net profit area , in cents

TABLE 4 (Est. credit: +9.6¢ +9.6¢ –1.0¢ = +18.2¢)

changes in the soybean future's price in 25¢ increments	weeks to expiration				
	8	6	4	2	0
+125	-57.9	-57.2	-56.8	-56.8	-56.8
+100	-37.1	-35.3	-32.9	-31.9	-31.8
+75	-20.5	-17.1	-12.4	-8.2	-6.8
+50	-9.3	-4.8	2.5	8.9	18.2
+25	-2.3	2.5	8.9	16.1	18.2
0	-1.0	3.6	10.0	17.2	18.2
-25	-2.3	2.5	8.9	16.1	18.2
-50	-9.3	-4.8	1.4	8.8	18.2
-75	-20.5	-17.1	-12.4	-8.2	-6.8
-100	-37.1	-35.3	-32.9	-31.9	-31.8
-125	-57.9	-57.2	-56.8	-56.8	-56.8

net profit area , in cents

TABLE 2 (Est. credit: +2.7¢ +2.7¢ –1.0¢ = +4.4¢)

changes in the soybean future's price in 25¢ increments	weeks to expiration				
	8	6	4	2	0
+125	-70.6	-70.6	-70.6	-70.6	-70.6
+100	-46.2	-45.9	-45.7	-45.6	-45.6
+75	-24.4	-23.2	-21.9	-21.0	-20.6
+50	-9.6	-7.4	-4.6	-1.0	4.4
+25	-2.2	0.1	2.5	3.6	4.4
0	-1.0	1.4	3.6	4.4	4.4
-25	-2.2	0.1	2.5	3.6	4.4
-50	-9.6	-7.4	-4.6	-1.0	4.4
-75	-24.4	-23.2	-21.9	-21.0	-20.6
-100	-46.2	-45.9	-45.7	-45.6	-45.6
-125	-70.6	-70.6	-70.6	-70.6	-70.6

net profit area , in cents

Wm Grandmill (1985) Ltd.

SELL A STRANGLE – #2

SELL A CALL AT $1.00 OUT OF THE MONEY
and SELL A PUT AT $1.00 OUT OF THE MONEY

TABLE 8

changes in the soybean future's price in 25¢ increments	weeks to expiration				
	8	6	4	2	0
+125	-23.4	-17.9	-10.0	-0.1	6.4
+100	-13.4	-6.8	2.1	14.1	31.4
+75	-5.3	1.5	10.6	23.3	31.4
+50	-0.8	6.5	15.8	26.2	31.4
+25	-2.0	6.4	17.5	28.7	31.4
0	-1.0	7.6	17.8	28.0	31.4
-25	-2.0	6.4	17.5	28.7	31.4
-50	-0.8	6.5	15.8	26.2	31.4
-75	-5.3	1.5	10.6	22.3	31.4
-100	-13.4	-6.8	2.1	14.1	31.4
-125	-23.4	-17.9	-10.0	-0.1	6.4

net profit area , in cents

Est.credit:+16.2¢+16.2¢-1.0¢=+31.4¢

TABLE 8

changes in the soybean future's price in 25¢ increments	weeks to expiration				
	8	6	4	2	0
+125	-27.5	-23.5	-17.7	-10.8	-7.2
+100	-16.0	-11.1	-4.5	4.5	17.8
+75	-7.9	-2.6	4.1	12.3	17.8
+50	-2.9	2.1	8.4	15.3	17.8
+25	-1.4	4.1	11.0	16.9	17.8
0	-1.0	4.4	10.8	17.0	17.8
-25	-1.4	4.1	11.0	16.9	17.8
-50	-2.9	2.1	8.4	15.3	17.8
-75	-7.9	-2.6	4.1	12.3	17.8
-100	-16.0	-11.1	-4.5	4.5	17.8
-125	-27.5	-23.5	-17.7	-10.8	-7.2

net profit area , in cents

Est.credit:+9.4¢+9.4¢-1.0¢=+17.8¢

TABLE 4

changes in the soybean future's price in 25¢ increments	weeks to expiration				
	8	6	4	2	0
+125	-29.5	-26.9	-23.3	-19.4	-18.0
+100	-16.5	-13.3	-8.7	-2.4	7.0
+75	-7.9	-4.9	-0.7	4.9	7.0
+50	-3.1	-0.6	2.9	6.5	7.0
+25	-0.9	1.8	5.1	7.0	7.0
0	-1.0	1.6	4.8	7.0	7.0
-25	-0.9	1.8	5.1	7.0	7.0
-50	-3.1	-0.6	2.9	6.5	7.0
-75	-7.9	-4.9	-0.7	4.9	7.0
-100	-16.5	-13.3	-8.7	-2.4	7.0
-125	-29.5	-26.9	-23.3	-19.4	-18.0

net profit area , in cents

Est.credit:+4.0¢+4.0¢-1.0¢=+7.0¢

TABLE 2/0

changes in the soybean future's price in 25¢ increments	weeks to expiration				
	8	6	4	2	0
+125	-28.7	-27.6	-26.3	-25.4	-25.0
+100	-13.5	-11.7	-9.0	-5.4	0.0
+75	-5.7	-4.0	-1.9	0.0	0.0
+50	-2.7	-1.4	-0.4	0.0	0.0
+25	-0.9	-0.3	0.0	0.0	0.0
0	-1.0	-0.2	0.0	0.0	0.0
-25	-0.9	-0.3	0.0	0.0	0.0
-50	-2.7	-1.4	-0.4	0.0	0.0
-75	-5.7	-4.0	-1.9	0.0	0.0
-100	-13.5	-11.7	-9.0	-5.4	0.0
-125	-28.7	-27.6	-26.3	-25.4	-25.0

net profit area , in cents

Est.credit:+0.5¢+0.5¢-1.0¢=0.0¢

Wm Grandmill (1985) Ltd.

BUY A CALL or BUY A PUT

AT THE MONEY

Table (Est. cost:-48.2¢ prem.-0.5¢ com.=-48.7¢)

changes in the soybean future's price in 25¢ increments	weeks to expiration					
	10	8	6	4	2	0
+125	82.0	78.9	76.6	76.3	76.3	76.3
+100	58.3	55.8	53.1	51.7	51.3	51.3
+75	38.0	35.2	32.3	28.9	26.4	26.3
+50	23.7	19.9	15.3	9.4	3.0	1.3
+25	9.9	5.7	0.4	-7.3	-17.2	-23.7
0	-0.5	-5.2	-11.1	-19.7	-31.4	-48.7
-25	-9.9	-14.5	-20.3	-28.7	-39.6	-48.7
-50	-18.3	-22.5	-27.8	-34.8	-43.5	-48.7
-75	-22.3	-26.8	-32.0	-39.1	-46.5	-48.7
-100	-28.7	-32.5	-36.8	-41.9	-47.0	-48.7
-125	-34.2	-37.2	-40.4	-44.4	-48.2	-48.7

net profit area

Table (Est. cost:-26.0¢ prem.-0.5¢ com.=-26.5¢)

changes in the soybean future's price in 25¢ increments	weeks to expiration					
	10	8	6	4	2	0
+125	98.5	98.5	98.5	98.5	98.5	98.5
+100	73.6	73.5	73.5	73.5	73.5	73.5
+75	50.2	49.5	48.9	48.5	48.5	48.5
+50	29.8	28.3	26.7	24.6	23.6	23.5
+25	12.3	10.0	7.4	3.8	-0.1	-1.5
0	-0.5	-3.0	-6.2	-10.8	-17.1	-26.5
-25	-9.2	-11.7	-14.6	-18.8	-24.4	-26.5
-50	-14.9	-16.9	-19.2	-22.4	-26.0	-26.5
-75	-19.0	-20.8	-22.7	-24.9	-26.5	-26.5
-100	-21.2	-22.5	-23.8	-25.4	-26.5	-26.5
-125	-23.4	-24.3	-25.2	-26.2	-26.5	-26.5

net profit area

Table (Est. cost:-37.1¢ prem.-0.5¢ com.=-37.6¢)

changes in the soybean future's price in 25¢ increments	weeks to expiration					
	10	8	6	4	2	0
+125	87.6	87.4	87.4	87.4	87.4	87.4
+100	64.1	63.3	62.7	62.4	62.4	62.4
+75	43.1	41.6	39.9	38.1	37.4	37.4
+50	26.0	23.4	20.4	16.6	12.9	12.4
+25	11.0	7.7	3.7	-2.1	-9.0	-12.6
0	-0.5	-4.2	-8.7	-15.3	-24.3	-37.6
-25	-9.7	-13.3	-17.7	-23.9	-32.1	-37.6
-50	-17.1	-20.3	-23.8	-28.9	-35.1	-37.6
-75	-21.4	-24.6	-28.1	-32.6	-36.8	-37.6
-100	-26.0	-28.2	-30.9	-34.1	-37.2	-37.6
-125	-29.6	-31.4	-33.4	-35.8	-37.5	-37.6

net profit area

Table (Est. cost:-14.9¢ prem.-0.5¢ com.=-15.4¢)

changes in the soybean future's price in 25¢ increments	weeks to expiration					
	10	8	6	4	2	0
+125	109.6	109.6	109.6	109.6	109.6	109.6
+100	84.6	84.6	84.6	84.6	84.6	84.6
+75	59.6	59.6	59.6	59.6	59.6	59.6
+50	35.5	35.2	34.9	34.7	34.6	34.6
+25	14.4	13.3	12.2	10.9	10.0	9.6
0	-0.5	-1.9	-3.7	-6.4	-10.0	-15.4
-25	-8.4	-9.7	-11.4	-13.5	-14.6	-15.4
-50	-11.8	-12.8	-14.0	-15.0	-15.4	-15.4
-75	-14.1	-14.5	-15.1	-15.1	-15.4	-15.4
-100	-14.5	-14.9	-15.3	-15.4	-15.4	-15.4
-125	-15.2	-15.3	-15.4	-15.4	-15.4	-15.4

net profit area , in cents

Wm Grandmill (1985) Ltd.

BUY A CALL or BUY A PUT
AT 50¢ OUT OF THE MONEY

10 weeks to expiration

TABLE 0

changes in the soybean future's price in 25¢ increments	weeks to expiration 10	8	6	4	2	0 net profit
+125	55.8	53.0	50.1	46.7	44.2	44.1
+100	41.5	37.7	33.1	27.2	20.8	19.1
+75	27.7	23.6	18.2	10.5	0.6	-5.9
+50	17.3	12.6	6.7	-1.9	-13.6	-30.9
+25	7.9	3.3	-2.5	-10.9	-21.8	-30.9
0	-0.5	-4.7	-10.0	-17.0	-25.6	-30.9
-25	-4.5	-9.0	-14.5	-21.3	-28.7	-30.9
-50	-10.9	-14.7	-19.0	-24.1	-29.2	-30.9
-75	-16.4	-19.4	-22.6	-26.6	-30.4	-30.9
-100	-22.9	-24.8	-26.9	-29.2	-30.9	-30.9
-125	-27.2	-28.4	-29.5	-30.1	-30.9	-30.9

Est. cost:-30.4¢ prem.-0.5¢ com.= -30.9¢

TABLE 0

changes in the soybean future's price in 25¢ increments	weeks to expiration 10	8	6	4	2	0 net profit
+125	59.7	58.2	56.5	54.7	54.0	54.0
+100	42.6	40.0	37.0	33.2	29.5	29.0
+75	27.6	24.3	20.3	14.5	7.6	4.0
+50	16.1	12.4	7.9	1.3	-7.7	-21.0
+25	6.9	3.3	-1.1	-7.3	-15.5	-21.0
0	-0.5	-3.7	-7.2	-12.3	-18.5	-21.0
-25	-4.8	-8.0	-11.5	-16.0	-20.2	-21.0
-50	-9.4	-11.6	-14.3	-17.5	-20.6	-21.0
-75	-13.0	-14.8	-16.8	-19.2	-20.9	-21.0
-100	-16.3	-17.6	-19.1	-20.3	-21.0	-21.0
-125	-18.6	-19.6	-20.5	-21.0	-21.0	-21.0

Est. cost:-20.5¢ prem. -0.5¢ com. = -21.0¢

TABLE 0

changes in the soybean future's price in 25¢ increments	weeks to expiration 10	8	6	4	2	0 net profit
+125	64.6	63.9	63.3	62.9	62.9	62.9
+100	44.2	42.7	41.1	39.0	38.0	37.9
+75	26.7	24.4	21.8	18.2	14.3	12.9
+50	13.9	11.4	8.2	3.6	-2.7	-12.1
+25	5.2	2.7	-0.2	-4.4	-10.0	-12.1
0	-0.5	-2.5	-4.8	-8.0	-11.6	-12.1
-25	-4.6	-6.4	-8.3	-10.5	-12.1	-12.1
-50	-6.8	-8.1	-9.4	-11.0	-12.1	-12.1
-75	-9.0	-9.8	-10.7	-11.8	-12.1	-12.1
-100	-11.3	-11.6	-11.8	-12.1	-12.1	-12.1
-125	-11.9	-12.0	-12.1	-12.1	-12.1	-12.1

Est. cost:-11.6¢ prem.-0.5¢ com. = -12.1¢

TABLE 2

changes in the soybean future's price in 25¢ increments	weeks to expiration 10	8	6	4	2	0 net profit
+125	70.9	70.9	70.9	70.9	70.9	70.9
+100	46.8	46.5	46.2	46.0	45.9	45.9
+75	24.7	23.6	22.5	21.7	21.3	20.9
+50	10.8	9.4	7.6	4.9	1.3	-4.1
+25	2.9	1.6	-0.1	-2.2	-3.3	-4.1
0	-0.5	-1.5	-2.7	-3.7	-4.1	-4.1
-25	-2.8	-3.2	-3.8	-4.1	-4.1	-4.1
-50	-3.2	-3.6	-4.0	-4.1	-4.1	-4.1
-75	-3.9	-4.0	-4.1	-4.1	-4.1	-4.1
-100	-4.1	-4.1	-4.1	-4.1	-4.1	-4.1
-125	-4.1	-4.1	-4.1	-4.1	-4.1	-4.1

Est. cost:-3.6¢ prem.-0.5¢ com. = -4.1¢

Wm Grandmill (1985) Ltd.

SELL A CALL or SELL A PUT

AT THE MONEY

TABLE 10

changes in the soybean future's price in 25¢ increments	10	8	6	4	2	0
				weeks to expiration		
+125	-83.0	-79.9	-77.6	-77.3	-77.3	-77.3
+100	-59.3	-56.8	-54.1	-52.7	-52.3	-52.3
+75	-39.0	-36.2	-33.3	-29.9	-27.4	-27.3
+50	-24.7	-20.9	-16.3	-10.4	-4.0	-2.3
+25	-10.9	-6.7	-1.4	6.3	16.2	22.7
0	-0.5	4.2	10.1	18.7	30.4	47.7
-25	8.9	13.5	19.3	27.7	38.6	47.7
-50	17.3	21.5	26.8	33.8	42.5	47.7
-75	21.3	25.8	31.0	38.1	45.5	47.7
-100	27.7	31.5	35.8	40.9	46.0	47.7
-125	33.2	37.1	39.4	43.4	47.2	47.7

net profit area , in cents

Est. credit:+48.2¢ prem.-0.5¢ com.=+47.7¢

TABLE 8

changes in the soybean future's price in 25¢ increments	10	8	6	4	2	0
				weeks to expiration		
+125	-88.6	-88.4	-88.4	-88.4	-88.4	-88.4
+100	-65.1	-64.4	-63.7	-63.4	-63.4	-63.4
+75	-44.1	-42.6	-40.9	-39.1	-38.4	-38.4
+50	-27.0	-24.4	-21.4	-17.6	-13.9	-13.4
+25	-12.0	-8.7	-4.7	1.1	8.0	11.6
0	-0.5	3.2	7.7	14.3	23.3	36.6
-25	8.7	12.3	16.7	22.9	31.1	36.6
-50	16.1	19.3	22.8	27.9	34.1	36.6
-75	20.4	23.6	27.1	31.6	35.8	36.6
-100	25.0	27.2	29.9	33.1	36.2	36.6
-125	28.6	30.4	32.4	34.8	36.5	36.6

net profit area , in cents

Est. credit:+37.1¢ prem.-0.5¢ com.=+36.6¢

TABLE 4

changes in the soybean future's price in 25¢ increments	10	8	6	4	2	0
				weeks to expiration		
+125	-99.5	-99.5	-99.5	-99.5	-99.5	-99.5
+100	-74.6	-74.5	-74.5	-74.5	-74.5	-74.5
+75	-51.2	-50.5	-49.9	-49.5	-49.5	-49.5
+50	-30.8	-29.3	-27.7	-25.6	-24.6	-24.5
+25	-13.3	-11.0	-8.4	-4.8	-0.9	0.5
0	-0.5	2.0	5.2	9.8	16.1	25.5
-25	8.2	10.7	13.6	17.8	23.4	25.5
-50	13.9	15.9	18.2	21.4	25.0	25.5
-75	18.0	19.8	21.7	23.9	25.2	25.5
-100	20.2	21.5	22.8	24.4	25.5	25.5
-125	22.4	23.3	24.2	25.2	25.5	25.5

net profit area , in cents

Est. credit:+26.0¢ prem.-0.5¢ com.=+25.5¢

TABLE 2

changes in the soybean future's price in 25¢ increments	10	8	6	4	2	0
				weeks to expiration		
+125	-110.6	-110.6	-110.6	-110.6	-110.6	-110.6
+100	-85.6	-85.6	-85.6	-85.6	-85.6	-85.6
+75	-60.6	-60.6	-60.6	-60.6	-60.6	-60.6
+50	-36.5	-36.2	-35.9	-35.7	-35.6	-35.6
+25	-15.4	-14.3	-13.2	-11.9	-11.0	-10.6
0	-0.5	0.9	2.7	5.4	9.0	14.4
-25	7.4	8.7	10.4	12.5	13.6	14.4
-50	10.8	11.8	13.0	14.0	14.4	14.4
-75	13.1	13.5	14.1	14.4	14.4	14.4
-100	13.5	13.9	14.3	14.4	14.4	14.4
-125	14.2	14.3	14.4	14.4	14.4	14.4

net profit area , in cents

Est. credit:+14.9¢ prem.-0.5¢ com.=+14.4¢

Wm Grandmill (1985) Ltd.

SELL A CALL or SELL A PUT

AT 50¢ OUT OF THE MONEY

10 weeks to expiration

TABLE 0

changes in the soybean future's price in 25¢ increments

	10	8	6	4	2	0
+125	-56.8	-54.0	-51.1	-47.7	-45.2	-45.1
+100	-42.5	-38.7	-34.1	-28.2	-21.8	-20.1
+75	-28.7	-24.6	-19.2	-11.5	-1.6	4.9
+50	-18.3	-13.6	-7.7	0.9	12.6	29.9
+25	-8.9	-4.3	1.5	9.9	20.8	29.9
0	-0.5	3.7	9.0	16.0	24.6	29.9
-25	3.5	8.0	13.5	20.3	27.7	29.9
-50	9.9	13.7	18.0	23.1	28.2	29.9
-75	15.4	18.4	21.6	25.6	29.4	29.9
-100	21.9	23.8	25.9	28.2	29.9	29.9
-125	26.2	27.4	28.5	29.1	29.9	29.9

weeks to expiration — net profit area, in cents

Est. credit:+30.4¢ prem.-0.5¢ com.=+29.9¢

TABLE 8

changes in the soybean future's price in 25¢ increments

	10	8	6	4	2	0
+125	-60.7	-59.2	-57.5	-55.7	-55.0	-55.0
+100	-43.6	-41.0	-38.0	-34.2	-30.5	-30.0
+75	-28.6	-25.3	-21.3	-15.5	-8.6	-5.0
+50	-17.1	-13.4	-8.9	-2.3	6.7	20.0
+25	-7.9	-4.3	0.1	6.3	14.5	20.0
0	-0.5	2.7	6.2	11.3	17.5	20.0
-25	3.8	7.0	10.5	15.0	19.2	20.0
-50	8.4	10.6	13.3	16.5	19.6	20.0
-75	12.0	13.8	15.8	18.2	19.9	20.0
-100	15.3	16.6	18.1	19.3	20.0	20.0
-125	17.6	18.6	19.5	20.0	20.0	20.0

weeks to expiration — net profit area, in cents

Est. credit:+20.5¢ prem.-0.5¢ com.=+20.0¢

TABLE 4

changes in the soybean future's price in 25¢ increments

	10	8	6	4	2	0
+125	-65.6	-64.9	-64.3	-63.9	-63.9	-63.9
+100	-45.2	-44.3	-43.7	-42.1	-40.0	-39.0
+75	-27.7	-25.4	-22.8	-19.2	-15.3	-13.9
+50	-14.9	-12.4	-9.2	-4.6	1.7	9.0
+25	-6.2	-3.7	-0.8	3.4	9.0	11.1
0	-0.5	1.5	3.8	7.0	10.6	11.1
-25	3.6	5.4	7.3	9.5	11.1	11.1
-50	5.8	7.1	8.4	10.0	11.1	11.1
-75	8.0	8.8	9.7	10.8	11.1	11.1
-100	10.3	10.6	10.8	11.1	11.1	11.1
-125	10.9	11.0	11.1	11.1	11.1	11.1

weeks to expiration — net profit area, in cents

Est. credit:+11.6¢ prem.-0.5¢ com.=+11.1¢

TABLE 2

changes in the soybean future's price in 25¢ increments

	10	8	6	4	2	0
+125	-71.9	-71.9	-71.9	-71.9	-71.9	-71.9
+100	-47.8	-47.5	-47.2	-47.0	-46.9	-46.9
+75	-25.7	-24.6	-23.5	-22.7	-22.3	-21.9
+50	-11.8	-10.4	-8.6	-5.9	-2.3	3.1
+25	-3.9	-2.6	-1.1	1.2	2.3	3.1
0	-0.5	0.5	1.7	2.7	3.1	3.1
-25	1.8	2.2	2.8	3.1	3.1	3.1
-50	2.2	2.6	3.0	3.1	3.1	3.1
-75	2.9	3.0	3.1	3.1	3.1	3.1
-100	3.1	3.1	3.1	3.1	3.1	3.1
-125	3.1	3.1	3.1	3.1	3.1	3.1

weeks to expiration — net profit area, in cents

Est. credit:+3.6¢ prem.-0.5¢ com.=+3.1¢

Wm Grandmill (1985) Ltd.

BULL or BEAR SPREAD – #1

BUY A CALL AT THE MONEY
and SELL A CALL AT 25¢ OUT OF THE MONEY

OR

BUY A PUT AT THE MONEY
and SELL A PUT AT 25¢ OUT OF THE MONEY

10 weeks to expiration

TABLE

changes in the soybean future's price in 25¢ increments	10	8	6	4	2	0
				weeks to expiration		
+125	13.6	13.8	14.0	14.2	14.6	14.6
+100	9.8	10.5	11.0	13.0	14.6	14.6
+75	6.4	7.0	8.0	9.6	13.0	14.6
+50	3.3	3.8	4.5	6.3	9.8	14.6
+25	1.0	1.1	1.3	2.0	3.8	14.6
0	-1.0	-1.1	-1.2	-1.4	-2.4	-10.4
-25	-2.0	-2.4	-3.1	-4.3	-6.5	-10.4
-50	-2.9	-3.5	-4.4	-5.5	-7.4	-10.4
-75	-4.0	-4.8	-5.8	-6.8	-8.4	-10.4
-100	-4.8	-5.7	-6.8	-7.9	-9.2	-10.4
-125	-5.2	-6.4	-7.6	-8.9	-9.9	-10.4

net profit area, in cents

Est. cost: -48.2¢ +38.8¢ -1.0¢ = -10.4¢

TABLE

changes in the soybean future's price in 25¢ increments	10	8	6	4	2	0
				weeks to expiration		
+125	13.6	14.0	14.5	14.8	14.8	14.8
+100	10.8	11.5	12.6	14.1	14.8	14.8
+75	7.3	8.0	9.3	11.3	14.3	14.8
+50	4.8	5.5	6.5	8.5	11.7	14.8
+25	1.3	1.7	2.2	3.0	5.1	14.8
0	-1.0	-1.1	-1.2	-1.7	-2.4	-10.2
-25	-2.8	-3.2	-4.1	-5.2	-7.2	-10.2
-50	-4.2	-4.8	-5.5	-6.5	-8.5	-10.2
-75	-5.6	-6.6	-7.4	-8.5	-9.8	-10.2
-100	-6.6	-7.0	-7.7	-8.6	-9.9	-10.2
-125	-6.9	-7.4	-7.9	-8.9	-10.1	-10.2

Est. cost: -37.1¢ +27.9¢ -1.0¢ = -10.2¢

TABLE

changes in the soybean future's price in 25¢ increments	10	8	6	4	2	0
				weeks to expiration		
+125	15.2	15.3	15.3	15.3	15.3	15.3
+100	13.7	14.3	14.9	15.3	15.3	15.3
+75	10.7	11.5	12.5	13.2	14.0	15.3
+50	7.8	8.6	9.6	11.1	14.0	15.3
+25	3.1	3.3	3.9	4.9	7.3	15.3
0	-1.0	-1.1	-1.3	-1.7	-2.5	-9.7
-25	-4.0	-4.5	-5.1	-6.1	-8.1	-9.7
-50	-5.6	-5.8	-6.2	-7.2	-9.2	-9.7
-75	-7.4	-7.7	-8.1	-8.5	-9.7	-9.7
-100	-7.5	-7.9	-8.4	-8.9	-9.7	-9.7
-125	-7.7	-8.1	-8.6	-9.4	-9.7	-9.7

net profit area, in cents

Est. cost: -26.0¢ +17.3¢ -1.0¢ = -9.7¢

TABLE

changes in the soybean future's price in 25¢ increments	10	8	6	4	2	0
				weeks to expiration		
+125	16.1	16.1	16.1	16.1	16.1	16.1
+100	15.2	15.5	15.8	16.0	16.1	16.1
+75	12.2	13.0	13.8	14.9	15.7	16.1
+50						
+25	6.0	6.3	7.0	8.4	11.1	16.1
0	-1.0	-1.1	-1.2	-1.8	-2.3	-8.9
-25	-5.5	-5.9	-6.3	-7.4	-8.3	-8.9
-50	-6.6	-7.1	-7.8	-8.5	-8.9	-8.9
-75	-7.4	-8.0	-8.7	-8.9	-8.9	-8.9
-100	-8.2	-8.5	-8.8	-8.9	-8.9	-8.9
-125	-8.7	-8.8	-8.9	-8.9	-8.9	-8.9

net profit area, in cents

Est. cost: -14.9¢ +7.0¢ -1.0¢ = -8.9¢

Wm Grandmill (1985) Ltd.

BULL or BEAR SPREAD – #2

BUY A CALL AT THE MONEY
and SELL 2 CALLS AT 50¢ OUT OF THE MONEY
OR
BUY A PUT AT THE MONEY
and SELL 2 PUTS AT 50¢ OUT OF THE MONEY

weeks to expiration: 10

TABLE 0 — changes in the soybean future's price in 25¢ increments

price change	| weeks to expiration |					
	10	8	6	4	2	0
+125	-31.6	-29.1	-25.6	-19.1	-14.1	-13.9
+100	-26.7	-21.6	-15.1	-6.0	1.5	11.1
+75	-19.4	-13.8	-6.1	5.9	18.4	36.1
+50	-12.9	-7.3	-0.1	11.2	28.2	61.1
+25	-7.9	-2.9	3.4	12.5	24.4	36.1
0	-1.5	2.2	6.9	12.3	18.0	11.1
-25	1.5	4.9	8.2	11.9	15.8	11.1
-50	8.5	10.0	11.2	12.1	12.9	11.1
-75	12.7	13.2	13.3	12.8	11.9	11.1
-100	13.3	15.8	13.6	13.6	11.1	11.1
-125	18.6	19.6	18.4	13.6	11.1	11.1

net profit area , in cents

Est. credit: -48.2¢ + 30.4¢ + 30.4¢ - 1.5¢ = +11.1¢

TABLE 8 — changes in the soybean future's price in 25¢ increments

price change	| weeks to expiration |					
	10	8	6	4	2	0
+125	-33.8	-31.0	-27.6	-24.0	-22.6	-22.6
+100	-23.1	-18.7	-13.3	-6.0	-2.1	2.4
+75	-14.1	-9.0	-2.7	7.1	1.4	27.4
+50	-8.2	-3.4	2.6	12.0	26.3	52.4
+25	-4.8	-0.9	3.9	10.5	20.0	27.4
0	-1.5	1.2	3.7	7.3	10.7	2.4
-25	-2.1	0.7	3.3	6.1	6.3	2.4
-50	-0.3	1.1	2.8	4.1	4.1	2.4
-75	2.6	3.0	3.5	3.8	4.0	2.4
-100	4.0	4.2	4.5	4.0	3.3	2.4
-125	5.6	5.8	5.6	4.2	2.5	2.4

net profit area , in cents

Est. credit: -37.1¢ + 20.5¢ + 20.5¢ - 1.5¢ = +2.4¢

TABLE 4 — changes in the soybean future's price in 25¢ increments

price change	| weeks to expiration |					
	10	8	6	4	2	0
+125	-32.7	-31.3	-30.1	-29.3	-29.3	-29.3
+100	-16.8	-13.4	-10.7	-6.5	-4.5	-4.3
+75	-5.2	-1.3	3.3	10.1	17.9	20.7
+50	0.0	2.6	5.8	15.4	27.0	45.7
+25	-0.1	2.6	5.8	10.6	17.9	20.7
0	-1.5	0.1	1.4	3.2	4.1	-4.3
-25	-2.0	-0.9	0.0	-0.1	-2.2	-4.3
-50	-3.3	-2.7	-2.5	-2.4	-3.8	-4.3
-75	-3.0	-3.1	-3.3	-3.4	-4.3	-4.3
-100	-2.2	-2.6	-3.1	-3.9	-4.3	-4.3
-125	-1.6	-2.3	-2.9	-4.0	-4.3	-4.3

net profit area

Est. cost: -26.0¢ + 11.0¢ + 11.0¢ - 1.5¢ = -4.3¢

TABLE 2 — changes in the soybean future's price in 25¢ increments

price change	| weeks to expiration |					
	10	8	6	4	2	0
+125	-34.2	-34.2	-34.2	-34.2	-34.2	-34.2
+100	-11.0	-10.4	-9.8	-9.4	-9.2	-9.2
+75	6.2	8.4	10.6	13.2	15.0	15.8
+50	11.9	14.4	17.7	22.7	29.8	40.8
+25	6.6	8.2	10.4	13.0	14.6	15.8
0	-1.5	-1.1	-0.3	-0.6	-3.8	-9.2
-25	-4.8	-5.3	-5.8	-7.3	-8.4	-9.2
-50	-7.4	-7.6	-8.0	-8.8	-9.2	-9.2
-75	-8.3	-8.5	-8.9	-9.0	-9.2	-9.2
-100	-8.6	-8.8	-9.0	-9.2	-9.2	-9.2
-125	-9.0	-9.1	-9.2	-9.2	-9.2	-9.2

net profit area

Est. cost: -14.0¢ + 3.6¢ + 3.6¢ - 1.5¢ = -9.2¢

Wm Grandmill (1985) Ltd.

TABLE 0

changes in the soybean future's price in 25¢ increments	weeks to expiration					
	10	8	6	4	2	0
+125	-49.8	-43.7	-38.2	-33.9	-30.1	-29.6
+100	-31.6	-25.3	-18.3	-11.8	-6.3	-4.6
+75	-17.7	-10.4	-2.3	8.2	18.1	20.4
+50	-7.4	0.6	10.5	23.4	38.5	45.4
+25	-2.0	6.8	17.9	34.0	54.8	70.4
0	-1.0	8.4	20.8	37.4	60.8	95.4
-25	-2.0	6.8	17.9	34.4	54.8	70.4
-50	-7.4	0.6	10.5	23.4	38.5	45.4
-75	-17.7	-10.4	-2.3	8.2	18.1	20.4
-100	-31.6	-25.3	-18.3	-11.8	-6.3	-4.6
-125	-49.8	-43.7	-38.2	-33.9	-30.1	-29.6

net profit area , in cents

Est. credit: +48.2¢ +48.2¢ -1.0¢= +95.4¢

TABLE 0

changes in the soybean future's price in 25¢ increments	weeks to expiration					
	10	8	6	4	2	0
+125	-60.0	-58.0	-56.0	-53.6	-51.9	-51.8
+100	-40.1	-37.1	-33.8	-30.3	-27.2	-26.8
+75	-23.7	-19.0	-13.8	-7.5	-2.6	-1.8
+50	-10.9	-5.1	1.7	10.3	20.2	23.2
+25	-3.3	3.6	12.0	24.0	39.1	48.2
0	-1.0	6.4	15.4	28.6	46.6	73.2
-25	-3.3	3.6	12.0	24.0	39.1	48.2
-50	-10.9	-5.1	1.7	10.3	20.2	23.2
-75	-23.7	-19.0	-13.8	-7.5	-2.6	-1.8
-100	-40.1	-37.1	-33.8	-30.3	-27.2	-26.8
-125	-60.0	-58.0	-56.0	-53.6	-51.9	-51.8

net profit area , in cents

Est. credit: +37.1¢+37.1¢-1.0¢= +73.2¢

TABLE 4

changes in the soybean future's price in 25¢ increments	weeks to expiration					
	10	8	6	4	2	0
+125	-77.1	-76.2	-75.3	-74.3	-74.0	-74.0
+100	-54.4	-53.0	-51.6	-50.1	-49.0	-49.0
+75	-33.1	-30.7	-28.2	-25.6	-24.0	-24.0
+50	-16.9	-13.4	-9.5	-4.2	0.4	1.0
+25	-5.1	-0.3	5.2	13.0	22.5	26.0
0	-1.0	4.0	10.4	19.6	33.2	51.0
-25	-5.1	-0.3	5.2	13.0	22.5	26.0
-50	-16.9	-13.4	-9.5	-4.2	0.4	1.0
-75	-33.1	-30.7	-28.2	-25.6	-24.0	-24.0
-100	-54.4	-53.0	-51.6	-50.1	-49.0	-49.0
-125	-77.1	-76.2	-75.3	-74.3	-74.0	-74.0

net profit area , in cents

Est. credit: +26.0¢+26.0¢-1.0¢= +51.0¢

TABLE 2

changes in the soybean future's price in 25¢ increments	weeks to expiration					
	10	8	6	4	2	0
+125	-96.4	-96.3	-96.2	-96.2	-96.2	-96.2
+100	-72.1	-71.7	-71.3	-71.2	-71.2	-71.2
+75	-47.5	-47.-	-46.5	-46.2	-46.2	-46.2
+50	-25.7	-24.4	-22.9	-21.7	-21.2	-21.2
+25	-8.0	-5.6	-2.8	0.6	3.3	3.8
0	-1.0	1.8	5.4	10.8	18.0	28.8
-25	-8.0	-5.6	-2.8	0.6	3.3	3.8
-50	-25.7	-24.4	-22.9	-21.7	-21.2	-21.2
-75	-47.5	-47.-	-46.5	-46.2	-46.2	-46.2
-100	-72.1	-71.7	-71.3	-71.2	-71.2	-71.2
-125	-96.4	-96.3	-96.2	-96.2	-96.2	-96.2

net profit area

Est. credit: +14.9¢+14.9¢-1.0¢= +28.8¢

Wm Grandmill (1985) Ltd.

SELL A CALL AT 50¢ OUT OF THE MONEY
and SELL A PUT AT 50¢ OUT OF THE MONEY

weeks to **10** expiration

TABLE

changes in the soybean future's price in 25¢ increments

	weeks to expiration					
	10	8	6	4	2	0
+125	-30.6	-26.6	-22.7	-18.6	-15.3	-15.2
+100	-20.6	-14.8	-8.2	0.0	8.1	9.8
+75	-13.0	-6.1	2.4	14.1	27.8	34.8
+50	-8.4	0.1	10.3	24.0	40.8	59.8
+25	-5.4	3.7	14.7	30.2	48.5	59.8
0	-1.0	7.4	18.0	32.0	49.4	59.8
-25	-5.4	3.7	14.7	30.2	48.5	59.8
-50	-8.4	0.1	10.3	24.0	40.8	59.8
-75	-13.0	-6.1	2.4	14.1	27.8	34.8
-100	-20.6	-14.8	-8.2	0.0	8.1	9.8
-125	-30.6	-26.6	-22.7	-18.6	-15.3	-15.2

net profit area , in cents

Est. credit: +30.4¢ +30.4¢ -1.0¢ = +59.8¢

TABLE

changes in the soybean future's price in 25¢ increments

	weeks to expiration					
	10	8	6	4	2	0
+125	-43.1	-40.6	-38.0	-35.7	-35.0	-35.0
+100	-28.3	-24.4	-19.9	-14.9	-10.5	-10.0
+75	-16.6	-11.5	-5.5	2.7	11.3	15.0
+50	-8.7	-2.8	4.4	14.2	26.3	40.0
+25	-4.1	2.7	10.6	21.3	33.7	40.0
0	-1.0	5.4	12.4	22.6	35.0	40.0
-25	-4.1	2.7	10.6	21.3	33.7	40.0
-50	-8.7	-2.8	4.4	14.2	26.3	40.0
-75	-16.6	-11.5	-5.5	2.7	11.3	15.0
-100	-28.3	-24.4	-19.9	-14.9	-10.5	-10.0
-125	-43.1	-40.6	-38.0	-35.7	-35.0	-35.0

net profit area , in cents

Est. credit: +20.5¢ +20.5¢ -1.0¢ = +40.0¢

TABLE

changes in the soybean future's price in 25¢ increments

	weeks to expiration					
	10	8	6	4	2	0
+125	-54.7	-53.9	-53.1	-52.8	-52.8	-52.8
+100	-34.9	-33.1	-31.3	-28.9	-27.9	-27.8
+75	-19.7	-16.5	-13.1	-8.4	-4.2	-2.8
+50	-9.1	-5.3	-0.8	5.4	12.8	22.2
+25	-2.6	1.7	6.5	12.9	20.1	22.2
0	-1.0	3.0	7.6	14.0	21.2	22.2
-25	-2.6	1.7	6.5	12.9	20.1	22.2
-50	-9.1	-5.3	-0.8	5.4	12.8	22.2
-75	-19.7	-16.5	-13.1	-8.4	-4.2	-2.8
-100	-34.9	-33.1	-31.3	-28.9	-27.9	-27.8
-125	-54.7	-53.9	-53.1	-52.8	-52.8	-52.8

net profit area , in cents

Est. credit: +11.6¢ +11.6¢ -1.0¢ = +22.2¢

TABLE

changes in the soybean future's price in 25¢ increments

	weeks to expiration					
	10	8	6	4	2	0
+125	-68.8	-68.8	-68.8	-68.8	-68.8	-68.8
+100	-44.7	-44.4	-44.1	-43.9	-43.8	-43.8
+75	-23.8	-22.6	-21.4	-20.1	-19.2	-18.8
+50	-9.6	-7.8	-5.6	-2.8	0.8	6.2
+25	-2.1	-0.4	1.9	5.4	6.2	6.2
0	-1.0	0.8	3.4	5.4	6.2	6.2
-25	-2.1	-0.4	1.9	5.4	6.2	6.2
-50	-9.6	-7.8	-5.6	-2.8	0.8	6.2
-75	-23.8	-22.6	-21.4	-20.1	-19.2	-18.8
-100	-44.7	-44.4	-44.1	-43.9	-43.8	-43.8
-125	-68.8	-68.8	-68.8	-68.8	-68.8	-68.8

net profit area , in cents

Est. credit: +3.6¢ +3.6¢ -1.0¢ = +6.2¢

Wm Grandmill (1985) Ltd.

SELL A STRANGLE – #2

SELL A CALL AT $1.00 OUT OF THE MONEY
and SELL A PUT AT $1.00 OUT OF THE MONEY

weeks to expiration

10

TABLE 0

changes in the soybean future's price in 25¢ increments	weeks to expiration					
	10	8	6	4	2	0
+125	-20.2	-15.8	-10.3	-2.4	7.5	14.0
+100	-11.0	-5.8	0.8	9.7	21.7	39.0
+75	-3.3	2.3	9.1	18.2	29.9	39.0
+50	0.6	6.8	14.1	23.4	33.8	39.0
+25	-1.9	5.6	14.0	25.1	36.3	39.0
0	-1.0	6.6	15.2	25.4	35.6	39.0
-25	-1.9	5.6	14.0	25.1	36.3	39.0
-50	0.6	6.8	14.1	23.4	33.8	39.0
-75	-3.3	2.3	9.1	18.2	29.9	39.0
-100	-11.0	-5.8	0.8	9.7	21.7	39.0
-125	-20.2	-15.8	-10.3	-2.4	7.5	14.0

net profit area , in cents

Est. credit: +20.0¢ +20.0¢ -1.0¢ = +39.0¢

TABLE 8

changes in the soybean future's price in 25¢ increments	weeks to expiration					
	10	8	6	4	2	0
+125	-26.6	-23.1	-19.1	-13.3	-6.4	-2.8
+100	-15.7	-13.6	-6.7	-0.1	8.9	22.2
+75	-8.1	-3.5	1.8	8.5	16.7	22.2
+50	-3.0	1.5	6.5	12.8	19.7	22.2
+25	-2.0	3.0	8.5	15.4	21.3	22.2
0	-1.0	3.4	8.8	15.2	21.4	22.2
-25	-2.0	3.0	8.5	15.4	21.3	22.2
-50	-3.0	1.5	6.5	12.8	19.7	22.2
-75	-8.1	-3.5	1.8	8.5	16.7	22.2
-100	-15.7	-13.6	-6.7	-0.1	8.9	22.2
-125	-26.6	-23.1	-19.1	-13.3	-6.4	-2.8

net profit area , in cents

Est. credit: +11.0¢ +11.0¢ -1.0¢ = +22.2¢

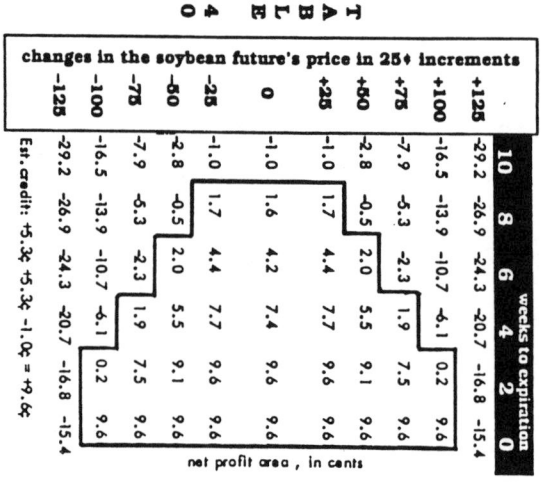

TABLE 4

changes in the soybean future's price in 25¢ increments	weeks to expiration					
	10	8	6	4	2	0
+125	-29.2	-26.9	-24.3	-20.7	-16.8	-15.4
+100	-16.5	-13.9	-10.7	-6.1	0.2	9.6
+75	-7.9	-5.3	-2.3	1.9	7.5	9.6
+50	-2.8	-0.5	2.0	5.5	9.1	9.6
+25	-1.0	1.7	4.4	7.7	9.6	9.6
0	-1.0	1.6	4.2	7.4	9.6	9.6
-25	-1.0	1.7	4.4	7.7	9.6	9.6
-50	-2.8	-0.5	2.0	5.5	9.1	9.6
-75	-7.9	-5.3	-2.3	1.9	7.5	9.6
-100	-16.5	-13.9	-10.7	-6.1	0.2	9.6
-125	-29.2	-26.9	-24.3	-20.7	-16.8	-15.4

net profit area , in cents

Est. credit: +5.3¢ +5.3¢ -1.0¢ = +9.6¢

TABLE 2

changes in the soybean future's price in 25¢ increments	weeks to expiration					
	10	8	6	4	2	0
+125	-29.0	-27.9	-26.8	-25.5	-24.6	-24.2
+100	-14.1	-12.7	-10.9	-8.2	-4.6	0.8
+75	-6.2	-4.9	-3.2	-1.1	0.1	0.8
+50	-2.8	-1.9	-0.6	0.4	0.8	0.8
+25	-0.7	-0.1	0.5	0.8	0.8	0.8
0	-1.0	-0.2	0.6	0.8	0.8	0.8
-25	-0.7	-0.1	0.5	0.8	0.8	0.8
-50	-2.8	-1.9	-0.6	0.4	0.8	0.8
-75	-6.2	-4.9	-3.2	-1.1	0.1	0.8
-100	-14.1	-12.7	-10.9	-8.2	-4.6	0.8
-125	-29.0	-27.9	-26.8	-25.5	-24.6	-24.2

net profit area , in cents

Est. credit: +0.9¢ +0.9¢ -1.0¢ = +0.8¢

Wm Grandmill (1985) Ltd.

TABLE — changes in the soybean future's price in 25¢ increments

changes	weeks to expiration						
	12	10	8	6	4	2	0
+125	80.8	78.0	74.9	72.8	72.3	72.3	72.4
+100	57.0	54.3	51.8	49.1	47.7	47.3	47.3
+75	36.6	34.0	31.2	28.3	24.9	22.4	22.3
+50	23.1	19.7	15.9	11.3	5.4	-1.0	-2.7
+25	9.8	5.9	1.7	-3.6	-11.3	-21.2	-27.7
0	-0.5	-4.5	-9.2	-15.1	-23.7	-35.4	-52.7
-25	-10.0	-13.9	-18.5	-24.3	-32.7	-43.6	-52.7
-50	-18.6	-22.3	-26.5	-31.8	-38.8	-47.5	-52.7
-75	-22.6	-26.3	-30.8	-36.0	-43.1	-50.5	-52.7
-100	-29.2	-32.7	-36.5	-40.8	-45.9	-51.0	-52.7
-125	-35.6	-38.2	-41.2	-44.4	-48.4	-52.2	-52.7

net profit area

Est. cost: -52.2¢ premium - 0.5¢ comm. = -52.7¢

TABLE — changes in the soybean future's price in 25¢ increments

changes	weeks to expiration						
	12	10	8	6	4	2	0
+125	96.3	96.3	96.3	96.3	96.3	96.3	96.3
+100	71.6	71.4	71.3	71.3	71.3	71.3	71.3
+75	48.6	48.0	47.3	46.7	46.3	46.3	46.3
+50	28.9	27.6	26.1	24.5	22.4	21.4	21.3
+25	12.0	10.1	7.8	5.2	1.6	-2.3	-3.7
0	-0.5	-2.7	-5.2	-8.4	-13.0	-19.3	-28.7
-25	-9.5	-11.4	-13.9	-16.8	-21.0	-26.6	-28.7
-50	-15.5	-17.1	-19.1	-21.4	-24.6	-28.2	-28.7
-75	-19.7	-21.2	-23.0	-24.9	-27.1	-28.7	-28.7
-100	-22.3	-23.4	-24.7	-26.0	-27.6	-28.7	-28.7
-125	-24.8	-25.6	-26.5	-27.4	-28.4	-28.7	-28.7

net profit area

Est. cost: -28.2¢ premium - 0.5¢ comm. = -28.7¢

TABLE — changes in the soybean future's price in 25¢ increments

changes	weeks to expiration						
	12	10	8	6	4	2	0
+125	108.3	108.3	108.3	108.3	108.3	108.3	108.3
+100	83.3	83.3	83.3	83.3	83.3	83.3	83.3
+75	58.4	58.3	58.3	58.3	58.3	58.3	58.3
+50	34.6	34.2	33.9	33.6	33.4	33.3	33.3
+25	14.0	13.1	12.0	10.9	9.6	8.7	8.3
0	-0.5	-1.8	-3.2	-5.0	-7.7	-11.3	-16.7
-25	-8.6	-9.7	-11.0	-12.7	-14.8	-15.9	-16.7
-50	-12.2	-13.1	-14.1	-15.3	-16.3	-16.7	-16.7
-75	-15.0	-15.4	-15.8	-16.4	-16.7	-16.7	-16.7
-100	-15.4	-15.8	-16.2	-16.6	-16.7	-16.7	-16.7
-125	-16.3	-16.5	-16.6	-16.7	-16.7	-16.7	-16.7

net profit area , in cents

Est. cost: -16.2¢ premium - 0.5¢ comm. = -16.7¢

Wm Grandmill (1985) Ltd.

BUY A CALL or BUY A PUT
AT 50¢ OUT OF THE MONEY

TABLE

changes in the soybean future's price in 25¢ increments	12	10	8	6	4	2	0
							weeks to expiration
+125	54.7	52.1	49.3	46.4	43.0	40.5	40.4
+100	41.2	37.8	34.0	29.4	23.5	17.1	15.4
+75	27.9	24.0	19.9	14.5	6.8	-3.1	-9.6
+50	17.6	13.6	8.9	3.0	-5.6	-17.3	-34.6
+25	8.1	4.2	-0.4	-6.2	-14.6	-25.5	-34.6
0	-0.5	-4.2	-8.4	-13.7	-20.7	-29.3	-34.6
-25	-4.5	-8.2	-12.7	-18.2	-25.0	-32.4	-34.6
-50	-11.1	-14.6	-18.4	-22.7	-27.8	-32.9	-34.6
-75	-17.5	-20.1	-23.1	-26.3	-30.3	-34.1	-34.6
-100	-24.7	-26.6	-28.5	-30.6	-32.9	-34.6	-34.6
-125	-29.3	-30.9	-32.1	-33.2	-33.8	-34.6	-34.6

net profit

Est. cost: -34.1¢ premium -0.5¢ comm. = -34.6¢

TABLE

changes in the soybean future's price in 25¢ increments	12	10	8	6	4	2	0
							weeks to expiration
+125	58.5	57.0	55.5	53.8	52.0	51.3	51.3
+100	42.2	39.9	37.3	34.3	30.5	26.8	26.3
+75	27.7	24.9	21.6	17.6	11.8	4.9	1.3
+50	16.5	13.4	9.7	5.2	-1.4	-10.4	-23.7
+25	7.2	4.2	0.6	-3.8	-10.0	-18.2	-23.7
0	-0.5	-3.2	-6.4	-9.9	-15.0	-21.2	-23.7
-25	-4.8	-7.5	-10.7	-14.2	-18.7	-22.9	-23.7
-50	-10.0	-12.1	-14.3	-17.0	-20.2	-23.3	-23.7
-75	-14.1	-15.7	-17.5	-19.5	-21.9	-23.6	-23.7
-100	-17.8	-19.0	-20.3	-21.8	-23.0	-23.7	-23.7
-125	-20.5	-21.3	-22.3	-23.2	-23.7	-23.7	-23.7

net profit

Est. cost: -23.2¢ premium -0.5¢ comm. = -23.7¢

TABLE

changes in the soybean future's price in 25¢ increments	12	10	8	6	4	2	0
							weeks to expiration
+125	63.6	63.0	62.3	61.7	61.3	61.3	61.3
+100	43.9	42.6	41.1	39.5	37.4	36.4	36.3
+75	27.0	25.1	22.8	20.2	16.6	12.7	11.3
+50	14.5	12.3	9.8	6.6	2.0	-4.3	-13.7
+25	5.5	3.6	1.1	-1.8	-6.0	-11.6	-13.7
0	-0.5	-2.1	-4.1	-6.4	-9.6	-13.2	-13.7
-25	-4.7	-6.2	-8.0	-9.9	-12.1	-13.7	-13.7
-50	-7.3	-8.4	-9.7	-11.0	-12.6	-13.7	-13.7
-75	-9.8	-10.6	-11.5	-12.3	-13.4	-13.7	-13.7
-100	-12.4	-12.9	-13.2	-13.4	-13.7	-13.7	-13.7
-125	-13.4	-13.5	-13.6	-13.6	-13.7	-13.7	-13.7

net profit

Est. cost: -13.2¢ premium - 0.5¢ comm. = -13.7¢

TABLE

changes in the soybean future's price in 25¢ increments	12	10	8	6	4	2	0
							weeks to expiration
+125	70.1	70.0	70.0	70.0	70.0	70.0	70.0
+100	46.3	45.9	45.6	45.3	45.1	45.0	45.0
+75	24.7	23.8	22.7	21.6	20.8	20.4	20.0
+50	11.2	9.9	8.5	6.7	4.0	0.4	-5.0
+25	3.1	2.0	0.7	-1.0	-3.1	-4.2	-5.0
0	-0.5	-1.4	-2.4	-3.6	-4.6	-5.0	-5.0
-25	-3.3	-3.7	-4.1	-4.7	-5.0	-5.0	-5.0
-50	-3.7	-4.1	-4.5	-4.9	-5.0	-5.0	-5.0
-75	-5.4	-5.2	-5.1	-5.0	-5.0	-5.0	-5.0
-100	-5.1	-5.0	-5.0	-5.0	-5.0	-5.0	-5.0
-125	-5.0	-5.0	-5.0	-5.0	-5.0	-5.0	-5.0

net profit

Est. cost: -4.5¢ premium - 0.5¢ comm. = - 5.0¢

Wm Grandmill (1985) Ltd.

SELL A CALL or SELL A PUT

AT THE MONEY

weeks to expiration

12

TABLE 8

changes in the soybean future's price in 25¢ increments	12	10	8	6	4	2	0
+125	-81.8	-79.0	-75.9	-73.6	-73.3	-73.3	-73.3
+100	-58.0	-55.3	-52.8	-50.1	-48.7	-48.3	-48.3
+75	-37.6	-35.0	-32.2	-29.7	-25.9	-23.4	-23.3
+50	-24.1	-20.7	-16.9	-12.3	-6.4	0.0	1.7
+25	-10.8	-6.9	-2.7	2.6	10.3	20.2	26.7
0	-0.5	3.5	8.2	14.1	22.7	34.4	51.7
-25	9.0	12.9	17.5	23.3	31.7	42.6	51.7
-50	17.6	21.3	25.5	30.8	37.8	46.5	51.7
-75	21.6	25.7	29.8	35.0	42.1	49.5	51.7
-100	28.2	31.7	35.5	39.8	44.9	50.0	51.7
-125	34.6	37.2	40.2	43.4	47.4	51.1	51.7

weeks to expiration — net profit area, in cents

Est. credit: +52.2¢ premium -0.5¢ comm. = +51.7¢

TABLE 6

changes in the soybean future's price in 25¢ increments	12	10	8	6	4	2	0
+125	-86.2	-85.5	-85.3	-85.3	-85.3	-85.3	-85.3
+100	-62.8	-62.0	-61.2	-60.6	-60.3	-60.3	-60.3
+75	-42.5	-41.0	-39.5	-37.8	-36.0	-35.3	-35.3
+50	-24.2	-23.9	-21.3	-18.3	-14.5	-10.8	-10.3
+25	-11.7	-8.9	-5.6	-1.6	4.2	11.1	14.7
0	-0.5	2.6	6.3	10.8	17.4	26.4	39.7
-25	8.8	11.8	15.4	19.8	26.0	34.2	39.7
-50	16.5	19.2	22.4	25.9	31.0	37.2	39.7
-75	20.8	23.5	26.7	30.2	34.7	38.9	39.7
-100	26.0	28.1	30.3	33.0	36.2	39.3	39.7
-125	30.1	31.7	33.5	35.5	37.9	39.6	39.7

weeks to expiration — net profit area, in cents

Est. credit: +40.2¢ premium - 0.5¢ comm.=+39.7¢

TABLE 4

changes in the soybean future's price in 25¢ increments	12	10	8	6	4	2	0
+125	-97.3	-97.3	-97.3	-97.3	-97.3	-97.3	-97.3
+100	-72.6	-72.4	-72.3	-72.3	-72.3	-72.3	-72.3
+75	-49.6	-49.0	-48.3	-47.7	-47.3	-47.3	-47.3
+50	-29.9	-28.6	-27.1	-25.5	-23.4	-22.4	-22.3
+25	-13.0	-11.1	-8.8	-6.2	-2.6	1.3	2.7
0	-0.5	1.7	4.2	7.4	12.0	18.3	27.7
-25	8.5	10.4	12.9	15.8	20.4	25.6	27.7
-50	14.5	16.1	18.1	20.4	23.6	27.2	27.7
-75	18.7	20.2	22.0	23.9	26.1	27.7	27.7
-100	21.3	22.4	23.7	25.0	26.6	27.7	27.7
-125	23.8	24.6	25.5	26.4	27.4	27.7	27.7

weeks to expiration — net profit area, in cents

Est. credit: +28.2¢ premium -0.5¢ comm. = +27.7¢

TABLE 2

changes in the soybean future's price in 25¢ increments	12	10	8	6	4	2	0
+125	-109.3	-109.3	-109.3	-109.3	-109.3	-109.3	-109.3
+100	-84.3	-84.3	-84.3	-84.3	-84.3	-84.3	-84.3
+75	-59.4	-59.3	-59.3	-59.3	-59.3	-59.3	-59.3
+50	-35.6	-35.2	-34.9	-34.6	-34.4	-34.3	-34.3
+25	-15.0	-14.1	-13.0	-11.9	-10.6	-9.7	-9.3
0	-0.5	0.8	2.2	4.0	6.7	10.3	15.7
-25	7.6	8.7	10.0	11.7	13.8	14.9	15.7
-50	11.2	12.1	13.1	14.3	15.3	15.7	15.7
-75	14.0	14.4	14.8	15.4	15.7	15.7	15.7
-100	14.4	14.8	15.2	15.6	15.7	15.7	15.7
-125	15.3	15.5	15.6	15.7	15.7	15.7	15.7

weeks to expiration — net profit area, in cents

Est. credit: +16.2¢ premium -0.5¢ comm. = +15.7¢

Wm Grandmill (1985) Ltd.

SELL A CALL or SELL A PUT

AT 50¢ OUT OF THE MONEY

TABLE 8 / 0

changes in the soybean future's price in 25¢ increments	weeks to expiration						
	12	10	8	6	4	2	0
+125	-55.7	-53.1	-50.3	-47.4	-44.0	-41.5	-41.4
+100	-42.2	-38.8	-35.0	-30.4	-24.5	-18.1	-16.4
+75	-28.9	-25.0	-20.9	-15.5	-7.8	2.1	8.6
+50	-18.6	-14.6	-9.9	-4.0	4.6	16.3	24.5
+25	-9.1	-5.2	-0.6	5.2	13.6	24.5	33.6
0	-0.5	3.2	7.4	12.7	19.7	28.3	33.6
-25	3.5	7.2	11.7	17.7	24.0	31.4	33.6
-50	10.1	13.6	17.4	21.7	26.8	31.9	33.6
-75	16.5	19.1	22.1	25.3	29.3	33.1	33.6
-100	23.7	25.6	27.5	29.6	31.9	33.6	33.6
-125	28.3	29.9	31.1	32.2	32.8	33.6	33.6

net profit area , in cents

Est. credit: +34.1¢ premium -0.5¢ comm. = +33.6¢

TABLE 6 / 0

changes in the soybean future's price in 25¢ increments	weeks to expiration						
	12	10	8	6	4	2	0
+125	-59.5	-58.0	-56.5	-54.8	-53.0	-52.3	-52.3
+100	-43.2	-40.9	-38.3	-35.3	-31.5	-27.8	-27.3
+75	-28.7	-25.9	-22.6	-18.6	-12.8	-5.9	-2.3
+50	-17.5	-14.4	-10.7	-6.2	0.4	9.4	22.7
+25	-8.2	-5.2	-1.6	2.8	9.0	17.2	22.7
0	-0.5	2.2	5.4	8.9	14.0	20.2	22.7
-25	3.8	6.5	9.7	13.2	17.7	21.9	22.7
-50	9.0	11.1	13.3	16.0	19.2	22.3	22.7
-75	13.1	14.7	16.5	18.5	20.9	22.6	22.7
-100	16.8	18.0	19.3	20.8	22.0	22.7	22.7
-125	19.5	20.3	21.3	22.2	22.7	22.7	22.7

net profit area , in cents

Est. credit: +23.2¢ premium -0.5¢ comm. = +22.7¢

TABLE 4 / 0

changes in the soybean future's price in 25¢ increments	weeks to expiration						
	12	10	8	6	4	2	0
+125	-64.6	-64.0	-63.3	-62.7	-62.3	-62.3	-62.3
+100	-44.9	-43.6	-42.1	-40.5	-38.4	-37.4	-37.3
+75	-28.0	-26.1	-23.8	-21.2	-17.6	-13.7	-12.3
+50	-15.5	-13.3	-10.8	-7.6	-3.0	3.3	12.7
+25	-6.5	-4.6	-2.1	0.8	5.0	10.6	12.7
0	-0.5	1.1	3.1	5.4	8.6	12.7	12.7
-25	3.7	5.2	7.0	8.9	11.1	12.7	12.7
-50	6.3	7.4	8.7	10.0	11.6	12.7	12.7
-75	8.8	9.6	10.5	11.3	12.4	12.7	12.7
-100	11.4	11.9	12.2	12.4	12.7	12.7	12.7
-125	12.4	12.5	12.6	12.7	12.7	12.7	12.7

net profit area , in cents

Est. credit: +13.2¢ premium -0.5¢ comm. = +12.7¢

TABLE 2 / 0

changes in the soybean future's price in 25¢ increments	weeks to expiration						
	12	10	8	6	4	2	0
+125	-71.1	-71.0	-71.0	-71.0	-71.0	-71.0	-71.0
+100	-47.3	-46.9	-46.6	-46.3	-46.1	-46.0	-46.0
+75	-25.7	-24.8	-23.7	-22.6	-21.8	-21.4	-21.0
+50	-12.2	-10.9	-9.5	-7.7	-5.0	-1.4	4.0
+25	-4.1	-3.0	-1.7	0.0	2.1	3.2	4.0
0	-0.5	0.4	1.4	2.6	3.6	4.0	4.0
-25	2.3	2.7	3.1	3.7	4.0	4.0	4.0
-50	2.7	3.1	3.5	3.9	4.0	4.0	4.0
-75	3.6	4.2	4.0	4.0	4.0	4.0	4.0
-100	4.1	4.0	4.0	4.0	4.0	4.0	4.0
-125	4.0	4.0	4.0	4.0	4.0	4.0	4.0

net profit area , in cents

Est. credit: +4.5¢ premium -0.5¢ comm. = +4.0¢

Wm Grandmill (1985) Ltd.

BULL or BEAR SPREAD – #1

BUY A CALL AT THE MONEY
and SELL A CALL AT 25¢ OUT OF THE MONEY
OR
BUY A PUT AT THE MONEY
and SELL A PUT AT 25¢ OUT OF THE MONEY

TABLE 8

changes in the soybean future's price in 25¢ increments	weeks to expiration						
	12	10	8	6	4	2	0
+125	13.3	13.5	13.7	13.9	14.1	14.5	14.5
+100	9.2	9.7	10.4	10.9	12.9	14.5	14.5
+75	5.8	6.3	6.9	7.9	9.5	12.9	14.5
+50	2.8	3.2	3.7	4.4	6.2	9.7	14.5
+25	0.8	0.9	1.0	1.2	1.9	3.7	14.5
0	-1.0	-1.1	-1.2	-1.3	-1.5	-2.5	-10.5
-25	-1.9	-2.1	-2.5	-3.2	-4.4	-6.6	-10.5
-50	-2.6	-3.0	-3.6	-4.5	-5.6	-7.5	-10.5
-75	-3.3	-4.1	-4.9	-5.9	-6.9	-8.5	-10.5
-100	-4.1	-4.9	-5.8	-6.9	-8.0	-9.3	-10.5
-125	-4.5	-5.3	-6.5	-7.7	-9.0	-10.0	-10.5
						net profit area , in cents	

Est. cost: -52.2¢ prem. +42.7¢ prem. -1.0¢ = -10.5¢

TABLE 4

changes in the soybean future's price in 25¢ increments	weeks to expiration						
	12	10	8	6	4	2	0
+125	14.7	14.9	15.0	15.0	15.0	15.0	15.0
+100	13.0	13.4	14.0	14.6	15.0	15.0	15.0
+75	9.7	10.4	11.2	12.2	12.9	13.7	15.0
+50	6.9	7.5	8.3	9.3	10.8	13.7	15.0
+25	2.5	2.8	3.0	3.6	4.6	7.0	15.0
0	-1.0	-1.2	-1.4	-1.6	-2.0	-2.8	-10.0
-25	-4.0	-4.3	-4.8	-5.4	-6.4	-8.4	-10.0
-50	-5.8	-5.9	-6.1	-6.5	-7.5	-9.5	-10.0
-75	-7.4	-7.7	-8.0	-8.4	-8.8	-9.7	-10.0
-100	-7.6	-7.8	-8.2	-8.7	-9.2	-10.0	-10.0
-125	-7.7	-8.0	-8.4	-8.9	-9.7	-10.0	-10.0
						net profit area , in cents	

Est. cost: -28.2¢ prem. +19.2¢ prem. -1.0¢= -10.0¢

TABLE 6

changes in the soybean future's price in 25¢ increments	weeks to expiration						
	12	10	8	6	4	2	0
+125	13.3	13.5	13.9	14.4	14.7	14.7	14.7
+100	10.2	10.7	11.4	12.5	14.0	14.7	14.7
+75	6.9	7.2	7.9	9.2	11.2	14.2	14.7
+50	4.3	4.7	5.4	6.4	8.4	11.6	14.7
+25	0.9	1.2	1.6	2.1	2.9	5.0	14.7
0	-1.0	-1.1	-1.2	-1.3	-1.7	-2.5	-10.3
-25	-2.6	-2.9	-3.3	-4.2	-5.3	-7.3	-10.3
-50	-3.9	-4.3	-4.9	-5.6	-6.6	-8.6	-10.3
-75	-5.1	-5.7	-6.7	-7.5	-8.6	-9.9	-10.3
-100	-6.2	-6.7	-7.1	-7.8	-8.7	-10.0	-10.3
-125	-6.6	-7.0	-7.5	-8.0	-9.0	-10.2	-10.3

Est. cost: -40.2¢ prem. +30.9¢ prem. -1.0¢ = -10.3¢

TABLE 2

changes in the soybean future's price in 25¢ increments	weeks to expiration						
	12	10	8	6	4	2	0
+125	15.9	15.9	15.9	15.9	15.9	15.9	15.9
+100	15.8	15.9	15.9	15.9	15.9	15.9	15.9
+75	14.7	15.0	15.3	15.6	15.8	15.9	15.9
+50	11.5	12.0	12.8	13.6	14.7	15.5	15.9
+25	5.4	5.8	6.1	6.8	8.2	10.9	15.9
0	-1.0	-1.2	-1.3	-1.4	-2.0	-2.5	-9.1
-25	-5.5	-5.7	-6.1	-6.5	-7.6	-8.5	-9.1
-50	-6.3	-6.8	-7.3	-8.0	-8.9	-9.1	-9.1
-75	-7.3	-7.6	-8.2	-8.9	-9.0	-9.1	-9.1
-100	-8.2	-8.4	-8.7	-9.0	-9.1	-9.1	-9.1
-125	-8.8	-8.9	-9.0	-9.1	-9.1	-9.1	-9.1
						net profit area , in cents	

Est. cost: -16.2¢ prem. +8.1¢ prem. -1.0¢= -9.1¢

Wm Grandmill (1985) Ltd.

BULL or BEAR SPREAD – #2

BUY A CALL AT THE MONEY
and SELL 2 CALLS AT 50¢ OUT OF THE MONEY
OR
BUY A PUT AT THE MONEY
and SELL 2 PUTS AT 50¢ OUT OF THE MONEY

TABLE (8 · 0)

changes in the soybean future's price in 25¢ increments

Δ price	12	10	8	6	4	2	0
+125	-30.6	-28.2	-25.7	-22.2	-15.7	-10.7	-10.5
+100	-27.4	-23.3	-18.2	-11.7	-1.3	11.1	14.5
+75	-21.2	-16.0	-10.4	-2.7	9.3	26.6	39.5
+50	-14.1	-9.5	-3.9	3.3	14.6	31.6	64.5
+25	-8.4	-4.5	0.5	6.8	15.9	27.7	39.5
0	-1.5	1.7	5.4	10.1	15.5	21.4	14.5
-25	-3.0	0.5	4.9	9.5	15.3	19.2	14.5
-50	1.6	4.9	8.3	11.6	14.8	16.3	14.5
-75	10.4	11.9	13.4	14.6	15.5	15.7	14.5
-100	15.0	16.1	16.6	16.7	16.2	15.3	14.5
-125	21.0	22.1	23.0	21.8	19.2	17.0	14.5

weeks to expiration — net profit area, in cents

Est credit-52.2¢ +34.1¢ +34.1¢ -1.5¢ com.=+14.5¢

TABLE (6 · 0)

changes in the soybean future's price in 25¢ increments

Δ price	12	10	8	6	4	2	0
+125	-33.8	-31.5	-28.7	-25.3	-21.7	-20.3	-20.3
+100	-24.6	-20.8	-16.4	-11.0	-3.7	11.1	4.7
+75	-15.9	-11.8	-6.7	-0.4	9.4	22.5	29.7
+50	-9.8	-5.9	-1.1	4.9	14.3	28.6	54.7
+25	-5.7	-2.5	1.4	6.2	12.8	22.3	29.7
0	-1.5	0.8	3.5	6.0	9.6	13.0	4.7
-25	-2.2	0.2	3.0	5.6	8.4	8.6	4.7
-50	0.5	2.0	3.4	5.1	6.4	6.4	4.7
-75	4.4	4.9	5.3	5.8	6.1	6.3	4.7
-100	6.0	6.3	6.5	6.8	6.3	5.6	4.7
-125	7.9	7.9	8.1	7.9	6.5	4.8	4.7

weeks to expiration — net profit area, in cents

Est credit-40.2¢+23.2¢+23.2¢-1.5¢ com. = +4.7¢

TABLE (4 · 0)

changes in the soybean future's price in 25¢ increments

Δ price	12	10	8	6	4	2	0
+125	-32.9	-31.7	-30.3	-29.1	-28.3	-28.3	-28.3
+100	-18.2	-15.8	-12.9	-9.7	-5.5	-3.5	-3.3
+75	-7.4	-4.2	-0.3	4.3	11.1	18.9	21.7
+50	-2.1	1.0	4.5	9.3	16.4	28.0	46.7
+25	-1.0	0.9	3.6	6.8	11.6	18.9	21.7
0	-1.5	-0.5	0.1	1.0	2.4	5.1	-3.3
-25	-2.1	-2.1	-2.3	-2.4	-2.8	-3.0	-3.3
-50	-2.9	-2.3	-1.7	-1.5	-1.4	-1.2	-3.3
-75	-0.7	-1.2	-1.6	-2.1	-2.9	-3.0	-3.3
-100	-0.6	-1.3	-1.9	-3.0	-3.3	-3.3	-3.3
-125	-0.1	-0.6	-1.2	-1.9	-3.0	-3.3	-3.3

weeks to expiration — net profit area

Est. cost:-28.2¢ +13.2¢+13.2¢-1.5¢ com.= -3.3¢

TABLE (2 · 0)

changes in the soybean future's price in 25¢ increments

Δ price	12	10	8	6	4	2	0
+125	-33.8	-33.7	-33.7	-33.7	-33.7	-33.7	-33.7
+100	-11.3	-10.5	-9.9	-9.3	-8.9	-8.7	-8.7
+75	5.0	6.7	8.9	11.1	13.7	15.5	16.3
+50	10.2	12.4	14.9	18.2	23.4	30.5	41.3
+25	5.8	7.1	8.7	10.9	13.5	15.1	16.3
0	-1.5	-1.2	-0.6	0.2	-0.1	-0.1	-8.7
-25	-4.0	-4.3	-4.8	-5.5	-6.8	-7.9	-8.7
-50	-6.8	-6.9	-7.1	-7.5	-8.3	-8.7	-8.7
-75	-7.7	-7.8	-8.0	-8.4	-8.7	-8.7	-8.7
-100	-7.9	-8.1	-8.3	-8.5	-8.7	-8.7	-8.7
-125	-8.3	-8.5	-8.6	-8.7	-8.7	-8.7	-8.7

weeks to expiration — net profit area

Est. cost:-16.2¢ +4.5¢ +4.5¢ -1.5¢ com. = -8.7¢

Wm Grandmill (1985) Ltd.

SELL A STRADDLE
SELL A CALL AT THE MONEY
and SELL A PUT AT THE MONEY

TABLE 8

changes in the soybean future's price in 25¢ increments	weeks to expiration						
	12	10	8	6	4	2	0
+125	-47.2	-41.8	-35.7	-30.2	-25.9	-22.1	-21.6
+100	-29.8	-23.6	-17.3	-10.3	-3.8	1.7	3.4
+75	-16.0	-9.7	-2.4	5.7	16.2	26.1	28.4
+50	-6.5	0.6	8.6	18.5	31.4	46.5	53.4
+25	-1.8	6.0	14.8	25.9	42.0	62.8	78.4
0	-1.0	7.0	16.4	28.2	45.4	68.8	103.4
-25	-1.8	6.0	14.8	25.9	42.0	62.8	78.4
-50	-6.5	0.6	8.6	18.5	31.4	46.5	53.4
-75	-16.0	-9.7	-2.4	5.7	16.2	26.1	28.4
-100	-29.8	-23.6	-17.3	-10.3	-3.8	1.7	3.4
-125	-47.2	-41.8	-35.7	-30.2	-25.9	-22.1	-21.6

net profit area , in cents

Est. credit: +52.2¢ +52.2¢ prems. -1.0¢ = +103.4¢

TABLE 0

changes in the soybean future's price in 25¢ increments	weeks to expiration						
	12	10	8	6	4	2	0
+125	-56.1	-53.8	-51.8	-49.8	-47.4	-45.7	-45.6
+100	-36.8	-33.9	-30.9	-27.6	-24.1	-21.0	-20.6
+75	-21.7	-17.5	-12.8	-7.6	-1.3	3.6	4.4
+50	-9.7	-4.7	1.1	7.9	16.5	26.4	29.4
+25	-2.9	2.9	9.8	18.2	30.2	45.3	54.5
0	-1.0	5.2	12.6	21.6	34.8	52.8	79.4
-25	-2.9	2.9	9.8	18.2	30.2	45.3	54.4
-50	-9.7	-4.7	1.1	7.9	16.5	26.4	29.4
-75	-21.7	-17.5	-12.8	-7.6	-1.3	3.6	4.4
-100	-36.8	-33.9	-30.9	-27.6	-24.1	-21.0	-20.6
-125	-56.1	-53.8	-51.8	-49.8	-47.4	-45.7	-45.6

net profit area , in cents

Est. credit: +40.2¢+40.2¢ prems.-1.0¢= +79.4¢

TABLE 4

changes in the soybean future's price in 25¢ increments	weeks to expiration						
	12	10	8	6	4	2	0
+125	-73.5	-72.7	-71.8	-70.9	-69.9	-69.6	-69.6
+100	-51.3	-50.0	-48.6	-47.2	-45.7	-44.6	-44.6
+75	-30.9	-28.7	-26.3	-23.8	-21.2	-19.6	-19.6
+50	-15.4	-12.5	-9.0	-5.1	0.2	4.8	5.4
+25	-4.5	-0.7	4.1	9.6	17.4	26.9	30.4
0	-1.0	3.4	8.4	14.8	24.0	36.6	55.4
-25	-4.5	-0.7	4.1	9.6	17.4	26.9	30.4
-50	-15.4	-12.5	-9.0	-5.1	0.2	4.8	5.4
-75	-30.9	-28.7	-26.3	-23.8	-21.2	-19.6	-19.6
-100	-51.3	-50.0	-48.6	-47.2	-45.7	-44.6	-44.6
-125	-73.5	-72.7	-71.8	-70.9	-69.9	-69.6	-69.6

net profit area , in cents

Est. credit +28.2¢ +28.2¢ prems. -1.0¢ = +55.4¢

TABLE 2

changes in the soybean future's price in 25¢ increments	weeks to expiration						
	12	10	8	6	4	2	0
+125	-94.0	-93.8	-93.7	-93.6	-93.6	-93.6	-93.6
+100	-69.9	-69.5	-69.1	-68.7	-68.6	-68.6	-68.6
+75	-45.4	-44.9	-44.4	-43.9	-43.6	-43.6	-43.6
+50	-24.4	-23.1	-21.8	-20.3	-19.1	-18.6	-18.6
+25	-7.4	-5.4	-3.0	-0.2	3.2	5.9	6.4
0	-1.0	1.6	4.4	8.0	13.4	20.6	31.4
-25	-7.4	-5.4	-3.0	-0.2	3.2	5.9	6.4
-50	-24.4	-23.1	-21.8	-20.3	-19.1	-18.6	-18.6
-75	-45.4	-44.9	-44.4	-43.9	-43.6	-43.6	-43.6
-100	-69.9	-69.5	-69.1	-68.7	-68.6	-68.6	-68.6
-125	-94.0	-93.8	-93.7	-93.6	-93.6	-93.6	-93.6

net profit area

Est. credit: +16.2¢ +16.2¢ prems. -1.0¢ = +31.4¢

Wm Grandmill (1985) Ltd.

SELL A STRANGLE – #1

SELL A CALL AT 50¢ OUT OF THE MONEY
and SELL A PUT AT 50¢ OUT OF THE MONEY

TABLE 0

changes in the soybean future's price in 25¢ increments	12	10	8	6	4	2	0
+125	-27.4	-23.2	-19.2	-15.3	-11.2	-7.9	-7.8
+100	-18.9	-13.2	-7.4	-0.8	7.4	15.5	17.2
+75	-12.4	-5.6	1.3	9.8	21.5	35.2	42.2
+50	-8.5	-1.0	7.5	17.7	31.4	48.2	67.2
+25	-5.6	2.0	11.1	22.1	37.6	55.9	67.2
0	-1.0	6.4	14.8	25.4	39.4	56.8	67.2
-25	-5.6	2.0	11.1	22.1	37.6	55.9	67.2
-50	-8.5	-1.0	7.5	17.7	31.4	48.2	67.2
-75	-12.4	-5.6	1.3	9.8	21.5	35.2	42.2
-100	-18.9	-13.2	-7.4	-0.8	7.4	15.5	17.2
-125	-27.4	-23.2	-19.2	-15.3	-11.2	-7.9	-7.8

weeks to expiration — net profit area, in cents

Est. credit: +34.1¢ +34.1¢ prems. -1.0¢= +67.2¢

TABLE 0

changes in the soybean future's price in 25¢ increments	12	10	8	6	4	2	0
+125	-40.0	-37.7	-35.2	-32.6	-30.3	-29.6	-29.6
+100	-26.4	-22.9	-19.0	-14.5	-9.5	-5.1	-4.6
+75	-15.6	-11.2	-6.1	-0.1	8.1	16.7	20.4
+50	-8.5	-3.3	2.6	9.8	19.6	31.7	45.4
+25	-4.4	1.3	8.1	16.0	26.7	39.1	45.4
0	-1.0	4.4	10.8	17.8	28.0	40.4	45.4
-25	-4.4	1.3	8.1	16.0	26.7	39.1	45.4
-50	-8.5	-3.3	2.6	9.8	19.6	31.7	45.4
-75	-15.6	-11.2	-6.1	-0.1	8.1	16.7	20.4
-100	-26.4	-22.9	-19.0	-14.5	-9.5	-5.1	-4.6
-125	-40.0	-37.7	-35.2	-32.6	-30.3	-29.6	-29.6

weeks to expiration — net profit area, in cents

Est. credit: +23.2¢ +23.2¢ prems. -1.0¢ +45.4¢

TABLE 0

changes in the soybean future's price in 25¢ increments	12	10	8	6	4	2	0
+125	-52.2	-51.5	-50.7	-50.0	-49.6	-49.6	-49.6
+100	-33.5	-31.7	-29.9	-28.1	-25.7	-24.7	-24.6
+75	-19.2	-16.5	-13.3	-9.9	-5.2	-1.0	0.4
+50	-9.2	-5.9	-2.1	2.4	8.6	13.0	25.4
+25	-2.8	0.6	4.9	9.7	16.1	23.3	25.4
0	-1.0	2.2	6.2	10.8	17.2	24.4	25.4
-25	-2.8	0.6	4.9	9.7	16.1	23.3	25.4
-50	-9.2	-5.9	-2.1	2.4	8.6	13.0	25.4
-75	-19.2	-16.5	-13.3	-9.9	-5.2	-1.0	0.4
-100	-33.5	-31.7	-29.9	-28.1	-25.7	-24.7	-24.6
-125	-52.2	-51.5	-50.7	-49.6	-49.6	-49.6	-24.6

weeks to expiration — net profit area, in cents

Est. credit: +13.1¢ +13.1¢ prems. -1.0¢ = +25.4¢

TABLE 0

changes in the soybean future's price in 25¢ increments	12	10	8	6	4	2	0
+125	-67.1	-67.0	-67.0	-67.0	-67.0	-67.0	-67.0
+100	-43.4	-42.9	-42.6	-42.3	-42.1	-42.0	-42.0
+75	-23.1	-22.0	-20.8	-19.6	-18.3	-17.4	-17.0
+50	-9.5	-7.8	-6.0	-3.8	-1.0	2.6	8.0
+25	-1.8	-0.3	1.4	3.7	6.1	7.2	8.0
0	-1.0	0.8	2.6	5.2	7.2	8.0	8.0
-25	-1.8	-0.3	1.4	3.7	6.1	7.2	8.0
-50	-9.5	-7.8	-6.0	-3.8	-1.0	2.6	8.0
-75	-23.1	-22.0	-20.8	-19.6	-18.3	-17.4	-17.0
-100	-43.4	-42.9	-42.6	-42.3	-42.1	-42.0	-42.0
-125	-67.1	-67.0	-67.0	-67.0	-67.0	-67.0	-67.0

weeks to expiration — net profit area, in cents

Est. credit: +4.5¢ +4.5¢ prems. -1.0¢ + 8.0¢

Wm Grandmill (1985) Ltd.

124

SELL A STRANGLE – #2

SELL A CALL AT $1.00 OUT OF THE MONEY
and SELL A PUT AT $1.00 OUT OF THE MONEY

weeks to expiration

12

TABLE 8 — changes in the soybean future's price in 25¢ increments

	12	10	8	6	4	2	0
+125	-17.3	-13.2	-8.8	-3.3	4.6	14.5	21.0
+100	-8.7	-4.0	1.2	7.8	16.7	28.7	46.0
+75	-2.0	3.7	9.3	16.1	25.2	36.9	46.0
+50	1.7	7.6	13.8	21.1	30.4	40.8	46.0
+25	-1.2	5.1	12.6	21.0	32.1	43.3	46.0
0	-1.0	6.0	13.6	22.2	32.4	42.6	46.0
-25	-1.2	5.1	12.6	21.0	32.1	43.3	46.0
-50	1.7	7.6	13.8	21.1	30.4	40.8	46.0
-75	-2.0	3.7	9.3	16.1	25.2	36.9	46.0
-100	-8.7	-4.0	1.2	7.8	16.7	28.7	46.0
-125	-17.3	-13.2	-8.8	-3.3	4.6	14.5	21.0

weeks to expiration — net profit area , in cents

Est. credit: +23.5¢ +23.5¢ prems. -1.0¢= +46.0¢

TABLE — changes in the soybean future's price in 25¢ increments

	12	10	8	6	4	2	0
+125	-25.6	-22.4	-18.9	-14.9	-9.1	-2.2	1.4
+100	-15.2	-11.5	-7.4	-2.5	4.1	13.1	26.4
+75	-7.7	-3.9	1.2	6.0	12.7	20.9	26.4
+50	-2.7	1.2	5.7	10.7	17.0	23.9	26.4
+25	-2.1	2.2	7.2	12.7	19.6	25.5	26.4
0	-1.0	3.2	7.6	13.0	19.4	25.6	26.4
-25	-2.1	2.2	7.2	12.7	19.6	25.5	26.4
-50	-2.7	1.2	5.7	10.7	17.0	23.9	26.4
-75	-7.7	-3.9	1.2	6.0	12.7	20.9	26.4
-100	-15.2	-11.5	-7.4	-2.5	4.1	13.1	26.4
-125	-25.6	-22.4	-18.9	-14.9	-9.1	-2.2	1.4

weeks to expiration — net profit area , in cents

Est. credit: +13.7¢ +13.7¢ prems. -1.0¢ = +26.4¢

TABLE 4 — changes in the soybean future's price in 25¢ increments

	12	10	8	6	4	2	0
+125	-28.9	-27.0	-24.7	-22.1	-18.5	-14.6	-13.2
+100	-16.5	-14.3	-11.7	-8.5	-3.9	2.4	11.8
+75	-7.7	-5.7	-3.1	-0.1	4.1	9.7	11.8
+50	-2.7	-0.6	1.7	4.2	7.7	11.3	11.8
+25	-1.1	1.2	3.9	6.6	9.9	11.8	11.8
0	-1.0	1.2	3.8	6.4	9.6	11.8	11.8
-25	-1.1	1.2	3.9	6.6	9.9	11.8	11.8
-50	-2.7	-0.6	1.7	4.2	7.7	11.3	11.8
-75	-7.7	-5.7	-3.1	-0.1	4.1	9.7	11.8
-100	-16.5	-14.3	-11.7	-8.5	-3.9	2.4	11.8
-125	-28.9	-27.0	-24.7	-22.1	-18.5	-14.6	-13.2

weeks to expiration — net profit area , in cents

Est. credit: +6.4¢ +6.4¢ prems. -1.0¢ com.= +11.8¢

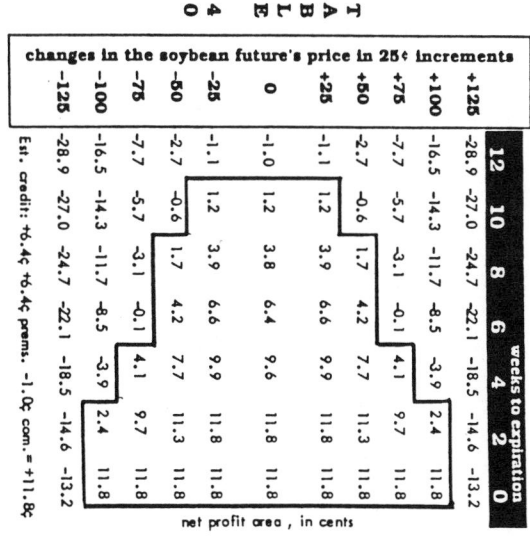

TABLE 2 — changes in the soybean future's price in 25¢ increments

	12	10	8	6	4	2	0
+125	-29.1	-28.2	-27.1	-26.0	-24.7	-23.8	-23.4
+100	-14.6	-13.3	-11.9	-10.1	-7.4	-3.8	1.6
+75	-6.5	-5.4	-4.1	-2.4	-0.3	0.8	1.6
+50	-2.9	-2.0	-1.1	0.2	1.2	1.6	1.6
+25	-0.6	0.1	0.7	1.3	1.6	1.6	1.6
0	-1.0	-0.2	0.6	1.4	1.6	1.6	1.6
-25	-0.6	0.1	0.7	1.3	1.6	1.6	1.6
-50	-2.9	-2.0	-1.1	0.2	1.2	1.6	1.6
-75	-6.5	-5.4	-4.1	-2.4	-0.3	0.8	1.6
-100	-14.6	-13.3	-11.9	-10.1	-7.4	-3.8	1.6
-125	-29.1	-28.2	-27.1	-26.0	-24.7	-23.8	-23.4

weeks to expiration — net profit area , in cents

Est. credit: +1.3¢ +1.3¢ prems. -1.0¢ com.= +1.6¢

Wm Grandmill (1985) Ltd.

BUY A CALL or BUY A PUT

AT THE MONEY

14 weeks to expiration

TABLE 8

changes in the soybean future's price in 25¢ increments

	weeks to expiration							
	14	12	10	8	6	4	2	0
+125	79.8	77.4	74.6	71.5	69.2	68.9	68.9	68.0
+100	56.3	53.6	50.9	48.4	45.7	44.3	43.9	43.9
+75	35.6	33.2	30.6	27.8	24.9	21.5	19.0	18.9
+50	22.8	19.7	16.3	12.5	7.9	2.0	-4.4	-6.1
+25	9.8	6.4	2.5	-1.7	-7.0	-14.7	-24.6	-31.1
0	-0.5	-3.9	-7.9	-12.6	-18.5	-27.1	-38.8	-56.1
-25	-10.1	-13.4	-17.3	-21.9	-27.7	-36.1	-47.0	-56.1
-50	-18.7	-22.0	-25.7	-29.9	-35.2	-42.2	-50.9	-56.1
-75	-22.7	-26.0	-29.7	-34.2	-39.4	-46.5	-53.9	-66.1
-100	-29.5	-32.6	-36.1	-39.9	-44.2	-49.3	-54.4	-66.1
-125	-36.6	-39.0	-41.6	-44.6	-47.8	-51.8	-55.6	-56.1

Est. cost is: -55.6¢ premium -0.5¢ comm. = -56.1¢

net profit area

TABLE 6

changes in the soybean future's price in 25¢ increments

	weeks to expiration							
	14	12	10	8	6	4	2	0
+125	83.9	82.6	81.9	81.7	81.7	81.7	81.7	81.7
+100	60.3	59.2	58.4	57.6	57.0	56.7	56.7	56.7
+75	40.3	38.9	37.4	35.9	34.2	31.7	31.7	31.7
+50	24.7	22.6	20.3	17.7	14.7	10.9	7.2	6.7
+25	10.4	8.1	5.3	2.0	-2.0	-7.8	-14.7	-18.3
0	-0.5	-3.1	-6.7	-9.9	-14.4	-21.0	-30.0	-43.3
-25	-9.9	-12.4	-15.4	-19.0	-23.4	-29.6	-37.8	-43.3
-50	-17.7	-20.1	-22.8	-26.0	-29.5	-34.6	-40.8	-43.3
-75	-22.0	-24.4	-27.1	-30.3	-33.8	-38.3	-42.5	-43.3
-100	-27.6	-29.6	-31.7	-33.9	-36.6	-39.8	-42.9	-43.3
-125	-32.2	-33.7	-35.3	-37.1	-39.1	-41.5	-43.2	-43.3

Estimated cost is: -42.8¢ premium - 0.5¢ comm. = -43.3¢

net profit area

TABLE 4

changes in the soybean future's price in 25¢ increments

	weeks to expiration							
	14	12	10	8	6	4	2	0
+125	94.5	94.5	94.5	94.5	94.5	94.5	94.5	94.5
+100	70.0	69.8	69.6	69.5	69.5	69.5	69.5	69.5
+75	47.4	46.8	46.2	45.5	44.9	44.5	44.5	44.5
+50	28.2	27.1	25.8	24.3	22.7	20.6	19.6	19.5
+25	11.8	10.2	8.3	6.0	3.4	-0.2	-4.1	-5.5
0	-0.5	-2.3	-4.5	-7.0	-10.2	-14.8	-21.1	-30.5
-25	-9.6	-11.3	-13.2	-15.7	-18.6	-22.8	-28.4	-30.5
-50	-15.9	-17.3	-18.9	-20.9	-23.2	-26.4	-30.0	-30.5
-75	-20.1	-21.5	-23.0	-24.8	-26.7	-28.9	-30.5	-30.5
-100	-23.2	-24.1	-25.2	-26.5	-27.8	-29.4	-30.2	-30.5
-125	-25.8	-26.6	-27.4	-28.3	-29.2	-30.2	-30.5	-30.5

Estimated cost: -30.0¢ premium - 0.5¢ comm. = -30.5¢

net profit area

TABLE 2

changes in the soybean future's price in 25¢ increments

	weeks to expiration							
	14	12	10	8	6	4	2	0
+125	107.3	107.3	107.3	107.3	107.3	107.3	107.3	107.3
+100	82.3	82.3	82.3	82.3	82.3	82.3	82.3	82.3
+75	57.4	57.4	57.3	57.3	57.3	57.3	57.3	57.3
+50	34.0	33.6	33.2	32.9	32.6	32.4	32.3	32.3
+25	13.8	13.0	12.1	11.0	9.9	8.6	7.7	7.3
0	-0.5	-1.5	-2.8	-4.2	-6.0	-8.7	-12.3	-17.7
-25	-8.7	-9.6	-10.7	-12.0	-13.7	-15.8	-16.9	-17.7
-50	-12.5	-13.2	-14.1	-15.1	-16.3	-17.3	-17.7	-17.7
-75	-15.5	-16.0	-16.4	-16.8	-17.4	-17.7	-17.7	-17.7
-100	-16.1	-16.4	-16.8	-17.2	-17.6	-17.7	-17.7	-17.7
-125	-17.2	-17.3	-17.5	-17.6	-17.7	-17.7	-17.7	-17.7

Estimated cost: -17.2¢ premium - 0.5¢ comm. = -17.7¢

net profit area , in cents

Wm Grandmill (1985) Ltd.

BUY A CALL or BUY A PUT
AT 50¢ OUT OF THE MONEY

TABLE 08

changes in the soybean future's price in 25¢ increments

	weeks to expiration							net profit
	14	12	10	8	6	4	2	0
+125	53.8	51.4	48.8	46.0	43.1	39.7	37.2	37.1
+100	41.0	37.9	34.5	30.7	26.1	20.2	13.8	12.1
+75	28.0	24.6	20.7	16.6	11.2	3.5	-6.4	-12.9
+50	17.7	14.3	10.3	5.6	-0.3	-8.9	-20.6	-37.9
+25	8.1	4.8	0.9	-3.7	-9.5	-17.9	-28.8	-37.9
0	-0.5	-3.8	-7.5	-11.7	-17.0	-24.0	-32.6	-37.9
-25	-4.5	-7.8	-11.5	-16.0	-21.5	-28.3	-35.7	-37.9
-50	-11.3	-14.4	-17.9	-21.7	-26.0	-31.1	-36.2	-37.9
-75	-18.4	-20.8	-23.4	-26.4	-29.6	-33.6	-37.4	-37.9
-100	-25.4	-28.0	-29.9	-31.8	-33.9	-36.2	-37.9	-37.9
-125	-30.8	-32.6	-34.2	-35.4	-36.5	-37.1	-37.9	-37.9

Estimated cost: -37.4¢ premium - 0.5¢ comm. = -37.9¢

TABLE 06

changes in the soybean future's price in 25¢ increments

	weeks to expiration							net profit
	14	12	10	8	6	4	2	0
+125	57.5	56.1	54.6	53.1	51.4	49.6	48.9	48.9
+100	41.9	39.8	37.5	34.9	31.9	28.1	24.4	23.9
+75	27.6	25.3	22.5	19.2	15.2	9.4	2.5	-1.1
+50	16.7	14.1	11.0	7.3	2.8	-3.8	-12.8	-26.1
+25	7.3	4.8	1.8	-1.8	-6.2	-12.4	-20.6	-26.1
0	-0.5	-2.9	-5.6	-8.8	-12.3	-17.4	-23.6	-26.1
-25	-4.8	-7.2	-9.9	-13.1	-16.6	-21.1	-25.3	-26.1
-50	-10.5	-12.4	-14.5	-16.7	-19.4	-22.6	-25.7	-26.1
-75	-15.0	-16.5	-18.1	-19.9	-21.9	-24.3	-26.0	-26.1
-100	-19.1	-20.2	-21.4	-22.7	-24.2	-25.4	-26.1	-26.1
-125	-22.1	-22.9	-23.7	-24.7	-25.6	-26.1	-26.1	-26.1

Estimated cost: -25.6¢ premium -0.5¢ comm. = -26.1¢

TABLE 04

changes in the soybean future's price in 25¢ increments

	weeks to expiration							net profit
	14	12	10	8	6	4	2	0
+125	62.8	62.2	61.6	60.9	60.3	59.9	59.9	59.9
+100	43.6	42.5	41.2	39.7	38.1	36.0	35.0	34.9
+75	27.2	25.6	23.7	21.4	18.8	15.2	11.3	9.9
+50	14.9	13.1	10.9	8.4	5.2	0.6	-5.7	-15.1
+25	5.8	4.1	2.2	-0.3	-3.2	-7.4	-13.0	-15.1
0	-0.5	-1.9	-3.5	-5.5	-7.8	-11.0	-14.6	-15.1
-25	-4.7	-6.1	-7.6	-9.4	-11.3	-13.5	-15.1	-15.1
-50	-7.8	-8.7	-9.8	-11.1	-12.4	-14.0	-15.1	-15.1
-75	-10.4	-11.2	-12.0	-12.9	-13.7	-14.8	-15.1	-15.1
-100	-13.1	-13.8	-14.3	-14.6	-14.8	-15.1	-15.1	-15.1
-125	-14.7	-14.8	-14.9	-15.0	-15.1	-15.1	-15.1	-15.1

Estimated cost: -14.6¢ premium - 0.5¢ comm. = -15.1¢

TABLE 02

changes in the soybean future's price in 25¢ increments

	weeks to expiration							net profit
	14	12	10	8	6	4	2	0
+125	69.4	69.4	69.3	69.3	69.3	69.3	69.3	69.3
+100	46.0	45.6	45.2	44.9	44.6	44.4	44.3	44.3
+75	24.8	24.0	23.1	22.0	20.9	20.1	19.7	19.3
+50	11.5	10.5	9.2	7.8	6.0	3.3	-0.3	-5.7
+25	3.3	2.4	1.3	0.0	-1.7	-3.8	-4.9	-5.7
0	-0.5	-1.2	-2.1	-3.1	-4.3	-5.3	-5.7	-5.7
-25	-3.5	-4.0	-4.8	-5.4	-5.7	-5.7	-5.7	-5.7
-50	-4.1	-4.4	-4.8	-5.2	-5.6	-5.7	-5.7	-5.7
-75	-5.2	-5.3	-5.5	-5.6	-5.7	-5.7	-5.7	-5.7
-100	-5.6	-5.6	-5.7	-5.7	-5.7	-5.7	-5.7	-5.7
-125	-5.7	-5.7	-5.7	-5.7	-5.7	-5.7	-5.7	-5.7

Estimated cost: -5.2¢ premium - 0.5¢ comm. = -5.7¢

Wm Grandmill (1985) Ltd.

SELL A CALL or SELL A PUT

AT THE MONEY

TABLE 8

changes in the soybean future's price in 25¢ increments

	weeks to expiration							
	14	12	10	8	6	4	2	0
+125	-80.8	-78.4	-75.6	-72.5	-70.2	-69.9	-69.9	-69.9
+100	-57.3	-54.6	-51.9	-49.4	-46.7	-45.3	-44.9	-44.9
+75	-36.6	-34.2	-31.6	-28.8	-25.9	-22.5	-20.0	-19.9
+50	-23.8	-20.7	-17.3	-13.5	-8.9	-3.0	3.4	5.1
+25	-10.8	-7.4	-3.5	0.7	6.0	13.7	23.6	30.1
0	-0.5	2.9	6.9	11.6	17.5	26.1	37.8	55.1
-25	9.1	12.4	16.3	20.9	26.7	35.1	46.0	55.1
-50	17.7	21.0	24.7	28.9	34.2	41.2	49.9	55.1
-75	21.7	25.0	28.7	33.2	38.4	45.5	52.9	55.1
-100	28.5	31.6	35.1	38.9	43.2	48.3	53.4	55.1
-125	35.6	38.4	40.6	43.6	46.8	50.8	54.6	55.1

The estimated credit: +55.6¢ premium -0.5¢ comm.=+55.1¢

net profit area , in cents

TABLE 6

changes in the soybean future's price in 25¢ increments

	weeks to expiration							
	14	12	10	8	6	4	2	0
+125	-84.9	-83.6	-82.9	-82.7	-82.7	-82.7	-82.7	-82.7
+100	-61.3	-60.2	-59.4	-58.6	-58.0	-57.7	-57.7	-57.7
+75	-41.3	-39.9	-38.4	-36.9	-35.2	-33.4	-32.7	-32.7
+50	-25.7	-23.6	-21.3	-18.7	-15.7	-11.9	-8.2	-7.7
+25	-11.4	-9.1	-6.3	-3.0	1.0	6.8	13.7	17.3
0	-0.5	2.1	5.7	8.9	13.4	20.0	29.0	42.3
-25	8.9	11.4	14.4	18.0	22.4	28.6	36.8	42.3
-50	16.7	19.1	21.8	25.0	28.5	33.6	39.8	42.3
-75	21.0	23.4	26.1	29.3	32.8	37.3	41.5	42.3
-100	26.6	28.6	30.7	32.9	35.6	38.8	41.9	42.3
-125	31.2	32.7	34.3	36.1	38.1	40.5	42.2	42.3

Estimated credit: + 42.8¢ premium -0.5¢ comm. = + 42.3¢

net profit area , in cents

TABLE 4

changes in the soybean future's price in 25¢ increments

	weeks to expiration							
	14	12	10	8	6	4	2	0
+125	-95.5	-95.5	-95.5	-95.5	-95.5	-95.5	-95.5	-95.5
+100	-71.0	-70.8	-70.6	-70.5	-70.5	-70.5	-70.5	-70.5
+75	-48.4	-47.8	-47.2	-46.5	-45.9	-45.5	-45.5	-45.5
+50	-29.2	-28.1	-26.8	-25.3	-23.7	-21.6	-20.6	-20.5
+25	-12.8	-11.2	-9.3	-7.0	-4.4	-0.8	3.1	4.5
0	-0.5	1.3	3.5	6.0	9.2	13.8	20.1	29.5
-25	8.6	10.3	12.2	14.7	17.6	21.8	27.4	29.5
-50	14.9	16.3	17.9	19.9	22.2	25.4	29.0	29.5
-75	19.1	20.5	22.0	23.8	25.7	27.9	29.2	29.5
-100	22.2	23.1	24.2	25.5	26.8	28.2	29.2	29.5
-125	24.8	25.6	26.4	27.3	28.2	29.2	29.5	29.5

Estimated credit: + 30.0¢ premium -0.5¢ comm. = + 29.5¢

net profit area , in cents

TABLE 2

changes in the soybean future's price in 25¢ increments

	weeks to expiration							
	14	12	10	8	6	4	2	0
+125	-108.3	-108.3	-108.3	-108.3	-108.3	-108.3	-108.3	-108.3
+100	-83.3	-83.3	-83.3	-83.3	-83.3	-83.3	-83.3	-83.3
+75	-58.4	-58.4	-58.3	-58.3	-58.3	-58.3	-58.3	-58.3
+50	-35.0	-34.6	-34.2	-33.9	-33.6	-33.4	-33.3	-33.3
+25	-14.8	-14.0	-13.1	-12.0	-10.9	-9.6	-8.7	-8.3
0	-0.5	0.5	1.8	3.2	5.0	7.7	11.3	16.7
-25	7.7	8.6	9.7	11.0	12.7	14.8	15.9	16.7
-50	11.5	12.2	13.1	14.1	15.3	16.3	16.7	16.7
-75	14.5	15.0	15.4	15.8	16.4	16.7	16.7	16.7
-100	15.1	15.4	15.8	16.2	16.6	16.7	16.7	16.7
-125	16.2	16.3	16.5	16.6	16.7	16.7	16.7	16.7

Estimated credit: +17.2¢ premium -0.5¢ comm. = +16.7¢

net profit area , in cents

Wm Grandmill (1985) Ltd.

SELL A CALL or SELL A PUT
AT 50¢ OUT OF THE MONEY

weeks to expiration **14**

TABLE 0 (8)

changes in the soybean future's price in 25¢ increments	14	12	10	8	6	4	2	0
					weeks to expiration			
+125	-54.8	-52.4	-49.8	-47.0	-44.1	-40.7	-38.2	-38.1
+100	-42.0	-38.9	-35.5	-31.7	-27.1	-21.2	-14.8	-13.1
+75	-29.0	-25.6	-21.7	-17.6	-12.2	-4.5	5.4	11.9
+50	-18.7	-15.3	-11.3	-6.6	-0.7	7.9	19.6	36.9
+25	-9.1	-5.8	-1.9	2.7	8.5	16.9	27.8	36.9
0	-0.5	2.8	6.5	10.7	16.0	23.0	31.6	36.9
-25	3.5	6.8	10.5	15.0	20.5	27.3	34.7	36.9
-50	10.3	13.4	16.9	20.7	25.0	30.1	35.2	36.9
-75	17.4	19.8	22.4	25.4	28.6	32.6	36.4	36.9
-100	24.4	27.0	28.9	30.8	32.9	35.2	36.9	36.9
-125	29.8	31.6	33.2	34.4	35.5	36.1	36.9	36.9

net profit area , in cents

Estimated credit: +37.4¢ premium -0.5¢ comn. = +36.9¢

TABLE 0 (6)

changes in the soybean future's price in 25¢ increments	14	12	10	8	6	4	2	0
					weeks to expiration			
+125	-58.5	-57.1	-55.6	-54.1	-52.4	-50.6	-49.9	-49.9
+100	-42.9	-40.8	-38.5	-35.9	-32.9	-29.1	-25.4	-24.9
+75	-28.6	-26.3	-23.5	-20.2	-16.2	-10.4	-3.5	0.1
+50	-17.7	-15.1	-12.0	-8.3	-3.8	2.8	11.8	25.1
+25	-8.3	-5.8	-2.8	0.8	5.2	11.4	19.6	25.1
0	-0.5	1.9	4.6	7.8	11.3	16.4	22.6	25.1
-25	3.8	6.2	8.9	12.1	15.6	20.1	24.3	25.1
-50	9.5	11.4	13.5	15.7	18.4	21.6	24.7	25.1
-75	14.0	15.5	17.1	18.8	20.9	23.3	25.0	25.1
-100	18.1	19.2	20.4	21.7	23.2	24.4	25.1	25.1
-125	21.1	21.9	22.7	23.7	24.6	25.1	25.1	25.1

net profit area, in cents

Estimated credit: +25.6¢ premium -0.5¢ comn. = +25.1¢

TABLE 0 (4)

changes in the soybean future's price in 25¢ increments	14	12	10	8	6	4	2	0
					weeks to expiration			
+125	-63.8	-63.2	-62.6	-61.9	-61.3	-60.9	-60.9	-60.9
+100	-44.6	-43.5	-42.2	-40.7	-39.1	-37.0	-36.0	-35.9
+75	-28.2	-26.6	-24.7	-22.4	-19.8	-16.2	-12.3	-10.9
+50	-15.9	-14.1	-11.9	-9.4	-6.2	-1.6	4.7	14.1
+25	-6.8	-5.1	-3.2	-0.7	2.2	6.4	12.0	14.1
0	-0.5	0.9	2.5	4.5	6.8	10.0	13.6	14.1
-25	3.7	5.1	6.6	8.4	10.3	12.5	14.1	14.1
-50	6.8	7.7	8.8	10.1	11.4	13.0	14.1	14.1
-75	9.4	10.2	11.0	11.9	12.7	13.8	14.1	14.1
-100	12.1	12.8	13.3	13.6	13.8	14.1	14.1	14.1
-125	13.7	13.8	13.9	14.0	14.1	14.1	14.1	14.1

net profit area , in cents

Estimated credit: +14.6¢ premium - 0.5¢ comn. = +14.1¢

TABLE 0 (2)

changes in the soybean future's price in 25¢ increments	14	12	10	8	6	4	2	0
					weeks to expiration			
+125	-70.4	-70.4	-70.3	-70.3	-70.3	-70.3	-70.3	-70.3
+100	-47.0	-46.6	-46.2	-45.9	-45.6	-45.4	-45.3	-45.3
+75	-25.8	-25.0	-24.1	-23.0	-21.9	-20.7	-20.3	-20.3
+50	-12.5	-11.5	-10.2	-8.8	-7.0	-4.3	-0.7	4.7
+25	-4.3	-3.4	-2.3	-1.0	0.7	2.8	3.9	4.7
0	-0.5	0.2	1.1	2.1	3.3	4.3	4.7	4.7
-25	2.5	3.0	3.4	3.8	4.4	4.7	4.7	4.7
-50	3.1	3.4	3.8	4.2	4.6	4.7	4.7	4.7
-75	4.2	4.3	4.5	4.6	4.7	4.7	4.7	4.7
-100	4.6	4.6	4.7	4.7	4.7	4.7	4.7	4.7
-125	4.7	4.7	4.7	4.7	4.7	4.7	4.7	4.7

net profit area, in cents

Estimated credit is: + 5.2¢ premium - 0.5¢ comn. = + 4.7¢

Wm Grandmill (1985) Ltd.

BULL or BEAR SPREAD – #1

BUY A CALL AT THE MONEY
and SELL A CALL AT 25¢ OUT OF THE MONEY

OR

BUY A PUT AT THE MONEY
and SELL A PUT AT 25¢ OUT OF THE MONEY

14 weeks to expiration

TABLE 8

changes in the soybean future's price in 25¢ increments	14	12	10	8	6	4	2	0
+125	13.1	13.2	13.4	13.6	13.8	14.0	14.4	14.4
+100	8.6	9.1	9.6	10.3	10.8	12.8	14.4	14.4
+75	5.3	5.7	6.2	6.8	7.8	9.4	12.8	14.4
+50	2.4	2.7	3.1	3.6	4.3	6.1	9.6	14.4
+25	0.6	0.7	0.8	0.9	1.1	1.8	3.6	14.4
0	-1.0	-1.1	-1.2	-1.3	-1.4	-1.6	-2.6	-10.6
-25	-2.0	-2.0	-2.2	-2.6	-3.3	-4.5	-6.7	-10.6
-50	-2.4	-2.7	-3.1	-3.7	-4.6	-5.7	-7.6	-10.6
-75	-2.8	-3.4	-4.2	-5.0	-6.0	-7.0	-8.6	-10.6
-100	-3.5	-4.2	-5.0	-5.9	-7.0	-8.1	-9.4	-10.6
-125	-3.8	-4.6	-5.4	-6.6	-7.8	-9.1	-10.1	-10.6

weeks to expiration — net profit area , in cents

Est. cost:-55.6¢ prem.+46.0¢ com.=-1.0¢

TABLE 6

changes in the soybean future's price in 25¢ increments	14	12	10	8	6	4	2	0
+125	13.1	13.2	13.4	13.8	13.8	14.6	14.6	14.6
+100	9.7	10.1	10.6	11.3	12.4	13.9	14.6	14.6
+75	6.5	6.8	7.1	7.8	9.1	11.1	14.1	14.6
+50	3.9	4.2	4.6	5.3	6.3	8.3	11.5	14.6
+25	0.5	0.8	1.1	1.5	2.0	2.8	4.9	14.6
0	-1.0	-1.1	-1.2	-1.3	-1.4	-1.8	-2.6	-10.4
-25	-2.5	-2.7	-3.0	-3.4	-4.3	-5.4	-7.4	-10.4
-50	-3.7	-4.0	-4.4	-5.0	-5.7	-6.7	-8.7	-10.4
-75	-4.8	-5.2	-5.8	-6.8	-7.6	-8.9	-10.0	-10.4
-100	-5.9	-6.3	-6.8	-7.2	-7.9	-8.8	-10.1	-10.4
-125	-6.3	-6.7	-7.1	-7.6	-8.1	-9.1	-10.3	-10.4

weeks to expiration — net profit area , in cents

Est. cost:-42.8¢ prem.+33.4¢ com. = -10.4¢

TABLE 4

changes in the soybean future's price in 25¢ increments	14	12	10	8	6	4	2	0
+125	14.4	14.6	14.8	14.9	14.9	14.9	14.9	14.9
+100	12.5	12.9	13.3	13.9	14.5	14.9	14.9	14.9
+75	9.1	9.6	10.3	11.1	12.1	12.8	13.6	14.9
+50	6.3	6.8	7.4	8.2	9.2	10.7	13.6	14.9
+25	2.2	2.4	2.7	2.8	3.5	4.5	6.9	14.9
0	-1.0	-1.1	-1.3	-1.5	-1.7	-2.1	-2.9	-10.1
-25	-3.8	-4.1	-4.4	-4.9	-5.5	-6.5	-8.5	-10.1
-50	-5.8	-5.9	-6.0	-6.2	-6.6	-7.6	-9.6	-10.1
-75	-7.1	-7.5	-7.8	-8.1	-8.5	-8.9	-10.1	-10.1
-100	-7.6	-7.8	-7.9	-8.3	-8.8	-9.3	-10.1	-10.1
-125	-7.6	-7.8	-8.1	-9.5	-9.8	-10.1	-10.1	-10.1

weeks to expiration — net profit area , in cents

Est. cost:-30.0¢ prem.+20.9¢ com.=-10.1¢

TABLE 2

changes in the soybean future's price in 25¢ increments	14	12	10	8	6	4	2	0
+125	15.8	15.8	15.8	15.8	15.8	15.8	15.8	15.8
+100	15.6	15.7	15.7	15.8	15.8	15.8	15.8	15.8
+75	14.2	14.6	14.9	15.2	15.5	15.7	15.8	15.8
+50	11.0	11.4	11.9	12.7	13.5	14.6	15.4	15.8
+25	5.1	5.3	5.7	6.0	6.7	8.1	10.8	15.8
0	-1.0	-1.1	-1.3	-1.4	-1.5	-2.1	-2.6	-9.2
-25	-5.4	-5.6	-5.8	-6.2	-6.7	-7.7	-8.6	-9.2
-50	-6.2	-6.4	-6.9	-7.4	-8.1	-8.8	-9.2	-9.2
-75	-7.2	-7.4	-7.7	-8.3	-9.0	-9.2	-9.2	-9.2
-100	-8.1	-8.3	-8.5	-8.8	-9.1	-9.2	-9.2	-9.2
-125	-8.8	-8.9	-9.0	-9.1	-9.2	-9.2	-9.2	-9.2

weeks to expiration — net profit area , in cents

Est. cost: -17.2¢ prem.+9.0¢ prem.-1.0¢ com. = -9.2¢

Wm Grandmill (1985) Ltd.

BULL or BEAR SPREAD – #2

**BUY A CALL AT THE MONEY
and SELL 2 CALLS AT 50¢ OUT OF THE MONEY
OR
BUY A PUT AT THE MONEY
and SELL 2 PUTS AT 50¢ OUT OF THE MONEY**

weeks to expiration

14

TABLE 8

changes in the soybean future's price in 25¢ increments	14	12	10	8	6	4	2	0
+125	-29.8	-27.4	-25.0	-22.5	-19.0	-12.5	-7.5	-7.3
+100	-27.7	-24.2	-20.1	-15.0	-8.5	1.9	14.3	17.7
+75	-22.4	-18.0	-12.8	-7.2	0.5	12.5	29.8	42.7
+50	-14.6	-10.9	-6.3	-0.7	6.5	19.1	34.8	67.7
+25	-8.4	-5.2	-1.3	3.7	10.0	17.8	31.0	42.7
0	-1.5	1.7	5.1	8.8	13.5	18.9	24.6	17.7
-25	-3.1	0.2	3.7	8.1	12.7	18.5	22.4	17.7
-50	1.9	4.8	8.1	11.5	14.8	19.5	19.5	17.7
-75	12.1	13.6	15.1	16.6	17.8	18.7	17.7	17.7
-100	17.0	18.2	19.3	19.8	19.8	19.4	18.5	17.7
-125	23.0	24.2	25.2	26.2	25.0	22.4	20.2	17.7

weeks to expiration — net profit area, in cents

Est. cost:-55.6¢ prem.+37.4¢+37.4¢ prem.-1.5¢ com.=+17.7¢

TABLE 6

changes in the soybean future's price in 25¢ increments	14	12	10	8	6	4	2	0
+125	-33.1	-31.6	-29.3	-26.5	-23.1	-19.5	-18.1	-18.1
+100	-25.6	-22.4	-18.6	-14.2	-8.8	-1.5	5.9	6.9
+75	-16.9	-13.7	-9.6	-4.5	1.8	11.6	24.7	31.9
+50	-10.7	-7.6	-3.7	1.1	7.1	16.5	30.8	56.9
+25	-6.2	-3.5	-0.3	3.6	8.4	15.0	24.5	31.9
0	-1.5	0.7	3.0	5.7	8.2	11.8	15.2	6.9
-25	-2.1	0.0	2.4	5.2	7.8	10.6	10.8	6.9
-50	1.2	2.7	4.2	5.6	7.3	8.6	8.6	6.9
-75	6.0	6.6	7.1	7.5	8.0	8.3	8.5	6.9
-100	7.8	8.2	8.5	8.7	9.0	8.5	7.8	6.9
-125	10.0	10.1	10.1	10.3	10.1	8.7	7.0	6.9

net profit area, in cents

Est. cost: -42.8¢ prem.+25.6¢+25.6¢ -1.5¢com.=+6.9¢

TABLE 4

changes in the soybean future's price in 25¢ increments	14	12	10	8	6	4	2	0
+125	-33.1	-31.9	-30.7	-29.3	-28.1	-27.3	-27.3	-27.3
+100	-19.2	-17.2	-14.8	-11.9	-8.7	-4.5	-2.5	-2.3
+75	-9.0	-6.4	-3.2	0.7	5.3	12.1	19.9	22.7
+50	-3.6	-1.1	2.0	5.5	10.3	17.4	29.0	47.7
+25	-1.8	0.0	1.9	4.6	7.8	12.6	19.9	22.7
0	-1.5	-0.5	0.5	2.0	3.4	5.2	6.1	-2.3
-25	-2.2	-1.1	0.0	1.1	2.0	2.2	-0.2	-2.3
-50	-2.4	-1.9	-1.3	-0.7	-0.5	-0.4	-1.8	-2.3
-75	-1.3	-1.1	-1.0	-1.1	-1.3	-1.4	-2.3	-2.3
-100	-0.8	-0.3	-0.2	-0.6	-0.9	-1.9	-2.3	-2.3
-125	-1.6	-1.0	-0.4	-0.3	-0.9	-2.0	-2.3	-2.3

weeks to expiration — net profit area

Est. cost:-30.0¢ prem.+14.6¢+14.6¢-1.5¢ cc.m.=-2.3¢

TABLE 2

changes in the soybean future's price in 25¢ increments	14	12	10	8	6	4	2	0
+125	-33.5	-33.4	-33.3	-33.3	-33.3	-33.3	-33.3	-33.3
+100	-11.7	-10.9	-10.1	-9.5	-8.9	-8.5	-8.3	-8.3
+75	3.8	5.4	7.1	9.3	11.5	14.1	16.9	16.7
+50	9.0	10.6	12.8	15.3	18.6	23.8	30.9	41.7
+25	5.2	6.2	7.5	9.1	11.3	13.9	15.5	16.7
0	-1.5	-1.1	-0.8	-0.2	0.6	0.3	-2.9	-8.3
-25	-3.7	-3.8	-4.1	-4.6	-5.3	-6.6	-7.5	-8.3
-50	-6.3	-6.4	-6.5	-6.7	-7.1	-7.9	-8.3	-8.3
-75	-7.2	-7.3	-7.4	-7.6	-8.0	-8.1	-8.3	-8.3
-100	-7.4	-7.5	-7.7	-7.9	-7.9	-8.1	-8.3	-8.3
-125	-7.8	-7.9	-8.1	-8.2	-8.3	-8.3	-8.3	-8.3

weeks to expiration — net profit area

Est. cost:-17.2¢ prem.+5.2¢+5.2¢ -1.5¢ com.= -8.3¢

Wm Grandmill (1985) Ltd.

SELL A STRADDLE
SELL A CALL AT THE MONEY and SELL A PUT AT THE MONEY

weeks to expiration

14

Table 8

changes in the soybean future's price in 25¢ increments

	14	12	10	8	6	4	2	0
+125	-45.2	-40.4	-35.0	-28.9	-23.4	-19.1	-15.3	-14.8
+100	-28.8	-23.0	-16.8	-10.5	-3.5	3.0	8.5	10.2
+75	-14.9	-9.2	-2.9	4.4	12.5	23.0	32.9	35.2
+50	-6.1	0.3	7.4	15.4	25.3	38.2	53.3	60.2
+25	-1.7	5.0	12.8	21.6	32.7	48.8	69.6	85.2
0	-1.0	5.8	13.8	23.2	35.0	52.2	75.6	110.2
-25	-1.7	5.0	12.8	21.6	32.7	48.8	69.6	85.2
-50	-6.1	0.3	7.4	15.4	25.3	38.2	53.3	60.2
-75	-14.9	-9.2	-2.9	4.4	12.5	23.0	32.9	35.2
-100	-28.8	-23.0	-16.8	-10.5	-3.5	3.0	8.5	10.2
-125	-45.2	-40.4	-35.0	-28.9	-23.4	-19.1	-15.3	-14.8

weeks to expiration — net profit area, in cents

Est. credit: -55.6¢ prem. +55.6¢ prem. -1.0¢ com.=+110.2¢

Table 6

changes in the soybean future's price in 25¢ increments

	14	12	10	8	6	4	2	0
+125	-53.7	-50.9	-48.6	-46.6	-44.6	-42.2	-40.5	-40.4
+100	-34.6	-31.6	-28.7	-25.7	-22.4	-18.9	-15.8	-15.4
+75	-20.3	-16.5	-12.3	-7.6	-2.4	3.9	8.8	9.6
+50	-9.0	-4.5	0.5	6.3	13.1	21.7	31.6	34.6
+25	-2.5	2.3	8.1	15.0	23.4	35.4	50.5	59.6
0	-1.0	4.2	10.4	17.8	26.8	40.0	58.0	84.6
-25	-2.5	2.3	8.1	15.0	23.4	35.4	50.5	59.6
-50	-9.0	-4.5	0.5	6.3	13.1	21.7	31.6	34.6
-75	-20.3	-16.5	-12.3	-7.6	-2.4	3.9	8.8	9.6
-100	-34.6	-31.6	-28.7	-25.7	-22.4	-18.9	-15.8	-15.4
-125	-53.7	-50.9	-48.6	-46.6	-44.6	-42.2	-40.5	-40.4

weeks to expiration — net profit area, in cents

Est. credit: +42.8¢ prem. +42.8¢ prem. -1.0¢ com.=+84.6¢

Table 4

changes in the soybean future's price in 25¢ increments

	14	12	10	8	6	4	2	0
+125	-70.7	-69.9	-69.1	-68.2	-67.3	-66.3	-66.0	-66.0
+100	-48.8	-47.7	-46.4	-45.0	-43.6	-42.1	-41.0	-41.0
+75	-31.3	-27.3	-25.1	-22.7	-20.2	-17.6	-16.0	-16.0
+50	-14.3	-11.8	-8.9	-5.4	-1.5	3.8	8.4	9.0
+25	-4.2	-0.9	2.9	7.7	13.2	21.0	30.5	34.0
0	-1.0	2.6	7.0	12.0	18.4	27.6	40.2	59.0
-25	-4.2	-0.9	2.9	7.7	13.2	21.0	30.5	34.0
-50	-14.3	-11.8	-8.9	-5.4	-1.5	3.8	8.4	9.0
-75	-31.3	-27.3	-25.1	-22.7	-20.2	-17.6	-16.0	-16.0
-100	-48.8	-47.7	-46.4	-45.0	-43.6	-42.1	-41.0	-41.0
-125	-70.7	-69.9	-69.1	-68.2	-67.3	-66.3	-66.0	-66.0

weeks to expiration — net profit area, in cents

Est. credit: +30.0¢ prem +30.0¢ prem. -1.0¢ com. = +59.0¢

Table 2

changes in the soybean future's price in 25¢ increments

	14	12	10	8	6	4	2	0
+125	-92.1	-92.0	-91.8	-91.7	-91.6	-91.6	-91.6	-91.6
+100	-68.2	-67.9	-67.5	-67.1	-66.7	-66.6	-66.6	-66.6
+75	-43.9	-43.4	-42.9	-42.4	-41.9	-41.6	-41.6	-41.6
+50	-23.5	-22.4	-21.1	-19.8	-18.3	-17.1	-16.6	-16.6
+25	-7.1	-5.4	-3.4	-1.0	1.8	5.2	7.9	8.4
0	-1.0	1.0	3.6	6.4	10.0	15.4	22.6	33.4
-25	-7.1	-5.4	-3.4	-1.0	1.8	5.2	7.9	8.4
-50	-23.5	-22.4	-21.1	-19.8	-18.3	-17.1	-16.6	-16.6
-75	-43.9	-43.4	-42.9	-42.4	-41.9	-41.6	-41.6	-41.6
-100	-68.2	-67.9	-67.5	-67.1	-66.7	-66.6	-66.6	-66.6
-125	-92.1	-92.0	-91.8	-91.7	-91.6	-91.6	-91.6	-91.6

weeks to expiration — net profit area

Est. credit: +17.2¢ prem.+17.2¢ prem.-1.0¢ comm.= +33.4¢

Wm Grandmill (1985) Ltd.

SELL A STRANGLE – #1

SELL A CALL AT 50¢ OUT OF THE MONEY and SELL A PUT AT 50¢ OUT OF THE MONEY

14 weeks to expiration

TABLE

changes in the soybean future's price in 25¢ increments — net profit area, in cents

price change	14	12	10	8	6	4	2	0
+125	-25.0	-20.8	-16.6	-12.6	-8.7	-4.7	-1.3	-1.2
+100	-17.6	-12.3	-6.6	-0.8	5.8	14.0	22.1	23.8
+75	-11.6	-5.8	1.0	7.9	16.4	28.1	41.8	48.8
+50	-8.4	-1.9	5.6	14.1	24.3	38.0	54.8	73.8
+25	-5.6	1.0	8.6	17.7	28.7	44.2	62.5	73.8
0	-1.0	5.6	13.0	21.4	32.0	46.0	63.4	73.8
-25	-5.6	1.0	8.6	17.7	28.7	44.2	62.5	73.8
-50	-8.4	-1.9	5.6	14.1	24.3	38.0	54.8	73.8
-75	-11.6	-5.8	1.0	7.9	16.4	28.1	41.8	48.8
-100	-17.6	-12.3	-6.6	-0.8	5.8	14.0	22.1	23.8
-125	-25.0	-20.8	-16.6	-12.6	-8.7	-4.7	-1.3	-1.2

Est. credit: +37.4¢ prem. +37.4¢ prem. -1.0¢ com. = +73.8¢

TABLE

changes in the soybean future's price in 25¢ increments — net profit area, in cents

price change	14	12	10	8	6	4	2	0
+125	-37.4	-35.2	-32.9	-30.4	-27.8	-25.5	-24.8	-24.8
+100	-24.8	-21.6	-18.1	-14.2	-9.7	-4.7	-0.3	0.2
+75	-14.6	-10.8	-6.4	-1.3	4.7	12.9	21.5	25.2
+50	-8.2	-3.7	1.5	7.4	14.6	24.4	36.5	50.2
+25	-4.5	0.4	6.1	12.9	20.8	31.5	43.9	50.2
0	-1.0	3.8	9.2	15.6	22.6	32.8	45.2	50.2
-25	-4.5	0.4	6.1	12.9	20.8	31.5	43.9	50.2
-50	-8.2	-3.7	1.5	7.4	14.6	24.4	36.5	50.2
-75	-14.6	-10.8	-6.4	-1.3	4.7	12.9	21.5	25.2
-100	-24.8	-21.6	-18.1	-14.2	-9.7	-4.7	-0.3	0.2
-125	-37.4	-35.2	-32.9	-30.4	-27.8	-25.5	-24.8	-24.8

Est. credit: +25.6¢ prem. +25.6¢ prem. -1.0¢ com. = +50.2¢

TABLE

changes in the soybean future's price in 25¢ increments — net profit area, in cents

price change	14	12	10	8	6	4	2	0
+125	-50.1	-49.4	-48.7	-47.9	-47.2	-46.8	-46.8	-46.8
+100	-32.5	-30.7	-28.9	-27.1	-25.3	-22.9	-21.9	-21.8
+75	-18.8	-16.4	-13.7	-10.5	-7.1	-2.4	1.8	3.2
+50	-9.1	-6.4	-3.1	0.7	5.2	11.4	18.8	28.2
+25	-3.1	0.0	3.4	7.7	12.5	18.9	26.1	28.2
0	-1.0	1.8	5.0	9.0	13.6	20.0	27.2	28.2
-25	-3.1	0.0	3.4	7.7	12.5	18.9	26.1	28.2
-50	-9.1	-6.4	-3.1	0.7	5.2	11.4	18.8	28.2
-75	-18.8	-16.4	-13.7	-10.5	-7.1	-2.4	1.8	3.2
-100	-32.5	-30.7	-28.9	-27.1	-25.3	-22.9	-21.9	-21.8
-125	-50.1	-49.4	-48.7	-47.9	-47.2	-46.8	-46.8	-46.8

Est. credit: +14.6¢ prem. +14.6¢ prem. -1.0¢ com. = +28.2¢

TABLE

changes in the soybean future's price in 25¢ increments — net profit area, in cents

price change	14	12	10	8	6	4	2	0
+125	-65.7	-65.7	-65.6	-65.6	-65.6	-65.6	-65.6	-65.6
+100	-42.4	-42.0	-41.5	-41.2	-40.9	-40.7	-40.6	-40.6
+75	-22.6	-21.7	-20.6	-19.4	-18.2	-16.9	-16.0	-15.6
+50	-10.4	-9.1	-6.4	-4.6	-2.4	0.4	4.0	9.4
+25	-1.8	-0.4	1.1	2.8	5.1	7.5	8.6	9.4
0	-1.0	0.4	2.2	4.0	6.6	8.6	9.4	9.4
-25	-1.8	-0.4	1.1	2.8	5.1	7.5	8.6	9.4
-50	-10.4	-9.1	-6.4	-4.6	-2.4	0.4	4.0	9.4
-75	-22.6	-21.7	-20.6	-19.4	-18.2	-16.9	-16.0	-15.6
-100	-42.4	-42.0	-41.5	-41.2	-40.9	-40.7	-40.6	-40.6
-125	-65.7	-65.7	-65.6	-65.6	-65.6	-65.6	-65.6	-65.6

Est. credit: +5.2¢ prem. +5.2¢ prem. -1.0¢ com. = +9.4¢

Wm Grandmill (1985) Ltd.

TABLE 8

changes in the soybean future's price in 25¢ increments — weeks to expiration — net profit area, in cents

price change	14	12	10	8	6	4	2	0
+125	-14.8	-11.1	-7.0	-2.6	2.9	10.8	20.7	27.2
+100	-6.8	-0.9	4.2	7.4	14.0	22.9	34.9	52.2
+75	2.3	7.9	9.9	15.5	22.3	31.4	47.0	52.2
+50	5.0	11.3	13.8	20.0	27.3	36.6	47.0	52.2
+25	-0.7	5.0	11.3	18.8	27.2	38.3	48.8	52.2
0	-1.0	5.2	12.2	19.8	28.4	38.6	49.5	52.2
-25	-0.7	5.0	11.3	18.8	27.2	38.3	48.8	52.2
-50	5.0	11.3	13.8	20.0	27.3	36.6	47.0	52.2
-75	2.3	7.9	9.9	15.5	22.3	31.4	47.0	52.2
-100	-6.8	-0.9	4.2	7.4	14.0	22.9	34.9	52.2
-125	-14.8	-11.1	-7.0	-2.6	2.9	10.8	20.7	27.2

Est. credit: +26.6¢ prem.+26.6¢ prem.-1.0¢ com. = +52.2¢

TABLE 6

changes in the soybean future's price in 25¢ increments — weeks to expiration — net profit area, in cents

price change	14	12	10	8	6	4	2	0
+125	-24.3	-21.8	-18.6	-15.1	-11.1	-5.3	1.6	5.2
+100	-14.6	-11.4	-7.6	-3.6	1.3	7.9	16.9	30.2
+75	-7.1	-3.9	-0.1	4.5	9.8	16.5	24.7	30.2
+50	-2.4	1.1	5.0	9.5	14.5	20.8	27.7	30.2
+25	-2.2	1.7	6.0	11.0	16.5	23.4	29.3	30.2
0	-1.0	2.8	7.0	11.4	16.8	23.2	29.4	30.2
-25	-2.2	1.7	6.0	11.0	16.5	23.4	29.3	30.2
-50	-2.4	1.1	5.0	9.5	14.5	20.8	27.7	30.2
-75	-7.1	-3.9	-0.1	4.5	9.8	16.5	24.7	30.2
-100	-14.6	-11.4	-7.6	-3.6	1.3	7.9	16.9	30.2
-125	-24.3	-21.8	-18.6	-15.1	-11.1	-5.3	1.6	5.2

Est. credit: +15.6¢ prem.+15.6¢ prem.-1.0¢ com. = +30.2¢

TABLE 4

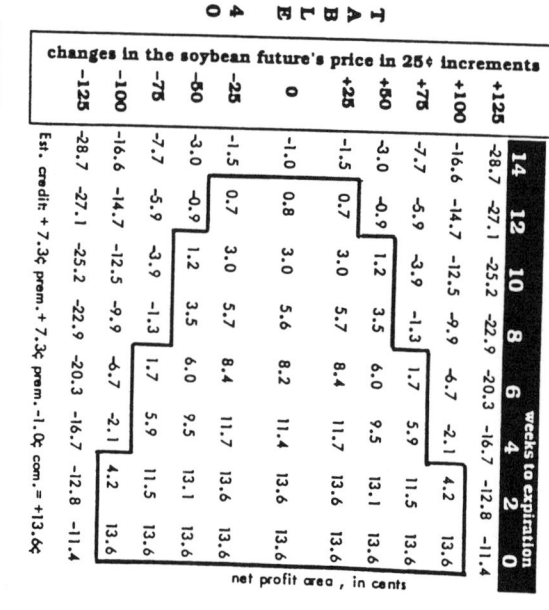

changes in the soybean future's price in 25¢ increments — weeks to expiration — net profit area, in cents

price change	14	12	10	8	6	4	2	0
+125	-28.7	-27.1	-25.2	-22.9	-20.3	-16.7	-12.8	-11.4
+100	-16.6	-14.7	-12.5	-9.9	-6.7	-2.1	4.2	13.6
+75	-7.7	-5.9	-3.9	-1.3	1.7	5.9	11.5	13.6
+50	-3.0	-0.9	1.2	3.5	6.0	9.5	13.1	13.6
+25	-1.5	0.7	3.0	5.7	8.4	11.7	13.6	13.6
0	-1.0	0.8	3.0	5.6	8.2	11.4	13.6	13.6
-25	-1.5	0.7	3.0	5.7	8.4	11.7	13.6	13.6
-50	-3.0	-0.9	1.2	3.5	6.0	9.5	13.1	13.6
-75	-7.7	-5.9	-3.9	-1.3	1.7	5.9	11.5	13.6
-100	-16.6	-14.7	-12.5	-9.9	-6.7	-2.1	4.2	13.6
-125	-28.7	-27.1	-25.2	-22.9	-20.3	-16.7	-12.8	-11.4

Est. credit: +7.3¢ prem.+7.3¢ prem.-1.0¢ com. = +13.6¢

TABLE 2

changes in the soybean future's price in 25¢ increments — weeks to expiration — net profit area, in cents

price change	14	12	10	8	6	4	2	0
+125	-29.3	-28.5	-27.6	-26.5	-25.4	-24.1	-23.2	-22.8
+100	-15.0	-14.0	-12.7	-11.3	-9.5	-6.8	-3.2	2.2
+75	-6.8	-5.9	-4.8	-3.5	-1.8	0.3	1.4	2.2
+50	-3.1	-2.3	-1.4	-0.5	0.8	1.8	2.2	2.2
+25	-0.5	0.1	0.7	1.3	1.9	2.0	2.2	2.2
0	-1.0	-0.4	0.4	1.2	2.0	2.2	2.2	2.2
-25	-0.5	0.1	0.7	1.3	1.9	2.0	2.2	2.2
-50	-3.1	-2.3	-1.4	-0.5	0.8	1.8	2.2	2.2
-75	-6.8	-5.9	-4.8	-3.5	-1.8	0.3	1.4	2.2
-100	-15.0	-14.0	-12.7	-11.3	-9.5	-6.8	-3.2	2.2
-125	-29.3	-28.5	-27.6	-26.5	-25.4	-24.1	-23.2	-22.8

Est. credit: +1.6¢ prem.+1.6¢ prem.-1.0¢ com. = +2.2¢

Wm Grandmill (1985) Ltd.

BUY A CALL or BUY A PUT
AT THE MONEY

16 weeks to expiration

TABLE 8

changes in the soybean future's price in 25¢ increments

Est. cost is: -58.5¢ premium -0.5¢ comm. = -59.0¢

	16	14	12	10	8	6	4	2	0
							weeks to expiration		
+125	79.3	76.9	74.5	71.7	68.6	66.3	66.0	66.0	66.0
+100	55.7	53.4	50.7	48.0	45.5	42.8	41.4	41.0	41.0
+75	35.0	32.7	30.3	27.7	24.9	22.0	18.6	16.1	16.0
+50	22.5	19.9	16.8	13.4	9.6	5.0	-0.9	-7.3	-9.0
+25	10.0	6.9	3.5	-0.4	-4.6	-9.9	-17.6	-27.5	-34.0
0	-0.5	-3.4	-6.8	-10.8	-15.5	-21.4	-30.0	-41.7	-59.0
-25	-10.1	-13.0	-16.3	-20.2	-24.8	-30.6	-39.0	-49.9	-59.0
-50	-18.8	-21.6	-24.9	-28.6	-32.8	-38.1	-45.1	-53.8	-59.0
-75	-22.7	-25.6	-28.9	-32.6	-37.1	-42.3	-49.4	-56.8	-59.0
-100	-29.6	-32.4	-35.5	-39.0	-42.8	-47.1	-52.2	-57.3	-59.0
-125	-37.2	-39.5	-41.9	-44.5	-47.5	-50.7	-54.7	-68.5	-59.0

net profit

TABLE 0

changes in the soybean future's price in 25¢ increments

Est cost is: -45.0¢ premium -0.5¢ comm. = -45.5¢

	16	14	12	10	8	6	4	2	0
							weeks to expiration		
+125	83.0	81.7	80.4	79.7	79.5	79.5	79.5	79.5	79.5
+100	59.5	58.7	57.3	56.2	55.4	54.8	54.5	54.5	54.5
+75	39.3	38.1	36.7	35.2	33.7	32.0	30.2	29.5	29.5
+50	24.4	22.5	20.4	18.1	15.5	12.5	8.7	5.0	4.5
+25	10.3	8.2	5.9	3.1	-0.2	-4.2	-10.0	-16.9	-20.5
0	-0.5	-2.7	-5.3	-8.4	-12.1	-16.6	-23.2	-32.2	-45.5
-25	-9.8	-12.1	-14.6	-17.6	-21.2	-25.6	-31.8	-40.0	-45.5
-50	-17.9	-19.9	-22.3	-25.0	-28.2	-31.7	-36.8	-43.0	-45.5
-75	-22.2	-24.2	-26.6	-29.3	-32.5	-36.0	-40.5	-44.7	-45.5
-100	-27.9	-29.8	-31.8	-33.9	-36.1	-38.8	-42.0	-45.1	-45.5
-125	-33.0	-34.4	-35.9	-37.5	-39.3	-41.3	-43.7	-45.4	-45.5

net profit area

TABLE 4

changes in the soybean future's price in 25¢ increments

Est. cost is: -31.0¢ premium -0.5¢ comm. = -32.1¢

	16	14	12	10	8	6	4	2	0
							weeks to expiration		
+125	92.9	92.9	92.9	92.9	92.9	92.9	92.9	92.9	92.9
+100	68.6	68.4	68.2	68.0	67.9	67.9	67.9	67.9	67.9
+75	46.4	45.8	45.2	44.6	43.9	43.3	42.9	42.9	42.9
+50	27.6	26.6	25.5	24.2	22.7	21.1	19.0	18.0	17.9
+25	11.7	10.2	8.6	6.7	4.4	1.8	-1.8	-5.7	-7.1
0	-0.5	-2.1	-3.9	-6.1	-8.6	-11.8	-16.4	-22.7	-32.1
-25	-9.6	-11.2	-12.9	-14.8	-17.3	-20.2	-24.4	-30.0	-32.1
-50	-16.2	-17.5	-18.9	-20.5	-22.5	-24.8	-28.0	-31.6	-32.1
-75	-20.5	-21.7	-23.1	-24.6	-26.4	-28.3	-30.5	-32.1	-32.1
-100	-23.8	-24.8	-25.7	-26.8	-28.1	-29.4	-31.0	-32.1	-32.1
-125	-26.7	-27.4	-28.2	-29.0	-29.9	-30.8	-31.8	-32.1	-32.1

net profit area

TABLE 2

changes in the soybean future's price in 25¢ increments

Estimated cost: -18.1¢ premium -0.5¢ comm. = -18.6¢

	16	14	12	10	8	6	4	2	0
							weeks to expiration		
+125	106.4	106.4	106.4	106.4	106.4	106.4	106.4	106.4	106.4
+100	81.4	81.4	81.4	81.4	81.4	81.4	81.4	81.4	81.4
+75	56.6	56.5	56.5	56.4	56.4	56.4	56.4	56.4	56.4
+50	33.5	33.1	32.7	32.3	32.0	31.7	31.5	31.4	31.4
+25	13.6	12.9	12.1	11.2	10.1	9.0	7.7	6.8	6.4
0	-0.5	-1.4	-2.4	-3.7	-5.1	-6.9	-9.6	-13.2	-18.4
-25	-8.8	-9.6	-10.5	-11.6	-12.9	-14.6	-16.7	-17.8	-18.6
-50	-12.8	-13.4	-14.1	-15.0	-16.0	-17.2	-18.2	-18.6	-18.6
-75	-15.9	-16.4	-16.9	-17.3	-17.7	-18.3	-18.6	-18.6	-18.6
-100	-16.7	-17.0	-17.3	-17.7	-18.1	-18.5	-18.6	-18.6	-18.6
-125	-17.9	-18.1	-18.2	-18.4	-18.6	-18.6	-18.6	-18.6	-18.6

net profit area , in cents

Wm Grandmill (1985) Ltd.

TABLE 8

changes in the soybean future's price in 25¢ increments	weeks to expiration								
	16	14	12	10	8	6	4	2	0
+125	53.4	51.0	48.6	46.0	43.2	40.3	36.9	34.4	34.2
+100	40.8	37.2	35.1	31.7	27.9	23.3	17.4	11.0	9.3
+75	28.3	25.2	21.8	17.9	13.8	8.4	0.7	-9.2	-15.7
+50	17.8	14.9	11.5	7.5	2.8	-3.1	-11.7	-23.4	-40.7
+25	8.2	5.3	2.0	-1.9	-6.5	-12.3	-20.7	-31.6	-40.7
0	-0.5	-3.3	-6.6	-10.3	-14.5	-19.8	-26.8	-35.4	-40.7
-25	-4.4	-7.3	-10.6	-14.3	-18.8	-24.3	-31.1	-38.5	-40.7
-50	-11.3	-14.1	-17.2	-20.7	-24.5	-28.8	-33.9	-39.0	-40.7
-75	-18.9	-21.2	-23.6	-26.2	-29.2	-32.4	-36.4	-40.2	-40.7
-100	-25.7	-28.2	-30.8	-32.7	-34.6	-36.7	-39.3	-40.7	-40.7
-125	-31.9	-33.6	-35.4	-37.0	-38.2	-39.3	-39.9	-40.7	-40.7

net profit

Est. cost is: - 40.2¢ premium - 0.5¢ comm. = -40.7¢

TABLE 6

changes in the soybean future's price in 25¢ increments	weeks to expiration								
	16	14	12	10	8	6	4	2	0
+125	56.7	55.5	54.1	52.6	51.1	49.4	47.6	46.9	46.9
+100	41.8	39.9	37.8	35.5	32.9	29.9	26.1	22.4	21.9
+75	27.7	25.6	23.3	20.5	17.2	13.2	7.4	0.5	-3.1
+50	16.9	14.7	12.1	9.0	5.3	0.8	-5.8	-14.8	-28.1
+25	7.6	5.3	2.8	-0.2	-3.8	-8.2	-14.4	-22.6	-28.1
0	-0.5	-2.5	-4.9	-7.6	-10.8	-14.3	-19.4	-25.6	-28.1
-25	-4.8	-6.8	-9.2	-11.9	-15.1	-18.6	-23.1	-27.3	-28.1
-50	-10.6	-12.5	-11.4	-13.5	-15.7	-18.4	-21.6	-24.7	-28.0
-75	-15.6	-17.0	-18.5	-20.1	-21.9	-23.9	-26.3	-28.0	-28.1
-100	-19.9	-21.1	-22.2	-23.4	-24.7	-26.2	-27.4	-28.1	-28.1
-125	-23.3	-24.1	-24.9	-25.7	-26.7	-27.6	-28.1	-28.1	-28.1

Estimated cost is: -27.6¢ premium - 0.5¢ comm. = - 28.1¢

TABLE 4

changes in the soybean future's price in 25¢ increments	weeks to expiration								
	16	14	12	10	8	6	4	2	0
+125	62.1	61.5	60.9	60.3	59.6	59.0	58.6	58.6	58.6
+100	43.3	42.3	41.2	39.9	38.4	36.8	34.7	33.7	33.6
+75	27.4	26.9	25.3	23.4	20.1	17.5	13.9	10.0	8.6
+50	15.2	13.6	11.8	9.6	7.1	3.9	-0.7	-7.0	-16.4
+25	6.1	4.5	2.8	0.9	-1.6	-4.5	-8.7	-14.3	-16.4
0	-0.5	-1.8	-3.2	-4.8	-6.8	-9.1	-12.3	-15.9	-16.4
-25	-4.8	-6.0	-7.4	-8.9	-10.7	-12.6	-14.8	-16.4	-16.4
-50	-8.1	-9.1	-10.0	-11.1	-12.4	-13.7	-15.3	-16.4	-16.4
-75	-11.1	-11.7	-12.5	-13.3	-14.2	-15.0	-16.1	-16.4	-16.4
-100	-13.8	-14.4	-15.1	-15.6	-15.9	-16.1	-16.3	-16.4	-16.4
-125	-15.8	-16.0	-16.1	-16.2	-16.3	-16.4	-16.4	-16.4	-16.4

net profit area

Estimated cost is: - 15.9¢ premium - 0.5¢ comm. = -16.4¢

TABLE 2

changes in the soybean future's price in 25¢ increments	weeks to expiration								
	16	14	12	10	8	6	4	2	0
+125	68.9	68.8	68.8	68.7	68.7	68.7	68.7	68.7	68.7
+100	45.8	45.4	45.0	44.6	44.3	44.0	43.8	43.7	43.7
+75	24.9	24.2	23.4	22.5	21.4	20.3	19.5	19.1	18.7
+50	11.8	10.9	9.9	8.6	7.2	5.4	2.7	-0.9	-6.3
+25	3.5	2.7	1.8	0.7	-0.6	-2.3	-4.4	-5.5	-6.3
0	-0.5	-1.1	-1.8	-2.7	-3.7	-4.9	-5.9	-6.3	-6.3
-25	-3.6	-4.1	-4.6	-5.0	-5.4	-6.0	-6.3	-6.3	-6.3
-50	-4.4	-4.7	-5.0	-5.4	-5.8	-6.2	-6.3	-6.3	-6.3
-75	-5.6	-5.8	-5.9	-6.1	-6.2	-6.3	-6.3	-6.3	-6.3
-100	-6.1	-6.2	-6.2	-6.3	-6.3	-6.3	-6.3	-6.3	-6.3
-125	-6.3	-6.3	-6.3	-6.3	-6.3	-6.3	-6.3	-6.3	-6.3

net profit area

Estimated cost is: - 5.8¢ premium - 0.5¢ comm. = - 6.3¢

Wm Grandmill (1985) Ltd.

136

TABLE 8

changes in the soybean future's price in 25¢ increments

	weeks to expiration 16	14	12	10	8	6	4	2	0
+125	-80.3	-77.9	-75.5	-72.7	-69.6	-67.3	-67.0	-67.0	-67.0
+100	-56.7	-53.4	-51.7	-49.0	-46.5	-43.8	-42.4	-42.0	-42.0
+75	-36.0	-33.7	-31.3	-28.7	-25.9	-23.0	-19.6	-17.1	-17.0
+50	-23.5	-20.9	-17.8	-14.4	-10.6	-6.0	-0.1	6.3	8.0
+25	-11.0	-7.9	-4.5	-0.6	3.6	8.9	16.6	26.5	33.0
0	-0.5	2.4	5.8	9.8	14.5	20.4	29.0	40.7	58.0
-25	9.1	12.0	15.3	19.2	23.8	29.6	38.0	48.9	58.0
-50	17.8	20.6	23.9	27.6	31.8	37.1	44.1	52.8	58.0
-75	21.7	24.6	27.9	31.5	36.0	41.3	48.4	55.8	58.0
-100	28.6	31.4	34.5	38.0	41.8	46.1	51.2	56.3	58.0
-125	36.2	38.5	40.9	43.5	46.5	49.7	53.7	57.5	58.0

net profit area , in cents

Estimated credit is: +58.5¢ premium - 0.5¢ comm. = +58.0¢

TABLE 6

changes in the soybean future's price in 25¢ increments

	weeks to expiration 16	14	12	10	8	6	4	2	0
+125	-84.0	-82.7	-81.4	-80.7	-80.5	-80.5	-80.5	-80.5	-80.5
+100	-60.5	-59.7	-58.3	-57.2	-56.4	-55.8	-55.5	-55.5	-55.5
+75	-40.3	-39.1	-37.7	-36.2	-34.7	-33.0	-31.2	-30.5	-30.5
+50	-25.4	-23.5	-21.4	-19.1	-16.5	-13.5	-9.7	-6.0	-5.5
+25	-11.3	-9.2	-6.9	-4.1	-0.8	3.2	9.0	15.9	19.5
0	-0.5	1.7	4.3	7.4	11.1	15.6	22.2	31.2	44.5
-25	8.9	11.1	13.6	16.6	20.2	24.6	30.8	39.0	44.5
-50	16.9	18.9	21.3	24.0	27.2	30.7	35.8	42.0	44.5
-75	21.2	23.2	25.6	28.3	31.5	35.0	39.5	43.7	44.5
-100	26.9	28.8	30.8	32.9	35.1	37.8	41.0	44.1	44.5
-125	32.0	33.4	34.9	36.5	38.3	40.3	42.7	44.4	44.5

net profit area , in cents

Estimated credit is: +45.0¢ premium - 0.5¢ comm. = +44.5¢

TABLE 4

changes in the soybean future's price in 25¢ increments

	weeks to expiration 16	14	12	10	8	6	4	2	0
+125	-93.9	-93.9	-93.9	-93.9	-93.9	-93.9	-93.9	-93.9	-93.9
+100	-69.6	-69.4	-69.2	-69.0	-68.9	-68.9	-68.9	-68.9	-68.9
+75	-47.4	-46.8	-46.2	-45.6	-44.9	-44.3	-43.9	-43.9	-43.9
+50	-28.6	-27.6	-26.5	-25.2	-23.7	-22.1	-20.0	-19.0	-18.9
+25	-12.7	-11.2	-9.6	-7.7	-5.4	-2.8	0.8	4.7	6.1
0	-0.5	1.1	2.9	5.1	7.6	10.8	15.4	21.7	31.1
-25	8.6	10.2	11.9	13.8	16.3	19.2	23.4	29.0	31.1
-50	15.2	16.5	17.9	19.5	21.5	23.8	27.0	30.6	31.1
-75	19.5	20.7	22.1	23.6	25.4	27.3	29.5	31.1	31.1
-100	22.8	23.8	24.7	25.8	27.1	28.4	30.0	31.1	31.1
-125	25.7	26.4	27.2	28.0	28.9	29.8	30.8	31.1	31.1

net profit area , in cents

Estimated credit is: +31.6¢ premium - 0.5¢ comm. = +31.1¢

TABLE 2

changes in the soybean future's price in 25¢ increments

	weeks to expiration 16	14	12	10	8	6	4	2	0
+125	-107.4	-107.4	-107.4	-107.4	-107.4	-107.4	-107.4	-107.4	-107.4
+100	-82.4	-82.4	-82.4	-82.4	-82.4	-82.4	-82.4	-82.4	-82.4
+75	-57.6	-57.5	-57.5	-57.4	-57.4	-57.4	-57.4	-57.4	-57.4
+50	-34.5	-34.1	-33.7	-33.3	-33.0	-32.7	-32.5	-32.4	-32.4
+25	-14.6	-13.9	-13.3	-12.2	-11.1	-10.0	-8.7	-7.8	-7.4
0	-0.5	0.4	1.4	2.7	4.1	5.9	8.6	12.2	17.6
-25	7.8	8.6	9.5	10.6	11.9	13.6	15.7	16.8	17.6
-50	11.8	12.4	13.1	14.0	15.0	16.2	17.2	17.6	17.6
-75	14.9	15.4	15.9	16.3	16.7	17.3	17.6	17.6	17.6
-100	15.7	16.0	16.3	16.7	17.1	17.5	17.6	17.6	17.6
-125	16.9	17.1	17.2	17.4	17.5	17.6	17.6	17.6	17.6

net profit area , in cents

Estimated credit is: +18.1¢ premium - 0.5¢ comm. = +17.6¢

16 weeks to expiration

Wm Grandmill (1985) Ltd.

TABLE 8

changes in the soybean future's price in 25¢ increments

	weeks to expiration								
	16	14	12	10	8	6	4	2	0
+125	-54.4	-52.0	-49.6	-47.0	-44.2	-41.3	-37.9	-35.4	-35.3
+100	-41.8	-38.2	-36.1	-32.7	-28.9	-24.3	-18.4	-12.0	-10.3
+75	-29.3	-26.2	-22.8	-18.9	-14.8	-9.4	-1.7	8.2	14.7
+50	-18.8	-15.9	-12.5	-8.5	-3.8	2.1	10.7	22.4	39.7
+25	-9.2	-6.3	-3.0	0.9	5.5	11.3	19.7	30.6	39.7
0	-0.5	2.3	5.6	9.3	13.5	18.8	25.8	34.4	39.7
-25	3.4	6.3	9.6	13.3	17.8	23.3	30.1	37.5	39.7
-50	17.9	20.2	22.6	25.2	28.2	31.4	35.4	39.2	39.7
-75	24.7	27.2	29.8	31.7	33.6	35.7	38.0	39.2	39.7
-100	30.9	32.6	34.4	36.0	37.2	38.3	38.9	39.7	39.7

Estimated credit is: + 40.2¢ premium - 0.5¢ comm. = + 39.7¢

net profit area , in cents

TABLE 6

changes in the soybean future's price in 25¢ increments

	weeks to expiration								
	16	14	12	10	8	6	4	2	0
+125	-57.7	-56.5	-55.1	-53.6	-52.1	-50.4	-48.6	-47.9	-47.9
+100	-42.8	-40.9	-38.8	-36.5	-33.9	-30.9	-27.1	-23.4	-22.9
+75	-28.7	-26.6	-24.3	-21.5	-18.2	-14.2	-8.4	-1.5	2.1
+50	-17.9	-15.7	-13.1	-10.0	-6.3	-1.8	4.8	13.8	27.1
+25	-8.6	-6.3	-3.8	-0.8	2.8	7.2	13.4	21.6	27.1
0	-0.5	1.5	3.9	6.6	9.8	13.3	18.4	24.6	27.1
-25	3.8	5.8	8.2	10.9	14.1	17.6	22.1	26.3	27.1
-50	9.6	11.5	12.5	14.7	17.4	20.6	23.7	27.1	27.1
-75	14.6	16.0	17.5	19.1	20.9	22.9	25.3	27.0	27.1
-100	18.9	20.1	21.2	22.4	23.7	25.2	26.4	27.1	27.1
-125	22.3	23.1	23.9	24.7	25.7	26.6	27.1	27.1	27.1

Estimated credit is: + 27.6¢ premium - 0.5¢ comm. = + 27.1¢

net profit area , in cents

TABLE 4

changes in the soybean future's price in 25¢ increments

	weeks to expiration								
	16	14	12	10	8	6	4	2	0
+125	-63.1	-62.5	-61.9	-61.3	-60.6	-60.0	-59.6	-59.6	-59.6
+100	-44.3	-43.3	-42.2	-40.9	-39.4	-37.8	-35.7	-34.7	-34.6
+75	-28.4	-27.9	-26.3	-24.4	-21.1	-18.5	-14.9	-11.0	-9.6
+50	-16.2	-14.6	-12.8	-10.6	-8.1	-4.9	-0.3	6.0	15.4
+25	-7.1	-5.5	-3.8	-1.9	0.6	3.5	7.7	13.3	15.4
0	-0.5	0.8	2.2	3.8	5.8	8.1	11.3	14.9	15.4
-25	3.8	5.0	6.4	7.9	9.7	11.6	13.8	15.4	15.4
-50	7.1	8.1	9.0	10.1	11.4	12.7	14.3	15.4	15.4
-75	10.1	10.7	11.5	12.3	13.2	14.0	15.1	15.4	15.4
-100	12.8	13.4	14.1	14.6	14.9	15.1	15.4	15.4	15.4
-125	14.8	15.0	15.1	15.2	15.3	15.4	15.4	15.4	15.4

Estimated credit is: + 15.9¢ premium - 0.5¢ comm. = - 15.4¢

net profit area , in cents

TABLE 2

changes in the soybean future's price in 25¢ increments

	weeks to expiration								
	16	14	12	10	8	6	4	2	0
+125	-69.9	-69.8	-69.8	-69.7	-69.7	-69.7	-69.7	-69.7	-69.7
+100	-46.8	-46.4	-46.0	-45.6	-45.3	-45.0	-44.8	-44.7	-44.7
+75	-25.9	-25.2	-24.4	-23.5	-22.4	-21.3	-20.5	-20.1	-19.7
+50	-12.8	-11.9	-10.9	-9.6	-8.2	-6.4	-3.7	-0.1	5.3
+25	-4.5	-3.7	-2.8	-1.7	-0.4	1.3	3.4	4.5	5.3
0	-0.5	0.1	0.8	1.7	2.7	3.9	4.9	5.3	5.3
-25	2.6	3.1	3.6	4.0	4.4	5.0	5.3	5.3	5.3
-50	3.4	3.7	4.0	4.4	4.8	5.2	5.3	5.3	5.3
-75	4.6	4.8	4.9	5.1	5.2	5.3	5.3	5.3	5.3
-100	5.1	5.2	5.2	5.3	5.3	5.3	5.3	5.3	5.3
-125	5.3	5.3	5.3	5.3	5.3	5.3	5.3	5.3	5.3

Estimated credit is: + 5.8¢ premium - 0.5¢ comm. = + 5.3¢

net profit area , in cents

Wm Grandmill (1985) Ltd.

BULL or BEAR SPREAD – #1

**BUY A CALL AT THE MONEY
and SELL A CALL AT 25¢ OUT OF THE MONEY
OR
BUY A PUT AT THE MONEY
and SELL A PUT AT 25¢ OUT OF THE MONEY**

weeks to expiration: **16**

TABLE 0

changes in the soybean future's price in 25¢ increments	weeks to expiration 16	14	12	10	8	6	4	2	0
+125	13.0	13.1	13.2	13.4	13.6	13.8	14.0	14.4	14.4
+100	8.2	8.6	9.1	9.6	10.3	10.8	12.8	14.4	14.4
+75	5.0	5.3	5.7	6.2	6.8	7.8	9.4	12.8	14.4
+50	2.2	2.4	2.7	3.1	3.6	4.3	6.1	9.6	14.4
+25	0.6	0.6	0.7	0.8	0.9	1.1	1.8	3.6	14.4
0	-1.0	-1.0	-1.1	-1.2	-1.3	-1.4	-1.6	-2.6	-10.6
-25	-1.9	-2.0	-2.0	-2.2	-2.6	-3.3	-4.5	-6.7	-10.6
-50	-2.2	-2.2	-2.4	-2.7	-3.1	-3.7	-4.6	-7.6	-10.6
-75	-2.6	-2.6	-2.8	-3.4	-3.7	-5.0	-6.0	-8.6	-10.6
-100	-3.0	-3.0	-3.5	-4.2	-5.0	-6.0	-7.0	-9.4	-10.6
-125	-3.2	-3.2	-3.8	-4.6	-5.4	-6.6	-7.8	-10.1	-10.6

net profit area, in cents

Est. cost: -58.5¢ premium +48.9¢ prem. -1.0¢ comm.= -10.6¢

TABLE 0

changes in the soybean future's price in 25¢ increments	weeks to expiration 16	14	12	10	8	6	4	2	0
+125	13.2	13.2	13.3	13.5	13.9	14.4	14.7	14.7	14.7
+100	9.4	9.8	10.2	10.7	11.4	12.5	14.0	14.7	14.7
+75	6.3	6.6	6.9	7.2	7.9	9.2	11.2	14.2	14.7
+50	3.8	4.0	4.3	4.7	5.4	6.4	8.4	11.6	14.7
+25	0.4	0.6	0.9	1.2	1.6	2.1	2.9	5.0	14.7
0	-1.0	-1.0	-1.1	-1.2	-1.2	-1.3	-1.7	-2.5	-10.3
-25	-2.2	-2.4	-2.6	-2.9	-3.3	-4.5	-5.3	-7.3	-10.3
-50	-3.3	-3.6	-3.9	-4.3	-4.9	-5.6	-6.6	-8.6	-10.3
-75	-4.4	-4.7	-5.1	-5.7	-6.7	-7.5	-8.6	-9.9	-10.3
-100	-5.4	-5.8	-6.2	-6.7	-7.1	-7.8	-8.7	-10.0	-10.3
-125	-5.9	-6.2	-6.6	-7.0	-7.5	-8.0	-9.0	-10.2	-10.3

net profit area, in cents

Est. cost: -45.0¢ prem. +35.7¢ prem. -1.0¢ comm. = -10.3¢

TABLE 0

changes in the soybean future's price in 25¢ increments	weeks to expiration 16	14	12	10	8	6	4	2	0
+125	14.2	14.4	14.6	14.8	14.9	14.9	14.9	14.9	14.9
+100	12.1	12.5	12.9	13.3	13.9	14.5	14.9	14.9	14.9
+75	8.7	9.1	9.6	10.3	11.1	12.1	13.9	14.9	14.9
+50	5.8	6.3	6.8	7.4	8.2	9.2	11.1	13.6	14.9
+25	2.1	2.2	2.4	2.7	2.9	3.5	4.5	6.9	14.9
0	-1.0	-1.1	-1.1	-1.3	-1.5	-1.7	-2.1	-2.9	-10.1
-25	-3.5	-3.8	-4.1	-4.4	-4.9	-5.5	-6.5	-8.5	-10.1
-50	-5.7	-5.8	-5.9	-6.0	-6.2	-6.6	-7.6	-9.6	-10.1
-75	-6.8	-7.1	-7.5	-7.8	-8.1	-8.5	-8.9	-9.8	-10.1
-100	-7.2	-7.4	-7.7	-7.9	-8.3	-8.8	-9.3	-10.1	-10.1
-125	-7.4	-7.6	-7.8	-8.1	-8.5	-9.0	-9.8	-10.1	-10.1

net profit area, in cents

Est. cost: -31.6¢ prem. +22.5¢ prem. -1.0¢ comm. = -10.1¢

TABLE 2

changes in the soybean future's price in 25¢ increments	weeks to expiration 16	14	12	10	8	6	4	2	0
+125	15.7	15.7	15.7	15.7	15.7	15.7	15.7	15.7	15.7
+100	15.5	15.6	15.6	15.7	15.7	15.7	15.7	15.7	15.7
+75	13.8	14.1	14.5	14.8	15.1	15.4	15.6	15.7	15.7
+50	10.6	10.9	11.3	11.8	12.6	13.4	14.5	15.3	15.7
+25	4.8	5.0	5.2	5.6	5.9	6.6	8.0	10.7	15.7
0	-1.0	-1.1	-1.2	-1.4	-1.5	-1.6	-2.2	-2.7	-9.3
-25	-5.3	-5.5	-5.7	-5.9	-6.3	-6.7	-7.8	-8.7	-9.3
-50	-6.2	-6.3	-6.5	-7.0	-7.5	-8.1	-8.9	-9.3	-9.3
-75	-7.1	-7.3	-7.5	-7.8	-8.4	-9.1	-9.2	-9.3	-9.3
-100	-8.0	-8.2	-8.4	-8.6	-8.9	-9.2	-9.3	-9.3	-9.3
-125	-8.8	-8.9	-9.0	-9.1	-9.2	-9.3	-9.3	-9.3	-9.3

net profit area, in cents

Est. cost: -18.1¢ prem. +9.8¢ premium -1.0¢ comm. = -9.3¢

BULL or BEAR SPREAD – #2

BUY A CALL AT THE MONEY
and SELL 2 CALLS AT 50¢ OUT OF THE MONEY
OR
BUY A PUT AT THE MONEY
and SELL 2 PUTS AT 50¢ OUT OF THE MONEY

16 weeks to expiration

TABLE (net profit area, in cents)

changes in the soybean future's price in 25¢ increments

price change	weeks to expiration 16	14	12	10	8	6	4	2	0
+125	-29.4	-27.1	-25.0	-22.3	-19.8	-16.3	-9.8	-4.8	-4.6
+100	-27.9	-25.0	-21.5	-17.4	-12.3	-5.8	4.6	17.0	20.4
+75	-23.6	-19.7	-15.3	-10.1	-4.5	3.2	15.2	32.5	45.4
+50	-15.1	-11.9	-8.2	-3.6	2.0	9.2	10.5	37.5	70.4
+25	-8.4	-5.7	-2.5	1.4	6.4	12.7	21.8	33.7	45.4
0	-1.5	1.2	4.4	7.8	11.5	16.2	21.6	27.3	20.4
-25	-3.3	-0.4	2.9	6.4	10.8	15.4	21.2	25.1	20.4
-50	1.8	4.6	7.5	10.8	14.2	17.5	20.7	22.2	20.4
-75	13.1	14.8	16.3	17.8	19.3	20.5	21.4	21.6	20.4
-100	18.2	19.7	20.9	22.0	22.5	22.6	22.1	21.2	20.4
-125	24.6	25.7	26.9	27.9	26.9	25.7	23.1	20.9	20.4

Est. credit: -58.5¢ prem. +40.2¢ prem. +40.2¢ prem. -1.5¢ com. =20.4¢

TABLE (net profit area, in cents)

changes in the soybean future's price in 25¢ increments

price change	weeks to expiration 16	14	12	10	8	6	4	2	0
+125	-32.4	-31.3	-29.8	-27.5	-24.7	-21.3	-17.7	-16.3	-16.3
+100	-26.1	-23.8	-20.6	-16.8	-12.4	-7.0	0.3	7.7	8.7
+75	-18.0	-15.1	-11.9	-7.8	-2.7	3.6	13.4	26.5	33.7
+50	-11.4	-8.9	-5.8	-1.9	2.9	8.9	18.3	32.6	58.7
+25	-6.9	-4.4	-1.7	1.5	5.4	10.2	13.4	26.3	33.7
0	-1.5	0.3	2.5	4.8	7.5	10.0	13.6	17.0	8.7
-25	-2.2	-0.3	1.8	4.2	7.0	9.6	12.6	17.0	8.7
-50	1.3	3.0	4.5	6.0	7.4	9.1	10.4	10.4	8.7
-75	7.0	7.8	8.4	8.9	9.3	9.8	10.1	10.3	8.7
-100	9.2	9.6	10.0	10.3	10.5	10.8	10.3	9.6	8.7
-125	11.6	11.8	11.9	12.0	12.1	11.9	10.5	8.8	8.7

Est. credit: -45.0¢ pre. +27.6¢ pre. +27.6¢ pre. -1.5¢ com. =+8.7¢

TABLE (net profit area)

changes in the soybean future's price in 25¢ increments

price change	weeks to expiration 16	14	12	10	8	6	4	2	0
+125	-33.3	-32.1	-30.9	-29.7	-28.3	-27.1	-26.3	-26.3	-26.3
+100	-20.0	-18.2	-16.2	-13.8	-10.9	-7.7	-3.5	-1.5	-1.3
+75	-10.4	-8.0	-5.4	-2.2	1.7	6.3	13.1	20.9	23.7
+50	-2.5	-0.8	1.0	3.2	5.6	8.8	13.6	30.2	48.7
+25	-2.5	-0.8	0.1	1.5	3.0	5.6	11.5	18.6	23.7
0	-1.5	-0.1	0.0	0.3	0.5	0.6	0.8	0.8	-1.3
-25	-2.0	-1.6	-1.3	-0.9	-0.4	-0.1	-0.3	-0.8	-1.3
-50	-2.0	-2.0	-1.4	-0.9	-0.3	0.3	0.5	0.6	-1.3
-75	-2.0	-1.8	-1.7	-1.6	-1.3	-0.9	-0.4	-0.1	-1.3
-100	-1.8	-1.8	-1.8	-1.8	-1.8	-1.3	-0.7	-0.3	-1.3
-125	-2.8	-2.6	-2.6	-2.0	-2.0	-1.6	-1.3	-1.3	-1.3

Est. cost: -31.6¢ prem. +15.9¢ prem. +15.9¢ prem. -1.5¢ com. =-1.3¢

TABLE (net profit area)

changes in the soybean future's price in 25¢ increments

price change	weeks to expiration 16	14	12	10	8	6	4	2	0
+125	-33.4	-33.2	-33.2	-33.0	-33.0	-33.0	-33.0	-33.0	-33.0
+100	-12.2	-11.4	-10.6	-9.8	-9.2	-8.6	-8.2	-8.0	-8.0
+75	2.6	4.1	5.7	7.4	9.6	11.8	14.4	16.2	17.0
+50	7.9	9.3	10.9	13.1	15.6	18.9	24.1	31.2	42.0
+25	4.6	5.5	6.5	7.8	9.4	11.6	14.2	15.8	17.0
0	-1.5	-1.2	-0.8	-0.5	0.1	0.9	0.6	-2.6	-8.0
-25	-3.4	-3.4	-3.5	-3.8	-4.3	-5.0	-6.3	-7.2	-8.0
-50	-6.0	-6.0	-6.1	-6.2	-6.4	-6.8	-7.6	-8.0	-8.0
-75	-6.8	-6.9	-7.0	-7.1	-7.3	-7.7	-7.8	-8.0	-8.0
-100	-7.0	-7.1	-7.2	-7.4	-7.6	-7.8	-8.0	-8.0	-8.0
-125	-7.4	-7.5	-7.6	-7.8	-7.9	-8.0	-8.0	-8.0	-8.0

Est. cost: -18.1¢ prem. +5.8¢ prem. +5.8¢ prem. -1.5¢ com. =-8.0¢

SELL A STRADDLE

SELL A CALL AT THE MONEY
and SELL A PUT AT THE MONEY

TABLE 0

changes in the soybean future's price in 25¢ increments

	16	14	12	10	8	6	4	2	0
+125	-44.1	-39.4	-34.6	-29.2	-23.1	-17.6	-13.3	-9.5	-9.0
+100	-28.1	-23.0	-17.2	-11.0	-4.7	2.3	8.8	14.3	16.0
+75	-14.3	-9.1	-3.4	2.9	10.2	18.3	28.8	38.7	41.0
+50	-5.7	-0.3	6.1	13.2	21.2	31.1	44.0	59.1	66.0
+25	-1.9	4.1	10.8	18.6	27.4	38.5	54.6	75.4	91.0
0	-1.0	4.8	11.6	19.6	29.0	40.8	58.0	81.4	116.0
-25	-1.9	4.1	10.8	18.6	27.4	38.5	54.6	75.4	91.0
-50	-5.7	-0.3	6.1	13.2	21.2	31.1	44.0	59.1	66.0
-75	-14.3	-9.1	-3.4	2.9	10.2	18.3	28.8	38.7	41.0
-100	-28.1	-23.0	-17.2	-11.0	-4.7	2.3	8.8	14.3	16.0
-125	-44.1	-39.4	-34.6	-29.2	-23.1	-17.6	-13.3	-9.5	-9.0

weeks to expiration · net profit area , in cents

Estimated credit: +58.5¢ prem. + 58.5¢ prem. -1.0¢ comm. =+116.0¢

TABLE 0

changes in the soybean future's price in 25¢ increments

	16	14	12	10	8	6	4	2	0
+125	-51.0	-47.3	-45.5	-44.2	-42.2	-40.2	-37.8	-36.1	-36.0
+100	-33.5	-30.2	-27.2	-24.3	-21.3	-18.0	-14.5	-11.4	-11.0
+75	-19.1	-15.9	-12.1	-7.9	-3.2	2.0	8.3	13.2	14.0
+50	-8.5	-4.6	-0.1	4.9	10.7	17.5	26.1	36.0	39.0
+25	-2.5	1.9	6.7	12.5	19.4	27.8	39.8	54.9	64.0
0	-1.0	3.4	8.6	14.8	22.2	31.2	44.4	62.4	89.0
-25	-2.5	1.9	6.7	12.5	19.4	27.8	39.8	54.9	64.0
-50	-8.5	-4.6	-0.1	4.9	10.7	17.5	26.1	36.0	39.0
-75	-19.1	-15.9	-12.1	-7.9	-3.2	2.0	8.3	13.2	14.0
-100	-33.5	-30.2	-27.2	-24.3	-21.3	-18.0	-14.5	-11.4	-11.0
-125	-51.0	-47.3	-45.5	-44.2	-42.2	-40.2	-37.8	-36.1	-36.0

weeks to expiration · net profit area , in cents

Est. credit: +45.0¢ prem. +45.0¢ prem. -1.0¢ comm. =+89.0¢

TABLE 4

changes in the soybean future's price in 25¢ increments

	16	14	12	10	8	6	4	2	0
+125	-68.1	-67.5	-66.7	-65.9	-65.0	-64.1	-63.1	-62.8	-62.8
+100	-46.8	-45.6	-44.5	-43.2	-41.8	-40.4	-38.9	-37.8	-37.8
+75	-27.9	-26.1	-24.1	-21.9	-19.5	-17.0	-14.4	-12.8	-12.8
+50	-13.4	-11.1	-8.6	-5.7	-2.2	1.7	7.0	11.6	12.2
+25	4.1	-1.0	2.3	6.1	10.9	16.4	24.2	33.7	37.2
0	-1.0	2.2	5.8	10.2	15.2	21.6	30.8	43.4	62.2
-25	4.1	-1.0	2.3	6.1	10.9	16.4	24.2	33.7	37.2
-50	-13.4	-11.1	-8.6	-5.7	-2.2	1.7	7.0	11.6	12.2
-75	-27.9	-26.1	-24.1	-21.9	-19.5	-17.0	-14.4	-12.8	-12.8
-100	-46.8	-45.6	-44.5	-43.2	-41.8	-40.4	-38.9	-37.8	-37.8
-125	-68.1	-67.5	-66.7	-65.9	-65.0	-64.1	-63.1	-62.8	-62.8

weeks to expiration · net profit area , in cents

Est. credit: +31.6¢ prem. + 31.6¢ prem. -1.0¢ comm. = + 62.2¢

TABLE 2

changes in the soybean future's price in 25¢ increments

	16	14	12	10	8	6	4	2	0
+125	-90.5	-90.3	-90.2	-90.0	-89.9	-89.8	-89.8	-89.8	-89.8
+100	-66.7	-66.4	-66.1	-65.7	-65.3	-64.9	-64.8	-64.8	-64.8
+75	-42.6	-42.1	-41.6	-41.1	-40.6	-40.1	-39.8	-39.8	-39.8
+50	-22.7	-21.7	-20.6	-19.3	-18.0	-16.5	-15.3	-14.8	-14.8
+25	-6.8	-5.3	-3.6	-1.6	0.8	3.6	7.0	9.7	10.2
0	-1.0	0.8	2.8	5.4	8.2	11.8	17.2	24.4	35.2
-25	-6.8	-5.3	-3.6	-1.6	0.8	3.6	7.0	9.7	10.2
-50	-22.7	-21.7	-20.6	-19.3	-18.0	-16.5	-15.3	-14.8	-14.8
-75	-42.6	-42.1	-41.6	-41.1	-40.6	-40.1	-39.8	-39.8	-39.8
-100	-66.7	-66.4	-66.1	-65.7	-65.3	-64.9	-64.8	-64.8	-64.8
-125	-90.5	-90.3	-90.2	-90.0	-89.9	-89.8	-89.8	-89.8	-89.8

weeks to expiration · net profit area

Est. credit: +18.1¢ prem. +18.1¢ prem. -1.0¢ comm. = +35.2¢

Wm Grandmill (1985) Ltd.

SELL A STRANGLE – #1

SELL A CALL AT 50¢ OUT OF THE MONEY and SELL A PUT AT 50¢ OUT OF THE MONEY

TABLE

changes in the soybean future's price in 25¢ increments

	16	14	12	10	8	6	4	2	0
+125	-23.4	-19.4	-15.2	-11.0	-7.0	-3.1	1.0	4.3	4.4
+100	-17.1	-12.0	-6.7	-1.0	4.8	11.4	19.6	27.7	29.4
+75	-11.4	-6.0	-0.2	6.6	13.5	22.0	33.7	47.4	54.4
+50	-8.5	-2.8	3.7	11.2	19.7	29.9	43.6	60.4	79.4
+25	-5.8	0.0	6.6	14.2	23.3	34.3	49.8	68.1	79.4
0	-1.0	4.6	11.2	18.6	27.0	37.6	51.6	69.0	79.4
-25	-5.8	0.0	6.6	14.2	23.3	34.3	49.8	68.1	79.4
-50	-8.5	-2.8	3.7	11.2	19.7	29.9	43.6	60.4	79.4
-75	-11.4	-6.0	-0.2	6.6	13.5	22.0	33.7	47.4	54.4
-100	-17.1	-12.0	-6.7	-1.0	4.8	11.4	19.6	27.7	29.4
-125	-23.4	-19.4	-15.2	-11.0	-7.0	-3.1	1.0	4.3	4.4

weeks to expiration — net profit area, in cents

Est. credit: +40.2¢ prem. + 40.2¢ prem. -1.0¢ com. = +79.4¢

TABLE

changes in the soybean future's price in 25¢ increments

	16	14	12	10	8	6	4	2	0
+125	-35.4	-33.4	-31.2	-28.9	-26.4	-23.8	-21.5	-20.8	-20.8
+100	-23.9	-20.8	-17.6	-14.1	-10.2	-5.7	-0.7	3.7	4.2
+75	-14.1	-10.4	-6.8	-2.4	2.7	8.7	16.9	25.5	29.2
+50	-8.3	-4.2	0.3	5.5	11.4	18.6	28.4	40.5	54.2
+25	-4.8	-0.5	4.4	10.1	16.9	24.8	35.5	47.9	54.2
0	-1.0	3.0	7.8	13.2	19.6	26.6	36.8	49.2	54.2
-25	-4.8	-0.5	4.4	10.1	16.9	24.8	35.5	47.9	54.2
-50	-8.3	-4.2	0.3	5.5	11.4	18.6	28.4	40.5	54.2
-75	-14.1	-10.4	-6.8	-2.4	2.7	8.7	16.9	25.5	29.2
-100	-23.9	-20.8	-17.6	-14.1	-10.2	-5.7	-0.7	3.7	4.2
-125	-35.4	-33.4	-31.2	-28.9	-26.4	-23.8	-21.5	-20.8	-20.8

weeks to expiration — net profit area, in cents

Est. credit: +27.6¢ prem. +27.6¢ prem. -1.0¢ com. = +54.2¢

TABLE

changes in the soybean future's price in 25¢ increments

	16	14	12	10	8	6	4	2	0
+125	-48.3	-47.5	-46.8	-46.1	-45.3	-44.6	-44.2	-44.2	-44.2
+100	-31.5	-29.9	-28.1	-26.3	-24.5	-22.7	-20.3	-19.3	-19.2
+75	-18.3	-16.2	-13.8	-11.1	-7.9	-4.5	0.2	4.4	5.8
+50	-9.0	-6.4	-3.7	-0.4	3.4	7.9	14.1	21.5	30.8
+25	-3.3	-0.5	2.6	6.0	10.3	15.1	21.5	28.7	30.8
0	-1.0	1.6	4.4	7.6	11.6	16.2	22.6	29.8	30.8
-25	-3.3	-0.5	2.6	6.0	10.3	15.1	21.5	28.7	30.8
-50	-9.0	-6.4	-3.7	-0.4	3.4	7.9	14.1	21.5	30.8
-75	-18.3	-16.2	-13.8	-11.1	-7.9	-4.5	0.2	4.4	5.8
-100	-31.5	-29.9	-28.1	-26.3	-24.5	-22.7	-20.3	-19.3	-19.2
-125	-48.3	-47.5	-46.8	-46.1	-45.3	-44.6	-44.2	-44.2	-44.2

weeks to expiration — net profit area, in cents

Est. credit: +15.9¢ prem. +15.9¢ prem. -1.0¢ com. = +30.8¢

TABLE

changes in the soybean future's price in 25¢ increments

	16	14	12	10	8	6	4	2	0
+125	-64.6	-64.5	-64.5	-64.4	-64.4	-64.4	-64.4	-64.4	-64.4
+100	-41.7	-41.2	-40.8	-40.3	-39.7	-39.5	-39.4	-39.4	-39.4
+75	-22.3	-21.4	-20.5	-19.4	-18.2	-17.0	-15.7	-14.8	-14.4
+50	-9.4	-8.2	-6.9	-5.2	-3.4	-1.2	1.6	5.2	10.6
+25	-1.9	-0.6	0.8	2.3	4.0	6.3	8.7	9.8	10.6
0	-1.0	0.2	1.6	3.4	5.2	7.8	9.8	9.8	10.6
-25	-1.9	-0.6	0.8	2.3	4.0	6.3	8.7	9.8	10.6
-50	-9.4	-8.2	-6.9	-5.2	-3.4	-1.2	1.6	5.2	10.6
-75	-22.3	-21.4	-20.5	-19.4	-18.2	-17.0	-15.7	-14.8	-14.4
-100	-41.7	-41.2	-40.8	-40.3	-39.7	-39.5	-39.4	-39.4	-39.4
-125	-64.6	-64.5	-64.5	-64.4	-64.4	-64.4	-64.4	-64.4	-64.4

weeks to expiration — net profit area, in cents

Est. credit: +5.8¢ prem. + 5.8¢ prem. -1.0¢ com. = +10.6¢

Wm Grandmill (1985) Ltd.

SELL A STRANGLE – #2

SELL A CALL AT $1.00 OUT OF THE MONEY
and SELL A PUT AT $1.00 OUT OF THE MONEY

16 weeks to expiration

TABLE 8

changes in the soybean future's price in 25¢ increments

	weeks to expiration								
	16	14	12	10	8	6	4	2	0
+125	-12.7	-9.2	-5.5	-1.4	3.0	8.5	16.4	26.3	32.8
+100	-5.0	-1.2	3.1	7.8	13.0	19.6	28.5	40.5	57.8
+75	0.1	4.7	9.8	15.5	21.1	27.9	37.0	48.7	57.8
+50	2.6	7.9	13.5	19.4	25.6	32.9	42.2	52.6	57.8
+25	-0.3	4.9	10.6	16.9	24.4	32.8	43.9	55.1	57.8
0	-1.0	4.6	10.8	17.8	25.4	34.0	44.2	54.4	57.8
-25	-0.3	4.9	10.6	16.9	24.4	32.8	43.9	55.1	57.8
-50	2.6	7.9	13.5	19.4	25.6	32.9	42.2	52.6	57.8
-75	0.1	4.7	9.8	15.5	21.1	27.9	37.0	48.7	57.8
-100	-5.0	-1.2	3.1	7.8	13.0	19.6	28.5	40.5	57.8
-125	-12.7	-9.2	-5.5	-1.4	3.0	8.5	16.4	26.3	32.8

net profit area , in cents

Est. credit: +29.4¢ prem. +29.4¢ prem. -1.0¢ comm. = +57.8¢

TABLE 6

changes in the soybean future's price in 25¢ increments

	weeks to expiration								
	16	14	12	10	8	6	4	2	0
+125	-22.8	-20.5	-18.0	-14.8	-11.3	-7.3	-1.5	5.4	9.0
+100	-13.3	-10.8	-7.6	-3.9	0.2	5.1	11.7	20.7	34.0
+75	-6.5	-3.4	-0.1	3.7	8.3	13.6	20.3	28.5	34.0
+50	-1.8	1.4	4.9	8.8	13.3	18.3	24.6	31.5	34.0
+25	-1.8	1.6	5.5	9.8	14.8	20.3	27.2	33.1	34.0
0	-1.0	2.8	6.6	10.8	15.2	20.6	27.0	33.2	34.0
-25	-1.8	1.6	5.5	9.8	14.8	20.3	27.2	33.1	34.0
-50	-1.8	1.4	4.9	8.8	13.3	18.3	24.6	31.5	34.0
-75	-6.5	-3.4	-0.1	3.7	8.3	13.6	20.3	28.5	34.0
-100	-13.3	-10.8	-7.6	-3.9	0.2	5.1	11.7	20.7	34.0
-125	-22.8	-20.5	-18.0	-14.8	-11.3	-7.3	-1.5	5.4	9.0

net profit area , in cents

Est. credit: +17.5¢ prem. +17.5¢ prem. -1.0¢ comm. = +34.0¢

TABLE 4

changes in the soybean future's price in 25¢ increments

	weeks to expiration								
	16	14	12	10	8	6	4	2	0
+125	-28.3	-26.7	-25.1	-23.2	-20.9	-18.3	-14.7	-10.8	-9.4
+100	-16.3	-14.6	-12.7	-10.5	-7.9	-4.7	-0.1	6.2	15.6
+75	-7.5	-5.7	-3.9	-1.9	0.7	3.7	7.9	13.5	15.6
+50	-2.9	-1.0	1.1	3.2	5.5	8.0	11.5	15.1	15.6
+25	-1.3	0.5	2.7	5.0	7.7	10.4	13.7	15.6	15.6
0	-1.0	1.0	2.8	5.0	7.6	10.2	13.4	15.6	15.6
-25	-1.3	0.5	2.7	5.0	7.7	10.4	13.7	15.6	15.6
-50	-2.9	-1.0	1.1	3.2	5.5	8.0	11.5	15.1	15.6
-75	-7.5	-5.7	-3.9	-1.9	0.7	3.7	7.9	13.5	15.6
-100	-16.3	-14.6	-12.7	-10.5	-7.9	-4.7	-0.1	6.2	15.6
-125	-28.3	-26.7	-25.1	-23.2	-20.9	-18.3	-14.7	-10.8	-9.4

net profit area , in cents

Est. credit: + 8.3¢ prem. + 8.3¢ prem. – 1.0¢ comm. = + 15.6¢

TABLE 2

changes in the soybean future's price in 25¢ increments

	weeks to expiration								
	16	14	12	10	8	6	4	2	0
+125	-29.4	-28.7	-27.9	-27.0	-25.9	-24.8	-23.5	-22.6	-22.2
+100	-15.3	-14.4	-13.4	-12.1	-10.7	-8.9	-6.2	-2.6	2.8
+75	-7.0	-6.2	-5.3	-4.2	-2.9	-1.2	0.9	2.0	2.8
+50	-3.2	-2.5	-1.7	-0.8	0.1	1.4	2.4	2.8	2.8
+25	-0.6	0.1	0.7	1.3	1.9	2.5	2.8	2.8	2.8
0	-1.0	-0.4	0.2	1.0	1.8	2.6	2.8	2.8	2.8
-25	-0.6	0.1	0.7	1.3	1.9	2.5	2.8	2.8	2.8
-50	-3.2	-2.5	-1.7	-0.8	0.1	1.4	2.4	2.8	2.8
-75	-7.0	-6.2	-5.3	-4.2	-2.9	-1.2	0.9	2.0	2.8
-100	-15.3	-14.4	-13.4	-12.1	-10.7	-8.9	-6.2	-2.6	2.8
-125	-29.4	-28.7	-27.9	-27.0	-25.9	-24.8	-23.5	-22.6	-22.2

net profit area , in cents

Est. credit: + 1.9¢ premium + 1.9¢ prem. -1.0¢ comm. = +2.8¢

Wm Grandmill (1985) Ltd.

BUY A CALL or BUY A PUT

AT THE MONEY

weeks to expiration: 18

TABLE 08

changes in the soybean future's price in 25¢ increments	weeks to expiration									
	18	16	14	12	10	8	6	4	2	0
+125	79.0	76.5	74.1	71.7	68.9	65.8	63.5	63.2	63.2	63.2
+100	55.5	52.9	50.6	47.9	45.2	42.7	40.0	38.6	38.2	38.2
+75	34.7	32.2	29.9	27.5	24.9	22.1	19.2	15.8	13.3	13.2
+50	22.3	19.7	17.1	14.0	10.6	6.8	2.2	-3.7	-10.1	-11.8
+25	10.3	7.2	4.1	0.7	-3.2	-7.4	-12.7	-20.4	-30.3	-36.8
0	-0.5	-3.3	-6.2	-9.6	-13.6	-18.3	-24.2	-32.8	-44.5	-61.8
-25	-10.1	-12.9	-15.8	-19.1	-23.0	-27.6	-33.4	-41.8	-52.7	-61.8
-50	-18.9	-21.6	-24.4	-27.7	-31.4	-35.6	-40.9	-47.9	-56.6	-61.8
-75	-22.9	-25.5	-28.4	-31.7	-35.4	-39.9	-45.1	-52.2	-59.6	-61.8
-100	-29.8	-32.4	-35.2	-38.3	-41.8	-45.6	-49.9	-55.0	-60.1	-61.8
-125	-37.6	-40.0	-42.3	-44.7	-47.3	-50.3	-53.5	-57.5	-61.3	-61.8

net profit

Estimated cost is: -61.3¢ premium - 0.5¢ comm. = -61.8¢

TABLE 06

changes in the soybean future's price in 25¢ increments	weeks to expiration									
	18	16	14	12	10	8	6	4	2	0
+125	82.3	80.8	79.5	78.2	77.5	77.3	77.3	77.3	77.3	77.3
+100	58.7	57.3	55.9	54.8	54.0	53.2	52.6	52.3	52.3	52.3
+75	38.4	37.1	35.6	34.5	33.0	31.5	29.8	28.0	27.3	27.3
+50	23.9	22.2	20.3	18.2	15.9	13.3	10.3	6.5	2.8	2.3
+25	10.0	8.1	6.0	3.7	0.9	-2.4	-6.4	-12.2	-19.1	-22.7
0	-0.5	-2.7	-4.9	-7.5	-10.6	-14.3	-18.8	-25.4	-34.4	-47.7
-25	-9.9	-12.0	-14.3	-16.8	-19.8	-23.4	-27.8	-34.0	-42.2	-47.7
-50	-18.2	-20.1	-22.1	-24.5	-27.2	-30.4	-33.9	-39.0	-45.2	-47.7
-75	-22.3	-24.4	-26.4	-28.8	-31.5	-34.7	-38.2	-42.7	-46.9	-47.7
-100	-28.4	-30.1	-32.0	-34.4	-36.1	-38.3	-41.0	-44.2	-47.3	-47.7
-125	-33.8	-35.2	-36.6	-38.1	-39.7	-41.5	-43.5	-45.9	-47.6	-47.7

net profit area

Estimated cost is: -47.2¢ premium - 0.5¢ comm. = -47.7¢

TABLE 04

changes in the soybean future's price in 25¢ increments	weeks to expiration									
	18	16	14	12	10	8	6	4	2	0
+125	91.4	91.4	91.4	91.4	91.4	91.4	91.4	91.4	91.4	91.4
+100	67.3	67.1	66.9	66.7	66.5	66.4	66.4	66.4	66.4	66.4
+75	45.5	44.9	44.3	43.7	43.1	42.4	41.8	41.4	41.4	41.4
+50	27.2	26.1	25.1	24.0	22.7	21.2	19.6	17.5	16.5	16.4
+25	11.4	10.2	8.7	7.1	5.2	2.9	0.3	-3.3	-7.2	-8.6
0	-0.5	-2.0	-3.6	-5.4	-7.6	-10.1	-13.3	-17.9	-24.2	-33.6
-25	-9.6	-11.1	-12.7	-14.4	-16.3	-18.8	-21.7	-25.9	-31.5	-33.6
-50	-16.5	-17.7	-19.0	-20.4	-22.0	-24.0	-26.3	-29.5	-33.1	-33.6
-75	-20.8	-22.0	-23.2	-24.6	-26.1	-27.9	-29.8	-32.0	-33.3	-33.6
-100	-24.4	-25.3	-26.3	-27.2	-28.3	-29.6	-30.9	-32.5	-33.6	-33.6
-125	-27.6	-28.2	-28.9	-29.7	-30.5	-31.4	-32.3	-33.3	-33.6	-33.6

net profit area

Estimated cost is: -33.1¢ premium - 0.5¢ comm. = -33.6¢

TABLE 02

changes in the soybean future's price in 25¢ increments	weeks to expiration									
	18	16	14	12	10	8	6	4	2	0
+125	105.5	105.5	105.5	105.5	105.5	105.5	105.5	105.5	105.5	105.5
+100	80.5	80.5	80.5	80.5	80.5	80.5	80.5	80.5	80.5	80.5
+75	55.8	55.7	55.6	55.6	55.5	55.5	55.5	55.5	55.5	55.5
+50	33.1	32.6	32.2	31.8	31.4	31.1	30.8	30.6	30.5	30.5
+25	13.4	12.7	12.0	11.2	10.3	9.2	8.1	6.8	5.9	5.5
0	-0.5	-1.4	-2.3	-3.3	-4.6	-6.0	-7.8	-10.5	-14.1	-19.5
-25	-8.8	-9.7	-10.5	-11.4	-12.5	-13.8	-15.5	-17.6	-18.7	-19.5
-50	-13.1	-13.7	-14.3	-15.0	-15.9	-16.9	-18.1	-19.1	-19.5	-19.5
-75	-16.3	-16.8	-17.3	-17.8	-18.2	-18.6	-19.2	-19.4	-19.5	-19.5
-100	-17.3	-17.6	-17.9	-18.2	-18.6	-19.0	-19.4	-19.5	-19.5	-19.5
-125	-18.5	-18.8	-19.0	-19.1	-19.3	-19.4	-19.5	-19.5	-19.5	-19.5

net profit area , in cents

Estimated cost is: -19.0¢ premium - 0.5¢ comm. = -19.5¢

Wm Grandmill (1985) Ltd.

BUY A CALL or BUY A PUT
AT 50¢ OUT OF THE MONEY

TABLE 0

changes in the soybean future's price in 25¢ increments	weeks to expiration									
	18	16	14	12	10	8	6	4	2	0
+125	53.1	50.7	48.3	45.9	43.3	40.5	37.6	34.2	31.7	31.6
+100	40.7	38.1	35.5	32.4	29.0	25.2	20.6	14.7	8.3	6.6
+75	28.7	25.6	22.5	19.1	15.2	11.1	5.7	-2.0	-11.9	-18.4
+50	17.9	15.1	12.2	8.8	4.8	0.1	-5.8	-14.4	-26.1	-43.4
+25	8.3	5.5	2.6	-0.7	-4.6	-9.2	-15.0	-23.4	-34.2	-43.4
0	-0.5	-3.2	-6.0	-9.3	-13.0	-17.2	-22.5	-29.5	-38.1	-43.4
-25	-4.5	-7.1	-10.0	-13.3	-17.0	-21.7	-27.0	-33.8	-41.2	-43.4
-50	-11.4	-14.0	-16.8	-19.9	-23.4	-27.2	-31.5	-36.6	-41.7	-43.4
-75	-19.2	-21.6	-23.9	-26.3	-28.9	-31.9	-35.1	-39.1	-42.9	-43.4
-100	-26.5	-28.4	-30.9	-33.5	-35.4	-37.3	-39.4	-41.7	-43.4	-43.4
-125	-33.0	-34.6	-36.3	-38.1	-39.7	-40.9	-42.0	-42.6	-43.4	-43.4

net profit — Estimated cost is: - 42.9¢ premium - 0.5¢ comm. = - 43.4¢

TABLE (8)

changes in the soybean future's price in 25¢ increments	weeks to expiration									
	18	16	14	12	10	8	6	4	2	0
+125	56.1	54.8	53.6	52.2	50.7	49.2	47.5	45.7	45.0	45.0
+100	41.6	39.9	38.0	35.9	33.6	31.0	28.0	24.2	20.5	20.0
+75	27.7	25.8	23.7	21.4	18.6	15.3	11.3	5.5	-1.4	-5.0
+50	17.2	15.0	12.8	10.2	7.1	3.4	-1.1	-7.7	-16.7	-30.0
+25	7.8	5.7	3.4	0.9	-2.1	-5.7	-10.1	-16.3	-24.5	-30.0
0	-0.5	-2.4	-4.4	-6.8	-9.5	-12.7	-16.2	-21.3	-27.5	-30.0
-25	-4.6	-6.7	-8.7	-11.1	-13.8	-17.0	-20.5	-25.0	-29.2	-30.0
-50	-10.8	-12.5	-14.4	-16.3	-18.4	-20.6	-23.3	-26.5	-29.6	-30.0
-75	-16.1	-17.5	-18.9	-20.4	-22.0	-23.8	-25.8	-28.2	-29.9	-30.0
-100	-20.7	-21.8	-23.0	-24.1	-25.3	-26.6	-28.1	-29.3	-30.0	-30.0
-125	-24.4	-25.2	-26.0	-26.8	-27.6	-28.6	-29.5	-30.0	-30.0	-30.0

Estimated cost is: - 29.5¢ premium - 0.5¢ comm. = - 30.0¢

TABLE (4)

changes in the soybean future's price in 25¢ increments	weeks to expiration									
	18	16	14	12	10	8	6	4	2	0
+125	61.5	60.9	60.3	59.7	59.1	58.4	57.8	57.4	57.4	57.4
+100	43.2	42.1	41.1	40.0	38.7	37.2	35.6	33.5	32.5	32.4
+75	27.4	26.2	24.7	23.1	21.2	18.9	16.3	12.7	8.8	7.4
+50	15.5	14.0	12.4	10.6	8.4	5.9	2.7	-1.9	-8.2	-17.6
+25	6.4	4.9	3.3	1.6	-0.3	-2.8	-5.7	-9.9	-15.5	-17.6
0	-0.5	-1.7	-3.0	-4.4	-6.0	-8.0	-10.3	-13.5	-17.1	-17.6
-25	-4.8	-6.0	-7.2	-8.6	-10.1	-11.9	-13.8	-16.0	-17.6	-17.6
-50	-8.4	-9.3	-10.3	-11.2	-12.3	-13.6	-14.9	-16.5	-17.6	-17.6
-75	-11.6	-12.3	-12.9	-13.7	-14.5	-15.4	-16.2	-17.3	-17.6	-17.6
-100	-14.4	-15.0	-15.6	-16.3	-16.8	-17.1	-17.3	-17.6	-17.6	-17.6
-125	-16.7	-17.0	-17.2	-17.3	-17.4	-17.5	-17.6	-17.6	-17.6	-17.6

net profit — Estimated cost is: -17.1¢ premium - o.5¢ comm. = -17.6¢

TABLE (2)

changes in the soybean future's price in 25¢ increments	weeks to expiration									
	18	16	14	12	10	8	6	4	2	0
+125	68.4	68.3	68.2	68.2	68.1	68.1	68.1	68.1	68.1	68.1
+100	45.7	45.2	44.8	44.4	44.0	43.7	43.4	43.2	43.1	43.1
+75	25.0	24.3	23.6	22.8	21.9	20.8	19.7	18.9	18.5	18.1
+50	12.1	11.2	10.3	9.3	8.0	6.6	4.8	2.1	-1.5	-6.9
+25	3.8	2.9	2.1	1.2	0.1	-1.2	-2.9	-5.0	-6.1	-6.9
0	-0.5	-1.1	-1.7	-2.4	-3.3	-4.3	-5.5	-6.5	-6.9	-6.9
-25	-3.7	-4.2	-4.7	-5.2	-5.6	-6.0	-6.6	-6.6	-6.9	-6.9
-50	-4.7	-5.0	-5.3	-5.6	-6.0	-6.4	-6.8	-6.9	-6.9	-6.9
-75	-5.9	-6.2	-6.4	-6.5	-6.7	-6.8	-6.9	-6.9	-6.9	-6.9
-100	-6.6	-6.7	-6.8	-6.8	-6.9	-6.9	-6.9	-6.9	-6.9	-6.9
-125	-6.9	-6.9	-6.9	-6.9	-6.9	-6.9	-6.9	-6.9	-6.9	-6.9

net profit — Estimated cost is: - 6.4¢ premium - o.5¢ comm. = - 6.9¢

Wm Grandmill (1985) Ltd.

SELL A CALL or SELL A PUT
AT THE MONEY

18 weeks to expiration

TABLE 0

changes in the soybean future's price in 25¢ increments

	18	16	14	12	10	8	6	4	2	0
+125	-80.0	-77.5	-75.1	-72.7	-69.9	-66.8	-64.5	-64.2	-64.2	-64.2
+100	-56.5	-53.9	-51.6	-48.9	-46.2	-43.7	-41.0	-39.6	-39.2	-39.2
+75	-35.7	-33.2	-30.9	-28.5	-25.9	-23.1	-20.2	-16.8	-14.3	-14.2
+50	-23.3	-20.7	-18.1	-15.0	-11.6	-7.8	-3.2	2.7	9.1	10.8
+25	-11.3	-8.2	-5.1	-1.7	2.2	6.4	11.7	19.4	29.3	35.8
0	-0.5	2.3	5.2	8.6	12.6	17.3	23.2	31.8	43.5	60.8
-25	9.1	11.9	14.8	18.1	22.0	26.6	32.4	40.8	51.7	60.8
-50	17.9	20.6	23.4	26.7	30.4	34.6	39.9	46.9	55.6	60.8
-75	21.9	24.5	27.4	30.7	34.4	38.9	44.1	51.1	58.6	60.8
-100	28.8	31.4	34.2	37.3	40.8	44.6	48.9	54.0	59.1	60.8
-125	36.6	39.0	41.3	43.7	46.3	49.3	52.5	56.5	60.3	60.8

weeks to expiration — net profit area, in cents

Estimated credit: + 61.3¢ premium - 0.5¢ comm. = + 60.8¢

TABLE 0

changes in the soybean future's price in 25¢ increments

	18	16	14	12	10	8	6	4	2	0
+125	-83.3	-81.8	-80.5	-79.2	-78.5	-78.3	-78.3	-78.3	-78.3	-78.3
+100	-59.7	-58.3	-56.9	-55.8	-55.0	-54.2	-53.6	-53.3	-53.3	-53.3
+75	-39.4	-38.1	-36.9	-35.5	-34.0	-32.5	-30.8	-29.0	-28.3	-28.3
+50	-24.9	-23.2	-21.3	-19.2	-16.9	-14.3	-11.3	-7.5	-3.8	-3.3
+25	-11.0	-9.1	-7.0	-4.7	-1.9	1.4	5.4	11.2	18.1	21.7
0	-0.5	1.7	3.9	6.5	9.6	13.3	17.8	24.4	33.4	46.7
-25	8.9	11.0	13.3	15.8	18.8	22.4	26.8	33.0	41.2	46.7
-50	17.2	19.1	21.1	23.5	26.2	29.4	32.9	38.0	44.2	46.7
-75	21.3	23.4	25.4	27.8	30.5	33.7	37.2	41.7	45.9	46.7
-100	27.4	29.1	31.0	33.0	35.1	37.3	40.0	43.2	45.9	46.7
-125	32.8	34.2	35.6	37.1	38.7	40.5	42.5	44.9	46.3	46.7

net profit area, in cents

Estimated credit is: + 47.2¢ premium - 0.5¢ comm. = + 46.7¢

TABLE 4

changes in the soybean future's price in 25¢ increments

	18	16	14	12	10	8	6	4	2	0
+125	-92.4	-92.4	-92.4	-92.4	-92.4	-92.4	-92.4	-92.4	-92.4	-92.4
+100	-68.3	-68.1	-67.9	-67.7	-67.5	-67.4	-67.4	-67.4	-67.4	-67.4
+75	-46.5	-45.9	-45.3	-44.7	-44.1	-43.4	-42.8	-42.4	-42.4	-42.4
+50	-28.2	-27.1	-26.1	-25.0	-23.7	-22.2	-20.6	-18.5	-17.5	-17.4
+25	-12.4	-11.2	-9.7	-8.1	-6.2	-3.9	-1.3	2.3	6.2	7.6
0	-0.5	1.0	2.6	4.4	6.6	9.1	12.3	16.9	23.2	32.6
-25	8.6	10.1	11.7	13.4	15.3	17.8	20.7	24.9	30.5	32.6
-50	15.5	16.7	18.0	19.4	21.0	23.0	25.3	28.5	32.1	32.6
-75	19.8	21.0	22.2	23.6	25.1	26.9	28.8	31.0	32.6	32.6
-100	23.4	24.3	25.3	26.2	27.3	28.6	29.9	31.5	32.6	32.6
-125	26.5	27.2	27.9	28.7	29.5	30.4	31.3	32.3	32.6	32.6

weeks to expiration — net profit area, in cents

Estimated credit is: + 33.1¢ premium - 0.5¢ comm. = + 32.6¢

TABLE 2

changes in the soybean future's price in 25¢ increments

	18	16	14	12	10	8	6	4	2	0
+125	-106.5	-106.5	-106.5	-106.5	-106.5	-106.5	-106.5	-106.5	-106.5	-106.5
+100	-81.5	-81.5	-81.5	-81.5	-81.5	-81.5	-81.5	-81.5	-81.5	-81.5
+75	-56.8	-56.7	-56.6	-56.6	-56.5	-56.5	-56.5	-56.5	-56.5	-56.5
+50	-34.1	-33.6	-33.2	-32.8	-32.4	-32.1	-31.9	-31.6	-31.5	-31.5
+25	-14.4	-13.7	-13.0	-12.2	-11.3	-10.2	-9.1	-7.8	-6.9	-6.5
0	-0.5	0.4	1.3	2.3	3.6	5.0	6.8	9.5	13.1	18.5
-25	7.8	8.7	9.5	10.4	11.5	12.8	14.5	16.6	17.7	18.5
-50	12.1	12.7	13.3	14.0	14.9	15.9	17.1	18.1	18.5	18.5
-75	15.3	15.8	16.3	16.8	17.2	17.6	18.0	18.2	18.5	18.5
-100	16.3	16.6	16.9	17.2	17.6	18.0	18.4	18.5	18.5	18.5
-125	17.5	17.8	18.0	18.1	18.3	18.4	18.5	18.5	18.5	18.5

weeks to expiration — net profit area, in cents

Estimated credit is: + 19.0¢ premium - 0.5¢ comm. = + 18.5¢

Wm Grandmill (1985) Ltd.

SELL A CALL or SELL A PUT
AT 50¢ OUT OF THE MONEY

18 weeks to expiration

TABLE

changes in the soybean future's price in 25¢ increments	weeks to expiration									
	18	16	14	12	10	8	6	4	2	0
+125	-54.1	-51.7	-49.3	-46.9	-44.3	-41.5	-38.6	-35.2	-32.7	-32.6
+100	-41.7	-39.1	-36.5	-33.4	-30.0	-26.2	-21.6	-15.7	-9.3	-7.6
+75	-29.7	-26.6	-23.5	-20.1	-16.2	-12.1	-6.7	1.0	10.9	17.4
+50	-18.9	-16.1	-13.2	-9.8	-5.8	-1.1	4.8	13.4	25.1	42.4
+25	-9.3	-6.5	-3.6	-0.3	3.6	8.2	14.0	22.4	33.3	42.4
0	-0.5	2.2	5.0	8.3	12.0	16.2	21.5	28.5	37.1	42.4
-25	3.5	6.1	9.0	12.3	16.0	20.5	26.0	32.8	40.2	42.4
-50	10.4	13.0	15.8	18.9	22.4	26.2	30.5	35.6	40.7	42.4
-75	18.2	20.6	22.9	25.3	27.9	30.9	34.1	38.1	41.9	42.4
-100	26.5	27.4	29.9	32.5	34.4	36.3	38.4	40.7	42.4	42.4
-125	32.0	33.6	35.2	37.1	38.7	39.9	41.0	41.6	42.4	42.4

net profit area , in cents

Estimated credit is: +42.9¢ premium − 0.5¢ comm. = +42.4¢

TABLE

changes in the soybean future's price in 25¢ increments	weeks to expiration									
	18	16	14	12	10	8	6	4	2	0
+125	-57.1	-55.8	-54.6	-53.2	-51.7	-50.2	-48.5	-46.7	-46.0	-46.0
+100	-42.6	-40.9	-39.0	-36.9	-34.6	-32.0	-29.0	-25.2	-21.5	-21.0
+75	-28.7	-26.8	-24.7	-22.4	-19.6	-16.3	-12.3	-6.5	0.4	-21.0
+50	-18.2	-16.0	-13.8	-11.2	-8.1	-4.4	0.1	6.7	15.7	4.0
+25	-8.8	-6.7	-4.4	-1.9	1.1	4.7	9.1	15.3	23.5	29.0
0	-0.5	1.4	3.4	5.8	8.5	11.7	15.2	20.3	26.5	29.0
-25	3.6	5.7	7.7	10.1	12.8	16.0	19.5	24.0	28.2	29.0
-50	9.8	11.5	13.4	15.3	17.4	19.6	22.3	25.5	28.6	29.0
-75	15.1	16.5	17.9	19.4	21.0	22.8	24.8	27.2	28.9	29.0
-100	19.7	20.8	22.0	23.1	24.3	25.6	27.1	28.3	29.0	29.0
-125	23.4	24.2	25.0	25.8	26.6	27.6	28.5	29.0	29.0	29.0

net profit area , in cents

Estimated credit is: +29.5¢ premium − 0.5¢ comm. = +29.0¢

TABLE

changes in the soybean future's price in 25¢ increments	weeks to expiration									
	18	16	14	12	10	8	6	4	2	0
+125	-62.5	-61.9	-61.3	-60.7	-60.1	-59.4	-58.4	-58.4	-58.4	-58.4
+100	-44.2	-43.1	-42.1	-41.0	-39.7	-38.2	-36.6	-34.5	-33.5	-33.4
+75	-28.4	-27.2	-25.7	-24.1	-22.2	-19.9	-17.3	-13.7	-9.8	-8.4
+50	-16.5	-15.0	-13.4	-11.6	-9.4	-6.9	-3.7	0.9	7.2	16.6
+25	-7.4	-5.9	-4.3	-2.6	-0.7	1.8	4.7	8.9	14.5	16.6
0	-0.5	0.7	2.0	3.4	5.0	7.0	9.3	12.5	16.1	16.6
-25	3.8	5.0	6.2	7.6	9.1	11.3	13.9	16.0	16.6	16.6
-50	7.4	8.3	9.3	10.2	11.3	12.6	15.5	16.3	16.6	16.6
-75	10.6	11.3	11.9	12.7	13.5	14.4	15.2	16.6	16.6	16.6
-100	13.4	14.0	14.6	15.3	15.8	16.1	16.3	16.6	16.6	16.6
-125	15.7	16.0	16.2	16.3	16.4	16.5	16.6	16.6	16.6	16.6

net profit area , in cents

Estimated credit is: +17.1¢ premium − 0.5¢ comm. = +16.6¢

TABLE

changes in the soybean future's price in 25¢ increments	weeks to expiration									
	18	16	14	12	10	8	6	4	2	0
+125	-69.4	-69.3	-69.2	-69.2	-69.1	-69.1	-69.1	-69.1	-69.1	-69.1
+100	-46.7	-46.2	-46.2	-45.8	-45.4	-45.0	-44.7	-44.4	-44.2	-44.1
+75	-26.0	-25.3	-24.6	-23.8	-22.9	-21.8	-20.7	-19.9	-19.5	-19.1
+50	-13.1	-12.2	-11.3	-10.3	-9.0	-7.6	-5.8	-3.1	0.5	5.9
+25	-4.8	-3.9	-3.1	-2.2	-1.1	0.2	1.9	4.0	5.1	5.9
0	-0.5	0.1	0.7	1.4	2.3	3.3	4.5	5.5	5.9	5.9
-25	2.7	3.2	3.7	4.2	4.6	5.0	5.6	5.9	5.9	5.9
-50	3.7	4.0	4.3	4.6	5.0	5.4	5.8	5.9	5.9	5.9
-75	4.9	5.2	5.4	5.5	5.7	5.8	5.9	5.9	5.9	5.9
-100	5.6	5.7	5.8	5.8	5.9	5.9	5.9	5.9	5.9	5.9
-125	5.9	5.9	5.9	5.9	5.9	5.9	5.9	5.9	5.9	5.9

net profit area , in cents

Estimated credit is: +6.4¢ premium − 0.5¢ comm. = +5.9¢

Wm Grandmill (1985) Ltd.

BULL or BEAR SPREAD – #1

BUY A CALL AT THE MONEY
and SELL A CALL AT 25¢ OUT OF THE MONEY
OR
BUY A PUT AT THE MONEY
and SELL A PUT AT 25¢ OUT OF THE MONEY

18 weeks to expiration

TABLE 0 (top left)

changes in the soybean future's price in 25¢ increments

	18	16	14	12	10	8	6	4	2	0
+125	12.9	13.0	13.1	13.1	13.2	13.8	14.3	14.6	14.6	14.6
+100	8.9	9.3	9.7	10.1	10.6	11.3	12.4	13.9	14.6	14.6
+75	6.0	6.2	6.5	6.8	7.1	7.8	9.1	11.1	14.1	14.6
+50	3.5	3.7	3.9	4.2	4.6	5.3	6.3	8.3	11.5	14.6
+25	0.1	0.3	0.5	0.8	1.1	1.5	2.0	2.8	4.9	14.6
0	-1.0	-1.0	-1.0	-1.1	-1.2	-1.3	-1.4	-1.8	-2.6	-10.4
-25	-2.1	-2.3	-2.5	-2.7	-3.0	-3.4	-4.3	-5.4	-7.4	-10.4
-50	-3.2	-3.4	-3.7	-4.0	-4.4	-5.0	-5.7	-6.7	-8.7	-10.4
-75	-4.2	-4.5	-4.8	-5.2	-5.8	-6.8	-7.6	-8.7	-10.0	-10.4
-100	-5.1	-5.5	-5.9	-6.3	-6.8	-7.2	-7.9	-8.8	-10.1	-10.4
-125	-5.7	-6.0	-6.3	-6.7	-7.1	-7.6	-8.1	-9.1	-10.3	-10.4

weeks to expiration — net profit area, in cents

Est. cost is: -47.2¢ premium +37.8¢ premium -1.0¢ comm.= -10.4¢

TABLE 0 (top right)

changes in the soybean future's price in 25¢ increments

	18	16	14	12	10	8	6	4	2	0
+125	12.9	13.0	13.1	13.2	13.4	13.6	13.8	14.0	14.4	14.4
+100	7.8	8.2	8.6	9.1	9.6	10.3	10.8	12.8	14.0	14.4
+75	4.7	5.0	5.3	5.7	6.2	6.8	7.8	9.4	12.8	14.4
+50	2.1	2.2	2.4	2.7	3.1	3.6	4.3	6.1	9.6	14.4
+25	0.5	0.6	0.6	0.7	0.8	0.9	1.1	1.8	3.6	14.4
0	-1.0	-1.0	-1.0	-1.1	-1.2	-1.3	-1.4	-1.6	-2.6	-10.6
-25	-1.8	-1.9	-2.0	-2.0	-2.2	-2.6	-3.3	-4.5	-6.7	-10.6
-50	-2.1	-2.2	-2.4	-2.7	-3.1	-3.7	-4.6	-5.7	-7.6	-10.6
-75	-2.5	-2.6	-2.8	-3.4	-4.2	-5.0	-6.0	-7.0	-8.6	-10.6
-100	-2.7	-3.0	-3.5	-4.2	-5.0	-5.9	-7.0	-8.1	-9.4	-10.6
-125	-3.0	-3.2	-3.8	-4.6	-5.4	-6.6	-7.8	-9.1	-10.1	-10.6

weeks to expiration — net profit area, in cents

Estimated cost is: -61.3¢ prem. +51.7¢ prem. -1.0¢ comm.= -10.6¢

TABLE 2 (bottom left)

changes in the soybean future's price in 25¢ increments

	18	16	14	12	10	8	6	4	2	0
+125	15.7	15.7	15.7	15.7	15.7	15.7	15.7	15.7	15.7	15.7
+100	15.4	15.5	15.6	15.6	15.7	15.7	15.7	15.7	15.7	15.7
+75	13.4	13.8	14.1	14.5	14.9	15.1	15.4	15.6	15.7	15.7
+50	10.3	10.6	10.9	11.3	11.8	12.6	13.4	14.5	15.3	15.7
+25	4.7	4.8	5.0	5.2	5.6	5.9	6.6	8.0	10.7	15.7
0	-1.0	-1.0	-1.0	-1.1	-1.2	-1.4	-1.5	-1.7	-2.7	-9.3
-25	-5.0	-5.3	-5.5	-5.7	-5.9	-6.3	-6.7	-7.5	-8.4	-9.3
-50	-6.1	-6.2	-6.3	-6.5	-6.5	-7.0	-7.5	-8.2	-8.9	-9.3
-75	-7.0	-7.1	-7.3	-7.5	-7.8	-8.4	-8.6	-9.1	-9.2	-9.3
-100	-7.9	-8.0	-8.2	-8.4	-8.6	-8.9	-9.2	-9.3	-9.3	-9.3
-125	-8.6	-8.8	-8.9	-9.0	-9.1	-9.2	-9.3	-9.3	-9.3	-9.3

weeks to expiration — net profit area, in cents

Est. cost is: -19.0¢ premium +10.7¢ premium -1.0¢ comm.= -9.3¢

TABLE 4 (bottom right)

changes in the soybean future's price in 25¢ increments

	18	16	14	12	10	8	6	4	2	0
+125	14.0	14.2	14.4	14.6	14.8	14.9	14.9	14.9	14.9	14.9
+100	11.8	12.1	12.5	12.9	13.3	13.9	14.5	14.9	14.9	14.9
+75	8.2	8.7	9.1	9.6	10.3	11.1	12.1	13.6	14.9	14.9
+50	5.7	5.8	6.3	6.8	7.4	8.2	9.1	10.7	13.6	14.9
+25	1.9	2.1	2.2	2.4	2.7	2.9	3.5	4.5	6.9	14.9
0	-1.0	-1.0	-1.0	-1.1	-1.3	-1.5	-1.7	-2.1	-2.9	-10.1
-25	-3.2	-3.5	-3.8	-4.1	-4.4	-4.9	-5.5	-6.5	-8.5	-10.1
-50	-5.5	-5.7	-5.8	-5.9	-6.0	-6.2	-6.6	-7.6	-9.6	-10.1
-75	-6.5	-6.8	-7.1	-7.5	-7.8	-8.1	-8.5	-8.9	-9.8	-10.1
-100	-6.9	-7.2	-7.5	-7.7	-7.9	-8.3	-8.8	-9.0	-9.3	-10.1
-125	-7.3	-7.4	-7.6	-7.8	-8.1	-8.5	-9.0	-9.3	-10.1	-10.1

weeks to expiration — net profit area, in cents

Est. cost is: -33.1 premium +24.0¢ premium -1.0¢ comm.= -10.1¢

BULL or BEAR SPREAD – #2

BUY A CALL AT THE MONEY
and SELL 2 CALLS AT 50¢ OUT OF THE MONEY
OR
BUY A PUT AT THE MONEY
and SELL 2 PUTS AT 50¢ OUT OF THE MONEY

weeks to
| 18 |
expiration

TABLE (net credit = +23.0¢)

changes in the soybean future's price in 25¢ increments

price change	weeks to expiration 18	16	14	12	10	8	6	4	2	0
+125	-29.1	-26.8	-24.5	-22.1	-19.7	-17.2	-13.7	-7.2	-2.2	-2.0
+100	-27.9	-25.3	-22.4	-18.9	-14.8	-9.7	-3.2	7.2	19.6	23.0
+75	-24.7	-21.0	-17.1	-12.7	-7.5	-1.9	5.8	17.8	35.1	48.0
+50	-15.5	-12.5	-9.3	-5.6	-1.0	4.6	11.8	23.1	40.1	73.0
+25	-8.3	-5.8	-3.1	0.1	4.0	9.0	15.3	24.4	36.3	48.0
0	-1.5	1.1	3.8	7.0	10.4	14.1	18.8	24.2	29.9	23.0
-25	-3.1	-0.7	2.2	5.5	9.0	13.4	18.0	23.8	27.7	23.0
-50	1.9	4.4	7.2	10.1	13.4	16.8	20.1	23.3	24.8	23.0
-75	13.5	15.7	17.4	18.9	20.4	21.9	23.1	24.0	24.2	23.0
-100	19.3	20.8	22.3	23.5	24.6	25.1	25.2	24.7	23.8	23.0
-125	26.4	27.2	28.3	29.5	30.5	31.5	30.3	27.7	25.5	23.0

net profit area , in cents

Est. credit: -61.3¢ prem. + 42.9¢ prem. + 42.9¢ prem. -1.5¢ com. = +23.0¢

TABLE (net credit = +10.3¢)

changes in the soybean future's price in 25¢ increments

price change	weeks to expiration 18	16	14	12	10	8	6	4	2	0
+125	-31.9	-30.9	-29.7	-28.2	-25.9	-23.1	-19.7	-16.1	-14.7	-14.7
+100	-26.5	-24.5	-22.2	-19.0	-15.2	-10.8	-5.4	1.9	9.3	10.3
+75	-19.0	-16.4	-13.5	-10.3	-6.2	-1.1	5.2	15.0	28.1	35.3
+50	-12.5	-9.8	-7.3	-4.2	-0.3	4.5	10.5	19.9	24.2	60.3
+25	-7.6	-5.3	-2.8	-0.1	3.1	7.0	11.8	18.4	27.9	35.3
0	-1.5	0.1	1.9	4.1	6.4	9.1	11.6	15.2	18.6	10.3
-25	-2.7	-0.6	1.3	3.4	5.8	8.6	11.2	14.0	14.2	10.3
-50	1.4	2.9	4.6	6.1	7.6	9.0	10.7	12.0	12.0	10.3
-75	7.9	8.6	9.4	10.0	10.5	10.9	11.4	11.7	11.9	10.3
-100	10.3	10.8	11.2	11.6	11.9	12.1	12.4	12.0	11.9	10.3
-125	13.0	13.2	13.4	13.5	13.7	13.5	13.5	12.1	11.2	10.3

net profit area , in cents

Est. credit: -47.2¢ prem. +29.5¢ prem. +29.5¢ prem. -1.5¢ com. = +10.3¢

TABLE (net credit = -0.4¢)

changes in the soybean future's price in 25¢ increments

price change	weeks to expiration 18	16	14	12	10	8	6	4	2	0
+125	-33.6	-32.4	-31.1	-30.0	-28.8	-27.4	-26.2	-25.4	-25.4	-25.4
+100	-20.9	-19.1	-17.3	-15.3	-12.9	-10.0	-6.8	-2.6	-0.6	-0.4
+75	-11.4	-9.5	-7.1	-4.5	-1.3	2.6	7.4	14.0	21.8	24.6
+50	-5.8	-3.9	-1.6	1.9	3.9	6.5	12.1	19.2	30.9	49.6
+25	-0.6	0.4	1.4	2.4	3.9	5.3	7.1	8.0	14.5	24.6
0	-2.0	-1.7	-1.1	-0.5	0.0	0.6	1.2	1.4	1.5	-0.4
-25	-1.5	-1.1	-0.3	0.8	1.9	3.0	3.9	4.1	1.7	-0.4
-50	0.4	0.5	0.6	0.8	0.9	0.8	0.6	0.5	0.1	-0.4
-75	2.6	2.7	2.7	2.7	2.3	1.6	1.0	0.5	0.0	-0.4
-100	3.8	3.7	3.5	2.9	2.3	1.6	1.0	-0.1	-0.4	-0.4
-125	3.8	3.7	3.5	2.9	2.3	1.6	1.0	-0.4	-0.4	-0.4

net profit area

Est. credit: -33.1¢ prem +17.1¢ prem. +17.1¢ prem. -1.5¢ com. = -0.4¢

TABLE (net cost = -7.7¢)

changes in the soybean future's price in 25¢ increments

price change	weeks to expiration 18	16	14	12	10	8	6	4	2	0
+125	-33.3	-33.1	-32.9	-32.8	-32.7	-32.7	-32.7	-32.7	-32.7	-32.7
+100	-12.9	-11.9	-11.1	-10.3	-9.5	-8.9	-8.3	-7.9	-7.7	-7.7
+75	1.6	2.9	4.4	6.0	7.7	9.9	12.1	14.7	16.5	17.3
+50	6.9	8.2	9.6	11.2	13.4	15.9	19.2	24.4	31.5	42.3
+25	3.9	4.9	5.8	6.8	8.1	9.7	11.9	14.5	16.1	17.3
0	-1.5	-1.2	-0.9	-0.5	-0.2	0.4	1.2	0.9	-2.3	-7.7
-25	-3.4	-3.1	-3.1	-3.2	-3.5	-4.0	-4.7	-6.0	-6.9	-7.7
-50	-5.7	-5.7	-5.7	-5.8	-5.9	-6.1	-6.5	-6.9	-7.3	-7.7
-75	-6.5	-6.5	-6.6	-6.7	-6.8	-7.0	-7.1	-7.4	-7.5	-7.7
-100	-6.7	-6.7	-6.8	-6.9	-7.1	-7.3	-7.4	-7.5	-7.6	-7.7
-125	-7.0	-7.1	-7.2	-7.3	-7.5	-7.6	-7.7	-7.7	-7.7	-7.7

net profit area

Est. cost: -19.0¢ prem + 6.4¢ prem + 6.4¢ prem. -1.5¢ com. = -7.7¢

SELL A STRADDLE

SELL A CALL AT THE MONEY
and SELL A PUT AT THE MONEY

weeks to expiration: 18

TABLE 0

changes in the soybean future's price in 25¢ increments

	18	16	14	12	10	8	6	4	2	0
+125	-43.4	-38.5	-33.8	-29.0	-23.6	-17.5	-12.0	-7.7	-3.9	-3.4
+100	-27.7	-22.5	-17.4	-11.6	-5.4	0.9	7.9	14.4	19.9	21.6
+75	-13.8	-8.7	-3.5	2.2	8.5	15.8	23.9	34.4	44.3	46.6
+50	-5.4	-0.1	5.3	11.7	18.8	26.8	36.7	49.6	64.7	71.6
+25	-2.2	3.7	9.7	16.4	24.2	33.0	44.1	60.2	81.0	96.6
0	-1.0	4.6	10.4	17.2	24.2	34.6	46.4	63.6	87.0	121.6
-25	-2.2	3.7	9.7	16.4	24.2	33.0	44.1	60.2	81.0	96.6
-50	-5.4	-0.1	5.3	11.7	18.8	26.8	36.7	49.6	64.7	71.6
-75	-13.8	-8.7	-3.5	2.2	8.5	15.8	23.9	34.4	44.3	46.6
-100	-27.7	-22.5	-17.4	-11.6	-5.4	0.9	7.9	14.4	19.9	21.6
-125	-43.4	-38.5	-33.8	-29.0	-23.6	-17.5	-12.0	-7.7	-3.9	-3.4

weeks to expiration. net profit area, in cents

Est. credit is: +61.3¢ premium + 61.3¢ premium -1.0¢ comm.= +121.6¢

TABLE 0

changes in the soybean future's price in 25¢ increments

	18	16	14	12	10	8	6	4	2	0
+125	-50.5	-47.6	-44.9	-42.1	-39.8	-37.8	-35.8	-33.4	-31.7	-31.6
+100	-32.2	-29.1	-25.8	-22.8	-19.9	-16.9	-13.6	-10.1	-7.0	-6.6
+75	-18.1	-14.7	-11.5	-7.7	-3.5	1.2	6.4	12.7	17.6	18.4
+50	-7.7	-4.1	-0.2	4.3	9.3	15.1	21.9	30.5	40.4	43.4
+25	-2.1	1.9	6.3	11.1	16.9	23.8	32.2	44.2	59.3	68.4
0	-1.0	3.4	7.8	13.0	19.2	26.6	35.6	48.8	66.8	93.4
-25	-2.1	1.9	6.3	11.1	16.9	23.8	32.2	44.2	59.3	68.4
-50	-7.7	-4.1	-0.2	4.3	9.4	15.1	21.9	30.5	40.4	43.4
-75	-18.1	-14.7	-11.5	-7.7	-3.5	1.2	6.4	12.7	17.6	18.4
-100	-32.2	-29.1	-25.8	-22.8	-19.9	-16.9	-13.6	-10.1	-7.0	-6.6
-125	-50.5	-47.6	-44.9	-42.1	-39.8	-37.8	-35.8	-33.4	-31.7	-31.6

net profit area, in cents

Est. credit: +47.2¢ premium + 47.2¢ premium -1.0¢ comm.= +93.4¢

TABLE 4

changes in the soybean future's price in 25¢ increments

	18	16	14	12	10	8	6	4	2	0
+125	-65.8	-65.1	-64.5	-63.7	-62.9	-62.0	-61.1	-60.1	-59.8	-59.8
+100	-44.9	-43.8	-42.6	-41.5	-40.2	-38.8	-37.4	-35.9	-34.8	-34.8
+75	-26.7	-24.9	-23.1	-21.1	-18.9	-16.5	-14.0	-11.4	-9.8	-9.8
+50	-12.7	-10.4	-8.1	-5.6	-2.7	0.8	4.7	10.0	14.6	15.2
+25	-3.8	-1.1	2.0	5.3	9.1	13.9	19.4	27.2	36.7	40.2
0	-1.0	2.0	5.2	8.8	13.2	18.2	24.6	33.8	46.4	65.2
-25	-3.8	-1.1	2.0	5.3	9.1	13.9	19.4	27.2	36.7	40.2
-50	-12.7	-10.4	-8.1	-5.6	-2.7	0.8	4.7	10.0	14.6	15.2
-75	-26.7	-24.9	-23.1	-21.1	-18.9	-16.5	-14.0	-11.4	-9.8	-9.8
-100	-44.9	-43.8	-42.6	-41.5	-40.2	-38.8	-37.4	-35.9	-34.8	-34.8
-125	-65.8	-65.1	-64.5	-63.7	-62.9	-62.0	-61.1	-60.1	-59.8	-59.8

weeks to expiration. net profit area, in cents

Est. credit: +33.1¢ premium + 33.1¢ premium -1.0¢ comm.= +65.2¢

TABLE 2

changes in the soybean future's price in 25¢ increments

	18	16	14	12	10	8	6	4	2	0
+125	-89.0	-88.7	-88.5	-88.4	-88.2	-88.1	-88.0	-88.0	-88.0	-88.0
+100	-65.2	-64.9	-64.6	-64.3	-63.9	-63.5	-63.1	-63.0	-63.0	-63.0
+75	-41.4	-40.8	-40.3	-39.8	-39.3	-38.8	-38.3	-38.0	-38.0	-38.0
+50	-22.0	-20.9	-19.9	-18.8	-17.5	-16.2	-14.7	-13.5	-13.0	-13.0
+25	-6.7	-5.0	-3.5	-1.8	0.2	2.6	5.4	8.8	11.5	12.0
0	-1.0	0.8	2.6	4.6	7.2	10.0	13.6	19.0	26.2	37.0
-25	-6.7	-5.0	-3.5	-1.8	0.2	2.6	5.4	8.8	11.5	12.0
-50	-22.0	-20.9	-19.9	-18.8	-17.5	-16.2	-14.7	-13.5	-13.0	-13.0
-75	-41.4	-40.8	-40.3	-39.8	-39.3	-38.8	-38.3	-38.0	-38.0	-38.0
-100	-65.2	-64.9	-64.6	-64.3	-63.9	-63.5	-63.1	-63.0	-63.0	-63.0
-125	-89.0	-88.7	-88.5	-88.4	-88.2	-88.1	-88.0	-88.0	-88.0	-88.0

weeks to expiration. net profit area

Est. credit: +19.0¢ premium + 19.0¢ premium -1.0¢ comm.= 37.0¢

Wm Grandmill (1985) Ltd.

SELL A CALL AT 50¢ OUT OF THE MONEY
and SELL A PUT AT 50¢ OUT OF THE MONEY

weeks to | 18 | expiration

TABLE (18 weeks)

changes in the soybean future's price in 25¢ increments

	18	16	14	12	10	8	6	4	2	0
+125	-22.1	-18.0	-14.0	-9.8	-5.6	-1.6	2.3	6.4	9.7	9.8
+100	-16.3	-11.7	-6.6	-1.3	4.4	10.2	16.8	25.0	33.1	34.8
+75	-11.5	-6.0	-0.6	5.2	12.0	18.9	27.4	42.8	65.8	84.8
+50	-8.5	-3.1	2.6	9.1	16.6	25.1	35.3	49.0	84.8	84.8
+25	-5.8	-0.4	5.4	12.0	19.6	28.7	39.7	55.2	73.5	84.8
0	-1.0	4.4	10.0	16.6	24.0	28.4	43.0	57.0	74.4	84.8
-25	-5.8	-0.4	5.4	12.0	19.6	28.7	39.7	55.2	73.5	84.8
-50	-8.5	-3.1	2.6	9.1	16.6	25.1	35.3	49.0	65.8	84.8
-75	-11.5	-6.0	-0.6	5.2	12.0	18.9	27.4	29.1	42.8	59.8
-100	-16.3	-11.7	-6.6	-1.3	4.4	10.2	16.8	25.0	33.1	34.8
-125	-22.1	-18.0	-14.0	-9.8	-5.6	-1.6	2.3	6.4	9.7	9.8

weeks to expiration

net profit area , in cents

Est. credit is: +42.9¢ premium +42.9¢ premium -1.0¢ comm.=+ 84.8¢

TABLE (8 weeks)

changes in the soybean future's price in 25¢ increments

	18	16	14	12	10	8	6	4	2	0
+125	-33.7	-31.6	-29.6	-27.4	-25.1	-22.6	-20.0	-17.7	-17.0	-17.0
+100	-22.9	-20.1	-17.0	-13.8	-10.3	-6.4	-1.9	3.1	7.5	8.0
+75	-13.6	-10.3	-6.8	-3.0	1.4	6.5	12.5	20.7	29.3	33.0
+50	-8.4	-4.5	-0.4	4.1	9.3	15.2	22.4	32.2	44.3	58.0
+25	-5.2	-1.0	3.3	8.2	13.9	20.7	28.6	39.3	51.7	58.0
0	-1.0	2.8	6.8	11.6	17.0	23.4	30.4	40.6	53.0	58.0
-25	-5.2	-1.0	3.3	8.2	13.9	20.7	28.6	39.3	51.7	58.0
-50	-8.4	-4.5	-0.4	4.1	9.3	15.2	22.4	32.2	44.3	58.0
-75	-13.6	-10.3	-6.8	-3.0	1.4	6.5	12.5	20.7	29.3	33.0
-100	-22.9	-20.1	-17.0	-13.8	-10.3	-6.4	-1.9	3.1	7.5	8.0
-125	-33.7	-31.6	-29.6	-27.4	-25.1	-22.6	-20.0	-17.7	-17.0	-17.0

net profit area , in cents

Est. credit: + 29.5¢ premium +29.5¢ premium -1.0¢ comm. = +58.0¢

TABLE (4 weeks)

changes in the soybean future's price in 25¢ increments

	18	16	14	12	10	8	6	4	2	0
+125	-46.8	-45.9	-45.1	-44.4	-43.7	-42.9	-42.2	-41.8	-41.8	-41.8
+100	-30.8	-29.1	-27.5	-25.7	-23.9	-22.1	-20.3	-17.9	-16.9	-16.8
+75	-17.8	-15.9	-13.8	-11.4	-8.7	-5.5	-2.1	2.6	6.8	8.2
+50	-9.1	-6.7	-4.1	-1.4	1.9	5.7	10.2	16.4	23.8	33.2
+25	-3.6	-0.9	1.9	5.0	8.4	12.7	17.5	23.9	31.1	33.2
0	-1.0	1.4	4.0	6.8	10.0	14.0	18.6	25.0	32.2	33.2
-25	-3.6	-0.9	1.9	5.0	8.4	12.7	17.5	23.9	31.1	33.2
-50	-9.1	-6.7	-4.1	-1.4	1.9	5.7	10.2	16.4	23.8	33.2
-75	-17.8	-15.9	-13.8	-11.4	-8.7	-5.5	-2.1	2.6	6.8	8.2
-100	-30.8	-29.1	-27.5	-25.7	-23.9	-22.1	-20.3	-17.9	-16.9	-16.8
-125	-46.8	-45.9	-45.1	-44.4	-43.7	-42.9	-42.2	-41.8	-41.8	-41.8

weeks to expiration

net profit area , in cents

Est. credit: +17.1¢ premium +17.1¢ premium -1.0¢ comm. = + 33.2¢

TABLE (2 weeks)

changes in the soybean future's price in 25¢ increments

	18	16	14	12	10	8	6	4	2	0
+125	-63.5	-63.4	-63.3	-63.3	-63.2	-63.2	-63.2	-63.2	-63.2	-63.2
+100	-41.1	-40.5	-40.0	-39.6	-39.1	-38.8	-38.5	-38.3	-38.2	-38.2
+75	-22.1	-21.1	-20.2	-19.3	-18.2	-17.0	-15.8	-14.5	-13.6	-13.2
+50	-9.4	-8.2	-7.0	-5.7	-4.0	-2.2	0.0	2.8	6.4	11.8
+25	-2.1	-0.7	0.6	2.0	3.5	5.2	7.5	9.9	11.0	11.8
0	-1.0	0.2	1.4	2.8	4.6	6.4	9.0	11.0	11.8	11.8
-25	-2.1	-0.7	0.6	2.0	3.5	5.2	7.5	9.9	11.0	11.8
-50	-9.4	-8.2	-7.0	-5.7	-4.0	-2.2	0.0	2.8	6.4	11.8
-75	-22.1	-21.1	-20.2	-19.3	-18.2	-17.0	-15.8	-14.5	-13.6	-13.2
-100	-41.1	-40.5	-40.0	-39.6	-39.1	-38.8	-38.5	-38.3	-38.2	-38.2
-125	-63.5	-63.4	-63.3	-63.3	-63.2	-63.2	-63.2	-63.2	-63.2	-63.2

weeks to expiration

net profit area , in cents

Est. credit: + 6.4¢ premium + 6.4¢ premium -1.0¢ comm. = +11.8¢

Wm Grandmill (1985) Ltd.

SELL A STRANGLE – #2

SELL A CALL AT $1.00 OUT OF THE MONEY and SELL A PUT AT $1.00 OUT OF THE MONEY

weeks to expiration

18

TABLE 8 — changes in the soybean future's price in 25¢ increments

changes	weeks to expiration 18	16	14	12	10	8	6	4	2	0
+125	-21.5	-19.4	-17.1	-14.6	-11.4	-7.9	-3.9	1.9	8.8	12.4
+100	-12.5	-9.9	-7.4	-4.2	-0.5	3.6	8.5	15.1	24.1	37.4
+75	-6.0	-3.1	0.0	3.3	7.1	11.7	17.0	23.7	31.9	37.4
+50	-1.4	1.6	4.8	8.3	12.2	16.7	21.7	28.0	34.9	37.4
+25	-1.9	1.6	5.0	8.9	13.2	18.2	23.7	30.6	36.5	37.4
0	-1.0	2.4	6.2	10.0	14.2	18.6	24.0	30.6	36.5	37.4
-25	-1.9	1.6	5.0	8.9	13.2	18.2	23.7	30.6	36.5	37.4
-50	-1.4	1.6	4.8	8.3	12.2	16.7	21.7	28.0	34.9	37.4
-75	-6.0	-3.1	0.0	3.3	7.1	11.7	17.0	23.7	31.9	37.4
-100	-12.5	-9.9	-7.4	-4.2	-0.5	3.6	8.5	15.1	24.1	37.4
-125	-21.5	-19.4	-17.1	-14.6	-11.4	-7.9	-3.9	1.9	8.8	12.4

Est. credit: +19.1¢ premium + 19.1¢ premium -1.0¢ comm.= + 37.4¢

net profit area , in cents

TABLE 8 — changes in the soybean future's price in 25¢ increments

changes	weeks to expiration 18	16	14	12	10	8	6	4	2	0
+125	-11.0	-7.5	-4.0	-0.3	3.8	8.2	13.7	21.6	31.5	38.0
+100	-3.5	0.2	4.0	8.3	13.0	18.2	24.8	33.7	45.7	63.0
+75	0.9	5.3	9.9	15.0	20.7	26.3	33.1	42.2	53.9	63.0
+50	3.1	7.8	13.1	18.7	24.6	30.8	38.1	47.8	57.8	63.0
+25	-0.1	4.9	10.1	15.8	22.1	29.6	38.0	49.1	60.3	63.0
0	-1.0	4.2	9.8	16.0	23.0	30.6	39.2	49.4	59.6	63.0
-25	-0.1	4.9	10.1	15.8	22.1	29.6	38.0	49.1	60.3	63.0
-50	3.1	7.8	13.1	18.7	24.6	30.8	38.1	47.8	57.8	63.0
-75	0.9	5.3	9.9	15.0	20.7	26.3	33.1	42.2	53.9	63.0
-100	-3.5	0.2	4.0	8.3	13.0	18.2	24.8	33.7	45.7	63.0
-125	-11.0	-7.5	-4.0	-0.3	3.8	8.2	13.7	21.6	31.5	38.0

Est. credit: + 32.0¢ premium + 32.0¢ premium -1.0¢ comm.= + 63.0¢

net profit area , in cents

TABLE 2 — changes in the soybean future's price in 25¢ increments

changes	weeks to expiration 18	16	14	12	10	8	6	4	2	0
+125	-29.6	-28.8	-28.1	-27.3	-26.4	-25.3	-24.2	-22.9	-22.0	-21.6
+100	-15.6	-14.7	-13.8	-12.8	-11.5	-10.1	-8.3	-5.6	-2.0	3.4
+75	-7.3	-6.4	-5.6	-4.7	-3.6	-2.3	-0.6	1.5	2.6	3.4
+50	-3.3	-2.6	-1.9	-1.1	-0.2	0.7	2.0	3.0	3.4	3.4
+25	-0.7	0.0	0.7	1.3	1.9	2.5	3.1	3.4	3.4	3.4
0	-1.0	-0.4	0.2	0.8	1.6	2.4	3.2	3.4	3.4	3.4
-25	-0.7	0.0	0.7	1.3	1.9	2.5	3.1	3.4	3.4	3.4
-50	-3.3	-2.6	-1.9	-1.1	-0.2	0.7	2.0	3.0	3.4	3.4
-75	-7.3	-6.4	-5.6	-4.7	-3.6	-2.3	-0.6	1.5	2.6	3.4
-100	-15.6	-14.7	-13.8	-12.8	-11.5	-10.1	-8.3	-5.6	-2.0	3.4
-125	-29.6	-28.8	-28.1	-27.3	-26.4	-25.3	-24.2	-22.9	-22.0	-21.6

Est. credit is: + 2.2¢ premium + 2.2¢ premium -1.0¢ comm.= + 3.4¢

net profit area , in cents

TABLE 4 — changes in the soybean future's price in 25¢ increments

changes	weeks to expiration 18	16	14	12	10	8	6	4	2	0
+125	-27.8	-26.5	-24.9	-23.3	-21.4	-19.1	-16.5	-12.9	-9.0	-7.6
+100	-16.2	-14.5	-12.8	-10.9	-8.7	-6.1	-2.9	1.7	8.0	17.4
+75	-7.5	-5.7	-3.9	-2.1	-0.1	2.5	5.5	9.7	15.3	17.4
+50	-1.4	0.5	2.9	5.0	7.3	9.8	13.3	16.9	17.4	17.4
+25	-1.0	0.8	2.3	4.5	6.8	9.4	12.0	15.2	17.4	17.4
0	-1.4	0.5	2.8	4.6	6.8	9.5	12.2	15.5	17.4	17.4
-25	-1.0	0.8	2.3	4.5	6.8	9.4	12.0	15.2	17.4	17.4
-50	-1.4	0.5	2.9	5.0	7.3	9.8	13.3	16.9	17.4	17.4
-75	-7.5	-5.7	-3.9	-2.1	-0.1	2.5	5.5	9.7	15.3	17.4
-100	-16.2	-14.5	-12.8	-10.9	-8.7	-6.1	-2.9	1.7	8.0	17.4
-125	-27.8	-26.5	-24.9	-23.3	-21.4	-19.1	-16.5	-12.9	-9.0	-7.6

Est. credit is: + 9.2¢ premium + 9.2¢ premium -1.0¢ comm.= + 17.4¢

net profit area , in cents

Wm Grandmill (1985) Ltd.

BUY A CALL or BUY A PUT

AT THE MONEY

weeks to expiration: **20**

Table (net profit) — estimated cost: - 63.8¢ - 0.5 comm. = - 64.3¢

changes in the soybean future's price in 25¢ increments	20	18	16	14	12	10	8	6	4	2	0
+125	79.0	76.5	74.0	71.6	69.2	66.4	63.3	61.0	60.7	60.7	60.7
+100	55.5	53.0	50.4	48.1	45.4	42.7	40.2	37.5	36.1	35.7	35.7
+75	34.5	32.2	29.7	27.4	25.0	22.4	19.6	16.7	13.3	10.8	10.7
+50	22.3	19.8	17.2	14.6	11.5	8.1	4.3	-0.3	-6.2	-12.6	-14.3
+25	10.5	7.8	4.7	1.6	-1.8	-5.7	-9.9	-15.2	-22.9	-32.8	-39.3
0	-0.5	-3.0	-5.8	-8.7	-12.1	-16.1	-20.8	-26.7	-35.3	-47.0	-64.3
-25	-10.1	-12.6	-15.4	-18.3	-21.6	-25.5	-30.1	-35.9	-44.3	-55.2	-64.3
-50	-18.9	-21.4	-24.1	-26.9	-30.2	-33.9	-38.1	-43.4	-50.4	-59.1	-64.3
-75	-22.9	-25.4	-28.0	-30.9	-34.2	-37.6	-42.4	-47.6	-54.7	-62.1	-64.3
-100	-29.9	-32.3	-34.9	-37.7	-40.8	-44.3	-48.1	-52.4	-57.5	-62.6	-64.3
-125	-37.8	-40.1	-42.5	-44.8	-47.2	-49.8	-52.8	-56.0	-60.0	-63.8	-64.3

weeks to expiration / net profit

Table (net profit area) — estimated cost: - 49.2¢ premium - 0.5¢ comm. = -49.7¢

changes in the soybean future's price in 25¢ increments	20	18	16	14	12	10	8	6	4	2	0
+125	81.7	80.3	78.8	77.5	76.2	75.5	75.3	75.3	75.3	75.3	75.3
+100	57.9	56.7	55.3	53.9	52.0	51.2	50.6	50.3	50.3	50.3	50.3
+75	37.6	36.4	35.1	33.9	32.5	31.0	29.5	27.8	26.0	25.3	25.3
+50	23.6	21.9	20.2	18.3	16.2	13.9	11.3	8.3	4.5	0.8	0.3
+25	9.8	8.0	6.1	4.0	1.7	-1.1	-4.4	-8.4	-14.2	-21.1	-24.7
0	-0.5	-2.5	-4.7	-6.9	-9.5	-12.6	-16.3	-20.8	-27.4	-36.4	-49.7
-25	-10.0	-11.9	-14.0	-16.3	-18.8	-21.8	-25.4	-29.8	-36.0	-44.2	-49.7
-50	-18.4	-20.2	-22.1	-24.1	-26.5	-29.2	-32.4	-35.9	-41.0	-47.2	-49.7
-75	-22.4	-24.3	-26.4	-28.4	-30.8	-33.5	-36.7	-40.2	-44.7	-48.9	-49.7
-100	-28.9	-30.4	-32.1	-34.0	-36.0	-38.1	-40.3	-43.0	-46.2	-49.3	-49.7
-125	-34.6	-35.8	-37.2	-38.6	-40.1	-41.7	-43.5	-45.5	-47.9	-49.6	-49.7

Table (net profit area) — estimated cost: - 34.5¢ premium - 0.5¢ comm. = - 35.0¢

changes in the soybean future's price in 25¢ increments	20	18	16	14	12	10	8	6	4	2	0
+125	90.0	90.0	90.0	90.0	90.0	90.0	90.0	90.0	90.0	90.0	90.0
+100	66.2	65.9	65.7	65.5	65.3	65.1	65.0	65.0	65.0	65.0	65.0
+75	44.6	44.1	43.5	42.9	42.3	41.7	41.0	40.4	40.0	40.0	40.0
+50	26.7	25.8	24.7	23.7	22.6	21.3	19.8	18.2	16.1	15.1	15.0
+25	11.3	10.0	8.8	7.3	5.7	3.8	1.5	-1.1	-4.7	-8.6	-10.0
0	-0.5	-1.9	-3.4	-5.0	-6.8	-9.0	-11.5	-14.7	-19.3	-25.6	-35.0
-25	-9.7	-11.0	-12.5	-14.1	-15.8	-17.7	-20.2	-23.1	-27.3	-32.9	-35.0
-50	-16.7	-17.9	-19.1	-20.4	-21.8	-23.4	-25.4	-27.7	-30.9	-34.5	-35.0
-75	-21.0	-22.2	-23.4	-24.6	-26.0	-27.5	-29.3	-31.2	-33.7	-35.0	-35.0
-100	-25.0	-25.8	-26.7	-27.7	-28.6	-29.7	-31.0	-32.3	-33.9	-34.7	-35.0
-125	-28.3	-29.0	-29.6	-30.3	-31.1	-31.9	-32.8	-33.7	-34.7	-35.0	-35.0

weeks to expiration / net profit area

Table (net profit area, in cent) — estimated cost: -19.8¢ premium - 0.5¢ comm. = - 20.3¢

changes in the soybean future's price in 25¢ increments	20	18	16	14	12	10	8	6	4	2	0
+125	104.7	104.7	104.7	104.7	104.7	104.7	104.7	104.7	104.7	104.7	104.7
+100	79.7	79.7	79.7	79.7	79.7	79.7	79.7	79.7	79.7	79.7	79.7
+75	55.1	55.0	54.9	54.8	54.8	54.7	54.7	54.7	54.7	54.7	54.7
+50	32.7	32.3	31.8	31.4	31.0	30.6	30.3	30.0	29.8	29.7	29.7
+25	13.3	12.6	11.9	11.2	10.4	9.5	8.4	7.3	6.0	5.1	4.7
0	-0.5	-1.3	-2.2	-3.1	-4.1	-5.4	-6.8	-8.6	-11.3	-14.9	-20.3
-25	-8.8	-9.6	-10.5	-11.3	-12.2	-13.3	-14.6	-16.3	-18.4	-19.5	-20.3
-50	-13.3	-13.9	-14.5	-15.1	-15.8	-16.7	-17.7	-18.9	-19.5	-19.9	-20.3
-75	-16.7	-17.1	-17.6	-18.1	-18.6	-19.0	-19.4	-20.0	-20.3	-20.3	-20.3
-100	-17.8	-18.1	-18.4	-18.7	-19.0	-19.4	-19.8	-20.2	-20.3	-20.3	-20.3
-125	-19.1	-19.3	-19.6	-19.8	-19.9	-20.1	-20.2	-20.3	-20.3	-20.3	-20.3

weeks to expiration / net profit area , in cent

BUY A CALL or BUY A PUT
AT 50¢ OUT OF THE MONEY

TABLE 80

changes in the soybean future's price in 25¢ increments

	weeks to expiration										
	20	18	16	14	12	10	8	6	4	2	0
+125	52.9	50.6	48.2	45.8	43.4	40.8	38.0	35.1	31.7	29.2	29.1
+100	40.7	38.2	35.6	33.0	29.9	26.5	22.7	18.1	12.2	5.8	4.1
+75	28.9	26.2	23.1	20.0	16.6	12.7	8.6	3.2	-4.5	-14.4	-20.9
+50	17.9	15.4	12.6	9.7	6.3	2.3	-2.4	-8.3	-16.9	-28.6	-45.9
+25	8.3	5.8	3.0	0.1	-3.2	-7.1	-11.7	-17.5	-25.9	-36.8	-45.9
0	-0.5	-3.0	-5.7	-8.5	-11.8	-15.5	-19.7	-25.0	-32.0	-40.6	-45.9
-25	-4.5	-7.0	-9.6	-12.5	-15.8	-19.5	-24.0	-29.5	-36.3	-44.2	-45.9
-50	-11.5	-13.9	-16.5	-19.3	-22.4	-25.9	-29.7	-34.0	-39.1	-44.2	-45.9
-75	-19.4	-21.7	-24.1	-26.4	-28.8	-31.4	-34.4	-37.6	-41.6	-45.4	-45.9
-100	-26.9	-29.0	-30.9	-33.4	-36.0	-37.9	-39.8	-41.9	-44.2	-45.9	-45.9
-125	-33.7	-35.5	-37.1	-38.8	-40.6	-42.2	-43.4	-44.5	-45.1	-45.9	-45.9

net profit

The estimated cost is: 45.4¢ premium - 0.5¢ comm. = 45.9¢

TABLE 40

changes in the soybean future's price in 25¢ increments

	weeks to expiration										
	20	18	16	14	12	10	8	6	4	2	0
+125	60.8	60.3	59.7	59.1	58.5	57.9	57.2	56.6	56.2	56.2	56.2
+100	42.9	42.0	40.9	39.9	38.8	37.5	36.0	34.4	32.3	31.3	31.2
+75	27.5	26.2	25.0	23.5	21.9	20.0	17.7	15.1	11.5	7.6	6.2
+50	15.7	14.3	12.8	11.2	9.4	7.2	4.7	1.5	-3.1	-9.4	-18.8
+25	6.5	5.2	3.7	2.1	0.4	-1.5	-4.0	-6.9	-11.1	-16.7	-18.8
0	-0.5	-1.7	-2.9	-4.2	-5.6	-7.2	-9.2	-11.5	-14.7	-18.3	-18.8
-25	-4.8	-6.0	-7.2	-8.4	-9.8	-11.3	-13.1	-15.0	-17.2	-18.8	-18.8
-50	-8.8	-9.6	-10.5	-11.5	-12.4	-13.5	-14.8	-16.1	-17.7	-18.8	-18.8
-75	-12.1	-12.8	-13.5	-14.1	-14.9	-15.7	-16.6	-17.4	-18.5	-18.8	-18.8
-100	-14.9	-15.6	-16.2	-16.8	-17.5	-18.0	-18.3	-18.5	-18.8	-18.8	-18.8
-125	-17.5	-17.9	-18.2	-18.4	-18.5	-18.6	-18.7	-18.8	-18.8	-18.8	-18.8

net profit area

The estimated cost is: -18.3¢ premium - 0.5¢ comm. = -18.8¢

TABLE 80

changes in the soybean future's price in 25¢ increments

	20	18	16	14	12	10	8	6	4	2	0
+125	55.5	54.3	53.0	51.8	50.4	48.9	447.4	45.7	43.9	43.2	43.2
+100	41.5	39.8	38.1	36.2	34.1	31.8	29.2	26.2	22.4	18.7	18.2
+75	27.7	25.9	24.0	21.9	19.6	16.8	13.5	9.5	3.7	-3.2	-6.8
+50	17.4	15.4	13.2	11.0	8.4	5.3	1.6	-2.9	-9.5	-18.5	-31.8
+25	7.9	6.0	3.9	1.6	-0.9	-3.9	-7.5	-11.9	-18.1	-26.3	-31.8
0	-0.5	-2.3	-4.2	-6.2	-8.6	-11.3	-14.5	-18.0	-23.1	-29.3	-31.8
-25	-4.5	-6.4	-8.5	-10.5	-12.9	-15.6	-18.8	-22.3	-26.8	-31.0	-31.8
-50	-11.0	-12.6	-14.3	-16.2	-18.1	-20.2	-22.4	-25.1	-28.3	-31.0	-31.8
-75	-16.7	-17.9	-19.3	-20.7	-22.2	-23.8	-25.6	-27.6	-30.0	-31.7	-31.8
-100	-21.7	-22.5	-23.6	-24.8	-25.9	-27.1	-28.4	-29.9	-31.1	-31.8	-31.8
-125	-25.5	-26.2	-27.0	-27.8	-28.6	-29.4	-30.4	-31.3	-31.8	-31.8	-31.8

The estimated cost is: -31.3¢ premium - 0.5¢ comm. = -31.8¢

TABLE 20

changes in the soybean future's price in 25¢ increments

	weeks to expiration										
	20	18	16	14	12	10	8	6	4	2	0
+125	68.0	67.8	67.7	67.6	67.6	67.5	67.5	67.5	67.5	67.5	67.5
+100	45.5	45.1	44.6	44.2	43.8	43.4	43.1	42.8	42.6	42.5	42.5
+75	25.1	24.4	23.7	23.0	22.2	21.3	20.2	19.1	18.3	17.9	17.5
+50	12.3	11.5	10.6	9.7	8.7	7.4	6.0	4.2	1.5	-2.1	-7.5
+25	4.0	3.2	2.3	1.5	0.6	-0.5	-1.8	-3.5	-5.6	-6.7	-7.5
0	-0.5	-1.1	-1.7	-2.3	-3.0	-3.9	-4.9	-6.1	-7.1	-7.5	-7.5
-25	-3.9	-4.3	-4.8	-5.3	-5.8	-6.2	-6.6	-7.2	-7.1	-7.5	-7.5
-50	-5.0	-5.3	-5.6	-5.9	-6.2	-6.6	-7.0	-7.4	-7.5	-7.5	-7.5
-75	-6.3	-6.5	-6.8	-7.0	-7.1	-7.3	-7.4	-7.5	-7.5	-7.5	-7.5
-100	-7.1	-7.2	-7.3	-7.4	-7.5	-7.5	-7.5	-7.5	-7.5	-7.5	-7.5
-125	-7.4	-7.5	-7.5	-7.5	-7.5	-7.5	-7.5	-7.5	-7.5	-7.5	-7.5

net profit area

The estimated cost is: -7.0¢ premium - 0.5¢ comm. = -7.5¢

Wm Grandmill (1985) Ltd.

SELL A CALL or SELL A PUT

AT THE MONEY

weeks to
20
expiration

TABLE 080 (estimated credit: +63.8¢ premium − 0.5¢ comm. = +63.3¢)

changes in the soybean future's price in 25¢ increments	weeks to expiration 20	18	16	14	12	10	8	6	4	2	0
+125	-80.0	-77.5	-75.0	-72.6	-70.2	-67.4	-64.3	-62.0	-61.7	-61.7	-61.7
+100	-56.5	-54.0	-51.4	-49.1	-44.4	-43.7	-41.2	-38.5	-37.1	-36.7	-36.7
+75	-35.5	-33.2	-30.7	-28.4	-26.0	-23.4	-20.6	-17.7	-14.3	-11.8	-11.7
+50	-23.3	-20.8	-18.2	-15.6	-12.5	-9.1	-5.3	-0.7	5.2	11.6	13.3
+25	-11.5	-8.8	-5.7	-2.6	0.8	4.7	8.9	14.7	21.9	31.8	38.3
0	-0.5	2.0	4.8	7.7	11.1	15.1	19.8	25.7	34.3	46.0	63.3
-25	9.1	11.6	14.4	17.3	20.6	24.5	29.1	34.9	43.3	54.2	63.3
-50	17.9	20.4	23.1	25.0	29.2	32.9	37.1	42.4	49.4	58.1	63.3
-75	21.9	24.4	27.0	29.9	33.2	36.6	41.4	46.6	53.7	61.1	63.3
-100	28.9	31.3	33.9	36.6	39.8	43.3	47.1	51.4	56.5	61.6	63.3
-125	36.8	39.1	41.5	43.8	46.2	48.8	51.8	55.0	59.0	62.8	63.3

net profit area, in cents

TABLE 080 (estimated credit: +49.2¢ premium − 0.5¢ comm. = +48.7¢)

changes in the soybean future's price in 25¢ increments	weeks to expiration 20	18	16	14	12	10	8	6	4	2	0
+125	-82.7	-81.3	-79.8	-78.5	-77.2	-76.5	-76.3	-76.3	-76.3	-76.3	-76.3
+100	-58.9	-57.7	-56.3	-54.9	-53.8	-53.0	-52.2	-51.6	-51.3	-51.3	-51.3
+75	-38.6	-37.4	-36.1	-34.9	-33.5	-32.0	-30.5	-28.8	-27.0	-26.3	-26.3
+50	-24.6	-22.9	-21.2	-19.3	-17.2	-14.9	-12.3	-9.3	-5.5	-1.8	-1.3
+25	-10.8	-9.0	-7.1	-5.0	-2.7	0.1	3.4	7.4	13.2	20.1	23.7
0	-0.5	1.5	3.7	5.9	8.5	11.6	15.3	19.8	26.4	35.4	48.7
-25	9.0	10.9	13.0	15.3	17.8	20.8	24.4	28.8	35.0	43.2	48.7
-50	17.4	19.2	21.1	23.1	25.5	28.2	31.4	34.9	40.0	46.2	48.7
-75	21.4	23.3	25.4	27.4	29.8	32.5	35.7	39.2	43.7	47.9	48.7
-100	27.9	29.4	31.1	33.0	35.0	37.1	39.3	42.0	45.2	48.3	48.7
-125	33.6	34.8	36.2	37.6	39.1	40.7	42.5	44.5	46.9	48.6	48.7

net profit area, in cents

TABLE 040 (estimated credit: +34.5¢ premium − 0.5¢ comm. = +34.0¢)

changes in the soybean future's price in 25¢ increments	weeks to expiration 20	18	16	14	12	10	8	6	4	2	0
+125	-91.0	-91.0	-91.0	-91.0	-91.0	-91.0	-91.0	-91.1	-91.0	-91.0	-91.0
+100	-67.2	-66.9	-66.7	-66.5	-66.3	-66.1	-66.0	-66.0	-66.0	-66.0	-66.0
+75	-45.6	-45.1	-44.5	-43.9	-43.3	-42.7	-42.0	-41.4	-41.0	-41.0	-41.0
+50	-27.7	-26.8	-25.7	-24.7	-23.6	-22.7	-20.8	-19.2	-17.1	-16.1	-16.0
+25	-12.3	-11.0	-9.8	-8.3	-6.7	-4.8	-2.5	0.1	3.7	7.6	9.0
0	-0.5	0.9	2.4	4.0	5.8	8.0	10.5	13.7	18.3	24.6	34.0
-25	8.7	10.0	11.5	13.1	14.8	16.7	19.2	22.1	26.3	31.9	34.0
-50	15.7	16.9	18.1	19.4	20.8	22.4	24.4	26.7	29.9	33.5	34.0
-75	20.0	21.2	22.4	23.6	25.0	26.5	28.3	30.2	32.4	34.0	34.0
-100	24.0	24.8	25.7	26.7	27.6	28.7	30.0	31.3	32.9	34.0	34.0
-125	27.3	28.0	28.6	29.3	30.1	30.9	31.8	32.7	33.7	34.0	34.0

net profit area, in cents

TABLE 020 (estimated credit: +19.8¢ premium − 0.5¢ comm. = +19.3¢)

changes in the soybean future's price in 25¢ increments	weeks to expiration 20	18	16	14	12	10	8	6	4	2	0
+125	-105.7	-105.7	-105.7	-105.7	-105.7	-105.7	-105.7	-105.7	-105.5	-105.7	-105.7
+100	-80.7	-80.7	-80.7	-80.7	-80.7	-80.7	-80.7	-80.7	-80.7	-80.7	-80.7
+75	-56.1	-56.0	-55.9	-55.8	-55.8	-55.7	-55.7	-55.7	-55.7	-55.7	-55.7
+50	-33.7	-33.3	-32.8	-32.4	-32.0	-31.6	-31.3	-31.0	-30.8	-30.7	-30.7
+25	-14.3	-13.6	-12.9	-12.2	-11.4	-10.5	-9.4	-8.3	-7.0	-6.1	-5.7
0	-0.5	0.3	1.2	2.1	3.1	4.4	5.8	7.6	10.3	13.9	19.3
-25	7.8	8.6	9.5	10.3	11.2	12.3	13.6	15.3	17.4	18.5	19.3
-50	12.3	12.9	13.5	14.1	14.8	15.7	16.7	17.9	18.9	19.3	19.3
-75	15.7	16.1	16.6	17.1	17.6	18.0	18.4	18.9	19.3	19.3	19.3
-100	16.8	17.1	17.4	17.7	18.0	18.4	18.8	19.2	19.3	19.3	19.3
-125	18.1	18.3	18.6	18.8	18.9	19.1	19.2	19.3	19.3	19.3	19.3

net profit area, in cents

Wm Grandmill (1985) Ltd.

SELL A CALL or SELL A PUT
AT 50¢ OUT OF THE MONEY

weeks to expiration: **20**

TABLE 08

changes in the soybean future's price in 25¢ increments — weeks to expiration

	20	18	16	14	12	10	8	6	4	2	0
+125	-53.9	-51.6	-49.2	-46.8	-44.4	-41.8	-39.0	-36.1	-32.7	-30.2	-30.1
+100	-41.7	-39.2	-36.6	-34.0	-30.9	-27.5	-23.7	-19.1	-13.2	-6.8	-5.1
+75	-29.9	-27.2	-24.1	-21.0	-17.6	-13.7	-9.6	-4.2	3.5	13.4	19.9
+50	-18.9	-15.4	-10.7	-7.3	-3.3	1.4	7.3	15.9	24.9	35.8	44.9
+25	-9.3	-6.8	-4.0	-1.1	2.2	6.1	10.7	16.5	24.0	35.8	44.9
0	-0.5	2.0	4.7	7.5	10.8	14.5	18.7	24.0	31.0	40.6	44.9
-25	3.5	6.0	8.6	11.5	14.8	18.5	23.0	28.5	35.3	42.7	44.9
-50	10.5	12.9	15.5	18.3	21.4	24.9	28.7	33.0	38.1	43.2	44.9
-75	18.4	20.7	23.1	25.4	27.8	30.4	33.4	36.6	40.6	44.4	44.9
-100	25.9	28.0	29.9	32.4	35.0	36.9	38.7	40.9	43.2	44.9	44.9
-125	32.7	34.5	36.1	37.8	39.6	41.2	42.4	43.5	44.1	44.9	44.9

net profit area, in cents

The estimated credit is: +45.4¢ premium - 0.5¢ comm. = +44.9¢

TABLE 08

changes in the soybean future's price in 25¢ increments — weeks to expiration

	20	18	16	14	12	10	8	6	4	2	0
+125	-56.5	-55.3	-54.0	-52.8	-51.4	-49.9	-48.4	-46.7	-44.9	-44.2	-44.2
+100	-42.5	-40.8	-39.1	-37.2	-35.1	-32.8	-30.2	-27.2	-23.4	-19.7	-19.2
+75	-28.7	-26.9	-25.0	-22.9	-20.6	-17.8	-14.5	-10.5	-4.7	2.2	5.8
+50	-18.4	-16.4	-14.2	-12.0	-9.4	-6.3	-2.6	1.9	8.5	17.5	30.8
+25	-8.9	-7.0	-4.9	-2.6	-0.1	2.9	6.5	10.9	17.1	25.3	30.8
0	-0.5	1.3	3.2	5.2	7.6	10.3	13.5	17.0	22.1	28.3	30.8
-25	3.5	5.4	7.5	9.5	11.9	14.5	17.8	21.3	25.8	30.0	30.8
-50	10.0	11.6	13.3	15.2	17.1	19.2	21.4	24.1	27.3	30.4	30.8
-75	15.7	16.9	18.3	19.7	21.2	22.8	24.6	26.6	29.0	30.7	30.8
-100	20.7	21.5	22.6	23.8	24.9	26.1	27.4	28.9	30.1	30.8	30.8
-125	24.5	25.2	26.0	26.8	27.6	28.4	29.4	30.3	30.8	30.8	30.8

net profit area, in cents

The estimated credit is: +31.3¢ premium - 0.5¢ comm. = +30.8¢

TABLE 04

changes in the soybean future's price in 25¢ increments — weeks to expiration

	20	18	16	14	12	10	8	6	4	2	0
+125	-61.8	-61.3	-60.7	-60.1	-59.5	-58.9	-58.2	-57.6	-57.2	-57.2	-57.2
+100	-44.0	-43.0	-41.9	-40.9	-39.8	-38.7	-37.0	-35.4	-33.3	-32.3	-32.2
+75	-28.5	-27.2	-26.0	-24.5	-22.9	-21.0	-18.7	-16.1	-12.5	-8.6	-7.2
+50	-16.7	-15.3	-13.8	-12.2	-10.4	-8.2	-5.7	-2.5	2.1	8.4	17.8
+25	-7.5	-6.2	-4.7	-3.1	-1.4	0.5	3.0	5.9	10.1	15.7	17.8
0	-0.5	0.7	1.9	3.2	4.6	6.2	8.2	10.5	13.7	17.3	17.8
-25	3.8	5.0	6.2	7.4	8.8	10.3	12.1	14.0	16.2	17.5	17.8
-50	7.8	8.6	9.5	10.5	11.4	12.5	13.8	15.1	17.0	17.8	17.8
-75	11.1	11.8	12.5	13.1	13.9	14.7	15.6	16.4	17.5	17.8	17.8
-100	13.9	14.6	15.2	15.8	16.5	17.0	17.3	17.5	17.8	17.8	17.8
-125	16.5	16.9	17.2	17.4	17.5	17.6	17.7	17.8	17.8	17.8	17.8

net profit area, in cents

The estimated credit is: +18.3¢ premium - 0.5¢ comm. = +17.8¢

TABLE 02

changes in the soybean future's price in 25¢ increments — weeks to expiration

	20	18	16	14	12	10	8	6	4	2	0
+125	-69.0	-68.8	-68.7	-68.6	-68.6	-68.5	-68.5	-68.5	-68.5	-68.5	-68.5
+100	-46.5	-46.1	-45.6	-45.2	-44.8	-44.4	-44.1	-43.8	-43.6	-43.5	-43.5
+75	-26.1	-25.4	-24.7	-24.0	-23.2	-22.3	-21.2	-20.1	-19.3	-18.9	-18.5
+50	-13.3	-12.5	-11.6	-10.7	-9.7	-8.4	-7.0	-5.2	-2.5	1.1	6.5
+25	-5.0	-4.2	-3.3	-2.5	-1.6	-0.5	0.8	2.5	4.6	5.7	6.5
0	-0.5	0.1	0.7	1.3	2.0	2.9	3.9	5.1	6.1	6.5	6.5
-25	2.9	3.3	3.8	4.3	4.8	5.6	6.2	6.5	6.5	6.5	6.5
-50	4.0	4.3	4.6	4.9	5.2	6.0	6.4	6.5	6.5	6.5	6.5
-75	5.3	5.5	5.8	6.0	6.1	6.3	6.4	6.5	6.5	6.5	6.5
-100	6.1	6.2	6.3	6.4	6.5	6.5	6.5	6.5	6.5	6.5	6.5
-125	6.4	6.5	6.5	6.5	6.5	6.5	6.5	6.5	6.5	6.5	6.5

net profit area, in cents

The estimated credit is: +7.0¢ premium - 0.5¢ comm. = +6.5¢

Wm Grandmill (1985) Ltd.

BULL or BEAR SPREAD – #1

BUY A CALL AT THE MONEY
and SELL A CALL AT 25¢ OUT OF THE MONEY
OR
BUY A PUT AT THE MONEY
and SELL A PUT AT 25¢ OUT OF THE MONEY

weeks to expiration: 20

TABLE 0

changes in the soybean future's price in 25¢ increments	weeks to expiration										
	20	18	16	14	12	10	8	6	4	2	0
+125	12.8	12.9	13.0	13.1	13.2	13.4	13.6	13.8	14.0	14.4	14.4
+100	7.4	7.8	8.2	8.6	9.1	9.6	10.3	10.8	12.8	14.4	14.4
+75	4.4	4.7	5.0	5.3	5.7	6.2	6.8	7.8	9.4	12.8	14.4
+50	2.0	2.1	2.2	2.4	2.7	3.1	3.6	4.3	6.1	9.6	14.4
+25	0.5	0.5	0.6	0.6	0.7	0.8	0.9	1.1	1.8	3.6	14.4
0	-1.0	-1.0	-1.0	-1.0	-1.1	-1.2	-1.3	-1.4	-1.6	-2.6	-10.6
-25	-1.8	-1.8	-1.9	-2.0	-2.0	-2.2	-2.6	-3.3	-4.5	-6.7	-10.6
-50	-2.1	-2.1	-2.2	-2.4	-2.7	-3.1	-3.7	-4.6	-5.7	-7.6	-10.6
-75	-2.4	-2.5	-2.6	-2.8	-3.4	-4.2	-5.0	-6.0	-7.0	-8.6	-10.6
-100	-2.6	-2.7	-3.0	-3.5	-4.2	-5.0	-5.9	-7.0	-8.1	-9.4	-10.6
-125	-2.8	-3.0	-3.2	-3.8	-4.6	-5.4	-6.6	-7.8	-9.1	-10.1	-10.6

net profit area , in cents

Estimated cost is:-63.8¢ premium + 54.2¢ premium -1.0¢ comm. = -10.6¢

TABLE 8

changes in the soybean future's price in 25¢ increments	weeks to expiration										
	20	18	16	14	12	10	8	6	4	2	0
+125	13.0	13.0	13.0	13.0	13.1	13.3	13.7	14.2	14.5	14.5	14.5
+100	8.5	8.8	9.2	9.6	10.0	10.5	11.2	12.3	13.8	14.5	14.5
+75	5.7	5.9	6.1	6.4	6.7	7.0	7.7	9.0	11.0	14.0	14.5
+50	3.3	3.4	3.6	3.8	4.1	4.5	5.2	6.2	8.2	11.4	14.5
+25	0.0	0.0	0.2	0.5	0.7	1.0	1.4	1.9	2.7	4.8	14.5
0	-1.0	-1.1	-1.1	-1.1	-1.2	-1.3	-1.4	-1.5	-1.9	-2.7	-10.5
-25	-2.1	-2.2	-2.4	-2.6	-2.8	-3.1	-3.5	-4.4	-5.5	-7.5	-10.5
-50	-3.1	-3.3	-3.5	-3.8	-4.1	-4.5	-5.1	-5.8	-6.8	-8.8	-10.5
-75	-4.0	-4.3	-4.6	-4.9	-5.3	-5.9	-6.9	-7.7	-8.8	-10.1	-10.5
-100	-4.8	-5.2	-5.6	-6.0	-6.4	-6.9	-7.3	-8.0	-8.9	-10.2	-10.5
-125	-5.5	-5.8	-6.1	-6.4	-6.8	-7.2	-7.7	-8.2	-9.2	-10.4	-10.5

Estimated cost is:-49.2¢ prem. +39.7¢ prem. - 0.5¢ comm. = -10.5¢

TABLE 4

changes in the soybean future's price in 25¢ increments	weeks to expiration										
	20	18	16	14	12	10	8	6	4	2	0
+125	13.6	13.9	14.1	14.3	14.5	14.7	14.8	14.8	14.8	14.8	14.8
+100	11.4	11.7	12.0	12.4	12.8	13.2	13.8	14.4	14.8	14.8	14.8
+75	7.7	8.1	8.6	9.0	9.5	10.2	11.0	12.0	13.5	14.8	14.8
+50	5.2	5.4	5.7	6.2	6.7	7.3	8.1	9.1	10.6	13.5	14.8
+25	1.6	1.8	2.0	2.1	2.3	2.6	2.8	3.4	4.4	6.8	14.8
0	-1.0	-1.1	-1.1	-1.1	-1.2	-1.4	-1.6	-1.8	-2.2	-3.0	-10.2
-25	-3.1	-3.3	-3.6	-3.9	-4.2	-4.5	-5.0	-5.6	-6.6	-8.6	-10.2
-50	-5.3	-5.6	-5.8	-6.0	-6.3	-6.7	-7.2	-7.7	-8.6	-9.7	-10.2
-75	-6.2	-6.6	-6.9	-7.2	-7.6	-7.9	-8.2	-9.0	-9.4	-10.2	-10.2
-100	-6.8	-7.0	-7.3	-7.6	-7.8	-8.0	-8.4	-8.9	-9.2	-9.9	-10.2
-125	-7.2	-7.4	-7.5	-7.7	-7.9	-8.2	-8.6	-9.1	-9.4	-10.2	-10.2

net profit area , in cents

Estimated cost is: -34.5¢ premium + 25.3¢ premium - 1.0¢ comm. = -10.2¢

TABLE 2

changes in the soybean future's price in 25¢ increments	weeks to expiration										
	20	18	16	14	12	10	8	6	4	2	0
+125	15.7	15.7	15.7	15.7	15.7	15.7	15.7	15.7	15.7	15.7	15.7
+100	15.3	15.4	15.5	15.6	15.6	15.7	15.7	15.7	15.7	15.7	15.7
+75	13.1	13.4	13.8	14.1	14.5	15.1	15.4	15.6	15.7	15.7	15.7
+50	10.1	10.3	10.6	10.9	11.3	11.8	12.6	13.4	14.5	15.6	15.7
+25	4.5	4.7	4.8	5.0	5.2	5.6	5.9	6.6	8.0	10.7	15.7
0	-1.0	-1.0	-1.0	-1.1	-1.2	-1.4	-1.5	-1.6	-2.2	-2.7	-9.3
-25	-4.8	-5.0	-5.3	-5.5	-5.7	-5.9	-6.3	-6.7	-7.7	-8.7	-9.3
-50	-5.9	-6.1	-6.2	-6.5	-6.7	-7.0	-7.5	-8.2	-8.9	-9.3	-9.3
-75	-6.9	-7.0	-7.1	-7.3	-7.5	-7.8	-8.4	-9.1	-9.3	-9.3	-9.3
-100	-7.8	-7.9	-8.0	-8.2	-8.6	-8.9	-9.2	-9.3	-9.3	-9.3	-9.3
-125	-8.5	-8.6	-8.8	-8.9	-8.9	-9.1	-9.3	-9.3	-9.3	-9.3	-9.3

net profit area , in cents

Estimated cost is: -19.8¢ premium +11.5¢ premium -1.0¢ comm. = -9.3¢

BULL or BEAR SPREAD – #2

BUY A CALL AT THE MONEY
and SELL 2 CALLS AT 50¢ OUT OF THE MONEY
OR
BUY A PUT AT THE MONEY
and SELL 2 PUTS AT 50¢ OUT OF THE MONEY

weeks to expiration: 20

TABLE 80

changes in the soybean future's price in 25¢ increments

	weeks to expiration										
	20	18	16	14	12	10	8	6	4	2	0
+125	-28.8	-26.6	-24.3	-22.0	-19.6	-17.2	-14.7	-11.2	-4.7	0.3	0.5
+100	-27.9	-25.4	-22.8	-19.9	-16.4	-12.3	-7.2	-0.7	9.7	22.1	25.5
+75	-25.3	-22.2	-18.5	-14.6	-10.2	-5.0	0.6	8.3	20.3	37.6	50.5
+50	-15.5	-13.0	-10.0	-6.8	-3.1	1.5	7.1	14.3	25.6	42.6	75.5
+25	-8.1	-5.8	-3.3	-0.6	2.6	6.5	11.5	17.8	26.9	38.8	50.5
0	-1.5	1.0	3.6	6.3	9.5	12.9	16.6	21.3	26.7	32.4	25.5
-25	-3.1	-0.6	1.8	4.7	8.0	11.5	15.9	20.5	26.3	30.2	25.5
-50	2.1	4.4	6.9	9.7	12.6	15.9	19.3	22.6	25.8	27.3	25.5
-75	13.9	16.0	18.2	19.9	21.4	22.9	24.4	25.6	26.5	26.7	25.5
-100	20.1	21.8	23.3	24.8	26.0	27.1	27.6	27.7	27.2	26.3	25.5
-125	28.0	28.9	29.7	30.8	32.0	33.0	34.0	32.8	30.2	28.0	25.5

Est. credit is: -63.8¢ prem. +45.4¢ prem. +45.4¢ prem. -1.5¢ comm. = +25.5¢

net profit area, in cents

TABLE 60

changes in the soybean future's price in 25¢ increments

	weeks to expiration										
	20	18	16	14	12	10	8	6	4	2	0
+125	-31.3	-30.3	-29.3	-28.1	-26.6	-24.3	-21.5	-18.1	-14.5	-13.1	-13.1
+100	-27.1	-24.9	-22.9	-20.6	-17.4	-13.6	-9.2	-3.8	3.3	9.5	11.9
+75	-19.8	-17.4	-14.8	-11.9	-8.7	-4.6	0.5	6.8	16.6	29.7	36.9
+50	-13.2	-10.9	-8.2	-5.7	-2.6	1.3	6.1	12.1	21.5	35.8	61.9
+25	-8.0	-6.0	-3.7	-1.2	0.5	4.7	8.6	13.4	20.0	29.5	36.9
0	-1.5	0.1	1.0	1.7	3.5	5.7	8.0	10.9	13.4	16.8	11.9
-25	-3.0	-1.1	1.0	2.9	5.0	7.4	10.2	12.8	15.6	15.8	11.9
-50	1.6	3.0	4.5	6.2	7.7	9.2	10.6	12.3	13.6	13.6	11.9
-75	9.0	9.5	10.2	11.0	11.6	12.1	12.5	13.3	13.6	13.6	11.9
-100	11.5	11.9	12.4	12.8	13.2	13.5	13.7	14.0	13.5	12.8	11.9
-125	14.4	14.6	14.8	15.0	15.1	15.1	15.3	15.1	13.7	12.0	11.9

Est. credit is: -49.2¢ prem. +31.3¢ prem. +31.3¢ prem. -1.5¢ comm. = +11.9¢

net profit area, in cents

TABLE 40

changes in the soybean future's price in 25¢ increments

	weeks to expiration										
	20	18	16	14	12	10	8	6	4	2	0
+125	-33.6	-32.6	-31.4	-30.2	-29.9	-27.8	-26.4	-25.2	-24.4	-24.4	-24.4
+100	-21.6	-19.9	-18.1	-16.3	-14.3	-11.9	-9.0	-5.8	-1.6	0.4	0.6
+75	-12.4	-10.4	-8.5	-6.1	-3.5	-0.3	3.6	8.2	15.0	22.8	25.6
+50	-6.7	-4.8	-2.9	-0.7	1.8	4.9	7.5	13.2	20.3	31.9	50.6
+25	-4.1	-2.4	-0.6	1.1	2.9	4.8	6.3	8.2	15.5	22.8	25.6
0	-1.5	-1.0	-0.5	0.2	1.0	1.6	2.2	2.5	2.5	1.1	0.6
-25	-2.1	-1.0	-0.1	0.7	1.6	2.2	2.4	2.4	1.5	0.9	0.6
-50	-1.1	-0.7	0.5	1.0	1.6	1.8	1.8	1.6	1.0	0.6	0.6
-75	1.2	1.4	1.6	1.8	1.9	1.8	1.6	1.0	0.9	0.6	0.6
-100	3.5	3.6	3.7	3.2	2.7	2.3	2.0	0.9	0.6	0.6	0.6
-125	4.7	4.8	4.7	4.5	3.9	3.3	2.7	2.0	0.9	0.6	0.6

Est. credit is: -34.5¢ prem. +18.3¢ prem. +18.3¢ prem. -1.5¢ comm. = +0.6¢

net profit area, in cents

TABLE 20

changes in the soybean future's price in 25¢ increments

	weeks to expiration										
	20	18	16	14	12	10	8	6	4	2	0
+125	-33.1	-32.9	-32.7	-32.5	-32.4	-32.3	-32.3	-32.3	-32.3	-32.3	-32.3
+100	-13.3	-12.5	-11.5	-10.7	-9.9	-9.1	-9.5	-7.9	-7.5	-7.3	-7.3
+75	0.9	2.0	3.3	4.8	6.4	8.1	10.3	12.5	15.1	16.9	17.7
+50	6.1	7.3	8.6	10.0	11.6	13.8	16.3	19.6	24.8	31.9	42.7
+25	3.3	4.3	5.3	6.2	7.2	8.5	10.1	12.3	14.9	16.5	17.7
0	-1.5	-1.1	-0.8	-0.5	-0.1	0.2	0.8	1.6	1.3	0.8	-7.3
-25	-3.1	-3.0	-2.7	-2.7	-2.8	-3.1	-3.6	-4.3	-5.6	-6.5	-7.3
-50	-5.3	-5.3	-5.3	-5.4	-5.5	-5.7	-6.1	-6.9	-7.0	-7.3	-7.3
-75	-6.1	-6.1	-6.1	-6.1	-6.2	-6.4	-6.6	-7.0	-7.1	-7.3	-7.3
-100	-6.2	-6.3	-6.3	-6.4	-6.7	-6.9	-7.1	-7.2	-7.3	-7.3	-7.3
-125	-6.5	-6.6	-6.7	-6.8	-6.9	-7.1	-7.2	-7.3	-7.3	-7.3	-7.3

Est. cost is: -19.8¢ prem. + 7.0¢ prem. + 7.0¢ prem. -1.5¢ comm. = -7.3¢

net profit

SELL A STRADDLE

SELL A CALL AT THE MONEY and SELL A PUT AT THE MONEY

weeks to expiration: **20**

TABLE (weeks to expiration = 8)

changes in the soybean future's price in 25¢ increments

weeks to expiration →	20	18	16	14	12	10	8	6	4	2	0
+125	-43.1	-38.4	-33.5	-28.8	-24.0	-18.6	-12.5	-7.0	-2.7	1.1	1.6
+100	-27.6	-22.7	-17.5	-12.4	-6.6	-0.4	5.9	12.9	19.4	24.9	26.6
+75	-13.6	-8.8	-3.7	1.5	7.2	13.5	20.8	28.9	39.4	49.3	51.6
+50	-5.4	-0.4	4.9	10.3	16.7	23.8	31.8	41.7	54.6	69.7	76.6
+25	-2.4	2.8	8.7	14.7	21.4	29.2	38.0	49.1	65.2	86.0	101.6
0	-1.0	4.0	9.6	15.4	22.2	30.2	39.6	51.4	68.6	92.0	126.6
-25	-2.4	2.8	8.7	14.7	21.4	29.2	38.0	49.1	65.2	86.0	101.6
-50	-5.4	-0.4	4.9	10.3	16.7	23.8	31.8	41.7	54.6	69.7	76.6
-75	-13.6	-8.8	-3.7	1.5	7.2	13.5	20.8	28.9	39.4	49.3	51.6
-100	-27.6	-22.7	-17.5	-12.4	-6.6	-0.4	5.9	12.9	19.4	24.9	26.6
-125	-43.2	-38.4	-33.5	-28.8	-24.0	-18.6	-12.5	-7.0	-2.7	1.1	1.6

net profit area, in cents

Estimated credit is: +63.8¢ premium + 63.8¢ premium -1.0¢ comm. =+126.6¢

TABLE (weeks to expiration = 0)

changes in the soybean future's price in 25¢ increments

weeks to expiration →	20	18	16	14	12	10	8	6	4	2	0
+125	-49.1	-46.5	-43.6	-40.9	-38.1	-35.8	-33.8	-31.8	-29.4	-27.7	-27.6
+100	-31.0	-28.2	-25.1	-21.8	-18.8	-15.9	-12.9	-9.6	-6.1	-3.0	-2.6
+75	-17.2	-14.1	-10.7	-7.5	-3.7	0.5	5.2	10.4	16.7	21.6	22.4
+50	-7.2	-3.7	-0.1	3.8	8.3	13.3	19.1	25.9	34.5	44.4	47.4
+25	-1.8	1.9	5.9	10.3	15.1	20.9	27.8	36.2	48.2	63.3	72.4
0	-1.0	3.0	7.4	11.8	17.0	23.2	30.6	39.6	52.8	70.8	97.4
-25	-1.8	1.9	5.9	10.3	15.1	20.9	27.8	36.2	48.2	63.3	72.4
-50	-7.2	-3.7	-0.1	3.8	8.3	13.3	19.1	25.9	34.5	44.4	47.4
-75	-17.2	-14.1	-10.7	-7.5	-3.7	0.5	5.2	10.4	16.7	21.6	22.4
-100	-31.0	-28.2	-25.1	-21.8	-18.8	-15.9	-12.9	-9.6	-6.1	-3.0	-2.6
-125	-49.1	-46.5	-43.6	-40.9	-38.1	-35.8	-33.8	-31.8	-29.4	-27.7	-27.6

net profit area, in cents

Est. credit is: +49.2¢ prem. + 49.2¢ prem. - 1.0¢ comm. = +97.4¢

TABLE (weeks to expiration = 4)

changes in the soybean future's price in 25¢ increments

weeks to expiration →	20	18	16	14	12	10	8	6	4	2	0
+125	-63.7	-63.0	-62.3	-61.7	-60.9	-60.1	-59.2	-58.3	-57.3	-57.0	-57.0
+100	-43.2	-42.1	-41.0	-39.8	-38.7	-37.4	-36.0	-34.6	-33.1	-32.0	-32.0
+75	-25.4	-23.9	-22.1	-20.3	-18.3	-16.1	-13.7	-11.2	-8.6	-7.0	-7.0
+50	-12.0	-9.9	-7.6	-5.3	-2.8	0.1	3.6	7.5	12.8	17.4	18.0
+25	-3.6	-1.0	1.7	4.8	8.1	11.9	16.7	22.2	30.0	39.5	43.0
0	-1.0	1.8	4.8	8.0	11.6	16.0	21.0	27.4	36.6	49.2	68.0
-25	-3.6	-1.0	1.7	4.8	8.1	11.9	16.7	22.2	30.0	39.5	43.0
-50	-12.0	-9.9	-7.6	-5.3	-2.8	0.1	3.6	7.5	12.8	17.4	18.0
-75	-25.4	-23.9	-22.1	-20.3	-18.3	-16.1	-13.7	-11.2	-8.6	-7.0	-7.0
-100	-43.2	-42.1	-41.0	-39.8	-38.7	-37.4	-36.0	-34.6	-33.1	-32.0	-32.0
-125	-63.7	-63.0	-62.3	-61.7	-60.9	-60.1	-59.2	-58.3	-57.3	-57.0	-57.0

net profit area, in cents

Est. credit is: +34.5¢ prem. + 34.5¢ prem. -1.0¢ comm. = +68.0¢

TABLE (weeks to expiration = 2 0)

changes in the soybean future's price in 25¢ increments

weeks to expiration →	20	18	16	14	12	10	8	6	4	2	0
+125	-87.6	-87.4	-87.1	-86.9	-86.8	-86.6	-86.5	-86.4	-86.4	-86.4	-86.4
+100	-63.9	-63.6	-63.3	-63.0	-62.7	-62.3	-61.9	-61.5	-61.4	-61.4	-61.4
+75	-40.4	-39.8	-39.2	-38.7	-38.2	-37.7	-37.2	-36.7	-36.4	-36.4	-36.4
+50	-21.4	-20.4	-19.3	-18.3	-17.2	-15.9	-14.6	-13.1	-11.9	-11.4	-11.4
+25	-6.5	-5.1	-3.4	-1.9	-0.2	1.8	4.2	7.0	10.4	13.1	13.6
0	-1.0	0.6	2.4	4.2	6.2	8.8	11.6	15.2	20.6	27.8	38.6
-25	-6.5	-5.1	-3.4	-1.9	-0.2	1.8	4.2	7.0	10.4	13.1	13.6
-50	-21.4	-20.4	-19.3	-18.3	-17.2	-15.9	-14.6	-13.1	-11.9	-11.4	-11.4
-75	-40.4	-39.8	-39.2	-38.7	-38.2	-37.7	-37.2	-36.7	-36.4	-36.4	-36.4
-100	-63.9	-63.6	-63.3	-63.0	-62.7	-62.3	-61.9	-61.5	-61.4	-61.4	-61.4
-125	-87.6	-87.4	-87.1	-86.9	-86.8	-86.6	-86.5	-86.4	-86.4	-86.4	-86.4

net profit area

Estimated credit is: +19.8¢ premium +19.8¢ premium -1.0¢ comm. = +38.0¢

Wm Grandmill (1985) Ltd.

SELL A STRANGLE - #1

SELL A CALL AT 50¢ OUT OF THE MONEY
and SELL A PUT AT 50¢ OUT OF THE MONEY

TABLE 8

changes in the soybean future's price in 25¢ increments

	weeks to expiration										
	20	18	16	14	12	10	8	6	4	2	0
+125	-21.0	-17.1	-13.0	-9.0	-4.8	-0.6	3.4	7.3	11.4	14.7	14.8
+100	-15.8	-11.3	-6.7	-1.6	3.7	9.4	15.2	21.8	30.0	38.1	39.8
+75	-11.5	-6.5	-1.0	4.4	10.2	17.0	23.9	32.4	44.1	57.8	64.8
+50	-5.8	-0.8	4.6	10.4	17.0	24.6	33.7	44.7	54.0	70.8	89.8
+25	-1.0	4.0	9.4	15.0	21.6	29.0	37.4	48.0	60.2	78.5	89.8
0	-5.8	-0.8	4.6	10.4	17.0	24.6	33.7	44.7	54.0	70.8	89.8
-25	-8.4	-3.5	1.9	7.6	14.1	21.6	30.1	40.3	54.0	70.8	64.8
-50	-11.5	-6.5	-1.0	4.4	10.2	17.0	23.9	32.4	44.1	57.8	39.8
-75	-15.8	-11.3	-6.5	-1.6	3.7	9.4	15.2	21.8	30.0	38.1	14.8
-100	-21.0	-17.1	-13.0	-9.0	-4.8	-0.6	3.4	11.4	14.7	14.7	14.8
-125	-21.0	-17.1	-13.0	-9.0	-4.8	-0.6	3.4	7.3	11.4	14.7	14.8

net profit area , in cents

Est. credit is: +45.4¢ premium +45.4¢ premium -1.0¢ comm. = +89.8¢

TABLE 6

changes in the soybean future's price in 25¢ increments

	weeks to expiration										
	20	18	16	14	12	10	8	6	4	2	0
+125	-32.0	-30.1	-28.0	-26.0	-23.8	-21.5	-19.0	-16.4	-14.1	-13.4	-13.4
+100	-21.8	-19.3	-16.5	-13.4	-10.2	-6.7	-2.8	1.7	6.7	11.1	11.6
+75	-13.0	-10.0	-6.7	-3.2	0.6	5.0	10.1	16.1	24.3	32.9	36.6
+50	-8.4	-4.8	-0.9	3.2	7.7	12.9	18.8	26.0	35.8	47.9	61.6
+25	-5.4	-1.6	2.6	6.9	11.8	17.5	24.3	32.2	42.9	55.3	61.6
0	-1.0	2.6	5.4	9.4	14.2	20.6	27.0	34.0	44.2	56.6	61.6
-25	-5.4	-1.6	2.6	6.9	11.8	17.5	24.3	32.2	42.9	47.9	36.6
-50	-8.4	-4.8	-0.9	3.2	7.7	12.9	18.8	26.0	35.8	32.9	11.6
-75	-13.0	-10.0	-6.7	-3.2	0.6	5.0	10.1	16.1	24.3	11.1	-13.4
-100	-21.8	-19.3	-16.5	-13.4	-10.2	-6.7	-2.8	1.7	6.7	-13.4	-13.4
-125	-32.0	-30.1	-28.0	-26.0	-23.8	-21.5	-19.0	-16.4	-14.1	-13.4	-13.4

net profit area , in cents

Est. credit is: +31.3¢ premium +31.3¢ premium -1.0¢ comm. = +61.6¢

TABLE 4

changes in the soybean future's price in 25¢ increments

	weeks to expiration										
	20	18	16	14	12	10	8	6	4	2	0
+125	-45.3	-44.4	-43.5	-42.7	-42.0	-41.3	-40.5	-39.8	-39.4	-39.4	-39.4
+100	-30.0	-28.4	-26.7	-25.1	-23.3	-21.5	-19.7	-17.9	-15.5	-14.5	-14.4
+75	-17.4	-15.4	-13.5	-11.4	-9.0	-6.3	-3.1	0.3	5.0	9.2	10.6
+50	-8.9	-6.7	-4.3	-1.7	1.0	4.3	8.1	12.6	18.8	26.3	35.6
+25	-3.7	-1.2	1.5	4.3	7.4	10.8	15.1	19.9	26.3	33.5	35.6
0	-1.0	1.4	3.8	6.4	9.2	12.4	16.4	21.0	27.4	34.6	35.6
-25	-3.7	-1.2	1.5	4.3	7.4	10.8	15.1	19.9	26.3	33.5	10.6
-50	-8.9	-6.7	-4.3	-1.7	1.0	4.3	8.1	12.6	18.8	16.2	-14.4
-75	-17.4	-15.4	-13.5	-11.4	-9.0	-6.3	-3.1	0.3	5.0	9.2	-39.4
-100	-30.0	-28.4	-26.7	-25.1	-23.3	-21.5	-19.7	-17.9	-15.5	-14.5	-39.4
-125	-45.3	-44.4	-43.5	-42.7	-42.0	-41.3	-40.5	-39.8	-39.4	-39.4	-39.4

net profit area , in cents

Est. credit is: +18.3¢ premium +18.3¢ premium -1.0¢ comm. = +35.6¢

TABLE 2

changes in the soybean future's price in 25¢ increments

	weeks to expiration										
	20	18	16	14	12	10	8	6	4	2	0
+125	-62.5	-62.3	-62.2	-62.1	-62.1	-62.0	-62.0	-62.0	-62.0	-62.0	-62.0
+100	-40.4	-39.3	-38.8	-38.4	-37.9	-37.6	-37.3	-37.1	-37.0	-37.0	-37.0
+75	-21.8	-20.9	-19.9	-19.0	-18.1	-17.0	-15.8	-14.6	-13.3	-12.4	-12.0
+50	-9.3	-8.2	-7.0	-5.8	-4.5	-2.8	-1.0	1.2	4.0	7.6	13.0
+25	-2.1	-0.9	0.5	1.8	3.2	4.7	6.4	8.7	11.1	12.2	13.0
0	-1.0	0.2	1.4	2.6	4.0	5.8	7.6	10.2	12.2	13.0	13.0
-25	-2.1	-0.9	0.5	1.8	3.2	4.7	6.4	8.7	11.1	12.2	13.0
-50	-9.3	-8.2	-7.0	-5.8	-4.5	-2.8	-1.0	1.2	4.0	7.6	13.0
-75	-21.8	-20.9	-19.9	-19.0	-18.1	-17.0	-15.8	-14.6	-13.3	-12.4	-12.0
-100	-40.4	-39.3	-38.8	-38.4	-37.9	-37.6	-37.3	-37.1	-37.0	-37.0	-37.0
-125	-62.5	-62.3	-62.2	-62.1	-62.1	-62.0	-62.0	-62.0	-62.0	-62.0	-62.0

net profit area , in cents

Estimated credit is: +7.0¢ premium +7.0¢ premium -1.0¢ comm. = +13.0¢

Wm Grandmill (1985) Ltd.

SELL A STRANGLE – #2

SELL A CALL AT $1.00 OUT OF THE MONEY and SELL A PUT AT $1.00 OUT OF THE MONEY

20 weeks to expiration

TABLE

changes in the soybean future's price in 25¢ increments

price change	20	18	16	14	12	10	8	6	4	2	0
+125	-9.3	-6.2	-2.7	0.8	4.5	8.6	13.0	18.5	26.4	36.3	42.8
+100	-2.1	1.3	5.0	8.8	13.1	17.8	23.0	29.6	38.5	50.5	67.8
+75	1.6	5.7	10.1	14.7	19.8	25.5	31.1	37.9	47.0	58.7	67.8
+50	3.4	7.9	12.6	17.9	23.5	29.4	35.6	42.9	52.2	62.6	67.8
+25	-0.1	4.7	9.7	14.9	20.6	26.9	34.4	42.8	53.9	65.1	67.8
0	-1.0	3.8	9.0	14.6	20.8	27.8	35.4	44.0	54.2	64.4	67.8
-25	-0.1	4.7	9.7	14.9	20.6	26.9	34.4	42.8	53.9	65.1	67.8
-50	3.4	7.9	12.6	17.9	23.5	29.4	35.6	42.9	52.2	62.6	67.8
-75	1.6	5.7	10.1	14.7	19.8	25.5	31.1	37.9	47.0	58.7	67.8
-100	-2.1	1.3	5.0	8.8	13.1	17.8	23.0	29.6	38.5	50.5	67.8
-125	-9.3	-6.2	-2.7	0.8	4.5	8.6	13.0	18.5	26.4	36.3	42.8

weeks to expiration; net profit area, in cents

Est. credit is: +34.4¢ premium + 34.4¢ premium -1.0¢ comm. = + 67.8¢

TABLE

changes in the soybean future's price in 25¢ increments

price change	20	18	16	14	12	10	8	6	4	2	0
+125	-20.4	-18.3	-16.2	-13.9	-11.4	-8.2	-4.7	-0.7	5.1	12.0	15.6
+100	-11.7	-9.3	-6.7	-4.2	-1.0	2.7	6.8	11.7	18.3	27.3	40.6
+75	-5.4	-2.8	0.1	3.2	6.5	10.3	14.9	20.2	26.9	35.1	40.6
+50	-0.8	1.8	4.8	8.0	11.5	15.4	19.9	24.9	31.2	38.1	40.6
+25	-1.8	1.3	4.8	8.2	12.1	16.4	21.4	26.9	33.8	39.7	40.6
0	-1.0	2.2	5.6	9.4	13.2	17.4	21.8	27.2	33.6	39.8	40.6
-25	-1.8	1.3	4.8	8.2	12.1	16.4	21.4	26.9	33.8	39.7	40.6
-50	-0.8	1.8	4.8	8.0	11.5	15.4	19.9	24.9	31.2	38.1	40.6
-75	-5.4	-2.8	0.1	3.2	6.5	10.3	14.9	20.2	26.9	35.1	40.6
-100	-11.7	-9.3	-6.7	-4.2	-1.0	2.7	6.8	11.7	18.3	27.3	40.6
-125	-20.4	-18.3	-16.2	-13.9	-11.4	-8.2	-4.7	-0.7	5.1	12.0	15.6

weeks to expiration; net profit area, in cents

Est. credit is: +20.8¢ premium + 20.8¢ premium -1.0¢ comm. = +40.6¢

---

weeks to expiration: 20

TABLE

changes in the soybean future's price in 25¢ increments

price change	20	18	16	14	12	10	8	6	4	2	0
+125	-27.6	-26.2	-24.9	-23.3	-21.7	-19.8	-17.5	-14.9	-11.3	-7.4	-6.0
+100	-16.2	-14.6	-12.9	-11.2	-9.3	-7.1	-4.5	-1.3	3.3	9.6	19.0
+75	-7.6	-5.9	-4.1	-2.3	-0.5	1.5	4.1	7.1	11.3	16.9	19.0
+50	-3.2	-1.3	0.5	2.4	4.5	6.6	8.9	11.4	14.9	18.5	19.0
+25	-1.7	0.2	2.1	3.9	6.1	8.4	11.1	13.8	17.1	19.0	19.0
0	-1.0	0.6	2.4	4.4	6.2	8.4	11.0	13.6	16.8	19.0	19.0
-25	-1.7	0.2	2.1	3.9	6.1	8.4	11.1	13.8	17.1	19.0	19.0
-50	-3.2	-1.3	0.5	2.4	4.5	6.6	8.9	11.4	14.9	18.5	19.0
-75	-7.6	-5.9	-4.1	-2.3	-0.5	1.5	4.1	7.1	11.3	16.9	19.0
-100	-16.2	-14.6	-12.9	-11.2	-9.3	-7.1	-4.5	-1.3	3.3	9.6	19.0
-125	-27.6	-26.2	-24.9	-23.3	-21.7	-19.8	-17.5	-14.9	-11.3	-7.4	-6.0

weeks to expiration; net profit area, in cents

Est. credit is: +10.0¢ premium +10.0¢ premium -1.0¢ comm. = +19.0¢

TABLE

changes in the soybean future's price in 25¢ increments

price change	20	18	16	14	12	10	8	6	4	2	0
+125	-29.8	-29.0	-28.2	-27.5	-26.7	-25.8	-24.7	-23.6	-22.3	-21.4	-21.0
+100	-15.8	-15.0	-14.1	-13.2	-12.2	-10.9	-9.5	-7.7	-5.0	-1.4	4.0
+75	-7.6	-6.7	-5.8	-5.0	-4.1	-3.0	-1.7	0.0	2.1	3.2	4.0
+50	-3.4	-2.6	-2.0	-1.3	-0.5	0.4	1.3	2.6	3.6	4.0	4.0
+25	-0.8	-0.1	0.6	1.3	1.9	2.5	3.1	3.7	4.0	4.0	4.0
0	-1.0	-0.4	0.2	0.8	1.4	2.2	3.0	3.8	4.0	4.0	4.0
-25	-0.8	-0.1	0.6	1.3	1.9	2.5	3.1	3.7	4.0	4.0	4.0
-50	-3.4	-2.6	-2.0	-1.3	-0.5	0.4	1.3	2.6	3.6	4.0	4.0
-75	-7.6	-6.7	-5.8	-5.0	-4.1	-3.0	-1.7	0.0	2.1	3.2	4.0
-100	-15.8	-15.0	-14.1	-13.2	-12.2	-10.9	-9.5	-7.7	-5.0	-1.4	4.0
-125	-29.8	-29.0	-28.2	-27.5	-26.7	-25.8	-24.7	-23.6	-22.3	-21.4	-21.0

weeks to expiration; net profit area, in cents

Estimated credit is: +2.5¢ premium + 2.5¢ premium -1.0¢ comm. = +4.0¢

Wm Grandmill (1985) Ltd.

BUY A CALL or BUY A PUT

AT THE MONEY

weeks to expiration: 25

TABLE 8

changes in the soybean future's price in 25¢ increments

	25	20	18	16	14	12	10	8	6	4	2	0
+125	79.3	73.7	71.2	68.7	66.3	63.9	61.1	58.0	55.7	55.4	55.4	55.4
+100	56.0	50.2	47.7	45.1	42.8	40.1	37.4	34.9	32.2	30.8	30.4	30.4
+75	34.5	29.2	26.9	24.4	22.1	19.7	17.1	14.3	11.4	8.0	5.5	5.4
+50	22.3	17.0	14.5	11.9	9.3	6.2	2.8	-1.0	-5.6	-11.5	-17.9	-19.6
+25	11.1	5.2	2.5	-0.6	-3.7	-7.1	-11.0	-15.2	-20.5	-28.2	-38.1	-44.6
0	-0.5	-5.8	-8.3	-11.1	-14.0	-17.4	-21.4	-26.1	-32.0	-40.6	-52.3	-69.6
-25	-10.1	-15.4	-17.9	-20.7	-23.6	-26.9	-30.8	-35.4	-41.2	-49.6	-60.5	-69.6
-50	-19.0	-24.2	-26.7	-29.4	-32.2	-35.5	-39.2	-43.4	-48.7	-55.7	-64.4	-69.6
-75	-23.0	-28.2	-30.7	-33.3	-36.2	-39.5	-43.2	-47.7	-52.9	-60.0	-67.4	-69.6
-100	-30.1	-35.2	-37.6	-40.2	-43.0	-46.1	-49.6	-53.4	-57.7	-62.8	-67.9	-69.6
-125	-38.2	-43.1	-45.4	-47.8	-50.1	-52.5	-55.1	-58.1	-61.3	-65.3	-69.4	-69.6

weeks to expiration

The estimated cost is: -69.1¢ premium -0.5¢ comm. = -69.6¢

net profit

TABLE 4

changes in the soybean future's price in 25¢ increments

	25	20	18	16	14	12	10	8	6	4	2	0
+125	87.3	87.2	87.2	87.2	87.2	87.2	87.2	87.2	87.2	87.2	87.2	87.2
+100	63.9	63.4	63.1	62.9	62.7	62.5	62.3	62.2	62.2	62.2	52.2	62.2
+75	43.0	41.8	41.3	40.7	40.1	39.5	38.9	38.2	37.6	37.2	37.2	37.2
+50	26.0	23.9	23.0	21.9	20.9	19.8	18.5	17.0	15.4	13.3	12.3	12.2
+25	11.0	8.5	7.2	6.0	4.5	2.9	1.0	-1.3	-3.9	-7.5	-11.4	-12.8
0	-0.5	-3.3	-4.7	-6.2	-7.8	-9.6	-11.8	-14.3	-17.5	-22.1	-28.4	-37.8
-25	-9.7	-12.5	-13.8	-15.3	-16.9	-18.6	-20.5	-23.0	-25.9	-30.1	-35.7	-37.8
-50	-17.2	-19.5	-20.7	-21.9	-23.2	-24.6	-26.2	-28.2	-30.5	-33.7	-37.3	-37.8
-75	-21.4	-23.8	-25.0	-26.2	-27.4	-28.8	-30.3	-32.1	-34.0	-36.2	-37.8	-37.8
-100	-26.1	-27.8	-28.6	-29.5	-30.5	-31.4	-32.5	-33.8	-35.1	-36.7	-37.8	-37.8
-125	-29.7	-31.1	-31.8	-32.4	-33.1	-33.9	-34.7	-35.6	-36.5	-37.5	-37.8	-37.8

weeks to expiration

The estimated cost is: -37.3¢ premium -0.5¢ comm. = -37.8¢

net profit area

TABLE 0

changes in the soybean future's price in 25¢ increments

	25	20	18	16	14	12	10	8	6	4	2	0
+125	80.5	77.7	76.3	74.8	73.5	72.2	71.5	71.3	71.3	71.3	71.3	71.3
+100	56.8	53.9	52.7	51.3	49.9	48.8	48.0	47.2	46.6	46.3	46.3	46.3
+75	36.3	33.6	32.4	31.1	29.9	28.5	27.0	25.5	23.8	22.0	21.3	21.3
+50	23.0	19.6	17.9	16.2	14.3	12.2	9.9	7.3	4.3	0.5	-3.2	-3.7
+25	9.8	5.8	4.0	2.1	0.0	-2.3	-5.1	-8.4	-12.4	-18.2	-25.1	-28.7
0	-0.5	-4.5	-6.5	-8.7	-10.9	-13.5	-16.6	-20.3	-24.8	-31.4	-40.4	-53.7
-25	-10.1	-14.0	-15.9	-18.0	-20.3	-22.8	-25.8	-29.4	-33.8	-40.0	-48.2	-53.7
-50	-18.6	-22.4	-24.2	-26.1	-28.1	-30.5	-33.2	-36.4	-39.9	-45.0	-51.2	-53.7
-75	-22.6	-26.4	-28.3	-30.4	-32.4	-34.8	-37.5	-40.7	-44.7	-48.7	-52.9	-53.7
-100	-29.4	-32.9	-34.4	-36.1	-38.0	-40.0	-42.1	-44.3	-47.0	-50.2	-53.3	-53.7
-125	-35.9	-38.6	-39.8	-41.2	-42.6	-44.1	-45.7	-47.5	-49.5	-51.9	-53.6	-53.7

The estimated cost is: -53.2¢ premium -0.5¢ comm. = -53.7¢

net profit

TABLE 2

changes in the soybean future's price in 25¢ increments

	25	20	18	16	14	12	10	8	6	4	2	0
+125	103.1	103.1	103.1	103.1	103.1	103.1	103.1	103.1	103.1	103.1	103.1	103.1
+100	78.1	78.1	78.1	78.1	78.1	78.1	78.1	78.1	78.1	78.1	78.1	78.1
+75	53.7	53.5	53.4	53.3	53.2	53.1	53.1	53.1	53.1	53.1	53.1	53.1
+50	31.9	31.1	30.7	30.2	29.8	29.4	29.0	28.7	28.4	28.2	28.1	28.1
+25	12.9	11.7	11.0	10.3	9.6	8.8	7.9	6.8	5.7	4.4	3.5	3.1
0	-0.5	-2.1	-2.9	-3.8	-4.7	-5.7	-7.0	-8.4	-10.2	-12.9	-16.5	-21.9
-25	-9.0	-10.4	-11.2	-12.1	-12.9	-13.8	-14.9	-16.2	-17.9	-20.0	-21.1	-21.9
-50	-13.8	-14.9	-15.5	-16.1	-16.7	-17.4	-18.3	-19.3	-20.5	-21.5	-21.9	-21.9
-75	-17.4	-18.3	-18.7	-19.2	-19.7	-20.2	-20.6	-21.0	-21.6	-21.8	-21.9	-21.9
-100	-18.8	-19.4	-19.7	-20.0	-20.3	-20.6	-21.0	-21.4	-21.8	-21.9	-21.9	-21.9
-125	-20.3	-20.7	-20.9	-21.2	-21.4	-21.5	-21.7	-21.8	-21.9	-21.9	-21.9	-21.9

weeks to expiration

The estimated cost is: -21.4¢ premium -0.5¢ comm. = -21.9¢

net profit area , in cents

Wm Grandmill (1985) Ltd.

BUY A CALL or BUY A PUT
AT 50¢ OUT OF THE MONEY

weeks to expiration: 25

TABLE (The estimated cost is: -50.6¢ premium -0.5¢ comm. = -51.1¢)

changes in the soybean future's price in 25¢ increments	\[weeks to expiration\] 25	20	18	16	14	12	10	8	6	4	2	0
+125	53.0	47.7	45.4	43.0	40.6	38.2	35.6	32.8	29.9	26.5	24.0	23.9
+100	40.8	35.5	33.0	30.4	27.8	24.7	21.3	17.5	12.9	7.0	0.6	-1.1
+75	29.6	23.7	21.0	17.9	14.8	11.4	7.5	3.4	-2.0	-9.7	-19.6	-26.1
+50	18.0	12.7	10.2	7.4	4.5	1.1	-2.9	-7.6	-13.5	-22.1	-33.8	-51.1
+25	8.4	3.1	0.6	-2.2	-5.1	-8.4	-12.3	-16.9	-22.7	-31.1	-42.0	-51.1
0	-0.5	-5.7	-8.2	-10.9	-13.7	-17.0	-20.7	-24.9	-30.2	-37.2	-45.8	-51.1
-25	-4.5	-9.7	-12.2	-14.8	-17.7	-21.0	-24.7	-29.2	-34.7	-41.5	-48.9	-51.1
-50	-11.6	-16.7	-19.1	-21.7	-24.5	-27.6	-31.1	-34.9	-39.2	-44.3	-49.4	-51.1
-75	-19.7	-24.6	-26.9	-29.3	-31.6	-34.0	-36.6	-39.6	-42.8	-46.8	-50.6	-51.1
-100	-28.1	-32.1	-34.2	-36.1	-38.6	-41.2	-43.1	-45.0	-47.1	-49.4	-51.1	-51.1
-125	-35.0	-38.9	-40.7	-42.3	-44.0	-45.8	-47.4	-48.6	-49.7	-50.3	-51.1	-51.1

prof

TABLE (The estimated cost is: -35.1¢ premium -0.5¢ comm. = -35.6¢)

changes in the soybean future's price in 25¢ increments	\[weeks to expiration\] 25	20	18	16	14	12	10	8	6	4	2	0
+125	54.4	51.7	50.5	49.2	48.0	46.6	45.1	43.6	41.9	40.1	39.4	39.4
+100	41.1	37.7	36.0	34.3	32.0	30.3	28.0	25.4	22.4	18.6	14.9	14.4
+75	27.9	23.9	22.1	20.2	18.1	15.8	13.0	9.7	5.7	-0.1	-7.0	-10.6
+50	17.6	13.6	11.6	9.4	7.2	4.6	1.5	-2.2	-6.7	-13.3	-22.3	-35.6
+25	8.0	4.1	2.2	0.1	-2.2	-4.7	-7.7	-11.3	-15.7	-21.9	-30.1	-35.6
0	-0.5	-4.3	-6.1	-8.0	-10.0	-12.4	-15.1	-18.3	-21.8	-26.9	-33.1	-35.6
-25	-4.5	-8.3	-10.2	-12.3	-14.3	-16.7	-19.4	-22.6	-26.1	-30.6	-34.8	-35.6
-50	-11.2	-14.8	-16.4	-18.1	-20.0	-21.9	-24.0	-26.2	-28.9	-32.1	-35.2	-35.6
-75	-17.8	-20.5	-21.7	-23.1	-24.5	-26.0	-27.6	-29.4	-31.4	-33.8	-35.5	-35.6
-100	-23.6	-25.5	-26.3	-27.4	-28.6	-29.7	-30.9	-32.2	-33.7	-34.9	-35.6	-35.6
-125	-27.6	-29.3	-30.0	-30.8	-31.6	-32.4	-33.2	-34.2	-35.1	-35.6	-35.6	-35.6

net profit

TABLE (The estimated cost is: -20.6¢ premium -0.5¢ comm. = -21.1¢)

changes in the soybean future's price in 25¢ increments	\[weeks to expiration\] 25	20	18	16	14	12	10	8	6	4	2	0
+125	59.7	58.5	58.0	57.4	56.8	56.2	55.6	54.9	54.3	53.9	53.9	53.9
+100	42.7	40.6	39.7	38.6	37.6	36.5	35.2	33.7	32.1	30.0	29.0	28.9
+75	27.7	25.2	23.9	22.7	21.2	19.6	17.7	15.4	12.8	9.2	5.3	3.9
+50	16.2	13.4	12.0	10.5	8.9	7.1	4.9	2.4	-0.8	-5.4	-11.7	-21.1
+25	7.0	4.2	2.9	1.4	-0.2	-1.9	-3.8	-6.3	-9.2	-13.4	-19.0	-21.1
0	-0.5	-2.8	-4.0	-5.2	-6.5	-7.9	-9.5	-11.5	-13.8	-17.0	-20.6	-21.1
-25	-4.7	-7.1	-8.3	-9.5	-10.7	-12.1	-13.6	-15.4	-17.3	-19.5	-21.1	-21.1
-50	-9.4	-11.1	-11.9	-12.8	-13.8	-14.7	-15.8	-17.1	-18.4	-20.0	-21.1	-21.1
-75	-13.0	-14.4	-15.1	-15.8	-16.4	-17.2	-18.0	-18.9	-19.7	-20.8	-21.1	-21.1
-100	-16.2	-17.2	-17.9	-18.5	-19.1	-19.8	-20.3	-20.6	-20.8	-21.1	-21.1	-21.1
-125	-19.0	-19.8	-20.2	-20.5	-20.7	-20.8	-20.9	-21.0	-21.0	-21.1	-21.1	-21.1

net profit area

TABLE (The estimated cost is: -8.1¢ premium -0.5¢ comm. = -8.6¢)

changes in the soybean future's price in 25¢ increments	\[weeks to expiration\] 25	20	18	16	14	12	10	8	6	4	2	0
+125	67.1	66.9	66.7	66.6	66.5	66.5	66.4	66.4	66.4	66.4	66.4	66.4
+100	45.2	44.4	44.0	43.5	43.1	42.7	42.3	42.0	41.7	41.5	41.4	41.4
+75	25.2	24.0	23.3	22.6	21.9	21.1	20.2	19.1	18.0	17.2	16.8	16.4
+50	12.8	11.2	10.4	9.5	8.6	7.6	6.3	4.9	3.1	0.4	-3.2	-8.6
+25	4.3	2.9	2.1	1.2	0.4	-0.5	-1.6	-2.9	-4.6	-6.7	-7.8	-8.6
0	-0.5	-1.6	-2.2	-2.8	-3.4	-4.1	-5.0	-6.0	-7.2	-8.2	-8.6	-8.6
-25	-4.1	-5.0	-5.4	-5.9	-6.4	-6.9	-7.3	-7.7	-8.3	-8.6	-8.6	-8.6
-50	-5.5	-6.1	-6.4	-6.7	-7.0	-7.3	-7.7	-8.1	-8.5	-8.6	-8.6	-8.6
-75	-7.0	-7.4	-7.6	-7.9	-8.1	-8.2	-8.4	-8.5	-8.6	-8.6	-8.6	-8.6
-100	-8.0	-8.2	-8.3	-8.4	-8.5	-8.5	-8.6	-8.6	-8.6	-8.6	-8.6	-8.6
-125	-8.4	-8.5	-8.6	-8.6	-8.6	-8.6	-8.6	-8.6	-8.6	-8.6	-8.6	-8.6

net profit

Wm Grandmill (1985) Ltd.

SELL A CALL or SELL A PUT

AT THE MONEY

weeks to expiration: 25

TABLE 80

changes in the soybean future's price in 25¢ increments

	25	20	18	16	14	12	10	8	6	4	2	0
+125	-80.3	-74.7	-72.2	-69.7	-67.3	-64.9	-62.2	-59.0	-56.7	-56.4	-56.4	-56.4
+100	-57.0	-51.2	-48.8	-46.1	-43.8	-41.1	-38.4	-35.9	-33.2	-31.8	-31.4	-31.4
+75	-35.5	-30.2	-27.9	-25.4	-23.1	-20.7	-18.1	-15.3	-12.4	-9.9	-6.5	-6.4
+50	-23.3	-18.0	-15.5	-12.9	-10.3	-7.2	-3.8	0.0	4.6	10.5	16.9	18.6
+25	-12.1	-6.2	-3.5	-0.4	2.7	6.1	10.0	14.2	19.5	27.2	37.1	43.6
0	-0.5	4.8	7.3	10.1	13.0	16.4	20.4	25.1	31.0	39.6	51.3	68.6
-25	9.1	14.4	16.9	19.7	22.6	25.9	29.8	34.4	40.2	48.6	59.5	68.6
-50	18.0	23.2	25.7	28.4	31.2	34.5	38.2	42.4	47.7	54.7	63.4	68.6
-75	22.0	27.2	29.7	32.3	35.2	38.5	42.2	46.7	51.9	59.0	66.4	68.6
-100	29.1	34.2	36.6	39.2	42.0	45.1	48.6	52.4	56.7	61.8	66.9	68.6
-125	37.2	42.1	44.4	46.8	49.1	51.5	54.1	57.1	60.3	64.3	68.4	68.6

weeks to expiration — net profit area, in cents

The estimated credit is: + 69.1¢ premium - 0.5¢ comm. = + 68.6¢

TABLE 40

changes in the soybean future's price in 25¢ increments

	25	20	18	16	14	12	10	8	6	4	2	0
+125	-88.4	-88.2	-88.2	-88.2	-88.2	-88.2	-88.2	-88.2	-88.2	-88.2	-88.2	-88.2
+100	-64.9	-64.4	-64.1	-63.9	-63.7	-63.5	-63.3	-63.2	-63.2	-63.2	-63.2	-63.2
+75	-44.0	-42.8	-42.3	-41.7	-41.1	-40.5	-39.9	-39.2	-38.6	-38.2	-38.2	-38.2
+50	-27.0	-24.9	-24.0	-22.9	-21.9	-20.8	-19.5	-18.0	-16.4	-14.3	-13.3	-13.2
+25	-12.0	-9.5	-8.2	-7.0	-5.5	-3.9	-2.0	0.3	2.9	6.5	10.4	11.8
0	-0.5	2.3	3.7	5.2	6.8	8.6	10.8	13.3	16.5	21.1	27.4	36.8
-25	8.7	11.5	12.8	14.3	15.9	17.6	19.5	22.0	24.9	29.1	34.7	36.8
-50	16.2	18.5	19.7	20.9	22.2	23.6	25.2	27.2	29.5	32.7	36.2	36.8
-75	20.4	22.8	24.0	25.2	26.4	27.8	29.3	31.1	33.0	35.2	36.8	36.8
-100	25.1	26.8	27.6	28.5	29.5	30.4	31.5	32.8	34.1	35.7	36.8	36.8
-125	28.7	30.1	30.8	31.4	32.1	32.9	33.7	34.6	35.5	36.2	36.8	36.8

weeks to expiration — net profit area, in cents

The estimated credit is: = 37.3¢ premium - 0.5¢ comm. = + 36.8¢

TABLE 08

changes in the soybean future's price in 25¢ increments

	25	20	18	16	14	12	10	8	6	4	2	0
+125	-81.5	-78.7	-77.3	-75.8	-74.5	-73.2	-72.5	-72.3	-72.3	-72.3	-72.3	-72.3
+100	-57.8	-54.9	-53.7	-52.3	-50.9	-49.8	-49.0	-48.2	-47.6	-47.3	-47.3	-47.3
+75	-37.3	-34.6	-32.1	-30.9	-29.5	-28.0	-26.5	-24.8	-23.0	-22.3	-22.3	-22.3
+50	-24.0	-20.6	-18.9	-17.2	-15.3	-13.2	-10.9	-8.3	-6.3	-1.5	2.2	2.7
+25	-10.8	-6.8	-5.0	-3.1	-1.0	1.3	4.1	7.4	11.4	17.2	24.1	27.7
0	-0.5	3.5	5.5	7.7	9.9	12.5	15.6	19.3	23.8	30.4	39.4	52.7
-25	9.1	13.0	14.9	17.0	19.3	21.8	24.8	28.4	32.8	39.4	47.2	52.7
-50	17.6	21.4	23.2	25.1	27.1	29.5	32.2	35.4	38.9	44.0	50.2	52.7
-75	21.6	25.4	27.3	29.4	31.4	33.8	36.5	39.7	43.2	47.7	51.9	52.7
-100	28.4	31.9	33.4	35.1	37.0	39.0	41.1	43.3	46.0	49.2	52.3	52.7
-125	34.9	37.6	38.8	40.2	41.6	43.1	44.7	46.5	48.5	50.9	52.6	52.7

weeks to expiration — net profit area, in cents

The estimated credit is: + 53.2¢ premium - 0.5¢ comm. = + 52.7¢

TABLE 20

changes in the soybean future's price in 25¢ increments

	25	20	18	16	14	12	10	8	6	4	2	0
+125	-104.1	-104.1	-104.1	-104.1	-104.1	-104.1	-104.1	-104.1	-104.1	-104.1	-104.1	-104.1
+100	-79.1	-79.1	-79.1	-79.1	-79.1	-79.1	-79.1	-79.1	-79.1	-79.1	-79.1	-79.1
+75	-54.7	-54.5	-54.4	-54.3	-54.2	-54.2	-54.1	-54.1	-54.1	-54.1	-54.1	-54.1
+50	-33.9	-32.9	-32.1	-31.7	-31.2	-30.8	-30.4	-30.0	-29.7	-29.4	-29.1	-29.1
+25	-13.9	-12.7	-12.0	-11.3	-10.6	-9.8	-8.9	-7.8	-6.7	-5.4	-4.5	-4.1
0	1.1	1.9	2.8	3.7	4.7	6.0	7.4	9.2	11.9	15.5	20.9	20.9
-25	8.0	9.4	10.2	11.1	11.9	12.8	13.9	15.2	16.9	19.0	20.1	20.9
-50	12.8	13.9	14.5	15.1	15.7	16.4	17.3	18.3	19.5	20.5	20.9	20.9
-75	16.4	17.3	17.7	18.2	18.7	19.2	19.6	20.0	20.6	20.9	20.9	20.9
-100	17.8	18.4	18.7	19.0	19.3	19.6	20.0	20.4	20.8	20.9	20.9	20.9
-125	19.3	19.7	19.9	20.2	20.4	20.5	20.7	20.8	20.9	20.9	20.9	20.9

weeks to expiration — net profit area, in cents

The estimated credit is: + 21.4¢ premium - 0.5¢ comm. = + 20.9¢

SELL A CALL or SELL A PUT
AT 50¢ OUT OF THE MONEY

weeks to **25** expiration

TABLE 8

changes in the soybean future's price in 25¢ increments	25	20	18	16	14	12	10	8	6	4	2	0
+125	-54.0	-48.8	-46.4	-44.0	-41.6	-39.2	-36.6	-33.8	-30.9	-27.5	-25.0	-24.9
+100	-41.8	-36.5	-34.0	-31.4	-28.8	-25.7	-22.3	-18.5	-13.9	-8.0	-1.6	0.1
+75	-30.6	-24.7	-22.0	-18.9	-15.8	-12.4	-8.5	-4.4	1.0	8.7	18.6	25.1
+50	-19.0	-13.7	-11.2	-8.4	-5.5	-2.1	1.9	6.6	12.5	21.1	32.8	50.1
+25	-9.4	-4.1	-1.6	1.2	4.1	7.4	11.3	15.9	21.7	30.1	41.0	50.1
0	-0.5	4.7	7.2	9.9	12.7	16.0	19.7	23.9	29.2	36.2	44.6	50.1
-25	3.5	8.7	11.2	13.8	16.7	20.0	23.7	28.2	33.7	40.5	47.9	50.1
-50	10.6	15.7	18.1	20.7	23.5	26.6	30.1	33.9	38.2	43.3	48.4	50.1
-75	18.7	23.6	25.9	28.3	30.6	33.0	35.6	38.6	41.8	45.8	49.6	50.1
-100	27.1	31.1	33.2	35.1	37.6	40.2	42.1	44.0	46.1	48.4	50.1	50.1
-125	34.0	37.9	39.7	41.3	43.0	44.8	46.4	47.6	48.1	49.3	50.1	50.1

weeks to expiration — net profit area , in cents

The estimated credit is: + 50.6¢ premium - 0.5¢ comm. = + 50.1¢

TABLE 6

changes in the soybean future's price in 25¢ increments	25	20	18	16	14	12	10	8	6	4	2	0
+125	-55.4	-52.7	-51.5	-50.2	-49.0	-47.6	-46.1	-44.6	-42.9	-41.1	-40.4	-40.4
+100	-42.1	-38.7	-37.0	-35.3	-33.4	-31.3	-29.0	-26.4	-23.4	-19.6	-15.9	-15.4
+75	-28.9	-24.9	-23.1	-21.2	-19.1	-16.8	-14.0	-10.7	-6.7	-0.9	6.0	9.6
+50	-18.6	-14.6	-12.6	-10.4	-8.2	-5.6	-2.5	1.2	5.7	12.8	21.3	34.6
+25	-9.0	-5.1	-3.2	-1.1	1.2	3.7	6.7	10.3	14.7	20.9	29.1	34.6
0	-0.5	3.3	5.1	7.0	9.0	11.4	14.1	17.3	20.8	25.9	32.1	34.6
-25	3.5	7.3	9.2	11.3	13.3	15.7	18.4	21.6	25.1	29.6	33.8	34.6
-50	10.2	13.8	15.4	17.1	19.0	21.0	23.0	25.2	27.9	31.1	34.2	34.6
-75	16.8	20.7	22.1	23.5	25.0	26.6	28.4	30.4	32.8	34.5	34.6	34.6
-100	22.6	24.5	25.3	26.4	27.6	28.7	29.9	31.2	32.7	33.9	34.6	34.6
-125	26.6	28.3	29.0	29.8	30.6	31.4	32.2	33.2	34.1	34.6	34.6	34.6

net profit area , in cents

The estimated credit is: + 35.1¢ premium - 0.5¢ comm. = + 34.6¢

TABLE 4

changes in the soybean future's price in 25¢ increments	25	20	18	16	14	12	10	8	6	4	2	0
+125	-60.7	-59.5	-59.0	-58.4	-57.8	-57.2	-56.6	-55.9	-55.3	-54.9	-54.9	-54.9
+100	-43.7	-41.6	-40.7	-39.6	-38.6	-37.5	-36.2	-34.7	-33.1	-31.0	-30.0	-29.9
+75	-28.7	-26.2	-25.0	-23.7	-22.2	-20.6	-18.7	-16.4	-13.8	-10.2	-6.3	-4.9
+50	-17.2	-14.4	-13.0	-11.5	-9.9	-8.1	-5.9	-3.4	-0.2	4.4	10.7	18.0
+25	-8.0	-5.2	-3.9	-2.4	-0.8	0.9	2.8	5.3	8.2	12.4	18.0	20.1
0	-0.5	1.8	3.0	4.2	5.5	6.9	8.5	10.5	12.8	16.0	19.6	20.1
-25	3.7	6.1	7.3	8.5	9.7	11.1	12.6	14.4	16.3	18.5	20.1	20.1
-50	8.4	10.1	10.9	11.8	12.8	13.7	14.8	16.1	17.4	19.0	20.1	20.1
-75	12.0	13.4	14.1	14.8	15.4	16.2	17.0	17.9	18.7	19.8	20.1	20.1
-100	15.2	16.2	16.9	17.5	18.1	18.8	19.3	19.6	20.0	20.1	20.1	20.1
-125	18.0	18.8	19.2	19.5	19.7	19.8	19.9	20.0	20.1	20.1	20.1	20.1

weeks to expiration — net profit area , in cents

The estimated credit is: + 20.6¢ premium - 0.5¢ comm. = + 20.1¢

TABLE 2

changes in the soybean future's price in 25¢ increments	25	20	18	16	14	12	10	8	6	4	2	0
+125	-68.1	-67.9	-67.7	-67.7	-67.5	-67.5	-67.4	-67.4	-67.4	-67.4	-67.4	-67.4
+100	-46.2	-45.4	-45.0	-44.5	-44.1	-43.7	-43.3	-43.0	-42.7	-42.5	-42.4	-42.4
+75	-26.2	-25.0	-24.3	-23.6	-22.9	-22.1	-21.2	-20.1	-19.0	-18.2	-17.8	-17.4
+50	-13.8	-12.2	-11.4	-10.5	-9.6	-8.6	-7.3	-5.9	-4.1	-1.4	2.2	7.6
+25	-5.4	-3.9	-3.1	-2.2	-1.4	-0.5	0.6	1.9	3.6	5.7	6.8	7.6
0	-0.5	0.6	1.2	1.8	2.4	3.1	4.0	5.0	6.2	7.2	7.6	7.6
-25	3.1	4.0	4.4	4.9	5.4	5.9	6.3	6.7	7.3	7.6	7.6	7.6
-50	4.5	5.1	5.4	5.7	6.0	6.3	6.7	7.1	7.5	7.6	7.6	7.6
-75	6.0	6.4	6.6	6.9	7.1	7.2	7.4	7.5	7.6	7.6	7.6	7.6
-100	7.0	7.2	7.3	7.4	7.5	7.6	7.6	7.6	7.6	7.6	7.6	7.6
-125	7.4	7.5	7.6	7.6	7.6	7.6	7.6	7.6	7.6	7.6	7.6	7.6

weeks to expiration — net profit area , in cents

The estimated credit is: + 8.1¢ premium - 0.5¢ comm. = + 7.6¢

Wm Grandmill (1985) Ltd.

BULL or BEAR SPREAD – #1

BUY A CALL AT THE MONEY
and SELL A CALL AT 25¢ OUT OF THE MONEY
OR
BUY A PUT AT THE MONEY
and SELL A PUT AT 25¢ OUT OF THE MONEY

25 weeks to expiration

TABLE 0 (upper right)

net profit area, in cents

changes in price (25¢ incr.)	25	20	18	16	14	12	10	8	6	4	2	0
+125	12.7	12.8	12.9	13.0	13.1	13.2	13.4	13.6	13.8	14.0	14.4	14.4
+100	7.0	7.4	7.8	8.2	8.6	9.1	9.6	10.3	10.8	12.8	14.4	14.4
+75	4.2	4.4	4.7	5.0	5.3	5.7	6.2	6.8	7.8	9.4	12.8	14.4
+50	1.9	2.0	2.1	2.2	2.4	2.7	3.1	3.6	4.3	6.1	9.6	14.4
+25	0.4	0.5	0.5	0.6	0.6	0.7	0.8	0.9	1.1	1.8	3.6	14.4
0	-1.0	-1.0	-1.0	-1.0	-1.0	-1.1	-1.2	-1.3	-1.4	-1.6	-2.6	-10.6
-25	-1.7	-1.8	-1.8	-1.9	-2.0	-2.0	-2.2	-2.6	-3.3	-4.5	-6.7	-10.6
-50	-2.0	-2.1	-2.1	-2.2	-2.4	-2.7	-3.1	-3.7	-4.6	-6.0	-7.6	-10.6
-75	-2.3	-2.4	-2.5	-2.6	-2.8	-3.4	-4.2	-5.0	-6.0	-7.0	-8.6	-10.6
-100	-2.5	-2.6	-2.7	-3.0	-3.5	-4.2	-5.0	-5.9	-7.0	-8.1	-9.4	-10.6
-125	-2.7	-2.8	-3.0	-3.2	-3.8	-4.6	-5.4	-6.6	-7.8	-9.1	-10.1	-10.6

The estimated cost is: -69.1¢ premium +59.5¢ premium -1.0¢ comm. = -10.6¢

TABLE 0 (upper left)

net profit area, in cents

changes in price (25¢ incr.)	25	20	18	16	14	12	10	8	6	4	2	0
+125	12.7	12.9	12.9	12.9	12.9	13.0	13.2	13.6	14.1	14.4	14.4	14.4
+100	8.1	8.4	8.7	9.1	9.5	9.9	10.4	11.1	12.2	13.7	13.9	14.4
+75	5.1	5.6	5.8	6.0	6.3	6.6	6.9	7.6	8.9	10.9	13.9	14.4
+50	2.6	3.2	3.3	3.5	3.7	4.0	4.4	5.1	6.1	8.1	11.3	14.6
+25	-0.1	-0.1	-0.1	0.1	0.3	0.6	0.9	1.3	1.8	2.6	4.7	14.4
0	-1.0	-1.1	-1.2	-1.2	-1.3	-1.4	-1.5	-1.6	-2.0	-2.8	-5.6	-10.6
-25	-2.1	-2.2	-2.3	-2.5	-2.7	-2.9	-3.2	-3.6	-4.5	-5.6	-7.6	-10.6
-50	-3.1	-3.2	-3.4	-3.6	-3.9	-4.2	-4.6	-5.2	-5.9	-6.9	-8.9	-10.6
-75	-3.9	-4.1	-4.4	-4.7	-5.0	-5.4	-6.0	-7.0	-7.8	-8.9	-10.2	-10.6
-100	-4.4	-4.9	-5.3	-5.7	-6.1	-6.5	-7.0	-7.4	-8.1	-9.0	-10.3	-10.6
-125	-4.8	-5.6	-5.9	-6.2	-6.5	-6.9	-7.3	-7.8	-8.3	-9.3	-10.5	-10.6

The estimated cost is: -53.2¢ premium +43.6¢ premium -1.0¢ comm. = -10.6¢

TABLE 0 (lower right)

net profit area, in cents

changes in price (25¢ incr.)	25	20	18	16	14	12	10	8	6	4	2	0
+125	13.4	13.6	13.9	14.1	14.3	14.5	14.7	14.8	14.8	14.8	14.8	14.8
+100	10.7	11.4	11.7	12.0	12.4	12.8	13.2	13.8	14.4	14.8	14.8	14.8
+75	6.8	7.7	8.1	8.6	9.0	9.5	10.2	11.0	12.0	12.7	13.5	14.8
+50	4.8	5.2	5.5	5.8	6.2	6.7	7.3	8.1	9.1	10.6	13.5	14.8
+25	1.3	1.6	1.8	2.0	2.1	2.3	2.6	2.8	3.4	4.4	6.8	14.8
0	-1.0	-1.0	-1.1	-1.1	-1.1	-1.2	-1.4	-1.6	-1.8	-2.2	-3.0	-10.2
-25	-2.8	-3.1	-3.3	-3.6	-3.9	-4.2	-4.5	-5.0	-5.6	-6.6	-8.6	-10.2
-50	-5.0	-5.3	-5.6	-5.8	-5.9	-6.0	-6.1	-6.3	-6.7	-7.7	-9.7	-10.2
-75	-5.6	-5.9	-6.2	-6.6	-6.9	-7.2	-7.6	-7.9	-8.6	-9.0	-9.7	-10.2
-100	-6.3	-6.8	-7.0	-7.3	-7.6	-7.8	-8.0	-8.4	-8.9	-9.4	-10.2	-10.2
-125	-7.0	-7.2	-7.4	-7.5	-7.7	-7.9	-8.2	-8.6	-9.1	-9.4	-9.7	-10.2

The estimated cost is: -37.3¢ premium +28.1¢ premium -1.0¢ comm. = -10.2¢

TABLE 2 (lower left)

net profit area, in cents

changes in price (25¢ incr.)	25	20	18	16	14	12	10	8	6	4	2	0
+125	15.5	15.5	15.5	15.5	15.5	15.5	15.5	15.5	15.5	15.5	15.5	15.5
+100	14.9	15.1	15.2	15.3	15.4	15.4	15.5	15.5	15.5	15.5	15.5	15.5
+75	12.3	13.0	13.2	13.6	13.9	14.3	14.7	14.9	15.2	15.4	15.5	15.5
+50	9.5	9.9	10.1	10.3	10.7	11.1	11.6	12.4	13.2	14.3	15.1	15.5
+25	3.9	4.3	4.5	4.6	4.8	5.0	5.4	5.7	6.4	7.8	10.5	15.5
0	-1.0	-1.1	-1.2	-1.2	-1.3	-1.4	-1.6	-1.7	-1.8	-2.4	-2.9	-9.5
-25	-4.7	-5.0	-5.2	-5.5	-5.7	-5.9	-6.1	-6.5	-6.9	-7.6	-8.9	-9.5
-50	-5.9	-6.1	-6.3	-6.4	-6.5	-6.7	-7.2	-7.7	-8.4	-9.1	-9.5	-9.5
-75	-7.0	-7.1	-7.2	-7.3	-7.5	-7.7	-8.0	-8.4	-9.3	-9.5	-9.5	-9.5
-100	-7.7	-7.9	-8.0	-8.1	-8.2	-8.4	-8.6	-8.8	-9.1	-9.4	-9.5	-9.5
-125	-8.6	-8.7	-8.8	-9.0	-9.1	-9.2	-9.3	-9.4	-9.5	-9.5	-9.5	-9.5

The estimated cost is: -21.4¢ premium +12.9¢ premium -1.0¢ comm. = -9.5¢

BULL or BEAR SPREAD – #2

**BUY A CALL AT THE MONEY
and SELL 2 CALLS AT 50¢ OUT OF THE MONEY
OR
BUY A PUT AT THE MONEY
and SELL 2 PUTS AT 50¢ OUT OF THE MONEY**

weeks to
expiration

25

TABLE (top-left)

changes in the soybean future's price in 25¢ increments

change	25	20	18	16	14	12	10	8	6	4	2	0
+125	-30.3	-27.7	-26.7	-25.7	-24.5	-23.0	-20.7	-17.9	-14.5	-10.9	-9.5	-9.5
+100	-27.4	-23.5	-21.3	-19.3	-17.0	-13.8	-10.0	-5.6	-0.2	7.1	14.5	15.5
+75	-21.5	-16.2	-13.8	-11.2	-8.3	-5.1	-1.0	4.1	10.4	20.2	33.3	40.5
+50	-14.2	-9.6	-7.3	-4.6	-2.1	1.0	4.9	9.7	15.7	25.1	39.4	65.5
+25	-8.2	-4.4	-2.4	-0.1	2.4	5.1	8.3	12.2	17.0	23.6	33.1	40.5
0	-1.5	2.4	3.7	5.3	7.1	9.3	11.6	14.3	16.8	20.4	23.8	15.5
-25	-3.1	0.6	2.5	4.6	6.5	8.6	11.0	13.8	16.4	19.2	17.2	15.5
-50	1.8	5.2	6.6	8.1	9.8	11.3	12.8	14.2	15.9	17.2	17.2	15.5
-75	11.0	12.6	13.1	13.8	14.6	15.2	15.7	16.1	16.6	17.1	16.4	15.5
-100	13.8	15.1	15.5	16.0	16.4	16.8	17.3	17.6	17.6	17.1	16.4	15.5
-125	17.4	18.0	18.2	18.4	18.6	18.7	18.8	18.9	18.7	17.3	15.6	15.5

weeks to expiration — net profit area, in cents

The estimated credit is: -53.2¢ prem. + 35.1¢ prem. + 35.1¢ prem. - 1.5¢ com. = +15.5¢

TABLE (top-right)

changes in the soybean future's price in 25¢ increments

change	25	20	18	16	14	12	10	8	6	4	2	0
+125	-28.7	-27.6	-23.7	-21.5	-19.2	-17.7	-14.8	-12.1	-9.6	-6.1	0.4	5.6
+100	-26.7	-22.8	-20.2	-17.1	-13.4	-11.3	-7.2	-2.1	4.4	14.8	27.2	30.6
+75	-15.7	-10.4	-7.9	-4.9	-1.7	2.0	6.6	13.4	19.4	25.4	42.7	55.6
+50	-7.7	-3.0	-0.7	1.8	4.5	7.7	11.6	16.6	22.9	32.0	43.9	80.6
+25	-1.5	3.6	6.1	8.7	11.4	14.6	18.0	21.7	26.4	31.8	37.5	55.6
0	3.6	7.2	9.5	12.0	14.8	17.7	21.0	24.4	27.7	30.9	32.4	30.6
-25	2.2	2.0	4.5	6.9	9.8	13.1	16.6	21.0	25.6	31.4	35.3	30.6
-50	-3.1	7.2	9.5	12.0	14.8	17.7	21.0	24.4	27.7	30.9	32.4	30.6
-75	14.4	19.0	21.1	23.3	25.0	26.5	28.0	29.5	30.7	31.6	31.8	30.6
-100	21.6	25.2	26.9	28.4	29.9	31.1	32.2	32.7	32.8	32.3	31.4	30.6
-125	30.0	33.1	34.0	34.8	35.9	37.1	38.1	39.1	37.9	35.3	33.1	30.6

weeks to expiration — net profit area, in cents

The estimated credit is: -69.1¢ premium +50.6¢ premium +50.6¢ premium -1.5¢ com. = 30.6¢

TABLE (bottom-left)

changes in the soybean future's price in 25¢ increments

change	25	20	18	16	14	12	10	8	6	4	2	0
+125	-5.8	-5.6	-5.4	-4.8	-4.7	-4.7	-5.1	-5.8	-6.4	-6.7	-6.7	-6.7
+100	-5.6	-5.6	-5.5	-5.5	-4.7	-4.7	-4.8	-5.6	-6.3	-6.5	-6.7	-6.7
+75	-5.4	-5.4	-5.5	-5.6	-5.6	-5.7	-5.8	-6.0	-6.4	-6.7	-6.7	-6.7
+50	-4.8	-4.7	-4.7	-4.7	-4.8	-4.9	-5.1	-5.5	-6.3	-6.7	-6.7	-6.7
+25	-2.8	-2.5	-2.4	-2.1	-2.2	-2.5	-3.0	-3.7	-5.0	-5.9	-6.7	-6.7
0	-1.5	-0.9	-0.5	-0.2	0.1	0.5	0.8	1.4	1.9	-1.3	-6.7	-6.7
+25	2.3	3.9	4.9	5.9	6.8	7.8	9.1	10.7	12.9	15.5	17.1	18.3
+50	-8.2?	4.9	5.9	6.8	7.8	9.1	10.7	12.9	15.5	17.1	17.5	43.3
-75	11.0	12.6	13.1	13.8	14.6	15.2	15.7	16.1	16.6	17.1	16.4	18.3
-100	13.8	15.1	15.5	16.0	16.4	16.8	17.3	17.6	17.6	17.1	16.4	15.5
-125	17.4	18.0	18.2	18.4	18.6	18.7	18.8	18.9	18.7	17.3	15.6	15.5

weeks to expiration — net profit area

The estimated cost is: -21.4¢ prem. +8.1¢ prem. +8.1¢ prem. -1.5¢ com. = -6.7¢

TABLE (bottom-right)

changes in the soybean future's price in 25¢ increments

change	25	20	18	16	14	12	10	8	6	4	2	0
+125	-34.0	-32.9	-31.8	-32.1	-31.9	-31.8	-31.7	-31.7	-31.7	-31.7	-31.7	-22.6
+100	-23.5	-30.8	-29.6	-28.4	-27.2	-26.0	-24.6	-23.4	-22.6	-22.6	-22.6	-22.6
+75	-14.4	-19.8	-18.1	-16.3	-14.5	-12.5	-10.1	-7.2	-4.0	0.2	2.2	2.4
+50	-5.0	-8.4	-10.6	-6.7	-4.3	-1.7	1.5	5.4	10.0	16.8	24.6	27.4
+25	2.3	4.3	6.7	7.9	9.2	10.6	12.2	14.4	16.9	20.2	25.4	33.7
0	-0.7	-1.5	3.9	5.4	7.0	8.7	10.9	13.1	15.0	17.3	22.1	17.5
-25	0.3	1.3	2.2	3.2	4.2	5.2	6.7	8.1	9.9	10.8	2.4	2.4
-50	2.6	3.0	3.2	3.3	3.4	3.6	3.7	3.6	3.4	3.3	2.7	2.4
-75	0.7	1.1	1.7	2.3	2.8	3.4	4.0	4.2	4.3	2.9	2.4	2.4
-100	-0.4	5.3	5.4	5.5	5.5	5.0	4.5	4.1	3.6	2.4	2.4	2.4
-125	6.2	6.5	6.6	6.5	6.3	5.7	5.1	4.4	3.8	2.7	2.4	2.4

weeks to expiration — net profit area, in cents

The estimated credit is: -37.4¢ prem. +20.6¢ prem. +20.6¢ prem. -1.5¢ com. = 2.4¢

SELL A CALL AT THE MONEY and SELL A PUT AT THE MONEY — 25 weeks to expiration (TABLE 0)

The estimated credit is: + 69.1¢ premium + 69.1¢ premium - 1.0¢ comm. = + 137.2¢

changes in the soybean future's price in 25¢ increments	weeks to expiration											
	25	20	18	16	14	12	10	8	6	4	2	0
+125	-43.1	-32.6	-27.8	-22.9	-18.2	-13.4	-8.0	-1.9	3.6	7.9	11.7	12.2
+100	-27.9	-17.0	-12.1	-6.9	-1.8	4.0	10.2	16.5	23.5	30.0	35.5	37.2
+75	-13.5	-3.0	1.8	6.9	12.1	17.8	24.1	31.4	39.5	50.0	59.9	62.2
+50	-5.3	5.2	10.2	15.5	20.9	27.3	34.4	42.3	52.3	65.2	80.3	87.2
+25	-3.0	8.2	13.4	19.3	25.3	32.0	39.8	48.6	59.7	75.8	96.9	112.2
0	-1.0	9.6	14.6	20.2	26.0	32.8	40.8	50.2	62.0	79.2	102.6	137.2
-25	-3.0	8.2	13.4	19.3	25.3	32.0	39.8	48.6	59.7	75.8	96.9	112.2
-50	-5.3	5.2	10.2	15.5	20.9	27.3	34.4	42.3	52.3	65.2	80.3	87.2
-75	-13.5	-3.0	1.8	6.9	12.1	17.8	24.1	31.4	39.5	50.0	59.9	62.2
-100	-27.9	-17.0	-12.1	-6.9	-1.8	4.0	10.2	16.5	23.5	30.0	35.5	37.2
-125	-43.1	-32.6	-27.8	-22.9	-18.2	-13.4	-8.0	-1.9	3.6	7.9	11.7	12.2

net profit area , in cents

SELL A CALL AT THE MONEY and SELL A PUT AT THE MONEY — 25 weeks to expiration (TABLE 4 / TABLE 2)

The estimated credit is: + 37.3¢ premium + 37.3¢ premium - 1.0¢ comm. = + 73.6¢

changes in the soybean future's price in 25¢ increments	weeks to expiration											
	25	20	18	16	14	12	10	8	6	4	2	0
+125	-59.7	-58.1	-57.4	-56.7	-56.1	-55.3	-54.5	-53.6	-52.7	-51.7	-51.4	-51.4
+100	-39.8	-37.8	-36.7	-35.6	-34.2	-33.1	-31.8	-30.4	-29.0	-27.5	-26.4	-26.4
+75	-23.6	-19.8	-18.3	-16.5	-14.7	-12.7	-10.5	-8.1	-5.6	-3.0	-1.4	-1.4
+50	-10.8	-6.4	-4.3	-2.0	0.3	2.8	5.7	9.2	13.1	18.4	23.0	23.6
+25	-3.3	2.0	4.6	7.3	10.4	13.7	17.5	22.3	27.8	35.6	45.1	48.6
0	-1.0	4.6	7.4	10.4	13.6	17.2	21.6	26.6	33.0	42.2	54.8	73.6
-25	-3.3	2.0	4.6	7.3	10.4	13.7	17.5	22.3	27.8	35.6	45.1	48.6
-50	-10.8	-6.4	-4.3	-2.0	0.3	2.8	5.7	9.2	13.1	18.4	23.0	23.6
-75	-23.6	-19.8	-18.3	-16.5	-14.7	-12.7	-10.5	-8.1	-5.6	-3.0	-1.4	-1.4
-100	-39.8	-37.8	-36.7	-35.6	-34.2	-33.1	-31.8	-30.4	-29.0	-27.5	-26.4	-26.4
-125	-59.7	-58.1	-57.4	-56.7	-56.1	-55.3	-54.5	-53.6	-52.7	-51.7	-51.4	-51.4

net profit area , in cents

SELL A STRADDLE — 25 weeks to expiration (TABLE 0)

The estimated credit is: + 53.2¢ premium + 52.2¢ premium - 1.0¢ comm. = + 105.4¢

changes in the soybean future's price in 25¢ increments	weeks to expiration											
	25	20	18	16	14	12	10	8	6	4	2	0
+125	-46.6	-41.1	-38.5	-35.6	-32.9	-30.1	-27.8	-25.8	-23.8	-21.4	-19.7	-19.6
+100	-29.5	-23.0	-20.2	-17.1	-13.8	-10.8	-7.9	-4.9	-1.6	1.9	5.0	5.4
+75	-15.7	-9.2	-6.1	-2.7	0.5	4.3	8.5	13.2	18.4	24.7	29.6	30.4
+50	-6.4	0.8	4.3	7.9	11.8	16.3	21.3	27.1	33.9	42.5	52.4	55.4
+25	-1.7	5.2	8.9	12.9	17.3	23.1	28.9	35.8	44.2	56.2	71.3	80.4
0	-1.0	7.0	11.0	15.4	19.8	25.0	31.2	38.6	47.6	60.8	78.8	105.4
-25	-1.7	5.2	8.9	12.9	17.3	23.1	28.9	35.8	44.2	56.2	71.3	80.4
-50	-6.4	0.8	4.3	7.9	11.8	16.3	21.3	27.1	33.9	42.5	52.4	55.4
-75	-15.7	-9.2	-6.1	-2.7	0.5	4.3	8.5	13.2	18.4	24.7	29.6	30.4
-100	-29.5	-23.0	-20.2	-17.1	-13.8	-10.8	-7.9	-4.9	-1.6	1.9	5.0	5.4
-125	-46.6	-41.1	-38.5	-35.6	-32.9	-30.1	-27.8	-25.8	-23.8	-21.4	-19.7	-19.6

net profit area , in cents

SELL A STRADDLE — 25 weeks to expiration (TABLE 2 / TABLE 0)

The estimated credit is: + 21.4¢ premium + 21.4¢ premium - 1.0¢ comm. = + 41.8¢

changes in the soybean future's price in 25¢ increments	weeks to expiration											
	25	20	18	16	14	12	10	8	6	4	2	0
+125	-84.8	-84.5	-84.2	-83.9	-83.7	-83.6	-83.4	-83.3	-83.2	-83.2	-83.2	-83.2
+100	-61.3	-60.7	-60.4	-60.1	-59.8	-59.5	-59.1	-58.7	-58.3	-58.2	-58.2	-58.2
+75	-38.3	-37.2	-36.6	-36.0	-35.5	-35.0	-34.5	-34.0	-33.5	-33.2	-33.2	-33.2
+50	-20.1	-18.2	-17.2	-16.1	-15.1	-14.0	-12.7	-11.4	-9.9	-8.7	-8.2	-8.2
+25	-5.9	-3.3	-1.9	-0.2	1.3	3.0	5.0	7.4	10.2	13.6	16.3	16.8
0	-1.0	2.2	3.8	5.6	7.4	9.4	12.0	14.8	18.4	23.8	31.0	41.8
-25	-5.9	-3.3	-1.9	-0.2	1.3	3.0	5.0	7.4	10.2	13.6	16.3	16.8
-50	-20.1	-18.2	-17.2	-16.1	-15.1	-14.0	-12.7	-11.4	-9.9	-8.7	-8.2	-8.2
-75	-38.3	-37.2	-36.6	-36.0	-35.5	-35.0	-34.5	-34.0	-33.5	-33.2	-33.2	-33.2
-100	-61.3	-60.7	-60.4	-60.1	-59.8	-59.5	-59.1	-58.7	-58.3	-58.2	-58.2	-58.2
-125	-84.8	-84.5	-84.2	-83.9	-83.7	-83.6	-83.4	-83.3	-83.2	-83.2	-83.2	-83.2

net profit

Wm Grandmill (1985) Ltd.

SELL A STRANGLE – #1

SELL A CALL AT 50¢ OUT OF THE MONEY and SELL A PUT AT 50¢ OUT OF THE MONEY

weeks to expiration: 25

TABLE (estimated credit: + 50.6¢ premium + 50.6¢ premium – 1.0¢ comm. = + 100.2¢)

changes in the soybean future's price in 25¢ increments	25	20	18	16	14	12	10	8	6	4	2	0
+125	-19.9	-10.6	-6.7	-2.6	1.4	5.6	9.8	13.8	17.7	21.8	25.1	25.2
+100	-14.7	-5.4	-0.9	3.7	8.8	14.1	19.8	25.6	32.2	40.4	48.5	50.2
+75	-11.9	-1.1	3.9	9.4	14.4	20.6	27.4	34.3	42.8	54.5	68.2	75.2
+50	-8.4	2.0	6.9	12.3	18.0	24.5	32.0	40.5	50.7	64.4	81.2	100.2
+25	-5.9	4.6	9.6	15.0	20.8	27.4	35.0	44.1	55.1	70.6	88.9	100.2
0	-1.0	9.4	14.4	19.8	25.4	32.0	39.4	47.8	58.4	72.4	89.8	100.2
-25	-5.9	4.6	9.6	15.0	20.8	27.4	35.0	44.1	55.1	70.6	88.9	100.2
-50	-8.4	2.0	6.9	12.3	18.0	24.5	32.0	40.5	50.7	64.4	81.2	100.2
-75	-11.9	-1.1	3.9	9.4	14.8	20.6	27.4	34.3	42.8	54.5	68.2	75.2
-100	-14.7	-5.4	-0.9	3.7	8.8	14.1	19.8	25.6	32.2	40.4	48.5	50.2
-125	-19.9	-10.6	-6.7	-2.6	1.4	5.6	9.8	13.8	17.7	21.8	25.1	25.2

weeks to expiration — net profit area, in cents

TABLE (estimated credit is: +35.1¢ premium +35.1¢ premium – 1.0¢ comm. = +69.2¢)

changes in the soybean future's price in 25¢ increments	25	20	18	16	14	12	10	8	6	4	2	0
+125	-28.8	-24.4	-22.5	-20.4	-18.4	-16.2	-13.9	-11.4	-8.8	-6.5	-5.8	-5.8
+100	-19.5	-14.2	-11.7	-8.9	-5.8	-2.6	0.9	4.8	9.3	14.3	18.7	19.2
+75	-12.1	-5.4	-2.4	0.9	4.4	8.2	12.6	17.7	23.7	31.9	40.5	44.2
+50	-8.4	-0.8	2.8	6.7	10.8	15.3	20.5	26.4	33.6	43.4	55.5	69.2
+25	-5.5	2.2	6.0	10.2	14.5	19.4	25.1	31.9	39.8	50.5	62.9	69.2
0	-1.0	6.6	10.2	14.0	18.0	22.8	28.2	34.6	41.6	51.8	64.2	69.2
-25	-5.5	2.2	6.0	10.2	14.5	19.4	25.1	31.9	39.8	50.5	62.9	69.2
-50	-8.4	-0.8	2.8	6.7	10.8	15.3	20.5	26.4	33.6	43.4	55.5	69.2
-75	-12.1	-5.4	-2.4	0.9	4.4	8.2	12.6	17.7	23.7	31.9	40.5	44.2
-100	-19.5	-14.2	-11.7	-8.9	-5.8	-2.6	0.9	4.8	9.3	14.3	18.7	19.2
-125	-28.8	-24.4	-22.5	-20.4	-18.4	-16.2	-13.9	-11.4	-8.8	-6.5	-5.8	-5.8

net profit area, in cents

TABLE (estimated credit is: + 20.6¢ premium + 20.6¢ premium – 1.0¢ comm. = + 40.2¢)

changes in the soybean future's price in 25¢ increments	25	20	18	16	14	12	10	8	6	4	2	0
+125	-42.7	-40.7	-39.8	-38.1	-37.4	-36.7	-35.9	-35.2	-34.9	-34.8	-34.8	-34.8
+100	-28.5	-25.3	-23.7	-22.1	-20.5	-18.7	-16.9	-15.1	-13.3	-10.9	-9.9	-9.8
+75	-16.7	-12.8	-10.8	-8.9	-6.8	-4.4	-1.7	1.5	4.9	9.6	13.8	15.2
+50	-8.8	-4.3	-2.1	0.3	2.9	5.6	8.9	12.7	17.2	23.4	30.8	40.2
+25	-4.3	0.9	3.4	6.1	8.9	12.0	15.4	19.7	24.5	30.9	37.9	40.2
0	-1.0	3.6	6.0	8.4	11.0	13.8	17.0	21.0	25.6	32.0	39.2	40.2
-25	-4.3	0.9	3.4	6.1	8.9	12.0	15.4	19.7	24.5	30.9	37.9	40.2
-50	-8.8	-4.3	-2.1	0.3	2.9	5.6	8.9	12.7	17.2	23.4	30.8	40.2
-75	-16.7	-12.8	-10.8	-8.9	-6.8	-4.4	-1.7	1.5	4.9	9.6	13.8	15.2
-100	-28.5	-25.3	-23.7	-22.1	-20.5	-18.7	-16.9	-15.1	-13.3	-10.9	-9.9	-9.8
-125	-42.7	-40.7	-39.8	-38.1	-37.4	-36.7	-35.9	-35.2	-34.8	-34.8	-34.8	-34.8

weeks to expiration — net profit area, in cents

TABLE (estimated credit is: + 8.1¢ premium + 8.1¢ premium – 1.0¢ comm. = + 15.2¢)

changes in the soybean future's price in 25¢ increments	25	20	18	16	14	12	10	8	6	4	2	0
+125	-60.6	-60.3	-60.1	-60.0	-59.9	-59.9	-59.8	-59.8	-59.8	-59.8	-59.8	-59.8
+100	-39.3	-38.2	-37.7	-37.1	-36.6	-36.2	-35.7	-35.4	-35.1	-34.9	-34.8	-34.8
+75	-21.2	-19.6	-18.7	-17.7	-16.8	-15.9	-14.8	-13.6	-12.4	-11.1	-10.2	-9.8
+50	-9.3	-7.1	-6.0	-4.8	-3.6	-2.3	-0.6	1.2	3.4	6.2	9.8	15.2
+25	-2.2	0.1	1.3	2.7	4.0	5.4	6.9	8.6	10.9	13.3	14.4	15.2
0	-1.0	1.2	2.4	3.6	4.8	6.2	8.0	9.8	12.4	14.4	15.2	15.2
-25	-2.2	0.1	1.3	2.7	4.0	5.4	6.9	8.6	10.9	13.3	14.4	15.2
-50	-9.3	-7.1	-6.0	-4.8	-3.6	-2.3	-0.6	1.2	3.4	6.2	9.8	15.2
-75	-21.2	-19.8	-18.7	-17.7	-16.8	-15.9	-14.8	-13.6	-12.4	-11.1	-10.2	-9.8
-100	-39.3	-38.2	-37.1	-36.6	-36.2	-35.7	-35.4	-35.1	-34.9	-34.8	-34.8	-34.8
-125	-60.6	-60.3	-60.1	-60.0	-59.9	-59.9	-59.8	-59.8	-59.8	-59.8	-59.8	-59.8

net profit area, in cents

Wm Grandmill (1985) Ltd.

SELL A STRANGLE – #2

SELL A CALL AT $1.00 OUT OF THE MONEY and SELL A PUT AT $1.00 OUT OF THE MONEY

weeks to expiration: 25

TABLE 0

changes in the soybean future's price in 25¢ increments — weeks to expiration

	25	20	18	16	14	12	10	8	6	4	2	0
+125	-17.6	-13.2	-11.1	-9.0	-6.7	-4.2	-1.0	2.5	6.5	12.3	19.2	22.8
+100	-9.4	-4.5	-2.1	0.5	3.0	6.2	9.9	14.0	18.9	25.5	34.5	47.8
+75	-3.8	1.8	4.4	7.3	10.4	13.7	17.5	22.1	27.4	34.1	42.3	47.8
+50	0.7	6.4	9.0	12.0	15.2	18.7	22.6	27.1	32.1	38.4	45.3	47.8
+25	-3.8	5.5	8.6	12.1	15.4	19.3	23.6	28.6	34.1	41.0	46.9	47.8
0	-1.0	6.2	9.4	12.8	16.6	20.4	24.6	29.0	34.4	40.8	47.0	47.8
-25	-1.1	5.5	8.6	12.1	15.4	19.3	23.6	28.6	34.1	41.0	46.9	47.8
-50	0.7	6.4	9.0	12.0	15.2	18.7	22.6	27.1	32.1	38.4	45.3	47.8
-75	-3.8	1.8	4.4	7.3	10.4	13.7	17.5	22.1	27.4	34.1	42.3	47.8
-100	-9.4	-4.5	-2.1	0.5	3.0	6.2	9.9	14.0	18.9	25.5	34.5	47.8
-125	-17.6	-13.1	-11.0	-9.0	-6.7	-4.2	-1.0	2.5	6.5	12.3	19.2	22.8

net profit area, in cents

The estimated credit is: +24.4¢ premium + 24.4¢ premium - 1.0¢ comm. = + 47.8¢

TABLE 8

changes in the soybean future's price in 25¢ increments — weeks to expiration

	25	20	18	16	14	12	10	8	6	4	2	0
+125	-6.0	0.9	4.0	7.5	11.0	14.7	18.8	23.2	28.7	36.6	46.5	53.0
+100	0.6	8.1	11.5	15.2	19.0	23.3	28.0	33.2	39.8	48.7	60.7	78.0
+75	2.5	11.8	15.9	20.3	24.9	30.0	35.7	41.3	48.1	57.2	68.9	78.0
+50	4.4	13.6	18.1	22.8	28.1	33.7	39.6	45.8	53.1	62.4	72.8	78.0
+25	0.0	10.1	14.9	19.9	25.1	30.8	37.1	44.6	53.0	64.4	75.3	78.0
0	-1.0	9.2	14.0	19.2	24.8	31.0	38.0	45.6	54.2	64.1	74.6	78.0
-25	0.0	10.1	14.9	19.9	25.1	30.8	37.1	44.6	53.0	64.4	75.3	78.0
-50	4.4	13.6	18.1	22.8	28.1	33.7	39.6	45.8	53.1	62.4	72.8	78.0
-75	2.5	11.8	15.9	20.3	24.9	30.0	35.7	41.3	48.1	57.2	68.9	78.0
-100	0.6	8.1	11.5	15.2	19.0	23.3	28.0	33.2	39.8	48.7	60.7	78.0
-125	-6.0	0.9	4.0	7.5	11.0	14.7	18.8	23.2	28.7	36.6	46.5	53.0

net profit area, in cents

The estimated credit is: +39.5¢ premium + 39.5¢ premium - 1.0¢ comm. = + 78.0¢

TABLE 2

changes in the soybean future's price in 25¢ increments — weeks to expiration

	25	20	18	16	14	12	10	8	6	4	2	0
+125	-29.6	-28.4	-27.8	-27.0	-26.3	-25.5	-24.6	-23.5	-22.4	-21.1	-20.2	-19.8
+100	-16.3	-14.6	-13.8	-12.9	-12.0	-11.0	-9.7	-8.3	-6.5	-3.8	-0.2	5.2
+75	-9.7	-7.9	-5.5	-4.6	-3.8	-2.9	-1.8	-0.5	1.2	3.3	4.4	5.2
+50	-3.6	-2.2	-1.5	-0.8	-0.1	0.7	1.6	2.5	3.8	4.8	5.2	5.2
+25	-0.9	0.4	1.1	1.8	2.5	3.1	3.7	4.3	4.9	5.2	5.2	5.2
0	-1.0	0.2	0.8	1.4	2.0	2.6	3.4	4.2	5.0	5.2	5.2	5.2
-25	-0.9	0.4	1.1	1.8	2.5	3.1	3.7	4.3	4.9	5.2	5.2	5.2
-50	-3.6	-2.2	-1.5	-0.8	-0.1	0.7	1.6	2.5	3.8	4.8	5.2	5.2
-75	-9.7	-7.9	-5.5	-4.6	-3.8	-2.9	-1.8	-0.5	1.2	3.3	4.4	5.2
-100	-16.3	-14.6	-13.8	-12.9	-12.0	-11.0	-9.7	-8.3	-6.5	-3.8	-0.2	5.2
-125	-29.6	-28.4	-27.8	-27.0	-26.3	-25.5	-24.6	-23.5	-22.4	-21.1	-20.2	-19.8

net profit area, in cents

The estimated credit is: +3.1¢ premium + 3.1¢ premium - 1.0¢ comm. = + 5.2¢

TABLE 4

changes in the soybean future's price in 25¢ increments — weeks to expiration

	25	20	18	16	14	12	10	8	6	4	2	0
+125	-27.0	-24.2	-22.8	-21.5	-19.9	-18.3	-16.4	-14.1	-11.5	-7.9	-4.0	-2.6
+100	-16.1	-12.8	-11.2	-9.5	-7.8	-5.9	-3.7	-1.1	2.1	6.7	13.0	22.4
+75	-7.8	-4.2	-2.7	-0.7	1.1	2.9	4.9	7.5	10.5	14.7	20.3	22.4
+50	-3.1	0.2	2.1	3.9	5.8	7.9	10.0	12.3	14.8	18.3	21.9	22.4
+25	-2.1	1.7	3.6	5.5	7.3	9.5	11.8	14.5	17.2	20.5	22.4	22.4
0	-1.0	2.4	4.0	5.8	7.8	9.6	11.8	14.4	17.0	20.2	22.4	22.4
-25	-2.1	1.7	3.6	5.5	7.3	9.5	11.8	14.5	17.2	20.5	22.4	22.4
-50	-3.1	0.2	2.1	3.9	5.8	7.9	10.0	12.3	14.8	18.3	21.9	22.4
-75	-7.8	-4.2	-2.7	-0.7	1.1	2.9	4.9	7.5	10.5	14.7	20.3	22.4
-100	-16.1	-12.8	-11.2	-9.5	-7.8	-5.9	-3.7	-1.1	2.1	6.7	13.0	22.4
-125	-27.0	-24.2	-22.8	-21.5	-19.9	-18.3	-16.4	-14.1	-11.5	-7.9	-4.0	-2.6

net profit area, in cents

The estimated credit is: +11.7¢ premium +11.7¢ premium -1.0¢ comm. = + 22.4¢

Wm Grandmill (1985) Ltd.

BUY A CALL or BUY A PUT

AT THE MONEY

weeks to expiration: 30

TABLE (top-right) — "net profit"

changes in the soybean future's price in 25¢ increments — weeks to expiration

change	30	25	20	18	16	14	12	10	8	6	4	2	0
+125	79.3	75.0	69.4	66.9	64.4	62.0	59.6	56.8	53.7	51.4	51.1	51.1	51.1
+100	56.3	51.7	45.9	43.4	40.8	38.5	35.8	30.6	27.9	26.5	26.1	26.1	26.1
+75	34.7	30.2	24.9	22.6	20.1	17.8	15.4	10.0	7.1	3.7	1.2	1.1	1.1
+50	22.3	18.0	12.7	10.2	7.6	5.0	1.9	-1.5	-5.3	-9.9	-15.8	-22.2	-23.9
+25	11.2	6.8	0.9	-1.8	-4.9	-8.0	-11.4	-15.3	-19.5	-24.8	-32.5	-42.4	-48.9
0	-0.5	-4.8	-9.9	-12.6	-15.4	-18.3	-21.7	-25.7	-30.4	-36.3	-44.9	-56.6	-73.9
-25	-10.1	-14.4	-19.7	-22.2	-25.0	-27.9	-31.2	-35.1	-39.7	-45.5	-53.9	-67.2	-73.9
-50	-19.1	-23.3	-27.3	-31.0	-33.7	-36.5	-39.8	-43.5	-47.7	-53.0	-60.0	-68.7	-73.9
-75	-23.3	-27.3	-32.5	-35.0	-37.6	-40.5	-43.8	-47.5	-52.0	-57.2	-64.3	-71.7	-73.9
-100	-30.7	-34.4	-39.5	-41.9	-44.5	-47.3	-50.4	-53.9	-57.7	-62.0	-67.1	-72.2	-73.9
-125	-23.5	-27.3	-32.5	-35.0	-37.6	-40.5	-43.8	-47.5	-52.0	-57.2	-64.3	-71.7	-73.9

The estimated cost is: –73.4¢ premium – 0.5¢ comm. = –73.9¢

TABLE (bottom-right) — "net profit area"

changes in the soybean future's price in 25¢ increments — weeks to expiration

change	30	25	20	18	16	14	12	10	8	6	4	2	0
+125	85.6	85.1	84.9	84.9	84.9	84.9	84.9	84.9	84.9	84.9	84.9	84.9	84.9
+100	62.1	61.6	61.1	60.8	60.6	60.4	60.2	60.0	59.9	59.9	59.9	59.9	59.9
+75	41.9	40.7	39.5	39.0	38.4	37.8	37.2	36.6	35.9	35.3	34.9	34.9	34.9
+50	25.4	23.7	21.6	20.7	19.6	18.6	17.5	16.2	14.7	13.1	11.0	10.0	9.9
+25	10.8	8.7	6.2	4.9	3.7	2.2	0.6	-1.3	-3.6	-6.2	-9.8	-13.7	-15.1
0	-0.5	-2.8	-5.6	-7.0	-8.5	-10.1	-11.9	-14.1	-16.6	-19.8	-24.4	-30.7	-40.1
-25	-9.8	-12.0	-14.8	-16.1	-17.6	-19.2	-20.9	-22.8	-25.3	-28.2	-32.4	-38.0	-40.1
-50	-17.4	-19.5	-21.8	-23.0	-24.2	-25.5	-26.9	-28.5	-30.5	-32.8	-36.0	-39.6	-40.1
-75	-21.7	-23.7	-26.1	-27.3	-28.5	-29.7	-31.1	-32.6	-34.4	-36.3	-38.5	-40.1	-40.1
-100	-26.7	-28.4	-30.1	-30.9	-31.8	-32.8	-33.7	-34.8	-36.1	-37.4	-39.0	-40.1	-40.1
-125	-30.8	-32.0	-33.4	-34.1	-34.7	-35.4	-36.2	-37.0	-37.9	-38.8	-39.8	-40.1	-40.1

The estimated cost is: –39.6¢ premium –0.5¢ comm. = –40.1¢

TABLE (top-left) — "net profit"

changes in the soybean future's price in 25¢ increments — weeks to expiration

change	30	25	20	18	16	14	12	10	8	6	4	2	0
+125	79.6	77.1	74.3	72.9	71.4	70.1	68.8	67.9	67.9	67.9	67.9	67.9	67.9
+100	56.1	53.4	50.5	49.3	47.9	46.5	45.4	43.8	43.2	42.9	42.9	42.9	42.9
+75	35.4	32.9	30.2	29.0	27.7	26.5	25.1	23.6	22.1	20.4	18.6	17.9	17.9
+50	22.7	19.6	16.2	14.5	12.8	10.9	8.8	6.5	3.9	0.9	-2.9	-6.6	-7.1
+25	9.8	6.4	2.4	0.6	-1.3	-3.4	-5.7	-8.5	-11.8	-15.8	-21.6	-28.5	-32.1
0	-0.5	-3.9	-7.9	-9.9	-12.1	-14.3	-16.9	-20.0	-23.7	-28.2	-34.8	-43.8	-57.1
-25	-10.1	-13.5	-17.4	-19.3	-21.4	-23.7	-26.2	-29.2	-32.8	-37.2	-43.4	-51.6	-57.1
-50	-18.8	-22.0	-25.8	-27.6	-29.5	-31.5	-33.9	-36.6	-39.8	-43.3	-48.4	-54.6	-57.1
-75	-22.7	-26.0	-29.8	-31.7	-33.8	-35.8	-38.2	-40.9	-44.1	-47.6	-52.1	-56.3	-57.1
-100	-29.5	-32.8	-36.3	-37.8	-39.5	-41.4	-43.4	-45.5	-47.7	-50.4	-53.6	-56.7	-57.1
-125	-36.8	-39.3	-42.0	-43.2	-44.6	-46.0	-47.5	-49.1	-50.9	-52.9	-55.7	-57.0	-57.1

The estimated cost is: –56.6¢ premium – 0.5¢ comm. = – 57.1¢

TABLE (bottom-left) — "net profit area , in cents"

changes in the soybean future's price in 25¢ increments — weeks to expiration

change	30	25	20	18	16	14	12	10	8	6	4	2	0
+125	101.7	101.7	101.7	101.7	101.7	101.7	101.7	101.7	101.7	101.7	101.7	101.7	101.7
+100	76.7	76.7	76.7	76.7	76.7	76.7	76.7	76.7	76.7	76.7	76.7	76.7	76.7
+75	52.5	52.3	52.1	52.0	51.9	51.8	51.8	51.7	51.7	51.7	51.7	51.7	51.7
+50	31.2	30.5	29.7	29.3	28.8	28.4	28.0	27.6	27.3	27.0	26.8	26.7	26.7
+25	12.7	11.5	10.3	9.6	8.9	8.2	7.4	6.5	5.4	4.3	3.0	2.1	1.7
0	-0.5	-1.9	-3.5	-4.3	-5.2	-6.1	-7.1	-8.4	-9.8	-11.6	-14.3	-17.9	-23.3
-25	-9.1	-10.4	-11.8	-12.6	-13.5	-14.3	-15.2	-16.3	-17.6	-19.3	-21.4	-22.5	-23.3
-50	-14.2	-15.2	-16.3	-16.9	-17.5	-18.1	-18.8	-19.7	-20.7	-21.9	-22.9	-23.3	-23.3
-75	-18.0	-18.8	-19.7	-20.1	-20.6	-21.1	-21.6	-22.0	-22.4	-23.0	-23.0	-23.3	-23.3
-100	-19.6	-20.2	-20.8	-21.1	-21.4	-21.7	-22.0	-22.4	-22.8	-23.2	-23.3	-23.3	-23.3
-125	-21.3	-21.7	-22.1	-22.3	-22.6	-22.9	-23.1	-23.2	-23.3	-23.3	-23.3	-23.3	-23.3

The estimated cost is: – 22.8¢ premium –0.5¢ comm. = – 23.3¢

Wm Grandmill (1985) Ltd.

BUY A CALL or BUY A PUT
AT 50¢ OUT OF THE MONEY

weeks to expiration: 30

TABLE 0 — changes in the soybean future's price in 25¢ increments

price change	30	25	20	18	16	14	12	10	8	6	4	2	0
+125	53.3	48.8	43.5	41.2	38.8	36.4	34.0	31.4	28.6	25.7	22.3	19.8	19.7
+100	40.9	36.6	31.3	28.8	26.2	23.6	20.5	17.1	13.3	8.7	2.8	-3.6	-5.3
+75	29.8	25.4	19.5	16.8	13.7	10.6	7.2	3.3	-0.8	-6.2	-13.9	-23.8	-30.3
+50	18.1	13.8	8.5	6.0	3.2	0.3	-3.1	-7.1	-11.8	-17.7	-26.3	-38.0	-55.3
+25	8.5	4.2	-1.1	-3.6	-6.4	-9.3	-12.6	-16.5	-21.1	-26.9	-35.3	-46.2	-55.3
0	-0.5	-4.7	-9.9	-12.4	-15.1	-17.9	-21.2	-24.9	-29.1	-34.4	-41.4	-50.0	-55.3
-25	-4.9	-8.7	-13.9	-16.4	-19.0	-21.9	-25.2	-28.9	-33.4	-38.9	-45.7	-53.1	-55.3
-50	-12.1	-15.8	-20.9	-23.3	-25.9	-28.7	-31.8	-35.3	-39.1	-43.4	-48.5	-53.6	-55.3
-75	-20.1	-23.9	-28.8	-31.1	-33.5	-35.8	-38.2	-40.8	-43.8	-47.0	-51.0	-54.8	-55.3
-100	-29.3	-32.3	-36.3	-38.4	-40.3	-42.8	-45.4	-47.3	-49.2	-51.3	-53.6	-55.3	-55.3
-125	-36.2	-39.2	-43.1	-44.9	-46.5	-48.2	-50.0	-51.6	-52.8	-53.9	-54.5	-55.3	-55.3

weeks to expiration — profit

The estimated cost is: -54.8¢ premium - 0.5¢ comm. = -55.3¢

TABLE 8 — changes in the soybean future's price in 25¢ increments

price change	30	25	20	18	16	14	12	10	8	6	4	2	0
+125	53.7	51.2	48.5	47.3	46.0	44.8	43.4	41.9	40.4	38.7	36.9	36.2	36.2
+100	41.0	38.9	35.8	32.4	30.7	29.0	27.1	24.8	22.2	19.2	15.4	11.7	11.2
+75	28.1	24.7	20.7	18.9	17.0	14.9	12.6	9.8	6.5	2.5	-3.3	-10.2	-13.8
+50	17.8	14.4	10.4	8.4	6.2	4.0	1.4	-1.7	-5.4	-9.9	-16.5	-25.5	-38.8
+25	8.2	4.8	0.9	-1.0	-3.1	-5.4	-7.9	-10.9	-14.5	-18.9	-25.1	-33.3	-33.8
0	-0.5	-3.7	-7.5	-9.3	-11.2	-13.2	-15.6	-18.3	-21.5	-25.0	-30.1	-36.3	-38.8
-25	-4.4	-7.7	-11.5	-13.4	-15.5	-17.5	-19.9	-22.6	-25.8	-29.3	-33.8	-38.0	-38.8
-50	-11.2	-14.4	-18.0	-19.6	-21.3	-23.2	-25.1	-27.2	-29.4	-32.1	-35.3	-38.4	-38.8
-75	-18.5	-21.0	-23.7	-24.9	-26.3	-27.7	-29.2	-30.8	-32.6	-34.6	-37.0	-38.7	-38.8
-100	-24.8	-26.8	-28.7	-29.5	-30.6	-31.8	-32.9	-34.1	-35.4	-36.9	-38.1	-38.8	-38.8
-125	-29.3	-30.8	-32.5	-33.2	-34.0	-34.8	-35.6	-36.4	-37.4	-38.3	-38.8	-38.8	-38.8

net profit

The estimated cost is: -38.3¢ premium - 0.5¢ comm. = -38.8¢

TABLE 4 — changes in the soybean future's price in 25¢ increments

price change	30	25	20	18	16	14	12	10	8	6	4	2	0
+125	58.8	57.6	56.4	55.9	55.3	54.7	54.1	53.5	52.8	52.2	51.8	51.8	51.8
+100	42.3	40.6	38.5	37.6	36.5	35.5	34.4	33.1	31.6	30.0	27.9	26.9	26.8
+75	27.7	25.6	23.1	21.8	20.6	19.1	17.5	15.6	13.3	10.7	7.1	3.2	1.8
+50	16.4	14.1	11.3	9.9	8.4	6.8	5.0	2.8	0.3	-2.9	-7.5	-13.8	-23.2
+25	7.1	4.9	2.1	0.8	-0.7	-2.3	-4.0	-5.9	-8.4	-11.3	-15.9	-21.1	-23.2
0	-0.5	-2.6	-4.9	-6.1	-7.3	-8.6	-10.0	-11.6	-13.6	-15.9	-19.1	-22.7	-23.2
-25	-4.8	-6.8	-9.2	-10.4	-11.6	-12.8	-14.2	-16.0	-17.9	-20.1	-21.7	-23.2	-23.2
-50	-9.8	-11.5	-13.2	-14.0	-14.9	-15.9	-16.8	-17.9	-19.2	-20.5	-22.1	-23.2	-23.2
-75	-13.9	-15.1	-16.5	-17.2	-17.9	-18.5	-19.3	-20.1	-21.0	-21.8	-22.9	-23.2	-23.2
-100	-17.3	-18.3	-19.3	-20.0	-20.6	-21.2	-21.9	-22.4	-22.7	-22.9	-23.2	-23.2	-23.2
-125	-20.3	-21.1	-21.9	-22.3	-22.6	-22.8	-22.9	-23.0	-23.1	-23.2	-23.2	-23.2	-23.2

weeks to expiration — net profit area

The estimated cost is: -22.7¢ premium - 0.5¢ comm. = -23.2¢

TABLE 2 — changes in the soybean future's price in 25¢ increments

price change	30	25	20	18	16	14	12	10	8	6	4	2	0
+125	66.3	66.1	65.9	65.7	65.6	65.5	65.5	65.4	65.4	65.4	65.4	65.4	65.4
+100	44.9	44.2	43.4	42.5	42.1	41.7	41.3	41.0	40.7	40.5	40.4	40.4	40.4
+75	25.4	24.2	23.1	21.6	20.9	20.1	19.2	18.1	17.0	16.2	15.8	15.4	15.4
+50	13.2	11.7	10.1	9.3	8.4	7.6	6.6	5.3	3.9	2.1	-0.6	-4.2	-9.6
+25	4.6	3.3	1.9	1.1	0.2	-0.6	-1.5	-2.6	-3.9	-5.6	-7.7	-8.8	-9.6
0	-0.5	-1.5	-2.6	-3.2	-3.8	-4.4	-5.1	-6.0	-7.0	-8.2	-9.2	-9.6	-9.6
-25	-4.3	-5.1	-6.0	-6.4	-6.9	-7.4	-7.9	-8.3	-8.7	-9.3	-9.6	-9.6	-9.6
-50	-5.9	-6.5	-7.1	-7.4	-7.7	-8.0	-8.3	-8.7	-9.1	-9.5	-9.6	-9.6	-9.6
-75	-7.6	-8.0	-8.4	-8.6	-8.9	-9.1	-9.2	-9.4	-9.5	-9.6	-9.6	-9.6	-9.6
-100	-8.7	-9.0	-9.2	-9.3	-9.4	-9.5	-9.5	-9.6	-9.6	-9.6	-9.6	-9.6	-9.6
-125	-9.2	-9.4	-9.5	-9.6	-9.6	-9.6	-9.6	-9.6	-9.6	-9.6	-9.6	-9.6	-9.6

weeks to expiration — net profit area

The estimated cost is: -9.1¢ premium - 0.5¢ comm. = -9.6¢

Wm Grandmill (1985) Ltd.

TABLE 8 0

changes in the soybean future's price in 25¢ increments	weeks to expiration												
	30	25	20	18	16	14	12	10	8	6	4	2	0
+125	-80.3	-76.0	-70.4	-67.9	-65.4	-63.0	-60.6	-57.8	-64.7	-52.4	-52.1	-52.1	-52.1
+100	-57.3	-52.7	-46.9	-44.4	-41.8	-39.5	-36.8	-34.1	-31.6	-28.9	-27.5	-27.1	-27.1
+75	-35.7	-31.2	-25.9	-23.6	-21.1	-18.8	-16.4	-13.8	-11.0	-8.1	-4.7	-2.2	-2.1
+50	-23.3	-19.0	-13.7	-11.2	-8.6	-6.0	-2.9	0.5	4.3	8.9	14.8	21.2	22.9
+25	-12.2	-7.8	-1.9	0.8	3.9	7.0	10.4	14.3	18.5	23.8	31.5	41.4	47.9
0	-0.5	3.8	8.9	11.6	14.4	17.3	20.7	24.7	29.4	35.3	43.9	55.6	72.9
-25	9.1	13.4	18.7	21.2	24.0	26.9	30.2	34.1	38.7	44.5	52.9	63.8	72.9
-50	18.1	22.3	27.5	30.0	32.7	35.5	38.8	42.5	46.7	52.0	59.0	67.7	72.9
-75	22.5	26.3	31.5	34.0	36.6	39.5	42.8	46.5	51.0	56.2	63.3	70.7	72.9
-100	29.7	33.4	38.5	40.9	43.5	46.3	49.4	52.9	56.7	61.6	66.1	71.2	72.9
-125	37.7	41.5	46.4	48.7	51.1	53.4	55.8	58.4	61.4	64.6	68.6	72.4	72.9

The estimated credit is: +73.4¢ premium -0.5¢ comm. = +72.9¢

net profit area , in cents

TABLE 6 0

changes in the soybean future's price in 25¢ increments	weeks to expiration												
	30	25	20	18	16	14	12	10	8	6	4	2	0
+125	-80.6	-78.1	-75.3	-73.9	-72.4	-71.1	-69.9	-69.1	-68.9	-68.9	-68.9	-68.9	-68.9
+100	-57.1	-54.4	-51.5	-50.3	-48.9	-47.5	-46.4	-45.6	-44.8	-43.9	-43.9	-43.9	-43.9
+75	-36.4	-33.9	-31.2	-30.0	-28.7	-27.5	-26.1	-24.6	-23.1	-21.4	-19.6	-18.9	-18.9
+50	-23.7	-20.6	-17.2	-15.5	-13.8	-11.9	-9.8	-7.5	-4.9	-1.9	1.9	5.6	6.1
+25	-10.8	-7.4	-3.4	-1.6	0.3	2.4	4.7	7.5	10.8	14.8	20.6	27.5	31.1
0	-0.5	2.9	6.9	8.9	11.1	13.3	15.9	19.0	22.7	27.2	33.8	42.8	56.1
-25	9.1	12.5	16.4	18.3	20.4	22.7	25.2	28.2	31.8	36.2	42.4	50.6	56.1
-50	17.8	21.0	24.8	26.6	28.5	30.5	32.9	35.6	38.8	42.3	47.4	53.6	56.1
-75	21.7	25.0	28.8	30.7	32.8	34.8	37.2	39.9	43.1	46.6	51.1	55.3	56.1
-100	28.5	31.8	35.3	36.8	38.5	40.4	42.4	44.5	46.7	49.4	52.6	55.7	56.1
-125	35.8	38.3	41.0	42.2	43.6	45.0	46.5	48.1	49.9	51.7	54.3	56.0	56.1

The estimated credit is: +56.6¢ premium - 0.5¢ comm. = +56.1¢

net profit area , in cents

TABLE 4 0

changes in the soybean future's price in 25¢ increments	weeks to expiration												
	30	25	20	18	16	14	12	10	8	6	4	2	0
+125	-86.6	-86.1	-85.9	-85.9	-85.9	-85.9	-85.9	-85.9	-85.9	-85.9	-85.9	-85.9	-85.9
+100	-63.1	-62.6	-62.1	-61.8	-61.6	-61.4	-61.2	-61.0	-60.9	-60.9	-60.9	-60.9	-60.9
+75	-42.9	-41.7	-40.5	-40.0	-39.4	-38.8	-38.2	-37.6	-36.9	-36.3	-35.9	-35.9	-35.9
+50	-26.4	-24.7	-22.6	-21.7	-20.6	-19.6	-18.5	-17.2	-15.7	-14.1	-12.0	-11.0	-10.9
+25	-11.8	-9.7	-7.2	-5.9	-4.7	-3.2	-1.6	0.3	2.6	5.2	8.8	12.7	14.1
0	-0.5	1.8	4.6	6.0	7.5	9.1	10.9	13.1	15.6	18.8	23.4	29.7	39.1
-25	8.8	11.0	13.8	15.1	16.6	18.2	19.9	21.8	24.3	27.2	31.4	37.0	39.1
-50	16.4	18.5	20.8	22.0	23.2	24.5	25.9	27.5	29.5	31.8	35.0	38.6	39.1
-75	20.7	22.7	25.1	26.3	27.5	28.7	30.1	31.6	33.4	35.3	37.5	39.1	39.1
-100	25.7	27.4	29.1	29.9	30.8	31.8	32.7	33.8	35.1	36.4	38.0	39.1	39.1
-125	29.8	31.0	32.4	33.1	33.7	34.4	35.2	36.0	36.9	37.8	38.8	39.1	39.1

The estimated credit is: +39.6¢ premium - 0.5¢ comm. = +39.1¢

net profit area , in cents

TABLE 2 0

changes in the soybean future's price in 25¢ increments	weeks to expiration												
	30	25	20	18	16	14	12	10	8	6	4	2	0
+125	-102.7	-102.7	-102.7	-102.7	-102.7	-102.7	-102.7	-102.7	-102.7	-102.7	-102.7	-102.7	-102.7
+100	-77.7	-77.7	-77.7	-77.7	-77.7	-77.7	-77.7	-77.7	-77.7	-77.7	-77.7	-77.7	-77.7
+75	-53.5	-53.3	-53.3	-53.1	-53.0	-52.9	-52.8	-52.7	-52.7	-52.7	-52.7	-52.7	-52.7
+50	-32.2	-31.5	-30.7	-30.3	-29.8	-29.4	-29.0	-28.6	-28.3	-28.0	-27.8	-27.7	-27.7
+25	-13.7	-12.5	-11.3	-10.6	-9.9	-9.2	-8.4	-7.5	-6.4	-5.3	-4.0	-3.1	-2.7
0	-0.5	0.9	2.5	3.3	4.2	5.1	6.1	7.4	8.8	10.6	13.3	16.9	22.3
-25	8.1	9.4	10.8	11.6	12.5	13.3	14.2	15.3	16.6	18.3	20.4	21.5	22.3
-50	13.2	14.2	15.3	15.9	16.5	17.1	17.8	18.7	19.7	20.9	21.9	22.3	22.3
-75	17.0	17.8	18.7	19.1	19.6	20.1	20.6	21.0	21.5	22.0	22.3	22.3	22.3
-100	18.6	19.2	19.8	20.1	20.4	20.7	21.0	21.4	21.8	22.2	22.3	22.3	22.3
-125	20.3	20.7	21.1	21.3	21.6	21.8	21.9	22.1	22.2	22.3	22.3	22.3	22.3

The estimated credit is: +22.8¢ premium - 0.5¢ comm. = +22.3¢

net profit area , in cents

Wm Grandmill (1985) Ltd.

SELL A CALL or SELL A PUT

AT 50¢ OUT OF THE MONEY

weeks to expiration: 30

TABLE 8

changes in the soybean future's price in 25¢ increments — weeks to expiration — net profit area, in cents

The estimated credit is: +54.8¢ premium −0.5¢ comm. = +54.3¢

price change	30	25	20	18	16	14	12	10	8	6	4	2	0
+125	-54.3	-49.8	-44.5	-42.2	-39.8	-37.4	-35.0	-32.4	-29.6	-26.7	-23.3	-20.8	-20.7
+100	-41.9	-37.6	-32.3	-29.8	-27.2	-24.6	-21.5	-18.1	-14.3	-9.7	-3.8	2.6	4.3
+75	-30.8	-26.4	-20.5	-17.8	-14.7	-11.6	-8.2	-4.3	-0.2	5.2	12.9	22.8	29.3
+50	-19.1	-14.8	-7.0	-4.2	-1.3	2.1	6.1	10.8	16.7	25.3	37.0	45.2	54.3
+25	-9.5	-5.2	0.1	2.6	5.4	8.3	11.6	15.5	20.1	25.9	34.3	49.0	54.3
0	-0.5	3.7	8.9	11.4	14.1	16.9	20.2	23.9	28.1	33.4	40.4	49.0	54.3
-25	3.9	7.7	12.9	15.4	18.0	20.9	24.2	27.9	32.4	37.9	44.7	52.1	54.3
-50	11.1	14.8	19.9	22.3	24.9	27.7	30.8	34.3	38.1	42.4	47.5	52.6	54.3
-75	19.1	22.9	27.8	30.1	32.5	34.8	37.2	39.8	42.8	47.5	52.6	53.8	54.3
-100	28.3	31.3	35.3	37.4	39.3	41.8	44.4	46.3	48.2	50.3	52.6	54.3	54.3
-125	35.2	39.1	42.1	43.9	45.5	47.2	49.0	50.6	51.8	52.9	53.5	54.3	54.3

TABLE 0

changes in the soybean future's price in 25¢ increments — weeks to expiration — net profit area, in cents

The estimated credit is: +38.3¢ premium −0.5¢ comm. = +37.8¢

price change	30	25	20	18	16	14	12	10	8	6	4	2	0
+125	-54.7	-52.2	-49.5	-48.3	-47.0	-45.8	-44.4	-42.9	-41.4	-39.7	-37.7	-37.2	-37.2
+100	-42.0	-39.9	-36.9	-33.4	-30.0	-28.1	-25.8	-23.2	-20.2	-16.4	-12.7	-12.7	-12.2
+75	-29.1	-25.7	-21.7	-19.9	-18.0	-15.9	-13.6	-10.8	-7.5	-3.5	2.3	9.2	12.8
+50	-18.8	-15.4	-11.4	-9.4	-7.2	-5.0	-2.4	0.7	4.4	8.9	15.5	24.5	37.8
+25	-9.2	-5.8	-1.9	0.0	2.1	4.4	8.9	9.9	13.5	17.9	24.1	35.3	37.8
0	-0.5	2.7	6.5	8.3	10.2	12.2	14.6	17.3	20.5	24.0	29.1	37.1	37.8
-25	3.4	6.7	10.5	12.4	14.5	16.5	18.9	21.6	24.8	28.3	32.8	37.8	37.8
-50	10.2	13.4	17.0	18.6	20.3	22.2	24.1	26.2	28.4	31.1	34.3	37.8	37.8
-75	17.5	20.0	22.7	23.9	25.3	26.7	28.2	29.8	31.6	33.6	36.0	37.8	37.8
-100	23.8	25.8	27.7	28.5	29.6	30.8	31.9	33.1	34.4	35.9	37.1	37.8	37.8
-125	28.3	29.8	31.5	32.2	33.0	33.8	34.6	35.4	36.4	37.3	37.8	37.8	37.8

TABLE 4

changes in the soybean future's price in 25¢ increments — weeks to expiration — net profit area, in cents

The estimated credit is: +22.7¢ premium −0.5¢ comm. = +22.2¢

price change	30	25	20	18	16	14	12	10	8	6	4	2	0
+125	-59.8	-58.6	-57.4	-56.9	-56.3	-55.7	-55.1	-54.5	-53.8	-53.2	-52.8	-52.8	-52.8
+100	-43.3	-41.6	-39.5	-38.6	-37.5	-36.5	-35.4	-34.1	-32.6	-31.0	-28.9	-27.9	-27.8
+75	-28.7	-26.6	-24.1	-22.8	-21.6	-20.1	-18.5	-16.6	-14.3	-11.7	-8.1	-4.2	-2.8
+50	-17.4	-15.1	-12.3	-10.9	-9.4	-7.8	-6.0	-3.8	-1.3	1.9	6.5	12.8	22.2
+25	-8.1	-5.9	-3.1	-1.8	-0.3	1.3	3.0	4.9	7.4	10.3	14.5	20.1	22.2
0	-0.5	1.6	3.9	5.1	6.3	7.6	9.0	10.6	12.6	14.9	18.1	21.6	22.2
-25	3.8	5.8	8.2	9.4	10.6	11.8	13.2	15.0	16.9	19.1	20.7	22.2	22.2
-50	8.8	10.5	12.2	13.0	13.9	14.9	15.8	16.9	18.2	19.5	21.1	22.2	22.2
-75	12.9	14.1	15.5	16.2	16.9	17.5	18.3	19.1	20.0	20.8	21.9	22.2	22.2
-100	16.3	17.3	18.3	19.0	19.6	20.2	20.9	21.4	21.7	21.9	22.2	22.2	22.2
-125	19.3	20.1	20.9	21.3	21.6	21.8	21.9	22.0	22.1	22.2	22.2	22.2	22.2

TABLE 2

changes in the soybean future's price in 25¢ increments — weeks to expiration — net profit area, in cents

The estimated credit is: +9.1¢ premium −0.5¢ comm. = +8.6¢

price change	30	25	20	18	16	14	12	10	8	6	4	2	0
+125	-67.3	-67.1	-66.9	-66.7	-66.6	-66.5	-66.4	-66.4	-66.4	-66.4	-66.4	-66.4	-66.4
+100	-45.9	-45.2	-44.4	-44.0	-43.5	-43.1	-42.7	-42.3	-42.0	-41.7	-41.5	-41.4	-41.4
+75	-26.4	-25.2	-24.0	-23.3	-22.6	-21.9	-21.1	-20.2	-19.1	-18.0	-17.2	-16.8	-16.4
+50	-14.2	-12.7	-11.1	-10.3	-9.4	-8.6	-7.6	-6.3	-4.9	-3.1	-0.4	3.2	8.6
+25	-5.6	-4.3	-2.9	-2.1	-1.2	-0.4	0.5	1.6	2.9	4.6	6.7	8.6	8.6
0	-0.5	0.5	1.6	2.2	2.8	3.4	4.1	5.0	6.0	7.2	7.8	8.6	8.6
-25	3.3	4.1	5.0	5.4	5.9	6.4	6.9	7.3	7.7	8.3	8.6	8.6	8.6
-50	4.9	5.5	6.1	6.4	6.7	7.0	7.3	7.7	8.1	8.5	8.6	8.6	8.6
-75	6.6	7.0	7.4	7.6	7.9	8.1	8.2	8.4	8.5	8.6	8.6	8.6	8.6
-100	7.7	8.0	8.2	8.3	8.4	8.5	8.6	8.6	8.6	8.6	8.6	8.6	8.6
-125	8.2	8.4	8.5	8.6	8.6	8.6	8.6	8.6	8.6	8.6	8.6	8.6	8.6

Wm Grandmill (1985) Ltd.

BULL or BEAR SPREAD – #1

BUY A CALL AT THE MONEY
and SELL A CALL AT 25¢ OUT OF THE MONEY

OR

BUY A PUT AT THE MONEY
and SELL A PUT AT 25¢ OUT OF THE MONEY

weeks to
30
expiration

TABLE (− 56.6¢ premium)

changes in the soybean future's price in 25¢ increments

	|						weeks to expiration						
	30	25	20	18	16	14	12	10	8	6	4	2	0
+125	12.9	12.9	12.9	12.9	13.0	13.1	13.2	13.6	14.1	14.4	14.4	14.4	14.4
+100	7.8	8.1	8.4	8.7	9.1	9.4	9.9	10.4	11.1	12.2	14.0	14.4	14.4
+75	4.7	5.1	5.6	6.0	6.3	6.6	6.9	7.6	8.9	10.9	13.9	14.4	14.4
+50	2.0	2.6	3.2	3.3	3.7	4.0	4.4	5.1	6.1	8.1	11.3	14.4	14.4
+25	0.1	0.1	0.1	0.1	0.1	0.3	0.6	0.9	1.3	1.8	2.6	4.7	14.4
0	-1.0	-1.1	-1.1	-1.2	-1.2	-1.2	-1.3	-1.4	-1.5	-1.6	-2.0	-2.8	-10.6
-25	-1.9	-2.1	-2.2	-2.3	-2.5	-2.7	-2.9	-3.2	-3.6	-4.5	-5.6	-7.6	-10.6
-50	-2.9	-3.1	-3.2	-3.4	-3.6	-3.9	-4.2	-4.6	-5.2	-5.9	-6.7	-8.9	-10.6
-75	-3.8	-3.9	-4.1	-4.4	-4.7	-5.0	-5.4	-6.0	-7.0	-7.8	-8.9	-10.2	-10.6
-100	-4.1	-4.4	-4.9	-5.3	-5.7	-6.1	-6.5	-7.0	-7.4	-8.1	-9.0	-10.3	-10.6
-125	-4.3	-4.8	-5.6	-5.9	-6.2	-6.5	-6.9	-7.3	-7.8	-8.3	-9.3	-10.5	-10.6

net profit area , in cents

The estimated cost is: − 56.6¢ premium + 47.0¢ premium − 1.0¢ comm. = − 10.6¢

TABLE (− 73.4¢ premium)

changes in the soybean future's price in 25¢ increments

							weeks to expiration						
	30	25	20	18	16	14	12	10	8	6	4	2	0
+125	12.6	12.7	12.8	12.9	13.0	13.1	13.2	13.4	13.6	13.8	14.0	14.4	14.4
+100	6.7	7.0	7.4	7.8	8.2	8.6	9.1	9.6	10.3	10.8	12.8	14.0	14.4
+75	4.0	4.2	4.4	4.7	5.0	5.3	5.7	6.2	6.8	7.8	9.4	12.8	14.4
+50	1.9	1.9	2.0	2.1	2.2	2.4	2.7	3.1	3.6	4.4	6.1	9.6	14.4
+25	0.4	0.4	0.5	0.5	0.6	0.6	0.7	0.8	0.9	1.1	1.8	3.6	14.4
0	-1.0	-1.0	-1.0	-1.0	-1.0	-1.0	-1.1	-1.2	-1.3	-1.4	-1.6	-2.6	-10.6
-25	-1.6	-1.7	-1.8	-1.8	-1.9	-2.0	-2.0	-2.2	-2.6	-3.3	-4.5	-6.7	-10.6
-50	-1.9	-2.0	-2.1	-2.1	-2.2	-2.4	-2.7	-3.1	-3.7	-4.6	-6.0	-8.1	-10.6
-75	-2.2	-2.3	-2.4	-2.5	-2.6	-2.8	-3.0	-3.4	-4.2	-5.0	-7.0	-8.6	-10.6
-100	-2.4	-2.5	-2.6	-2.7	-3.0	-3.2	-3.5	-4.2	-5.0	-5.9	-7.0	-9.1	-10.6
-125	-2.6	-2.7	-2.8	-3.0	-3.2	-3.4	-4.6	-5.0	-5.9	-6.6	-8.0	-9.4	-10.6

net profit area , in cents

The estimated cost is: − 73.4¢ premium + 63.8¢ premium − 1.0¢ comm. = − 10.6¢

TABLE (− 22.8¢ premium)

changes in the soybean future's price in 25¢ increments

							weeks to expiration						
	30	25	20	18	16	14	12	10	8	6	4	2	0
+125	15.4	15.4	15.4	15.4	15.4	15.4	15.4	15.4	15.4	15.4	15.4	15.4	15.4
+100	14.6	14.8	15.0	15.1	15.2	15.3	15.4	15.4	15.4	15.4	15.4	15.4	15.4
+75	11.7	12.2	12.8	13.1	13.5	13.8	14.2	14.5	14.7	15.1	15.3	15.4	15.4
+50	8.9	9.4	9.8	10.0	10.3	10.6	11.0	11.5	12.3	13.1	14.2	15.0	15.4
+25	3.6	3.8	4.2	4.4	4.5	4.7	4.9	5.3	5.6	6.3	7.7	10.4	15.4
0	-1.0	-1.1	-1.2	-1.3	-1.3	-1.4	-1.5	-1.7	-1.8	-1.9	-2.5	-3.0	-9.6
-25	-4.5	-4.7	-5.1	-5.3	-5.6	-5.8	-6.0	-6.2	-6.6	-7.0	-8.1	-9.6	-9.6
-50	-5.8	-6.0	-6.2	-6.4	-6.5	-6.6	-6.8	-7.3	-7.8	-8.5	-9.2	-9.6	-9.6
-75	-6.9	-7.1	-7.2	-7.3	-7.4	-7.6	-7.8	-8.1	-8.7	-9.4	-9.6	-9.6	-9.6
-100	-7.9	-8.0	-8.1	-8.2	-8.3	-8.5	-8.7	-8.9	-9.2	-9.5	-9.6	-9.6	-9.6
-125	-8.6	-8.7	-8.8	-8.9	-9.1	-9.2	-9.3	-9.4	-9.5	-9.6	-9.6	-9.6	-9.6

net profit area , in cents

The estimated cost is: − 22.8¢ premium + 14.2¢ premium − 1.0¢ comm. = − 9.6¢

TABLE (− 39.6¢ premium)

changes in the soybean future's price in 25¢ increments

							weeks to expiration						
	30	25	20	18	16	14	12	10	8	6	4	2	0
+125	13.2	13.3	13.5	13.8	14.0	14.2	14.4	14.6	14.7	14.7	14.7	14.7	14.7
+100	9.9	10.6	11.3	11.6	11.9	12.3	12.7	13.1	13.7	14.3	14.7	14.7	14.7
+75	6.2	6.7	7.6	8.0	8.5	8.9	9.4	10.1	10.9	11.9	13.4	14.7	14.7
+50	4.3	4.7	5.1	5.4	5.6	6.1	6.6	7.2	8.0	9.0	10.5	13.4	14.7
+25	1.0	1.2	1.5	1.7	1.9	2.0	2.2	2.5	2.7	3.3	4.3	6.7	14.7
0	-1.0	-1.1	-1.1	-1.2	-1.2	-1.2	-1.3	-1.5	-1.7	-1.9	-2.3	-3.1	-10.3
-25	-2.7	-2.9	-3.2	-3.4	-3.7	-4.0	-4.3	-4.6	-5.1	-5.7	-6.7	-8.7	-10.3
-50	-4.9	-5.1	-5.4	-5.7	-5.9	-6.0	-6.1	-6.2	-6.4	-6.8	-7.8	-9.8	-10.3
-75	-5.3	-5.7	-6.3	-6.7	-7.0	-7.3	-7.7	-8.0	-8.1	-8.3	-8.7	-9.1	-10.3
-100	-6.0	-6.4	-6.9	-7.1	-7.4	-7.7	-7.9	-8.1	-8.3	-8.7	-9.0	-9.5	-10.3
-125	-6.8	-7.1	-7.3	-7.5	-7.6	-7.8	-8.0	-8.3	-8.7	-9.2	-10.0	-10.3	-10.3

net profit area , in cents

The estimated cost is: − 39.6¢ premium + 30.3¢ premium − 1.0¢ comm. = − 10.3¢

BULL or BEAR SPREAD – #2

BUY A CALL AT THE MONEY
and SELL 2 CALLS AT 50¢ OUT OF THE MONEY

OR

BUY A PUT AT THE MONEY
and SELL 2 PUTS AT 50¢ OUT OF THE MONEY

30 weeks to expiration

TABLE (upper right) — net profit area, in cents

changes in the soybean future's price in 25¢ increments

price change	30	25	20	18	16	14	12	10	8	6	4	2	0
+125	-29.3	-24.6	-19.6	-17.4	-15.1	-12.8	-10.4	-8.0	-5.5	-2.0	4.5	9.5	9.7
+100	-27.5	-23.5	-18.7	-16.2	-13.6	-10.7	-7.2	-3.1	2.0	8.5	18.9	31.3	34.7
+75	-26.9	-22.6	-16.1	-13.0	-9.3	-5.4	-1.0	4.2	10.7	17.5	29.5	46.8	59.7
+50	-15.9	-11.6	-6.3	-3.8	-1.8	2.4	6.1	10.7	16.3	23.5	33.8	51.8	84.7
+25	-7.8	-3.6	1.1	3.4	5.9	8.6	11.8	15.7	20.7	27.0	36.1	48.0	59.7
0	-1.5	2.6	7.7	10.2	12.8	15.5	18.7	22.1	25.8	30.5	35.9	41.6	34.7
-25	-2.3	1.0	6.1	8.6	11.0	13.9	17.2	20.7	25.1	29.7	35.5	39.4	34.7
-50	3.1	6.3	11.3	13.6	16.1	18.9	21.8	25.1	28.5	31.8	35.0	36.5	34.7
-75	14.7	18.5	23.1	25.2	27.4	29.1	30.6	32.1	33.6	34.8	35.7	35.9	34.7
-100	22.9	25.7	29.3	31.0	32.5	34.0	35.2	36.3	36.8	36.9	36.4	35.5	34.7
-125	31.9	34.1	37.2	38.1	38.9	40.0	41.2	42.2	41.2	40.0	37.4	35.2	34.7

The estimated credit is: −73.4¢ premium + 54.8¢ premium + 54.8¢ premium − 1.5¢ comm. = +34.7¢

TABLE (upper left) — net profit area, in cents

changes in the soybean future's price in 25¢ increments

price change	30	25	20	18	16	14	12	10	8	6	4	2	0
+125	-29.3	-27.3	-24.7	-23.7	-22.7	-21.5	-20.0	-17.7	-14.9	-11.5	-7.9	-6.5	-6.5
+100	-27.9	-24.4	-20.5	-18.3	-16.3	-14.0	-10.8	-7.0	-2.6	2.8	10.1	17.5	18.5
+75	-22.8	-18.5	-13.2	-10.8	-8.2	-5.3	-2.1	2.0	7.1	13.4	23.2	36.3	43.5
+50	-14.9	-11.2	-6.6	-4.3	-1.6	0.9	4.0	7.9	12.7	18.7	26.1	32.4	68.5
+25	-8.6	-5.2	-1.4	0.6	2.9	5.4	8.1	11.3	15.2	20.0	26.6	36.1	43.5
0	-1.5	1.5	5.4	6.7	8.3	10.1	12.3	14.6	17.3	19.8	23.4	26.8	18.5
-25	-3.3	-0.1	3.6	5.5	7.6	9.5	11.6	14.0	16.8	19.4	22.2	22.4	18.5
-50	1.6	4.8	8.2	9.6	11.1	12.8	14.0	15.8	17.2	18.9	20.2	20.2	18.5
-75	12.3	14.0	15.6	16.1	16.8	17.6	18.2	18.7	19.1	19.6	19.9	20.1	18.5
-100	15.3	16.8	18.1	18.5	19.0	19.4	19.8	20.1	20.3	20.6	20.1	19.4	18.5
-125	19.8	20.4	21.0	21.2	21.4	21.6	21.7	21.8	21.9	21.7	20.3	18.6	18.5

The estimated credit is: −56.6¢ premium +38.3¢ +38.3¢ premium − 1.5¢ comm. = +18.5¢

TABLE (lower right) — net profit area, in cents

changes in the soybean future's price in 25¢ increments

price change	30	25	20	18	16	14	12	10	8	6	4	2	0
+125	-34.0	-32.1	-29.9	-28.9	-27.7	-26.5	-25.3	-24.1	-22.7	-21.5	-20.7	-20.7	-20.7
+100	-24.5	-21.6	-17.9	-16.2	-14.4	-12.6	-10.6	-8.2	-6.3	-2.1	2.1	4.1	4.3
+75	-15.5	-12.5	-8.7	-6.7	-4.8	-2.4	0.2	3.4	7.3	11.9	18.7	26.5	29.3
+50	-9.4	-6.5	-3.0	-1.1	0.2	3.0	5.5	8.6	12.1	16.9	24.0	35.6	54.3
+25	-5.4	-3.1	-0.4	0.8	3.0	4.8	6.6	8.5	11.2	14.4	19.2	26.5	29.3
0	-1.5	0.4	2.2	3.2	4.1	5.1	6.1	7.1	8.6	10.0	11.8	12.7	4.3
-25	-2.2	-0.4	1.6	2.7	3.6	4.4	5.5	6.6	7.7	8.6	8.8	6.4	4.3
-50	0.2	1.5	2.6	3.0	3.6	4.2	4.7	5.3	5.9	6.1	6.2	4.8	4.3
-75	4.1	4.5	4.9	5.1	5.2	5.3	5.5	5.6	5.5	5.3	5.2	4.6	4.3
-100	6.6	6.9	7.2	7.3	7.4	6.9	6.4	6.0	5.5	5.3	4.7	4.3	4.3
-125	7.8	8.1	8.4	8.5	8.4	8.2	7.6	7.0	6.3	5.7	4.6	4.3	4.3

The estimated credit is: − 39.6¢ premium +22.7¢ +22.7¢ premiums −1.5¢ comm. = + 4.3¢

TABLE (lower left) — net profit area, in cents

changes in the soybean future's price in 25¢ increments

price change	30	25	20	18	16	14	12	10	8	6	4	2	0
+125	-32.7	-32.3	-31.9	-31.7	-31.5	-31.3	-31.2	-31.1	-31.1	-31.1	-31.1	-31.1	-31.1
+100	-15.1	-13.7	-12.1	-11.3	-10.3	-9.5	-8.7	-7.9	-7.3	-6.7	-6.3	-6.3	-6.1
+75	-2.3	-0.1	2.1	3.2	4.5	6.0	7.6	9.3	11.5	13.7	16.3	18.1	18.9
+50	2.8	4.9	7.3	8.3	9.8	11.2	12.8	15.0	17.5	20.8	26.0	33.1	43.9
+25	1.5	2.9	4.5	5.5	6.5	7.4	8.4	9.7	11.3	13.3	16.1	17.6	18.9
0	-1.5	-0.9	0.1	0.4	0.7	1.1	1.4	2.0	2.8	2.5	-0.7	-6.1	-6.1
-25	-2.5	-2.2	-1.9	-1.8	-1.6	-1.5	-1.4	-1.7	-2.2	-2.9	-4.2	-5.3	-6.1
-50	-4.8	-4.4	-4.8	-4.1	-4.1	-4.1	-4.2	-4.3	-4.5	-4.6	-5.7	-6.1	-6.1
-75	-4.8	-4.8	-4.9	-4.9	-5.0	-5.0	-5.1	-5.2	-5.4	-5.8	-6.1	-6.1	-6.1
-100	-4.9	-5.0	-5.3	-5.1	-5.2	-5.3	-5.4	-5.5	-5.7	-5.9	-6.1	-6.1	-6.1
-125	-5.1	-5.2	-5.3	-5.4	-5.5	-5.6	-5.7	-5.9	-6.0	-6.1	-6.1	-6.1	-6.1

The estimated cost is: −22.8¢ premium +9.1¢ + 9.1¢ premium − 1.5¢ comm. = −6.1¢

SELL A STRADDLE

SELL A CALL AT THE MONEY and SELL A PUT AT THE MONEY

weeks to expiration: 30

TABLE 0 (30 weeks to expiration)

changes in the soybean future's price in 25¢ increments	30	25	20	18	16	14	12	10	8	6	4	2	0
+125	-42.6	-34.5	-24.0	-19.2	-14.3	-9.6	-4.8	0.6	6.7	12.2	16.5	20.3	20.8
+100	-27.6	-19.3	-8.4	-3.5	1.7	6.8	12.6	18.8	25.1	32.1	38.6	44.1	45.8
+75	-13.2	-4.9	5.6	10.4	15.5	20.7	26.4	32.7	40.0	48.1	58.6	68.5	70.8
+50	-5.2	3.3	13.8	18.8	24.1	29.5	35.9	43.0	51.0	60.9	73.8	88.9	95.8
+25	-3.1	5.6	16.8	22.0	27.9	33.9	40.6	48.4	57.2	68.3	84.4	105.2	120.8
0	-1.0	7.6	18.2	23.2	28.8	34.6	41.4	49.4	58.8	70.6	87.8	111.2	145.8
-25	-3.1	5.6	16.8	22.0	27.9	33.9	40.6	48.4	57.2	68.3	84.4	105.2	120.8
-50	-5.2	3.3	13.8	18.8	24.1	29.5	35.9	43.0	51.0	60.9	73.8	88.9	95.8
-75	-13.2	-4.9	5.6	10.4	15.5	20.7	26.4	32.7	40.0	48.1	58.6	68.5	70.8
-100	-27.6	-19.3	-8.4	-3.5	1.7	6.8	12.6	18.8	25.1	32.1	38.6	44.1	45.8
-125	-42.6	-34.5	-24.0	-19.2	-14.3	-9.6	-4.8	0.6	6.7	12.2	16.5	20.3	20.8

weeks to expiration / net profit area, in cents

The estimated credit is: +73.4¢ premium +73.4¢ premium - 1.0¢ comm. = +145.8¢

TABLE 0 (30 weeks to expiration)

changes in the soybean future's price in 25¢ increments	30	25	20	18	16	14	12	10	8	6	4	2	0
+125	-44.8	-39.8	-34.3	-31.7	-28.8	-26.1	-23.3	-21.0	-19.0	-17.0	-14.6	-12.9	-12.8
+100	-28.6	-22.7	-16.2	-13.4	-10.3	-7.0	-4.0	-1.1	1.9	5.2	8.7	11.8	12.2
+75	-14.7	-8.9	-2.4	0.7	4.1	7.3	11.1	15.3	20.0	25.2	31.5	36.4	37.2
+50	-5.9	0.4	7.6	11.1	14.7	18.6	23.1	28.1	33.9	40.7	49.3	59.2	62.2
+25	-1.7	5.1	13.0	16.7	20.7	25.1	29.9	35.7	42.6	51.0	63.0	78.1	87.2
0	-1.0	5.8	13.8	17.8	22.2	26.6	31.8	38.0	45.4	54.4	67.6	85.6	112.2
-25	-1.7	5.1	13.0	16.7	20.7	25.1	29.9	35.7	42.6	51.0	63.0	78.1	87.2
-50	-5.9	0.4	7.6	11.1	14.7	18.6	23.1	28.1	33.9	40.7	49.3	59.2	62.2
-75	-14.7	-8.9	-2.4	0.7	4.1	7.3	11.1	15.3	20.0	25.2	31.5	36.4	37.2
-100	-28.6	-22.7	-16.2	-13.4	-10.3	-7.0	-4.0	-1.1	1.9	5.2	8.7	11.8	12.2
-125	-44.8	-39.8	-34.3	-31.7	-28.8	-26.1	-23.3	-21.0	-19.0	-17.0	-14.6	-12.9	-12.8

weeks to expiration / net profit area, in cents

The estimated credit is: +56.6¢ premium +56.6¢ premium - 1.0¢ comm. = +112.2¢

TABLE 0 (4 weeks to expiration)

changes in the soybean future's price in 25¢ increments	30	25	20	18	16	14	12	10	8	6	4	2	0
+125	-56.8	-55.1	-53.5	-52.8	-52.1	-51.5	-50.7	-49.9	-49.0	-48.1	-47.1	-46.8	-46.8
+100	-37.4	-35.2	-33.0	-31.9	-30.8	-29.6	-28.5	-27.2	-25.8	-24.4	-22.9	-21.8	-21.8
+75	-22.2	-19.0	-15.2	-13.7	-11.9	-10.1	-8.1	-5.9	-3.5	-1.0	1.6	3.2	3.2
+50	-9.6	-6.2	-1.8	0.3	2.6	4.9	7.4	10.3	13.8	17.7	23.0	27.6	28.2
+25	-3.0	1.3	6.6	9.2	11.9	15.0	18.3	22.1	26.9	32.4	40.2	49.7	53.2
0	-1.0	3.6	9.2	12.0	15.0	18.2	21.8	26.2	31.2	37.6	46.8	59.4	78.2
-25	-3.0	1.3	6.6	9.2	11.9	15.0	18.3	22.1	26.9	32.4	40.2	49.7	53.2
-50	-9.6	-6.2	-1.8	0.3	2.6	4.9	7.4	10.3	13.8	17.7	23.0	27.6	28.2
-75	-22.2	-19.0	-15.2	-13.7	-11.9	-10.1	-8.1	-5.9	-3.5	-1.0	1.6	3.2	3.2
-100	-37.4	-35.2	-33.0	-31.9	-30.8	-29.6	-28.5	-27.2	-25.8	-24.4	-22.9	-21.8	-21.8
-125	-56.8	-55.1	-53.5	-52.8	-52.1	-51.5	-50.7	-49.9	-49.0	-48.1	-47.1	-46.8	-46.8

weeks to expiration / net profit area, in cents

The estimated credit is: +39.6¢ premium +39.6¢ premium - 1.0¢ comm. = +78.2¢

TABLE 0 (2 weeks to expiration)

changes in the soybean future's price in 25¢ increments	30	25	20	18	16	14	12	10	8	6	4	2	0
+125	-82.4	-82.0	-81.7	-81.4	-81.1	-80.9	-80.8	-80.6	-80.5	-80.4	-80.4	-80.4	-80.4
+100	-59.0	-58.3	-57.9	-57.6	-57.3	-57.0	-56.7	-56.3	-55.9	-55.5	-55.4	-55.4	-55.4
+75	-36.3	-35.5	-34.4	-33.8	-33.2	-32.7	-32.2	-31.7	-31.2	-30.7	-30.4	-30.4	-30.4
+50	-19.0	-17.3	-15.4	-14.4	-13.3	-12.3	-11.2	-9.9	-8.6	-7.1	-5.9	-5.4	-5.4
+25	-5.6	-3.1	-0.5	0.9	2.6	4.1	5.8	7.8	10.2	13.0	16.4	19.1	19.6
0	-1.0	1.8	5.0	6.6	8.4	10.2	12.2	14.8	17.6	21.2	26.6	33.8	44.6
-25	-5.6	-3.1	-0.5	0.9	2.6	4.1	5.8	7.8	10.2	13.0	16.4	19.1	19.6
-50	-19.0	-17.3	-15.4	-14.4	-13.3	-12.3	-11.2	-9.9	-8.6	-7.1	-5.9	-5.4	-5.4
-75	-36.3	-35.5	-34.4	-33.8	-33.2	-32.7	-32.2	-31.7	-31.2	-30.7	-30.4	-30.4	-30.4
-100	-59.0	-58.3	-57.9	-57.6	-57.3	-57.0	-56.7	-56.3	-55.9	-55.5	-55.4	-55.4	-55.4
-125	-82.4	-82.0	-81.7	-81.4	-81.1	-80.9	-80.8	-80.6	-80.5	-80.4	-80.4	-80.4	-80.4

weeks to expiration / net profit area

The estimated credit is: +22.8¢ premium +22.8¢ premium - 1.0¢ comm. = +44.6¢

Wm Grandmill (1985) Ltd.

SELL A STRANGLE – #1

SELL A CALL AT 50¢ OUT OF THE MONEY and SELL A PUT AT 50¢ OUT OF THE MONEY

weeks to **30** expiration

TABLE 0

changes in the soybean future's price in 25¢ increments

	30	25	20	18	16	14	12	10	8	6	4	2	0
+125	-19.0	-11.5	-2.2	1.7	5.8	9.8	14.0	18.2	22.2	26.1	30.2	33.5	33.6
+100	-13.6	-6.6	2.7	7.5	12.1	17.2	22.5	28.2	34.0	40.6	48.8	56.9	58.6
+75	-11.7	-3.5	7.3	12.3	17.8	23.2	29.0	35.8	42.7	51.2	62.9	76.6	83.6
+50	-8.0	0.0	10.4	15.3	20.7	26.4	32.9	40.4	48.9	59.1	72.8	89.7	108.6
+25	-5.6	2.5	12.7	18.0	23.4	29.2	35.8	43.4	52.5	63.5	79.0	97.3	108.6
0	-1.0	7.4	17.8	22.8	28.2	33.8	40.4	48.1	56.5	66.8	80.8	98.2	108.6
-25	-5.6	2.5	12.7	18.0	23.4	29.2	35.8	43.4	52.5	63.5	79.0	97.3	108.6
-50	-8.0	0.0	10.4	15.3	20.7	26.4	32.9	40.4	48.9	59.1	72.8	89.7	108.6
-75	-11.7	-3.5	7.3	12.3	17.8	23.2	29.0	35.8	42.7	51.2	62.9	76.6	83.6
-100	-13.6	-6.6	2.7	7.5	12.1	17.2	22.5	28.2	34.0	40.6	48.8	56.9	58.6
-125	-19.0	-11.5	-2.2	1.7	5.8	9.8	14.0	18.2	22.2	26.1	30.2	33.5	33.6

weeks to expiration

The estimated credit is: +54.8¢ premium +54.8¢ premium -1.0¢ comm. = +108.6¢

net profit area, in cents

TABLE 0

changes in the soybean future's price in 25¢ increments

	30	25	20	18	16	14	12	10	8	6	4	2	0
+125	-26.4	-22.6	-18.2	-16.3	-14.2	-12.0	-9.8	-7.5	-5.0	-2.4	-0.1	0.6	
+100	-18.2	-13.1	-7.8	-5.3	-2.5	0.6	3.8	7.3	11.2	15.7	20.7	25.1	25.6
+75	-11.6	-5.7	1.0	4.0	7.3	10.8	14.6	19.0	24.1	30.1	38.3	46.9	50.6
+50	-8.6	-2.0	5.6	9.2	13.1	17.2	21.7	26.9	32.8	40.0	49.8	61.9	75.6
+25	-5.8	0.9	8.6	12.4	16.6	20.9	25.8	31.5	38.3	46.2	56.9	69.3	75.6
0	-1.0	5.4	13.0	16.6	20.4	24.4	29.2	34.6	41.0	48.0	58.2	60.6	75.6
-25	-5.8	0.9	8.6	12.4	16.6	20.9	25.8	31.5	38.3	46.2	56.9	69.3	75.6
-50	-8.6	-2.0	5.6	9.2	13.1	17.2	21.7	26.9	32.8	40.0	49.8	61.9	75.6
-75	-11.6	-5.7	1.0	4.0	7.3	10.8	14.6	19.0	24.1	30.1	38.3	46.9	50.6
-100	-18.2	-13.1	-7.8	-5.3	-2.5	0.6	3.8	7.3	11.2	15.7	20.7	25.1	25.6
-125	-26.4	-22.6	-18.2	-16.3	-14.2	-12.0	-9.8	-7.5	-5.0	-2.4	-0.1	0.6	

weeks to expiration

The estimated credit is: +38.3¢ premium +38.3¢ premium -1.0¢ comm. = +75.6¢

net profit area, in cents

TABLE 4

changes in the soybean future's price in 25¢ increments

	30	25	20	18	16	14	12	10	8	6	4	2	0
+125	-40.5	-38.5	-36.5	-35.6	-34.7	-33.9	-33.2	-32.5	-31.7	-31.0	-30.6	-30.6	-30.6
+100	-27.0	-24.3	-21.2	-19.6	-17.9	-16.3	-14.5	-12.7	-10.9	-9.1	-6.7	-5.7	-5.6
+75	-15.8	-12.5	-8.6	-6.6	-4.7	-2.6	-0.2	2.5	4.7	9.1	13.8	18.0	19.4
+50	-8.6	-4.3	-0.1	2.1	4.5	7.1	9.8	13.1	16.9	21.4	27.6	35.0	44.4
+25	-4.3	-0.1	5.1	7.6	10.3	13.1	16.2	19.6	23.9	28.7	35.1	42.3	44.4
0	-1.0	3.2	7.8	10.2	12.6	15.2	18.0	21.2	25.2	29.8	35.1	43.4	44.4
-25	-4.3	-0.1	5.1	7.6	10.3	13.1	16.2	19.6	23.9	28.7	35.1	42.3	44.4
-50	-8.6	-4.3	-0.1	2.1	4.5	7.1	9.8	13.1	16.9	21.4	27.6	35.0	44.4
-75	-15.8	-12.5	-8.6	-6.6	-4.7	-2.6	-0.2	2.5	5.7	9.1	13.8	18.0	19.4
-100	-27.0	-24.3	-21.2	-19.6	-17.9	-16.3	-14.5	-12.7	-10.9	-9.1	-6.7	-5.7	-5.6
-125	-40.5	-38.5	-36.5	-35.6	-34.7	-33.9	-33.2	-32.5	-31.7	-31.0	-30.6	-30.6	-30.6

weeks to expiration

The estimated credit is: +22.7¢ premium +22.7¢ premium -1.0¢ comm. = +44.4¢

net profit area, in cents

TABLE 2

changes in the soybean future's price in 25¢ increments

	30	25	20	18	16	14	12	10	8	6	4	2	0
+125	-59.1	-58.6	-58.3	-58.1	-58.1	-57.9	-57.9	-57.8	-57.8	-57.8	-57.8	-57.8	-57.8
+100	-38.3	-37.3	-36.2	-35.7	-35.1	-34.6	-34.2	-33.7	-33.4	-33.1	-32.9	-32.8	-32.8
+75	-20.8	-19.2	-17.6	-16.7	-15.7	-14.8	-13.9	-12.8	-11.6	-10.4	-9.1	-8.2	-7.8
+50	-9.3	-7.3	-5.1	-4.0	-2.8	-1.6	-0.3	1.4	3.2	5.4	8.2	11.8	17.2
+25	-2.3	-0.2	2.1	3.3	4.7	6.0	7.4	8.9	10.6	12.9	15.3	16.4	17.2
0	-1.0	1.0	3.2	4.4	5.6	7.4	8.2	10.0	11.8	14.4	16.4	17.2	17.2
-25	-2.3	-0.2	2.1	3.3	4.7	6.0	7.4	8.9	10.6	12.9	15.3	16.4	17.2
-50	-9.3	-7.3	-5.1	-4.0	-2.8	-1.6	-0.3	1.4	3.2	5.4	8.2	11.8	17.2
-75	-20.8	-19.2	-17.6	-16.7	-15.7	-14.8	-13.9	-12.8	-11.6	-10.4	-9.1	-8.2	-7.8
-100	-38.3	-37.3	-36.2	-35.7	-35.1	-34.6	-34.2	-33.7	-33.4	-33.1	-32.9	-32.8	-32.8
-125	-59.1	-58.6	-58.3	-58.1	-58.1	-57.9	-57.9	-57.8	-57.8	-57.8	-57.8	-57.8	-57.8

weeks to expiration

The estimated credit is: +9.1¢ premium +9.1¢ premium -1.0¢ comm. = +17.2¢

net profit area, in cents

Wm Grandmill (1985) Ltd.

SELL A STRANGLE – #2

SELL A CALL AT $1.00 OUT OF THE MONEY
and SELL A PUT AT $1.00 OUT OF THE MONEY

30 weeks to expiration

TABLE (estimated credit is: +43.2¢ premium +43.2¢ premium −1.0¢ comm. = +85.4¢)

changes in the soybean future's price in 25¢ increments — weeks to expiration

	30	25	20	18	16	14	12	10	8	6	4	2	0
+125	-3.9	1.4	8.3	11.4	14.9	18.4	22.1	26.2	30.6	36.1	44.0	53.9	60.4
+100	1.4	8.0	15.5	18.9	22.6	26.4	30.7	35.4	40.6	47.2	56.1	68.1	85.4
+75	2.6	9.9	19.2	23.3	27.7	32.3	37.4	43.1	48.7	55.5	64.6	76.3	85.4
+50	4.6	11.8	21.0	25.5	30.2	35.5	41.1	47.0	53.2	60.5	69.8	80.2	85.4
+25	-0.2	7.4	17.5	22.3	27.3	32.5	38.2	44.5	52.0	60.4	71.5	82.7	85.4
0	-1.0	6.4	16.6	21.4	26.6	32.2	38.4	45.4	53.0	61.6	71.8	82.0	85.4
-25	-0.2	7.4	17.5	22.3	27.3	32.5	38.2	44.5	52.0	60.4	71.5	82.7	85.4
-50	4.6	11.8	21.0	25.5	30.2	35.5	41.1	47.0	53.2	60.5	69.8	80.2	85.4
-75	2.6	9.9	19.2	23.3	27.7	32.3	37.4	43.1	48.7	55.5	64.6	76.3	85.4
-100	1.4	8.0	15.5	18.9	22.6	26.4	30.7	35.4	40.6	47.2	56.1	68.1	85.4
-125	-3.9	1.4	8.3	11.4	14.9	18.4	22.1	26.2	30.6	36.1	44.0	53.9	60.4

net profit area, in cents

TABLE (estimated credit is: +13.4¢ premium +13.4¢ premium −1.0¢ comm. = +25.8¢)

changes in the soybean future's price in 25¢ increments — weeks to expiration

	30	25	20	18	16	14	12	10	8	6	4	2	0
+125	-25.8	-23.6	-20.8	-19.4	-18.1	-16.5	-14.9	-13.0	-10.7	-8.1	-4.5	-0.6	0.8
+100	-15.3	-12.7	-9.4	-7.8	-6.1	-4.4	-2.5	-0.3	2.3	5.5	10.1	16.4	25.8
+75	-7.4	-4.4	-0.8	0.9	2.7	4.5	6.3	8.3	10.9	13.9	18.1	23.7	25.8
+50	-1.9	1.3	5.1	7.0	8.9	10.7	12.9	15.2	17.9	20.6	23.9	25.8	25.8
+25	-1.0	2.4	5.8	7.4	9.2	11.2	13.0	15.2	17.8	20.4	23.6	25.8	25.8
0	-1.0	2.4	5.8	7.4	9.2	11.2	13.0	15.2	17.8	20.4	23.6	25.8	25.8
-25	-1.0	2.4	5.8	7.4	9.2	11.2	13.0	15.2	17.8	20.4	23.6	25.8	25.8
-50	-1.9	1.3	5.1	7.0	8.9	10.7	12.9	15.2	17.9	20.6	23.9	25.8	25.8
-75	-7.4	-4.4	-0.8	0.9	2.7	4.5	6.3	8.3	10.9	13.9	18.1	23.7	25.8
-100	-15.3	-12.7	-9.4	-7.8	-6.1	-4.4	-2.5	-0.3	2.3	5.5	10.1	16.4	25.8
-125	-25.8	-23.6	-20.8	-19.4	-18.1	-16.5	-14.9	-13.0	-10.7	-8.1	-4.5	-0.6	0.8

net profit area, in cents

TABLE (estimated credit is: +27.6¢ premium +27.6¢ premium −1.0¢ comm. = +54.2¢)

changes in the soybean future's price in 25¢ increments — weeks to expiration

	30	25	20	18	16	14	12	10	8	6	4	2	0
+125	-15.1	-11.2	-6.8	-4.7	-2.6	-0.3	2.2	5.4	8.9	12.9	18.7	25.6	29.2
+100	-7.4	-3.0	1.9	4.3	6.9	9.4	12.6	16.3	20.4	25.3	31.9	40.9	54.2
+75	-2.3	1.9	8.2	10.8	13.7	16.8	20.1	23.9	28.5	33.8	40.5	48.7	54.2
+50	1.9	7.1	12.8	15.4	18.4	21.6	25.1	29.0	33.5	38.5	44.8	51.7	54.2
+25	-0.5	5.3	11.8	14.9	18.4	21.8	25.7	30.0	35.0	41.5	47.4	53.3	54.2
0	-1.0	5.4	12.6	15.8	19.2	23.0	26.8	31.0	35.4	40.8	47.2	53.4	54.2
-25	-0.5	5.3	11.8	14.9	18.4	21.8	25.7	30.0	35.0	41.5	47.4	53.3	54.2
-50	1.9	7.1	12.8	15.4	18.4	21.6	25.1	29.0	33.5	38.5	44.8	51.7	54.2
-75	-2.3	1.9	8.2	10.8	13.7	16.8	20.1	23.9	28.5	33.8	40.5	48.7	54.2
-100	-7.4	-3.0	1.9	4.3	6.9	9.4	12.6	16.3	20.4	25.3	31.9	40.9	54.2
-125	-15.1	-11.2	-6.8	-4.7	-2.6	-0.3	2.2	5.4	8.9	12.9	18.7	25.6	29.2

net profit area, in cents

TABLE (the estimated credit is: +3.7¢ premium +3.7¢ premium −1.0¢ comm. = +6.4¢)

changes in the soybean future's price in 25¢ increments — weeks to expiration

	30	25	20	18	16	14	12	10	8	6	4	2	0
+125	-29.7	-28.4	-27.2	-26.6	-25.8	-25.1	-24.3	-23.4	-22.3	-21.2	-19.9	-19.0	-18.6
+100	-16.6	-15.1	-13.4	-12.6	-11.7	-10.8	-9.8	-8.5	-7.1	-5.3	-2.6	1.0	6.4
+75	-8.3	-6.7	-5.2	-4.3	-3.4	-2.6	-1.7	-0.6	0.9	2.4	4.5	5.6	6.4
+50	-3.7	-2.4	-1.0	-0.1	0.4	1.1	1.9	2.8	3.7	5.0	6.0	6.4	6.4
+25	-0.9	0.3	1.6	2.3	3.0	3.7	4.3	4.9	5.5	6.1	6.4	6.4	6.4
0	-1.0	0.2	1.4	2.0	2.6	3.2	3.8	4.6	5.4	6.2	6.4	6.4	6.4
-25	-0.9	0.3	1.6	2.3	3.0	3.7	4.3	4.9	5.5	6.1	6.4	6.4	6.4
-50	-3.7	-2.4	-1.0	-0.1	0.4	1.1	1.9	2.8	3.7	5.0	6.0	6.4	6.4
-75	-8.3	-6.7	-5.2	-4.3	-3.4	-2.6	-1.7	-0.6	0.9	2.4	4.5	5.6	6.4
-100	-16.6	-15.1	-13.4	-12.6	-11.7	-10.8	-9.8	-8.5	-7.1	-5.3	-2.6	1.0	6.4
-125	-29.7	-28.4	-27.2	-26.6	-25.8	-25.1	-24.3	-23.4	-22.3	-21.2	-19.9	-19.0	-18.6

net profit area, in cents

30 weeks to expiration

Wm Grandmill (1985) Ltd.

BUY A CALL or BUY A PUT

AT THE MONEY

35 weeks to expiration

Table (estimated cost: -77.1¢ premium - 0.5¢ comm. = -77.6¢)

changes in the soybean future's price in 25¢ increments	weeks to expiration													
	35	30	25	20	18	16	14	12	10	8	6	4	2	0
+125	79.2	75.6	71.3	65.7	63.2	60.7	58.3	55.9	53.1	50.0	47.7	47.4	47.4	47.4
+100	56.5	52.6	48.0	42.2	39.7	37.1	34.8	32.1	29.4	26.9	24.2	22.8	22.4	22.4
+75	34.8	31.0	26.5	21.2	18.9	16.4	14.1	11.7	9.1	6.3	3.4	-2.5	-2.6	-2.6
+50	21.9	18.6	14.3	9.0	6.5	3.9	1.3	-1.8	-5.2	-9.0	-13.6	-19.5	-25.9	-27.6
+25	10.5	7.5	3.1	-2.8	-5.5	-8.6	-11.7	-15.1	-19.0	-24.2	-29.4	-36.2	-46.1	-52.6
0	-0.5	-4.4	-8.5	-13.6	-16.3	-19.1	-22.0	-25.4	-29.4	-34.1	-40.0	-48.6	-60.3	-77.6
-25	-10.5	-13.8	-18.1	-23.4	-25.9	-28.7	-31.6	-34.9	-38.8	-43.4	-49.2	-57.6	-68.5	-77.6
-50	-19.6	-22.8	-27.0	-32.2	-34.7	-37.4	-40.2	-43.5	-47.5	-51.4	-55.7	-63.7	-72.4	-77.6
-75	-24.4	-27.2	-31.0	-36.2	-38.7	-41.3	-44.2	-47.5	-51.2	-55.7	-60.9	-68.0	-75.4	-77.6
-100	-31.7	-34.4	-38.1	-43.2	-45.6	-48.2	-51.0	-54.1	-57.6	-61.4	-65.7	-70.8	-75.9	-77.6
-125	-39.8	-42.4	-46.2	-51.1	-53.4	-55.8	-58.1	-60.5	-63.1	-66.1	-69.3	-73.3	-77.1	-77.6

net profit

The estimated cost is: -77.1¢ premium - 0.5¢ comm. = -77.6¢

Table (estimated cost: -59.4¢ premium - 0.5¢ comm. = -59.9¢)

changes in the soybean future's price in 25¢ increments	weeks to expiration													
	35	30	25	20	18	16	14	12	10	8	6	4	2	0
+125	79.0	76.8	74.3	71.5	70.1	68.6	67.3	66.0	65.3	65.1	65.1	65.1	65.1	65.1
+100	55.8	53.3	50.6	47.7	46.5	45.1	43.7	42.6	41.8	41.0	40.1	40.1	40.1	40.1
+75	34.9	32.6	30.1	27.4	26.2	24.9	23.7	22.3	20.8	19.3	17.6	15.8	15.1	15.1
+50	22.8	19.9	16.8	13.4	11.7	10.0	8.1	6.0	3.7	1.1	-1.9	-5.7	-9.4	-9.9
+25	10.1	7.0	3.6	-0.4	-2.2	-4.1	-6.2	-8.5	-11.3	-14.6	-18.6	-24.4	-31.3	-34.9
0	-0.5	-3.3	-6.7	-10.7	-12.7	-14.9	-17.1	-19.7	-22.8	-26.5	-31.0	-37.6	-46.6	-59.9
-25	-9.9	-12.9	-16.3	-20.2	-22.1	-24.2	-26.5	-29.0	-32.0	-35.6	-40.0	-46.2	-54.4	-59.9
-50	-19.0	-21.6	-24.8	-28.6	-30.4	-32.3	-34.3	-36.7	-39.4	-42.6	-46.1	-51.4	-57.4	-59.9
-75	-22.6	-25.5	-28.8	-32.6	-34.5	-36.6	-38.6	-41.0	-43.7	-46.9	-50.4	-54.9	-59.1	-59.9
-100	-29.3	-32.3	-35.7	-39.7	-40.7	-42.4	-44.3	-46.2	-48.3	-50.5	-53.2	-56.4	-59.5	-59.9
-125	-37.3	-39.6	-42.1	-44.8	-46.0	-47.4	-48.8	-50.3	-51.9	-53.7	-55.7	-58.1	-59.8	-59.9

net profit area

The estimated cost is: -59.4¢ premium - 0.5¢ comm. = -59.9¢

Table (estimated cost: -41.5¢ premium - 0.5¢ comm. = -42.0¢)

changes in the soybean future's price in 25¢ increments	weeks to expiration													
	35	30	25	20	18	16	14	12	10	8	6	4	2	0
+125	84.4	83.7	83.2	83.0	83.0	83.0	83.0	83.0	83.0	83.0	83.0	83.0	83.0	83.0
+100	60.8	60.2	59.7	59.2	58.9	58.7	58.5	58.3	58.1	58.0	58.0	58.0	58.0	58.0
+75	41.3	40.0	38.8	37.6	37.1	36.5	35.9	35.3	34.7	34.0	33.4	33.0	33.0	33.0
+50	25.3	23.5	21.8	19.7	18.8	17.7	16.7	15.6	14.3	12.8	11.2	9.1	8.1	8.0
+25	11.0	8.9	6.8	4.3	3.0	1.8	0.3	-1.3	-3.2	-5.5	-8.1	-11.7	-15.6	-17.0
0	-0.5	-2.4	-4.7	-7.5	-8.9	-10.4	-12.0	-13.8	-16.0	-18.5	-21.7	-26.3	-32.2	-42.0
-25	-9.7	-11.7	-13.9	-16.7	-18.0	-19.5	-21.1	-23.0	-24.7	-27.2	-30.1	-34.3	-39.9	-42.0
-50	-17.3	-19.3	-21.4	-23.7	-24.9	-26.1	-27.4	-28.8	-30.4	-32.4	-34.7	-37.9	-41.5	-42.0
-75	-21.9	-23.6	-25.6	-27.3	-28.0	-29.2	-30.4	-31.6	-33.0	-34.5	-36.3	-38.2	-40.4	-42.0
-100	-27.0	-28.6	-30.3	-32.0	-32.8	-33.7	-34.7	-35.6	-36.7	-38.0	-39.3	-40.4	-41.7	-42.0
-125	-31.6	-32.7	-33.9	-35.3	-36.0	-36.7	-37.3	-38.1	-38.9	-39.8	-40.6	-41.5	-42.0	-42.0

net profit area

The estimated cost is: -41.5¢ premium - 0.5¢ comm. = -42.0¢

Table (estimated cost: -24.0 premium - 0.5 comm. = -24.5¢)

changes in the soybean future's price in 25¢ increments	weeks to expiration													
	35	30	25	20	18	16	14	12	10	8	6	4	2	0
+125	100.5	100.5	100.5	100.5	100.5	100.5	100.5	100.5	100.5	100.5	100.5	100.5	100.5	100.5
+100	75.5	75.5	75.5	75.5	75.5	75.5	75.5	75.5	75.5	75.5	75.5	75.5	75.5	75.5
+75	51.5	51.3	51.1	50.9	50.8	50.7	50.6	50.6	50.5	50.5	50.5	50.5	50.5	50.5
+50	30.6	30.0	29.3	28.5	28.1	27.6	27.2	26.8	26.4	26.1	25.8	25.6	25.5	25.5
+25	12.5	11.5	10.3	9.1	8.4	7.7	7.0	6.2	5.3	4.2	3.1	1.8	0.9	0.5
0	-0.5	-1.7	-3.1	-4.7	-5.5	-6.4	-7.3	-8.3	-9.6	-11.0	-12.8	-15.5	-19.1	-24.5
-25	-9.2	-10.3	-11.6	-13.0	-13.8	-14.7	-15.5	-16.4	-17.5	-18.8	-20.5	-22.6	-23.7	-24.5
-50	-14.5	-15.4	-16.4	-17.5	-18.1	-18.7	-19.3	-20.0	-20.9	-21.8	-23.1	-24.1	-24.1	-24.5
-75	-18.5	-19.2	-20.0	-20.9	-21.3	-21.9	-22.3	-22.8	-23.6	-24.0	-24.2	-24.3	-24.5	-24.5
-100	-20.3	-20.8	-21.4	-22.0	-22.3	-22.6	-23.2	-23.6	-24.0	-24.0	-24.4	-24.5	-24.5	-24.5
-125	-22.2	-22.5	-22.9	-23.3	-23.5	-23.8	-24.0	-24.1	-24.3	-24.4	-24.5	-24.5	-24.5	-24.5

net profit area, in cents

The estimated cost is: -24.0 premium - 0.5 comm. = -24.5¢

Wm Grandmill (1985) Ltd.

TABLE 8

The estimated cost is: -58.0¢ premium - 0.5¢ comm. = -58.5¢

changes in the soybean future's price in 25¢ increments — weeks to expiration

	35	30	25	20	18	16	14	12	10	8	6	4	2	0
+125	53.9	50.1	45.6	40.3	38.0	35.5	33.2	30.8	28.2	25.4	22.5	19.1	16.6	16.5
+100	41.0	37.7	33.4	28.1	25.6	23.0	20.4	17.3	13.9	10.1	5.5	-0.4	-6.8	-8.5
+75	30.0	26.6	22.2	16.3	13.6	10.5	7.4	4.0	0.1	-4.0	-9.4	-17.1	-27.0	-33.5
+50	18.3	14.9	10.6	5.3	2.8	0.0	-2.9	-6.3	-10.3	-15.0	-20.9	-29.5	-41.2	-58.5
+25	8.6	5.3	1.0	-4.3	-6.8	-9.6	-12.5	-15.8	-19.7	-24.3	-30.1	-38.5	-49.4	-58.5
0	-0.5	-3.7	-7.9	-13.1	-15.6	-18.3	-21.1	-24.4	-28.1	-32.3	-37.6	-44.6	-53.2	-58.5
-25	-5.3	-8.1	-11.9	-17.1	-19.6	-22.2	-25.1	-28.8	-32.1	-36.6	-41.8	-48.9	-56.3	-58.5
-50	-12.6	-15.3	-19.0	-24.1	-26.5	-29.1	-31.9	-35.0	-38.5	-42.3	-46.6	-51.7	-56.8	-58.5
-75	-20.6	-23.3	-27.1	-32.0	-34.3	-36.7	-39.0	-41.4	-44.0	-47.0	-50.2	-54.2	-58.0	-58.5
-100	-29.9	-32.5	-35.5	-39.5	-41.6	-43.5	-46.0	-48.1	-50.5	-52.4	-54.5	-56.8	-58.5	-58.5
-125	-37.0	-39.4	-42.4	-46.3	-48.1	-49.7	-51.4	-53.2	-55.0	-56.0	-57.1	-57.7	-58.5	-58.5

net profit

TABLE 6

The estimated cost is: -40.9¢ premium - 0.5¢ comm. = -41.4¢

changes in the soybean future's price in 25¢ increments

	35	30	25	20	18	16	14	12	10	8	6	4	2	0
+125	53.4	51.1	48.6	45.9	44.7	43.4	42.2	40.8	39.3	37.8	36.1	34.3	33.6	33.6
+100	41.4	38.4	35.3	31.9	30.2	28.5	26.6	24.5	22.2	19.6	16.6	12.8	9.1	8.6
+75	28.6	25.5	22.1	18.1	16.3	14.4	12.3	10.0	7.2	3.9	-0.1	-5.9	-12.8	-16.4
+50	18.0	15.2	11.8	7.8	5.8	3.6	1.4	-1.2	-4.3	-8.0	-12.5	-19.1	-28.1	-41.4
+25	8.6	5.6	2.2	-1.4	-3.6	-5.7	-8.0	-10.5	-13.5	-17.1	-21.5	-27.7	-35.9	-41.4
0	-0.5	-3.1	-6.3	-10.1	-11.9	-13.8	-15.8	-18.2	-20.9	-24.1	-27.6	-32.7	-38.9	-41.4
-25	-4.1	-7.0	-10.3	-14.1	-16.0	-18.1	-20.1	-22.5	-25.2	-28.4	-31.9	-36.4	-40.6	-41.4
-50	-10.8	-13.8	-17.0	-20.6	-22.2	-23.9	-25.8	-27.7	-30.3	-32.0	-34.7	-37.9	-41.0	-41.4
-75	-18.8	-21.1	-23.6	-26.3	-27.5	-28.9	-30.3	-31.8	-33.4	-35.2	-37.2	-39.6	-41.3	-41.4
-100	-25.6	-27.4	-29.4	-31.3	-32.1	-33.2	-34.4	-35.8	-36.7	-38.0	-39.5	-40.7	-41.4	-41.4
-125	-30.7	-31.9	-33.4	-35.1	-35.8	-36.6	-37.4	-38.2	-39.0	-40.0	-40.9	-41.4	-41.4	-41.4

TABLE 4

The estimated cost is: -24.7¢ premium - 0.5¢ comm. = -25.2¢

changes in the soybean future's price in 25¢ increments — weeks to expiration

	35	30	25	20	18	16	14	12	10	8	6	4	2	0
+125	58.1	56.8	55.6	54.4	53.9	53.3	52.7	52.0	51.5	50.8	50.2	49.8	49.8	49.8
+100	42.1	40.3	38.6	36.5	35.6	34.5	33.5	32.4	31.1	29.6	28.0	25.9	24.9	24.8
+75	27.8	25.7	23.6	21.1	19.8	18.6	17.1	15.5	13.6	11.3	8.7	5.1	1.2	-0.2
+50	16.3	14.4	12.1	9.3	7.9	6.4	4.8	3.0	0.8	-1.7	-4.9	-9.5	-15.8	-25.2
+25	7.1	5.1	2.9	0.1	-1.2	-2.7	-4.3	-6.0	-7.9	-10.4	-13.3	-17.9	-23.1	-25.2
0	-0.5	-2.5	-4.6	-6.9	-8.1	-9.3	-10.6	-12.0	-13.6	-15.6	-17.9	-21.1	-25.2	-25.2
-25	-5.1	-6.8	-8.8	-11.2	-12.4	-13.6	-14.8	-16.2	-17.7	-19.5	-21.4	-23.6	-25.2	-25.2
-50	-10.2	-11.8	-13.5	-15.2	-16.0	-16.9	-17.9	-18.8	-19.9	-21.2	-23.0	-24.1	-25.2	-25.2
-75	-14.8	-15.9	-17.1	-18.5	-19.2	-19.9	-20.5	-21.3	-22.1	-23.0	-23.8	-24.9	-25.2	-25.2
-100	-18.3	-19.3	-20.3	-21.2	-21.8	-22.0	-22.6	-23.2	-24.1	-24.4	-24.7	-25.1	-25.2	-25.2
-125	-21.6	-22.3	-23.1	-23.9	-24.2	-24.5	-24.8	-24.9	-25.0	-25.0	-25.1	-25.2	-25.2	-25.2

net profit

TABLE 2, 0

The estimated cost is: -10.0¢ premium - 0.5¢ comm. = -10.5¢

changes in the soybean future's price in 25¢ increments — weeks to expiration

	35	30	25	20	18	16	14	12	10	8	6	4	2	0
+125	65.5	65.3	65.1	64.9	64.8	64.7	64.6	64.5	64.5	64.5	64.5	64.5	64.5	64.5
+100	44.6	44.0	43.3	42.5	42.1	41.6	41.2	40.8	40.4	40.1	39.8	39.6	39.5	39.5
+75	26.5	25.5	24.3	23.1	22.4	21.7	21.0	20.2	19.3	18.2	17.1	15.3	14.9	14.5
+50	13.5	12.3	10.9	9.3	8.5	7.6	6.7	5.7	4.4	3.0	1.2	-1.5	-5.1	-10.5
+25	4.8	3.7	2.4	1.0	0.2	-0.7	-1.5	-2.4	-3.5	-4.8	-6.5	-8.6	-9.7	-10.5
0	-0.5	-1.4	-2.4	-3.5	-4.1	-4.7	-5.3	-6.0	-6.9	-7.9	-9.1	-10.1	-10.5	-10.5
-25	-4.5	-5.2	-6.0	-6.9	-7.3	-7.8	-8.3	-8.8	-9.2	-9.6	-10.2	-10.5	-10.5	-10.5
-50	-6.3	-6.8	-7.4	-8.0	-8.3	-8.6	-8.9	-9.2	-9.6	-10.0	-10.4	-10.5	-10.5	-10.5
-75	-8.2	-8.5	-8.9	-9.3	-9.5	-9.8	-10.0	-10.1	-10.3	-10.4	-10.5	-10.5	-10.5	-10.5
-100	-9.2	-9.5	-9.8	-10.1	-10.2	-10.3	-10.4	-10.4	-10.5	-10.5	-10.5	-10.5	-10.5	-10.5
-125	-9.8	-10.1	-10.3	-10.4	-10.5	-10.5	-10.5	-10.5	-10.5	-10.5	-10.5	-10.5	-10.5	-10.5

net profit area

Wm Grandmill (1985) Ltd.

TABLE 80 — changes in the soybean future's price in 25¢ increments | weeks to expiration | net profit area, in cents

	35	30	25	20	18	16	14	12	10	8	6	4	2	0
+125	-80.2	-76.6	-72.3	-66.7	-64.2	-61.7	-59.3	-56.9	-54.1	-51.6	-48.7	-48.4	-48.4	-48.4
+100	-57.5	-53.6	-49.0	-43.2	-40.7	-38.1	-35.8	-33.1	-30.4	-27.9	-25.2	-23.8	-23.4	-23.4
+75	-35.8	-32.0	-27.5	-22.2	-19.9	-17.4	-15.1	-12.7	-10.1	-7.3	-4.4	-1.0	1.5	1.6
+50	-22.9	-19.6	-15.3	-10.0	-7.5	-4.9	-2.3	0.8	4.2	8.0	12.6	18.5	24.9	26.6
+25	-11.5	-8.5	-4.1	1.8	4.5	7.6	10.7	14.1	18.0	22.2	27.5	35.2	45.1	51.6
0	-0.5	3.4	7.5	12.6	15.3	18.1	21.0	24.4	28.4	33.1	39.0	47.6	59.3	76.6
-25	9.5	12.8	17.1	22.4	24.9	27.7	30.6	33.9	37.8	42.4	48.2	56.6	67.5	76.6
-50	18.6	21.8	26.0	31.2	33.7	36.4	39.2	42.5	46.2	50.4	55.7	62.7	71.4	76.6
-75	23.4	26.2	30.0	35.2	37.7	40.3	43.2	46.5	50.2	54.7	59.9	67.0	74.4	76.6
-100	30.7	33.4	37.1	42.2	44.6	47.2	50.0	53.1	56.6	60.4	64.7	69.8	74.9	76.6
-125	38.8	41.4	45.2	50.1	52.4	54.8	57.1	59.5	62.1	65.1	68.3	72.3	76.1	76.6

The estimated credit is: +77.1 premium − 0.5 comm. = +76.6¢

TABLE 40 — changes in the soybean future's price in 25¢ increments | weeks to expiration | net profit area, in cents

	35	30	25	20	18	16	14	12	10	8	6	4	2	0
+125	-85.4	-84.7	-84.2	-84.0	-84.0	-84.0	-84.0	-84.0	-84.0	-84.0	-84.0	-84.0	-84.0	-84.0
+100	-61.8	-61.2	-60.7	-60.2	-59.9	-59.7	-59.5	-59.3	-59.1	-59.0	-59.0	-59.0	-59.0	-59.0
+75	-42.3	-41.0	-39.8	-38.6	-38.1	-37.5	-36.9	-36.3	-35.7	-35.0	-34.4	-34.0	-34.0	-34.0
+50	-26.3	-24.3	-22.8	-20.7	-19.8	-18.7	-17.7	-16.6	-15.3	-13.8	-12.2	-10.1	-9.1	-9.0
+25	-12.0	-9.9	-7.8	-5.3	-4.0	-2.8	-1.3	0.3	2.2	4.5	7.1	10.7	14.6	16.0
0	-0.5	1.4	3.7	6.5	7.9	9.4	11.0	12.8	15.0	17.5	20.7	25.3	31.6	41.0
-25	8.7	10.7	12.9	15.7	17.0	18.5	20.1	21.8	23.7	26.2	29.1	33.3	38.6	41.0
-50	16.3	18.3	20.4	22.7	23.9	25.1	26.4	27.8	29.4	31.4	34.3	36.9	40.5	41.0
-75	20.9	22.6	24.6	27.0	28.2	29.4	30.6	32.0	33.5	35.3	37.2	39.4	41.0	41.0
-100	26.0	27.6	29.3	31.0	31.8	32.7	33.7	34.6	35.7	37.0	38.3	39.9	41.0	41.0
-125	30.6	31.7	32.9	34.3	35.0	35.7	36.3	37.1	37.9	38.8	39.6	40.7	41.0	41.0

The estimated credit is: +41.5 premium − 0.5 comm. = +41.0¢

TABLE 80 — changes in the soybean future's price in 25¢ increments | weeks to expiration | net profit area, in cents

	35	30	25	20	18	16	14	12	10	8	6	4	2	0
+125	-80.2	-77.8	-75.3	-72.5	-71.1	-69.6	-68.3	-67.0	-66.3	-66.1	-66.1	-66.1	-66.1	-66.1
+100	-56.8	-54.3	-51.6	-48.7	-47.5	-46.1	-44.7	-43.6	-42.8	-42.0	-42.0	-41.4	-41.4	-41.4
+75	-35.9	-33.6	-31.1	-28.4	-27.2	-25.9	-24.7	-23.3	-21.8	-20.3	-18.6	-16.8	-16.1	-16.1
+50	-23.9	-20.9	-17.8	-14.4	-12.7	-11.0	-9.1	-7.0	-4.7	-2.1	0.9	4.7	8.4	8.9
+25	-11.1	-8.0	-4.6	-0.6	1.2	3.1	5.2	7.5	10.3	13.6	17.6	23.4	30.3	33.9
0	-0.5	2.3	5.7	9.7	11.7	13.9	16.1	18.7	21.8	25.5	30.0	36.6	45.6	58.9
-25	8.9	11.9	15.3	19.2	21.1	23.2	25.5	28.0	31.0	34.6	39.0	45.2	53.4	58.9
-50	18.0	20.6	23.8	27.6	29.4	31.3	33.3	35.7	38.4	41.6	45.1	50.2	56.4	58.9
-75	21.6	24.5	27.8	31.6	33.5	35.6	37.6	40.0	42.7	45.9	49.4	54.7	58.1	58.9
-100	28.3	31.3	34.7	38.7	39.7	41.4	43.3	45.2	47.3	49.5	52.2	55.4	58.5	58.9
-125	36.3	38.6	41.1	43.8	45.0	46.4	47.8	49.3	50.9	52.7	54.7	57.1	58.8	58.9

The estimated credit is: +59.4¢ premium − 0.5¢ comm. = +58.9¢

TABLE 20 — changes in the soybean future's price in 25¢ increments | weeks to expiration | net profit area, in cents

	35	30	25	20	18	16	14	12	10	8	6	4	2	0
+125	-101.5	-101.5	-101.5	-101.5	-101.5	-101.5	-101.5	-101.5	-101.5	-101.5	-101.5	-101.5	-101.5	-101.5
+100	-76.5	-76.5	-76.5	-76.5	-76.5	-76.5	-76.5	-76.5	-76.5	-76.5	-76.5	-76.5	-76.5	-76.5
+75	-52.5	-52.3	-52.1	-51.9	-51.8	-51.7	-51.6	-51.6	-51.5	-51.5	-51.5	-51.5	-51.5	-51.5
+50	-31.6	-31.0	-30.3	-29.5	-29.1	-28.6	-28.2	-27.8	-27.4	-27.1	-26.8	-26.6	-26.5	-26.5
+25	-13.5	-12.5	-11.3	-10.1	-9.4	-8.7	-8.0	-7.2	-6.3	-5.2	-4.1	-2.8	-1.9	-1.5
0	-0.5	0.7	2.1	3.7	5.4	6.3	7.3	8.6	10.0	11.8	14.5	18.1		23.5
-25	8.2	9.3	10.6	12.0	13.7	14.5	15.4	16.5	17.8	19.5	21.6	22.7		23.5
-50	13.5	14.4	15.4	16.5	17.1	17.7	18.3	19.0	19.9	20.8	22.1	23.1	23.5	23.5
-75	17.5	18.2	19.0	19.9	20.3	20.9	21.3	21.8	22.2	22.6	23.2	23.5	23.5	23.5
-100	19.3	19.8	20.4	21.0	21.3	21.6	21.8	22.2	22.6	23.2	23.4	23.5	23.5	23.5
-125	21.2	21.5	21.9	22.3	22.5	22.8	23.0	23.1	23.3	23.4	23.5	23.5	23.5	23.5

The estimated credit is: +24.0¢ premium − 0.5¢ comm. = +23.5¢

Wm Grandmill (1985) Ltd.

SELL A CALL or SELL A PUT
AT 50¢ OUT OF THE MONEY

TABLE 0 (top right)

The estimated credit is: +58.0¢ premium − 0.5¢ comm. = +57.5¢

changes in the soybean future's price in 25¢ increments

	weeks to expiration													
	35	30	25	20	18	16	14	12	10	8	6	4	2	0
+125	36.0	38.4	41.4	45.3	47.1	48.7	50.4	52.2	54.0	55.0	56.0	57.0	57.5	57.5
+100	28.9	31.5	34.5	38.5	40.6	42.5	45.0	47.9	49.5	51.4	53.5	55.8	57.5	57.5
+75	19.6	22.3	26.1	31.0	33.3	35.7	38.0	40.4	43.0	45.6	50.7	55.8	57.0	57.5
+50	11.6	14.3	18.0	23.1	25.5	28.1	30.9	34.0	37.5	41.3	45.6	50.7	55.8	57.5
+25	4.3	7.1	10.9	16.1	18.6	21.2	24.1	27.4	31.1	35.6	40.8	47.9	55.3	57.5
0	−0.5	2.7	6.9	12.1	14.6	17.3	20.1	23.4	27.1	31.3	36.6	43.6	52.2	57.5
−25	−9.6	−6.3	−2.0	3.3	5.8	8.6	11.5	14.8	18.7	23.3	29.1	37.5	48.4	57.5
−50	−19.3	−15.9	−11.6	−6.3	−3.8	−1.0	1.9	5.3	9.3	14.0	19.9	28.5	40.2	57.5
−75	−31.0	−27.6	−23.2	−17.3	−14.6	−11.5	−8.4	−5.0	−1.1	3.0	8.4	16.1	26.6	32.5
−100	−42.0	−38.7	−34.4	−29.1	−26.6	−24.0	−21.4	−18.3	−14.9	−11.1	−6.5	−0.6	5.8	7.5
−125	−54.9	−51.1	−46.6	−39.6	−36.5	−34.2	−31.8	−29.2	−26.4	−23.5	−20.1	−17.6	−17.5	−17.5

net profit area , in cents

TABLE 0 (top left)

The estimated credit is: +40.9¢ premium −0.5¢ comm. = +40.4¢

changes in the soybean future's price in 25¢ increments

	weeks to expiration													
	35	30	25	20	18	16	14	12	10	8	6	4	2	0
+125	29.7	30.9	32.4	34.1	34.8	35.6	36.4	37.2	38.0	39.0	39.9	40.4	40.4	40.4
+100	24.6	26.4	28.4	30.3	31.1	32.2	33.4	34.8	35.7	37.0	38.5	39.7	40.4	40.4
+75	17.8	20.1	22.6	25.3	26.5	27.9	29.3	30.8	32.4	34.2	36.2	38.6	40.3	40.4
+50	9.8	12.8	16.0	19.6	21.2	22.9	24.8	26.7	28.8	31.0	33.7	36.9	40.0	40.4
+25	3.1	6.0	9.3	13.1	15.0	17.1	19.1	21.5	24.2	27.4	30.9	35.4	39.6	40.4
0	−0.5	2.1	5.3	9.1	10.9	12.8	14.8	17.2	19.9	23.1	26.6	31.7	37.9	40.4
−25	−9.6	−6.6	−3.2	0.4	2.6	4.7	7.0	9.5	12.5	16.1	20.5	26.7	34.9	40.4
−50	−19.0	−16.2	−12.8	−8.8	−6.8	−4.6	−2.4	0.2	3.3	7.0	11.5	18.1	27.1	40.4
−75	−29.6	−26.5	−23.1	−19.1	−17.3	−15.4	−13.3	−11.0	−8.2	−4.9	−0.9	4.9	11.8	15.4
−100	−42.4	−39.4	−36.3	−32.9	−31.2	−29.5	−27.6	−25.5	−23.2	−20.6	−17.6	−13.8	−10.1	−9.6
−125	−54.4	−52.1	−49.6	−45.7	−44.4	−43.2	−41.8	−40.3	−38.8	−37.1	−35.3	−34.6	−34.6	−34.6

net profit area , in cents

TABLE 4 (bottom right)

The estimated credit is: +24.7¢ premium −0.5¢ comm. = +24.2¢

changes in the soybean future's price in 25¢ increments

	weeks to expiration													
	35	30	25	20	18	16	14	12	10	8	6	4	2	0
+125	20.6	21.3	22.1	22.9	23.2	23.5	23.8	23.9	24.0	24.1	24.2	24.2	24.2	24.2
+100	17.3	18.3	19.3	20.3	21.0	21.6	22.2	22.9	23.4	23.7	23.9	24.2	24.2	24.2
+75	13.8	14.9	16.1	17.5	18.2	18.9	19.5	20.3	21.1	22.0	22.8	23.6	24.2	24.2
+50	9.2	10.8	12.5	14.2	15.0	15.9	16.9	17.8	18.9	20.2	21.5	23.1	24.2	24.2
+25	4.1	5.8	7.8	10.2	11.4	12.6	13.8	15.2	16.7	18.5	20.4	22.6	24.2	24.2
0	−0.5	1.5	3.6	5.9	7.1	8.3	9.6	11.0	12.6	14.6	16.9	20.1	23.7	24.2
−25	−8.1	−6.1	−3.9	−1.1	0.2	1.7	3.3	5.0	6.9	9.4	12.3	16.5	22.1	24.2
−50	−17.3	−15.4	−13.1	−10.3	−8.9	−7.4	−5.8	−4.0	−1.8	0.7	3.9	8.5	14.8	24.2
−75	−28.8	−26.7	−24.6	−22.1	−20.8	−19.6	−18.1	−16.5	−14.6	−12.3	−9.7	−6.1	−2.2	−0.8
−100	−43.1	−41.3	−39.6	−37.5	−36.6	−35.5	−34.5	−33.4	−32.1	−30.6	−29.0	−26.9	−25.9	−25.8
−125	−59.1	−57.8	−56.6	−55.4	−54.9	−54.3	−53.7	−53.0	−52.5	−51.8	−51.2	−50.8	−50.8	−50.8

net profit area , in cents

TABLE 2 (bottom left)

The estimated credit is: +10.0¢ premium −0.5¢ comm. = +9.5¢

changes in the soybean future's price in 25¢ increments

	weeks to expiration													
	35	30	25	20	18	16	14	12	10	8	6	4	2	0
+125	8.8	9.1	9.3	9.4	9.5	9.5	9.5	9.5	9.5	9.5	9.5	9.5	9.5	9.5
+100	8.2	8.5	8.8	9.1	9.2	9.3	9.4	9.3	9.4	9.3	9.5	9.5	9.5	9.5
+75	7.2	7.5	7.9	8.3	8.5	8.8	9.0	9.1	9.2	9.4	9.4	9.5	9.5	9.5
+50	5.3	5.8	6.4	7.0	7.3	7.6	7.9	8.2	8.6	9.0	9.1	9.5	9.5	9.5
+25	3.5	4.2	5.0	5.9	6.3	6.8	7.3	7.8	8.2	8.6	9.2	9.5	9.5	9.5
0	−0.5	0.4	1.4	2.5	3.1	3.7	4.3	5.0	5.9	6.9	8.1	9.1	9.5	9.5
−25	−5.8	−4.7	−3.4	−2.0	−1.2	−0.3	0.5	1.4	2.5	3.8	5.5	7.6	8.7	9.5
−50	−14.5	−13.3	−11.9	−10.3	−9.5	−8.6	−7.7	−6.7	−5.4	−4.0	−2.2	0.5	4.1	9.5
−75	−27.5	−26.5	−25.3	−24.1	−23.4	−22.7	−22.0	−21.2	−20.3	−19.2	−18.1	−16.3	−15.9	−15.5
−100	−45.6	−45.0	−44.3	−43.5	−43.1	−42.6	−42.2	−41.8	−41.4	−41.1	−40.8	−40.6	−40.5	−40.5
−125	−66.5	−66.3	−66.1	−65.9	−65.8	−65.7	−65.6	−65.6	−65.5	−65.5	−65.5	−65.5	−65.5	−65.5

net profit area , in cents

Wm Grandmill (1985) Ltd.

BULL or BEAR SPREAD – #1

BUY A CALL AT THE MONEY
and SELL A CALL AT 25¢ OUT OF THE MONEY
OR
BUY A PUT AT THE MONEY
and SELL A PUT AT 25¢ OUT OF THE MONEY

35 weeks to expiration

TABLE

changes in the soybean future's price in 25¢ increments

	weeks to expiration													
	35	30	25	20	18	16	14	12	10	8	6	4	2	0
+125	12.4	12.6	12.7	12.8	12.9	13.0	13.1	13.2	13.4	13.6	13.8	14.0	14.4	14.4
+100	6.4	6.7	7.0	7.4	7.8	8.2	8.6	9.1	9.6	10.3	11.1	12.8	14.4	14.4
+75	3.8	4.0	4.2	4.4	4.7	5.0	5.3	5.7	6.2	6.8	7.8	9.4	12.8	14.4
+50	1.9	1.9	1.9	2.0	2.1	2.2	2.4	2.7	3.1	3.6	4.3	6.1	9.6	14.4
+25	0.3	0.4	0.4	0.5	0.5	0.6	0.6	0.7	0.8	0.9	1.1	1.8	3.6	14.4
0	-1.0	-1.0	-1.0	-1.0	-1.0	-1.0	-1.0	-1.1	-1.2	-1.3	-1.4	-1.6	-2.6	-10.6
-25	-1.5	-1.6	-1.7	-1.8	-1.8	-1.9	-2.0	-2.1	-2.2	-2.6	-3.3	-4.5	-6.7	-10.6
-50	-1.8	-1.9	-2.0	-2.1	-2.1	-2.2	-2.4	-2.7	-3.1	-3.7	-4.6	-6.0	-7.6	-10.6
-75	-2.1	-2.2	-2.3	-2.4	-2.5	-2.6	-2.8	-3.4	-4.2	-5.0	-5.9	-7.0	-8.1	-10.6
-100	-2.3	-2.4	-2.5	-2.6	-2.7	-3.0	-3.5	-4.2	-5.0	-5.9	-6.6	-8.1	-9.4	-10.6
-125	-2.5	-2.6	-2.7	-2.8	-3.0	-3.3	-3.8	-4.6	-5.4	-6.6	-7.8	-9.1	-10.1	-10.6

net profit area, in cents

The estimated cost is: -77.1¢ premium + 67.5¢ premium - 1.0¢ comm. = -10.6¢

TABLE

changes in the soybean future's price in 25¢ increments

	weeks to expiration													
	35	30	25	20	18	16	14	12	10	8	6	4	2	0
+125	13.2	13.3	13.4	13.6	13.9	14.1	14.3	14.5	14.7	14.8	14.8	14.8	14.8	14.8
+100	9.3	10.0	10.7	11.4	11.7	12.0	12.4	12.8	13.2	13.8	14.4	14.8	14.8	14.8
+75	6.0	6.3	6.8	7.4	8.0	8.6	9.0	9.5	10.2	11.0	12.0	13.5	14.8	14.8
+50	4.1	4.4	4.8	5.1	5.4	5.7	6.2	6.7	7.3	8.1	9.1	10.6	12.7	14.8
+25	0.9	1.1	1.3	1.6	1.8	2.0	2.1	2.3	2.6	2.8	3.4	4.4	6.8	14.8
0	-1.0	-1.0	-1.0	-1.0	-1.1	-1.1	-1.1	-1.2	-1.4	-1.6	-1.8	-2.2	-3.0	-10.2
-25	-2.4	-2.6	-2.8	-3.1	-3.3	-3.9	-4.2	-4.5	-5.0	-5.6	-6.6	-7.7	-8.6	-10.2
-50	-4.7	-4.8	-5.0	-5.3	-5.6	-5.9	-6.0	-6.1	-6.3	-6.7	-7.7	-8.6	-9.7	-10.2
-75	-5.6	-5.9	-6.3	-6.7	-7.0	-7.2	-7.5	-7.8	-8.1	-8.3	-8.6	-9.0	-9.4	-10.2
-100	-6.4	-6.7	-7.0	-7.2	-7.4	-7.6	-7.8	-8.0	-8.1	-8.3	-8.4	-8.9	-9.4	-10.2
-125	-6.7	-7.0	-7.2	-7.4	-7.6	-7.8	-8.0	-8.1	-8.3	-8.6	-9.1	-9.7	-10.2	-10.2

net profit area, in cents

The estimated cost is: -41.5¢ premium + 32.3¢ premium - 1.0¢ comm. = -10.2¢

TABLE

changes in the soybean future's price in 25¢ increments

	weeks to expiration													
	35	30	25	20	18	16	14	12	10	8	6	4	2	0
+125	13.0	13.1	13.1	13.1	13.1	13.1	13.1	13.2	13.4	13.8	14.3	14.6	14.6	14.6
+100	7.7	8.0	8.3	8.6	8.9	9.3	9.7	10.1	10.6	11.3	12.4	13.9	14.6	14.6
+75	4.5	4.9	5.3	5.8	6.0	6.2	6.5	6.8	7.1	7.8	9.1	11.1	13.9	14.6
+50	2.0	2.2	2.8	3.3	3.5	3.7	3.9	4.2	4.6	5.3	6.3	8.3	11.5	14.6
+25	0.1	0.1	0.1	0.1	0.1	0.3	0.5	0.8	1.1	1.5	2.0	2.8	4.9	14.6
0	-1.0	-1.0	-1.0	-1.0	-1.0	-1.0	-1.0	-1.1	-1.2	-1.3	-1.4	-1.8	-2.6	-10.4
-25	-1.5	-1.7	-1.9	-2.0	-2.1	-2.3	-2.5	-2.7	-3.0	-3.4	-4.3	-5.4	-7.4	-10.4
-50	-2.6	-2.7	-2.9	-3.0	-3.2	-3.4	-3.7	-4.0	-4.4	-5.0	-5.7	-6.7	-8.7	-10.4
-75	-3.5	-3.6	-3.7	-3.9	-4.2	-4.5	-4.8	-5.2	-5.9	-6.8	-7.6	-8.7	-10.0	-10.4
-100	-3.6	-3.9	-4.2	-4.7	-5.1	-5.5	-6.0	-6.3	-6.8	-7.2	-7.9	-8.8	-10.1	-10.4
-125	-3.7	-4.1	-4.6	-5.4	-5.7	-6.0	-6.3	-6.7	-7.1	-7.6	-8.1	-9.1	-10.3	-10.4

net profit area, in cents

The estimated cost is: -59.4¢ premium + 50.0¢ premium - 1.0¢ comm. = -10.4¢

TABLE

changes in the soybean future's price in 25¢ increments

	weeks to expiration													
	35	30	25	20	18	16	14	12	10	8	6	4	2	0
+125	15.3	15.3	15.3	15.3	15.3	15.3	15.3	15.3	15.3	15.3	15.3	15.3	15.3	15.3
+100	14.3	14.5	14.7	14.9	15.0	15.2	15.2	15.3	15.3	15.3	15.3	15.3	15.3	15.3
+75	11.2	11.6	12.1	12.7	13.0	13.4	13.7	14.1	14.4	14.7	15.0	15.2	15.3	15.3
+50	8.4	8.8	9.3	9.6	9.9	10.2	10.5	10.9	11.4	12.2	13.0	14.1	14.9	15.3
+25	3.3	3.5	3.7	4.0	4.3	4.4	4.6	4.8	5.1	5.5	6.2	7.6	10.3	15.3
0	-1.0	-1.1	-1.2	-1.3	-1.4	-1.4	-1.5	-1.6	-1.8	-1.9	-2.0	-2.6	-3.1	-9.7
-25	-4.4	-4.6	-4.9	-5.2	-5.4	-5.7	-5.9	-6.1	-6.3	-6.7	-7.1	-8.1	-8.6	-9.7
-50	-5.7	-5.9	-6.1	-6.3	-6.5	-6.6	-6.7	-6.9	-7.3	-7.9	-8.6	-9.3	-9.7	-9.7
-75	-6.9	-7.0	-7.2	-7.3	-7.4	-7.5	-7.7	-7.9	-8.2	-8.8	-9.0	-9.4	-9.7	-9.7
-100	-7.9	-8.0	-8.1	-8.2	-8.3	-8.4	-8.6	-8.8	-9.0	-9.3	-9.6	-9.7	-9.7	-9.7
-125	-8.7	-8.7	-8.8	-8.9	-9.0	-9.2	-9.3	-9.4	-9.5	-9.6	-9.7	-9.7	-9.7	-9.7

net profit area, in cents

The estimated cost is: -24.0¢ premium + 15.3¢ premium - 1.0¢ comm. = -9.7¢

Wm Grandmill (1985) Ltd.

BULL or BEAR SPREAD – #2

BUY A CALL AT THE MONEY
and SELL 2 CALLS AT 50¢ OUT OF THE MONEY
OR
BUY A PUT AT THE MONEY
and SELL 2 PUTS AT 50¢ OUT OF THE MONEY

weeks to expiration: **35**

TABLE (upper right) — changes in the soybean future's price in 25¢ increments

	35	30	25	20	18	16	14	12	10	8	6	4	2	0
+125	-30.6	-26.6	-21.9	-16.9	-14.7	-12.4	-10.1	-7.7	-5.3	-2.8	0.7	7.2	12.2	12.4
+100	-28.3	-24.8	-20.8	-16.0	-13.5	-10.9	-8.0	-4.5	-0.4	4.7	11.2	21.6	34.0	37.0
+75	-27.9	-24.2	-19.9	-13.4	-10.9	-6.6	-2.7	1.7	6.9	12.5	20.2	32.2	49.5	62.4
+50	-17.3	-13.2	-8.9	-3.6	-1.1	1.9	5.1	8.8	12.5	19.0	26.2	37.5	54.5	87.4
+25	-9.1	-5.1	-0.9	3.8	6.1	8.6	11.3	14.5	18.4	23.4	29.7	38.8	50.7	62.4
0	-1.5	1.2	5.3	10.4	12.9	15.5	18.2	21.4	24.8	28.5	33.2	38.6	42.1	37.4
-25	-1.5	0.4	3.7	8.8	11.3	13.7	16.6	19.9	23.4	27.8	32.4	38.2	43.9	37.4
-50	3.6	5.8	9.0	14.0	16.3	18.8	21.6	24.5	27.8	31.2	34.5	37.7	39.2	37.4
-75	14.8	17.4	21.2	25.8	27.9	30.1	31.8	34.8	36.3	37.5	38.4	38.6	38.6	37.4
-100	23.9	25.6	28.4	31.0	33.7	35.2	37.9	39.0	40.1	41.3	42.7	40.1	38.2	37.4
-125	32.8	34.6	36.8	38.9	40.8	41.8	42.8	43.9	44.9	43.9	42.7	37.9	37.4	37.4

weeks to expiration — net profit area, in cents

The estimated credit: -77.1¢ premium + 58.0¢ premium + 58.0¢ premium - 1.5¢ comm. = + 37.4¢

TABLE (upper left) — changes in the soybean future's price in 25¢ increments

	35	30	25	20	18	16	14	12	10	8	6	4	2	0
+125	21.7	22.2	22.8	23.2	23.6	23.8	24.0	24.1	24.2	24.3	24.1	24.2	21.0	20.9
+100	16.2	17.7	19.2	20.1	20.9	21.4	21.8	22.2	22.5	22.7	23.0	22.5	21.8	20.9
+75	13.0	14.7	16.4	17.8	18.5	19.2	20.0	20.6	21.1	21.5	22.0	22.6	22.5	20.9
+50	0.6	4.0	7.2	10.6	12.0	13.5	15.2	16.7	18.2	19.6	21.3	22.6	24.8	20.9
+25	-3.9	-0.7	2.3	6.0	7.9	10.0	11.9	14.0	16.4	19.2	21.8	24.6	24.8	20.9
0	-1.5	0.9	3.9	7.5	9.1	10.7	12.5	14.7	17.0	19.7	22.2	25.8	29.2	45.9
-25	13.7	15.1	15.1	17.6	19.2	21.1	21.3	22.4	29.0	38.5	45.9	—	—	—
-50	23.9	25.6	28.4	31.0	33.7	35.2	36.3	37.5	38.4	38.6	70.6	—	—	—
-75	45.9	—	—	—	—	—	—	—	—	—	45.9	—	—	—
-100	—	—	—	—	—	—	—	—	—	—	20.9	—	—	—
-125	—	—	—	—	—	—	—	—	—	—	-4.1	—	—	—

net profit area, in cents

The estimated credit is: -59.4¢ premium + 40.9¢ premium + 40.9¢ premium - 1.5¢ comm. = + 20.9¢

TABLE (lower right) — changes in the soybean future's price in 25¢ increments

	35	30	25	20	18	16	14	12	10	8	6	4	2	0
+125	-33.8	-31.9	-30.0	-27.8	-26.8	-25.6	-24.4	-23.2	-22.0	-20.6	-19.4	-18.6	-18.6	-18.6
+100	-25.4	-22.4	-19.5	-15.8	-14.1	-12.3	-10.5	-8.5	-6.1	-3.2	0.0	4.2	6.2	6.4
+75	-16.3	-13.4	-10.4	-6.6	-4.5	-2.7	-0.3	2.3	5.5	9.4	14.0	20.8	28.6	31.4
+50	-9.3	-7.3	-4.4	-0.3	1.0	2.9	5.1	7.6	10.7	13.3	16.5	21.3	37.7	56.4
+25	-5.2	-3.3	-1.0	1.7	2.9	5.1	6.9	8.7	10.6	13.3	16.5	21.4	26.6	31.4
0	-1.5	0.6	2.5	4.3	5.3	6.2	7.2	8.2	9.2	9.8	10.7	10.9	13.9	6.4
-25	-1.5	-0.1	1.7	3.7	4.8	5.7	6.3	6.8	7.4	8.0	8.3	8.3	6.9	6.4
-50	1.1	2.3	3.6	4.7	5.1	5.7	6.3	6.8	7.2	7.6	7.4	7.3	6.4	6.4
-75	5.8	6.2	6.6	7.0	7.2	7.3	7.4	7.6	7.7	7.6	7.4	6.4	6.4	6.4
-100	8.4	8.7	9.0	9.3	9.4	9.5	9.5	9.7	9.1	8.5	8.1	6.8	6.4	6.4
-125	9.6	9.9	10.2	10.5	10.6	10.5	10.3	10.3	9.0	8.1	7.8	6.7	6.4	6.4

weeks to expiration — net profit area, in cents

The estimated credit is: -41.5¢ premium + 24.7¢ premium + 24.7¢ premium - 1.5¢ comm. = +6.4¢

TABLE (lower left) — changes in the soybean future's price in 25¢ increments

	35	30	25	20	18	16	14	12	10	8	6	4	2	0
+125	-2.2	-1.9	-1.6	-1.3	-1.2	-0.9	-0.9	-0.8	-1.1	-1.6	-2.1	-3.6	-4.7	-5.5
+100	-1.5	-0.9	-0.3	0.3	0.7	1.0	1.3	1.7	2.2	2.6	3.1	3.4	-0.1	-5.5
+75	0.9	2.1	3.5	5.1	6.1	7.1	8.0	9.0	10.3	11.9	14.1	16.7	18.3	19.5
+50	—	—	—	—	—	—	—	—	—	—	—	33.7	44.5	44.5
+25	—	—	—	—	—	—	—	—	—	—	—	18.7	19.5	19.5
0	—	—	—	—	—	—	—	—	-5.3	-5.1	-5.2	-5.5	-5.5	-5.5
-25	-1.6	-1.3	-1.0	-0.9	-0.9	-0.9	-0.8	-1.1	-1.6	-2.1	-3.6	-4.7	-4.7	-5.5
-50	-3.8	-3.6	-3.5	-3.5	-3.5	-3.6	-3.7	-3.9	-4.3	-4.8	-5.1	-5.5	-5.5	-5.5
-75	-4.2	-4.4	-4.3	-4.4	-4.5	-4.6	-4.7	-4.9	-5.1	-5.3	-5.5	-5.5	-5.5	-5.5
-100	-4.3	-4.3	-4.4	-4.5	-4.6	-4.8	-5.0	-5.1	-5.4	-5.5	-5.5	-5.5	-5.5	-5.5
-125	-4.4	-4.5	-4.6	-4.7	-4.8	-4.9	-5.1	-5.3	-5.4	-5.5	-5.5	-5.5	-5.5	-5.5

net profit

The estimated cost is: -24.3¢ premium + 10.0¢ premium + 10.0¢ premium - 1.5¢ comm. = -5.5¢

Wm Grandmill (1985) Ltd.

SELL A STRADDLE

SELL A CALL AT THE MONEY and SELL A PUT AT THE MONEY

35 weeks to expiration

Table (credit +153.2¢)

changes in the soybean future's price in 25¢ increments	weeks to expiration 35	30	25	20	18	16	14	12	10	8	6	4	2	0
+125	-41.5	-35.2	-27.1	-16.6	-11.8	-6.9	-2.2	2.6	8.0	14.1	19.6	23.9	27.7	28.2
+100	-26.8	-20.2	-11.9	-1.0	3.9	9.1	14.2	20.0	26.2	32.5	39.5	46.0	51.5	53.2
+75	-12.4	-5.8	2.5	13.0	17.8	22.9	28.1	33.8	40.1	47.4	55.5	66.0	75.9	78.2
+50	-4.3	2.2	10.7	21.2	26.2	31.5	36.9	43.3	50.4	58.4	68.3	81.2	96.3	103.2
+25	-2.4	4.3	13.0	24.2	29.4	35.3	41.3	48.0	55.8	64.6	75.7	91.8	112.6	128.2
0	-1.0	6.4	15.0	25.6	30.6	36.2	42.0	48.8	56.8	66.2	78.0	95.2	118.6	153.2
-25	-2.4	4.3	13.0	24.2	29.4	35.3	41.3	48.0	55.8	64.6	75.7	91.8	112.6	128.2
-50	-4.3	2.2	10.7	21.2	26.2	31.5	36.9	43.3	50.4	58.4	68.3	81.2	96.3	103.2
-75	-12.4	-5.8	2.5	13.0	17.8	22.9	28.1	33.8	40.1	47.4	55.5	66.0	75.9	78.2
-100	-26.8	-20.2	-11.9	-1.0	3.9	9.1	14.2	20.0	26.2	32.5	39.5	46.0	51.5	53.2
-125	-41.5	-35.2	-27.1	-16.6	-11.8	-6.9	-2.2	2.6	8.0	14.1	19.6	23.9	27.7	28.2

The estimated credit is: +77.1¢ premium +77.1¢ premium - 1.0¢ comm. = +153.2¢

net profit area , in cents

Table (credit +117.8¢)

changes in the soybean future's price in 25¢ increments	35	30	25	20	18	16	14	12	10	8	6	4	2	0
+125	-43.7	-39.2	-34.2	-28.7	-26.1	-23.2	-20.5	-17.7	-15.4	-13.4	-11.4	-9.0	-7.3	-7.2
+100	-28.5	-23.0	-17.1	-10.6	-7.8	-4.7	-1.4	1.6	4.5	7.5	10.8	14.3	17.4	17.8
+75	-14.3	-9.1	-3.3	6.3	9.7	12.9	16.7	20.9	25.6	30.8	37.1	42.0	42.8	42.8
+50	-5.9	-0.3	3.2	13.2	16.7	20.3	24.2	28.7	33.7	39.5	46.3	54.9	64.8	67.8
+25	-1.7	3.9	10.7	18.6	22.3	26.3	30.7	35.5	41.3	48.2	56.6	68.6	83.7	92.8
0	-1.0	4.6	11.4	19.4	23.4	27.8	32.2	37.4	43.6	51.0	60.0	73.2	91.2	117.8
-25	-1.7	3.9	10.7	18.6	22.3	26.3	30.7	35.5	41.3	48.2	56.6	68.6	83.7	92.8
-50	-5.9	-0.3	3.2	13.2	16.7	20.3	24.2	28.7	33.7	39.5	46.3	54.9	64.8	67.8
-75	-14.3	-9.1	-3.3	6.3	9.7	12.9	16.7	20.9	25.6	30.8	37.1	42.0	42.8	42.8
-100	-28.5	-23.0	-17.1	-10.6	-7.8	-4.7	-1.4	1.6	4.5	7.5	10.8	14.3	17.4	17.8
-125	-43.7	-39.2	-34.2	-28.7	-26.1	-23.2	-20.5	-17.7	-15.4	-13.4	-11.4	-9.0	-7.3	-7.2

The estimated credit is: +59.4¢ premium +59.4¢ premium - 1.0¢ comm. = +117.8¢

net profit area , in cents

Table (credit +82.0¢)

changes in the soybean future's price in 25¢ increments	weeks to expiration 35	30	25	20	18	16	14	12	10	8	6	4	2	0
+125	-54.8	-53.0	-51.3	-49.7	-49.0	-48.3	-47.7	-46.9	-46.1	-45.2	-44.3	-43.3	-43.0	-43.0
+100	-35.8	-33.6	-31.4	-29.2	-28.1	-27.0	-25.8	-24.7	-23.4	-22.0	-20.6	-19.1	-18.0	-18.0
+75	-21.4	-18.4	-15.2	-11.4	-9.9	-8.1	-6.3	-4.3	-2.1	0.3	2.8	5.4	7.0	7.0
+50	-9.0	-5.8	-2.4	2.0	4.1	6.4	8.7	11.2	14.1	17.6	21.5	26.8	31.4	32.0
+25	-3.3	0.8	5.1	10.4	13.0	15.7	18.8	22.1	25.9	30.0	36.2	44.0	50.6	57.0
0	-1.0	2.8	7.4	13.0	15.8	18.8	22.0	25.6	30.0	35.0	41.4	50.6	63.2	82.0
-25	-3.3	0.8	5.1	10.4	13.0	15.7	18.8	22.1	25.9	30.0	36.2	44.0	50.6	57.0
-50	-9.0	-5.8	-2.4	2.0	4.1	6.4	8.7	11.2	14.1	17.6	21.5	26.8	31.4	32.0
-75	-21.4	-18.4	-15.2	-11.4	-9.9	-8.1	-6.3	-4.3	-2.1	0.3	2.8	5.4	7.0	7.0
-100	-35.8	-33.6	-31.4	-29.2	-28.1	-27.0	-25.8	-24.7	-23.4	-22.0	-20.6	-19.1	-18.0	-18.0
-125	-54.8	-53.0	-51.3	-49.7	-49.0	-48.3	-47.7	-46.9	-46.1	-45.2	-44.3	-43.3	-43.0	-43.0

The estimated credit is: +41.5¢ premium +41.5¢ premium - 1.0 comm. = +82.0¢

net profit area , in cents

Table (credit +47.0¢)

changes in the soybean future's price in 25¢ increments	35	30	25	20	18	16	14	12	10	8	6	4	2	0
+125	-80.3	-80.0	-79.6	-79.2	-79.0	-78.7	-78.5	-78.4	-78.2	-78.1	-78.0	-78.0	-78.0	-78.0
+100	-57.0	-56.6	-56.1	-55.5	-55.2	-54.9	-54.6	-54.3	-53.9	-53.5	-53.1	-53.0	-53.0	-53.0
+75	-34.9	-33.9	-33.0	-32.0	-31.4	-30.8	-30.3	-29.8	-29.3	-28.9	-28.3	-28.0	-28.0	-28.0
+50	-18.1	-16.6	-14.9	-13.0	-12.0	-10.9	-9.9	-8.8	-7.5	-6.2	-4.7	-3.5	-3.0	-3.0
+25	-5.3	-3.2	-0.7	1.9	3.3	5.0	6.5	8.2	10.2	12.6	15.4	18.8	21.5	22.0
0	-1.0	1.4	4.2	7.4	9.0	10.8	12.6	14.6	17.2	20.0	23.6	29.0	36.2	47.0
-25	-5.3	-3.2	-0.7	1.9	3.3	5.0	6.5	8.2	10.2	12.6	15.4	18.8	21.5	22.0
-50	-18.1	-16.6	-14.9	-13.0	-12.0	-10.9	-9.9	-8.8	-7.5	-6.2	-4.7	-3.5	-3.0	-3.0
-75	-34.9	-33.9	-33.0	-32.0	-31.4	-30.8	-30.3	-29.8	-29.3	-28.9	-28.3	-28.0	-28.0	-28.0
-100	-57.0	-56.6	-56.1	-55.5	-55.2	-54.9	-54.6	-54.3	-53.9	-53.5	-53.1	-53.0	-53.0	-53.0
-125	-80.3	-80.0	-79.6	-79.2	-79.0	-78.7	-78.5	-78.4	-78.2	-78.1	-78.0	-78.0	-78.0	-78.0

The estimated credit is: +24.0¢ premium +24.0¢ premium - 1.0¢ comm. = +47.0¢

net profit area

Wm Grandmill (1985) Ltd.

SELL A STRANGLE – #1

SELL A CALL AT 50¢ OUT OF THE MONEY and SELL A PUT AT 50¢ OUT OF THE MONEY

weeks to expiration

35

TABLE 0

changes in the soybean future's price in 25¢ increments

net profit area , in cents — weeks to expiration

changes	35	30	25	20	18	16	14	12	10	8	6	4	2	0
+125	-18.9	-12.6	-5.1	4.2	8.1	12.2	16.2	20.4	24.6	28.6	32.5	36.6	39.9	40.0
+100	-13.1	-7.2	0.1	9.4	13.9	18.5	23.6	28.9	34.6	40.4	47.0	55.2	63.3	65.0
+75	-11.0	-5.3	2.9	13.7	18.7	24.2	29.6	35.4	42.2	49.1	57.6	69.3	83.0	90.0
+50	-8.0	-1.6	6.4	16.8	21.7	27.1	32.8	39.3	46.8	55.3	65.5	79.2	96.0	115.0
+25	-5.7	0.8	8.9	19.4	24.4	29.8	35.6	42.2	49.8	58.9	69.9	85.4	103.7	115.0
0	-1.0	5.4	13.8	24.2	29.2	34.6	40.2	46.8	54.2	62.6	73.2	87.2	104.6	115.0
-25	-5.7	0.8	8.9	19.4	24.4	29.8	35.6	42.2	49.8	58.9	69.9	85.4	103.7	115.0
-50	-8.0	-1.6	6.4	16.8	21.7	27.1	32.8	39.3	46.8	55.3	65.5	79.2	96.0	115.0
-75	-11.0	-5.3	2.9	13.7	18.7	24.2	29.6	35.4	42.2	49.1	57.6	69.3	83.0	90.0
-100	-13.1	-7.2	0.1	9.4	13.9	18.5	23.6	28.9	34.6	40.4	47.0	55.2	63.3	65.0
-125	-18.9	-12.6	-5.1	4.2	8.1	12.2	16.2	20.4	24.6	28.6	32.5	36.6	39.9	40.0

The estimated credit is: + 58.0¢ premium + 58.0¢ premium - 1.0¢ comm. = + 115.0¢

TABLE 8

changes in the soybean future's price in 25¢ increments

net profit area

changes	35	30	25	20	18	16	14	12	10	8	6	4	2	0
+125	-24.7	-21.2	-17.2	-12.8	-10.9	-8.8	-6.8	-4.6	-2.3	0.2	2.8	5.1	5.8	5.8
+100	-17.8	-13.0	-7.9	-2.6	-0.1	2.7	5.8	9.0	12.5	16.4	20.9	25.9	30.3	30.8
+75	-11.8	-6.4	-0.5	6.2	9.2	12.5	16.0	19.8	24.2	29.3	35.3	43.5	52.1	55.8
+50	-9.2	-3.4	3.2	10.8	14.4	18.3	22.4	26.9	32.1	38.0	45.2	55.0	67.1	80.8
+25	-6.5	-0.6	6.1	13.8	17.6	21.8	26.1	31.0	36.7	43.5	51.4	62.1	74.5	80.8
0	-1.0	4.2	10.6	18.2	21.8	25.6	29.6	34.4	39.8	46.2	53.2	63.4	75.8	80.8
-25	-6.5	-0.6	6.1	13.8	17.6	21.8	26.1	31.0	36.7	43.5	51.4	62.1	74.5	80.8
-50	-9.2	-3.4	3.2	10.8	14.4	18.3	22.4	26.9	32.1	38.0	45.2	55.0	67.1	80.8
-75	-11.8	-6.4	-0.5	6.2	9.2	12.5	16.0	19.8	24.2	29.3	35.3	43.5	52.1	55.8
-100	-17.8	-13.0	-7.9	-2.6	-0.1	2.7	5.8	9.0	12.5	16.4	20.9	25.9	30.3	30.8
-125	-24.7	-21.2	-17.2	-12.8	-10.9	-8.8	-6.8	-4.6	-2.3	0.2	2.8	5.1	5.8	5.8

The estimated credit is: +40.0¢ premium + 40.0¢ premium - 1.0¢ comm. = + 80.8¢

TABLE 4

changes in the soybean future's price in 25¢ increments

net profit area , in cents — weeks to expiration

changes	35	30	25	20	18	16	14	12	10	8	6	4	2	0
+125	-38.5	-36.5	-34.5	-32.5	-31.6	-30.7	-29.9	-29.2	-28.5	-27.7	-27.0	-26.6	-26.6	-26.6
+100	-25.8	-23.0	-20.3	-17.2	-15.6	-13.9	-12.3	-10.5	-8.7	-6.9	-5.1	-2.7	-1.7	-1.6
+75	-15.0	-11.8	-8.5	-4.6	-2.6	-0.7	1.4	3.8	6.5	9.7	13.1	17.8	22.0	23.4
+50	-8.1	-4.6	-0.6	3.9	6.1	8.5	11.1	13.8	17.1	20.9	25.4	31.6	39.0	48.4
+25	-4.0	-0.3	3.9	9.1	11.6	14.3	17.1	20.2	23.6	27.9	32.7	39.1	46.3	48.4
0	-1.0	3.0	7.2	11.8	14.2	16.6	19.2	22.0	25.2	29.2	33.8	40.2	47.4	48.4
-25	-4.0	-0.3	3.9	9.1	11.6	14.3	17.1	20.2	23.6	27.9	32.7	39.1	46.3	48.4
-50	-8.1	-4.6	-0.6	3.9	6.1	8.5	11.1	13.8	17.1	20.9	25.4	31.6	39.0	48.4
-75	-15.0	-11.8	-8.5	-4.6	-2.6	-0.7	1.4	3.8	6.5	9.7	13.1	17.8	22.0	23.4
-100	-25.8	-23.0	-20.3	-17.2	-15.6	-13.9	-12.3	-10.5	-8.7	-6.9	-5.1	-2.7	-1.7	-1.6
-125	-38.5	-36.5	-34.5	-32.5	-31.6	-30.7	-29.9	-29.2	-28.5	-27.7	-27.0	-26.6	-26.6	-26.6

The estimated credit is: +24.7¢ premium + 24.7¢ premium - 1.0¢ comm. = +48.4¢

TABLE 2

changes in the soybean future's price in 25¢ increments

net profit area

changes	35	30	25	20	18	16	14	12	10	8	6	4	2	0
+125	-57.8	-57.3	-56.8	-56.5	-56.3	-56.2	-56.1	-56.1	-56.0	-56.0	-56.0	-56.0	-56.0	-56.0
+100	-37.4	-36.5	-35.5	-34.4	-33.9	-33.3	-32.8	-32.4	-31.9	-31.6	-31.3	-31.1	-31.0	-31.0
+75	-20.3	-19.0	-17.4	-15.8	-14.9	-13.9	-12.1	-11.0	-9.8	-8.6	-7.3	-6.4	-6.0	-6.0
+50	-9.0	-7.5	-5.5	-3.3	-2.2	-1.0	0.2	1.5	3.2	5.0	7.2	10.0	13.6	19.0
+25	-2.3	-0.5	1.6	3.9	5.1	6.5	7.8	9.2	10.7	12.4	14.7	17.1	18.2	19.0
0	-1.0	0.8	2.8	5.0	6.2	7.4	8.6	10.0	11.8	13.6	16.2	18.2	19.0	19.0
-25	-2.3	-0.5	1.6	3.9	5.1	6.5	7.8	9.2	10.7	12.4	14.7	17.1	18.2	19.0
-50	-9.0	-7.5	-5.5	-3.3	-2.2	-1.0	0.2	1.5	3.2	5.0	7.2	10.0	13.6	19.0
-75	-20.3	-19.0	-17.4	-15.8	-14.9	-13.9	-12.1	-11.0	-9.8	-8.6	-7.3	-6.4	-6.0	-6.0
-100	-37.4	-36.5	-35.5	-34.4	-33.9	-33.3	-32.8	-32.4	-31.9	-31.6	-31.3	-31.1	-31.0	-31.0
-125	-57.8	-57.3	-56.8	-56.5	-56.3	-56.2	-56.1	-56.1	-56.0	-56.0	-56.0	-56.0	-56.0	-56.0

The estimated credit is: + 10.0¢ premium + 10.0¢ premium - 1.0¢ comm. = + 19.0¢

Wm Grandmill (1985) Ltd.

SELL A STRANGLE – #2

SELL A CALL AT $1.00 OUT OF THE MONEY and SELL A PUT AT $1.00 OUT OF THE MONEY

35 weeks to expiration

TABLE 0 — 35 weeks to expiration

changes in the soybean future's price in 25¢ increments

	35	30	25	20	18	16	14	12	10	8	6	4	2	0
+125	-2.5	1.5	6.8	13.7	16.8	20.3	23.8	27.5	31.6	36.0	41.5	49.4	59.3	65.8
+100	0.8	6.8	13.4	20.9	24.3	28.0	31.8	36.1	40.8	46.0	52.6	61.5	73.5	90.8
+75	1.8	8.0	15.3	24.6	28.7	33.1	37.7	42.8	48.5	54.1	61.9	73.5	85.6	90.8
+50	4.2	10.0	17.2	26.4	30.9	35.6	40.9	46.5	52.4	58.6	65.9	75.2	85.6	90.8
+25	-0.3	5.2	12.8	22.9	27.7	32.7	37.9	43.6	49.9	57.4	65.8	76.9	88.1	90.8
0	-1.0	4.4	11.8	22.0	26.8	32.0	37.6	43.8	50.8	58.4	67.0	77.2	87.4	90.8
-25	-0.3	5.2	12.8	22.9	27.7	32.7	37.9	43.6	49.9	57.4	65.8	76.9	88.1	90.8
-50	4.2	10.0	17.2	26.4	30.9	35.6	40.9	46.5	52.4	58.6	65.9	75.2	85.6	90.8
-75	1.8	8.0	15.3	24.6	28.7	33.1	37.7	42.8	48.5	54.1	60.9	70.0	81.7	90.8
-100	0.8	6.8	13.4	20.9	24.3	28.0	31.8	36.1	40.8	46.0	52.6	61.5	73.5	90.8
-125	-2.5	1.5	6.8	13.7	16.8	20.3	23.8	27.5	31.6	36.0	41.5	49.4	59.3	65.8

weeks to expiration — net profit area, in cents

The estimated credit is: +45.9¢ premium +45.9¢ premium -1.0¢ comm. = +90.8¢

TABLE 0 — 30 weeks

changes in the soybean future's price in 25¢ increments

	35	30	25	20	18	16	14	12	10	8	6	4	2	0
+125	-12.8	-9.1	-5.2	-0.8	1.3	3.4	5.7	8.2	11.4	14.9	18.9	24.7	31.6	35.2
+100	-5.2	-1.4	3.0	7.9	10.3	12.9	15.4	18.6	22.3	26.4	31.3	37.9	46.9	60.2
+75	-0.5	3.7	8.6	14.2	16.8	19.7	22.8	26.1	29.9	34.5	39.8	46.5	54.7	60.2
+50	3.5	7.9	13.1	16.8	21.4	24.4	27.6	31.1	35.0	39.5	44.5	50.8	57.7	60.2
+25	-0.5	3.7	8.6	17.8	20.9	24.4	27.8	31.7	36.0	41.0	46.5	53.4	59.3	60.2
0	-1.0	5.0	11.4	18.6	21.8	25.2	29.0	32.8	37.0	41.4	46.8	53.2	59.4	60.2
-25	0.3	5.5	11.3	17.8	20.9	24.4	27.8	31.7	36.0	41.0	46.5	53.4	59.3	60.2
-50	3.5	7.9	13.1	18.8	21.4	24.4	27.6	31.1	35.0	39.5	44.5	50.8	57.7	60.2
-75	-0.5	3.7	8.6	14.2	16.8	19.7	22.8	26.1	29.9	34.5	39.8	46.5	54.7	60.2
-100	-5.2	-1.4	3.0	7.9	10.3	12.9	15.4	18.6	22.3	26.4	31.3	37.9	46.9	60.2
-125	-12.8	-9.1	-5.2	-0.8	1.3	3.4	5.7	8.2	11.4	14.9	18.9	24.7	31.6	35.2

weeks to expiration — net profit area, in cents

The estimated credit is: +30.0¢ premium +30.0¢ premium -1.0¢ comm. = +60.2¢

TABLE 4 weeks

changes in the soybean future's price in 25¢ increments

	35	30	25	20	18	16	14	12	10	8	6	4	2	0
+125	-24.9	-22.6	-20.4	-17.6	-16.2	-14.9	-13.3	-11.7	-9.8	-7.5	-4.9	-1.3	2.6	4.0
+100	-14.3	-12.1	-9.5	-6.2	-4.6	-2.9	-1.2	0.7	2.9	5.5	8.7	13.3	19.6	29.0
+75	-6.9	-4.2	-1.2	2.4	4.1	5.9	7.7	9.5	11.5	14.1	17.1	21.3	26.9	29.0
+50	-1.5	1.3	4.5	8.3	10.2	12.1	13.9	16.1	18.4	21.4	24.9	28.5	29.0	29.0
+25	-2.6	0.4	6.8	10.6	12.4	14.4	16.2	18.4	21.0	23.8	27.1	29.0	29.0	29.0
0	-1.0	2.2	5.6	9.0	10.5	12.4	13.9	16.6	18.9	21.4	23.6	26.8	29.0	29.0
-25	-1.5	1.3	4.5	8.3	10.2	12.1	14.5	16.1	18.4	21.1	23.8	27.1	29.0	29.0
-50	-2.6	0.4	3.5	6.8	8.7	10.5	12.4	14.5	16.9	18.9	21.4	24.9	28.5	29.0
-75	-6.9	-4.2	-1.2	2.4	4.1	5.9	7.7	9.5	11.5	14.1	17.1	21.4	26.9	29.0
-100	-14.3	-12.1	-9.5	-6.2	-4.6	-2.9	-1.2	0.7	2.9	5.5	8.7	13.3	19.6	29.0
-125	-24.9	-22.6	-20.4	-17.6	-16.2	-14.9	-13.3	-11.7	-9.8	-7.5	-4.9	-1.3	2.6	4.0

weeks to expiration — net profit area, in cents

The estimated credit is: +15.0¢ premium +15.0¢ premium -1.0¢ comm. = +29.0¢

TABLE 2 weeks

changes in the soybean future's price in 25¢ increments

	35	30	25	20	18	16	14	12	10	8	6	4	2	0
+125	-30.1	-29.1	-27.8	-26.6	-26.0	-25.2	-24.5	-23.7	-22.8	-21.7	-20.6	-19.3	-18.4	-18.0
+100	-17.3	-16.0	-14.5	-12.8	-12.0	-11.1	-10.2	-9.2	-7.9	-6.5	-4.7	-2.0	1.6	7.0
+75	-9.0	-7.7	-6.1	-4.6	-3.7	-2.8	-2.0	-1.1	0.0	1.3	3.0	5.1	6.2	7.0
+50	-4.3	-3.1	-1.8	-0.4	0.3	1.0	1.7	2.5	3.4	4.3	5.6	6.6	7.0	7.0
+25	-1.3	-0.3	0.9	2.2	2.9	3.6	4.3	4.9	5.5	6.1	6.7	7.0	7.0	7.0
0	-1.0	-0.4	0.8	2.0	2.6	3.2	3.8	4.4	5.2	6.0	6.8	7.0	7.0	7.0
-25	-1.3	-0.3	0.9	2.2	2.9	3.6	4.3	4.9	5.5	6.1	6.7	7.0	7.0	7.0
-50	-4.3	-3.1	-1.8	-0.4	0.3	1.0	1.7	2.5	3.4	4.3	5.6	6.6	7.0	7.0
-75	-9.0	-7.7	-6.1	-4.6	-3.7	-2.8	-2.0	-1.1	0.0	1.3	3.0	5.1	6.2	7.0
-100	-17.3	-16.0	-14.5	-12.8	-12.0	-11.1	-10.2	-9.2	-7.9	-6.5	-4.7	-2.0	1.6	7.0
-125	-30.1	-29.1	-27.8	-26.6	-26.0	-25.2	-24.5	-23.7	-22.8	-21.7	-20.6	-19.3	-18.4	-18.0

weeks to expiration — net profit area, in cents

The estimated credit is: +4.0¢ premium +4.0¢ premium -1.0¢ comm. = +7.0¢

Wm Grandmill (1985) Ltd.

188

PART IV

THE SAFETY CHARTS

How safe is your money?

WHY and HOW THE SAFETY CHARTS WERE MADE

WHY

So far we have learned that each of the 9 option positions outlined in this book is best suited for certain conditions.   For example, a long call option is best used in the short term when volatility is moderate or low.   Whereas, a strangle works best in the long or medium term when volatility is higher than average.

So far we have also seen the size of the net profit areas for different degrees of volatility and time.

We have also learned that safety is just as important as the profit.   This book urges that the safety of one's working capital be protected at all times because, if one loses his working capital, then he is out of the game.

But how is safety to be defined?   How safe should an option trade be? We know that the greater the risk, the greater the potential profit.   Therefore, if we opt for safety, then we must be satisfied with a smaller profit.

Where does this book stand?   Does it stand exactly halfway between extreme risk and extreme safety?   No - not quite, not exactly halfway.   This book leans a bit toward safety. One could say that the recommendations from this book are comprised of 60% safety and 40% risk.

This brings us to the charts in this section.   The charts here were designed to give you some idea of just how safe an option should be under the different variations of volatility, time and price.

Each option's estimated safety will be displayed for Tables 80,60,40, and 20 (representing different degrees of volatility). If you need the information for a table different from the four tables mentioned, then you must interpolate.

The charts for "buying a call or a put" are a bit different. They show when the call or put will make a profit and when it could lose money.

HOW

A small safety zone was built into each of the safety charts to keep you from a temporary loss due to price fluctuations.   Prices never move in a smooth line.   A upward trend, for example, will be a zig-zag pattern but with the average of the move trending upward.

The amount or size of the price fluctuations is caused mainly by the volatility rate, and to a lesser extent by the time period of the option i.e. long term or short term.

Price fluctuations themselves are caused by rumors, news, or some event which can influence prices.   Often a rumor will cause prices to move up today only to subside tomorrow.   But, in the meantime, much damage has been done to those traders who held a close up stop price - they are out of the market.

A typical rumor which always causes a price fluctuation is the rumor that the Russians will not be buying U.S. beans or meal but will buy from Brazil instead.   So the market reacts but will settle back about 3 days later. Often these rumors are false   A typical news item goes like this,"Mr. X, a well known weather forecaster, says that there will be a long,dry period in July ".

That kind of news is always good for a hefty price move. But, sometimes a few days later, a news item will appear on the news wire which says something like this, " The National Weather Service's long range forecast expects normal weather for the month of July ". Another price reaction. The summer months are prone to weather rumors.

A high volatility rate causes greater price fluctuations than does a low volatility rate. Also a long term, like 36 weeks to expiration, has more opprotunity for price fluctuations than does a short term, like 6 weeks.

A study of past price behavior was made to try to estimate the amount of a price fluctuation based on the volatility of the time, and for the long and short term. Below you see a table which contains the estimated price fluctuations under a variety of conditions. These amounts were incorporated into the safety charts so that , when you consulted the charts, you would get an indication of how safe the trade was, with the price fluctuations included.

wks to exp.	Tables 80	60	40	20
36	50¢	40¢	30¢	20¢
30	50¢	40¢	30¢	20¢
20	40¢	30¢	25¢	15¢
10	30¢	20¢	15¢	10¢
4	25¢	15¢	10¢	5¢

Example

If you bought a call at 30 weeks to expiration and if you were using Table 60 (moderately high volatility), you would pay a premium of about 57. 1¢ for the call. Therefore if prices rise by 57. 1¢, you would break even, no profit or loss at that point. But fluctuating prices could go against you by as much as 40¢ (see the chart above) and it means that you could lose money at the break even point just from fluctuating prices. Therefore the profit chart for buying a call has a built-in safety zone of 40¢ at that point for your protection against an unexpected loss. In other words, the profit chart in this section for buying a call will use a new break-even point of 97. 1¢ (57. 1¢ for the normal break-even point , plus the 40¢ safety zone). Do this. Look now at the "buy a call at the money" chart for Table 60. Look at the junction of "30 weeks to expiration" and the column of a 100¢ price change (i.e. 97. 1¢) and you see the word NO - which means,"do not take this call position because you could lose money". Now look at the junction of 30 weeks and a 110¢ price change, and you see the letter F. Look at the bottom of the chart and you see that "F" means a fair profit can be made here. You can see that the 40¢ injected into the Table 60 call in this example,is added protection from those annoying price fluctuations which can normally turn a borderline profit into a loss. To sum up ; you can use these safety tables as a tool to help you to decide which option position you would use - using the safety of your working capital and a moderate profit as your goal.

Another Example

A different chart will be used for this example. Let's say that you believe that soybean prices are going to rise in the weeks ahead. You decide to "Sell a put at 50¢ out of the money ".   The Forecasting Graphs indicate that prices could rise by 60¢.   The time to expiration is 14 weeks.   <u>Is it safe to do this trade?</u>

That's the question that you want an answer to.   Let's say that the volatility is Table 60. <u>Do this.</u>   Turn to the " Sell a call or a put at 50¢ out of the money " Table 60 chart in the pages just ahead.   Look at the junction of the 14 row and the 60¢ price change column.   You see a " VS " which means " Very Safe ".   If you have got the market direction right, then don't miss this one !

That is how the safety charts were constructed with a built- in safety zone.   In the pages just ahead each of the 9 options and its chart will be explained.

BUY A CALL OR A PUT - AT THE MONEY

Even though this is the most popular option, especially among those who are trading options for the first time, it is among the least profitable of options.

Look at the chart. You will need a large price change to earn a profit, except in the short term. Look at the 18th week row. According to this chart you will need a price move of over 80¢ just to earn only a "Fair" profit - likely less than 100%.

You will remember that one of our safety rules is to take a position only if one can earn a 100% profit or better.

BUY A CALL OR A PUT - AT 50¢ OUT OF THE MONEY

This option position is the least useful of all the 9 option positions which are outlined in this book.

Look at the profit chart and you will see that there is not much opportunity to make money here.

This position is superior to the " at the money " position above only when there is likely to be a large price change - like $1.50 for example.

SELL A CALL OR A PUT - AT THE MONEY

This is a nice, profitable option. Look at the safety chart. The secret of success here is to get the market direction right - and, if you do that, your success is almost assured.

You will remember that one should sell a call only if one expects prices to fall. And to sell a put when prices are expected to rise.

Those R's which you see at the front of the safety chart will remind you that the riskiest part of the option occurrs when there is little or no price movement. But with a normal price change, one should have no difficulty trading in the area of S's and VS's.

WHAT ARE MY CHANCES
FOR A GOOD PROFIT?

BUY A CALL or BUY A PUT

AT THE MONEY

wks to expir

	0¢	10	20	30	40	50	60	70	80	90	100	110	120
36	NO	NO	NO	NO	NO	NO	NO	NO	NO	NO	NO	F	F
34	NO	NO	NO	NO	NO	NO	NO	NO	NO	NO	NO	F	F
32	NO	NO	NO	NO	NO	NO	NO	NO	NO	NO	NO	F	F
30	NO	NO	NO	NO	NO	NO	NO	NO	NO	NO	NO	F	F
28	NO	NO	NO	NO	NO	NO	NO	NO	NO	NO	F	F	F
26	NO	NO	NO	NO	NO	NO	NO	NO	NO	NO	F	F	F
24	NO	NO	NO	NO	NO	NO	NO	NO	NO	F	F	F	F
22	NO	NO	NO	NO	NO	NO	NO	NO	NO	F	F	F	F
20	NO	NO	NO	NO	NO	NO	NO	NO	NO	F	F	F	F
18	NO	NO	NO	NO	NO	NO	NO	NO	NO	F	F	F	F
16	NO	NO	NO	NO	NO	NO	NO	NO	NO	F	F	F	G
14	NO	NO	NO	NO	NO	NO	NO	NO	F	F	F	G	G
12	NO	NO	NO	NO	NO	NO	NO	NO	F	F	F	G	G
10	NO	NO	NO	NO	NO	NO	NO	F	F	F	G	G	G
8	NO	NO	NO	NO	NO	NO	NO	F	F	G	G	G	E
6	NO	NO	NO	NO	NO	NO	F	F	G	G	G	E	E
4	NO	NO	NO	NO	NO	F	F	G	G	E	E	E	E

T A B L E 6 0

changes in the soybean future's price in 10¢ increments

Provided that you get the market direction right, then...

NO = don't take it, could lose money

F = fair profit, up to about 100%

G = good profit

E = excellent profit, the best

WHAT ARE MY CHANCES
FOR A GOOD PROFIT?

BUY A CALL or BUY A PUT

AT 50¢ OUT OF THE MONEY

wks to expir

T A B L E 6 0	0¢	10	20	30	40	50	60	70	80	90	100	110	120
36	NO	NO	NO	NO	NO	NO	NO	NO	NO	NO	NO	NO	F
34	NO	NO	NO	NO	NO	NO	NO	NO	NO	NO	NO	NO	F
32	NO	NO	NO	NO	NO	NO	NO	NO	NO	NO	NO	NO	F
30	NO	NO	NO	NO	NO	NO	NO	NO	NO	NO	NO	NO	F
28	NO	NO	NO	NO	NO	NO	NO	NO	NO	NO	NO	NO	F
26	NO	NO	NO	NO	NO	NO	NO	NO	NO	NO	NO	F	F
24	NO	NO	NO	NO	NO	NO	NO	NO	NO	NO	NO	F	F
22	NO	NO	NO	NO	NO	NO	NO	NO	NO	NO	NO	F	F
20	NO	NO	NO	NO	NO	NO	NO	NO	NO	NO	NO	F	F
18	NO	NO	NO	NO	NO	NO	NO	NO	NO	NO	NO	F	F
16	NO	NO	NO	NO	NO	NO	NO	NO	NO	NO	NO	F	F
14	NO	NO	NO	NO	NO	NO	NO	NO	NO	NO	F	F	G
12	NO	NO	NO	NO	NO	NO	NO	NO	NO	NO	F	F	G
10	NO	NO	NO	NO	NO	NO	NO	NO	NO	F	F	G	G
8	NO	NO	NO	NO	NO	NO	NO	NO	NO	F	G	G	E
6	NO	NO	NO	NO	NO	NO	NO	NO	F	G	G	E	E
4	NO	NO	NO	NO	NO	NO	NO	F	G	G	E	E	E

changes in the soybean future's price in 10¢ increments

Provided that you get the market direction right, then...
NO = don't take it, could lose money
F = fair profit, to about 100%
G = good profit
E = excellent profit, the best

SELL A CALL or SELL A PUT

AT THE MONEY

wks to
expir

	0¢	10	20	30	40	50	60	70	80	90	100	110	120
36	R	R	R	R	R	R	S	S	S	S	VS	VS	VS
34	R	R	R	R	R	R	S	S	S	S	VS	VS	VS
32	R	R	R	R	R	R	S	S	S	S	VS	VS	VS
30	R	R	R	R	R	S	S	S	S	VS	VS	VS	VS
28	R	R	R	R	R	S	S	S	S	VS	VS	VS	VS
26	R	R	R	R	R	S	S	S	S	VS	VS	VS	VS
24	R	R	R	R	R	S	S	S	S	VS	VS	VS	VS
22	R	R	R	R	R	S	S	S	S	VS	VS	VS	VS
20	R	R	R	R	S	S	S	S	S	VS	VS	VS	VS
18	R	R	R	R	S	S	S	S	S	VS	VS	VS	BS
16	R	R	R	R	S	S	S	S	S	VS	VS	VS	VS
14	R	R	R	R	S	S	S	S	S	VS	VS	VS	VS
12	R	R	R	S	S	S	S	S	VS	VS	VS	VS	VS
10	R	R	R	S	S	S	S	S	VS	VS	VS	VS	VS
8	R	R	R	S	S	S	S	S	VS	VS	VS	VS	VS
6	R	R	R	S	S	S	S	S	VS	VS	VS	VS	VS
4	R	R	R	S	S	S	S	VS	VS	VS	VS	VS	VS

T A B L E 6 0 (row label at left)

changes in the soybean future's price in 10¢ increments

Provided that you get the market direction right, then...
R = risky, price fluctuations could reduce or eliminate your profit
S = safe, your profit should be protected from price fluctuations
VS = very safe, here your profit is likely safe from any danger.

SELL A CALL OR A PUT - AT 50¢ OUT OF THE MONEY

This is the safest of all the 9 options and it is profitable, too. Look at the safety chart. See all those S's and VS's ! This could turn out to be your favorite option.

You may be wondering why this option is safer than selling a call or a put " at the money ".   The answer is this : you are selling at 50¢ out of the money - so that 50¢ acts as a buffer against a loss.   It's a great safety advantage.   It's almost like running the 100 yard dash and getting a 50 yard headstart.   The profit is naturally less than an "at the money" sale, but it is good.

BULL or BEAR SPREAD #1 - BUY A CALL AT THE MONEY and SELL A CALL AT 25¢ OUT OF MONEY
- BUY A PUT AT THE MONEY and SELL A PUT AT 25¢ OUT OF MONEY

This is a nice spread that is easy on the nerves because you know where you stand with this one - you will either earn about a 15¢ profit or you will lose about 10¢ - and that occurs no matter what the volatility is or whether you are trading long term or short term.

You can see by looking at the safety chart that the first 20¢ price change is the most dangerous place.

BULL or BEAR SPREAD #2 - BUY A CALL AT THE MONEY and SELL 2 CALLS AT 50¢ OUT OF MONEY
- BUY A PUT AT THE MONEY and SELL 2 PUTS AT 50¢ OUT OF MONEY

Look at the safety chart.   Note that the VS's are in the area where there is little or no price change.   But you know that the largest profit is made on the +50 line.   So you may be wondering why the best ratings in the chart are at the 0¢ to 20¢ line.

Well, the answer is this : it is true that the best profits are on the +50 line but this chart is not about profits - it's about safety and the profit is safer at the 0¢ line even though it is a smaller profit.

Note the NO at the 120¢ column.   That means that a too great a price change is worse than a small price change because a large price change will over - shoot the target which is the maximum profit on the +50 line .   This spread loses money with a large price change.

HOW SAFE IS
MY PROFIT?

SELL A CALL or SELL A PUT

AT 50¢ OUT OF THE MONEY

wks to
expir

T A B L E 6 0	wks	0¢	10	20	30	40	50	60	70	80	90	100	110	120
	36	R	S	S	S	S	VS	VS	VS	VS	VS	VS	VS	VS
	34	R	S	S	S	S	VS	VS	VS	VS	VS	VS	VS	VS
	32	R	S	S	S	S	VS	VS	VS	VS	VS	VS	VS	VS
	30	R	S	S	S	S	VS	VS	VS	VS	VS	VS	VS	VS
	28	R	S	S	S	S	VS	VS	VS	VS	VS	VS	VS	VS
	26	R	S	S	S	S	VS	VS	VS	VS	VS	VS	VS	VS
	24	R	S	S	S	S	VS	VS	VS	VS	VS	VS	VS	VS
	22	R	S	S	S	S	VS	VS	VS	VS	VS	VS	VS	VS
	20	R	S	S	S	S	VS	VS	VS	VS	VS	VS	VS	VS
	18	R	S	S	S	S	VS	VS	VS	VS	VS	VS	VS	VS
	16	R	S	S	S	S	VS	VS	VS	VS	VS	VS	VS	VS
	14	R	S	S	S	S	VS	VS	VS	VS	VS	VS	VS	VS
	12	R	S	S	S	S	VS	VS	VS	VS	VS	VS	VS	VS
	10	R	S	S	S	S	VS	VS	VS	VS	VS	VS	VS	VS
	8	R	S	S	S	S	VS	VS	VS	VS	VS	VS	VS	VS
	6	R	S	S	S	S	VS	VS	VS	VS	VS	VS	VS	VS
	4	R	S	S	S	S	VS	VS	VS	VS	VS	VS	VS	VS

changes in the soybean future's price in 10¢ increments

Provided that you get the market direction right, then...
R = risky, price fluctuations could reduce or eliminate your profit
S = safe, your profit should be protected from price fluctuations
VS = very safe, here your profit is likely safe from any danger.

HOW SAFE IS
MY PROFIT?

BULL or BEAR SPREAD – #1

BUY A CALL AT THE MONEY
and SELL A CALL AT 25¢ OUT OF THE MONEY
OR
BUY A PUT AT THE MONEY
and SELL A PUT AT 25¢ OUT OF THE MONEY

wks to expir	0¢	10	20	30	40	50	60	70	80	90	100	110	120
36	NO	NO	R	R	R	R	S	S	S	VS	VS	VS	VS
34	NO	NO	R	R	R	R	S	S	S	VS	VS	VS	VS
32	NO	NO	R	R	R	R	S	S	S	VS	VS	VS	VS
30	NO	NO	R	R	R	R	S	S	S	VS	VS	VS	VS
28	NO	NO	R	R	R	R	S	S	S	VS	VS	VS	VS
26	NO	NO	R	R	R	R	S	S	S	VS	VS	VS	VS
24	NO	NO	R	R	R	R	S	S	S	VS	VS	VS	VS
22	NO	NO	R	R	R	R	S	S	S	VS	VS	VS	VS
20	NO	NO	R	R	R	R	S	S	S	VS	VS	VS	VS
18	NO	NO	R	R	R	R	S	S	S	VS	VS	VS	VS
16	NO	NO	R	R	R	R	S	S	S	VS	VS	VS	VS
14	NO	NO	R	R	R	S	S	S	VS	VS	VS	VS	VS
12	NO	NO	R	R	R	S	S	S	VS	VS	VS	VS	VS
10	NO	NO	R	R	R	S	S	S	VS	VS	VS	VS	VS
8	NO	NO	R	R	S	S	S	VS	VS	VS	VS	VS	VS
6	NO	NO	R	R	S	S	S	VS	VS	VS	VS	VS	VS
4	NO	NO	R	R	S	S	VS	VS	VS	VS	VS	VS	VS

changes in the soybean future's price in 10¢ increments

Provided that you get the market direction right, then...
NO = don't take it, will likely lose money
R = risky, price fluctuations could reduce or eliminate your profit
S = safe, your profit is likely safe from price fluctuations here
VS = very safe, your profit is likely safe from any danger here

One chart will serve all tables because the profit
is about the same for any volatility.

HOW SAFE IS
MY PROFIT?

BULL or BEAR SPREAD – #2

BUY A CALL AT THE MONEY
and SELL 2 CALLS AT 50¢ OUT OF THE MONEY
OR
BUY A PUT AT THE MONEY
and SELL 2 PUTS AT 50¢ OUT OF THE MONEY

wks to expir

	0¢	10	20	30	40	50	60	70	80	90	100	110	120
36	VS	VS	VS	S	S	S	S	R	R	R	R	R	NO
34	VS	VS	VS	S	S	S	S	R	R	R	R	R	NO
32	VS	VS	VS	S	S	S	S	R	R	R	R	R	NO
30	VS	VS	VS	S	S	S	S	R	R	R	R	R	NO
28	VS	VS	VS	S	S	S	S	R	R	R	R	R	NO
26	VS	VS	VS	S	S	S	S	R	R	R	R	R	NO
24	VS	VS	VS	S	S	S	S	R	R	R	R	R	NO
22	VS	VS	VS	S	S	S	S	R	R	R	R	R	NO
20	VS	VS	VS	S	S	S	S	R	R	R	R	R	NO
18	VS	VS	VS	S	S	S	S	R	R	R	R	NO	NO
16	VS	VS	VS	S	S	S	S	R	R	R	R	NO	NO
14	VS	VS	VS	S	S	S	S	R	R	R	R	NO	NO
12	VS	VS	VS	S	S	S	S	R	R	R	R	NO	NO
10	VS	VS	VS	S	S	S	S	R	R	R	R	NO	NO
8	NO	R	R	R	S	S	S	R	R	R	NO	NO	NO
6	NO	NO	R	R	S	S	S	R	R	R	NO	NO	NO
4	NO	NO	R	R	R	S	R	R	R	NO	NO	NO	NO

TABLE 60

changes in the soybean future's price in 10¢ increments

Provided that you get the market direction right, then . . .
NO = don't take it, will likely lose money
R = risky, price fluctuations could reduce or eliminate your profit
S = safe, your profit is likely safe from price fluctuations here
VS = very safe, your profit is likely safe from any danger here

SELL A STRADDLE - SELL A CALL AT THE MONEY and SELL A PUT AT THE MONEY

The best situation here is to take this position when the Forecasting Graphs indicate that there will be little or no price movement, either up or down.

Look at the safety chart and you will see that the VS's are in the area where there is little or no price change. But look at the NO's. See where they are. This is another option which loses money when there is a large price change.

However, this option earns the largest percentage return on the investment of all the 9 options - but only when there is little or no price change.

SELL A STRANGLE #1 - SELL A CALL AT 50¢ OUT OF THE MONEY
- SELL A PUT AT 50¢ OUT OF THE MONEY

This is a reasonably safe option and it earns a good profit. Look at the safety chart. You can see that this option works best with a moderate price change or less. You can also see that it works well in the long term.

This option is much safer than the straddle above because the 50¢ out of the money acts as a safety buffer.

SELL A STRANGLE #2 - SELL A CALL AT $1.00 OUT OF THE MONEY
- SELL A PUT AT $1.00 OUT OF THE MONEY

This is a very safe option. Look at the chart and you will see that about half the chart contains VS's. The profit size, though, is less than the strangle above.

This may be a difficult option to take because it isn't easy to sell a call or a put which is so far out of the money. But if you can get it, your working capital will be safe no matter whether prices will be rising or falling - it makes no difference. You will earn a good moderate profit.

SELL A STRADDLE

SELL A CALL AT THE MONEY
and SELL A PUT AT THE MONEY

wks to expir

T A B L E 6 0	0¢	10	20	30	40	50	60	70	80	90	100	110	120
36	VS	VS	VS	S	S	S	S	R	R	R	R	R	NO
34	VS	VS	VS	S	S	S	S	R	R	R	R	R	NO
32	VS	VS	VS	S	S	S	S	R	R	R	R	R	NO
30	VS	VS	VS	S	S	S	S	R	R	R	R	R	NO
28	VS	VS	VS	S	S	S	S	R	R	R	R	R	NO
26	VS	VS	VS	S	S	S	S	R	R	R	R	R	NO
24	VS	VS	VS	S	S	S	S	R	R	R	R	NO	NO
22	VS	VS	S	S	S	S	S	R	R	R	R	NO	NO
20	VS	VS	S	S	S	S	S	R	R	R	R	NO	NO
18	VS	VS	S	S	S	S	R	R	R	R	NO	NO	NO
16	VS	VS	S	S	S	S	R	R	R	NO	NO	NO	NO
14	VS	VS	S	S	S	R	R	R	R	NO	NO	NO	NO
12	VS	S	S	S	S	R	R	R	NO	NO	NO	NO	NO
10	S	S	S	S	R	R	R	R	NO	NO	NO	NO	NO
8	S	S	S	R	R	R	R	NO	NO	NO	NO	NO	NO
6	S	S	R	R	R	R	NO	NO	NO	NO	NO	NO	NO
4	S	R	R	R	R	NO	NO	NO	NO	NO	NO	NO	NO

changes in the soybean future's price in 10¢ increments

Provided that you get the market direction right, then...
NO = don't take it, will likely lose money
R = risky, price fluctuations could reduce or eliminate your profit
S = safe, your profit is likely safe from price fluctuations here
VS = very safe, your profit is likely safe from any danger here

SELL A STRANGLE – #1

SELL A CALL AT 50¢ OUT OF THE MONEY and SELL A PUT AT 50¢ OUT OF THE MONEY

wks to expir

TABLE 60	0¢	10	20	30	40	50	60	70	80	90	100	110	120
36	VS	VS	VS	VS	VS	S	S	S	S	R	R	R	R
34	VS	VS	VS	VS	VS	S	S	S	S	R	R	R	R
32	VS	VS	VS	VS	VS	S	S	S	S	R	R	R	R
30	VS	VS	VS	VS	VS	S	S	S	S	R	R	R	R
28	VS	VS	VS	VS	VS	S	S	S	S	R	R	R	R
26	VS	VS	VS	VS	VS	S	S	S	S	R	R	R	R
24	VS	VS	VS	VS	S	S	S	S	R	R	R	R	R
22	VS	VS	VS	VS	S	S	S	S	R	R	R	R	NO
20	VS	VS	VS	VS	S	S	S	R	R	R	R	NO	NO
18	VS	VS	VS	S	S	S	S	R	R	R	R	NO	NO
16	VS	VS	VS	S	S	S	S	R	R	R	R	NO	NO
14	VS	VS	VS	S	S	S	R	R	R	R	NO	NO	NO
12	VS	VS	S	S	S	S	R	R	R	R	NO	NO	NO
10	VS	VS	S	S	S	R	R	R	R	NO	NO	NO	NO
8	VS	S	S	S	S	R	R	R	R	NO	NO	NO	NO
6	S	S	S	S	R	R	R	R	NO	NO	NO	NO	NO
4	S	S	S	R	R	R	R	NO	NO	NO	NO	NO	NO

changes in the soybean future's price in 10¢ increments

Provided that you get the market direction right, then...
NO = don't take it, will likely lose money
R = risky, price fluctuations could reduce or eliminate your profit
S = safe, your profit is likely safe from price fluctuations here
VS = very safe, your profit is likely safe from any danger

HOW SAFE IS
MY PROFIT?

SELL A STRANGLE – #2

SELL A CALL AT $1.00 OUT OF THE MONEY
and SELL A PUT AT $1.00 OUT OF THE MONEY

wks to
expir

	0¢	10	20	30	40	50	60	70	80	90	100	110	120
36	VS	VS	VS	VS	VS	VS	VS	VS	VS	S	S	S	S
34	VS	VS	VS	VS	VS	VS	VS	VS	VS	S	S	S	S
32	VS	VS	VS	VS	VS	VS	VS	VS	VS	S	S	S	S
30	VS	VS	VS	VS	VS	VS	VS	VS	S	S	S	S	R
28	VS	VS	VS	VS	VS	VS	VS	VS	S	S	S	S	R
26	VS	VS	VS	VS	VS	VS	VS	VS	S	S	S	R	R
24	VS	VS	VS	VS	VS	VS	VS	S	S	S	S	R	R
22	VS	VS	VS	VS	VS	VS	VS	S	S	S	S	R	R
20	VS	VS	VS	VS	VS	VS	VS	S	S	S	R	R	R
18	VS	VS	VS	VS	VS	VS	VS	S	S	S	R	R	R
16	VS	VS	VS	VS	VS	VS	S	S	S	R	R	R	R
14	VS	VS	VS	VS	VS	VS	S	S	S	R	R	R	R
12	VS	VS	VS	VS	VS	VS	S	S	S	R	R	R	R
10	VS	VS	VS	VS	VS	S	S	S	R	R	R	R	R
8	VS	VS	VS	VS	VS	S	S	S	R	R	R	R	NO
6	VS	VS	VS	VS	S	S	S	S	R	R	R	R	NO
4	VS	VS	VS	S	S	S	S	R	R	R	R	NO	NO

TABLE 60

changes in the soybean future's price in 10¢ increments

Provided that you get the market direction right, then...
NO = don't take it, will likely lose money
R = risky, price fluctuations could reduce or eliminate your profit
S = safe, your profit is likely safe from price fluctuations here
VS = very safe, your profit is likely safe from any danger

IS YOUR OPTION TRADE SAFE?

IS YOUR OPTION CALL GOING TO BE PROFITABLE?

That's what the next few pages will tell you.

(1) You can see if buying a call or buying a put will earn a good profit.

(2) You can see if your option profit will be safe from price fluctuations and dangers.

BUY A CALL or BUY A PUT
AT THE MONEY

WHAT ARE MY CHANCES FOR A GOOD PROFIT?

TABLE 20

wks to expir	0¢	10	20	30	40	50	60	70	80	90	100	110	120
36	NO	NO	NO	NO	F	F	F	G	E	E	E	E	E
34	NO	NO	NO	NO	F	F	F	G	E	E	E	E	E
32	NO	NO	NO	NO	F	F	F	G	E	E	E	E	E
30	NO	NO	NO	NO	F	F	G	G	E	E	E	E	E
28	NO	NO	NO	NO	F	F	G	G	E	E	E	E	E
26	NO	NO	NO	NO	F	F	G	G	E	E	E	E	E
24	NO	NO	NO	NO	F	F	G	E	E	E	E	E	E
22	NO	NO	NO	NO	F	F	G	E	E	E	E	E	E
20	NO	NO	NO	NO	F	G	G	E	E	E	E	E	E
18	NO	NO	NO	NO	F	G	G	E	E	E	E	E	E
16	NO	NO	NO	NO	F	G	G	E	E	E	E	E	E
14	NO	NO	NO	NO	F	G	E	E	E	E	E	E	E
12	NO	NO	NO	NO	F	G	E	E	E	E	E	E	E
10	NO	NO	NO	NO	F	G	E	E	E	E	E	E	E
8	NO	NO	NO	NO	F	G	E	E	E	E	E	E	E
6	NO	NO	NO	NO	F	G	E	E	E	E	E	E	E
4	NO	NO	NO	NO	F	G	E	E	E	E	E	E	E

changes in the soybean future's price in 10¢ increments

Provided that you get the market direction right, then...

NO = don't take it, could lose money
F = fair profit, up to about 100%
G = good profit
E = excellent profit, the best

TABLE 20

wks to expir	0¢	10	20	30	40	50	60	70	80	90	100	110	120
36	NO	NO	NO	NO	NO	NO	NO	F	F	F	F	F	G
34	NO	NO	NO	NO	NO	NO	NO	F	F	F	F	F	G
32	NO	NO	NO	NO	NO	NO	NO	F	F	F	F	G	G
30	NO	NO	NO	NO	NO	NO	NO	F	F	F	F	G	G
28	NO	NO	NO	NO	NO	NO	F	F	F	F	G	G	E
26	NO	NO	NO	NO	NO	NO	F	F	F	F	G	G	E
24	NO	NO	NO	NO	NO	F	F	F	F	G	G	E	E
22	NO	NO	NO	NO	NO	F	F	F	F	G	G	E	E
20	NO	NO	NO	NO	NO	F	F	F	G	G	E	E	E
18	NO	NO	NO	NO	NO	F	F	F	G	G	E	E	E
16	NO	NO	NO	NO	F	F	F	G	G	E	E	E	E
14	NO	NO	NO	NO	F	F	F	G	G	E	E	E	E
12	NO	NO	NO	NO	F	F	G	G	E	E	E	E	E
10	NO	NO	NO	NO	F	F	G	G	E	E	E	E	E
8	NO	NO	NO	F	F	G	G	E	E	E	E	E	E
6	NO	NO	NO	F	F	G	G	E	E	E	E	E	E
4	NO	NO	NO	F	F	G	E	E	E	E	E	E	E

changes in the soybean future's price in 10¢ increments

Wm Grandmill (1985) Ltd.

BUY A CALL or BUY A PUT
AT THE MONEY

WHAT ARE MY CHANCES FOR A GOOD PROFIT?

Provided that you get the market direction right, then....

NO = don't take it, could lose money
F = fair profit, up to about 100%
G = good profit
E = excellent profit, the best

TABLE 60

wks to expir	0¢	10	20	30	40	50	60	70	80	90	100	110	120
36	NO	NO	NO	NO	NO	NO	NO	NO	NO	NO	NO	F	F
34	NO	NO	NO	NO	NO	NO	NO	NO	NO	NO	F	F	F
32	NO	NO	NO	NO	NO	NO	NO	NO	NO	F	F	F	G
30	NO	NO	NO	NO	NO	NO	NO	NO	NO	F	F	G	G
28	NO	NO	NO	NO	NO	NO	NO	NO	F	F	F	G	G
26	NO	NO	NO	NO	NO	NO	NO	F	F	F	G	G	G
24	NO	NO	NO	NO	NO	NO	NO	F	F	F	G	G	G
22	NO	NO	NO	NO	NO	NO	F	F	F	G	G	G	E
20	NO	NO	NO	NO	NO	F	F	F	F	G	G	G	E
18	NO	NO	NO	NO	NO	F	F	F	F	G	G	E	E
16	NO	NO	NO	NO	F	F	F	G	G	G	G	E	E
14	NO	NO	NO	NO	F	F	F	G	G	G	E	E	E
12	NO	NO	NO	F	F	F	G	G	G	E	E	E	E
10	NO	NO	NO	F	F	G	G	G	E	E	E	E	E
8	NO	NO	NO	F	F	G	G	G	E	E	E	E	E
6	NO	NO	F	F	G	G	G	E	E	E	E	E	E
4	NO	F	F	G	G	E	E	E	E	E	E	E	E

changes in the soybean future's price in 10¢ increments

TABLE 80

wks to expir	0¢	10	20	30	40	50	60	70	80	90	100	110	120
36	NO	NO	NO	NO	NO	NO	NO	NO	NO	NO	NO	NO	NO
34	NO	NO	NO	NO	NO	NO	NO	NO	NO	NO	NO	NO	NO
32	NO	NO	NO	NO	NO	NO	NO	NO	NO	NO	NO	NO	F
30	NO	NO	NO	NO	NO	NO	NO	NO	NO	NO	NO	NO	F
28	NO	NO	NO	NO	NO	NO	NO	NO	NO	NO	NO	NO	NO
26	NO	NO	NO	NO	NO	NO	NO	NO	NO	NO	NO	NO	NO
24	NO	NO	NO	NO	NO	NO	NO	NO	NO	NO	NO	NO	F
22	NO	NO	NO	NO	NO	NO	NO	NO	NO	NO	NO	F	F
20	NO	NO	NO	NO	NO	NO	NO	NO	NO	NO	NO	F	F
18	NO	NO	NO	NO	NO	NO	NO	NO	NO	NO	F	F	F
16	NO	NO	NO	NO	NO	NO	NO	NO	NO	NO	F	F	F
14	NO	NO	NO	NO	NO	NO	NO	NO	NO	F	F	F	F
12	NO	NO	NO	NO	NO	NO	NO	NO	F	F	F	F	F
10	NO	NO	NO	NO	NO	NO	NO	F	F	F	F	G	G
8	NO	NO	NO	NO	NO	NO	NO	F	F	F	G	G	G
6	NO	NO	NO	NO	NO	NO	F	F	F	F	G	G	G
4	NO	NO	NO	NO	NO	F	F	F	G	G	G	G	G

changes in the soybean future's price in 10¢ increments

Wm Grandmill (1985) Ltd.

TABLE 20

wks to expir	0¢	10	20	30	40	50	60	70	80	90	100	110	120
36	NO	NO	NO	NO	NO	NO	F	F	G	E	E		
34	NO	NO	NO	NO	NO	NO	F	F	G	E	E		
32	NO	NO	NO	NO	NO	NO	F	G	G	E	E	E	
30	NO	NO	NO	NO	NO	F	F	G	E	E	E	E	
28	NO	NO	NO	NO	NO	F	F	G	E	E	E	E	
26	NO	NO	NO	NO	NO	F	G	G	E	E	E	E	
24	NO	NO	NO	NO	F	F	G	E	E	E	E	E	
22	NO	NO	NO	NO	F	G	G	E	E	E	E	E	
20	NO	NO	NO	NO	F	G	E	E	E	E	E	E	
18	NO	NO	NO	F	F	G	E	E	E	E	E	E	E
16	NO	NO	NO	F	G	E	E	E	E	E	E	E	E
14	NO	NO	NO	F	G	E	E	E	E	E	E	E	E
12	NO	NO	F	F	G	E	E	E	E	E	E	E	E
10	NO	NO	F	G	E	E	E	E	E	E	E	E	E
8	NO	NO	F	G	E	E	E	E	E	E	E	E	E
6	NO	F	G	E	E	E	E	E	E	E	E	E	E
4	NO	F	G	E	E	E	E	E	E	E	E	E	E

changes in the soybean future's price in 10¢ increments

Provided that you get the market direction right, then...
NO = don't take it, could lose money
F = fair profit, to about 100%
G = good profit
E = excellent profit, the best

TABLE 40

wks to expir	0¢	10	20	30	40	50	60	70	80	90	100	110	120
36	NO	NO	NO	NO	NO	NO	NO	NO	NO	NO	F	F	G
34	NO	NO	NO	NO	NO	NO	NO	NO	NO	F	F	G	G
32	NO	NO	NO	NO	NO	NO	NO	NO	NO	F	F	G	G
30	NO	NO	NO	NO	NO	NO	NO	NO	F	F	G	G	E
28	NO	NO	NO	NO	NO	NO	NO	NO	F	F	G	G	E
26	NO	NO	NO	NO	NO	NO	NO	F	F	G	G	E	E
24	NO	NO	NO	NO	NO	NO	NO	F	F	G	G	E	E
22	NO	NO	NO	NO	NO	NO	F	F	G	G	E	E	E
20	NO	NO	NO	NO	NO	NO	F	F	G	G	E	E	E
18	NO	NO	NO	NO	NO	F	F	G	G	E	E	E	E
16	NO	NO	NO	NO	NO	F	F	G	G	E	E	E	E
14	NO	NO	NO	NO	F	F	G	G	E	E	E	E	E
12	NO	NO	NO	NO	F	F	G	E	E	E	E	E	E
10	NO	NO	NO	F	F	G	E	E	E	E	E	E	E
8	NO	NO	NO	F	G	G	E	E	E	E	E	E	E
6	NO	NO	NO	F	G	E	E	E	E	E	E	E	E
4	NO	NO	F	G	E	E	E	E	E	E	E	E	E

changes in the soybean future's price in 10¢ increments

Wm Grandmill (1985) Ltd.

Table (upper) — BUY A CALL or BUY A PUT AT 50¢ OUT OF THE MONEY

wks to expir	0¢	10	20	30	40	50	60	70	80	90	100	110	120
36	NO	NO	NO	NO	NO	NO	NO	NO	NO	NO	NO	NO	F
34	NO	NO	NO	NO	NO	NO	NO	NO	NO	NO	NO	NO	F
32	NO	NO	NO	NO	NO	NO	NO	NO	NO	NO	NO	F	F
30	NO	NO	NO	NO	NO	NO	NO	NO	NO	NO	NO	F	F
28	NO	NO	NO	NO	NO	NO	NO	NO	NO	NO	NO	F	F
26	NO	NO	NO	NO	NO	NO	NO	NO	NO	NO	NO	F	F
24	NO	NO	NO	NO	NO	NO	NO	NO	NO	NO	F	F	F
22	NO	NO	NO	NO	NO	NO	NO	NO	NO	NO	F	F	F
20	NO	NO	NO	NO	NO	NO	NO	NO	NO	F	F	F	G
18	NO	NO	NO	NO	NO	NO	NO	NO	NO	F	F	G	G
16	NO	NO	NO	NO	NO	NO	NO	NO	F	F	G	G	E
14	NO	NO	NO	NO	NO	NO	NO	F	F	G	G	E	E
12	NO	NO	NO	NO	NO	NO	NO	F	F	G	G	E	E
10	NO	NO	NO	NO	NO	NO	F	F	G	G	E	E	E
8	NO	NO	NO	NO	NO	F	F	G	G	E	E	E	E
6	NO	NO	NO	NO	F	F	G	G	E	E	E	E	E
4	NO	NO	NO	F	F	G	G	E	E	E	E	E	E

changes in the soybean future's price in 10¢ increments

BUY A CALL or BUY A PUT

AT 50¢ OUT OF THE MONEY

Provided that you get the market direction right, then...

NO = don't take it, could lose money
F = fair profit, to about 100%
G = good profit
E = excellent profit, the best

Table (lower)

wks to expir	0¢	10	20	30	40	50	60	70	80	90	100	110	120
36	NO	NO	NO	NO	NO	NO	NO	NO	NO	NO	NO	NO	NO
34	NO	NO	NO	NO	NO	NO	NO	NO	NO	NO	NO	NO	NO
32	NO	NO	NO	NO	NO	NO	NO	NO	NO	NO	NO	NO	NO
30	NO	NO	NO	NO	NO	NO	NO	NO	NO	NO	NO	NO	NO
28	NO	NO	NO	NO	NO	NO	NO	NO	NO	NO	NO	NO	NO
26	NO	NO	NO	NO	NO	NO	NO	NO	NO	NO	NO	NO	NO
24	NO	NO	NO	NO	NO	NO	NO	NO	NO	NO	NO	NO	NO
22	NO	NO	NO	NO	NO	NO	NO	NO	NO	NO	NO	NO	NO
20	NO	NO	NO	NO	NO	NO	NO	NO	NO	NO	NO	NO	NO
18	NO	NO	NO	NO	NO	NO	NO	NO	NO	NO	NO	NO	NO
16	NO	NO	NO	NO	NO	NO	NO	NO	NO	NO	NO	NO	NO
14	NO	NO	NO	NO	NO	NO	NO	NO	NO	NO	NO	NO	NO
12	NO	NO	NO	NO	NO	NO	NO	NO	NO	NO	NO	NO	NO
10	NO	NO	NO	NO	NO	NO	NO	NO	NO	NO	NO	F	F
8	NO	NO	NO	NO	NO	NO	NO	NO	F	F	F	G	G
6	NO	NO	NO	NO	NO	NO	NO	F	F	G	G	G	G
4	NO	NO	NO	NO	NO	NO	F	F	G	G	G	G	E

changes in the soybean future's price in 10¢ increments

Wm Grandmill (1985) Ltd.

SELL A CALL or SELL A PUT
AT THE MONEY

HOW SAFE IS MY PROFIT?

TABLE 20

wks to expir	0¢	10	20	30	40	50	60	70	80	90	100	110	120
36	R	R	R	R	S	S	S	S	VS	VS	VS	VS	VS
34	R	R	R	R	S	S	S	S	VS	VS	VS	VS	VS
32	R	R	R	R	S	S	S	VS	VS	VS	VS	VS	VS
30	R	R	R	S	S	S	VS	VS	VS	VS	VS	VS	VS
28	R	R	R	S	S	S	VS	VS	VS	VS	VS	VS	VS
26	R	R	R	S	S	S	VS	VS	VS	VS	VS	VS	VS
24	R	R	R	S	S	VS	VS	VS	VS	VS	VS	VS	VS
22	R	R	R	R	S	S	VS	VS	VS	VS	VS	VS	VS
20	R	R	R	S	S	VS	VS	VS	VS	VS	VS	VS	VS
18	R	R	R	S	S	VS	VS	VS	VS	VS	VS	VS	VS
16	R	R	R	S	S	VS	VS	VS	VS	VS	VS	VS	VS
14	R	R	R	S	S	VS	VS	VS	VS	VS	VS	VS	VS
12	R	R	R	S	S	VS	VS	VS	VS	VS	VS	VS	VS
10	R	R	R	S	S	VS	VS	VS	VS	VS	VS	VS	VS
8	R	R	R	S	VS	VS	VS	VS	VS	VS	VS	VS	VS
6	R	R	R	S	VS	VS	VS	VS	VS	VS	VS	VS	VS
4	R	R	S	S	VS	VS	VS	VS	VS	VS	VS	VS	VS

changes in the soybean future's price in 10¢ increments

TABLE 40

wks to expir	0¢	10	20	30	40	50	60	70	80	90	100	110	120
36	R	R	R	R	R	R	S	S	S	VS	VS	VS	VS
34	R	R	R	R	R	R	S	S	S	VS	VS	VS	VS
32	R	R	R	R	R	R	S	S	VS	VS	VS	VS	VS
30	R	R	R	R	R	S	S	S	VS	VS	VS	VS	VS
28	R	R	R	R	R	S	S	VS	VS	VS	VS	VS	VS
26	R	R	R	R	R	S	S	VS	VS	VS	VS	VS	VS
24	R	R	R	R	S	S	VS	VS	VS	VS	VS	VS	VS
22	R	R	R	R	R	S	S	VS	VS	VS	VS	VS	VS
20	R	R	R	R	R	S	VS	VS	VS	VS	VS	VS	VS
18	R	R	R	R	S	S	VS	VS	VS	VS	VS	VS	VS
16	R	R	R	R	S	VS	VS	VS	VS	VS	VS	VS	VS
14	R	R	R	R	S	VS	VS	VS	VS	VS	VS	VS	VS
12	R	R	R	S	S	VS	VS	VS	VS	VS	VS	VS	VS
10	R	R	R	S	VS	VS	VS	VS	VS	VS	VS	VS	VS
8	R	R	S	S	VS	VS	VS	VS	VS	VS	VS	VS	VS
6	R	R	S	VS	VS	VS	VS	VS	VS	VS	VS	VS	VS
4	R	S	S	VS	VS	VS	VS	VS	VS	VS	VS	VS	VS

changes in the soybean future's price in 10¢ increments

Wm Grandmill (1985) Ltd.

SELL A CALL or SELL A PUT
AT THE MONEY

HOW SAFE IS MY PROFIT?

Provided that you get the market direction right, then...
R = risky, price fluctuations could reduce or eliminate your profit
S = safe, your profit should be protected from price fluctuations
VS = very safe, here your profit is likely safe from any danger.

TABLE 06

wks to expir	0¢	10	20	30	40	50	60	70	80	90	100	110	120
36	R	R	R	R	R	S	S	S	VS	VS	VS	VS	VS
34	R	R	R	R	R	S	S	S	VS	VS	VS	VS	VS
32	R	R	R	R	R	S	S	S	VS	VS	VS	VS	VS
30	R	R	R	R	S	S	S	VS	VS	VS	VS	VS	VS
28	R	R	R	R	S	S	S	VS	VS	VS	VS	VS	VS
26	R	R	R	S	S	S	VS	VS	VS	VS	VS	VS	VS
24	R	R	R	S	S	S	VS	VS	VS	VS	VS	VS	VS
22	R	R	R	S	S	VS	VS	VS	VS	VS	VS	VS	VS
20	R	R	S	S	S	VS	VS	VS	VS	VS	VS	VS	VS
18	R	R	S	S	VS	VS	VS	VS	VS	VS	VS	VS	BS
16	R	R	S	S	VS	VS	VS	VS	VS	VS	VS	VS	VS
14	R	R	S	S	VS	VS	VS	VS	VS	VS	VS	VS	VS
12	R	S	S	S	VS	VS	VS	VS	VS	VS	VS	VS	VS
10	R	S	S	S	VS	VS	VS	VS	VS	VS	VS	VS	VS
8	R	S	S	VS	VS	VS	VS	VS	VS	VS	VS	VS	VS
6	R	S	S	VS	VS	VS	VS	VS	VS	VS	VS	VS	VS
4	R	S	S	VS	VS	VS	VS	VS	VS	VS	VS	VS	VS

changes in the soybean future's price in 10¢ increments

TABLE 08

wks to expir	0¢	10	20	30	40	50	60	70	80	90	100	110	120
36	R	R	R	R	R	R	R	S	S	S	S	VS	VS
34	R	R	R	R	R	R	R	S	S	S	S	VS	VS
32	R	R	R	R	R	R	S	S	S	S	VS	VS	VS
30	R	R	R	R	R	R	S	S	S	S	VS	VS	VS
28	R	R	R	R	R	S	S	S	S	VS	VS	VS	VS
26	R	R	R	R	R	S	S	S	S	VS	VS	VS	VS
24	R	R	R	R	S	S	S	S	VS	VS	VS	VS	VS
22	R	R	R	R	S	S	S	S	VS	VS	VS	VS	VS
20	R	R	R	R	S	S	S	VS	VS	VS	VS	VS	VS
18	R	R	R	R	S	S	S	VS	VS	VS	VS	VS	VS
16	R	R	R	R	S	S	S	VS	VS	VS	VS	VS	VS
14	R	R	R	S	S	S	VS	VS	VS	VS	VS	VS	VS
12	R	R	R	S	S	S	VS	VS	VS	VS	VS	VS	VS
10	R	R	R	S	S	S	VS	VS	VS	VS	VS	VS	VS
8	R	R	R	S	S	VS	VS	VS	VS	VS	VS	VS	VS
6	R	R	R	S	S	VS	VS	VS	VS	VS	VS	VS	VS
4	R	R	R	S	S	VS	VS	VS	VS	VS	VS	VS	VS

changes in the soybean future's price in 10¢ increments

Wm Grandmill (1985) Ltd.

SELL A CALL or SELL A PUT
AT 50¢ OUT OF THE MONEY

HOW SAFE IS MY PROFIT?

Provided that you get the market direction right, then...

R = risky, price fluctuations could reduce or eliminate your profit
S = safe, your profit should be protected from price fluctuations
VS = very safe, here your profit is likely safe from any danger.

TABLE 20

wks to expir	0¢	10	20	30	40	50	60	70	80	90	100	110	120
36	R	R	S	S	S	S	VS	VS	VS	VS	VS	VS	VS
34	R	R	S	S	S	S	VS	VS	VS	VS	VS	VS	VS
32	R	R	S	S	S	S	VS	VS	VS	VS	VS	VS	VS
30	R	R	S	S	S	S	VS	VS	VS	VS	VS	VS	VS
28	R	R	S	S	S	S	VS	VS	VS	VS	VS	VS	VS
26	R	R	S	S	S	S	VS	VS	VS	VS	VS	VS	VS
24	R	R	S	S	S	S	VS	VS	VS	VS	VS	VS	VS
22	R	R	S	S	S	S	VS	VS	VS	VS	VS	VS	VS
20	R	R	S	S	S	S	VS	VS	VS	VS	VS	VS	VS
18	R	R	S	S	S	S	VS	VS	VS	VS	VS	VS	VS
16	R	R	S	S	S	S	VS	VS	VS	VS	VS	VS	VS
14	R	R	S	S	S	S	VS	VS	VS	VS	VS	VS	VS
12	R	R	S	S	S	S	VS	VS	VS	VS	VS	VS	VS
10	R	R	S	S	S	S	VS	VS	VS	VS	VS	VS	VS
8	R	R	S	S	S	S	VS	VS	VS	VS	VS	VS	VS
6	R	R	S	S	S	S	VS	VS	VS	VS	VS	VS	VS
4	A LOSS OCCURS HERE												

changes in the soybean future's price in 10¢ increments

TABLE 20

wks to expir	0¢	10	20	30	40	50	60	70	80	90	100	110	120
36	R	R	S	S	S	VS	VS	VS	VS	VS	VS	VS	VS
34	R	R	S	S	S	S	VS	VS	VS	VS	VS	VS	VS
32	R	R	S	S	S	S	VS	VS	VS	VS	VS	VS	VS
30	R	R	S	S	S	S	VS	VS	VS	VS	VS	VS	VS
28	R	R	S	S	S	S	VS	VS	VS	VS	VS	VS	VS
26	R	R	S	S	S	S	VS	VS	VS	VS	VS	VS	VS
24	R	R	S	S	S	S	VS	VS	VS	VS	VS	VS	VS
22	R	R	S	S	S	S	VS	VS	VS	VS	VS	VS	VS
20	R	R	S	S	S	S	VS	VS	VS	VS	VS	VS	VS
18	R	R	S	S	S	S	VS	VS	VS	VS	VS	VS	VS
16	R	R	S	S	S	S	VS	VS	VS	VS	VS	VS	VS
14	R	R	S	S	S	S	VS	VS	VS	VS	VS	VS	VS
12	R	R	S	S	S	S	VS	VS	VS	VS	VS	VS	VS
10	R	R	S	S	S	S	VS	VS	VS	VS	VS	VS	VS
8	R	R	S	S	S	S	VS	VS	VS	VS	VS	VS	VS
6	R	R	S	S	S	S	VS	VS	VS	VS	VS	VS	VS
4	R	R	S	S	S	S	VS	VS	VS	VS	VS	VS	VS

changes in the soybean future's price in 10¢ increments

Wm Grandmill (1985) Ltd.

SELL A CALL or SELL A PUT
AT 50¢ OUT OF THE MONEY

HOW SAFE IS MY PROFIT?

Provided that you get the market direction right, then...
R = risky, price fluctuations could reduce or eliminate your profit
S = safe, your profit should be protected from price fluctuations
VS = very safe, here your profit is likely safe from any danger.

T A B L E 0

wks to expir	0¢	10	20	30	40	50	60	70	80	90	100	110	120
36	R	S	S	S	S	S	VS	VS	VS	VS	VS	VS	VS
34	R	S	S	S	S	S	VS	VS	VS	VS	VS	VS	VS
32	R	S	S	S	S	S	VS	VS	VS	VS	VS	VS	VS
30	R	S	S	S	S	S	VS	VS	VS	VS	VS	VS	VS
28	R	S	S	S	S	S	VS	VS	VS	VS	VS	VS	VS
26	R	S	S	S	S	S	VS	VS	VS	VS	VS	VS	VS
24	R	S	S	S	S	S	VS	VS	VS	VS	VS	VS	VS
22	R	S	S	S	S	S	VS	VS	VS	VS	VS	VS	VS
20	R	S	S	S	S	S	VS	VS	VS	VS	VS	VS	VS
18	R	S	S	S	S	S	VS	VS	VS	VS	VS	VS	VS
16	R	S	S	S	S	S	VS	VS	VS	VS	VS	VS	VS
14	R	S	S	S	S	S	VS	VS	VS	VS	VS	VS	VS
12	R	S	S	S	S	S	VS	VS	VS	VS	VS	VS	VS
10	R	S	S	S	S	S	VS	VS	VS	VS	VS	VS	VS
8	R	S	S	S	S	S	VS	VS	VS	VS	VS	VS	VS
6	R	S	S	S	S	S	VS	VS	VS	VS	VS	VS	VS
4	R	S	S	S	S	S	VS	VS	VS	VS	VS	VS	VS

changes in the soybean future's price in 10¢ increments

T A B L E 0

wks to expir	0¢	10	20	30	40	50	60	70	80	90	100	110	120
36	S	S	S	S	VS	VS	VS	VS	VS	VS	VS	VS	VS
34	S	S	S	S	VS	VS	VS	VS	VS	VS	VS	VS	VS
32	S	S	S	S	VS	VS	VS	VS	VS	VS	VS	VS	VS
30	S	S	S	S	VS	VS	VS	VS	VS	VS	VS	VS	VS
28	S	S	S	S	VS	VS	VS	VS	VS	VS	VS	VS	VS
26	S	S	S	S	VS	VS	VS	VS	VS	VS	VS	VS	VS
24	S	S	S	S	VS	VS	VS	VS	VS	VS	VS	VS	VS
22	S	S	S	S	VS	VS	VS	VS	VS	VS	VS	VS	VS
20	S	S	S	S	VS	VS	VS	VS	VS	VS	VS	VS	VS
18	S	S	S	S	VS	VS	VS	VS	VS	VS	VS	VS	VS
16	S	S	S	S	VS	VS	VS	VS	VS	VS	VS	VS	VS
14	S	S	S	S	VS	VS	VS	VS	VS	VS	VS	VS	VS
12	S	S	S	S	VS	VS	VS	VS	VS	VS	VS	VS	VS
10	S	S	S	S	VS	VS	VS	VS	VS	VS	VS	VS	VS
8	S	S	S	S	VS	VS	VS	VS	VS	VS	VS	VS	VS
6	S	S	S	S	VS	VS	VS	VS	VS	VS	VS	VS	VS
4	S	S	S	S	VS	VS	VS	VS	VS	VS	VS	VS	VS

changes in the soybean future's price in 10¢ increments

Wm Grandmill (1985) Ltd.

BULL or BEAR SPREAD – #1

*BUY A CALL AT THE MONEY
and SELL A CALL AT 25¢ OUT OF THE MONEY
OR
BUY A PUT AT THE MONEY
and SELL A PUT AT 25¢ OUT OF THE MONEY*

wks to expir	0¢	10	20	30	40	50	60	70	80	90	100	110	120
36	NO	NO	R	R	R	R	S	S	S	VS	VS	VS	VS
34	NO	NO	R	R	R	R	S	S	S	VS	VS	VS	VS
32	NO	NO	R	R	R	R	S	S	S	VS	VS	VS	VS
30	NO	NO	R	R	R	R	S	S	S	VS	VS	VS	VS
28	NO	NO	R	R	R	R	S	S	S	VS	VS	VS	VS
26	NO	NO	R	R	R	R	S	S	S	VS	VS	VS	VS
24	NO	NO	R	R	R	R	S	S	S	VS	VS	VS	VS
22	NO	NO	R	R	R	R	S	S	S	VS	VS	VS	VS
20	NO	NO	R	R	R	R	S	S	S	VS	VS	VS	VS
18	NO	NO	R	R	R	R	S	S	S	VS	VS	VS	VS
16	NO	NO	R	R	R	R	S	S	S	VS	VS	VS	VS
14	NO	NO	R	R	R	S	S	S	VS	VS	VS	VS	VS
12	NO	NO	R	R	R	S	S	S	VS	VS	VS	VS	VS
10	NO	NO	R	R	R	S	S	S	VS	VS	VS	VS	VS
8	NO	NO	R	R	R	S	S	S	VS	VS	VS	VS	VS
6	NO	NO	R	R	R	S	S	S	VS	VS	VS	VS	VS
4	NO	NO	R	R	S	S	S	VS	VS	VS	VS	VS	VS

changes in the soybean future's price in 10¢ increments

Provided that you get the market direction right, then...
NO = don't take it, will likely lose money
R = risky, price fluctuations could reduce or eliminate your profit
S = safe, your profit is likely safe from price fluctuations here
VS = very safe, your profit is likely safe from any danger here

One chart will serve all tables because the profit
is about the same for any volatility.

Wm Grandmill (1985) Ltd.

BUY A CALL AT THE MONEY and SELL 2 CALLS AT 50¢ OUT OF THE MONEY
OR
BUY A PUT AT THE MONEY and SELL 2 PUTS AT 50¢ OUT OF THE MONEY

HOW SAFE IS MY PROFIT?

Provided that you get the market direction right, then....

NO = don't take it, will likely lose money
R = risky, price fluctuations could reduce or eliminate your profit
S = safe, your profit is likely safe from price fluctuations here
VS = very safe, your profit is likely safe from any danger

First table

wks to expir	0¢	10	20	30	40	50	60	70	80	90	100	110	120
36	NO	NO	R	R	R	R	R	R	R	NO	NO	NO	NO
34	NO	NO	R	R	R	R	R	R	R	NO	NO	NO	NO
32	NO	NO	R	R	R	R	R	R	R	NO	NO	NO	NO
30	NO	NO	R	R	R	R	R	R	R	NO	NO	NO	NO
28	NO	NO	R	R	R	R	R	R	R	NO	NO	NO	NO
26	NO	NO	R	R	R	R	R	R	R	NO	NO	NO	NO
24	NO	NO	R	R	R	R	R	R	R	NO	NO	NO	NO
22	NO	NO	R	R	R	R	R	R	R	NO	NO	NO	NO
20	NO	NO	R	R	R	R	R	R	R	NO	NO	NO	NO
18	NO	NO	R	R	R	R	R	R	R	NO	NO	NO	NO
16	NO	NO	R	R	R	R	R	R	R	NO	NO	NO	NO
14	NO	NO	R	R	R	R	R	R	R	NO	NO	NO	NO
12	NO	NO	R	R	R	R	R	R	R	NO	NO	NO	NO
10	NO	NO	R	R	R	R	R	R	R	NO	NO	NO	NO
8	NO	NO	R	R	R	R	R	R	R	NO	NO	NO	NO
6	NO	NO	R	R	R	R	R	R	R	NO	NO	NO	NO
4	NO	NO	R	R	R	R	R	R	R	NO	NO	NO	NO

(row label at left: **TABLE 20**)

changes in the soybean future's price in 10¢ increments

Second table

wks to expir	0¢	10	20	30	40	50	60	70	80	90	100	110	120
36	VS	VS	VS	VS	S	S	S	S	S	S	R	R	NO
34	VS	VS	VS	VS	S	S	S	S	S	S	R	R	NO
32	VS	VS	VS	S	S	S	S	S	S	S	R	R	NO
30	VS	VS	S	S	S	S	S	S	S	S	R	R	NO
28	VS	S	S	S	S	S	S	S	S	R	R	R	NO
26	S	S	S	S	S	S	S	S	S	R	R	R	NO
24	S	S	S	S	S	S	S	S	R	R	R	R	NO
22	S	S	S	S	S	S	S	R	R	R	R	R	NO
20	S	S	S	S	S	S	R	R	R	R	R	R	NO
18	NO	S	S	S	S	R	R	R	R	R	R	R	NO
16	NO	S	S	S	R	R	R	R	R	R	R	R	NO
14	NO	S	S	R	R	R	R	R	R	R	R	NO	NO
12	NO	S	R	R	R	R	R	R	R	R	R	NO	NO
10	NO	R	R	R	R	R	R	R	R	R	NO	NO	NO
8	NO	R	R	R	R	R	R	R	R	NO	NO	NO	NO
6	NO	R	R	R	R	S	S	S	R	R	NO	NO	NO
4	NO	NO	R	R	R	S	S	S	R	R	NO	NO	NO

(row label at left: **TABLE 40**)

changes in the soybean future's price in 10¢ increments

Wm Grandmill (1985) Ltd.

BULL or BEAR SPREAD – #2

BUY A CALL AT THE MONEY
and SELL 2 CALLS AT 50¢ OUT OF THE MONEY

OR

BUY A PUT AT THE MONEY
and SELL 2 PUTS AT 50¢ OUT OF THE MONEY

HOW SAFE IS MY PROFIT?

Provided that you get the market direction right, then…

NO = don't take it, will likely lose money
R = risky, price fluctuations could reduce or eliminate your profit here
S = safe, your profit is likely safe from price fluctuations here
VS = very safe, your profit is likely safe from any danger here

TABLE 0 (first)

wks to expir	0¢	10	20	30	40	50	60	70	80	90	100	110	120
36	VS	VS	VS	S	S	S	S	R	R	R	R	R	NO
34	VS	VS	VS	S	S	S	S	R	R	R	R	R	NO
32	VS	VS	VS	S	S	S	S	R	R	R	R	R	NO
30	VS	VS	VS	S	S	S	S	R	R	R	R	R	NO
28	VS	VS	VS	S	S	S	S	R	R	R	R	R	NO
26	VS	VS	VS	S	S	S	S	R	R	R	R	R	NO
24	VS	VS	VS	S	S	S	S	R	R	R	R	R	NO
22	VS	VS	S	S	S	S	S	R	R	R	R	R	NO
20	VS	VS	S	S	S	S	S	R	R	R	R	NO	NO
18	VS	VS	S	S	S	S	S	R	R	R	R	NO	NO
16	VS	VS	S	S	S	S	R	R	R	R	R	NO	NO
14	VS	VS	S	S	S	S	R	R	R	R	NO	NO	NO
12	VS	VS	S	S	S	R	R	R	R	R	NO	NO	NO
10	VS	VS	S	S	S	R	R	R	R	NO	NO	NO	NO
8	NO	R	R	R	R	R	R	R	R	NO	NO	NO	NO
6	NO	R	R	R	R	R	R	R	NO	NO	NO	NO	NO
4	NO	NO	R	R	R	R	R	R	NO	NO	NO	NO	NO

changes in the soybean future's price in 10¢ increments

TABLE 0 (second)

wks to expir	0¢	10	20	30	40	50	60	70	80	90	100	110	120
36	VS	VS	VS	S	S	S	S	R	R	R	R	R	R
34	VS	VS	VS	S	S	S	S	R	R	R	R	R	R
32	VS	VS	VS	S	S	S	S	R	R	R	R	R	R
30	VS	VS	VS	S	S	S	S	S	R	R	R	R	R
28	VS	VS	VS	S	S	S	S	S	R	R	R	R	R
26	VS	VS	VS	S	S	S	S	S	R	R	R	R	R
24	VS	VS	VS	S	S	S	S	S	R	R	R	R	R
22	VS	VS	VS	S	S	S	S	S	R	R	R	R	R
20	VS	VS	VS	S	S	S	S	S	S	R	R	R	R
18	VS	VS	VS	S	S	S	S	S	R	R	R	R	R
16	VS	VS	VS	S	S	S	S	S	R	R	R	R	NO
14	VS	VS	VS	S	S	S	S	S	R	R	R	R	NO
12	VS	VS	VS	S	S	S	S	S	R	R	R	R	NO
10	VS	VS	VS	S	S	S	S	S	R	R	R	NO	NO
8	VS	VS	VS	S	S	S	S	R	R	R	R	NO	NO
6	VS	VS	VS	S	S	S	R	R	R	R	R	NO	NO
4	NO	R	R	R	S	S	S	R	R	R	R	NO	NO

changes in the soybean future's price in 10¢ increments

Wm Grandmill (1985) Ltd.

SELL A STRADDLE

SELL A CALL AT THE MONEY and SELL A PUT AT THE MONEY

HOW SAFE IS MY PROFIT?

Provided that you get the market direction right, then...

NO = don't take it, will likely lose money
R = risky, price fluctuations could reduce or eliminate your profit
S = safe, your profit is likely safe from price fluctuations here
VS = very safe, your profit is likely safe from any danger

TABLE 20

wks to expir	0¢	10	20	30	40	50	60	70	80	90	100	110	120
36	R	R	NO	NO	NO	NO	NO	NO	NO	NO	NO	NO	NO
34	R	R	NO	NO	NO	NO	NO	NO	NO	NO	NO	NO	NO
32	R	R	NO	NO	NO	NO	NO	NO	NO	NO	NO	NO	NO
30	R	R	NO	NO	NO	NO	NO	NO	NO	NO	NO	NO	NO
28	R	R	NO	NO	NO	NO	NO	NO	NO	NO	NO	NO	NO
26	R	R	NO	NO	NO	NO	NO	NO	NO	NO	NO	NO	NO
24	R	R	NO	NO	NO	NO	NO	NO	NO	NO	NO	NO	NO
22	R	R	NO	NO	NO	NO	NO	NO	NO	NO	NO	NO	NO
20	R	R	NO	NO	NO	NO	NO	NO	NO	NO	NO	NO	NO
18	R	R	NO	NO	NO	NO	NO	NO	NO	NO	NO	NO	NO
16	R	R	NO	NO	NO	NO	NO	NO	NO	NO	NO	NO	NO
14	R	R	NO	NO	NO	NO	NO	NO	NO	NO	NO	NO	NO
12	R	R	NO	NO	NO	NO	NO	NO	NO	NO	NO	NO	NO
10	R	R	NO	NO	NO	NO	NO	NO	NO	NO	NO	NO	NO
8	R	R	NO	NO	NO	NO	NO	NO	NO	NO	NO	NO	NO
6	NO	NO	NO	NO	NO	NO	NO	NO	NO	NO	NO	NO	NO
4	NO	NO	NO	NO	NO	NO	NO	NO	NO	NO	NO	NO	NO

changes in the soybean future's price in 10¢ increments

TABLE 40

wks to expir	0¢	10	20	30	40	50	60	70	80	90	100	110	120
36	S	S	S	S	R	R	R	R	NO	NO	NO	NO	NO
34	S	S	S	S	R	R	R	R	NO	NO	NO	NO	NO
32	S	S	S	S	R	R	R	R	NO	NO	NO	NO	NO
30	S	S	S	S	R	R	R	R	NO	NO	NO	NO	NO
28	S	S	S	S	R	R	R	R	NO	NO	NO	NO	NO
26	S	S	S	S	R	R	R	R	NO	NO	NO	NO	NO
24	S	S	S	S	R	R	R	NO	NO	NO	NO	NO	NO
22	S	S	S	S	R	R	R	NO	NO	NO	NO	NO	NO
20	S	S	S	S	R	R	R	NO	NO	NO	NO	NO	NO
18	S	S	S	S	R	R	R	NO	NO	NO	NO	NO	NO
16	S	S	S	R	R	R	R	NO	NO	NO	NO	NO	NO
14	S	S	S	R	R	R	NO	NO	NO	NO	NO	NO	NO
12	S	S	R	R	R	R	NO	NO	NO	NO	NO	NO	NO
10	S	S	R	R	R	NO	NO	NO	NO	NO	NO	NO	NO
8	S	R	R	R	R	NO	NO	NO	NO	NO	NO	NO	NO
6	R	R	R	R	NO	NO	NO	NO	NO	NO	NO	NO	NO
4	R	R	R	NO	NO	NO	NO	NO	NO	NO	NO	NO	NO

changes in the soybean future's price in 10¢ increments

Wm Grandmill (1985) Ltd.

Wm Grandmill (1985) Ltd.

SELL A STRADDLE

SELL A CALL AT THE MONEY and SELL A PUT AT THE MONEY

wks to expir	0¢	10	20	30	40	50	60	70	80	90	100	110	120
36	VS	VS	VS	S	S	R	R	R	NO	NO	NO	NO	NO
34	VS	VS	VS	S	S	S	R	R	R	NO	NO	NO	NO
32	VS	VS	VS	S	S	S	R	R	R	R	NO	NO	NO
30	VS	VS	VS	S	S	S	S	R	R	R	NO	NO	NO
28	VS	VS	VS	S	S	S	S	R	R	R	R	NO	NO
26	VS	VS	VS	S	S	S	S	S	R	R	R	NO	NO
24	VS	VS	VS	VS	S	S	S	S	R	R	R	R	NO
22	VS	VS	VS	S	S	S	S	S	R	R	R	R	NO
T 20	VS	VS	S	S	S	S	S	R	R	R	R	R	NO
A 18	VS	VS	S	S	S	S	S	R	R	R	R	R	NO
B 16	VS	VS	S	S	S	S	R	R	R	R	R	NO	NO
L 14	VS	VS	S	S	S	R	R	R	R	R	NO	NO	NO
E 12	VS	S	S	S	R	R	R	R	R	NO	NO	NO	NO
10	S	S	S	R	R	R	R	NO	NO	NO	NO	NO	NO
8	S	S	R	R	R	R	NO	NO	NO	NO	NO	NO	NO
6	S	S	R	R	R	NO	NO	NO	NO	NO	NO	NO	NO
4	S	R	R	R	NO	NO	NO	NO	NO	NO	NO	NO	NO

changes in the soybean future's price in 10¢ increments

HOW SAFE IS MY PROFIT?

Provided that you get the market direction right, then...

NO = don't take it, will likely lose money
R = risky, price fluctuations could reduce or eliminate your profit here
S = safe, your profit is likely safe from price fluctuations here
VS = very safe, your profit is likely safe from any danger here

wks to expir	0¢	10	20	30	40	50	60	70	80	90	100	110	120
36	VS	VS	VS	VS	VS	VS	VS	VS	S	S	S	S	S
34	VS	VS	VS	VS	VS	VS	VS	VS	S	S	S	S	S
32	VS	VS	VS	VS	VS	VS	VS	S	S	S	S	S	S
30	VS	VS	VS	VS	VS	VS	S	S	S	S	S	S	R
28	VS	VS	VS	VS	VS	S	S	S	S	S	S	R	R
26	VS	VS	VS	VS	S	S	S	S	S	S	R	R	R
24	VS	VS	VS	VS	S	S	S	S	S	R	R	R	R
22	VS	VS	VS	S	S	S	S	S	R	R	R	R	R
T 20	VS	VS	VS	S	S	S	S	R	R	R	R	R	NO
A 18	VS	VS	S	S	S	S	R	R	R	R	R	NO	NO
B 16	VS	VS	S	S	S	R	R	R	R	R	NO	NO	NO
L 14	VS	VS	S	S	R	R	R	R	R	NO	NO	NO	NO
E 12	VS	VS	S	S	R	R	R	R	NO	NO	NO	NO	NO
10	VS	VS	S	S	R	R	R	NO	NO	NO	NO	NO	NO
8	VS	VS	S	R	R	R	NO	NO	NO	NO	NO	NO	NO
6	S	S	R	R	R	NO	NO	NO	NO	NO	NO	NO	NO
4	S	S	R	R	NO	NO	NO	NO	NO	NO	NO	NO	NO

changes in the soybean future's price in 10¢ increments

SELL A STRANGLE – #1

SELL A CALL AT 50¢ OUT OF THE MONEY and SELL A PUT AT 50¢ OUT OF THE MONEY

wks to expir	0¢	10¢	20¢	30¢	40¢	50¢	60¢	70¢	80¢	90¢	100¢	110¢	120¢
36	S	S	S	R	R	R	R	R	NO	NO	NO	NO	NO
34	S	S	S	R	R	R	R	R	NO	NO	NO	NO	NO
32	S	S	S	R	R	R	R	R	NO	NO	NO	NO	NO
30	S	S	S	R	R	R	R	R	NO	NO	NO	NO	NO
28	S	S	S	R	R	R	R	R	NO	NO	NO	NO	NO
26	S	S	S	R	R	R	R	NO	NO	NO	NO	NO	NO
24	S	S	S	R	R	R	R	NO	NO	NO	NO	NO	NO
22	S	S	S	R	R	R	R	NO	NO	NO	NO	NO	NO
20	S	S	S	R	R	R	R	NO	NO	NO	NO	NO	NO
18	S	S	R	R	R	R	R	NO	NO	NO	NO	NO	NO
16	S	S	R	R	R	R	NO	NO	NO	NO	NO	NO	NO
14	S	S	R	R	R	R	NO	NO	NO	NO	NO	NO	NO
12	S	S	R	R	R	R	NO	NO	NO	NO	NO	NO	NO
10	S	S	R	R	R	NO	NO	NO	NO	NO	NO	NO	NO
8	S	S	R	R	NO	NO	NO	NO	NO	NO	NO	NO	NO
6	NO	NO	NO	NO	NO	NO	NO	NO	NO	NO	NO	NO	NO
4	NO	NO	NO	NO	NO	NO	NO	NO	NO	NO	NO	NO	NO

(Left margin label: **TABLE 20**)

changes in the soybean future's price in 10¢ increments

HOW SAFE IS MY PROFIT?

Provided that you get the market direction right, then…

NO = don't take it, will likely lose money
R = risky, price fluctuations could reduce or eliminate your profit here
S = safe, your profit is likely safe from price fluctuations here
VS = very safe, your profit is likely safe from any danger here

wks to expir	0¢	10¢	20¢	30¢	40¢	50¢	60¢	70¢	80¢	90¢	100¢	110¢	120¢
36	VS	S	S	S	R	R	R	NO	NO	NO	NO	NO	NO
34	VS	S	S	S	R	R	R	NO	NO	NO	NO	NO	NO
32	VS	S	S	S	R	R	R	NO	NO	NO	NO	NO	NO
30	VS	S	S	S	R	R	R	NO	NO	NO	NO	NO	NO
28	VS	S	S	S	R	R	R	NO	NO	NO	NO	NO	NO
26	VS	S	S	S	R	R	R	NO	NO	NO	NO	NO	NO
24	VS	S	S	S	R	R	R	NO	NO	NO	NO	NO	NO
22	VS	S	S	S	R	R	R	NO	NO	NO	NO	NO	NO
20	VS	S	S	S	R	R	R	NO	NO	NO	NO	NO	NO
18	S	S	S	S	R	R	R	R	NO	NO	NO	NO	NO
16	S	S	S	R	R	R	R	NO	NO	NO	NO	NO	NO
14	S	S	S	R	R	R	R	NO	NO	NO	NO	NO	NO
12	S	S	S	R	R	R	NO	NO	NO	NO	NO	NO	NO
10	S	S	R	R	R	R	NO	NO	NO	NO	NO	NO	NO
8	S	S	R	R	R	NO	NO	NO	NO	NO	NO	NO	NO
6	S	S	R	R	NO	NO	NO	NO	NO	NO	NO	NO	NO
4	S	S	R	R	NO	NO	NO	NO	NO	NO	NO	NO	NO

(Left margin label: **TABLE 40**)

changes in the soybean future's price in 10¢ increments

Wm Grandmill (1985) Ltd.

SELL A STRANGLE – #1

SELL A CALL AT 50¢ OUT OF THE MONEY
and SELL A PUT AT 50¢ OUT OF THE MONEY

TABLE 60

wks to expir	0¢	10	20	30	40	50	60	70	80	90	100	110	120
36	VS	VS	VS	S	S	S	R	R	R	R	R	R	R
34	VS	VS	VS	S	S	S	R	R	R	R	R	R	R
32	VS	VS	VS	S	S	S	R	R	R	R	R	R	R
30	VS	VS	VS	S	S	S	R	R	R	R	R	R	NO
28	VS	VS	VS	S	S	S	S	R	R	R	R	R	NO
26	VS	VS	VS	S	S	S	S	R	R	R	R	NO	NO
24	VS	VS	VS	S	S	S	S	R	R	R	R	NO	NO
22	VS	VS	VS	S	S	S	S	R	R	R	NO	NO	NO
20	VS	VS	VS	VS	S	S	S	R	R	R	NO	NO	NO
18	VS	VS	VS	VS	S	S	S	R	R	NO	NO	NO	NO
16	VS	VS	VS	VS	S	S	R	R	R	NO	NO	NO	NO
14	VS	VS	VS	VS	S	S	R	R	NO	NO	NO	NO	NO
12	VS	VS	VS	VS	S	S	R	R	NO	NO	NO	NO	NO
10	VS	VS	VS	S	S	R	R	NO	NO	NO	NO	NO	NO
8	VS	VS	S	S	S	R	R	NO	NO	NO	NO	NO	NO
6	S	S	S	S	R	R	NO	NO	NO	NO	NO	NO	NO
4	S	S	S	R	R	NO	NO	NO	NO	NO	NO	NO	NO

changes in the soybean future's price in 10¢ increments

HOW SAFE IS MY PROFIT?

Provided that you get the market direction right, then…

NO = don't take it, will likely lose money
R = risky, price fluctuations could reduce or eliminate your profit
S = safe, your profit is likely safe from price fluctuations here
VS = very safe, your profit is likely safe from any danger

TABLE 80

wks to expir	0¢	10	20	30	40	50	60	70	80	90	100	110	120
36	VS	VS	VS	VS	VS	VS	VS	VS	VS	VS	VS	VS	S
34	VS	VS	VS	VS	VS	VS	VS	VS	VS	VS	VS	S	S
32	VS	VS	VS	VS	VS	VS	VS	VS	VS	VS	S	S	S
30	VS	VS	VS	VS	VS	VS	VS	VS	VS	S	S	S	S
28	VS	VS	VS	VS	VS	VS	VS	VS	S	S	S	S	R
26	VS	VS	VS	VS	VS	VS	VS	S	S	S	S	R	R
24	VS	VS	VS	VS	VS	VS	VS	S	S	S	R	R	R
22	VS	VS	VS	VS	VS	VS	S	S	S	R	R	R	R
20	VS	VS	VS	VS	VS	S	S	S	R	R	R	R	R
18	VS	VS	VS	VS	VS	VS	S	S	R	R	R	R	NO
16	VS	VS	VS	VS	VS	VS	R	R	R	R	R	NO	NO
14	VS	VS	VS	VS	VS	S	S	R	R	R	NO	NO	NO
12	VS	VS	VS	VS	S	S	R	R	R	NO	NO	NO	NO
10	VS	VS	VS	S	S	R	R	R	NO	NO	NO	NO	NO
8	VS	VS	VS	S	S	R	R	NO	NO	NO	NO	NO	NO
6	VS	VS	S	S	R	R	NO	NO	NO	NO	NO	NO	NO
4	S	S	S	R	R	NO	NO	NO	NO	NO	NO	NO	NO

changes in the soybean future's price in 10¢ increments

Wm Grandmill (1985) Ltd.

SELL A STRANGLE – #2

SELL A CALL AT $1.00 OUT OF THE MONEY and SELL A PUT AT $1.00 OUT OF THE MONEY

HOW SAFE IS MY PROFIT?

Provided that you get the market direction right, then...

NO = don't take it, will likely lose money
R = risky, price fluctuations could reduce or eliminate your profit
S = safe, your profit is likely safe from price fluctuations here
VS = very safe, your profit is likely safe from any danger here

TABLE 20

wks to expir	0¢	10	20	30	40	50	60	70	80	90	100	110	120
36	VS	S	S	S	S	S	S	NO	NO	NO	NO	NO	NO
34	VS	S	S	S	S	S	S	NO	NO	NO	NO	NO	NO
32	VS	S	S	S	S	S	S	R	NO	NO	NO	NO	NO
30	VS	S	S	S	S	S	S	R	NO	NO	NO	NO	NO
28	VS	S	S	S	S	S	S	R	R	NO	NO	NO	NO
26	VS	S	S	S	S	S	S	R	R	NO	NO	NO	NO
24	VS	S	S	S	S	S	S	R	R	R	NO	NO	NO
22	VS	S	S	S	S	S	S	R	R	R	NO	NO	NO
20	VS	S	S	S	S	S	S	R	R	R	R	NO	NO
18	VS	S	S	S	S	S	S	R	R	R	R	NO	NO
16	VS	S	S	S	S	S	R	R	R	R	R	NO	NO
14	VS	VS	S	S	S	S	R	R	R	R	NO	NO	NO
12	VS	VS	S	S	S	R	R	R	R	NO	NO	NO	NO
10	VS	VS	S	S	R	R	R	R	NO	NO	NO	NO	NO
8	NO	NO	NO	NO	NO	NO	NO	NO	NO	NO	NO	NO	NO
6	NO	NO	NO	NO	NO	NO	NO	NO	NO	NO	NO	NO	NO
4	NO	NO	NO	NO	NO	NO	NO	NO	NO	NO	NO	NO	NO

changes in the soybean future's price in 10¢ increments

TABLE 40

wks to expir	0¢	10	20	30	40	50	60	70	80	90	100	110	120
36	VS	VS	VS	VS	VS	VS	S	S	S	R	R	R	R
34	VS	VS	VS	VS	VS	VS	S	S	S	R	R	R	R
32	VS	VS	VS	VS	VS	VS	S	S	S	R	R	R	R
30	VS	VS	VS	VS	VS	VS	S	S	S	R	R	R	R
28	VS	VS	VS	VS	VS	S	S	S	S	R	R	R	R
26	VS	VS	VS	VS	VS	S	S	S	S	R	R	R	R
24	VS	VS	VS	VS	VS	S	S	S	R	R	R	R	NO
22	VS	VS	VS	VS	VS	S	S	S	R	R	R	R	NO
20	VS	VS	VS	VS	S	S	S	R	R	R	R	R	NO
18	VS	VS	VS	VS	S	S	S	R	R	R	R	R	NO
16	VS	VS	VS	S	S	S	R	R	R	R	R	NO	NO
14	VS	VS	VS	S	S	S	R	R	R	R	R	NO	NO
12	VS	VS	VS	S	S	R	R	R	R	R	NO	NO	NO
10	VS	VS	VS	S	S	R	R	R	R	R	NO	NO	NO
8	VS	VS	S	S	S	R	R	R	R	NO	NO	NO	NO
6	VS	VS	S	S	R	R	R	R	R	NO	NO	NO	NO
4	NO	NO	NO	NO	NO	NO	NO	NO	NO	NO	NO	NO	NO

changes in the soybean future's price in 10¢ increments

Wm Grandmill (1985) Ltd.

222

SELL A CALL AT $1.00 OUT OF THE MONEY and SELL A PUT AT $1.00 OUT OF THE MONEY

TABLE 0

changes in the soybean future's price in 10¢ increments

wks to expir	0¢	10	20	30	40	50	60	70	80	90	100	110	120
36	VS	VS	VS	VS	VS	VS	VS	VS	S	S	S	S	S
34	VS	VS	VS	VS	VS	VS	VS	VS	S	S	S	S	S
32	VS	VS	VS	VS	VS	VS	VS	VS	S	S	S	S	R
30	VS	VS	VS	VS	VS	VS	VS	S	S	S	S	R	R
28	VS	VS	VS	VS	VS	VS	VS	S	S	S	R	R	R
26	VS	VS	VS	VS	VS	VS	S	S	S	R	R	R	R
24	VS	VS	VS	VS	VS	VS	VS	S	S	R	R	R	R
22	VS	VS	VS	VS	VS	S	S	S	R	R	R	R	R
20	VS	VS	VS	VS	VS	S	S	R	R	R	R	R	R
18	VS	VS	VS	VS	S	S	S	R	R	R	R	R	R
16	VS	VS	VS	VS	S	S	R	R	R	R	R	R	R
14	VS	VS	VS	S	S	R	R	R	R	R	R	NO	NO
12	VS	VS	VS	S	S	R	R	R	R	R	R	NO	
10	VS	VS	S	S	S	R	R	R	R	R	NO	NO	
8	VS	VS	S	S	S	R	R	R	R	NO	NO		
6	VS	VS	S	S	S	R	R	R	NO	NO			
4	VS	VS	S	S	S	R	R	R	NO	NO			

Provided that you get the market direction right, then...

NO = don't take it, will likely lose money
R = risky, price fluctuations could reduce or eliminate your profit
S = safe, your profit is likely safe from price fluctuations here
VS = very safe, your profit is likely safe from any danger

TABLE 0

changes in the soybean future's price in 10¢ increments

wks to expir	0¢	10	20	30	40	50	60	70	80	90	100	110	120
36	VS	VS	VS	VS	VS	VS	VS	VS	VS	VS	VS	S	S
34	VS	VS	VS	VS	VS	VS	VS	VS	VS	VS	VS	S	S
32	VS	VS	VS	VS	VS	VS	VS	VS	VS	VS	VS	S	S
30	VS	VS	VS	VS	VS	VS	VS	VS	VS	VS	S	S	S
28	VS	VS	VS	VS	VS	VS	VS	VS	VS	VS	S	S	S
26	VS	VS	VS	VS	VS	VS	VS	VS	VS	S	S	S	S
24	VS	VS	VS	VS	VS	VS	VS	VS	VS	S	S	S	R
22	VS	VS	VS	VS	VS	VS	VS	VS	S	S	S	R	R
20	VS	VS	VS	VS	VS	VS	VS	VS	S	S	S	R	R
18	VS	VS	VS	VS	VS	VS	VS	S	S	S	R	R	R
16	VS	VS	VS	VS	VS	VS	VS	S	S	S	R	R	R
14	VS	VS	VS	VS	VS	VS	S	S	S	R	R	R	R
12	VS	VS	VS	VS	VS	S	S	S	S	R	R	R	R
10	VS	VS	VS	VS	VS	S	S	S	R	R	R	R	R
8	VS	VS	VS	VS	S	VS	S	S	R	R	R	R	R
6	VS	VS	VS	VS	S	S	S	S	R	R	R	R	R
4	VS	VS	VS	VS	S	S	S	S	R	R	R	R	NO

Wm Grandmill (1985) Ltd.

WHAT WORKS BEST WHERE?

<u>There are 3 principal factors</u> which affect the performance of an option. They are : <u>volatility, time, price</u>

  Nine different option positions have been outlined and illustrated in this book.   Some of them are more profitable when used with one or more of the 3 factors mentioned above ; volatility, time, and price. This page will show you which of the positions below are best used with one or more of the 3 factors.

    1. Buy a call or put at the money
    2. Buy a call or put at 50¢ out of the money
    3. Sell a call or put at the money
    4. Sell a call or put at 50¢ out of the money

    5. Bull spread #1
    6. Bull spread #2
    7. Sell a straddle
    8. Sell a strangle #1
    9. Sell a strangle #2

<u>VOLATILITY</u>- which of the 9 positions above perform well when there is...

    <u>high</u> volatility : 3, 4, 5, 6, 7, 8, 9

    <u>medium</u> " "   : 3, 4, 5, 6, 7, 8, 9

    <u>low</u>   " "   : 1, 2, 3, 4, 5, 9

<u>TIME</u> – which of the 9 option positions above perform well for the long term, medium term, short term...

    <u>long term</u> (36–24 wks. to exp.) : 3, 4, 5, 6, 7, 8, 9

    <u>medium term</u> (23 – 11 wks. to exp.) 3, 4, 5, 6, 7, 8, 9

    <u>short term</u> (10 – 4 wks. to exp.) : 1, 3, 4, 5, 8, 9

<u>PRICE</u> – which of the 9 option positions perform well when the Forecasting Graphs indicate that there will be a price move coming up which will be: a large price movement, medium, or no price change...

    <u>large</u> price change (60¢ to 120¢) : 1, 3, 4, 5, 6

    <u>medium</u> price change (30¢ to 60¢) : 3, 4, 6, 7, 8, 9

    <u>little or no</u> price change (0 to 30¢) : 4, 6, 7, 8, 9

  <u>The most frequently mentioned option position</u> mentioned above is number 4 (sell a call or a put, at 50¢ out of the money) .   Therefore you can look upon number 4 as being one of the safest and most reliable profit earners of all the nine positions outlined in this book. It is not the one which can earn the greatest % of profit, but it is likely the most consistent earner.   "Sell a call or a put at 50¢ out of the money" is mentioned in every one of the nine categories above.

  <u>The least mentioned option position</u> is number 2 (buy a call or a put at 50¢ out of the money). Therefore you will find that number 2 is the least useful of the 9 positions outlined above.

PART V

THE DECISION MAKER TABLES

This is where you select the safest and the most profitable of the 9 option positions.

THE DECISION MAKER TABLES

This is where you select the safest and the most profitable of the 9 option positions.

This section was constructed for those option traders who want the highest degree of safety for their working capital, plus a good to moderate return on their invested capital.

This section will tell you:
1. Which of the 9 selected option positions is the best one to trade under a variety of conditions as determined by the current rate of volatility, length of time to expiration, and the price.
2. Which of the 9 options will earn the best percentage return on your investment.
3. which of the 9 options have been rejected because they did not meet the high safety standards.

WHY and HOW THESE SAFETY and PROFIT TABLES WERE MADE

WHY

You have just read the previous section which contained the safety charts. In those charts, you saw such initials as "R, S, VS " which means "Risky, Safe, Very Safe ". The "safety " in those charts was arrived at by constructing a safety zone of 50¢ to 5¢, depending on the volatility.

This section goes further in 2 ways (1) the protective "safety zone" is more stringent than the safety zone in the previous section. (2) Also, you will see how much percentage profit you can expect from each of the 9 selected option positions.

The following tables were constructed especially for those traders and investors who are seeking the greatest amount of safety for their working capital. You will see below just how strict the safety standards are – and you will be surprised to see that even with those stringent standards, one can still earn a good profit. The secret of success is in selecting the correct option strategy. And that's what this section will do – it will show you which of the 9 options positions is the best one to use, based on the volatility and time and price of the soybean market at that particular moment.

HOW

Before the following tables were constructed, the author thought long and hard on the question, "How safe should 'very safe' be?" In other words, if a soybean trader is seeking a "very safe " trade, how extreme should he go without killing the trade altogether by being too careful?

Back in the previous section where the safety charts are located, a safety zone of 50¢ to 5¢ was used. But this section in which you are now, is constructed with an even greater protection, a much wider safety zone than in the previous section.

By studying previous long term price moves in the past, it was found that the average long term price move was about $1.00 to $1.25 from the lowest soybean price for the year to the highest price. This study was needed so that one could decide how wide a safety zone could be used.

Then it was necessary to decide which of the 3 major factors would be used as the basis for the safety standard i.e. the volatility, time. or price. It was decided to use time as the base. This is because of the theory that the longer you hold your option position, the more likely it will be that something will go wrong. For example, if you sell a call with a time period of 36 weeks to expiration, then all kind of things can happen in 36 weeks. A drought could occur or a bumper soybean crop could develop in that long time. All kinds of unexpected events could happen in 36 weeks. Therefore, a wide safety zone is needed when you trade for the long term so that an unexpected event will not cause a loss of money.

On the other hand, a 4 week (short term) option position is not as risky as a long term trade because you can foresee most of the events which will likely happen in the next month. For example, you will know if there is a drought building up, or you will know how the Brazilian soybean crop is coming along. Because the short term position is less risky, then a narrower safety zone will suffice.

The problem. The problem here is this: a safety zone of sufficient magnitude would have to be created which would be so safe that an extraordinary event would not cause a loss of one's working capital. On the other hand, the safety standards must not be too severe because a "too severe" safety standard would hinder the implementation of an option position.

For example, the average soybean price change between the lowest and highest prices is about $1 to $1.25. So if a safety zone of $1 was used, there would not be many opportunities to take a soybean position. In other words, all the fun of trading would be gone because several seasons might pass before you had an opportunity to take a position within the standards of safety. So the question is," How wide should the safety zone be, so that one's working capital is protected and yet there will be ample chances for taking a position?"

The solution. It was decided to use a 70¢ safety zone for the long term, narrowing down to 55¢ for the short term. Here's how it was allocated: (1) a safety zone of 70¢ for a time period of 20 weeks to expiration or longer (2) a 65¢ safety zone for a time period of 19 to 11 weeks (3) a 60¢ safety zone for a period of 10 weeks to 7 weeks to expiration (4) a 55¢ zone for periods of less than 7 weeks to expiration.

Schematically, it looks like this:

a normal profit and loss , 20 weeks to exp.

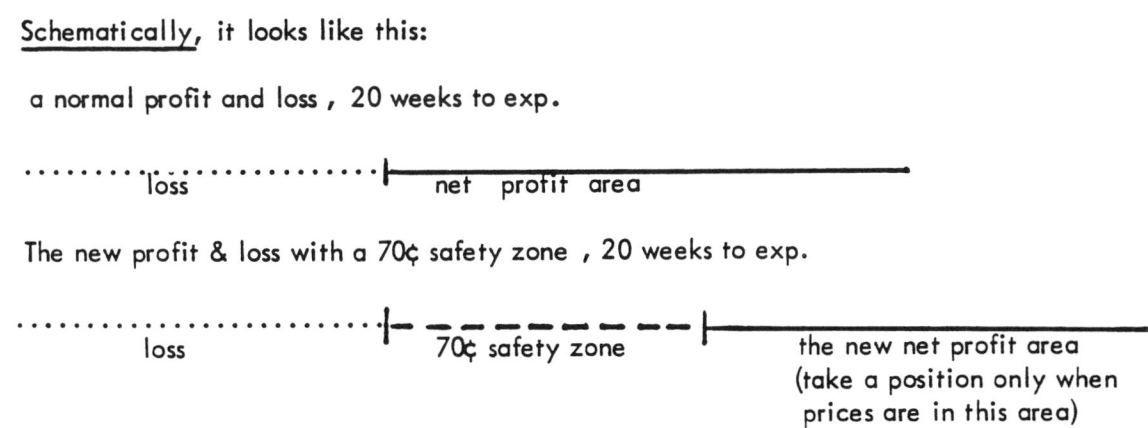

Here's the theory, using the diagram above. If you take the option only when prices are in the "new net profit area ", and if something goes wrong which could cause a price reversal, then your option would fall into the safety zone where you could get out with a small profit. If your option investment was long term, then prices would have to reverse by more than 70¢ before you would lose any money. It's not likely that you will encounter a price reversal of more than 70¢ very often. This is safe investing.

You might think that there would not be many option opportunities because the 70¢ zone might make it very difficult to find an option which meets those stringent safety standards and still produce a profit. Not so. You'll be surprised when you see the tables that there are usually 3 or 4 out of the 9 selected options which meet the strict standards and which also produce a good profit.

<u>But the safety zone has a different effect upon each of the 9 selected options.</u>
Two examples will show what is meant by the sentence above.

(1) <u>Buying a call at the money</u>, at 30 weeks to expiration , the premium is 30¢ .
    (a) The total cost is : 30¢ + 0.5¢ commission = a cost of 30.5¢.
    (b) Therefore you would need a price increase of 30.5¢ at expiration just to get your money back.
    (c) Then you add on 70¢ for the safety zone.
    (d) Therefore the Forecasting Graph would have to indicate a price rise of 100.5¢ or more before you would consider taking a long call option (30.5 + 70 = 100.5¢).

(2) <u>Selling a call at the money</u> , at 30 weeks to expiration , the premium is 30¢ .
    (a) Remember, you <u>sell</u> a call only when you expect prices to decline.
    (b) Your net profit from the sale is +29.5¢ (+30¢ - 0.5¢ commission = +29.5¢).
    (c) The safety zone is 70¢ (actually it is -70¢ because you expect prices to fall).
    (d) Therefore you would take this position only if the Forecasting Graph indicated that prices would fall by 40.5¢ or more (+29.5 - 70 = - 40.5¢).
    (e) Compare the price move here with the price move needed for the long call above. (40.5¢ vs 100.5¢)
    (f) You can see now that each of the 9 selected options will be affected differently by the size of the safety zone.

You might be wondering," Do I have to do calculations, like the calculation above, for each of the 9 options so that I can determine which one is the best one to use? It's a lot of work!"

<u>Answer</u>. No, you don't have to calculate anything. The author has done it for you. You need only to look at the appropriate table and you can see at a glance which is the best option position to use – and you can also see how much profit it will likely earn at the expiration date.

HOW THE FOLLOWING TABLES WERE MADE

The net profit was calculated for each of the 9 selected option positions, using this criteria:

(a) Each of the 9 options was tested for a time period of 36 wks. to exp. to 4 wks. to expiration.

(b) The safety zone of 70¢ to 55¢ was applied to each of the 9 options.

(c) A margin (which represents the amont of the investment) was applied to each "sell" position, and the amount of the margin varied from $800 for a low volatility position to $2500 for a high volatility position.

(d) The amount of the net profit for each of the 9 options was calculated for a price change from the Forecasting Graphs of 0¢ to 120¢, in 10¢ increments.

(e) The most profitable of the 9 options which met the stringent safety standards is listed first, followed by the second best option, followed by the third best, etc.

(f) The net profit at the expiration date is expressed as % (net profit $\div$ amount of investment x 100 = %)

(g) Even though each of the 9 selected option positions was tested, you will notice that some of them are missing from the table. That's because the missing options did not meet the strict safety standards.

It is time to take a look at a table. Each part will be explained.

Use this page when you expect soybean prices to *RISE*

1 BUY A CALL *AT THE MONEY*

2 BUY A CALL *AT 50¢ OUT OF THE MONEY*

3 SELL A PUT *AT THE MONEY*

4 SELL A PUT *AT 50¢ OUT OF THE MONEY*

5 BULL SPREAD
BUY A CALL AT THE MONEY
and SELL A CALL AT 25¢ OUT OF THE MONEY

6 REVERSE BULL SPREAD
BUY A PUT AT THE MONEY
and SELL 2 PUTS AT 50¢ OUT OF THE MONEY

7 SELL A STRADDLE
SELL A CALL AT THE MONEY
and SELL A PUT AT THE MONEY

8 SELL A STRANGLE – #1
SELL A CALL AT 50¢ OUT OF THE MONEY
and SELL A PUT AT 50¢ OUT OF THE MONEY

9 SELL A STRANGLE – #2
SELL A CALL AT $1.00 OUT OF THE MONEY
and SELL A PUT AT $1.00 OUT OF THE MONEY

weeks to
26
expiration

the amount of the estimated soybean price increase

Table No.	0¢	10¢	20¢	30¢	40¢	50¢	60¢	70¢	80¢	90¢	100¢	110¢	120¢
20	9=27	4=38 9=27	4=38 9=27	4=38 9=27	3=103 4=38 9=27	3=103 4=38	3=103 4=38	3=103 4=38	3=103 5=68 4=38	1=305 3=103 5=68 4=38	1=350 3=103 5=68 4=38	1=396 3=103 5=68 4=38	2=690 % 1=441 % 3=103 % 5=68 % 4=38 %
30	8=133 4=68 9=64	8=133 4=68 9=64	4=68 9=64	4=68 9=64	3=143 4=68 9=64	3=143 4=68	3=143 4=68	3=143 4=68	3=143 4=68 5=48	3=143 4=68 5=48	1=230 3=143 4=68 5=48	1=263 3=143 4=68 5=48	1=296 % 3=143 % 4=68 % 5=48 %
40	8=133 9=74 4=67 6=7	8=133 9=74 4=67 6=7	8=133 9=74 4=67 6=7	3=120 9=74 4=67 6=7	3=120 9=74 4=67 6=7	3=120 9=74 4=67	3=120 4=67	3=120 4=67	3=120 4=67 5=39	3=120 4=67 5=39	3=120 4=67 5=39	1=86 3=120 4=67 5=39	1=223 % 3=120 % 4=67 % 5=39 %
50	7=292 8=179 9=114 4=90 6=14	7=260 8=179 9=114 4=90 6=14	7=228 8=179 3=146 9=114 4=90 6=14	8=179 3=146 9=114 4=90 6=14	3=146 9=114 4=90 6=14	3=146 9=114 4=90	3=146 9=114 4=90	3=146 4=90	3=146 4=90 5=31	3=146 4=90 5=31	3=146 4=90 5=31	3=146 4=90 5=31	1=159 % 3=146 % 4=90 % 5=31 %
60	7=340 8=230 9=166 4=115 6=22	7=319 8=230 9=166 4=115 6=22	7=297 8=230 3=176 9=166 4=115 6=22	7=275 8=230 3=176 9=166 4=115 6=22	8=230 7=230 3=176 9=166 4=115 6=22	8=230 3=176 9=166 4=115 6=22	3=176 9=166 4=115	3=176 9=166 4=115 5=26	3=176 9=166 4=115 5=26	3=176 4=155 5=26	3=176 4=155 5=26	3=176 4=155 5=26	3=176 % 4=155 % 5=26 %
70	7=396 8=277 9=207 4=141 6=29	7=363 8=277 9=207 3=201 4=141 6=29	7=331 8=277 9=207 3=201 4=141 6=29	7=299 8=277 9=207 3=201 4=141 6=29	8=277 7=267 9=207 3=201 4=141 6=29	8=277 7=235 9=207 3=201 4=141 6=29	8=245 9=207 3=201 4=141	8=213 9=207 3=201 4=141	9=207 3=201 4=141 5=23	9=207 3=201 4=141 5=23	3=201 4=141 5=23	3=201 4=141 5=23	3=201 % 4=141 % 5=23 %
80	7=338 8=250 9=194 3=171 4=124 6=35	7=314 8=250 9=194 3=171 4=124 6=35	7=290 8=250 9=194 3=171 4=124 6=35	7=265 8=250 9=194 3=171 4=124 6=35	8=250 7=241 9=194 3=171 4=124 6=35	8=250 7=217 9=194 3=171 4=124 6=35	8=224 7=192 9=194 3=171 4=124 6=35	8=199 9=194 7=168 3=171 4=124	9=194 8=174 3=171 4=124 5=20	9=194 3=171 4=124 5=20	9=194 3=171 4=124 5=20	3=171 9=170 4=124 5=20	3=171 % 4=124 % 5=20 %

1. Look at the sample table above.

2. Note title,"Use this page when you expect soybean prices to RISE". There are 2 sections to these tables.
   (1) One section is used when the Forecasting Graphs indicate that prices will RISE.
   (2) The other section is used when the Forecasting Graphs indicate that prices will FALL.

3. Note that each of the 9 selected options has been assigned a number. For example, #4 represents "sell a put at 50¢ out of the money."

4. Look at the top line of the table. It shows the amount of the price rise as estimated by the Forecasting Graphs, in 10¢ increments.

5. Look at the margin at the left side. These are table numbers. As you already know, table 20 represents a low rate of volatility, table 80 represents a high rate of volatility.

6. Finally we arrive at the important part – the contents of the chart itself. The numbers here represent the option positions which are numbered above, plus the estimated profit %. The options shown here are the options which have met the safety standards. You will note that some of the 9 options are not listed in some places. That means that those missing options did not meet the safety standards for that price level.

7. Example: Follow this in the chart above.
   (a) Let's say that you wished to take an option position at 26 weeks to expiration.
   (b) Let's also say that the Forecasting Graph indicated a price rise of 70¢.
   (c) Let's say that the Table Finder page indicated table 50 as the current volatility.
   (d) Do this. Look down the 70¢ column until it meets the table 50 row. At that juncture you see 3=146 and 4=90. Look at the top of the page and you see that 3 represents "sell a put at the money", and it should earn an estimated 146% on the investment in 26 weeks. The number 4 represents "sell a put at 50¢ out of the money"and it should earn an estimated 90% in 26 weeks.

8. You will note that the numbers 3 and 4 are the only options which meet the safety standards when prices are expected to rise by 70¢ for table 50. But the profit is good.

9. But if you look along the table 50 row, you can see that other options become eligible to use. This shows that a different size of price increase will require a different option. For example, at 0¢ there are 5 options which meet the safety standards for table 50. You can see from this that various degrees of volatility, time, and price will require a different kind of option position.

10. You can see now that these tables are exactly what an option trader needs.
    (a) The options on the chart satisfy the strict safety standards.
    (b) You can see which option is the best one to use, as determined by the volatility, time, and price.
    (c) You can see what the estimated net profit % is likely to be.

11. One of the options listed at the top of the page should be explained. It is #6, "Reverse Bull Spread". This one is the reverse of "Bull Spread #2". Look back at the option charts which show a heavy black line around the net profit areas. Find the "Bull Spread #2" net profit area for the 25th week to exp., Table 60. Got it? Now look at the bottom half of the chart and note that profits here extend to infinity. This is an ultra safe area.
   Now think back again. Do you remember reading in a previous section that one could almost achieve "The 100% Sure Thing" by deliberately trying to get into this area, the bottom half of the Bull Spread #2? By deliberately trading in this area, you will have a position which is much safer than a

good blue chip stock. But the % profit is low.

Look again at our sample table with 26 wks. to exp. Locate the #6 trade for Table 50. You will se it at the bottom because the profit is small. Note the net profit of 14% in 26 weeks, or on an annual basis it is 28% which is a pretty good return on an almost "100% Sure Thing". To sum up, the #6 option deliberately projects your position into the safe bottom half of the Bull Spread #2.

But the use of this tactic is limited. To function best, it need a long term and an above average rate of volatility for best results. Look at all the #6 net profit percentages and you can see that a high volatility will give you a good annual rate of return with no risk, almost. The word "almost" was added to that last sentence because there is a saying in the commodity business that nothing is 100% certain - so let's say that #6 is 98% certain.

You might be wondering why #6 is included in our list of 9 options. The answer is that many people who trade in commodities still want security, want some trade which is safer than a good blue chip stock, safer than the average mutual fund, and nearly as secure as a T-bill and which will pay better than a stock, mutual fund, or a T-bill. The #6 option will do it with the right conditions of weeks to expiration and volatility.

12. Something should be pointed out on the sample chart with 26 wks. to exp. Look down the 70¢ column from the top at table 20. Look at the % return for #3 option. It starts at 103%, then 143%, then 120%. That 120% might seem like an error but it is not. What happened here is a change in the amount of margin needed (you need to deposit a margin into your account when you are "selling" an option). The amount of margin required increases as the volatility increases. In this book margins of $800 to $2500 were used. So a change in margin will affect the "rate" of profit, but it will not affect the amount of the profit. Look at the #3 trade in tables 70 and 80 and you will see a change from 201% to 171% in the 70¢ column. This was caused by a change in the amount of margin needed. With all things being equal, both the % profit and the "amount" of profit will increase as the volatility increases. But a change in margin will affect the % but not affect the amount of profit.

IT IS TIME TO DO A COMPLETE EXAMPLE - FROM BEGINNING TO END

1. The date is Oct. 21st and you think that soybeans are at or close to their harvest lows. You think that there may be a good profit in taking a May option. You calculate the time to expiration and you get 26 weeks.

2. The next step is to find out from the Forecasting Graphs whether May soybean prices will likely rise or fall. And by how much.
   (a) You look in the morning paper at yeaterday's closing price and you see that May beans closed at $6.
   (b) The current estimated carryover is 12%.
   (c) Using the May Forecasting Graph and the 12% carryover, you get an estimated $7.00 on May 1st.
   (d) Therefore, you estimate that bean prices will rise by $1 by May 1st.

3. The next step is to find the current volatility in the soybean market. This is accomplished by using the Table Finder page to find the table number which represents the volatility. (Remember, Table 20 represents a low rate of volatility, and Table 80 represents a high rate of volatility, and Tables 40 and 50 represent a moderate rate of volatility.)
   (a) You look at the soybean option quotes in the paper, and you see this:

		CALLS	
strike	Jan	Mar	May
550	56	70	85
575	32 1/2	49	60 1/2
600	21	33	45 3/4
625	17	23	30

(b) You want the "at the money" quote. The Table Finder pages use the "at the money" premium. The present price of May soybeans is $6.00. So you find 600 in the strike price column, look to the right under the May heading, and you get the "at the money" premium for May of <u>45 3/4 cents.</u>

(c) Turn to the Table Finder pages and search the 26 week column to locate 45 3/4 or 45.7. You find the closest, which is 45.8. Look to the right and you see that <u>Table 50</u> represents the volatility. You now have all the data you need – volatility, time, price.

4. Turn, now, to the pertinent page. (Remember there are two sections here : one section for rising prices, one section for falling prices.) Turn to the section for <u>rising</u> prices, and <u>locate Table 26 weeks to exp.</u>

(a) You are now at the "26 wks. to exp." page, for <u>rising</u> prices.

(b) The Forecasting Graph estimated that the May price would rise by $1.00.

(c) Look down the 100¢ column to intercept the Table 50 row.

(d) At the junction of the 100¢ column and the Table 50 row you see 3 options which meet the strict safety standards. They are #3, #4, and #5. The most profitable one is #3 which should earn about 146% on your investment at the expiration date in 26 weeks time. Looking at the top of the page you see that #3 represents " Sell a put at the money " (or as near the money as you can get).

5. That's all there is to it. What you have really done is to find the best and safest option position, based on the volatility, time, and price of the moment.

6. This was an easy example, with all the numbers coming out exact, with no interpolation needed. This was done deliberately for this example in order to keep it simple. The last thing that anyone needs when doing something for the first time, is unnecessary complications such as interpolations.

       But in real life, you will often have to interpolate between numbers such as finding the "at the money" option value, or , if you needed Table 43's values then you must interpolate between Tables 40 and 50, and so on.

7. Here are the steps again:

(a) Find the number of weeks to expiration.

(b) Use the Forecasting Graphs to find if prices will rise or fall, and by how much.

(c) Find the "at the money" value of the option from the option quote page.

(d) Use the "at the money" value with the "weeks to expiration" on the Table Finder pages in order to find the Table Number (which is actually the current volatility).

(e) Turn to the pertinent table which is signified by the "wks. to exp." number, but be sure it is in the correct section i.e. either the Rising <u>or</u> the Falling price section.

USE THE FOLLOWING TABLES WHEN YOU EXPECT SOYBEAN PRICES TO <u>RISE</u>

1. Calculate the "at the money" option value.

2. Find the "weeks to expiration".

3. Use the information found above to find the corresponding Table Number.

4. Turn to the nearest appropriate "weeks to expiration" page in the following pages.

5. Use the appropriate Forecasting Graph to get the amount of the estimated price rise.

6. Using the estimated price rise, and using the appropriate Table Number found above, interpolate to find the best soybean option trade.

Use this page when you expect soybean prices to *RISE*

1 BUY A CALL *AT THE MONEY*

2 BUY A CALL *AT 50¢ OUT OF THE MONEY*

3 SELL A PUT *AT THE MONEY*

4 SELL A PUT *AT 50¢ OUT OF THE MONEY*

5 BULL SPREAD
BUY A CALL AT THE MONEY
and *SELL A CALL AT 25¢ OUT OF THE MONEY*

6 REVERSE BULL SPREAD
BUY A PUT AT THE MONEY
and *SELL 2 PUTS AT 50¢ OUT OF THE MONEY*

7 SELL A STRADDLE
SELL A CALL AT THE MONEY
and *SELL A PUT AT THE MONEY*

8 SELL A STRANGLE – #1
SELL A CALL AT 50¢ OUT OF THE MONEY
and *SELL A PUT AT 50¢ OUT OF THE MONEY*

9 SELL A STRANGLE – #2
SELL A CALL AT $1.00 OUT OF THE MONEY
and *SELL A PUT AT $1.00 OUT OF THE MONEY*

weeks to

4

expiration

the amount of the estimated soybean price increase

Table No.	0¢	10¢	20¢	30¢	40¢	50¢	60¢	70¢	80¢	90¢	100¢	110¢	120¢
20	4=0 9=0	4=0 9=0	4=0 9=0	4=0 9=0	3=41 4=0	3=41 4=0	1=531 5=169 3=41 4=0	1=636 5=169 3=41 4=0	1=743 5=168 3=41 4=0	1=848 5=169 3=41 4=0	1=953 5=169 3=41 4=0	2=5900 1=1058 5=169 3=41	2=6900 % 1=1163 % 5=169 % 3=41 %
30	4=7 9=0	4=7 9=0	4=7 9=0	4=7 9=0	3=58 4=7 9=0	3=58 4=7	5=122 3=58 4=7	1=447 5=122 3=58 4=7	1=525 5=122 3=58 4=7	1=603 5=122 3=58 4=7	1=681 5=122 3=58 4=7	1=735 5=122 3=58 4=7	1=789 % 5=122 % 3=58 % 4=7 %
40	8=23 4=12 9=4	4=12 9=4	4=12 9=4	4=12 9=4	3=49 4=12 9=4	3=49 4=12	3=49 4=12	5=96 3=49 4=12	1=394 5=96 3=49 4=12	1=458 5=96 3=49 4=12	1=517 5=96 3=49 4=12	1=576 5=96 3=49 4=12	1=641 % 5=96 % 3=49 % 4=12 %
50	8=39 4=19 9=10	8=39 4=19 9=10	4=19 9=10	4=19 9=10	3=60 4=19 9=10	3=60 4=19 9=10	3=60 4=19	5=78 3=60 4=19	1=310 5=78 3=60 4=19	1=362 5=78 3=60 4=19	1=413 5=78 3=60 4=19	1=464 5=78 3=60 4=19	1=516 % 5=78 % 3=60 % 4=19 %
60	8=53 4=26 9=19	8=53 4=26 9=19	4=26 9=19	3=70 4=26 9=19	3=70 4=26 9=19	3=70 4=26 9=19	3=70 4=26	3=70 5=67 4=26	3=70 5=67 4=26	1=298 3=70 5=67 4=26	1=338 3=70 5=67 4=26	1=374 3=70 5=67 4=26	1=412 % 3=70 % 5=67 % 4=26 %
70	7=162 8=69 4=35 9=30	7=129 8=69 4=35 9=30	8=69 3=83 4=35 9=30	3=83 4=35 9=30	3=83 4=35 9=30	3=83 4=35 9=30	3=83 4=35 9=30	3=83 5=57 4=35	3=83 5=57 4=35	1=345 3=83 5=57 4=35	1=383 3=83 5=57 4=35	1=421 3=83 5=57 4=35	1=459 % 3=83 % 5=57 % 4=35 %
80	8=65 4=33 9=30	8=65 4=33 9=30	8=65 4=33 9=30	3=70 4=33 9=30	3=70 4=33 9=30	3=70 4=33 9=30	3=70 4=33 9=30	3=70 5=50 4=33	3=70 5=50 4=33	1=205 3=70 5=50 4=33	1=239 3=70 5=50 4=33	1=316 3=70 5=50 4=33	1=385 % 3=70 % 5=50 % 4=33 %

Wm Grandmill (1985) Ltd.

Use this page when you expect soybean prices to *RISE*

1 BUY A CALL *AT THE MONEY*

2 BUY A CALL *AT 50¢ OUT OF THE MONEY*

3 SELL A PUT *AT THE MONEY*

4 SELL A PUT *AT 50¢ OUT OF THE MONEY*

5 BULL SPREAD
BUY A CALL AT THE MONEY
and SELL A CALL AT 25¢ OUT OF THE MONEY

6 REVERSE BULL SPREAD
BUY A PUT AT THE MONEY
and SELL 2 PUTS AT 50¢ OUT OF THE MONEY

7 SELL A STRADDLE
SELL A CALL AT THE MONEY
and SELL A PUT AT THE MONEY

8 SELL A STRANGLE – #1
SELL A CALL AT 50¢ OUT OF THE MONEY
and SELL A PUT AT 50¢ OUT OF THE MONEY

9 SELL A STRANGLE – #2
SELL A CALL AT $1.00 OUT OF THE MONEY
and SELL A PUT AT $1.00 OUT OF THE MONEY

weeks to **6** expiration

the amount of the estimated soybean price increase

Table No.	0¢	10¢	20¢	30¢	40¢	50¢	60¢	70¢	80¢	90¢	100¢	110¢	120¢
20	9=0	4=0 9=0	4=0 9=0	4=0 9=0	4=0	3=55 4=0	3=55 4=0	1=474 5=128 3=55 4=0	1=555 5=128 3=55 4=0	1=637 5=128 3=55 4=0	1=720 5=128 3=55 4=0	2=3057 1=802 5=128 3=55 4=0	2=3583 % 1=884 % 5=128 % 3=55 % 4=0
30	4=19 9=7	4=19 9=7	4=19 9=7	4=19 9=7	3=76 4=19 9=7	3=76 4=19	3=76 5=93 4=19	1=324 5=93 3=76 4=19	1=384 5=93 3=76 4=19	1=444 5=93 3=76 4=19	1=506 5=93 3=76 4=19	1=567 5=93 3=76 4=19	1=628 % 5=93 % 3=76 % 4=19 %
40	8=44 4=22 9=14	4=22 9=14	4=22 9=14	4=22 9=14	3=64 4=22 9=14	3=64 4=22	3=64 4=22	5=73 3=64 4=22	1=284 5=73 3=64 4=22	1=332 5=73 3=64 4=22	1=380 5=73 3=64 4=22	1=428 5=73 3=64 4=22	1=476 % 5=73 % 3=64 % 4=22 %
50	8=65 4=32 9=26	8=65 4=32 9=26	4=32 9=26	3=78 4=32 9=26	3=78 4=32 9=26	3=78 4=32 9=26	3=78 4=32	3=78 5=59 4=32	1=219 3=78 5=59 4=32	1=259 3=78 5=59 4=32	1=298 3=78 5=59 4=32	1=338 3=78 5=59 4=32	1=378 % 3=78 % 5=59 % 4=32 %
60	8=85 4=43 9=40	8=85 4=43 9=40	8=85 4=43 9=40	3=91 4=43 9=40	3=91 4=43 9=40	3=91 4=43 9=40	3=91 4=43 9=40	3=91 5=51 4=43	3=91 5=51 4=43	1=212 3=91 5=51 4=43	1=240 3=91 5=51 4=43	1=268 3=91 5=51 4=43	1=296 % 3=91 % 5=51 % 4=43 %
70	7=212 8=108 9=57 4=55	7=179 8=108 9=57 4=55	8=108 3=108 9=57 4=55	8=108 3=108 9=57 4=55	3=108 9=57 4=55	3=108 9=57 4=55	3=108 9=57 4=55	3=108 4=55 5=43	3=108 4=55 5=43	1=267 3=108 4=55 5=43	1=296 3=108 4=55 5=43	1=325 3=108 4=55 5=43	1=354 % 3=108 % 4=55 % 5=43 %
80	7=181 8=100 9=56 4=50 6=5	7=156 8=100 9=56 4=50 6=5	7=132 8=100 3=92 9=56 4=50 6=5	8=100 3=92 9=56 4=50 6=5	3=92 9=56 4=50 6=5	3=92 9=56 4=50	3=92 9=56 4=50	3=92 4=50 5=38	3=92 4=50 5=38	1=136 3=92 4=50 5=38	1=162 3=92 4=50 5=38	1=188 3=92 4=50 5=38	1=215 % 3=92 % 4=50 % 5=38 %

Wm Grandmill (1985) Ltd.

Use this page when you expect soybean prices to *RISE*

1 BUY A CALL *AT THE MONEY*

2 BUY A CALL *AT 50¢ OUT OF THE MONEY*

3 SELL A PUT *AT THE MONEY*

4 SELL A PUT *AT 50¢ OUT OF THE MONEY*

5 BULL SPREAD
BUY A CALL AT THE MONEY
and *SELL A CALL AT 25¢ OUT OF THE MONEY*

6 REVERSE BULL SPREAD
BUY A PUT AT THE MONEY
and *SELL 2 PUTS AT 50¢ OUT OF THE MONEY*

7 SELL A STRADDLE
SELL A CALL AT THE MONEY
and *SELL A PUT AT THE MONEY*

8 SELL A STRANGLE – #1
SELL A CALL AT 50¢ OUT OF THE MONEY
and *SELL A PUT AT 50¢ OUT OF THE MONEY*

9 SELL A STRANGLE – #2
SELL A CALL AT $1.00 OUT OF THE MONEY
and *SELL A PUT AT $1.00 OUT OF THE MONEY*

weeks to

8

expiration

Table No.	0¢	10¢	20¢	30¢	40¢	50¢	60¢	70¢	80¢	90¢	100¢	110¢	120¢
20	9=0	4=11 9=0	4=11 9=0	4=11 9=0	4=11	3=63 4=11	3=63 4=11	1=400 5=112 3=63 4=11	1=471 5=112 3=63 4=11	1=542 5=112 3=63 4=11	1=614 5=112 3=63 4=11	2=1775 1=686 5=112 3=63 4=11	2=2088 % 1=757 % 5=112 % 3=63 % 4=11 %
30	4=25 9=15	4=25 9=15	4=25 9=15	4=25 9=15	3=88 4=25 9=15	3=88 4=25	3=88 4=25	3=88 4=25	1=321 3=88 4=25	1=376 3=88 4=25	1=428 3=88 4=25	1=478 3=88 4=25	1=532 % 3=88 % 4=25 %
40	8=59 4=29 9=29	8=59 4=29 9=29	4=29 9=29	4=29 9=29	3=74 4=29 9=29	3=74 4=29 9=29	3=74 4=29	3=74 5=62 4=29	1=233 3=74 5=62 4=29	1=274 3=74 5=62 4=29	1=317 3=74 5=62 4=29	1=358 3=74 5=62 4=29	1=400 % 3=74 % 5=62 % 4=29 %
50	8=83 4=42 9=39	8=83 4=42 9=39	4=42 9=39	3=90 4=42 9=39	3=90 4=42 9=39	3=90 4=42 3=39	3=90 4=42	3=90 5=50 4=42	3=90 5=50 4=42	1=211 3=90 5=50 4=42	1=244 3=90 5=50 4=42	1=279 3=90 5=50 4=42	1=314 % 3=90 % 5=50 %. 4=42 %
60	8=108 9=57 4=54	8=108 9=57 4=54	8=108 9=57 4=54	8=108 3=106 9=57 4=54	3=106 9=57 4=54	3=106 9=57 4=54	3=106 9=57 4=54	3=106 4=54 5=43	3=106 4=54 5=43	3=106 3=106 5=43	1=94 3=106 4=54 5=43	1=218 3=106 4=54 5=43	1=242 % 3=106 % 4=54 % 5=43 %
70	7=244 8=136 9=77 4=69 6=6	7=212 8=136 9=77 4=69 6=6	7=180 8=136 9=77 3=124 4=69 6=6	8=136 9=77 3=124 4=69 6=6	3=124 9=77 4=69 6=6	3=124 9=77 4=69	3=124 9=77 4=69	3=124 4=69 5=37	3=124 4=69 5=37	3=124 4=69 5=37	1=257 3=124 4=69 5=37	1=283 3=124 4=69 5=37	1=309 % 3=124 % 4=69 % 5=37 %
80	7=210 8=125 9=76 4=63 6=12	7=186 8=125 9=76 4=63 6=12	7=161 8=125 3=106 9=76 4=63 6=12	7=137 8=125 3=106 9=76 4=63 6=12	8=125 3=106 9=76 4=63 6=12	3=106 9=76 4=63 6=12	3=106 9=76 4=63	3=106 4=63 5=33	3=106 4=63 5=33	3=106 4=63 5=33	1=127 3=106 4=63 5=33	1=150 3=106 4=63 5=33	1=172 % 3=106 % 4=63 % 5=33 %

the amount of the estimated soybean price increase

Wm Grandmill (1985) Ltd.

Use this page when you expect soybean prices to *RISE*

1 BUY A CALL *AT THE MONEY*

2 BUY A CALL *AT 50¢ OUT OF THE MONEY*

3 SELL A PUT *AT THE MONEY*

4 SELL A PUT *AT 50¢ OUT OF THE MONEY*

5 BULL SPREAD
BUY A CALL AT THE MONEY
and *SELL A CALL AT 25¢ OUT OF THE MONEY*

6 REVERSE BULL SPREAD
BUY A PUT AT THE MONEY
and *SELL 2 PUTS AT 50¢ OUT OF THE MONEY*

7 SELL A STRADDLE
SELL A CALL AT THE MONEY
and *SELL A PUT AT THE MONEY*

8 SELL A STRANGLE – #1
SELL A CALL AT 50¢ OUT OF THE MONEY
and *SELL A PUT AT 50¢ OUT OF THE MONEY*

9 SELL A STRANGLE – #2
SELL A CALL AT $1.00 OUT OF THE MONEY
and *SELL A PUT AT $1.00 OUT OF THE MONEY*

the amount of the estimated soybean price increase

Table No.	0¢	10¢	20¢	30¢	40¢	50¢	60¢	70¢	80¢	90¢	100¢	110¢	120¢
20	9=0	4=16 9=0	4=16 9=0	4=16 9=0	4=16	3=70 4=16	3=70 4=16	1=355 5=100 3=70 4=16	1=419 5=100 3=70 4=16	1=485 5=100 3=70 4=16	1=549 5=100 3=70 4=16	2=1363 1=614 5=100 3=70 4=16	2=1607 % 1=680 % 5=100 % 3=70 % 4=16 %
30	4=34 9=22	4=34 9=22	4=34 9=22	4=34 9=22	3=98 4=34 9=22	3=98 4=34	3=98 4=34	3=98 5=72 4=34	1=281 3=98 5=72 4=34	1=329 3=98 5=72 4=34	1=376 3=98 5=72 4=34	1=424 3=98 5=72 4=34	1=471 % 3=98 % 5=72 % 4=34 %
40	8=72 4=36 9=31	8=72 4=36 9=31	4=36 9=31	4=36 9=31	3=82 4=36 9=31	3=82 4=36 9=31	3=82 4=36	3=82 5=57 4=36	3=82 5=57 4=36	1=239 3=82 5=57 4=36	1=277 3=82 5=57 4=36	1=315 3=82 5=57 4=36	1=353 % 3=82 % 5=57 % 4=36 %
50	8=100 9=50 4=50 6=0	8=100 9=50 4=50 6=0	8=100 9=50 4=50 6=0	3=100 9=50 4=50 6=0	3=100 9=50 4=50	3=100 9=50 4=50	3=100 4=50	3=100 4=50	3=100 4=50 5=45	1=180 3=100 4=50 5=45	1=212 3=100 4=50 5=45	1=234 3=100 4=50 5=45	1=274 % 3=100 % 4=50 % 5=45 %
60	7=236 8=129 9=71 4=67 6=4	7=209 8=129 9=71 4=67 6=4	8=129 9=71 4=67 6=4	8=129 3=122 9=71 4=67 6=4	3=122 9=71 4=67 6=4	3=122 9=71 4=67	3=122 9=71 4=67	3=122 4=67 5=39	3=122 4=67 5=39	3=122 4=67 5=39	1=166 3=122 4=67 5=39	1=188 3=122 4=67 5=39	1=210 % 3=122 % 4=67 % 5=39 %
70	7=272 8=160 9=97 4=82 6=11	7=239 8=160 9=97 4=82 6=11	7=207 8=160 3=138 9=97 6=11	8=160 3=138 9=97 4=82 6=11	8=160 3=138 9=97 4=82 6=11	3=138 9=97 4=82 6=11	3=138 9=97 4=82	3=138 9=97 4=82 5=33	3=138 4=82 5=33	3=138 4=82 5=33	1=232 3=138 4=82 5=33	1=255 3=138 4=82 5=33	1=279 % 3=138 % 4=82 % 5=33 %
80	7=233 8=146 9=95 4=74 6=16	7=208 8=146 3=117 9=95 4=74 6=16	7=183 8=146 3=117 9=95 4=74 6=16	7=159 8=146 3=117 9=95 4=74 6=16	8=146 7=135 3=117 9=95 4=74 6=16	8=146 3=117 9=95 4=74 6=16	3=117 9=95 4=74	3=117 9=95 4=74 5=30	3=117 9=95 4=74 5=30	3=117 4=74 5=30	3=117 4=74 5=30	1=124 3=117 4=74 5=30	1=146 % 3=117 % 4=74 % 5=30 %

Wm Grandmill (1985) Ltd.

Use this page when you expect soybean prices to *RISE*

1 BUY A CALL *AT THE MONEY*

2 BUY A CALL *AT 50¢ OUT OF THE MONEY*

3 SELL A PUT *AT THE MONEY*

4 SELL A PUT *AT 50¢ OUT OF THE MONEY*

5 BULL SPREAD
BUY A CALL AT THE MONEY
and SELL A CALL AT 25¢ OUT OF THE MONEY

6 REVERSE BULL SPREAD
BUY A PUT AT THE MONEY
and SELL 2 PUTS AT 50¢ OUT OF THE MONEY

7 SELL A STRADDLE
SELL A CALL AT THE MONEY
and SELL A PUT AT THE MONEY

8 SELL A STRANGLE – #1
SELL A CALL AT 50¢ OUT OF THE MONEY
and SELL A PUT AT 50¢ OUT OF THE MONEY

9 SELL A STRANGLE – #2
SELL A CALL AT $1.00 OUT OF THE MONEY
and SELL A PUT AT $1.00 OUT OF THE MONEY

weeks to
12
expiration

the amount of the estimated soybean price increase

Table No.	0¢	10¢	20¢	30¢	40¢	50¢	60¢	70¢	80¢	90¢	100¢	110¢	120¢
20	9=6	4=20 9=6	4=20 9=6	4=20 9=6	4=20	3=76 4=20	3=76 4=20	5=92 3=76 4=20	1=380 5=92 3=76 4=20	1=440 5=92 3=76 4=20	1=500 5=92 3=76 4=20	2=1100 1=560 5=92 3=76 4=20	2=1300 % 1=620 % 5=92 % 3=76 % 4=20 %
30	4=40 9=30	4=40 9=30	4=40 9=30	4=40 9=30	3=101 4=40 9=30	3=101 4=40	3=101 4=40	3=101 4=40	3=101 5=66 4=40	1=296 3=101 5=66 4=40	1=341 3=101 5=66 4=40	1=485 3=101 5=66 4=40	1=429 % 3=101 % 5=66 % 4=40 %
40	8=82 4=41 9=38	8=82 4=41 9=38	4=41 9=38	4=41 9=38	3=89 4=41 9=38	3=89 4=41 9=38	3=89 4=41	3=89 4=41	3=89 5=53 4=41	1=212 3=89 5=53 4=41	1=248 3=89 5=53 4=41	1=282 3=89 5=53 4=41	1=317 % 3=89 % 5=53 % 4=41 %
50	8=113 9=61 4=56 6=1	8=113 9=61 4=56 6=1	8=113 9=61 4=56 6=1	3=109 9=61 4=56 6=1	3=109 9=61 4=56	3=109 9=61 4=56	3=109 4=56	3=109 4=56 5=42	3=109 4=56 5=42	3=109 4=56 5=42	1=188 3=109 4=56 5=42	1=217 3=109 4=56 5=42	1=246 % 3=109 % 4=56 % 5=42 %
60	7=264 8=151 9=88 4=75 6=7	7=236 8=151 9=88 4=75 6=7	8=151 9=88 4=75 6=7	8=151 3=132 9=88 4=75 6=7	3=132 9=88 4=75 6=7	3=132 9=88 4=75	3=132 9=88 4=75	3=132 4=75	3=132 4=75 5=36	3=132 4=75 5=36	3=132 4=75 5=36	1=166 3=132 4=75 5=36	1=186 % 3=132 % 4=75 % 5=36 %
70	7=294 8=181 9=115 4=92 6=15	7=261 8=181 9=115 4=92 6=15	7=229 8=181 3=150 9=115 4=92 6=15	7=197 8=181 3=150 9=115 4=92 6=15	8=181 3=150 9=115 4=92 6=15	3=150 9=115 4=92 6=15	3=150 9=115 4=92	3=150 9=115 4=92	3=150 4=92 5=31	3=150 4=92 5=31	3=150 4=92 5=31	1=236 3=150 4=92 5=31	1=257 % 3=150 % 4=92 % 5=31 %
80	7=252 8=164 9=112 4=83 6=20	7=227 8=164 3=128 9=112 4=83 6=20	7=203 8=164 3=128 9=112 4=83 6=20	7=179 8=164 3=128 9=112 4=83 6=20	8=164 7=154 3=128 9=112 4=83 6=20	8=164 3=128 9=127 4=83	3=128 9=112 4=83	3=128 9=112 4=83 5=27	3=128 9=112 4=83 5=27	3=128 4=83 5=27	3=128 4=83 5=27	3=128 4=83 5=27	3=128 % 1=127 % 4=83 % 5=27 %

Wm Grandmill (1985) Ltd.

Use this page when you expect soybean prices to *RISE*

1 BUY A CALL *AT THE MONEY*

2 BUY A CALL *AT 50¢ OUT OF THE MONEY*

3 SELL A PUT *AT THE MONEY*

4 SELL A PUT *AT 50¢ OUT OF THE MONEY*

5 BULL SPREAD
BUY A CALL AT THE MONEY
and *SELL A CALL AT 25¢ OUT OF THE MONEY*

6 REVERSE BULL SPREAD
BUY A PUT AT THE MONEY
and *SELL 2 PUTS AT 50¢ OUT OF THE MONEY*

7 SELL A STRADDLE
SELL A CALL AT THE MONEY
and *SELL A PUT AT THE MONEY*

8 SELL A STRANGLE – #1
SELL A CALL AT 50¢ OUT OF THE MONEY
and *SELL A PUT AT 50¢ OUT OF THE MONEY*

9 SELL A STRANGLE – #2
SELL A CALL AT $1.00 OUT OF THE MONEY
and *SELL A PUT AT $1.00 OUT OF THE MONEY*

weeks to **14** expiration

the amount of the estimated soybean price increase

Table No.	0¢	10¢	20¢	30¢	40¢	50¢	60¢	70¢	80¢	90¢	100¢	110¢	120¢
20	9=10	4=23 9=10	4=23 9=10	4=23 9=10	4=23	3=81 4=23	3=81 4=23	5=87 3=81 4=23	1=352 5=87 3=81 4=23	1=408 5=87 3=81 4=23	1=465 5=87 3=81 4=23	1=521 5=87 3=81 4=23	2=1130 % 1=571 % 5=87 % 3=81 % 4=23 %
30	4=45 9=34	4=45 9=34	4=45 9=34	4=45 9=34	3=113 4=45 9=34	3=113 4=45	3=113 4=45	3=113 4=45	3=113 5=62 4=45	1=274 3=113 5=62 4=45	1=315 3=113 5=62 4=45	1=357 3=113 5=62 4=45	1=398 % 3=113 % 5=62 % 4=45 %
40	8=91 9=44 4=45	8=91 9=44 4=45	9=44 4=45	9=44 4=45	3=95 9=44 4=45	3=95 9=44 4=45	3=95 4=45	3=95 4=45	3=95 5=48 4=45	1=195 3=95 5=48 4=45	1=228 3=95 5=48 4=45	1=260 3=95 5=48 4=45	1=293 % 3=95 % 5=48 % 4=45 %
50	7=232 8=125 9=69 4=62 6=4	7=200 8=125 9=69 4=62 6=4	8=125 9=69 4=62 6=4	3=116 9=69 4=62 6=4	3=116 9=69 4=62 6=4	3=116 9=69 4=62	3=116 9=69 4=62	3=116 4=62	3=116 4=62 5=40	3=116 4=62 5=40	1=171 3=116 4=62 5=40	1=198 3=116 4=62 5=40	1=225 % 3=116 % 4=62 % 5=40 %
60	7=282 8=167 9=100 4=83 6=10	7=254 8=167 9=100 4=83 6=10	7=224 8=167 3=141 9=100 4=83 6=10	8=167 3=141 9=100 4=83 6=10	8=167 3=141 9=100 4=83 6=10	3=141 9=100 4=83	3=141 9=100 4=83	3=141 9=100 4=83	3=141 4=83 5=34	3=141 4=83 5=34	3=141 4=83 5=34	1=150 3=141 4=83 5=34	1=168 % 3=141 % 4=83 % 5=34 %
70	7=314 8=199 9=130 4=101 6=18	7=281 8=199 9=130 4=101 6=18	7=249 8=199 3=159 9=130 4=101 6=18	7=217 8=199 3=159 9=130 4=101 6=18	8=199 3=159 9=130 4=101 6=18	8=199 3=159 9=130 4=101 6=18	3=159 9=130 4=101	3=159 9=130 4=101	3=159 4=101 5=29	3=159 4=101 5=29	3=159 4=101 5=29	1=222 3=159 4=101 5=29	1=242 % 3=159 % 4=101 % 5=29 %
80	7=268 8=180 9=127 4=91 6=24	7=244 8=180 3=136 9=127 4=91 6=24	7=220 8=180 3=136 9=127 4=91 6=24	7=196 8=180 3=136 9=127 4=91 6=24	8=180 7=171 3=136 9=127 4=91 6=24	8=180 7=147 3=136 9=127 4=91 6=24	8=155 3=136 9=127 4=91	3=136 9=127 4=91 5=25	3=136 9=127 4=91 5=25	3=136 9=127 4=91 5=25	3=136 4=91 5=25	3=136 4=91 5=25	3=136 % 1=114 % 4=91 % 5=25

Wm Grandmill (1985) Ltd.

Use this page when you expect soybean prices to *RISE*

1 BUY A CALL *AT THE MONEY*

2 BUY A CALL *AT 50¢ OUT OF THE MONEY*

3 SELL A PUT *AT THE MONEY*

4 SELL A PUT *AT 50¢ OUT OF THE MONEY*

5 BULL SPREAD
BUY A CALL AT THE MONEY
and *SELL A CALL AT 25¢ OUT OF THE MONEY*

6 REVERSE BULL SPREAD
BUY A PUT AT THE MONEY
and *SELL 2 PUTS AT 50¢ OUT OF THE MONEY*

7 SELL A STRADDLE
SELL A CALL AT THE MONEY
and *SELL A PUT AT THE MONEY*

8 SELL A STRANGLE – #1
SELL A CALL AT 50¢ OUT OF THE MONEY
and *SELL A PUT AT 50¢ OUT OF THE MONEY*

9 SELL A STRANGLE – #2
SELL A CALL AT $1.00 OUT OF THE MONEY
and *SELL A PUT AT $1.00 OUT OF THE MONEY*

weeks to
16
expiration

the amount of the estimated soybean price increase

Table No.	0¢	10¢	20¢	30¢	40¢	50¢	60¢	70¢	80¢	90¢	100¢	110¢	120¢
20	9=13	4=26 9=13	4=26 9=13	4=26 9=13	4=26	3=86 4=26	3=86 4=26	3=86 5=82 4=26	1=330 3=86 5=82 4=26	1=384 3=86 5=82 4=26	1=438 3=86 5=82 4=26	1=492 3=86 5=82 4=26	2=1014 % 1=545 % 3=86 % 5=82 4=26
30	8=97 4=50 9=40	8=97 4=50 9=40	4=50 9=40	4=50 9=40	3=119 4=50 9=40	3=119 4=50	3=119 4=50	3=119 4=50	3=119 5=59 4=50	1=254 3=119 5=59 4=50	1=294 3=119 5=59 4=50	1=333 3=119 5=59 4=50	1=372 % 3=119 % 5=59 % 4=50 %
40	8=100 9=50 4=50	8=100 9=50 4=50	8=100 9=50 4=50	9=50 4=50	3=100 9=50 4=50	3=100 9=50 4=50	3=100 4=50	3=100 4=50	3=100 4=50 5=46	3=100 4=50 5=46	1=212 3=100 4=50 5=46	1=242 3=100 4=50 5=46	1=272 % 3=100 % 4=50 % 5=46 %
50	7=244 8=136 9=77 4=68 6=7	7=212 8=136 9=77 4=68 6=7	8=136 9=77 4=68 6=7	3=122 9=77 4=68 6=7	3=122 9=77 4=68 6=7	3=122 9=77 4=68	3=122 9=77 4=68	3=122 4=68	3=122 4=68 5=38	3=122 4=68 5=38	1=157 3=122 4=68 5=38	1=183 3=122 4=68 5=38	1=208 % 3=122 % 4=68 % 5=38 %
60	7=296 8=180 9=113 4=90 6=13	7=268 8=180 9=113 4=90 6=13	7=240 8=180 3=148 9=113 4=90 6=13	8=180 3=148 9=113 4=90 6=13	8=180 3=148 9-113 4=90 6=13	3=148 9=113 4=90	3=148 9=113 4=90	3=148 9=113 4=90	3=148 4=90 5=32	3=148 4=90 5=32	3=148 4=90 5=32	3=148 1=140 4=90 5=32	1=155 % 3=148 % 4=90 % 5=32
70	7=330 8=214 9=146 4=109 6=20	7=299 8=214 3=168 9=146 4=109 6=20	7=267 8=214 3=168 9=146 4=109 6=20	7=233 8=214 3=168 9=146 4=109 6=20	8=214 7=201 3=168 9=146 4=109 6=20	8=214 3=168 9=146 9=146 6=20	3=168 9=146 4=109	3=168 9=146 4=109	3=168 9=146 4=109 5=27	3=168 4=109 5=27	3=168 4=109 5=27	3=168 4=109 5=27	1=230 % 3=168 % 4=109 % 5=27 %
80	7=283 8=194 9=140 4=98 6=26	7=268 8=194 3=145 9=140 4=98 6=26	7=234 8=194 3=145 9=140 4=98 6=26	7=209 8=194 3=145 9=140 4=98 6=26	8=194 7=185 3=145 9=140 9=140 6=26	8=194 7=161 3=145 9=140 9=140 6=26	8=170 3=145 9=140 7=136 4=98	3=145 9=140 4=98 5=24	3=145 9=140 4=98 5=24	3=145 9=140 4=98 5=24	3=145 4=98 5=24	3=145 4=98 5=24	3=145 % 1=103 % 4=98 % 5=24 %

Wm Grandmill (1985) Ltd.

Use this page when you expect soybean prices to *RISE*

1 BUY A CALL *AT THE MONEY*

2 BUY A CALL *AT 50¢ OUT OF THE MONEY*

3 SELL A PUT *AT THE MONEY*

4 SELL A PUT *AT 50¢ OUT OF THE MONEY*

5 BULL SPREAD
BUY A CALL AT THE MONEY
and SELL A CALL AT 25¢ OUT OF THE MONEY

6 REVERSE BULL SPREAD
BUY A PUT AT THE MONEY
and SELL 2 PUTS AT 50¢ OUT OF THE MONEY

7 SELL A STRADDLE
SELL A CALL AT THE MONEY
and SELL A PUT AT THE MONEY

8 SELL A STRANGLE – #1
SELL A CALL AT 50¢ OUT OF THE MONEY
and SELL A PUT AT 50¢ OUT OF THE MONEY

9 SELL A STRANGLE – #2
SELL A CALL AT $1.00 OUT OF THE MONEY
and SELL A PUT AT $1.00 OUT OF THE MONEY

weeks to
18
expiration

the amount of the estimated soybean price increase

Table No.	0¢	10¢	20¢	30¢	40¢	50¢	60¢	70¢	80¢	90¢	100¢	110¢	120¢
20	9=16	4=29 9=16	4=29 9=16	4=29 9=16	4=29 4=29	3=90 4=29	3=90 4=29	3=90 5=79 4=29	1=311 3=90 5=79 4=29	1=362 3=90 5=79 4=29	1=413 3=90 5=79 4=29	1=466 3=90 5=79 4=29	2=915 % 1=518 % 3=90 % 5=79 % 4=29 %
30	8=105 4=54 9=46	8=105 4=54 9=46	4=54 9=46	4=54 9=46	3=125 4=54 9=46	3=125 4=54	3=125 4=54	3=125 4=54	3=125 5=56 4=54	1=239 3=125 5=56 4=54	1=277 3=125 5=56 4=54	1=314 3=125 5=56 4=54	1=351 % 3=125 % 5=56 % 4=54 %
40	8=107 9=56 4=54	8=107 9=56 4=54	8=107 9=56 4=54	9=56 4=54	3=105 9=56 4=54	3=105 9=56 4=54	3=105 4=54	3=105 4=54	3=105 4=54 5=44	3=105 4=54 5=44	1=98 3=105 4=54 5=44	1=228 3=105 4=54 5=44	1=257 % 3=105 % 4=54 % 5=44 %
50	7=256 8=146 9=86 4=73 6=9	7=223 8=146 9=86 4=73 6=9	8=146 9=86 4=73 6=9	8=146 3=128 9=86 4=73 6=9	3=128 9=86 4=73 6=9	3=128 9=86 4=73	3=128 9=86 4=73	3=128 4=73	3=128 4=73 5=36	3=128 4=73 5=36	3=128 4=73 5=36	1=171 3=128 4=73 5=36	1=195 % 3=128 % 4=73 % 5=36 %
60	7=310 8=193 9=125 4=97 6=15	7=268 8=193 9=125 4=97 6=15	7=230 8=193 3=158 9=125 4=97	8=193 3=158 9=125 4=97 6=15	8=193 3=158 9=125 4=97 6=15	3=158 9=125 4=97	3=158 9=125 4=97	3=158 9=125 4=97	3=158 4=97 5=31	3=158 4=97 5=31	3=158 4=97 5=31	3=158 4=97 5=31	3=158 % 1=144 % 4=97 % 5=31
70	7=346 8=230 9=160 4=117 6=22	7=314 8=230 3=176 9=160 4=117 6=22	7=282 8=230 3=176 9=160 4=117 6=22	7=250 8=230 3=176 9=160 4=117 6=22	8=230 7=217 3=176 9=160 4=117 6=22	8=230 3=176 9=160 4=117 6=22	8=197 3=176 9=160 4=117	3=176 9=160 4=117	3=176 9=160 4=117 5=26	3=176 4=117 5=26	3=176 4=117 5=26	3=176 4=117 5=26	1=219 % 3=176 % 4=117 % 5=26 %
80	7=296 8=207 9=154 4=105 6=28	7=272 8=207 9=154 3=151 4=105 6=28	7=248 8=207 9=154 3=151 4=105 6=28	7=224 8=207 9=154 3=151 4=105 6=28	8=207 7=200 9=154 3=151 4=105 6=28	8=207 7=175 9=154 3=151 4=105 6=28	8=182 7=161 9=154 3=151 4=105 6=28	8=158 9=154 3=151 4=105	9=154 3=151 4=105 5=23	9=154 3=151 4=105 5=23	9=154 3=151 4=105 5=23	3=151 4=105 5=23	3=151 % 4=105 % 5=23 %

Wm Grandmill (1985) Ltd.

Use this page when you expect soybean prices to *RISE*

1 BUY A CALL *AT THE MONEY*

2 BUY A CALL *AT 50¢ OUT OF THE MONEY*

3 SELL A PUT *AT THE MONEY*

4 SELL A PUT *AT 50¢ OUT OF THE MONEY*

5 BULL SPREAD
BUY A CALL AT THE MONEY
and SELL A CALL AT 25¢ OUT OF THE MONEY

6 REVERSE BULL SPREAD
BUY A PUT AT THE MONEY
and SELL 2 PUTS AT 50¢ OUT OF THE MONEY

7 SELL A STRADDLE
SELL A CALL AT THE MONEY
and SELL A PUT AT THE MONEY

8 SELL A STRANGLE – #1
SELL A CALL AT 50¢ OUT OF THE MONEY
and SELL A PUT AT 50¢ OUT OF THE MONEY

9 SELL A STRANGLE – #2
SELL A CALL AT $1.00 OUT OF THE MONEY
and SELL A PUT AT $1.00 OUT OF THE MONEY

weeks to
20
expiration

the amount of the estimated soybean price increase

Table No.	0¢	10¢	20¢	30¢	40¢	50¢	60¢	70¢	80¢	90¢	100¢	110¢	120¢
20	9=19	4=32 9=19	4=32 9=19	4=32 9=19	4=32 9=19	3=94 4=32	3=94 4=32	3=94 4=32	1=294 3=94 5=75 4=32	1=342 3=94 5=75 4=32	1=390 3=94 5=75 4=32	1=440 3=94 5=75 4=32	2=833 % 1=491 % 3=94 % 5=75 % 4=32 %
30	8=112 4=58 9=50	8=112 4=58 9=50	4=58 9=50	4=58 9=50	3=130 4=58 9=50	3=130 4=58	3=130 4=58	3=130 4=58	3=130 4=58 5=54	3=130 4=58 5=54	1=262 3=130 4=58 5=54	1=298 3=130 4=58 5=54	1=335 % 3=130 % 4=58 % 5=54 %
40	8=115 9=61 4=57	8=115 9=61 4=57	8-115 9=61 4=57	9=61 4=57	3=110 9=61 4=57	3=110 9=61 4=57	3=110 4=57	3=110 4=57	3=110 4=57 5=43	3=110 4=57 5=43	1=185 3=110 4=57 5=43	1=214 3=110 4=57 5=43	1=243 % 3=110 % 4=57 % 5=43 %
50	7=266 8=156 9=93 4=78 6=11	7=234 8=156 9=93 4=78 6=11	8=156 9=93 4=78 6=11	8=156 3=133 9=93 4=78 6=11	3=133 9=93 4=78 6=11	3=133 9=93 4=78	3=133 9=93 4=78	3=133 4=78	3=133 4=78 5=34	3=133 4=78 5=34	3=133 4=78 5=34	1=160 3=133 4=78 5=34	1=184 % 3=133 % 4=78 % 5=34 %
60	7=325 8=205 9=135 4=103 6=17	7=293 8=205 9=135 4=103 6=17	7=265 8=205 3=162 9=135 4=103 6=17	7=241 8=205 3=162 9=135 4=103 6=17	8=205 3=162 9=135 4=103 6=17	3=162 9=135 4=103	3=162 9=135 4=103	3=162 9=135 4=103	3=162 4=103 5=30	3=162 4=103 5=30	3=162 4=103 5=30	3=162 4=103 5=30	3=162 % 1=151 % 4=103 % 5=30 %
70	7=346 8=230 9=174 4=117 6=24	7=314 8=230 3=183 9=174 4=117 6=24	7=282 8=230 3=183 9=174 4=117 6=24	7=250 8=230 3=183 9=174 4=117 6=24	8=230 7=217 3=183 9=174 4=117	8=230 3=183 9=174 4=117 6=24	8=197 3=183 9=174 4=117	3=183 9=174 4=117	3=183 9=174 4=117 5=25	3=183 4=117 5=25	3=183 4=117 5=25	3=183 4=117 5=25	3=183 % 4=117 % 5=25 %
80	7=309 8=219 9=165 4=109 6=30	7=285 8=219 9=165 3=154 4=109 3=30	7=261 8=219 9=165 3=154 4=109 6=30	7=235 8=219 9=165 3=154 4=109 6=30	8=219 7=211 9=165 3=154 4=109 6=30	8=219 7=187 9=165 3=154 4=109 6=30	8=195 7=162 9=165 3=154 4=109 6=30	8=170 9=165 3=154 4=109 5=22	9=165 3=154 4=109 5=22	9=165 3=154 4=109 5=22	9=165 3=154 4=109 5=22	3=154 4=109 5=22	3=154 % 4=109 % 5=22 %

Wm Grandmill (1985) Ltd.

Use this page when you expect soybean prices to *RISE*

1 BUY A CALL *AT THE MONEY*

2 BUY A CALL *AT 50¢ OUT OF THE MONEY*

3 SELL A PUT *AT THE MONEY*

4 SELL A PUT *AT 50¢ OUT OF THE MONEY*

5 BULL SPREAD
BUY A CALL AT THE MONEY
and SELL A CALL AT 25¢ OUT OF THE MONEY

6 REVERSE BULL SPREAD
BUY A PUT AT THE MONEY
and SELL 2 PUTS AT 50¢ OUT OF THE MONEY

7 SELL A STRADDLE
SELL A CALL AT THE MONEY
and SELL A PUT AT THE MONEY

8 SELL A STRANGLE – #1
SELL A CALL AT 50¢ OUT OF THE MONEY
and SELL A PUT AT 50¢ OUT OF THE MONEY

9 SELL A STRANGLE – #2
SELL A CALL AT $1.00 OUT OF THE MONEY
and SELL A PUT AT $1.00 OUT OF THE MONEY

weeks to

22

expiration

the amount of the estimated soybean price increase

Table No.	0¢	10¢	20¢	30¢	40¢	50¢	60¢	70¢	80¢	90¢	100¢	110¢	120¢
20	9=23	4=34 9=23	4=34 9=23	4=34 9=23	4=34 9=23	3=97 4=34	3=97 4=34	3=97 4=34	1=283 3=97 5=73 4=34	1=330 3=97 5=73 4=34	1=383 3=97 5=73 4=34	1=425 3=97 5=73 4=34	2=785 % 1=475 % 3=97 % 5=73 % 4=34 %
30	8=120 4=61 9=55	8=120 4=61 9=55	4=61 9=55	4=61 9=55	3=135 4=61 9=55	3=135 4=61	3=135 4=61	3=135 4=61	3=135 4=61 5=52	3=135 4=61 5=52	1=250 3=135 4=61 5=52	1=285 3=135 4=61 5=52	1=320 % 3=135 % 4=61 % 5=52 %
40	8=121 9=65 4=60	8=121 9=65 4=60	8=121 9=65 4=60	3=113 9=65 4=60	3=113 9=65 4=60	3=113 9=65 4=60	3=113 4=60	3=113 4=60	3=113 4=60 5=42	3=113 4=60 5=42	1=176 3=113 4=60 5=42	1=205 3=113 4=60 5=42	1=232 % 3=113 % 4=60 % 5=42 %
50	7=276 8=164 9=100 4=82 6=12	7=243 8=164 9=100 4=82 6=12	7=211 8=164 9=100 4=82 6=12	8=164 3=138 9=100 4=82 6=12	3=138 9=100 4=82 6=12	3=138 9=100 4=82	3=138 9=100 4=82	3=138 4=82	3=138 4=82 5=33	3=138 4=82 5=33	3=138 4=82 5=33	1=151 3=138 4=82 5=33	1=174 % 3=138 % 4=82 % 5=33 %
60	7=330 8=213 9=142 4=106 6=19	7=304 8=213 9=142 4=106 6=19	7=279 8=213 3=167 9=142 4=106 6=19	7=254 8=213 3=167 9=142 4=106 6=19	8=213 3=167 9=142 4=106 6=19	3=167 9=142 4=106 6=19	3=167 9=142 4=106	3=167 9=142 4=106	3=167 4=106 5=28	3=167 4=106 5=28	3=167 4=106 5=28	3=167 4=106 5=28	3=167 % 4=106 % 5=28 %
70	7=374 8=256 9=186 4=130 6=26	7=342 8=256 3=190 9=186 4=130 6=26	7=310 8=256 3=190 9=186 4=130 6=26	7=278 8=256 3=190 9=186 4=130 6=26	8=256 7=245 3=190 9=186 4=130 6=26	8=256 7=213 3=190 9=186 4=130 6=26	8=223 3=190 9=186 4=130	3=190 9=186 4=130	3=190 9=186 4=130 5=24	3=190 9=186 4=130 5=24	3=190 4=130 5=24	3=190 4=130 5=24	3=190 % 4=130 % 5=24 %
80	7=319 8=230 9=175 4=114 6=32	7=295 8=230 9=175 3=159 4=114 6=32	7=271 8=230 9=175 3=159 4=114 6=32	7=245 8=230 9=175 3=159 4=114 6=32	8=230 7=221 9=175 3=159 4=114 6=32	8=230 7=197 9=175 3=159 4=114 6=32	8=205 7=172 9=175 3=159 4=114	8=180 3=159 3=159 4=114	9=175 3=159 4=114 5=21	9=175 3=159 4=114 5=21	9=175 3=159 4=114 5=21	3=159 4=114 5=21	3=159 % 4=114 % 5=21 %

Wm Grandmill (1985) Ltd.

Use this page when you expect soybean prices to *RISE*

1 **BUY A CALL** *AT THE MONEY*

2 **BUY A CALL** *AT 50¢ OUT OF THE MONEY*

3 **SELL A PUT** *AT THE MONEY*

4 **SELL A PUT** *AT 50¢ OUT OF THE MONEY*

5 **BULL SPREAD**
BUY A CALL AT THE MONEY
and SELL A CALL AT 25¢ OUT OF THE MONEY

6 **REVERSE BULL SPREAD**
BUY A PUT AT THE MONEY
and SELL 2 PUTS AT 50¢ OUT OF THE MONEY

7 **SELL A STRADDLE**
SELL A CALL AT THE MONEY
and SELL A PUT AT THE MONEY

8 **SELL A STRANGLE – #1**
SELL A CALL AT 50¢ OUT OF THE MONEY
and SELL A PUT AT 50¢ OUT OF THE MONEY

9 **SELL A STRANGLE – #2**
SELL A CALL AT $1.00 OUT OF THE MONEY
and SELL A PUT AT $1.00 OUT OF THE MONEY

weeks to
24
expiration

the amount of the estimated soybean price increase

Table No.	0¢	10¢	20¢	30¢	40¢	50¢	60¢	70¢	80¢	90¢	100¢	110¢	120¢
20	9=25	4=36	4=36	4=36	3=100	3=100	3=100	3=100	3=100	1=317	1=367	1=410	2=738 %
		9=25	9=25	9=25	4=36	4=36	4=36	4=36	5=70	3=100	3=100	3=100	1=458 %
					9=25				4=36	5=70	5=70	5=70	3=100 %
										4=36	4=36	4=36	5=70 %
													4=36 %
30	8=128	8=128	4=65	4=65	3=139	3=139	3=139	3=139	3=139	3=139	1=239	1=273	1=307 %
	4=65	4=65	9=60	9=60	4=65	4=65	4=65	4=65	4=65	4=65	3=139	3=139	3=139 %
	9=60	9=60			9=60				5=50	5=50	4=65	4=65	4=65 %
											5=50	5=50	5=50 %
40	8=127	8=127	8=127	3=117	3=117	3=117	3=117	3=117	3=117	3=117	3=117	1=195	1=222 %
	9=70	9=70	9=70	9=70	9=70	9=70	4=63	4=63	4=63	4=63	4=63	3=117	3=117 %
	4=63	4=63	4=63	4=63	4=63	4=63			5=40	5=40	5=40	4=63	4=63 %
												5=40	5=40 %
50	7=284	7=252	7=220	8=172	3=142	3=142	3=142	3=142	3=142	3=142	3=142	3=142	1=166 %
	8=172	8=172	8=172	3=142	9=107	9=107	9=107	4=86	4=86	4=86	4=86	4=86	3=142 %
	9=107	9=107	9=107	9=107	4=86	4=86	4=86		5=32	5=32	5=32	5=32	4=86 %
	4=86	4=86	4=86	4=86	6=13								5=32 %
	6=13	6=13	6=13	6=13									
60	7=335	7=311	7=289	7=267	8=221	8=221	3=172	3=172	3=172	3=172	3=172	3=172	3=172 %
	8=221	8=221	8=221	8=221	7=220	3=172	9=159	9=159	9=159	4=109	4=109	4=109	4=109 %
	9=159	9=159	3=172	3=172	3=172	9=159	4=109	4=109	4=109	5=27	5=27	5=27	5=27 %
	4=109	4=109	9=159	9=159	9=159	4=109			5=27				
	6=21	6=21	4=109	4=109	4=109	6=21							
			6=21	6=21	6=21								
70	7=386	7=353	7=321	7=289	8=267	8=267	8=234	9=197	9=197	9=197	3=196	3=196	3=196 %
	8=267	8=267	8=267	8=267	7=256	7=224	9=197	3=196	3=196	3=196	4=137	4=137	4=137 %
	9=197	9=197	9=197	9=197	9=197	9=197	3=196	4=137	4=137	4=137	5=23	5=23	5=23 %
	4=137	3=196	3=196	3=196	3=196	3=196	4=137		5=23	5=23			
	6=28	4=137	4=137	4=137	4=137	4=137							
		6=28	6=28	6=28	6=28	6=28							
80	7=329	7=305	7=281	7=255	8=241	8=241	8=215	8=190	9=195	9=185	9=185	3=166	3=166 %
	8=241	8=241	8=241	8=241	7=231	7=207	9=185	9=185	8=165	3=166	3=166	4=119	4=119 %
	9=185	9=185	9=185	9=185	9=185	9=185	7=182	3=166	3=166	4=119	4=119	5=21	5=21 %
	3=166	3=166	3=166	3=166	3=166	3=166	3=166	7=159	4=119	5=21	5=21		
	4=119	4=119	4=119	4=119	4=119	4=119	4=119	4=119	5=21				
	6=34	6=34	6=34	6=34	6=34	6=34	6=34						

Wm Grandmill (1985) Ltd.

244

Use this page when you expect soybean prices to RISE

1 BUY A CALL *AT THE MONEY*

2 BUY A CALL *AT 50¢ OUT OF THE MONEY*

3 SELL A PUT *AT THE MONEY*

4 SELL A PUT *AT 50¢ OUT OF THE MONEY*

5 BULL SPREAD
BUY A CALL AT THE MONEY
and *SELL A CALL AT 25¢ OUT OF THE MONEY*

6 REVERSE BULL SPREAD
BUY A PUT AT THE MONEY
and *SELL 2 PUTS AT 50¢ OUT OF THE MONEY*

7 SELL A STRADDLE
SELL A CALL AT THE MONEY
and *SELL A PUT AT THE MONEY*

8 SELL A STRANGLE – #1
SELL A CALL AT 50¢ OUT OF THE MONEY
and *SELL A PUT AT 50¢ OUT OF THE MONEY*

9 SELL A STRANGLE – #2
SELL A CALL AT $1.00 OUT OF THE MONEY
and *SELL A PUT AT $1.00 OUT OF THE MONEY*

weeks to **26** **expiration**

the amount of the estimated soybean price increase

Table No.	0¢	10¢	20¢	30¢	40¢	50¢	60¢	70¢	80¢	90¢	100¢	110¢	120¢
20	9=27	4=38 9=27	4=38 9=27	4=38 9=27	3=103 4=38 9=27	3=103 4=38	3=103 4=38	3=103 4=38	3=103 5=68 4=38	1=305 3=103 5=68 4=38	1=350 3=103 5=68 4=38	1=396 3=103 5=68 4=38	2=690 % 1=441 % 3=103 % 5=68 % 4=38 %
30	8=133 4=68 9=64	8=133 4=68 9=64	4=68 9=64	4=68 9=64	3=143 4=68 9=64	3=143 4=68	3=143 4=68	3=143 4=68	3=143 4=68 5=48	3=143 4=68 5=48	1=230 3=143 4=68 5=48	1=263 3=143 4=68 5=48	1=296 % 3=143 % 4=68 % 5=48 %
40	8=133 9=74 4=67 6=7	8=133 9=74 4=67 6=7	8=133 9=74 4=67 6=7	3=120 9=74 4=67 6=7	3=120 9=74 4=67 6=7	3=120 9=74 4=67	3=120 4=67	3=120 4=67	3=120 4=67 5=39	3=120 4=67 5=39	3=120 4=67 5=39	1=86 3=120 4=67 5=39	1=223 % 3=120 % 4=67 % 5=39 %
50	7=292 8=179 9=114 4=90 6=14	7=260 8=179 9=114 4=90 6=14	7=228 8=179 3=146 9=114 4=90 6=14	8=179 3=146 9=114 4=90 6=14	3=146 9=114 4=90 6=14	3=146 9=114 4=90	3=146 9=114 4=90	3=146 4=90	3=146 4=90 5=31	3=146 4=90 5=31	3=146 4=90 5=31	3=146 4=90 5=31	1=159 % 3=146 % 4=90 % 5=31 %
60	7=340 8=230 9=166 4=115 6=22	7=319 8=230 9=166 4=115 6=22	7=297 8=230 3=176 9=166 4=115 6=22	7=275 8=230 3=176 9=166 4=115 6=22	8=230 7=230 3=176 9=166 4=115 6=22	8=230 3=176 9=166 4=115	3=176 9=166 4=115	3=176 9=166 4=115 5=26	3=176 9=166 4=115 5=26	3=176 4=155 5=26	3=176 4=155 5=26	3=176 4=155 5=26	3=176 % 4=155 % 5=26 %
70	7=396 8=277 9=207 4=141 6=29	7=363 8=277 9=207 3=201 4=141 6=29	7=331 8=277 9=207 3=201 4=141 6=29	7=299 8=277 9=207 3=201 4=141 6=29	8=277 7=267 9=207 3=201 4=141 6=29	8=277 7=235 9=207 3=201 4=141 6=29	8=245 9=207 3=201 4=141	8=213 9=207 3=201 4=141	9=207 3=201 4=141 5=23	9=207 3=201 4=141 5=23	3=201 4=141 5=23	3=201 4=141 5=23	3=201 % 4=141 % 5=23 %
80	7=338 8=250 9=194 3=171 4=124 6=35	7=314 8=250 9=194 3=171 4=124 6=35	7=290 8=250 9=194 3=171 4=124 6=35	7=265 8=250 9=194 3=171 4=124 6=35	8=250 7=241 9=194 3=171 4=124 6=35	8=250 7=217 9=194 3=171 4=124 6=35	8=224 7=192 9=194 3=171 4=124 6=35	8=199 9=194 7=168 3=171 4=124	9=194 8=174 3=171 4=124 5=20	9=194 3=171 4=124 5=20	9=194 3=171 4=124 5=20	3=171 9=170 4=124	3=171 % 4=124 % 5=20 %

Wm Grandmill (1985) Ltd.

1 BUY A CALL *AT THE MONEY*

2 BUY A CALL *AT 50¢ OUT OF THE MONEY*

3 SELL A PUT *AT THE MONEY*

4 SELL A PUT *AT 50¢ OUT OF THE MONEY*

5 BULL SPREAD
BUY A CALL AT THE MONEY
and *SELL A CALL AT 25¢ OUT OF THE MONEY*

6 REVERSE BULL SPREAD
BUY A PUT AT THE MONEY
and *SELL 2 PUTS AT 50¢ OUT OF THE MONEY*

7 SELL A STRADDLE
SELL A CALL AT THE MONEY
and *SELL A PUT AT THE MONEY*

8 SELL A STRANGLE – #1
SELL A CALL AT 50¢ OUT OF THE MONEY
and *SELL A PUT AT 50¢ OUT OF THE MONEY*

9 SELL A STRANGLE – #2
SELL A CALL AT $1.00 OUT OF THE MONEY
and *SELL A PUT AT $1.00 OUT OF THE MONEY*

weeks to **28** expiration

the amount of the estimated soybean price increase

Table No.	0¢	10¢	20¢	30¢	40¢	50¢	60¢	70¢	80¢	90¢	100¢	110¢	120¢
20	9=28	4=40 9=28	4=40 9=28	4=40 9=28	3=106 4=4= 9=28	3=106 4=4=	3=106 4=40	3=106 4=40	3=106 5=67 4=40	1=294 3=106 5=67 4=40	1=340 3=106 5=67 4=40	1=383 3=106 5=67 4=40	1=427 % 3=106 % 5=67 % 4=40 %
30	8=139 4=71 9=69	8=139 4=71 9=69	4=71 9=69	4=71 9=69	3=147 4=71 9=69	3=147 4=71	3=147 4=71	3=147 4=71	3=147 4=71 5=47	3=147 4=71 5=47	1=222 3=147 5=47	1=254 3=147 4=71 5=47	1=286 % 3=147 % 4=71 % 5=47 %
40	8=138 9=79 4=69 6=9	8=138 9=79 4=69 6=9	8=138 9=79 4=69 6=9	3=123 9=79 4=69 6=9	3=123 9=79 4=69 6=9	3=123 9=79 4=69	3=123 9=79 4=69	3=123 4=69	3=123 4=69 5=37	3=123 4=69 5=37	3=123 4=69 5=37	1=180 3=123 4=69 5=37	1=212 % 3=123 % 4=69 % 5=37 %
50	7=300 8=186 9=119 4=93 6=16	7=267 8=186 9=119 4=93 6=16	7=235 8=186 3=150 9=119 4=93 6=16	8=186 3=150 9=119 4=93 6=16	8=186 3=150 9=119 4=93 6=16	3=150 9=119 4=93	3=150 9=119 4=93	3=150 9=119 4=93	3=150 4=93 5=30	3=150 4=93 5=30	3=150 4=93 5=30	3=150 4=93 5=30	1=152 % 3=150 % 4=93 % 5=30 %
60	7=345 8=237 9=173 4=120 6=23	7=325 8=237 9=173 4=120 6=23	7=304 8=237 3=181 9=173 4=120 6=23	7=273 8=237 3=181 9=173 4=120 6=23	8=237 7=237 3=181 9=173 4=120 6=23	8=237 3=181 9=173 4=120 6=23	3=181 9=173 4=120	3=181 9=173 4=120 5=26	3=181 9=166 4=120 5=26	3=181 4=120 5=26	3=181 4=120 5=26	3=181 4=120 5=26	3=181 % 4=120 % 5=26 %
70	7=406 8=288 9=217 4=146 6=30	7=374 8=288 9=217 3=206 4=146 6=30	7=342 8=288 9=217 3=206 4=146 6=30	7=309 8=288 9=217 3=206 4=146 6=30	8=288 7=277 9=217 3=206 4=146 6=30	8=288 7=245 9=217 3=206 4=146 6=30	8=255 9=217 7=213 3=206 4=146	8=223 9=217 3=206 4=146	9=217 3=206 4=146 5=22	9=217 3=206 4=146 5=22	3=206 4=146 5=22	3=206 4=146 5=22	3=206 % 4=146 % 5=22 %
80	7=347 8=258 9=202 3=175 4=133 6=36	7=323 8=258 9=202 3=175 4=133 6=36	7=298 8=258 9=202 3=175 4=133 6=36	7=274 8=258 9=202 3=175 4=133 6=36	8=258 7=250 9=202 3=175 4=133 6=36	8=258 7=226 9=202 3=175 4=133 6=36	8=233 7=201 9=202 3=175 4=133 6=36	8=208 9=202 7=180 3=175 4=133	9=202 8=183 3=175 7=156 4=133	9=202 3=175 8=172 4=133 5=19	9=202 3=175 4=133 5=19	9=177 3=175 4=133 5=19	3=175 % 4=133 % 5=19 %

Wm Grandmill (1985) Ltd.

Use this page when you expect soybean prices to RISE

1 BUY A CALL *AT THE MONEY*

2 BUY A CALL *AT 50¢ OUT OF THE MONEY*

3 SELL A PUT *AT THE MONEY*

4 SELL A PUT *AT 50¢ OUT OF THE MONEY*

5 BULL SPREAD
BUY A CALL AT THE MONEY
and *SELL A CALL AT 25¢ OUT OF THE MONEY*

6 REVERSE BULL SPREAD
BUY A PUT AT THE MONEY
and *SELL 2 PUTS AT 50¢ OUT OF THE MONEY*

7 SELL A STRADDLE
SELL A CALL AT THE MONEY
and *SELL A PUT AT THE MONEY*

8 SELL A STRANGLE – #1
SELL A CALL AT 50¢ OUT OF THE MONEY
and *SELL A PUT AT 50¢ OUT OF THE MONEY*

9 SELL A STRANGLE – #2
SELL A CALL AT $1.00 OUT OF THE MONEY
and *SELL A PUT AT $1.00 OUT OF THE MONEY*

weeks to
30
expiration

the amount of the estimated soybean price increase

Table No.	0¢	10¢	20¢	30¢	40¢	50¢	60¢	70¢	80¢	90¢	100¢	110¢	120¢
20	9=30	4=42 9=30	4=42 9=30	4=42 9=30	3=109 4=42 9=30	3=109 4=42	3=109 4=42	3=109 4=42	3=109 5=65 4=42	1=284 3=109 5=65 4=42	1=329 3=109 5=65 4=42	1=371 3=109 5=65 4=42	1=414 % 3=109 % 5=65 % 4=42 %
30	8=144 4=74 9=72	8=144 4=74 9=72	4=74 9=72	4=74 9=72	3=150 4=74 9=72	3=150 4=74	3=150 4=74	3=150 4=74	3=150 4=74 5=46	3=150 4=74 5=46	1=215 3=150 4=74 5=46	1=247 3=150 4=74 5=46	1=278 % 3=150 % 4=74 % 5=46 %
40	7=252 8=143 9=83 4=72 6=10	7=226 8=143 9=83 4=72 6=10	8=143 9=83 4=72 6=10	3=126 9=83 4=72 6=10	3=126 9=83 4=72 6=10	3-126 9=83 4=72	3=126 9=83 4=72	3=126 4=72	3=126 4=72 5=36	3=126 4=72 5=36	3=126 4=72 5=36	1=174 3=126 4=72 5=36	1=200 % 3=126 % 4=72 % 5=36 %
50	7=307 8=193 9=125 4=96 6=17	7=274 8=193 9=125 4=96 6=17	7=242 8=193 3=154 9=125 4=96 6=17	8=193 3=154 9=125 4=96 6=17	8=193 3=154 9=125 4=96 6=17	3=154 9=125 4=96	3=154 9=125 4=96	3=154 9=125 4=96	3=154 4=96 5=29	3=154 4=96 5=29	3=154 4=96 5=29	3=154 4=96 5=29	3=154 % 1=147 % 4=96 % 5=29 %
60	7=351 8=253 9=180 4=126 6=24	7=330 8=253 3=187 9=180 4=126 6=24	7=310 8=253 3=187 9=180 4=126 6=24	7=291 8=253 3=187 9=180 4=126 6=24	8=253 7=250 3=187 9=180 4=126 6=24	8=253 3=187 9=180 4=126	8=211 3=187 9=180 4=126	3=187 9=180 4=126	3=187 9=180 4=126 5=25	3=187 9=180 4=126 5=25	3=187 4=126 5=25	3=187 4=126 5=25	3=187 % 4=126 % 5=25 %
70	7=415 8=297 9=226 4=151 6=31	7=383 8=297 9=226 3=211 4=151 6=31	7=351 8=297 9=226 3=211 4=151 6=31	7=318 8=297 9=226 3=211 4=151 6=31	8=297 7=286 9=226 3=211 4=151 6=31	8=297 7=254 9=226 3=211 4=151 6=31	8=266 9=226 7=221 3=211 4=151	8=235 9=226 3=211 4=151	9=226 3=211 4=151 5=22	9=226 3=211 4=151 5=22	9=226 3=211 4=151 5=22	3=211 4=151 5=22	3=211 % 4=151 % 5=22 %
80	7=356 8=265 9=208 3=181 4=136 6=37	7=331 8=265 9=208 3=181 4=136 6=37	7=306 8=265 9=208 3=181 4=136 6=37	7=282 8=265 9=208 3=181 4=136 6=37	8=265 7=258 9=208 3=181 4=136 6=37	8=265 7=234 9=208 3=181 4=136 6=37	8=242 7=209 9=208 3=181 4=136 6=37	8=217 9=208 7=184 3=181 4=136 6=37	9=208 8=192 3=181 7=160 4=136	9=208 3=181 8=167 4=136 5=19	9=208 3=181 4=136 5=19	9=184 3=181 4=136 5=19	3=181 % 9=160 % 4=136 % 5=19 %

Wm Grandmill (1985) Ltd.

Use this page when you expect soybean prices to *RISE*

1 **BUY A CALL** *AT THE MONEY*

2 **BUY A CALL** *AT 50¢ OUT OF THE MONEY*

3 **SELL A PUT** *AT THE MONEY*

4 **SELL A PUT** *AT 50¢ OUT OF THE MONEY*

5 **BULL SPREAD**
BUY A CALL AT THE MONEY
and *SELL A CALL AT 25¢ OUT OF THE MONEY*

6 **REVERSE BULL SPREAD**
BUY A PUT AT THE MONEY
and *SELL 2 PUTS AT 50¢ OUT OF THE MONEY*

7 **SELL A STRADDLE**
SELL A CALL AT THE MONEY
and *SELL A PUT AT THE MONEY*

8 **SELL A STRANGLE – #1**
SELL A CALL AT 50¢ OUT OF THE MONEY
and *SELL A PUT AT 50¢ OUT OF THE MONEY*

9 **SELL A STRANGLE – #2**
SELL A CALL AT $1.00 OUT OF THE MONEY
and *SELL A PUT AT $1.00 OUT OF THE MONEY*

weeks to
32
expiration

the amount of the estimated soybean price increase

Table No.	0¢	10¢	20¢	30¢	40¢	50¢	60¢	70¢	80¢	90¢	100¢	110¢	120¢
20	9=30	4=43 9=30	4=43 9=30	4=43 9=30	3=111 4=43 9=30	3=111 4=43	3=111 4=43	3=111 4=43	3=111 5=65 4=43	1=278 3=111 5=65 4=43	1=321 3=111 5=65 4=43	1=363 3=111 5=65 4=43	1=404 % 3=111 % 5=65 % 4=43 %
30	8=149 4=76 9=76	8=149 4=76 9=76	4=76 9=76	4=76 9=76	3=153 4=76 9=76	3=153 4=76	3=153 4=76	3=153 4=76	3=153 4=76 5=44	3=153 4=76 5=44	1=210 3=153 4=76 5=44	1=241 3=153 4=76 5=44	1=275 % 3=153 % 4=76 % 5=44 %
40	7=256 8=148 9=87 4=74 6=12	7=224 8=148 9=87 4=74 6=12	8=148 9=87 4=74 6=12	3=128 9=87 4=74 6=12	3=128 9=87 4=74 6=12	3=128 9=87 4=74	3=128 9=87 4=74	3=128 4=74	3=128 4=74 5=36	3=128 4=74 5=36	3=128 4=74 5=36	1=170 3=128 4=74 5=36	1=190 % 3=128 % 4=74 % 5=36 %
50	7=314 8=199 9=130 4=100 6=18	7=272 8=199 9=130 4=100 6=18	7=240 8=199 3=157 9=130 4=100 6=18	8=199 3=157 9=130 4=100 6=18	8=199 3=157 9=130 4=100 6=18	3=157 9=130 4=100	3=157 9=130 4=100	3=157 9=130 4=100	3=157 4=100 5=29	3=157 4=100 5=29	3=157 4=100 5=29	3=157 4=100 5=29	3=157 % 4=100 % 5=29 %
60	7=364 8=269 9=186 4=110 6=25	7=340 8=269 3=190 9=186 4=110 6=25	7=318 8=269 3=190 9=186 4=110 6=25	7=297 8=269 3=190 9=186 4=110 6=25	8=269 7=256 3=190 9=186 4=110 6=25	8=269 7=226 3=190 9=186 4=110 6=25	8=216 3=190 9=186 4=110	3=190 9=186 4=110	3=190 9=186 4=110 5=25	3=190 9=186 4=110 5=25	3=190 4=110 5=25	3=190 4=110 5=25	3=190 % 4=110 % 5=25 %
70	7=425 8=305 9=234 3=216 4=155 6=32	7=392 8=305 9=234 3=216 4=155 6=32	7=360 8=305 9=234 3=216 4=155 6=32	7=327 8=305 9=234 3=216 4=155 6=32	8=305 7=295 9=234 3=216 4=155 6=32	8=305 7=263 9=234 3=216 4=155 6=32	8=273 9=234 7=230 3=216 4=155 6=32	8=241 9=234 3=216 4=155	9=234 3=216 4=155 5=21	9=234 3=216 4=155 5=21	9=234 3=216 4=155 5=21	3=216 4=155 5=21	3=216 % 4=155 % 5=21 %
80	7=363 8=271 9=213 3=185 4=139 6=37	7=338 8=271 9=213 3=185 4=139 6=37	7=313 8=271 9=213 3=185 4=139 6=37	7=289 8=271 9=213 3=185 4=139 6=37	8=271 7=265 9=213 3=185 4=139 6=37	8=271 7=241 9=213 3=185 4=139 6=37	8=248 7=216 9=213 3=185 4=139 6=37	8=223 9=213 7=191 3=185 4=139 6=37	9=213 8=198 3=185 7=164 4=139 5=19	9=213 3=185 8=174 4=139 5=19	9=213 3=185 4=139 5=19	9=189 3=185 4=139 5=19	3=185 % 9=164 % 4=139 % 5=19 %

Wm Grandmill (1985) Ltd.

Use this page when you expect soybean prices to *RISE*

weeks to
34
expiration

1 BUY A CALL *AT THE MONEY*

2 BUY A CALL *AT 50¢ OUT OF THE MONEY*

3 SELL A PUT *AT THE MONEY*

4 SELL A PUT *AT 50¢ OUT OF THE MONEY*

5 **BULL SPREAD**
BUY A CALL AT THE MONEY
and *SELL A CALL AT 25¢ OUT OF THE MONEY*

6 **REVERSE BULL SPREAD**
BUY A PUT AT THE MONEY
and *SELL 2 PUTS AT 50¢ OUT OF THE MONEY*

7 **SELL A STRADDLE**
SELL A CALL AT THE MONEY
and *SELL A PUT AT THE MONEY*

8 **SELL A STRANGLE – #1**
SELL A CALL AT 50¢ OUT OF THE MONEY
and *SELL A PUT AT 50¢ OUT OF THE MONEY*

9 **SELL A STRANGLE – #2**
SELL A CALL AT $1.00 OUT OF THE MONEY
and *SELL A PUT AT $1.00 OUT OF THE MONEY*

the amount of the estimated soybean price increase

Table No.	0¢	10¢	20¢	30¢	40¢	50¢	60¢	70¢	80¢	90¢	100¢	110¢	120¢
20	9=31	4=44 9-31	4=44 9-31	4=44 9=31	3=113 4=44 9=31	3=113 4=44	3=113 4=44	3=113 4=44	3=113 5=62	1=271 3=113 5=62 4=44	1=312 3=113 5=62 4=44	1=354 3=113 5=62 4=44	1=395 % 3=113 % 5=62 % 4=44 %
30	8=152 9=80 4=78	8=152 9=80 4=78	9=80 4=78	9=80 4=78	3=156 9=80 4=78	3=156 4=78	3=156 4=78	3=156 4=78	3=156 4=78 5=44	3=156 4=78 5=44	1=204 3=156 4=78 5=44	1=234 3=156 4=78 5=44	1=265 % 3=156 % 4=78 % 5=44 %
40	7=261 8=153 9=91 4=76 6=14	7=229 8-153 9=91 4=76 6=14	8=153 9=91 4=76 6=14	8=153 3=130 9=91 4=76 6=14	3=130 9=91 4=76 6=14	3=130 9=91 4=76	3=130 9=91 4=76	3=130 4=76	3=130 4=76 5=35	3=130 4=76 5=35	3=130 4=76 5=35	1=65 3=130 4=76 5=35	1=180 % 3=130 % 4=76 % 5=35 %
50	7=320 8=205 9=135 4=103 6=19	7=287 8=205 9=135 4=103 6=19	7=255 8=205 3=160 9=135 4=103 6=19	8=205 3=160 9=135 4=103 6=19	8=205 3=160 9=135 4=103 6=19	3=160 9=135 4=103	3=160 9=135 4=103	3=160 9=135 4=103	3=160 4=103 5=28	3=160 4=103 5=28	3=160 4=103 5=28	3=160 4=103 5=28	3=160 % 4=103 % 5=28 %
60	7=371 8=263 9=193 4=132 6=26	7=350 8=263 9=193 3=193 4=132 6=26	7=325 8=263 9=193 3=193 4=132 6=26	7=303 8=263 9=193 3=193 4=132 6=26	7=263 8=263 9=193 3=193 4=132 6=26	8=263 7=219 9=193 3=193 4=132 6=26	8=221 9=193 3=193 4=132	9=193 9=193 3=193 4=132	9=193 3=193 4=132 5=25	9=193 3=193 4=132 5=25	3=193 4=132 5=25	3=193 4=132 5=25	3=193 % 4=132 % 5=25%
70	7=432 8=313 9=242 3=220 4=159 6=33	7=400 8=313 9=242 3=220 4=159 6=33	7=368 8=313 9=242 3=220 4=159 6=33	7=335 8=313 9=242 3=220 4=159 6=33	8=313 7=303 9=242 3=220 4=159 6=33	8=313 7=271 9=242 3=220 4=159 6=33	8=28= 9=242 7=238 3=220 4=159 6=33	8=248 9=242 7=206 3=220 4=159	9=242 8=216 3=220 4=159 5=21	9=242 3=220 4=159 5=21	9=242 3=220 4=159 5=21	3=220 4=159 5=21	3=220 % 4=159 % 5=21 %
80	7=370 8=277 9=218 3=189 4=142 6=38	7=345 8=277 9=218 3=189 4=142 6=38	7=320 8=277 9=218 3=189 4=142 6=38	7=296 8=277 9=218 3=189 4=142 6=38	8=277 7=272 9=218 3=189 4=142 6=38	8=277 7=248 9=218 3=189 4=142 6=38	8=254 7=223 9=218 3=189 4=142 6=38	8=229 9=218 7=198 3=189 4=142 6=38	9=218 8=204 3=189 7=174 4=142 5=18	9=218 3=189 8=180 7=151 4=142 5=18	9=218 3=189 8=155 4=142 7=126 5=18	9=194 3=189 4=142 8=128 5=18	3=189 % 9=168 % 4=142 % 5=18 %

Wm Grandmill (1985) Ltd.

249

Use this page when you expect soybean prices to *RISE*

weeks to

36

expiration

1 BUY A CALL *AT THE MONEY*

2 BUY A CALL *AT 50¢ OUT OF THE MONEY*

3 SELL A PUT *AT THE MONEY*

4 SELL A PUT *AT 50¢ OUT OF THE MONEY*

5 BULL SPREAD
BUY A CALL AT THE MONEY
and SELL A CALL AT 25¢ OUT OF THE MONEY

6 REVERSE BULL SPREAD
BUY A PUT AT THE MONEY
and SELL 2 PUTS AT 50¢ OUT OF THE MONEY

7 SELL A STRADDLE
SELL A CALL AT THE MONEY
and SELL A PUT AT THE MONEY

8 SELL A STRANGLE – #1
SELL A CALL AT 50¢ OUT OF THE MONEY
and SELL A PUT AT 50¢ OUT OF THE MONEY

9 SELL A STRANGLE – #2
SELL A CALL AT $1.00 OUT OF THE MONEY
and SELL A PUT AT $1.00 OUT OF THE MONEY

the amount of the estimated soybean price increase

Table No.	0¢	10¢	20¢	30¢	40¢	50¢	60¢	70¢	80¢	90¢	100¢	110¢	120¢
20	9=32	4=46 9=32	4=46 9=32	4=46 9=32	3=115 4=46 9=32	3=115 4=46	3=115 4=46	3=115 4=46	3=115 5=61 4=46	1=264 3=115 5=61 4=46	1=304 3=115 5=61 4=46	1=345 3=115 5=61 4=46	1=385 % 3=115 % 5=61 % 4=46 %
30	8=156 9=82 4=80	8=156 9=82 4=80	9=82 4=80	9=82 4=80	3=158 9=82 4=80	3=158 4=80	3=158 4=80	3=158 4=80	3=158 4=80 5=44	3=158 4=80 5=44	1=199 3=158 4=80 5=44	1=229 3=158 4=80 5=44	1=259 % 3=158 % 4=80 % 5=44 %
40	7=266 8=158 9=96 4=78 6=15	7=234 8=158 9=96 4=78 6=15	8=158 9=96 4=78 6=15	8=158 3=131 9=96 4=78 6=15	3=131 9=96 4=78 6=15	3=131 9=96 4=78	3=131 9=96 4=78	3=131 4=78	3=131 4=78 5=35	3=131 4=78 5=35	3=131 4=78 5=35	1=160 3=131 4=78 5=35	1=169 % 3=131 % 4=78 % 5=35 %
50	8=211 9=140 4=106 6=19	8=211 9=140 4=106 6=19	8=211 3=163 9=140 4=106 6=19	8=211 3=163 9=140 4=106 6=19	8=211 3=163 9=140 4=106 6=19	3=163 9=140 4=106	3=163 9=140 4=106	3=163 9=140 4=106	3=163 4=106 5=28	3=163 4=106 5=28	3=163 4=106 5=28	3=163 4=106 5=28	3=163 % 4=106 % 5=28 %
60	7=390 8=269 9=200 4=135 6=27	7=363 8=269 9=200 3=196 4=135 6=27	7=336 8=269 9=200 3=196 4=135 6=27	7=309 8=269 9=200 3=196 4=135 6=27	8=269 7=268 9=200 3=196 4=135 6=27	8=269 7=226 9=200 3=196 4=135	8=227 9=200 3=196 4=135	9=200 3=196 4=135	9=200 3=196 4=135 5=25	9=200 3=196 4=135 5=25	3=196 4=135 5=25	3=196 4=135 5=25	3=196 % 4=135 % 5=25 %
70	7=440 8=321 9=250 3=224 4=163 6=33	7=407 8-321 9=250 3=224 4=163 6=33	7=375 8=321 9=250 3=224 4=163 6=33	7=343 8=321 9=250 3=224 4=163 6=33	8=321 7=310 9=250 3=224 4=163 6=33	8-321 7=279 9=250 3=224 4=163 6=33	8=288 9=250 7=246 3=224 4=163 6=33	8=256 9=250 7=214 3=224 4=163	9=250 8=224 3=224 4=163 5=21	9=250 3=224 4=163 5=21	9=250 3=224 4=163 5=21	3=224 4=163 4=163 5=21	3=224 % 4=163 % 4=163 % 5=21 %
80	7=374 8=280 9=221 3=192 4=144 6=38	7=349 8=280 9=221 3=192 4=144 6=38	7=324 8=280 9=221 3=192 4=144 6=38	7=300 8=280 9=221 3=192 4=144 6=38	8=280 7=276 9=221 3=192 4=144 6=38	8=280 7=252 9=221 3=192 4=144 6=38	8=256 7=227 9=221 3=192 4=144 6=38	8=232 9=221 7=203 3=192 4=144 6=38	9=221 8=207 3=192 7=178 4=144 5=18	9=221 3=192 8=182 4=144 5=18	9=221 3=192 4=144 5=18	9=196 3=192 4=144 5=18	3=192 % 9=172 % 4=144 % 5=18 %

Wm Grandmill (1985) Ltd.

USE THE FOLLOWING TABLES WHEN YOU EXPECT SOYBEAN PRICES TO <u>DECLINE</u>

1. Calculate the "at the money" option value.

2. Find the "weeks to expiration".

3. Use the information found above to find the corresponding Table Number.

4. Turn to the nearest appropriate "weeks to expiration" page in the following pages.

5. Use the appropriate Forecasting Graph to get the amount of the estimated price decline.

6. Using the estimated price decline, and using the Table Number found above, interpolate to find the best soybean option trade.

Use this page when you expect soybean prices to *FALL*

1 BUY A PUT *AT THE MONEY*

2 BUY A PUT *AT 50¢ OUT OF THE MONEY*

3 SELL A CALL *AT THE MONEY*

4 SELL A CALL *AT 50¢ OUT OF THE MONEY*

5 BEAR SPREAD
BUY A PUT AT THE MONEY
and SELL A PUT AT 25¢ OUT OF THE MONEY

6 REVERSE BEAR SPREAD
BUY A CALL AT THE MONEY
and SELL 2 CALLS AT 50¢ OUT OF THE MONEY

7 SELL A STRADDLE
SELL A CALL AT THE MONEY
and SELL A PUT AT THE MONEY

8 SELL A STRANGLE – #1
SELL A CALL AT 50¢ OUT OF THE MONEY
and SELL A PUT AT 50¢ OUT OF THE MONEY

9 SELL A STRANGLE – #2
SELL A CALL AT $1.00 OUT OF THE MONEY
and SELL A PUT AT $1.00 OUT OF THE MONEY

weeks to

4

expiration

the amount of the estimated soybean price decline

Table No.	0¢	10¢	20¢	30¢	40¢	50¢	60¢	70¢	80¢	90¢	100¢	110¢	120¢
20	4=0 9=0	4=0 9=0	4=0 9=0	4=0 9=0	3=41 4=0	3=41 4=0	1=531 5=169 3=41 4=0	1=636 5=169 3=41 4=0	1=743 5=168 3=41 4=0	1=848 5=169 3=41 4=0	1=953 5=169 3=41 4=0	2=5900 1=1058 5=169 3=41	2=6900 % 1=1163 % 5=169 % 3=41 %
30	4=7 9=0	4=7 9=0	4=7 9=0	4=7 9=0	3=58 4=7 9=0	3=58 4=7	5=122 3=58 4=7	1=447 5=122 3=58 4=7	1=525 5=122 3=58 4=7	1=603 5=122 3=58 4=7	1=681 5=122 3=58 4=7	1=735 5=122 3=58 4=7	1=789 % 5=122 % 3=58 % 4=7 %
40	8=23 4=12 9=4	4=12 9=4	4=12 9=4	4=12 9=4	3=49 4=12 9=4	3=49 4=12	3=49 4=12	5=96 3=49 4=12	1=394 5=96 3=49 4=12	1=458 5=96 3=49 4=12	1=517 5=96 3=49 4=12	1=576 5=96 3=49 4=12	1=641 % 5=96 % 3=49 % 4=12 %
50	8=39 4=19 9=10	8=39 4=19 9=10	4=19 9=10	4=19 9=10	3=60 4=19 9=10	3=60 4=19 9=10	3=60 4=19	5=78 3=60 4=19	1=310 5=78 3=60 4=19	1=362 5=78 3=60 4=19	1=413 5=78 3=60 4=19	1=464 5=78 3=60 4=19	1=516 % 5=78 % 3=60 % 4=19 %
60	8=53 4=26 9=19	8=53 4=26 9=19	4=26 9=19	3=70 4=26 9=19	3=70 4=26 9=19	3=70 4=26 9=19	3=70 4=26	3=70 5=67 4=26	3=70 5=67 4=26	1=298 3=70 5=67 4=26	1=338 3=70 5=67 4=26	1=374 3=70 5=67 4=26	1=412 % 3=70 % 5=67 % 4=26 %
70	7=162 8=69 4=35 9=30	7=129 8=69 4=35 9=30	8=69 3=83 4=35 9=30	3=83 4=35 9=30	3=83 4=35 9=30	3=83 4=35 9=30	3=83 4=35 9=30	3=83 5=57 4=35	3=83 5=57 4=35	1=345 3=83 5=57 4=35	1=383 3=83 5=57 4=35	1=421 3=83 5=57 4=35	1=459 % 3=83 % 5=57 % 4=35 %
80	8=65 4=33 9=30	8=65 4=33 9=30	8=65 4=33 9=30	3=70 4=33 9=30	3=70 4=33 9=30	3=70 4=33 9=30	3=70 4=33 9=30	3=70 5=50 4=33	3=70 5=50 4=33	1=205 3=70 5=50 4=33	1=239 3=70 5=50 4=33	1=316 3=70 5=50 4=33	1=385 % 3=70 % 5=50 % 4=33 %

Wm Grandmill (1985) Ltd.

Use this page when you expect soybean prices to *FALL*

1 BUY A PUT *AT THE MONEY*

2 BUY A PUT *AT 50¢ OUT OF THE MONEY*

3 SELL A CALL *AT THE MONEY*

4 SELL A CALL *AT 50¢ OUT OF THE MONEY*

5 BEAR SPREAD
BUY A PUT AT THE MONEY
and SELL A PUT AT 25¢ OUT OF THE MONEY

6 REVERSE BEAR SPREAD
BUY A CALL AT THE MONEY
and SELL 2 CALLS AT 50¢ OUT OF THE MONEY

7 SELL A STRADDLE
SELL A CALL AT THE MONEY
and SELL A PUT AT THE MONEY

8 SELL A STRANGLE – #1
SELL A CALL AT 50¢ OUT OF THE MONEY
and SELL A PUT AT 50¢ OUT OF THE MONEY

9 SELL A STRANGLE – #2
SELL A CALL AT $1.00 OUT OF THE MONEY
and SELL A PUT AT $1.00 OUT OF THE MONEY

weeks to
6
expiration

Table No.	0¢	10¢	20¢	30¢	40¢	50¢	60¢	70¢	80¢	90¢	100¢	110¢	120¢
20	9=0	4=0 9=0	4=0 9=0	4=0 9=0	4=0	3=55 4=0	3=55 4=0	1=474 5=128 3=55 4=0	1=555 5=128 3=55 4=0	1=637 5=128 3=55 4=0	1=720 5=128 3=55 4=0	2=3057 1=802 5=128 3=55 4=0	2=3583 % 1=884 % 5=128 % 3=55 % 4=0
30	4=19 9=7	4=19 9=7	4=19 9=7	4=19 9=7	3=76 4=19 9=7	3=76 4=19	3=76 5=93 4=19	1=324 5=93 3=76 4=19	1=384 5=93 3=76 4=19	1=444 5=93 3=76 4=19	1=506 5=93 3=76 4=19	1=567 5=93 3=76 4=19	1=628 % 5=93 % 3=76 % 4=19 %
40	8=44 4=22 9=14	4=22 9=14	4=22 9=14	4=22 9=14	3=64 4=22 9=14	3=64 4=22	3=64 4=22	5=73 3=64 4=22	1=284 5=73 3=64 4=22	1=332 5=73 3=64 4=22	1=380 5=73 3=64 4=22	1=428 5=73 3=64 4=22	1=476 % 5=73 % 3=64 % 4=22 %
50	8=65 4=32 9=26	8=65 4=32 9=26	4=32 9=26	3=78 4=32 9=26	3=78 4=32 9=26	3=78 4=32 9=26	3=78 4=32	3=78 5=59 4=32	1=219 3=78 5=59 4=32	1=259 3=78 5=59 4=32	1=298 3=78 5=59 4=32	1=338 3=78 5=59 4=32	1=378 % 3=78 % 5=59 % 4=32 %
60	8=85 4=43 9=40	8=85 4=43 9=40	8=85 4=43 9=40	3=91 4=43 9=40	3=91 4=43 9=40	3=91 4=43 9=40	3=91 4=43 9=40	3=91 5=51 4=43	3=91 5=51 4=43	1=212 3=91 5=51 4=43	1=240 3=91 5=51 4=43	1=268 3=91 5=51 4=43	1=296 % 3=91 % 5=51 % 4=43 %
70	7=212 8=108 9=57 4=55	7=179 8=108 9=57 4=55	8=108 3=108 9=57 4=55	8=108 3=108 9=57 4=55	3=108 9=57 4=55	3=108 9=57 4=55	3=108 9=57 4=55	3=108 4=55 5=43	3=108 4=55 5=43	1=267 3=108 4=55 5=43	1=296 3=108 4=55 5=43	1=325 3=108 4=55 5=43	1=354 % 3=108 % 4=55 % 5=43 %
80	7=181 8=100 9=56 4=50 6=5	7=156 8=100 9=56 4=50 6=5	7=132 8=100 3=92 9=56 4=50 6=5	8=100 3=92 9=56 4=50 6=5	3=92 9=56 4=50 6=5	3=92 9=56 4=50	3=92 9=56 4=50	3=92 4=50 5=38	3=92 4=50 5=38	1=136 3=92 4=50 5=38	1=162 3=92 4=50 5=38	1=188 3=92 4=50 5=38	1=215 % 3=92 % 4=50 % 5=38 %

the amount of the estimated soybean price decline

Wm Grandmill (1985) Ltd.

Use this page when you expect soybean prices to *FALL*

1 BUY A PUT *AT THE MONEY*

2 BUY A PUT *AT 50¢ OUT OF THE MONEY*

3 SELL A CALL *AT THE MONEY*

4 SELL A CALL *AT 50¢ OUT OF THE MONEY*

5 BEAR SPREAD
BUY A PUT AT THE MONEY
and SELL A PUT AT 25¢ OUT OF THE MONEY

6 REVERSE BEAR SPREAD
BUY A CALL AT THE MONEY
and SELL 2 CALLS AT 50¢ OUT OF THE MONEY

7 SELL A STRADDLE
SELL A CALL AT THE MONEY
and SELL A PUT AT THE MONEY

8 SELL A STRANGLE – #1
SELL A CALL AT 50¢ OUT OF THE MONEY
and SELL A PUT AT 50¢ OUT OF THE MONEY

9 SELL A STRANGLE – #2
SELL A CALL AT $1.00 OUT OF THE MONEY
and SELL A PUT AT $1.00 OUT OF THE MONEY

weeks to

8

expiration

the amount of the estimated soybean price decline

Table No.	0¢	10¢	20¢	30¢	40¢	50¢	60¢	70¢	80¢	90¢	100¢	110¢	120¢
20	9=0	4=11 9=0	4=11 9=0	4=11 9=0	4=11	3=63 4=11	3=63 4=11	1=400 5=112 3=63 4=11	1=471 5=112 3=63 4=11	1=542 5=112 3=63 4=11	1=614 5=112 3=63 4=11	2=1775 1=686 5=112 3=63 4=11	2=2088 % 1=757 % 5=112 % 3=63 % 4=11 %
30	4=25 9=15	4=25 9=15	4=25 9=15	4=25 9=15	3=88 4=25 9=15	3=88 4=25	3=88 4=25	3=88 4=25	1=321 3=88 4=25	1=376 3=88 4=25	1=428 3=88 4=25	1=478 3=88 4=25	1=532 % 3=88 % 4=25 %
40	8=59 4=29 9=29	8=59 4=29 9=29	4=29 9=29	4=29 9=29	3=74 4=29 9=29	3=74 4=29 9=29	3=74 4=29	3=74 5=62 4=29	1=233 3=74 5=62 4=29	1=274 3=74 5=62 4=29	1=317 3=74 5=62 4=29	1=358 3=74 5=62 4=29	1=400 % 3=74 % 5=62 % 4=29 %
50	8=83 4=42 9=39	8=83 4=42 9=39	4=42 9=39	3=90 4=42 9=39	3=90 4=42 9=39	3=90 4=42 3=39	3=90 4=42	3=90 5=50 4=42	3=90 5=50 4=42	1=211 3=90 5=50 4=42	1=244 3=90 5=50 4=42	1=279 3=90 5=50 4=42	1=314 % 3=90 % 5=50 % 4=42 %
60	8=108 9=57 4=54	8=108 9=57 4=54	8=108 9=57 4=54	8=108 3=106 9=57 4=54	3=106 9=57 4=54	3=106 9=57 4=54	3=106 9=57 4=54	3=106 4=54 5=43	3=106 4=54 5=43	3=106 3=106 5=43	1=94 3=106 4=54 5=43	1=218 3=106 4=54 5=43	1=242 % 3=106 % 4=54 % 5=43 %
70	7=244 8=136 9=77 4=69 6=6	7=212 8=136 9=77 4=69 6=6	7=180 8=136 9=77 3=124 4=69 6=6	8=136 9=77 3=124 4=69 6=6	3=124 9=77 4=69 6=6	3=124 9=77 4=69	3=124 9=77 4=69	3=124 4=69 5=37	3=124 4=69 5=37	3=124 4=69 5=37	1=257 3=124 4=69 5=37	1=283 3=124 4=69 5=37	1=309 % 3=124 % 4=69 % 5=37 %
80	7=210 8=125 9=76 4=63 6=12	7=186 8=125 9=76 4=63 6=12	7=161 8=125 3=106 9=76 4=63 6=12	7=137 8=125 3=106 9=76 4=63 6=12	8=125 3=106 9=76 4=63 6=12	3=106 9=76 4=63	3=106 9=76 4=63	3=106 4=63 5=33	3=106 4=63 5=33	3=106 4=63 5=33	1=127 3=106 4=63 5=33	1=150 3=106 4=63 5=33	1=172 % 3=106 % 4=63 % 5=33 %

Wm Grandmill (1985) Ltd.

Use this page when you expect soybean prices to *FALL*

1 **BUY A PUT** *AT THE MONEY*

2 **BUY A PUT** *AT 50¢ OUT OF THE MONEY*

3 **SELL A CALL** *AT THE MONEY*

4 **SELL A CALL** *AT 50¢ OUT OF THE MONEY*

5 **BEAR SPREAD**
BUY A PUT AT THE MONEY
and SELL A PUT AT 25¢ OUT OF THE MONEY

6 **REVERSE BEAR SPREAD**
BUY A CALL AT THE MONEY
and SELL 2 CALLS AT 50¢ OUT OF THE MONEY

7 **SELL A STRADDLE**
SELL A CALL AT THE MONEY
and SELL A PUT AT THE MONEY

8 **SELL A STRANGLE – #1**
SELL A CALL AT 50¢ OUT OF THE MONEY
and SELL A PUT AT 50¢ OUT OF THE MONEY

9 **SELL A STRANGLE – #2**
SELL A CALL AT $1.00 OUT OF THE MONEY
and SELL A PUT AT $1.00 OUT OF THE MONEY

weeks to **10** expiration

the amount of the estimated soybean price decline

Table No.	0¢	10¢	20¢	30¢	40¢	50¢	60¢	70¢	80¢	90¢	100¢	110¢	120¢
20	9=0	4=16 9=0	4=16 9=0	4=16 9=0	4=16	3=70 4=16	3=70 4=16	1=355 5=100 3=70 4=16	1=419 5=100 3=70 4=16	1=485 5=100 3=70 4=16	1=549 5=100 3=70 4=16	2=1363 1=614 5=100 3=70 4=16	2=1607 % 1=680 % 5=100 % 3=70 % 4=16 %
30	4=34 9=22	4=34 9=22	4=34 9=22	4=34 9=22	3=98 4=34 9=22	3=98 4=34	3=98 4=34	3=98 5=72 4=34	1=281 3=98 5=72 4=34	1=329 3=98 5=72 4=34	1=376 3=98 5=72 4=34	1=424 3=98 5=72 4=34	1=471 % 3=98 % 5=72 % 4=34 %
40	8=72 4=36 9=31	8=72 4=36 9=31	4=36 9=31	4=36 9=31	3=82 4=36 9=31	3=82 4=36 9=31	3=82 4=36	3=82 5=57 4=36	3=82 5=57 4=36	1=239 3=82 5=57 4=36	1=277 3=82 5=57 4=36	1=315 3=82 5=57 4=36	1=353 % 3=82 % 5=57 % 4=36 %
50	8=100 9=50 4=50 6=0	8=100 9=50 4=50 6=0	8=100 9=50 4=50 6=0	3=100 9=50 4=50 6=0	3=100 9=50 4=50	3=100 9=50 4=50	3=100 4=50	3=100 4=50	3=100 4=50 5=45	1=180 3=100 4=50 5=45	1=212 3=100 4=50 5=45	1=234 3=100 4=50 5=45	1=274 % 3=100 % 4=50 % 5=45 %
60	7=236 8=129 9=71 4=67 6=4	7=209 8=129 9=71 4=67 6=4	8=129 9=71 4=67 6=4	8=129 3=122 9=71 4=67	3=122 9=71 4=67 6=4	3=122 9=71 4=67	3=122 9=71 4=67	3=122 4=67 5=39	3=122 4=67 5=39	3=122 4=67 5=39	1=166 3=122 4=67 5=39	1=188 3=122 4=67 5=39	1=210 % 3=122 % 4=67 % 5=39 %
70	7=272 8=160 9=97 4=82 6=11	7=239 8=160 9=97 4=82 6=11	7=207 8=160 3=138 9=97 6=11	8=160 3=138 9=97 4=82 6=11	8=160 3=138 9=97 4=82 6=11	3=138 9=97 4=82 6=11	3=138 9=97 4=82	3=138 9=97 4=82 5=33	3=138 4=82 5=33	3=138 4=82 5=33	1=232 3=138 4=82 5=33	1=255 3=138 4=82 5=33	1=279 % 3=138 % 4=82 % 5=33 %
80	7=233 8=146 9=95 4=74 6=16	7=208 8=146 3=117 9=95 4=74 6=16	7=183 8=146 3=117 9=95 4=74 6=16	7=159 8=146 3=117 9=95 4=74 6=16	8=146 7=135 3=117 9=95 4=74 6=16	8=146 3=117 9=95 4=74 6=16	3=117 9=95 4=74	3=117 9=95 4=74 5=30	3=117 9=95 4=74 5=30	3=117 4=74 5=30	3=117 4=74 5=30	1=124 3=117 4=74 5=30	1=146 % 3=117 % 4=74 % 5=30 %

W.n Grandmill (1985) Ltd.

Use this page when you expect soybean prices to *FALL*

1 BUY A PUT *AT THE MONEY*

2 BUY A PUT *AT 50¢ OUT OF THE MONEY*

3 SELL A CALL *AT THE MONEY*

4 SELL A CALL *AT 50¢ OUT OF THE MONEY*

5 BEAR SPREAD
BUY A PUT AT THE MONEY
and SELL A PUT AT 25¢ OUT OF THE MONEY

6 REVERSE BEAR SPREAD
BUY A CALL AT THE MONEY
and SELL 2 CALLS AT 50¢ OUT OF THE MONEY

7 SELL A STRADDLE
SELL A CALL AT THE MONEY
and SELL A PUT AT THE MONEY

8 SELL A STRANGLE – #1
SELL A CALL AT 50¢ OUT OF THE MONEY
and SELL A PUT AT 50¢ OUT OF THE MONEY

9 SELL A STRANGLE – #2
SELL A CALL AT $1.00 OUT OF THE MONEY
and SELL A PUT AT $1.00 OUT OF THE MONEY

weeks to

12

expiration

the amount of the estimated soybean price decline

Table No.	0¢	10¢	20¢	30¢	40¢	50¢	60¢	70¢	80¢	90¢	100¢	110¢	120¢
20	9=6	4=20 9=6	4=20 9=6	4=20 9=6	4=20	3=76 4=20	3=76 4=20	5=92 3=76 4=20	1=380 5=92 3=76 4=20	1=440 5=92 3=76 4=20	1=500 5=92 3=76 4=20	2=1100 1=560 5=92 3=76 4=20	2=1300 % 1=620 % 5=92 % 3=76 % 4=20 %
30	4=40 9=30	4=40 9=30	4=40 9=30	4=40 9=30	3=101 4=40 9=30	3=101 4=40	3=101 4=40	3=101 4=40	3=101 5=66 4=40	1=296 3=101 5=66 4=40	1=341 3=101 5=66 4=40	1=485 3=101 5=66 4=40	1=429 % 3=101 % 5=66 % 4=40 %
40	8=82 4=41 9=38	8=82 4=41 9=38	4=41 9=38	4=41 9=38	3=89 4=41 9=38	3=89 4=41 9=38	3=89 4=41	3=89 4=41	3=89 5=53 4=41	1=212 3=89 5=53 4=41	1=248 3=89 5=53 4=41	1=282 3=89 5=53 4=41	1=317 % 3=89 % 5=53 % 4=41 %
50	8=113 9=61 4=56 6=1	8=113 9=61 4=56 6=1	8=113 9=61 4=56 6=1	3=109 9=61 4=56 6=1	3=109 9=61 4=56	3=109 9=61 4=56	3=109 4=56	3=109 4=56 5=42	3=109 4=56 5=42	3=109 4=56 5=42	1=188 3=109 4=56 5=42	1=217 3=109 4=56 5=42	1=246 % 3=109 % 4=56 % 5=42 %
60	7=264 8=151 9=88 4=75 6=7	7=236 8=151 9=88 4=75 6=7	8=151 9=88 4=75 6=7	8=151 3=132 9=88 4=75 6=7	3=132 9=88 4=75 6=7	3=132 9=88 4=75	3=132 9=88 4=75	3=132 4=75	3=132 4=75 5=36	3=132 4=75 5=36	3=132 4=75 5=36	1=166 3=132 4=75 5=36	1=186 % 3=132 % 4=75 % 5=36 %
70	7=294 8=181 9=115 4=92 6=15	7=261 8=181 9=115 4=92 6=15	7=229 8=181 3=150 9=115 4=92 6=15	7=197 8=181 3=150 9=115 4=92 6=15	8=181 3=150 9=115 4=92 6=15	3=150 9=115 4=92 6=15	3=150 9=115 4=92	3=150 9=115 4=92	3=150 4=92 5=31	3=150 4=92 5=31	3=150 4=92 5=31	1=236 3=150 4=92 5=31	1=257 % 3=150 % 4=92 % 5=31 %
80	7=252 8=164 9=112 4=83 6=20	7=227 8=164 3=128 9=112 4=83 6=20	7=203 8=164 3=128 9=112 4=83 6=20	7=179 8=164 3=128 9=112 4=83 6=20	8=164 7=154 3=128 9=112 4=83 6=20	8=164 3=128 9=127 4=83	3=128 9=112 4=83	3=128 9=112 4=83 5=27	3=128 9=112 4=83 5=27	3=128 4=83 5=27	3=128 4=83 5=27	3=128 4=83 5=27	3=128 % 1=127 % 4=83 % 5=27 %

Wm Grandmill (1985) Ltd.

Use this page when you expect soybean prices to *FALL*

1 BUY A PUT *AT THE MONEY*

2 BUY A PUT *AT 50¢ OUT OF THE MONEY*

3 SELL A CALL *AT THE MONEY*

4 SELL A CALL *AT 50¢ OUT OF THE MONEY*

5 BEAR SPREAD
BUY A PUT AT THE MONEY
and SELL A PUT AT 25¢ OUT OF THE MONEY

6 REVERSE BEAR SPREAD
BUY A CALL AT THE MONEY
and SELL 2 CALLS AT 50¢ OUT OF THE MONEY

7 SELL A STRADDLE
SELL A CALL AT THE MONEY
and SELL A PUT AT THE MONEY

8 SELL A STRANGLE – #1
SELL A CALL AT 50¢ OUT OF THE MONEY
and SELL A PUT AT 50¢ OUT OF THE MONEY

9 SELL A STRANGLE – #2
SELL A CALL AT $1.00 OUT OF THE MONEY
and SELL A PUT AT $1.00 OUT OF THE MONEY

weeks to

14

expiration

the amount of the estimated soybean price decline

Table No.	0¢	10¢	20¢	30¢	40¢	50¢	60¢	70¢	80¢	90¢	100¢	110¢	120¢
20	9=10	4=23 9=10	4=23 9=10	4=23 9=10	4=23	3=81 4=23	3=81 4=23	5=87 3=81 4=23	1=352 5=87 3=81 4=23	1=408 5=87 3=81 4=23	1=465 5=87 3=81 4=23	1=521 5=87 3=81 4=23	2=1130 % 1=571 % 5=87 % 3=81 % 4=23 %
30	4=45 9=34	4=45 9=34	4=45 9=34	4=45 9=34	3=113 4=45 9=34	3=113 4=45	3=113 4=45	3=113 4=45	3=113 5=62 4=45	1=274 3=113 5=62 4=45	1=315 3=113 5=62 4=45	1=357 3=113 5=62 4=45	1=398 % 3=113 % 5=62 % 4=45 %
40	8=91 9=44 4=45	8=91 9=44 4=45	9=44 4=45	9=44 4=45	3=95 9=44 4=45	3=95 9=44 4=45	3=95 4=45	3=95 4=45	3=95 5=48 4=45	1=195 3=95 5=48 4=45	1=228 3=95 5=48 4=45	1=260 3=95 5=48 4=45	1=293 % 3=95 % 5=48 % 4=45 %
50	7=232 8=125 9=69 4=62 6=4	7=200 8=125 9=69 4=62 6=4	8=125 9=69 4=62 6=4	3=116 9=69 4=62 6=4	3=116 9=69 4=62 6=4	3=116 9=69 4=62	3=116 9=69 4=62	3=116 4=62	3=116 4=62 5=40	3=116 4=62 5=40	1=171 3=116 4=62 5=40	1=198 3=116 4=62 5=40	1=225 % 3=116 % 4=62 % 5=40 %
60	7=282 8=167 9=100 4=83 6=10	7=254 8=167 9=100 4=83 6=10	7=224 8=167 3=141 9=100 4=83 6=10	8=167 3=141 9=100 4=83 6=10	8=167 3=141 9=100 4=83 6=10	3=141 9=100 4=83	3=141 9=100 4=83	3=141 9=100 4=83	3=141 4=83 5=34	3=141 4=83 5=34	3=141 4=83 5=34	1=150 3=141 4=83 5=34	1=168 % 3=141 % 4=83 % 5=34 %
70	7=314 8=199 9=130 4=101 6=18	7=281 8=199 9=130 4=101 6=18	7=249 8=199 3=159 9=130 4=101 6=18	7=217 8=199 3=159 9=130 4=101 6=18	8=199 3=159 9=130 4=101 6=18	8=199 3=159 9=130 4=101 6=18	3=159 9=130 4=101	3=159 9=130 4=101	3=159 4=101 5=29	3=159 4=101 5=29	3=159 4=101 5=29	1=222 3=159 4=101 5=29	1=242 % 3=159 % 4=101 % 5=29 %
80	7=268 8=180 9=127 4=91 6=24	7=244 8=180 3=136 9=127 4=91 6=24	7=220 8=180 3=136 9=127 4=91 6=24	7=196 8=180 3=136 9=127 4=91 6=24	8=180 7=171 3=136 9=127 4=91 6=24	8=180 7=147 3=136 9=127 4=91 6=24	8=155 3=136 9=127 4=91	3=136 9=127 4=91 5=25	3=136 9=127 4=91 5=25	3=136 9=127 4=91 5=25	3=136 4=91 5=25	3=136 4=91 5=25	3=136 % 1=114 % 4=91 % 5=25

Wm Grandmill (1985) Ltd.

Use this page when you expect soybean prices to *FALL*

1 BUY A PUT *AT THE MONEY*

2 BUY A PUT *AT 50¢ OUT OF THE MONEY*

3 SELL A CALL *AT THE MONEY*

4 SELL A CALL *AT 50¢ OUT OF THE MONEY*

5 BEAR SPREAD
BUY A PUT *AT THE MONEY*
and SELL A PUT *AT 25¢ OUT OF THE MONEY*

6 REVERSE BEAR SPREAD
BUY A CALL *AT THE MONEY*
and SELL 2 CALLS *AT 50¢ OUT OF THE MONEY*

7 SELL A STRADDLE
SELL A CALL AT THE MONEY
and SELL A PUT AT THE MONEY

8 SELL A STRANGLE – #1
SELL A CALL AT 50¢ OUT OF THE MONEY
and SELL A PUT AT 50¢ OUT OF THE MONEY

9 SELL A STRANGLE – #2
SELL A CALL AT $1.00 OUT OF THE MONEY
and SELL A PUT AT $1.00 OUT OF THE MONEY

weeks to
16
expiration

the amount of the estimated soybean price decline

Table No.	0¢	10¢	20¢	30¢	40¢	50¢	60¢	70¢	80¢	90¢	100¢	110¢	120¢
20	9=13	4=26 9=13	4=26 9=13	4=26 9=13	4=26	3=86 4=26	3=86 4=26	3=86 5=82 4=26	1=330 3=86 5=82 4=26	1=384 3=86 5=82 4=26	1=438 3=86 5=82 4=26	1=492 3=86 5=82 4=26	2=1014 % 1=545 % 3=86 % 5=82 4=26
30	8=97 4=50 9=40	8=97 4=50 9=40	4=50 9=40	4=50 9=40	3=119 4=50 9=40	3=119 4=50	3=119 4=50	3=119 4=50	3=119 5=59 4=50	1=254 3=119 5=59 4=50	1=294 3=119 5=59 4=50	1=333 3=119 5=59 4=50	1=372 % 3=119 % 5=59 % 4=50 %
40	8=100 9=50 4=50	8=100 9=50 4=50	8=100 9=50 4=50	9=50 4=50	3=100 9=50 4=50	3=100 9=50 4=50	3=100 4=50	3=100 4=50	3=100 4=50 5=46	3=100 4=50 5=46	1=212 3=100 4=50 5=46	1=242 3=100 4=50 5=46	1=272 % 3=100 % 4=50 % 5=46 %
50	7=244 8=136 9=77 4=68 6=7	7=212 8=136 9=77 4=68 6=7	8=136 9=77 4=68 6=7	3=122 9=77 4=68 6=7	3=122 9=77 4=68 6=7	3=122 9=77 4=68	3=122 9=77 4=68	3=122 4=68	3=122 4=68 5=38	3=122 4=68 5=38	1=157 3=122 4=68 5=38	1=183 3=122 4=68 5=38	1=208 % 3=122 % 4=68 % 5=38 %
60	7=296 8=180 9=113 4=90 6=13	7=268 8=180 9=113 4=90 6=13	7=240 8=180 3=148 9=113 4=90 6=13	8=180 3=148 9=113 4=90 6=13	8=180 3=148 9-113 4=90 6=13	3=148 9=113 4=90	3=148 9=113 4=90	3=148 9=113 4=90	3=148 4=90 5=32	3=148 4=90 5=32	3=148 4=90 5=32	3=148 1=140 4=90 5=32	1=155 % 3=148 % 4=90 % 5=32
70	7=330 8=214 9=146 4=109 6=20	7=299 8=214 3=168 9=146 4=109 6=20	7=267 8=214 3=168 9=146 4=109 6=20	7=233 8=214 3=168 9=146 4=109 6=20	8=214 7=201 3=168 9=146 4=109 6=20	8=214 3=168 9=146 6=20	3=168 9=146 4=109	3=168 9=146 4=109	3=168 9=146 4=109 5=27	3=168 4=109 5=27	3=168 4=109 5=27	3=168 4=109 5=27	1=230 % 3=168 % 4=109 % 5=27 %
80	7=283 8=194 9=140 4=98 6=26	7=268 8=194 3=145 9=140 4=98 6=26	7=234 8=194 3=145 9=140 4=98 6=26	7=209 8=194 3=145 9=140 4=98 6=26	8=194 7=185 3=145 9=140 4=98 6=26	8=194 7=161 3=145 9=140 4=98 6=26	8=170 3=145 9=140 7=136 4=98 6=26	3=145 9=140 4=98 5=24	3=145 9=140 4=98 5=24	3=145 9=140 4=98 5=24	3=145 4=98 5=24	3=145 4=98 5=24	3=145 % 1=103 % 4=98 % 5=24 %

Wm Grandmill (1985) Ltd.

Use this page when you expect soybean prices to *FALL*

1 BUY A PUT *AT THE MONEY*

2 BUY A PUT *AT 50¢ OUT OF THE MONEY*

3 SELL A CALL *AT THE MONEY*

4 SELL A CALL *AT 50¢ OUT OF THE MONEY*

5 BEAR SPREAD
BUY A PUT AT THE MONEY
and SELL A PUT AT 25¢ OUT OF THE MONEY

6 REVERSE BEAR SPREAD
BUY A CALL AT THE MONEY
and SELL 2 CALLS AT 50¢ OUT OF THE MONEY

7 SELL A STRADDLE
SELL A CALL AT THE MONEY
and SELL A PUT AT THE MONEY

8 SELL A STRANGLE – #1
SELL A CALL AT 50¢ OUT OF THE MONEY
and SELL A PUT AT 50¢ OUT OF THE MONEY

9 SELL A STRANGLE – #2
SELL A CALL AT $1.00 OUT OF THE MONEY
and SELL A PUT AT $1.00 OUT OF THE MONEY

weeks to
18
expiration

the amount of the estimated soybean price decline

Table No.	0¢	10¢	20¢	30¢	40¢	50¢	60¢	70¢	80¢	90¢	100¢	110¢	120¢
20	9=16	4=29 9=16	4=29 9=16	4=29 9=16	4=29 4=29	3=90 4=29	3=90 4=29	3=90 5=79 4=29	1=311 3=90 5=79 4=29	1=362 3=90 5=79 4=29	1=413 3=90 5=79 4=29	1=466 3=90 5=79 4=29	2=915 % 1=518 % 3=90 % 5=79 % 4=29 %
30	8=105 4=54 9=46	8=105 4=54 9=46	4=54 9=46	4=54 9=46	3=125 4=54 9=46	3=125 4=54	3=125 4=54	3=125 4=54	3=125 5=56 4=54	1=239 3=125 5=56 4=54	1=277 3=125 5=56 4=54	1=314 3=125 5=56 4=54	1=351 % 3=125 % 5=56 % 4=54 %
40	8=107 9=56 4=54	8=107 9=56 4=54	8=107 9=56 4=54	9=56 4=54	3=105 9=56 4=54	3=105 9=56 4=54	3=105 4=54	3=105 4=54	3=105 4=54 5=44	3=105 4=54 5=44	1=98 3=105 4=54 5=44	1=228 3=105 4=54 5=44	1=257 % 3=105 % 4=54 % 5=44 %
50	7=256 8=146 9=86 4=73 6=9	7=223 8=146 9=86 4=73 6=9	8=146 9=86 4=73 6=9	8=146 3=128 9=86 4=73 6=9	3=128 9=86 4=73 6=9	3=128 9=86 4=73	3=128 9=86 4=73	3=128 4=73	3=128 4=73 5=36	3=128 4=73 5=36	3=128 4=73 5=36	1=171 3=128 4=73 5=36	1=195 % 3=128 % 4=73 % 5=36 %
60	7=310 8=193 9=125 4=97 6=15	7=268 8=193 9=125 4=97 6=15	7=230 8=193 3=158 9=125 4=97	8=193 3=158 9=125 4=97 6=15	8=193 3=158 9=125 4=97 6=15	3=158 9=125 4=97	3=158 9=125 4=97	3=158 9=125 4=97	3=158 4=97 5=31	3=158 4=97 5=31	3=158 4=97 5=31	3=158 4=97 5=31	3=158 % 1=144 % 4=97 % 5=31
70	7=346 8=230 9=160 4=117 6=22	7=314 8=230 3=176 9=160 4=117 6=22	7=282 8=230 3=176 9=160 4=117 6=22	7=250 8=230 3=176 9=160 4=117 6=22	8=230 7=217 3=176 9=160 4=117 6=22	8=230 3=176 9=160 4=117	8=197 3=176 9=160 4=117	3=176 9=160 4=117	3=176 9=160 4=117 5=26	3=176 4=117 5=26	3=176 4=117 5=26	3=176 4=117 5=26	1=219 % 3=176 % 4=117 % 5=26 %
80	7=296 8=207 9=154 4=105 6=28	7=272 8=207 9=154 3=151 4=105 6=28	7=248 8=207 9=154 3=151 4=105 6=28	7=224 8=207 9=154 3=151 4=105 6=28	8=207 7=200 9=154 3=151 4=105 6=28	8=207 7=175 9=154 3=151 4=105 6=28	8=182 7=161 9=154 3=151 4=105 6=28	8=158 9=154 3=151 4=105	9=154 3=151 4=105 5=23	9=154 3=151 4=105 5=23	9=154 3=151 4=105 5=23	3=151 4=105 5=23	3=151 % 4=105 % 5=23 %

Wm Grandmill (1985) Ltd.

Use this page when you expect soybean prices to *FALL*

1 BUY A PUT *AT THE MONEY*

2 BUY A PUT *AT 50¢ OUT OF THE MONEY*

3 SELL A CALL *AT THE MONEY*

4 SELL A CALL *AT 50¢ OUT OF THE MONEY*

5 BEAR SPREAD
BUY A PUT AT THE MONEY
and SELL A PUT AT 25¢ OUT OF THE MONEY

6 REVERSE BEAR SPREAD
BUY A CALL AT THE MONEY
and SELL 2 CALLS AT 50¢ OUT OF THE MONEY

7 SELL A STRADDLE
SELL A CALL AT THE MONEY
and SELL A PUT AT THE MONEY

8 SELL A STRANGLE – #1
SELL A CALL AT 50¢ OUT OF THE MONEY
and SELL A PUT AT 50¢ OUT OF THE MONEY

9 SELL A STRANGLE – #2
SELL A CALL AT $1.00 OUT OF THE MONEY
and SELL A PUT AT $1.00 OUT OF THE MONEY

weeks to

20

expiration

the amount of the estimated soybean price decline

Table No.	0¢	10¢	20¢	30¢	40¢	50¢	60¢	70¢	80¢	90¢	100¢	110¢	120¢
20	9=19	4=32 9=19	4=32 9=19	4=32 9=19	4=32 9=19	3=94 4=32	3=94 4=32	3=94 4=32	1=294 3=94 5=75 4=32	1=342 3=94 5=75 4=32	1=390 3=94 5=75 4=32	1=440 3=94 5=75 4=32	2=833 % 1=491 % 3=94 % 5=75 % 4=32 %
30	8=112 4=58 9=50	8=112 4=58 9=50	4=58 9=50	4=58 9=50	3=130 4=58 9=50	3=130 4=58	3=130 4=58	3=130 4=58	3=130 4=58 5=54	3=130 4=58 5=54	1=262 3=130 4=58 5=54	1=298 3=130 4=58 5=54	1=335 % 3=130 % 4=58 % 5=54 %
40	8=115 9=61 4=57	8=115 9=61 4=57	8-115 9=61 4=57	9=61 4=57	3=110 9=61 4=57	3=110 9=61 4=57	3=110 4=57	3=110 4=57	3=110 4=57 5=43	3=110 4=57 5=43	1=185 3=110 4=57 5=43	1=214 3=110 4=57 5=43	1=243 % 3=110 % 4=57 % 5=43 %
50	7=266 8=156 9=93 4=78 6=11	7=234 8=156 9=93 4=78 6=11	8=156 9=93 4=78 6=11	8=156 3=133 9=93 4=78 6=11	3=133 9=93 4=78 6=11	3=133 9=93 4=78	3=133 9=93 4=78	3=133 4=78	3=133 4=78 5=34	3=133 4=78 5=34	3=133 4=78 5=34	1=160 3=133 4=78 5=34	1=184 % 3=133 % 4=78 % 5=34 %
60	7=325 8=205 9=135 4=103 6=17	7=293 8=205 9=135 4=103 6=17	7=265 8=205 3=162 9=135 4=103 6=17	7=241 8=205 3=162 9=135 4=103 6=17	8=205 3=162 9=135 4=103 6=17	3=162 9=135 4=103	3=162 9=135 4=103	3=162 9=135 4=103	3=162 4=103 5=30	3=162 4=103 5=30	3=162 4=103 5=30	3=162 4=103 5=30	3=162 % 1=151 % 4=103 % 5=30 %
70	7=346 8=230 9=174 4=117 6=24	7=314 8=230 3=183 9=174 4=117 6=24	7=282 8=230 3=183 9=174 4=117 6=24	7=250 8=230 3=183 9=174 4=117 6=24	8=230 7=217 3=183 9=174 4=117	8=230 3=183 9=174 4=117 6=24	8=197 3=183 9=174 4=117	3=183 9=174 4=117	3=183 9=174 4=117 5=25	3=183 4=117 5=25	3=183 4=117 5=25	3=183 4=117 5=25	3=183 % 4=117 % 5=25 %
80	7=309 8=219 9=165 4=109 6=30 6=30	7=285 8=219 9=165 3=154 4=109 3=30	7=261 8=219 9=165 3=154 4=109 6=30	7=235 8=219 9=165 3=154 4=109 6=30	8=219 7=211 9=165 3=154 4=109 6=30	8=219 7=187 9=165 3=154 4=109 6=30	8=195 7=162 9=165 3=154 4=109 6=30	8=170 9=165 3=154 4=109 5=22	9=165 3=154 4=109 5=22	9=165 3=154 4=109 5=22	9=165 3=154 4=109 5=22	3=154 4=109 5=22	3=154 % 4=109 % 5=22 %

Wm Grandmill (1985) Ltd.

Use this page when you expect soybean prices to FALL

1 BUY A PUT *AT THE MONEY*

2 BUY A PUT *AT 50¢ OUT OF THE MONEY*

3 SELL A CALL *AT THE MONEY*

4 SELL A CALL *AT 50¢ OUT OF THE MONEY*

5 BEAR SPREAD
BUY A PUT AT THE MONEY
and SELL A PUT AT 25¢ OUT OF THE MONEY

6 REVERSE BEAR SPREAD
BUY A CALL AT THE MONEY
and SELL 2 CALLS AT 50¢ OUT OF THE MONEY

7 SELL A STRADDLE
SELL A CALL AT THE MONEY
and SELL A PUT AT THE MONEY

8 SELL A STRANGLE – #1
SELL A CALL AT 50¢ OUT OF THE MONEY
and SELL A PUT AT 50¢ OUT OF THE MONEY

9 SELL A STRANGLE – #2
SELL A CALL AT $1.00 OUT OF THE MONEY
and SELL A PUT AT $1.00 OUT OF THE MONEY

the amount of the estimated soybean price decline

Table No.	0¢	10¢	20¢	30¢	40¢	50¢	60¢	70¢	80¢	90¢	100¢	110¢	120¢
20	9=23	4=34 9=23	4=34 9=23	4=34 9=23	4=34 9=23	3=97 4=34	3=97 4=34	3=97 4=34	1=283 3=97 5=73 4=34	1=330 3=97 5=73 4=34	1=383 3=97 5=73 4=34	1=425 3=97 5=73 4=34	2=785 % 1=475 % 3=97 % 5=73 % 4=34 %
30	8=120 4=61 9=55	8=120 4=61 9=55	4=61 9=55	4=61 9=55	3=135 4=61 9=55	3=135 4=61	3=135 4=61	3=135 4=61	3=135 4=61 5=52	3=135 4=61 5=52	1=250 3=135 4=61 5=52	1=285 3=135 4=61 5=52	1=320 % 3=135 % 4=61 % 5=52 %
40	8=121 9=65 4=60	8=121 9=65 4=60	8=121 9=65 4=60	3=113 9=65 4=60	3=113 9=65 4=60	3=113 9=65 4=60	3=113 4=60	3=113 4=60	3=113 4=60 5=42	3=113 4=60 5=42	1=176 3=113 4=60 5=42	1=205 3=113 4=60 5=42	1=232 % 3=113 % 4=60 % 5=42 %
50	7=276 8=164 9=100 4=82 6=12	7=243 8=164 9=100 4=82 6=12	7=211 8=164 9=100 4=82 6=12	8=164 3=138 9=100 4=82 6=12	3=138 9=100 4=82 6=12	3=138 9=100 4=82	3=138 9=100 4=82	3=138 4=82	3=138 4=82 5=33	3=138 4=82 5=33	3=138 4=82 5=33	1=151 3=138 4=82 5=33	1=174 % 3=138 % 4=82 % 5=33 %
60	7=330 8=213 9=142 4=106 6=19	7=304 8=213 9=142 4=106 6=19	7=279 8=213 3=167 9=142 4=106 6=19	7=254 8=213 3=167 9=142 4=106 6=19	8=213 3=167 9=142 4=106 6=19	3=167 9=142 4=106	3=167 9=142 4=106	3=167 9=142 4=106	3=167 4=106 5=28	3=167 4=106 5=28	3=167 4=106 5=28	3=167 4=106 5=28	3=167 % 4=106 % 5=28 %
70	7=374 8=256 9=186 4=130 6=26	7=342 8=256 3=190 9=186 4=130 6=26	7=310 8=256 3=190 9=186 4=130 6=26	7=278 8=256 3=190 9=186 4=130 6=26	8=256 7=245 3=190 9=186 4=130 6=26	8=256 7=213 3=190 9=186 4=130 6=26	8=223 3=190 9=186 4=130	3=190 9=186 4=130	3=190 9=186 4=130 5=24	3=190 9=186 4=130 5=24	3=190 4=130 5=24	3=190 4=130 5=24	3=190 % 4=130 % 5=24 %
80	7=319 8=230 9=175 4=114 6=32	7=295 8=230 9=175 3=159 4=114 6=32	7=271 8=230 9=175 3=159 4=114 6=32	7=245 8=230 9=175 3=159 4=114 6=32	8=230 7=221 9=175 3=159 4=114 6=32	8=230 7=197 9=175 3=159 4=114 6=32	8=205 7=172 9=175 3=159 4=114	8=180 3=159 3=159 4=114	9=175 3=159 4=114 5=21	9=175 3=159 4=114 5=21	9=175 3=159 4=114 5=21	3=159 4=114 5=21	3=159 % 4=114 % 5=21 %

Wm Grandmill (1985) Ltd.

Use this page when you expect soybean prices to *FALL*

1 BUY A PUT *AT THE MONEY*

2 BUY A PUT *AT 50¢ OUT OF THE MONEY*

3 SELL A CALL *AT THE MONEY*

4 SELL A CALL *AT 50¢ OUT OF THE MONEY*

5 BEAR SPREAD
BUY A PUT AT THE MONEY
and SELL A PUT AT 25¢ OUT OF THE MONEY

6 REVERSE BEAR SPREAD
BUY A CALL AT THE MONEY
and SELL 2 CALLS AT 50¢ OUT OF THE MONEY

7 SELL A STRADDLE
SELL A CALL AT THE MONEY
and SELL A PUT AT THE MONEY

8 SELL A STRANGLE – #1
SELL A CALL AT 50¢ OUT OF THE MONEY
and SELL A PUT AT 50¢ OUT OF THE MONEY

9 SELL A STRANGLE – #2
SELL A CALL AT $1.00 OUT OF THE MONEY
and SELL A PUT AT $1.00 OUT OF THE MONEY

24 weeks to expiration

the amount of the estimated soybean price decline

Table No.	0¢	10¢	20¢	30¢	40¢	50¢	60¢	70¢	80¢	90¢	100¢	110¢	120¢
20	9=25	4=36 9=25	4=36 9=25	4=36 9=25	3=100 4=36 9=25	3=100 4=36	3=100 4=36	3=100 4=36	3=100 5=70 4=36	1=317 3=100 5=70 4=36	1=367 3=100 5=70 4=36	1=410 3=100 5=70 4=36	2=738 % 1=458 % 3=100 % 5=70 % 4=36 %
30	8=128 4=65 9=60	8=128 4=65 9=60	4=65 9=60	4=65 9=60	3=139 4=65 9=60	3=139 4=65	3=139 4=65	3=139 4=65	3=139 4=65 5=50	3=139 4=65 5=50	1=239 3=139 4=65 5=50	1=273 3=139 4=65 5=50	1=307 % 3=139 % 4=65 % 5=50 %
40	8=127 9=70 4=63	8=127 9=70 4=63	8=127 9=70 4=63	3=117 9=70 4=63	3=117 9=70 4=63	3=117 9=70 4=63	3=117 4=63	3=117 4=63	3=117 4=63 5=40	3=117 4=63 5=40	3=117 4=63 5=40	1=195 3=117 4=63 5=40	1=222 % 3=117 % 4=63 % 5=40 %
50	7=284 8=172 9=107 4=86 6=13	7=252 8=172 9=107 4=86 6=13	7=220 8=172 9=107 4=86 6=13	8=172 3=142 9=107 4=86 6=13	3=142 9=107 4=86 6=13	3=142 9=107 4=86	3=142 9=107 4=86	3=142 4=86	3=142 4=86 5=32	3=142 4=86 5=32	3=142 4=86 5=32	3=142 4=86 5=32	1=166 % 3=142 % 4=86 % 5=32 %
60	7=335 8=221 9=159 4=109 6=21	7=311 8=221 9=159 4=109 6=21	7=289 8=221 3=172 9=159 4=109 6=21	7=267 8=221 3=172 9=159 4=109 6=21	8=221 7=220 3=172 9=159 4=109 6=21	8=221 3=172 9=159 4=109	3=172 9=159 4=109	3=172 9=159 4=109	3=172 9=159 4=109 5=27	3=172 4=109 5=27	3=172 4=109 5=27	3=172 4=109 5=27	3=172 % 4=109 % 5=27 %
70	7=386 8=267 9=197 4=137 6=28	7=353 8=267 9=197 3=196 4=137 6=28	7=321 8=267 9=197 3=196 4=137 6=28	7=289 8=267 9=197 3=196 4=137 6=28	8=267 7=256 9=197 3=196 4=137 6=28	8=267 7=224 9=197 3=196 4=137	8=234 9=197 3=196 4=137	9=197 3=196 4=137	9=197 3=196 4=137 5=23	9=197 3=196 4=137 5=23	3=196 4=137 5=23	3=196 4=137 5=23	3=196 % 4=137 % 5=23 %
80	7=329 8=241 9=185 3=166 4=119 6=34	7=305 8=241 9=185 3=166 4=119 6=34	7=281 8=241 9=185 3=166 4=119 6=34	7=255 8=241 9=185 3=166 4=119 6=34	8=241 7=231 9=185 3=166 4=119 6=34	8=241 7=207 9=185 3=166 4=119 6=34	8=215 9=185 7=182 3=166 4=119 6=34	8=190 9=185 3=166 7=159 4=119	9=195 8=165 3=166 4=119 5=21	9=185 3=166 4=119 5=21	9=185 3=166 4=119 5=21	3=166 4=119 5=21	3=166 % 4=119 % 5=21 %

Wm Grandmill (1985) Ltd.

Use this page when you expect soybean prices to *FALL*

1 BUY A PUT *AT THE MONEY*

2 BUY A PUT *AT 50¢ OUT OF THE MONEY*

3 SELL A CALL *AT THE MONEY*

4 SELL A CALL *AT 50¢ OUT OF THE MONEY*

5 BEAR SPREAD
BUY A PUT AT THE MONEY
and SELL A PUT AT 25¢ OUT OF THE MONEY

6 REVERSE BEAR SPREAD
BUY A CALL AT THE MONEY
and SELL 2 CALLS AT 50¢ OUT OF THE MONEY

7 SELL A STRADDLE
SELL A CALL AT THE MONEY
and SELL A PUT AT THE MONEY

8 SELL A STRANGLE – #1
SELL A CALL AT 50¢ OUT OF THE MONEY
and SELL A PUT AT 50¢ OUT OF THE MONEY

9 SELL A STRANGLE – #2
SELL A CALL AT $1.00 OUT OF THE MONEY
and SELL A PUT AT $1.00 OUT OF THE MONEY

the amount of the estimated soybean price decline

Table No.	0¢	10¢	20¢	30¢	40¢	50¢	60¢	70¢	80¢	90¢	100¢	110¢	120¢
20	9=27	4=38 9=27	4=38 9=27	4=38 9=27	3=103 4=38 9=27	3=103 4=38	3=103 4=38	3=103 4=38	3=103 5=68 4=38	1=305 3=103 5=68 4=38	1=350 3=103 5=68 4=38	1=396 3=103 5=68 4=38	2=690 % 1=441 % 3=103 % 5=68 % 4=38 %
30	8=133 4=68 9=64	8=133 4=68 9=64	4=68 9=64	4=68 9=64	3=143 4=68 9=64	3=143 4=68	3=143 4=68	3=143 4=68	3=143 4=68 5=48	3=143 4=68 5=48	1=230 3=143 4=68 5=48	1=263 3=143 4=68 5=48	1=296 % 3=143 % 4=68 % 5=48 %
40	8=133 9=74 4=67 6=7	8=133 9=74 4=67 6=7	8=133 9=74 4=67 6=7	3=120 9=74 4=67 6=7	3=120 9=74 4=67 6=7	3=120 9=74 4=67	3=120 4=67	3=120 4=67	3=120 4=67 5=39	3=120 4=67 5=39	3=120 4=67 5=39	1=86 3=120 4=67 5=39	1=223 % 3=120 % 4=67 % 5=39 %
50	7=292 8=179 9=114 4=90 6=14	7=260 8=179 9=114 4=90 6=14	7=228 8=179 3=146 9=114 4=90 6=14	8=179 3=146 9=114 4=90 6=14	3=146 9=114 4=90 6=14	3=146 9=114 4=90	3=146 9=114 4=90	3=146 4=90	3=146 4=90 5=31	3=146 4=90 5=31	3=146 4=90 5=31	3=146 4=90 5=31	1=159 % 3=146 % 4=90 % 5=31 %
60	7=340 8=230 9=166 4=115 6=22	7=319 8=230 9=166 4=115 6=22	7=297 8=230 3=176 9=166 4=115 6=22	7=275 8=230 3=176 9=166 4=115 6=22	8=230 7=230 3=176 9=166 4=115 6=22	8=230 3=176 9=166 4=115	3=176 9=166 4=115	3=176 9=166 4=115 5=26	3=176 9=166 4=115 5=26	3=176 4=155 5=26	3=176 4=155 5=26	3=176 4=155 5=26	3=176 % 4=155 % 5=26 %
70	7=396 8=277 9=207 4=141 6=29	7=363 8=277 9=207 3=201 4=141 6=29	7=331 8=277 9=207 3=201 4=141 6=29	7=299 8=277 9=207 3=201 4=141 6=29	8=277 7=267 9=207 3=201 4=141 6=29	8=277 7=235 9=207 3=201 4=141 6=29	8=245 9=207 3=201 4=141	8=213 9=207 3=201 4=141	9=207 3=201 4=141 5=23	9=207 3=201 4=141 5=23	3=201 4=141 5=23	3=201 4=141 5=23	3=201 % 4=141 % 5=23 %
80	7=338 8=250 9=194 3=171 4=124 6=35	7=314 8=250 9=194 3=171 4=124 6=35	7=290 8=250 9=194 3=171 4=124 6=35	7=265 8=250 9=194 3=171 4=124 6=35	8=250 7=241 9=194 3=171 4=124 6=35	8=250 7=217 9=194 3=171 4=124 6=35	8=224 7=192 9=194 3=171 4=124 6=35	8=199 9=194 7=168 3=171 4=124	9=194 8=174 3=171 4=124 5=20	9=194 3=171 4=124 5=20	9=194 3=171 4=124 5=20	3=171 9=170 4=124 5=20	3=171 % 4=124 % 5=20 %

Wm Grandmill (1985) Ltd.

Use this page when you expect soybean prices to *FALL*

1 BUY A PUT *AT THE MONEY*

2 BUY A PUT *AT 50¢ OUT OF THE MONEY*

3 SELL A CALL *AT THE MONEY*

4 SELL A CALL *AT 50¢ OUT OF THE MONEY*

5 BEAR SPREAD
BUY A PUT AT THE MONEY
and SELL A PUT AT 25¢ OUT OF THE MONEY

6 REVERSE BEAR SPREAD
BUY A CALL AT THE MONEY
and SELL 2 CALLS AT 50¢ OUT OF THE MONEY

7 SELL A STRADDLE
SELL A CALL AT THE MONEY
and SELL A PUT AT THE MONEY

8 SELL A STRANGLE – #1
SELL A CALL AT 50¢ OUT OF THE MONEY
and SELL A PUT AT 50¢ OUT OF THE MONEY

9 SELL A STRANGLE – #2
SELL A CALL AT $1.00 OUT OF THE MONEY
and SELL A PUT AT $1.00 OUT OF THE MONEY

weeks to
28
expiration

the amount of the estimated soybean price decline

Table No.	0¢	10¢	20¢	30¢	40¢	50¢	60¢	70¢	80¢	90¢	100¢	110¢	120¢
20	9=28	4=40	4=40	4=40	3=106	3=106	3=106	3=106	3=106	1=294	1=340	1=383	1=427 %
		9=28	9=28	9=28	4=4=	4=4=	4=40	4=40	5=67	3=106	3=106	3=106	3=106 %
					9=28				4=40	5=67	5=67	5=67	5=67 %
										4=40	4=40	4=40	4=40 %
30	8=139	8=139	4=71	4=71	3=147	3=147	3=147	3=147	3=147	3=147	1=222	1=254	1=286 %
	4=71	4=71	9=69	9=69	4=71	4=71	4=71	4=71	4=71	4=71	3=147	3=147	3=147 %
	9=69	9=69			9=69				5=47	5=47	4=71	4=71	4=71 %
											5=47	5=47	5=47 %
40	8=138	8=138	8=138	3=123	3=123	3=123	3=123	3=123	3=123	3=123	3=123	1=180	1=212 %
	9=79	9=79	9=79	9=79	9=79	9=79	9=79	4=69	4=69	4=69	4=69	3=123	3=123 %
	4=69	4=69	4=69	4=69	4=69	4=69	4=69		5=37	5=37	5=37	4=69	4=69 %
	6=9	6=9	6=9	6=9	6=9							5=37	5=37 %
50	7=300	7=267	7=235	8=186	8=186	3=150	3=150	3=150	3=150	3=150	3=150	3=150	1=152 %
	8=186	8=186	8=186	3=150	3=150	9=119	9=119	9=119	4=93	4=93	4=93	4=93	3=150 %
	9=119	9=119	3=150	9=119	9=119	4=93	4=93	4=93	5=30	5=30	5=30	5=30	4=93 %
	4=93	4=93	9=119	4=93	4=93								5=30 %
	6=16	6=16	4=93	6=16	6=16								
			6=16										
60	7=345	7=325	7=304	7=273	8=237	8=237	3=181	3=181	3=181	3=181	3=181	3=181	3=181 %
	8=237	8=237	8=237	8=237	7=237	3=181	9=173	9=173	9=166	4=120	4=120	4=120	4=120 %
	9=173	9=173	3=181	3=181	3=181	9=173	4=120	4=120	4=120	5=26	5=26	5=26	5=26 %
	4=120	4=120	9=173	9=173	9=173	4=120		5=26	5=26				
	6=23	6=23	4=120	4=120	4=120	6=23							
			6=23	6=23	6=23								
70	7=406	7=374	7=342	7=309	8=288	8=288	8=255	8=223	9=217	9=217	3=206	3=206	3=206 %
	8=288	8=288	8=288	8=288	7=277	7=245	9=217	9=217	3=206	3=206	4=146	4=146	4=146 %
	9=217	9=217	9=217	9=217	9=217	9=217	7=213	3=206	4=146	4=146	5=22	5=22	5=22 %
	4=146	3=206	3=206	3=206	3=206	3=206	3=206	4=146	5=22	5=22			
	6=30	4=146	4=146	4=146	4=146	4=146	4=146						
		6=30	6=30	6=30	6=30	6=30	6=30						
80	7=347	7=323	7=298	7=274	8=258	8=258	8=233	8=208	9=202	9=202	9=202	9=177	3=175 %
	8=258	8=258	8=258	8=258	7=250	7=226	7=201	9=202	8=183	3=175	3=175	3=175	4=133 %
	9=202	9=202	9=202	9=202	9=202	9=202	9=202	7=180	3=175	8=172	4=133	4=133	5=19 %
	3=175	3=175	3=175	3=175	3=175	3=175	3=175	3=175	7=156	4=133	5=19	5=19	
	4=133	4=133	4=133	4=133	4=133	4=133	4=133	4=133	5=19				
	6=36	6=36	6=36	6=36	6=36	6=36	6=36						

Wm Grandmill (1985) Ltd.

Use this page when you expect soybean prices to FALL

1 BUY A PUT *AT THE MONEY*

2 BUY A PUT *AT 50¢ OUT OF THE MONEY*

3 SELL A CALL *AT THE MONEY*

4 SELL A CALL *AT 50¢ OUT OF THE MONEY*

5 BEAR SPREAD
BUY A PUT AT THE MONEY
and SELL A PUT AT 25¢ OUT OF THE MONEY

6 REVERSE BEAR SPREAD
BUY A CALL AT THE MONEY
and SELL 2 CALLS AT 50¢ OUT OF THE MONEY

7 SELL A STRADDLE
SELL A CALL AT THE MONEY
and SELL A PUT AT THE MONEY

8 SELL A STRANGLE – #1
SELL A CALL AT 50¢ OUT OF THE MONEY
and SELL A PUT AT 50¢ OUT OF THE MONEY

9 SELL A STRANGLE – #2
SELL A CALL AT $1.00 OUT OF THE MONEY
and SELL A PUT AT $1.00 OUT OF THE MONEY

weeks to | **30** | **expiration**

the amount of the estimated soybean price decline

Table No.	0¢	10¢	20¢	30¢	40¢	50¢	60¢	70¢	80¢	90¢	100¢	110¢	120¢
20	9=30	4=42 9=30	4=42 9=30	4=42 9=30	3=109 4=42 9=30	3=109 4=42	3=109 4=42	3=109 4=42	3=109 5=65 4=42	1=284 3=109 5=65 4=42	1=329 3=109 5=65 4=42	1=371 3=109 5=65 4=42	1=414 % 3=109 % 5=65 % 4=42 %
30	8=144 4=74 9=72	8=144 4=74 9=72	4=74 9=72	4=74 9=72	3=150 4=74 9=72	3=150 4=74	3=150 4=74	3=150 4=74	3=150 4=74 5=46	3=150 4=74 5=46	1=215 3=150 4=74 5=46	1=247 3=150 4=74 5=46	1=278% 3=150 % 4=74 % 5=46 %
40	7=252 8=143 9=83 4=72 6=10	7=226 8=143 9=83 4=72 6=10	8=143 9=83 4=72 6=10	3=126 9=83 4=72 6=10	3=126 9=83 4=72 6=10	3-126 9=83 4=72	3=126 9=83 4=72	3=126 4=72	3=126 4=72 5=36	3=126 4=72 5=36	3=126 4=72 5=36	1=174 3=126 4=72 5=36	1=200 % 3=126 % 4=72 % 5=36 %
50	7=307 8=193 9=125 4=96 6=17	7=274 8=193 9=125 4=96 6=17	7=242 8=193 3=154 9=125 4=96 6=17	8=193 3=154 9=125 4=96 6=17	8=193 3=154 9=125 4=96 6=17	3=154 9=125 4=96	3=154 9=125 4=96	3=154 9=125 4=96	3=154 4=96 5=29	3=154 4=96 5=29	3=154 4=96 5=29	3=154 4=96 5=29	3=154 % 1=147 % 4=96 % 5=29 %
60	7=351 8=253 9=180 4=126 6=24	7=330 8=253 3=187 9=180 4=126 6=24	7=310 8=253 3=187 9=180 4=126 6=24	7=291 8=253 3=187 9=180 4=126 6=24	8=253 7=250 3=187 9=180 4=126 6=24	8=253 3=187 9=180 4=126 6=24	8=211 3=187 9=180 4=126	3=187 9=180 4=126	3=187 9=180 4=126 5=25	3=187 9=180 4=126 5=25	3=187 4=126 5=25	3=187 4=126 5=25	3=187 % 4=126 % 5=25 %
70	7=415 8=297 9=226 4=151 6=31	7=383 8=297 9=226 3=211 4=151 6=31	7=351 8=297 9=226 3=211 4=151 6=31	7=318 8=297 9=226 3=211 4=151 6=31	8=297 7=286 9=226 3=211 4=151 6=31	8=297 7=254 9=226 3=211 4=151 6=31	8=266 7=221 9=226 3=211 4=151 6=31	8=235 9=226 3=211 4=151	9=226 3=211 4=151 5=22	9=226 3=211 4=151 5=22	9=226 3=211 4=151 5=22	3=211 4=151 5=22	3=211 % 4=151 % 5=22 %
80	7=356 8=265 9=208 3=181 4=136 6=37	7=331 8=265 9=208 3=181 4=136 6=37	7=306 8=265 9=208 3=181 4=136 6=37	7=282 8=265 9=208 3=181 4=136 6=37	8=265 7=258 9=208 3=181 4=136 6=37	8=265 7=234 9=208 3=181 4=136 6=37	8=242 7=209 9=208 3=181 4=136 6=37	8=217 9=208 7=184 3=181 4=136 6=37	9=208 8=192 3=181 7=160 4=136	9=208 3=181 8=167 4=136 5=19	9=208 3=181 4=136 5=19	9=184 3=181 4=136 5=19	3=181 % 9=160 % 4=136 % 5=19 %

Wm Grandmill (1985) Ltd.

Use this page when you expect soybean prices to *FALL*

weeks to **32** expiration

1 BUY A PUT *AT THE MONEY*

2 BUY A PUT *AT 50¢ OUT OF THE MONEY*

3 SELL A CALL *AT THE MONEY*

4 SELL A CALL *AT 50¢ OUT OF THE MONEY*

5 BEAR SPREAD
BUY A PUT AT THE MONEY
and SELL A PUT AT 25¢ OUT OF THE MONEY

6 REVERSE BEAR SPREAD
BUY A CALL AT THE MONEY
and SELL 2 CALLS AT 50¢ OUT OF THE MONEY

7 SELL A STRADDLE
SELL A CALL AT THE MONEY
and SELL A PUT AT THE MONEY

8 SELL A STRANGLE – #1
SELL A CALL AT 50¢ OUT OF THE MONEY
and SELL A PUT AT 50¢ OUT OF THE MONEY

9 SELL A STRANGLE – #2
SELL A CALL AT $1.00 OUT OF THE MONEY
and SELL A PUT AT $1.00 OUT OF THE MONEY

the amount of the estimated soybean price decline

Table No.	0¢	10¢	20¢	30¢	40¢	50¢	60¢	70¢	80¢	90¢	100¢	110¢	120¢
20	9=30	4=43 9=30	4=43 9=30	4=43 9=30	3=111 4=43 9=30	3=111 4=43	3=111 4=43	3=111 4=43	3=111 5=65 4=43	1=278 3=111 5=65 4=43	1=321 3=111 5=65 4=43	1=363 3=111 5=65 4=43	1=404 % 3=111 % 5=65 % 4=43 %
30	8=149 4=76 9=76	8=149 4=76 9=76	4=76 9=76	4=76 9=76	3=153 4=76 9=76	3=153 4=76	3=153 4=76	3=153 4=76	3=153 4=76 5=44	3=153 4=76 5=44	1=210 3=153 4=76 5=44	1=241 3=153 4=76 5=44	1=275 % 3=153 % 4=76 % 5=44 %
40	7=256 8=148 9=87 4=74 6=12	7=224 8=148 9=87 4=74 6=12	8=148 9=87 4=74 6=12	3=128 9=87 4=74 6=12	3=128 9=87 4=74 6=12	3=128 9=87 4=74	3=128 9=87 4=74	3=128 4=74	3=128 4=74 5=36	3=128 4=74 5=36	3=128 4=74 5=36	1=170 3=128 4=74 5=36	1=190 % 3=128 % 4=74 % 5=36 %
50	7=314 8=199 9=130 4=100 6=18	7=272 8=199 9=130 4=100 6=18	7=240 8=199 3=157 9=130 4=100 6=18	8=199 3=157 9=130 4=100 6=18	8=199 3=157 9=130 4=100 6=18	3=157 9=130 4=100	3=157 9=130 4=100	3=157 9=130 4=100	3=157 4=100 5=29	3=157 4=100 5=29	3=157 4=100 5=29	3=157 4=100 5=29	3=157 % 4=100 % 5=29 %
60	7=364 8=269 9=186 4=110 6=25	7=340 8=269 3=190 9=186 4=110 6=25	7=318 8=269 3=190 9=186 4=110 6=25	7=297 8=269 3=190 9=186 4=110 6=25	8=269 7=256 3=190 9=186 4=110 6=25	8=269 7=226 3=190 9=186 4=110 6=25	8=216 3=190 9=186 4=110	3=190 9=186 4=110	3=190 9=186 4=110 5=25	3=190 9=186 4=110 5=25	3=190 4=110 5=25	3=190 4=110 5=25	3=190 % 4=110 % 5=25 %
70	7=425 8=305 9=234 3=216 4=155 6=32	7=392 8=305 9=234 3=216 4=155 6=32	7=360 8=305 9=234 3=216 4=155 6=32	7=327 8=305 9=234 3=216 4=155 6=32	8=305 7=295 9=234 3=216 4=155 6=32	8=305 7=263 9=234 3=216 4=155 6=32	8=273 9=234 7=230 3=216 4=155 6=32	8=241 9=234 3=216 4=155	9=234 3=216 4=155 5=21	9=234 3=216 4=155 5=21	9=234 3=216 4=155 5=21	3=216 4=155 5=21	3=216 % 4=155 % 5=21 %
80	7=363 8=271 9=213 3=185 4=139 6=37	7=338 8=271 9=213 3=185 4=139 6=37	7=313 8=271 9=213 3=185 4=139 6=37	7=289 8=271 9=213 3=185 4=139 6=37	8=271 7=265 9=213 3=185 4=139 6=37	8=271 7=241 9=213 3=185 4=139 6=37	8=248 7=216 9=213 3=185 4=139 6=37	8=223 9=213 7=191 3=185 4=139 6=37	9=213 8=198 3=185 7=164 4=139 5=19	9=213 3=185 8=174 4=139 5=19	9=213 3=185 4=139 5=19	9=189 3=185 4=139 5=19	3=185 % 9=164 % 4=139 % 5=19 %

Wm Grandmill (1985) Ltd.

Use this page when you expect soybean prices to FALL

1 BUY A PUT *AT THE MONEY*

2 BUY A PUT *AT 50¢ OUT OF THE MONEY*

3 SELL A CALL *AT THE MONEY*

4 SELL A CALL *AT 50¢ OUT OF THE MONEY*

5 BEAR SPREAD
BUY A PUT AT THE MONEY
and SELL A PUT AT 25¢ OUT OF THE MONEY

6 REVERSE BEAR SPREAD
BUY A CALL AT THE MONEY
and SELL 2 CALLS AT 50¢ OUT OF THE MONEY

7 SELL A STRADDLE
SELL A CALL AT THE MONEY
and SELL A PUT AT THE MONEY

8 SELL A STRANGLE – #1
SELL A CALL AT 50¢ OUT OF THE MONEY
and SELL A PUT AT 50¢ OUT OF THE MONEY

9 SELL A STRANGLE – #2
SELL A CALL AT $1.00 OUT OF THE MONEY
and SELL A PUT AT $1.00 OUT OF THE MONEY

the amount of the estimated soybean price decline

Table No.	0¢	10¢	20¢	30¢	40¢	50¢	60¢	70¢	80¢	90¢	100¢	110¢	120¢
20	9=31	4=44 9=31	4=44 9-31	4=44 9=31	3=113 4=44 9=31	3=113 4=44	3=113 4=44	3=113 4=44	3=113 5=62	1=271 3=113 5=62 4=44	1=312 3=113 5=62 4=44	1=354 3=113 5=62 4=44	1=395 % 3=113 % 5=62 % 4=44 %
30	8=152 9=80 4=78	8=152 9=80 4=78	9=80 4=78	9=80 4=78	3=156 9=80 4=78	3=156 4=78	3=156 4=78	3=156 4=78	3=156 4=78 5=44	3=156 4=78 5=44	1=204 3=156 4=78 5=44	1=234 3=156 4=78 5=44	1=265 % 3=156 % 4=78 % 5=44 %
40	7=261 8=153 9=91 4=76 6=14	7=229 8-153 9=91 4=76 6=14	8=153 9=91 4=76 6=14	8=153 3=130 9=91 4=76 6=14	3=130 9=91 4=76 6=14	3=130 9=91 4=76	3=130 9=91 4=76	3=130 4=76	3=130 4=76 5=35	3=130 4=76 5=35	3=130 4=76 5=35	1=65 3=130 4=76 5=35	1=180 % 3=130 % 4=76 % 5=35 %
50	7=320 8=205 9=135 4=103 6=19	7=287 8=205 9=135 4=103 6=19	7=255 8=205 3=160 9=135 4=103 6=19	8=205 3=160 9=135 4=103 6=19	8=205 3=160 9=135 4=103 6=19	3=160 9=135 4=103	3=160 9=135 4=103	3=160 9=135 4=103	3=160 4=103 5=28	3=160 4=103 5=28	3=160 4=103 5=28	3=160 4=103 5=28	3=160 % 4=103 % 5=28 %
60	7=371 8=263 9=193 4=132 6=26	7=350 8=263 9=193 3=193 4=132 6=26	7=325 8=263 9=193 3=193 4=132 6=26	7=303 8=263 9=193 3=193 4=132 6=26	7=263 8=263 9=193 3=193 4=132 6=26	8=263 7=219 9=193 3=193 4=132 6=26	8=221 9=193 3=193 4=132	9=193 9=193 3=193 4=132	9=193 3=193 4=132 5=25	9=193 3=193 4=132 5=25	3=193 4=132 5=25	3=193 4=132 5=25	3=193 % 4=132 % 5=25%
70	7=432 8=313 9=242 3=220 4=159 6=33	7=400 8=313 9=242 3=220 4=159 6=33	7=368 8=313 9=242 3=220 4=159 6=33	7=335 8=313 9=242 3=220 4=159 6=33	8=313 7=303 9=242 3=220 4=159 6=33	8=313 7=271 9=242 3=220 4=159 6=33	8=28= 9=242 7=238 3=220 4=159 6=33	8=248 9=242 7=206 3=220 4=159	9=242 8=216 3=220 4=159 5=21	9=242 3=220 4=159 5=21	9=242 3=220 4=159 5=21	3=220 4=159 5=21	3=220 % 4=159 % 5=21 %
80	7=370 8=277 9=218 3=189 4=142 6=38	7=345 8=277 9=218 3=189 4=142 6=38	7=320 8=277 9=218 3=189 4=142 6=38	7=296 8=277 9=218 3=189 4=142 6=38	8=277 7=272 9=218 3=189 4=142 6=38	8=277 7=248 9=218 3=189 4=142 6=38	8=254 7=223 9=218 3=189 4=142 6=38	8=229 9=218 7=198 3=189 4=142 6=38	9=218 8=204 3=189 7=174 4=142 5=18	9=218 3=189 8=180 7=151 4=142 5=18	9=218 3=189 8=155 4=142 7=126 5=18	9=194 3=189 4=142 8=128 5=18	3=189 % 9=168 % 4=142 % 5=18 %

Wm Grandmill (1985) Ltd.

Use this page when you expect soybean prices to *FALL*

1 BUY A PUT *AT THE MONEY*

2 BUY A PUT *AT 50¢ OUT OF THE MONEY*

3 SELL A CALL *AT THE MONEY*

4 SELL A CALL *AT 50¢ OUT OF THE MONEY*

5 BEAR SPREAD
*BUY A PUT AT THE MONEY
and SELL A PUT AT 25¢ OUT OF THE MONEY*

6 REVERSE BEAR SPREAD
*BUY A CALL AT THE MONEY
and SELL 2 CALLS AT 50¢ OUT OF THE MONEY*

7 SELL A STRADDLE
*SELL A CALL AT THE MONEY
and SELL A PUT AT THE MONEY*

8 SELL A STRANGLE – #1
*SELL A CALL AT 50¢ OUT OF THE MONEY
and SELL A PUT AT 50¢ OUT OF THE MONEY*

9 SELL A STRANGLE – #2
*SELL A CALL AT $1.00 OUT OF THE MONEY
and SELL A PUT AT $1.00 OUT OF THE MONEY*

weeks to
36
expiration

the amount of the estimated soybean price decline

Table No.	0¢	10¢	20¢	30¢	40¢	50¢	60¢	70¢	80¢	90¢	100¢	110¢	120¢
20	9=32	4=46 9=32	4=46 9=32	4=46 9=32	3=115 4=46 9=32	3=115 4=46	3=115 4=46	3=115 4=46	3=115 5=61 4=46	1=264 3=115 5=61 4=46	1=304 3=115 5=61 4=46	1=345 3=115 5=61 4=46	1=385 % 3=115 % 5=61 % 4=46 %
30	8=156 9=82 4=80	8=156 9=82 4=80	9=82 4=80	9=82 4=80	3=158 9=82 4=80	3=158 4=80	3=158 4=80	3=158 4=80	3=158 4=80 5=44	3=158 4=80 5=44	1=199 3=158 5=44	1=229 3=158 4=80 5=44	1=259 % 3=158 % 4=80 % 5=44 %
40	7=266 8=158 9=96 4=78 6=15	7=234 8=158 9=96 4=78 6=15	8=158 9=96 4=78 6=15	8=158 3=131 9=96 4=78 6=15	3=131 9=96 4=78 6=15	3=131 9=96 4=78	3=131 9=96 4=78	3=131 4=78	3=131 4=78 5=35	3=131 4=78 5=35	3=131 4=78 5=35	1=160 3=131 4=78 5=35	1=169 % 3=131 % 4=78 % 5=35 %
50	8=211 9=140 4=106 6=19	8=211 9=140 4=106 6=19	8=211 3=163 9=140 4=106 6=19	8=211 3=163 9=140 4=106 6=19	8=211 3=163 9=140 4=106 6=19	3=163 9=140 4=106	3=163 9=140 4=106	3=163 9=140 4=106	3=163 4=106 5=28	3=163 4=106 5=28	3=163 4=106 5=28	3=163 4=106 5=28	3=163 % 4=106 % 5=28 %
60	7=390 8=269 9=200 4=135 6=27	7=363 8=269 9=200 3=196 4=135 6=27	7=336 8=269 9=200 3=196 4=135 6=27	7=309 8=269 9=200 3=196 4=135 6=27	8=269 7=268 9=200 3=196 4=135 6=27	8=269 7=226 9=200 3=196 4=135 6=27	8=227 9=200 3=196 4=135	9=200 3=196 4=135	9=200 3=196 4=135 5=25	9=200 3=196 4=135 5=25	3=196 4=135 5=25	3=196 4=135 5=25	3=196 % 4=135 % 5=25 %
70	7=440 8=321 9=250 3=224 4=163 6=33	7=407 8-321 9=250 3=224 4=163 6=33	7=375 8=321 9=250 3=224 4=163 6=33	7=343 8=321 9=250 3=224 4=163 6=33	8=321 7=310 9=250 3=224 4=163 6=33	8-321 7=279 9=250 3=224 4=163 6=33	8=288 9=250 7=246 3=224 4=163 6=33	8=256 9=250 7=214 3=224 4=163	9=250 8=224 3=224 4=163 5=21	9=250 3=224 4=163 5=21	9=250 3=224 4=163 5=21	3=224 4=163 4=163 5=21	3=224 % 4=163 % 4=163 % 5=21 %
80	7=374 8=280 9=221 3=192 4=144 6=38	7=349 8=280 9=221 3=192 4=144 6=38	7=324 8=280 9=221 3=192 4=144 6=38	7=300 8=280 9=221 3=192 4=144 6=38	8=280 7=276 9=221 3=192 4=144 6=38	8=280 7=252 9=221 3=192 4=144 6=38	8=256 7=227 9=221 3=192 4=144 6=38	8=232 9=221 7=203 3=192 4=144 6=38	9=221 8=207 3=192 7=178 4=144 5=18	9=221 3=192 8=182 4=144 5=18	9=221 3=192 4=144 5=18	9=196 3=192 4=144 5=18	3=192 % 9=172 % 4=144 % 5=18 %

Wm Grandmill (1985) Ltd.